Using AutoCAD®

3rd Edition

Ralph Grabowski
with Tim Huddleston

QUE
CORPORATION
LEADING COMPUTER KNOWLEDGE

Using AutoCAD ®
3rd Edition

Library of Congress Catalog No.: 90-62080

ISBN No.: 0-88022-623-4

94 93 92 91   5 4 3 2 1

Interpretation of the printing code: the rightmost double-digit number is the year of the book's printing; the rightmost single-digit number is the number of the book's printing. For example, a printing code of 91-1 shows that the first printing of the book occurred in 1991.

Using AutoCAD, 3rd Edition, is based on AutoCAD Release 11. Commands and functions detailed in this book should work with other releases in which the pertinent features are available.

ABOUT THE AUTHORS

Ralph H. Grabowski holds a degree in civil engineering from the University of British Columbia. He is senior editor of *CADalyst*, a magazine devoted to AutoCAD systems management. Before becoming the magazine's senior editor, he was technical editor in charge of hardware and software testing. Mr. Grabowski also operates the CAD Management Group, an AutoCAD consulting firm specializing in technical writing and editing, training, and solving CAD management problems.

Tim Huddleston is a production editor at Que Corporation, and is product line director of Que's AutoCAD titles. During his tenure at Que, Mr. Huddleston edited and contributed to the development of a number of popular titles, including *Using UNIX, MS-DOS User's Guide*, Special Edition; *AutoCAD Quick Reference*, 2nd Edition; and *Using AutoCAD*, 2nd Edition.

Publisher

Lloyd Short

Publishing Director

David Paul Ewing

Acquisitions Editor

Terrie Lynn Solomon

Product Development Manager

Charles O. Stewart III

Product Director

Tim Huddleston

Managing Editor

Mary Bednarek

Editors

Tim Ryan
Gail Burlakoff
Sandra Blackthorn
Robert L. Knight
William R. Valaski
Diane L. Steele
Robin Drake

Technical Editor

Craig Spaid

Technical Support

Jerry Ellis

Acquisitions Editorial Assistant

Stacey Beheler

Editorial Secretary

Karen Opal

Indexer

Sharon Hilgenberg

Book Design and Production

Claudia Bell
Jeff Baker
Brad Chinn
Martin Coleman
Joelyn Gifford
Sandy Grieshop
Tami Hughes
Betty Kish
Bob LaRoche
Sarah Leatherman
Howard Peirce
Cindy L. Phipps
Tad Ringo
Dennis Sheehan
Louise Shinault
Johnna VanHoose
Mary Beth Wakefield
Lisa A. Wilson

Composed in Garamond and OCRB
by Que Corporation.

CONTENTS AT A GLANCE

Part VI   Reference

TABLE OF CONTENTS

I CAD and Computer Basics

1 Manual versus Computer Drafting 21

III Moving Beyond the Basics

10 Advanced Drawing Techniques 301

IV Customizing the AutoCAD Environment

11 Setting Up the Drawing Environment.............365

ACKNOWLEDGMENTS

Using AutoCAD, 3rd Edition, represents the collaborative efforts of many talented people. Que Corporation thanks the following individuals for their contributions to the development of this book.

Dave Ewing, for his guidance and invaluable advice through all phases of the project, and especially for his unwavering support and encouragement. Dave is representative of the commitment to quality that has made Que's books so popular.

Tim Huddleston, for his willingness to make great sacrifices to ensure that *Using AutoCad*, 3rd Edition, is the best AutoCAD book on the market. Tim provided developmental direction for the book and directed and coordinated the editors who worked on this project. Tim's many contributions to developing the content and structure of this book are deeply appreciated.

Gail Burlakoff, for her superb editing abilities and versatility. Gail wore many hats during the editing and production of this book, and she wore them all with great style.

Tim Ryan, for taking on a difficult task at a moment's notice, and for smiling all the while. Parts Five and Six benefited from Tim's skillful editing; we all benefited from his enthusiasm and good humor.

Jerry Ellis, for his can-do attitude and his willingess to pitch in wherever and whenever he was needed. Jerry's unbending resolve to make things right is apparent in this book's illustrations and technical accuracy.

Robert Knight and **William Valaski**, for their contributions to the development of Part Five of this book.

Craig Spaid, for his insightful technical review of the manuscript.

Mary Bednarek, for her patience and nurturing guidance. Mary tirelessly juggled schedules and resources to ensure the quality of this book.

Terrie Lynn Solomon, for being the consummate communicator, coordinator, and counselor.

Stacey Beheler, for tracking the innumerable pieces that went into this book, and for always being able to fit "just one more thing" into her hectic schedule.

Autodesk, Inc., and especially Gloria Bastidas, for providing advice, materials, and consolation throughout this project. Everyone in the computer industry should be inspired by Autodesk's commitment to its customers. The company's care and understanding were apparent in the many contributions Autodesk's staff members made to this book.

TRADEMARK
ACKNOWLEDGMENTS

Que Corporation has made every attempt to supply trademark information about company names, products, and services mentioned in this book. Trademarks indicated below were derived from various sources. Que Corporation cannot attest to the accuracy of this information.

1-2-3 and Lotus are registered trademarks of Lotus Development Corporation.

ACAD, ATC, AutoCAD 386, Autodesk Animator, Autodesk Animator Clips, AutoFlix, and DFX are trademarks of Autodesk, Inc.

AEGIS is a trademark of Apollo Computer, Inc.

Apple and Macintosh II are registered trademarks of Apple Computer, Inc.

AutoCAD, Autodesk, the Autodesk logo, AutoLISP, AutoShade, AutoSketch, and AutoSolid are registered trademarks of Autodesk, Inc.

CompuServe Information Service is a registered trademark of CompuServe Inc. and H&R Block, Inc.

Ashton-Tate and dBASE are registered trademarks of Ashton-Tate Corporation.

DEC is a registered trademark and VAX/VMS is a trademark of Digital Equipment Corporation.

EPSON is a registered trademark of Seiko Epson Corporation.

IBM and OS/2 are registered trademarks of International Business Machines Corporation.

Generic CADD is a trademark of Generic Software, an Autodesk company.

HP is a registered trademark and LaserJet is a trademark of Hewlett-Packard Co.

Microsoft, MS-DOS, and XENIX are registered trademarks of Microsoft Corporation.

Motorola is a registered trademark of Motorola, Inc.

NEC MultiSync is a registered trademark of NEC Home Electronics (USA) Inc.

PC Tools is a trademark of Central Point Software.

PostScript is a registered trademark of Adobe Systems Inc.

SideKick is a registered trademark of Borland International, Inc.

UNIX is a trademark of AT&T.

WordPerfect is a registered trademark of WordPerfect Corporation.

WordStar is a registered trademark of MicroPro International Corporation.

Xerox is a registered trademark of Xerox Corporation.

Trademarks of other products mentioned in this book are held by the companies producing them.

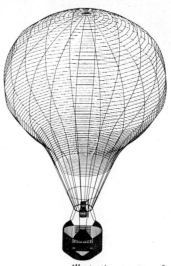

Introduction

*Illustration courtesy of
Autodesk, Inc., Sausalito, CA.*

Computer-aided drafting (or CAD) has taken designers and drafters a quantum leap beyond the T-square and the drafting table. From its beginnings as a simple drawing tool used exclusively on mainframe computer systems, CAD has evolved into a powerful drafting, design, and engineering environment. Now that CAD can be used on a PC, nearly everyone has access to CAD's design and drafting capabilities. As CAD-system hardware increases in power and decreases in price, CAD programs are still evolving.

A Brief History of CAD

The first *interactive* drawing system was developed in the early 1960s. The system was revolutionary because it enabled the user to see lines and circles as they were being drawn. Computer-aided drafting became a reality in the early 1970s, but the cost was high ($150,000 per station) because the only computers available were expensive mainframe and minicomputers. Only large companies could afford CAD, and then only if it was used 24 hours a day.

In the early 1980s, the advent of the microcomputer helped reduce the cost of a CAD system to $10,000 per station. Autodesk, Inc. unveiled the AutoCAD program in 1982. This early version was so rudimentary that it could barely be used for drafting and design. But Autodesk's programmers worked hard to improve AutoCAD, boasting that it had 80 percent of the functionality of the big CAD systems at only 20 percent of the cost. Since then, several companies have developed CAD software for personal computers. As the cost of computer hardware falls, almost anyone can purchase and use a CAD program, even at home. As a result, computer-

1

aided drafting is having an impact on society. CAD is being taught in schools, it is automating small manufacturing operations, and it helps people with disabilities to work more productively.

Now that the program is nearly 10 years old, AutoCAD boasts all the functionality of the larger systems it is replacing. AutoCAD Release 11 is capable of performing 2-D drafting, 3-D drafting, and solids modeling. The program's drawing capabilities are limited only by your computer's capacity.

AutoCAD Today

Today, AutoCAD is the leading CAD software package used on personal computers and workstations. AutoCAD's popularity continues to grow for many reasons, including the following:

- ❏ AutoCAD is an "open" program. You can learn to customize it for your own purposes.
- ❏ AutoCAD features a built-in programming language, AutoLISP, for design calculations and automatic drawing. Built-in "hooks" enable you to use more powerful programming languages, such as C, to solve more complex problems.
- ❏ Because of AutoCAD's openness and its programming languages, hundreds of additional programs are available that customize AutoCAD for specific purposes, or help make AutoCAD easier to use.
- ❏ If you ever have a problem with AutoCAD, help is easy to find. Hundreds of users' groups and training centers, dozens of books, and several publications are dedicated to AutoCAD.

In addition to AutoCAD, Autodesk offers the following software products, which can broaden your range of CAD capabilities and greatly enhance your CAD output:

- ❏ **Advanced Modeling Extension.** With AutoCAD's Advanced Modeling Extension (AME), you can turn 3-D wireframe models into solid models. These solid models contain attributes that help define properties such as center of gravity, weight, and volume. With AME's help, a designer can draw an object and then model the object and analyze its behavior in its intended use. You can use AME to build electronic models of your designs, eliminating the need for cardboard or plastic prototypes.
- ❏ **AutoShade.** AutoShade's rendering capabilities enable you to view your design's aesthetics and functionality on-

screen. You can present your projects to clients while still in the preliminary design stage.

❏ **Autodesk Animator and 3D Studio.** These programs enable you to deal with a project at any level. With Autodesk Animator, you can "walk" your client through a project. Autodesk 3D Studio enables you to create impressive three-dimensional animations of kinetic and dynamic motions.

Using AutoCAD, 3rd Edition, is written and designed to help both first-time and experienced CAD users become more proficient with the AutoCAD program. First-time users will quickly learn to use AutoCAD and to feel more comfortable with CAD equipment. Experienced users will learn to use the more advanced features of AutoCAD and to exploit the capabilities of Release 11. Users at all levels will appreciate the book's comprehensive reference sections.

Why Use AutoCAD?

Not only is AutoCAD an impressive drafting package, but it also forms the core for an entire design environment. Before the arrival of CAD, designers and drafters spent tedious hours painstakingly and repeatedly drawing the same projects by hand. With CAD, such repetitive chores are a thing of the past. Those who see AutoCAD in action are amazed at the ease with which an object—a gear, for example—can be drawn. That gear can be drawn in two or three dimensions, analyzed, and animated.

Why use AutoCAD rather than another computer-assisted design package? For the following reasons:

❏ Cost savings

❏ Compatibility

❏ Flexibility

❏ The industry standard

The following sections discuss each of these factors in turn.

Cost Savings

Economy is the main reason for buying a CAD system. You want to be more competitive, save time, and use your time more efficiently, thereby reducing drafting costs. Implemented correctly, a CAD system can help you achieve these cost-related goals.

A person's time is the most valuable resource a company has. CAD provides the design firm's employees with a multipurpose tool, and the ability to design, draw, and analyze an object or space in a fraction of the time it would take with an ordinary drafting table, T-square, and triangle. This efficient use of time results not only in lower design costs, but ultimately in better quality of design.

A computer system initially costs far more than a drafting table. CAD is such an efficient tool, however, that it can help you draw up to four times more efficiently than manual drafting. When you purchase a CAD system, you are substituting long-term capital for short-term cost.

The start-up cost of an AutoCAD system ranges from less than $5,000 to more than $50,000, depending on the type of computer and options you select.

AutoCAD Release 11 has a retail price of about $3,500, similar to competing CAD packages. Autodesk also sells two lower-priced CAD packages. The 2-D AutoSketch ($250) and the 3-D Generic CADD ($450) have fewer features than AutoCAD but may have enough functionality to work as a *front-end* to AutoCAD. A project manager (or an engineer working at home) can use AutoSketch or Generic CADD to draw up preliminary design ideas. The drawing files then can be transferred to AutoCAD for full implementation.

Of all the costs you must incur in setting up a CAD system, however, hardware costs vary the most. Here are a few examples:

- ❏ Computers: from less than $1,500 to more than $20,000
- ❏ Graphics subsystems (that display the drawing on the video screen): from less than $200 to more than $10,000
- ❏ Input devices (that help you draw on the screen): from less than $50 to more than $3,000
- ❏ Output devices (that print your drawing on paper): from less than $200 to more than $50,000
- ❏ Miscellaneous add-ons: scanners ($400 to $30,000), mass-storage devices ($300 to $20,000), add-on software (free to $5,000), networks ($300 to $1,500 per computer)

Fortunately, computers are *modular* so that you start out with a basic, low-cost system, and then add more parts as you need them.

When you purchase a complete CAD system, you can expect a package price that costs less than the sum of the individual components. Similarly, dealers often sell AutoCAD at a lower price if you buy several copies at a time.

Despite its popularity, AutoCAD is not the CAD package of choice in all design fields. Integrated circuit design and statewide mapping, for example, are applications to which other CAD packages are better adapted. In terms of its features, however, AutoCAD compares favorably with any competitive CAD package. It has the important advantage of being the most popular software in the CAD world, just as Lotus 1-2-3, WordPerfect, and dBASE are the leaders in the areas of spreadsheets, word processing, and databases, respectively.

Compatibility

Compatibility means that another user—using a different system—can easily work on a CAD drawing that you have developed. When you select a CAD drafting package, you should consider compatibility with clients and contractors who may need access to your work. Compatibility issues range from the type of computer you use to the CAD package's language. CAD users are most interested in *system compatibility* and *drawing compatibility*.

System compatibility with your clients is extremely important. If the systems are compatible, you can move information easily from computer to computer or between CAD systems. Even though AutoCAD runs on a variety of hardware platforms and under several operating systems, its drawing files are completely compatible regardless of their origin. You do not need to translate the files. This is not always true of other CAD software packages.

If you are looking for drawing compatibility, AutoCAD set the standard with its DXF (*Drawing Exchange Format*) translation. Generally, you can transfer an AutoCAD drawing to and from most CAD and graphics packages. Be aware, however, that the process of transferring drawings is not foolproof. You probably will lose small pieces of the drawing during translation. To solve the problem of incompatibility, you must either use the same CAD package as your clients (the better solution) or find out beforehand which entities are not common to both packages.

Flexibility

AutoCAD is a powerful tool for drafting and design work of all kinds. Unlike some CAD packages, which are written specifically for architects or electrical engineers, AutoCAD is a powerful "graphics engine." You decide what kind of vehicle you want to build around the engine. AutoCAD can be customized to fit your specific needs.

The program is easy to learn and use for standard drafting. AutoCAD prompts are easy to understand, and as you will see, editing is not difficult. To aid drawing, you can create temporary construction lines, which won't show in your final output. AutoCAD's menu systems enable you to access commands quickly and efficiently.

From a mechanical drafting standpoint, AutoCAD enables you to check clearances on parts that move together, or to design parts as complex as modified sine cams. From an architectural point of view, you can evaluate structures in perspective or isometric from any location, inside or outside the building. AutoCAD has the potential to be used as an exceptional design tool with the aid of the built-in AutoLISP programming language and the ADS (AutoCAD Development System) interface. Combined with your ingenuity and creativity, AutoCAD's power is almost unlimited.

The Industry Standard

In addition to being an excellent tool for drafting, a good tool for design, and an easy package to learn and use, AutoCAD is the industry standard for CAD systems. That is often reason enough to select AutoCAD.

AutoCAD has become such a strong standard for the following reasons:

- ❏ A strong network of users' groups
- ❏ A strongly supported network of training centers and a large selection of books
- ❏ Journals devoted specifically to its use and promotion
- ❏ An extensive array of dealers across the country

If you would like to talk with people who use AutoCAD, you can find AutoCAD users' groups all over the world. These groups share experiences with the program, and are an excellent source of advice if you encounter problems when using AutoCAD. (Part Six includes a complete listing of users' groups and other sources of information on AutoCAD.)

Autodesk certifies nearly 200 authorized training centers (called *ATCs*) around the world to provide training at different levels.

If you are new to AutoCAD, this book and others let you learn the program on your own, and supply you with additional information not provided in the manual. For a fast, easy-to-use guide to AutoCAD's commands, responses, and system variables, see *AutoCAD Quick Reference*, 2nd Edition, published by Que Corporation. More experienced users can learn advanced drawing and editing strategies and a variety of AutoLISP routines from *AutoCAD Advanced Techniques*, also published by Que Corporation.

Should you prefer a broader, more detailed analysis of the latest AutoCAD tips and tricks, *CADalyst* and *Cadence* are two periodicals devoted to AutoCAD. In Europe, look for the English-language *CAD User* and the German-language *AutoCAD Magazin*.

No matter what kind of question or problem you have, your AutoCAD dealer is your first line of support. Autodesk works hard to make its dealers the best and most informed in the industry. If you are experiencing difficulties, your dealer probably has already seen the problem or knows where to get the answer. If you have problems with your dealer, Autodesk can refer you to another in your area.

In addition to all this support, an Autodesk Forum is available on CompuServe. If you own a modem, this is your "direct line" to AutoCAD users and Autodesk personnel. Here you can get fast answers to your questions, find out the latest news, and download useful utility programs.

What Can You Do with AutoCAD?

Even if you are interested in AutoCAD for a specific purpose, you may be surprised at how others have used AutoCAD. Here are some ordinary (and some out-of-the-ordinary) examples.

AutoCAD was used to design the steel structures holding up the dinosaurs at Knotts Berry Farm and the fearsome King Kong at Universal Studios Tour. AutoCAD helps maintain city rail-transit systems, showing which track segments need repair. AutoCAD forms the graphics database for emergency response teams, pointing out the best route to a disaster and any potentially dangerous conditions. AutoCAD is used for log-home design, teaching art concepts to college students, designing printed circuit boards, and building architectural scale models.

Technical Illustration

AutoCAD's precision lends itself to illustrating technical documents. Volvo uses AutoCAD to prepare illustrations of its car parts. The drawings are merged with desktop publishing software to create owner and service manuals.

Road Design

Many surveyors use electronic data-gathering equipment for new road projects. The data is transferred by phone lines to a computer back at the home office, where an engineer uses AutoCAD to transform the data into a road design, showing the existing site conditions, elevations, and site services. Other software then can create a drive-through that lets the engineer "drive" along the new road to check sight distances and the safety of curves—months before construction begins.

NC Programming

The use of AutoCAD in NC (*numerical control*) programming has revolutionized the manufacturing industry. (The term *NC* refers to the use of a computer to control a lathe or milling machine.) With AutoCAD and AME, you can design a product—such as an engine block for next year's model of automobile—by using solids modeling (see fig. I-1). With a third-party program, you can perform stress and heat analysis on the engine block. With another third-party program, you can translate the engine block's final design into NC code. Finally, a milling machine reads the code and produces the engine block out of aluminum. The route from design to final product is entirely electronic; you don't need a single sheet of paper.

Fig. I.1.
An NC drawing, generated by AutoCAD.

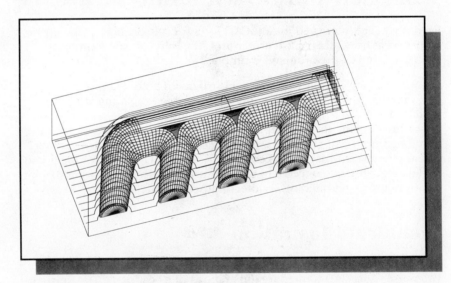

Landscape Architecture

AutoCAD has had a tremendous impact on the landscaping and landscape design industries (see fig. I.2). With AutoCAD and a third-party landscape architecture program, you can perform site analysis of any landscape or site development project, such as a new golf course. You can plan the golf links, the water courses, and the clubhouse. Using irrigation analysis, you can place the sprinkler system. Then, using Autodesk Animator, you can take your clients on a tour of the unbuilt course.

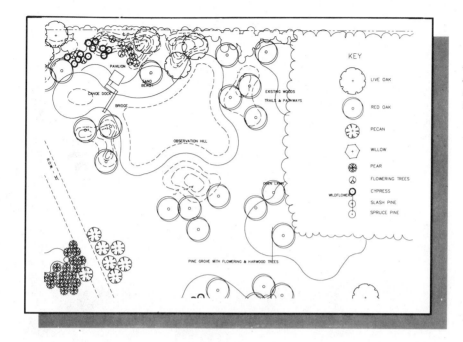

Fig. I.2.
A landscape
design, drawn
by AutoCAD.

After the golf course is built and operating, you can keep track of vegetation types and fertilizer rates by using AutoCAD and a database program.

Geographical Information Systems

Mapping may well be the most demanding application for any CAD system; detailed map files are easily the largest kind of drawing files. CAD makes it easy for organizations such as the U.S. Bureau of the Census to update their maps.

But drawing is only one aspect of mapping. A more powerful system of map use and control is GIS (*geographical information system*), which relates database information to a CAD-based map. Exxon and the state of Alaska, for example, used an AutoCAD-based GIS to keep track of the Valdez oil spill, the clean-up efforts, and the environmental impact. With the data entered into the GIS, operators could ask the database, for example, to display the hardest-hit seal birthing areas. By windowing an area on the AutoCAD screen, operators could obtain from the database a printout of oil density along a certain stretch of beach.

Many municipalities now use GIS to track the information they use for engineering services, law enforcement, land-use planning, and taxation (see fig. I.3).

*Fig. I.3.
A GIS map,
drawn in
AutoCAD.*

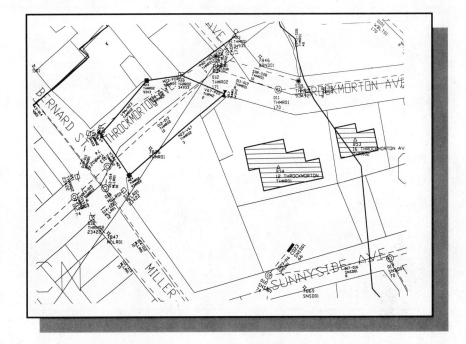

Custom Design

Using AutoCAD, a designer of stained glass can create designs on-screen and print them out on a pen plotter. AutoCAD becomes particularly useful when the design does not fit a customer's window. The designer then can have AutoCAD scale the design (both horizontally and vertically) for a tailored fit.

Taking custom design one step further, a tailor uses AutoCAD to create custom-fit trousers for people who have difficulty finding ready-made pants that fit properly. The tailor's son wrote several AutoLISP routines to automate the design process. The tailor simply tells AutoCAD the customer's measurements, and AutoCAD produces the pattern. Similarly, AutoCAD has been used for quilt design.

Underwater Archaeology

Possibly the most exotic application of AutoCAD is in the field of underwater archaeology. When an Australian team found the *HMS Pandora* (the ship sent to bring the *Bounty* mutineers back to England, but which sank off the Great Barrier Reef on its return trip), archaeologists used AutoCAD to keep track of the location of every find made during their dives.

Assumptions about the Reader

As this book was written, certain assumptions were made about you, the reader. The text assumes that you have AutoCAD Release 10 or 11, that you have the equipment necessary to run AutoCAD, and that you know basic computer-related information.

To run AutoCAD Release 11, you must have the following basic hardware:

❑ A 286, 386, or 486 IBM-compatible computer with at least 2M of RAM; a Macintosh II; or a workstation by Sun, Apollo, or DEC

❑ A math (numeric) coprocessor

❑ A hard disk (at least 40M)

❑ A monitor and graphics board

The following peripherals are optional but recommended:

❑ A digitizing pad or mouse

❑ A plotter or printer plotter

You must be familiar with computers, have a basic working knowledge of your operating system, directories, and files, and know how to reference different disk drives. The basic DOS and OS/2 commands useful for AutoCAD work are discussed in Chapter 3. For more information about DOS or OS/2, consult *Using DOS* or *Using OS/2*; both are published by Que Corporation.

Important software concepts in Chapters 1, 2, and 3 of *Using AutoCAD*, 3rd Edition, are not described elsewhere in the book. You should familiarize yourself with these concepts so that when they appear in later chapters, you will know what they mean.

About This Book

As you look through this book, you will notice certain conventions that show you at a glance what actions to take as you use the program. Examples of these conventions follow:

❑ AutoCAD commands begin with an uppercase letter: Line

❑ AutoCAD system variables appear in all uppercase letters: TILEMODE

❑ DOS and AutoCAD prompts and messages appear in a special typeface: `Command:`

❑ Information you type at the AutoCAD prompt is in **boldface**

❑ New terms are in italics: *entities*

So that you can learn the commands quickly, the text introduces the entire prompt sequence. Each command, listed as though you had typed it from the keyboard, is shown with all pertinent prompts. For example:

Prompt	Response	Explanation
`Command:`	**CIRCLE**	Starts the CIRCLE command
`3P/2P/TTR/`		
`<Center Point>:`	Move cross-hairs to circle's center point; pick it.	
`Diameter/<Radius>:`	.25	Indicates a radius of .25 inch

The text also provides explanations of the selections you can make at each prompt.

Examples accompany the explanations of most commands. As you read the text, you work through projects that make use of most of AutoCAD's commands. Each successive project builds on your knowledge of the commands covered earlier in the book.

Although this book covers AutoCAD Releases 10 and 11 (much of the text also applies to earlier releases of the program), some of the descriptions deal only with Release 11. If a passage applies to Release 11 alone, it is marked with a special icon in the margin, like the icon you see next to this paragraph.

What Is in This Book

Using AutoCAD, 3rd Edition, describes all drawing and editing commands. After reading this book, you should be able to create, edit, and plot to your specifications both a 2-D and a 3-D drawing. You will be able to set up and use a symbol library and create basic drawings on which to pattern other drawings. You will be able to customize AutoCAD to your working environment, and to program with AutoCAD's programming language, AutoLISP.

In this book, you will follow an example of drawing a one-bedroom apartment. You will learn how to draw the floor plan in two dimensions, add dimensioning and text, insert symbols, convert the drawing to three dimensions, and then produce a shaded rendering. As each chapter builds on the previous one, you will add more detail to the sample drawing.

Each chapter teaches you a new set of AutoCAD commands. You will learn all the options associated with each command and some of the system variables that affect it. The book includes notes, tips, and warnings that help you become more productive with AutoCAD.

Because *Using AutoCAD*, 3rd Edition, has been written for both the novice and the experienced AutoCAD user, your level of proficiency with AutoCAD should determine where you begin reading the book. In any case, you should supplement this book with the *AutoCAD Reference Manual* that comes with your copy of AutoCAD.

By starting with Chapter 1 and continuing through each chapter, you will establish a firm command of the concepts on which AutoCAD is based. If you are familiar with the equipment, DOS, and the computer environment, you can skip Part One. Instead, start with Chapter 4 ("A Quick Start in AutoCAD") and continue through the rest of the book. Experienced CAD users may want to try the AutoCAD quick start offered in Chapter 4, and then jump to Part Three ("Moving Beyond the Basics"). The book then expands into 3-D work, customizing AutoCAD, and programming with AutoLISP.

A complete reference section provides valuable information for users of all levels. The following synopses should help you decide where to begin reading and where to find specific information.

Part One: CAD and Computer Basics

Part One provides the basic information you need to know before you begin to work with AutoCAD. You will learn the benefits of using CAD compared with manual drafting. An overview of CAD equipment explains the functions of each peripheral, and a discussion of DOS shows you how to manage your AutoCAD files.

Chapter 1, "Manual versus Computer Drafting," looks at the differences between doing drafting and design by hand and by computer. This chapter describes the advantages and disadvantages of computer-aided drafting.

Chapter 2, "CAD Equipment," explains the computer equipment (the hardware) you need to run AutoCAD. Various hardware options are covered. The chapter ends with basic and recommended lists of hardware.

Chapter 3, "Operating Systems," discusses three of the operating systems—DOS, OS/2, and UNIX—on which AutoCAD can run. The chapter introduces the concepts of files and file management, and shows you how to organize the computer's hard disk.

Part Two: Learning To Use AutoCAD

This part shows you how to use AutoCAD. After a quick introductory tour of AutoCAD, you draw an apartment floor plan. You learn how to edit, view, and plot the drawing. Explanations are provided for all the AutoCAD commands used to perform the different tasks.

Chapter 4, "A Quick Start in AutoCAD," is a fast-paced tutorial that shows you how to use basic AutoCAD drawing commands. Basic examples take you step-by-step through starting AutoCAD and drawing a few simple shapes. The Main Menu options are fully explained.

Chapter 5, "Drawing Basics," guides you through all of AutoCAD's basic drawing commands. By the end of the chapter, you will have created a simple apartment floor plan.

Chapter 6, "Editing Basics," describes all of AutoCAD's basic editing commands. Once you have drawn something in AutoCAD, you should never need to draw it again. The chapter shows you how to copy, move, and erase objects in the drawing.

Chapter 7, "Viewing a Drawing," introduces you to all the different ways to view a two-dimensional drawing on-screen. The chapter shows you how to magnify and shrink the drawing to show more detail or more of the drawing. You also can store views and slides for display later.

Chapter 8, "Plotting a Drawing," guides you through the steps required to produce a copy of the drawing on paper, using your printer or plotter. The chapter includes tips for improving the look of the plotted output.

Part Three: Moving Beyond the Basics

Part Three is designed to make your work with AutoCAD quicker and more efficient. You learn the more advanced AutoCAD commands for drawing and editing by drawing the rest of the apartment suite.

Chapter 9, "Advanced Editing Techniques," describes AutoCAD's more involved editing commands, which enable you to change the properties of objects, and create and change drawing layers.

Chapter 10, "Advanced Drawing Techniques," shows you how to add details to any drawing. You add text, dimensions, and hatching to a drawing. You also learn how to use AutoCAD as a sketch pad.

Part Four: Customizing the AutoCAD Environment

You experience the true power of AutoCAD when you learn how to customize it. In Part Four, you learn how to set up the drawing environment and create your own symbol libraries. When you write custom menus and AutoLISP programs, you let AutoCAD do much of the drafting and design work for you.

Chapter 11, "Setting Up the Drawing Environment," explains how to set up AutoCAD to suit the way you draw. The chapter shows you how to draw more accurately and easily, and how to list the information AutoCAD stores about the drawing.

Chapter 12, "Creating a Symbol Library," concentrates on putting together a library of commonly used parts drawings. You find out how to extract information from the drawing for use by other programs, and how to access other drawings from within AutoCAD.

Chapter 13, "Customizing Basics," shows you how to be more effective with AutoCAD by reducing the number of keystrokes and commands you need to execute. Command aliases, script files, and menu macros help automate the drawing process.

Chapter 14, "An AutoLISP Primer," is a tutorial on AutoCAD's built-in programming language, AutoLISP. The chapter shows you how to enter AutoLISP commands at the keyboard, add AutoLISP to menu macros, and write your own AutoLISP programs.

Part Five: Drawing in Three Dimensions

With Release 10, AutoCAD gained true 3-D capabilities. Part Five discusses all the commands and functions that support three-dimensional drawing and editing, and examples show you how to use the 3-D commands. This part also introduces Autodesk's other graphics programs: the Advanced Modeling Extension, AutoShade, AutoFlix, Autodesk Animator, and Autodesk 3D Studio.

Chapter 15, "Understanding the Third Dimension," is an introduction to drawing in three dimensions. You learn how to create 3-D objects, how to view them from different angles, and how to make them look realistic. AutoCAD's User Coordinate System enables you to draw at any orientation in space.

Chapter 16, "Using AutoCAD's 3-D Drawing Tools," explains how to use the commands that reduce the effort required to draw in three dimensions. AutoCAD can automatically create a number of 3-D objects, including boxes, wedges, cylinders, spheres, and tori. The chapter shows you how to draw revolved and meshed surfaces.

Chapter 17, "Editing a 3-D Drawing," applies AutoCAD's 3-D editing commands to 3-D objects. The chapter shows you how to edit and break 3-D polylines and polymeshes.

Chapter 18, "Viewing a 3-D Drawing," illustrates AutoCAD's advanced viewing commands for 3-D drawings. You find out how to create perspective views and shaded renderings, and how to display the drawing in four different windows.

Chapter 19, "Plotting a 3-D Drawing," describes how AutoCAD Release 11 gives you complete flexibility for plotting several drawings on a single sheet of paper. The drawings can be 2-D or 3-D, with or without hidden lines removed.

Chapter 20, "Rendering and Animating," is an overview of other Autodesk graphical products, including AME for solids modeling, AutoShade and RenderMan for photo realistic shading and rendering, and AutoFlix, Animator, and 3D Studio for animation.

Part Six: Reference

AutoCAD Command Reference. This section is an alphabetical listing and explanation of the entire set of AutoCAD commands (excluding AutoLISP and ADE commands).

System Variable Reference. This section is a convenient reference to the variables that give you complete control over the AutoCAD drawing environment.

Where To Get Help. This section provides you with information on where to turn for help with AutoCAD. Here you will find a list of users' groups and ways to get answers if you run into trouble as you begin working with AutoCAD.

Troubleshooting Guide. This section identifies and offers solutions to problems you may encounter when using AutoCAD. When you are in trouble, this information can result in significant time savings.

Appendix A: Installing and Configuring AutoCAD. This appendix includes instructions for installing and configuring AutoCAD Release 11.

Appendix B: Useful Additional Programs. This is a list of supplemental programs that greatly enhance AutoCAD's power and flexibility.

Appendix C: Hatch Patterns. This appendix gives you graphical examples of the many hatch patterns available in AutoCAD. This information makes hatch selection much easier.

Appendix D: Linetypes. When you need to choose one of AutoCAD's linetypes for a certain portion of a drawing, this appendix can help you make the right selection.

Appendix E: Text Fonts. This appendix shows you samples of each of

AutoCAD's available text font styles, so that you can add various types of text to your drawings.

Appendix F: Button Assignments. This appendix lists the standard mouse and puck button assignments in AutoCAD.

Appendix G: File-name Extensions. AutoCAD makes use of several different file-name extensions. This appendix explains the meaning of each extension, to help you understand what each type of file contains.

Glossary. The glossary explains computer and CAD terms.

Summary

Using AutoCAD, 3rd Edition, is designed to help you become more productive in your use of AutoCAD. This book will familiarize you with CAD equipment and with AutoCAD's 2-D and 3-D commands. In addition, you will learn 3-D drafting and customization techniques, undoubtedly the most exciting aspects of AutoCAD.

Part One

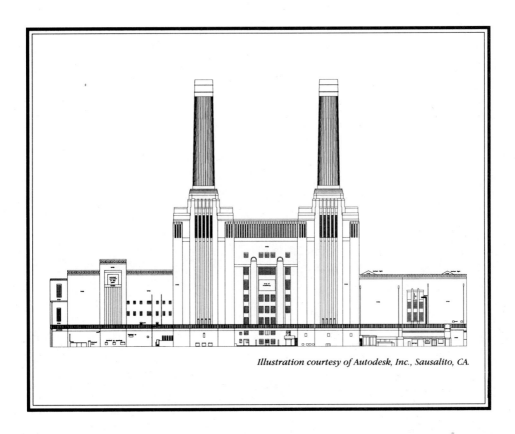

Illustration courtesy of Autodesk, Inc., Sausalito, CA.

CAD and Computer Basics

1

Manual versus Computer Drafting

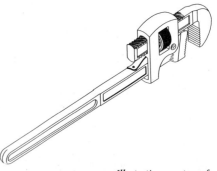

Illustration courtesy of Autodesk, Inc., Sausalito, CA.

Many firms are switching from manual drafting to computer-aided drafting (known as *CAD*). They are doing so for good reason. Computers offer many advantages over manual drafting tools. The differences between manual and computer drafting techniques are what make CAD productive for you and your company.

The purpose of this chapter is to illustrate the differences between manual and computer-aided drafting and to highlight the advantages CAD offers. To this end, this chapter discusses the following pros and cons of CAD:

❑ Flexibility

❑ Full-size drawing

❑ Precision drawing

❑ Design capabilities

❑ Templates and symbols

❑ Reusing previous work

❑ Quick changes

❑ Diversity and the multidiscipline drawing

❑ Final output

❑ Training

❑ Customization

When you have finished reading this chapter, you should be familiar with the similarities and differences between CAD and manual drafting, and the advantages each method offers.

Flexibility

One of the most important concepts in CAD is that it sets nothing in concrete, unlike the manual drawing process. If you need to change a drawing (or even the system itself), you can do so, and often in just seconds! AutoCAD is a dynamic environment, designed to be tailored to your specific needs. If you need to print detail drawings at different scales on the same sheet, AutoCAD can easily make the arrangement. If a building needs to be moved over a foot, you can move it in seconds. If a hatch pattern doesn't look right, you can modify it.

This flexibility places computer-aided drafting significantly ahead of manual drafting. As a result, electric erasers are going the way of slide rules. To create drawings, all you need is an understanding of the resources AutoCAD provides.

Full-Size Drawing

With manual drafting, the first thing you need to decide when you begin a new drawing is the scale. A gear may be drawn at a 5:1 scale, a floor plan at 1/8"=1'-0", a site plan at 1"=500'. In AutoCAD, you work with scale in two ways.

You can establish a drawing scale, as you would when drafting manually, if you want to draw details at different scales on one sheet. As you become more familiar with AutoCAD, however, you will find that drawing to scale does not take advantage of all the features CAD offers.

A better approach is to ignore the problem of scale and draw at 1:1, full size. If you choose this method, you don't have to worry about calculating the scaled measurements of everything you draw. When you are ready to plot your drawing, you tell AutoCAD the scale that will make the drawing fit the paper. If the scale doesn't matter, AutoCAD will fit the drawing to the paper for you.

You enjoy two advantages when you work at full scale. First, a full-scale drawing is easier to keep accurate than a scaled drawing. Say, for example, that you are creating a site plan for a house, and that you want to use a drawing scale of 1"=20'. If you draw at full scale, you tell AutoCAD to draw the garage wall 24'-4" long, and the wall is exactly 24'-4". If you were to draw to scale, you would first need to calculate how many inches 24'-4" would be at 1:240 scale (1.21666667 inches). Then you would have AutoCAD draw the line that length. Repeating such calculations over the course of an entire project becomes tiresome. It's far easier to let AutoCAD do the scaling for you at plotting time.

The second benefit has to do with what everyone else is doing. Most AutoCAD users have adopted the standard of working at full scale for all drawings. By doing so, they can take advantage of drawings and symbol libraries—which have been drawn at full scale created by other companies. If you work in something other than full-scale, you quickly isolate yourself from much of the AutoCAD community.

Precision Drawing

There are several conceptual differences between drawing by hand and drawing with a computer. One difference is drawing precision. Unless you take time to understand the concept, it can cause several problems when you begin working with AutoCAD.

When drawing manually, you probably start with a rough sketch and then fill in the details. Saying that a bolt will be about 1 inch long or that a wall will be about 16 feet long is good enough in manual drafting. You know that you will go back and finish the drawing with accurate dimensions. This method lets you produce a first draft quickly, but forces you to come back later to dimension your work. This takes time and, if a mistake slips through, can be costly. With a powerful tool like AutoCAD, you can do thumbnail sketches to have an idea of what you will draw, without running the risk of costly mistakes.

Drawing in AutoCAD is much easier if you draw precisely from the day you start using the program. AutoCAD is exact because it works to a precision of 16 decimal places (this system is called *double precision*). When you draw a 1-inch square in AutoCAD, it is exactly 1.0000000000000000 inches square. At the other extreme, AutoCAD's double precision enables you to work with very large drawings. If you want to draw the solar system full size, AutoCAD lets you. Not all CAD packages have this much accuracy and capacity.

As explained later in this chapter, CAD programs do not recognize lines and shapes in exactly the same manner as the human eye recognizes them. To AutoCAD, lines, shapes, and their many attributes are stored as numbers, calculations, and responses in a large database. When you draw a line, AutoCAD does not store or "see" the line itself; rather, the program sees the line as the product of a process, the results of which can be stored as data in the database. Certainly, this is an oversimplification of how a CAD program "thinks," but it should help you understand how AutoCAD can operate with such precision and at such an incredible capacity.

Because AutoCAD stores numbers so precisely within its database, the program accurately reflects any imperfections in your work. With AutoCAD, you can tell if one side of a 200-foot wall was drawn a fraction of an inch shorter than the other side, which is useful if you need to do clearance checking. Here are some advantages to such precision:

❑ Corner lines meet exactly.

❑ AutoCAD can dimension your drawing semiautomatically.

❑ Specific information, such as the square footage of office space, linear feet of steel beams, and the total number of bolts, can be extracted from the drawing.

❑ Conflicting elements are more obvious.

❑ Others can easily work with your drawings.

By taking advantage of AutoCAD's precision from the very first drawing, you will make your tasks much easier. The good news is that AutoCAD has many tools to help you draw precisely, and you will learn how to use these tools as you go through this book. You should not, however, let this knowledge keep you from using a sketch pad for your ideas. Many designers use pencil and paper for the creative process and then put their roughed-out ideas into AutoCAD, using precise dimensions. The more experienced you are as a designer and engineer, the easier you will find this method.

Design Capabilities

AutoCAD is much more than a computerized drafting machine. Auto-CAD's advanced modeling and dimensioning capabilities—as well as the ease with which it lets you "try and try again"—make the program an ideal tool for design work of all types.

AutoCAD's *undo* feature lets you try a new design and then erase it to try a variation, much like a "what-if" scenario on a spreadsheet. You can undo your work all the way back to the beginning of the design session.

AutoCAD also can draw *parametrically*, a process in which dimensions are replaced by variables. In a parametric drawing, the length, thickness, and radius of your design are not tied to specific measurements. Rather, you can give AutoCAD a list of dimensions and it redraws the design in different configurations.

With AutoCAD's three-dimensional and modeling capabilities, you can analyze your design visually and materially. Shadings and renderings make the proposed design look more realistic. All these capabilities take AutoCAD beyond ordinary drafting uses and into the realm of design.

Templates and Symbols

Every manual drafter uses dozens of plastic templates to produce accurate drawings quickly. Circle and ellipse templates, bathrooms and kitchens, steel shapes and shrubbery are all immortalized in plastic cutouts available from your local drafting supply store.

Every discipline has standard symbols: the center line of circles, the symbol that represents an electrical outlet, the pattern of a wooden parquet floor, a water valve, or a north arrow on a map are a few examples.

As you will see in Chapter 12, AutoCAD provides an easy way to insert predrawn graphic symbols within your drawings. You can create symbols yourself, or you can purchase libraries of symbols created by others. Symbol libraries are easier to use than the old-fashioned drafting templates because you no longer have to draw each symbol. You merely tell AutoCAD how big to draw the symbol and where to locate it.

Reusing Previous Work

When you use a computer-aided drafting system, one of the biggest boosts to your productivity is that you can reuse previous work in a new drawing. AutoCAD makes modifying an existing drawing easier than starting a new one. This saves hours of work, when compared with the manual method of redrawing previously drafted information.

Suppose, for example, that you are drawing the floor plans for a new 500-bed hospital, which contains two types of patient rooms—private and four-bed—and 100 rooms of each type. If you use AutoCAD, you need to draw each type of room only once. For each floor plan (and even for drawings of other hospitals), you can have AutoCAD redraw the rooms for you as often as necessary. You no longer need to redraw the same two rooms 100 times.

Tech Note . . .

A brief explanation of how AutoCAD sees drawings may help you understand how it can do this. AutoCAD stores drawings electronically. Every entity in the drawing is stored in a database as an individual piece of information. (An *entity* is a basic drawing element, such as a line, a circle, an arc, and so on.) When a line is stored in the program's database, for example, AutoCAD keeps track of the line's endpoints, its color, and line style. Information stored for a circle includes its center point and radius.

Tech Note (continued) . . .

Here is what the entity list for a circle looks like:

```
(
(-1 . <Entity name: 60000018>)
(0 . "CIRCLE")
(8 . "0")
(62 . 1)
(39 . 0.5)
(10 4.0 4.0 1.0)
(40 . 2.0)
)
```

This is the information AutoCAD reports for a circle on layer 0 drawn in red (color #1). The circle is 0.5 units thick and is centered at 4,4,1with a diameter of 2.0 units.

When you make changes to or duplicates of any part of a drawing, AutoCAD merely changes or duplicates the numbers associated with the affected entities. Until your drawing is plotted on paper, all the drawing information is simply a collection of electronic bits and bytes, held together by AutoCAD under a common file name (which may be as simple as ROOM-1.DWG). AutoCAD lets you reuse this electronic information in a tiny fraction of the time that would be required to redraw the drawing from scratch. Many examples similar to the hospital will become apparent as you work within the AutoCAD drawing environment.

Quick Changes

Things never go as smoothly as you would like. A drawing changes, notes are added, details are added and removed. After many revisions, you have spent a great deal of time on a single sheet of paper, compromising the quality of the final product.

A drawing in AutoCAD, on the other hand, can be changed quickly. If you want to change a detail that appears several times in a drawing, you can update every occurrence of the detail simultaneously. If you need to remove a detail, it is erased almost instantly. Parts can be moved around so that the drawing doesn't look cluttered. You can even alter the text size of notes with no disruption to the rest of the drawing. Manual drafting cannot duplicate the ease with which AutoCAD lets you modify your work and still produce a clean, easily read product.

Diversity and the Multidiscipline Drawing

A good drafter uses different line weights, unique text, and artistic license to make a drawing readable. In the early days of computer-aided drafting, drawings looked computer-generated. Now you can tailor AutoCAD to make drawings look hand-drawn or make them unusually clear to read. Undoubtedly, CAD excels in this area of drawing; one of its most important capabilities is its diversity.

CAD's diversity means that a drawing can contain any number of elements that best emphasize the ideas that you, the creator, are trying to convey. The typeface you use for titles can be different from that which you use for notes. You can use a hatch pattern that shows exactly how you want a brick sidewalk to look or to differentiate wood from stone.

As more firms of various disciplines (architecture, engineering, and others) collaborate on projects with AutoCAD, they find that they need to share electronic drawing files just as they used to share paper drawings. By using AutoCAD and by establishing common standards for all firms, everyone involved in the project builds on the same base of information. Large corporations and agencies now demand that contractors submit drawings in AutoCAD format and that the drawings follow their standards.

A *word about backing up your drawing files* . . .

Because AutoCAD stores drawings in the computer, they are "invisible" (at least until they are printed out on paper). There are times when you may lose the electronic form of a drawing, because you accidentally erase it, because your computer suffers a power outage or surge, or because part of the computer goes bad.

To prevent the possibility of losing your work, it is important to keep *backups*, or secondary copies of your drawing files. Fortunately, computers enable you to make additional copies of drawing files quickly and easily. Many firms create backups daily, storing the copies on floppy disks or computer tapes, and housing the backups somewhere off-site. Drawings on diskette (or other storage medium) take up less space and last longer than paper drawings. Further, electronic copies of drawings can be duplicated instantly; you can make a disk copy of a drawing and then make changes to it without making any paper copies, and without harming the original drawing in any way.

Even with backups, you can lose original work. If you ever lose an original disk file, you may be able to "get it back" by using one of several programs that attempt to recover erased and damaged drawing files (see Appendix B).

Final Output Considerations

Whether you are using AutoCAD or drafting manually, no drawing is complete until you hand it to the client. As an AutoCAD user, you have to be more sensitive to the timing involved. It is important that you schedule plotting jobs carefully, to avoid missing deadlines.

A difficult decision that a project manager must make is when to plot the project drawings. Some people think that the one plot produced at the end of the project will do. But because it's likely that your work will be reviewed during its development, and because people tend to be more comfortable looking at and scribbling on a paper drawing than they are with the video screen, you may have to produce check plots along the way.

In manual drafting, the drawing is complete when the drafter finishes with it. In CAD, because the drawing is still in electronic form when the drafter finishes, you have to allow for additional time before the end of the project to produce the final plots. Although plotters are getting faster, a pen plotter can take from 30 to 90 minutes to draw a complex drawing. The faster (and far more expensive) electrostatic plotter reduces this time to 5 minutes or less.

Several days may be required to plot a set of drawings for a large project. Remember to make allowances for final plotting as you schedule your project.

Training Considerations

The cost of training also must be taken into account when a company decides to set up a CAD system. A company should plan on making a substantial initial investment in training employees to use AutoCAD. Training can range from reading this book to taking week-long courses. Although there are many commercial training centers, in-house training is often better. Then there is the never-ending need to update this training to increase proficiency and incorporate AutoCAD's new features. Anyone who thinks "I already know everything I need to know about AutoCAD" is limiting his or her potential.

Training is available at Autodesk-accredited Authorized Training Centers, or you can hire an instructor to teach in your office. In either case, make sure that the instruction relates to your discipline. By reading books like this one, you can teach yourself time-saving techniques. The AutoCAD-specific magazines can keep you up to date with the latest advances in hardware and software.

Managers like to hear CAD users say that CAD can increase a drafter's productivity by 300 to 400 percent. Few managers can accept the fact, however, that about six months of training and practice are required to achieve the same level of productivity as realized in a manual drafting environment. For some kinds of drawings, productivity will remain at that level. Eventually, you may attain 4:1 productivity for drawings that use many repetitive elements or symbols. You should realize that, for a while, you probably will be faster on a drawing board than with AutoCAD.

As a rule, you can improve your productivity if you follow two concepts. First, concentrate on the basics. If you understand and feel comfortable with the commands you use frequently, you will be able to use AutoCAD effectively.

The second (and more important) way to improve productivity is customization. Learning to draw with a computer is more complex than learning to draw with a parallel bar and a triangle. AutoCAD's many tools make the drawing process semiautomatic. Because AutoCAD is faster and more accurate than you are, it makes sense that the more drawing AutoCAD can do for you, the more productive you will become.

Customization

AutoCAD has a great deal of built-in power, so you can use it "straight out of the box." More important, however, is the program's flexibility, which enables you to customize AutoCAD to the way you work.

You can make a single command do several things at once. You can rename commands. You can give commands different functions. You can create libraries of commonly used symbols that you simply add to your drawing without needing to redraw them. You can automate the drawing process so that you need only enter a part's dimensions and AutoCAD draws the part.

AutoCAD has so many settings and options that most people will never learn them all. Even this book does not attempt to explain everything about AutoCAD. For now, you should focus on the basics of AutoCAD. As you gain experience with the program, you may want to take advantage of its flexibility and openness, and create "your own" version of AutoCAD.

Summary

Almost anything you draw on a piece of paper can be drawn with a computer. As you have seen, computer-aided drafting can provide advantages that are not possible with a manual drawing system.

AutoCAD can draw frequently used symbols for you and can make quick changes to a drawing. Work that might take days of manual drafting can be reduced to hours with AutoCAD.

Nevertheless, don't let the outstanding advantages of AutoCAD blur your vision. You must weigh the advantages of high-technology drafting against the cost of the system, plotting time, and training considerations.

Chapter 2 looks more closely at the computer equipment used with AutoCAD.

2

CAD Equipment

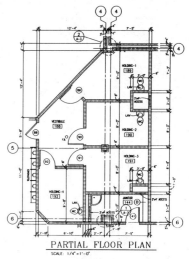

PARTIAL FLOOR PLAN
SCALE: 1/4" = 1'-0"

*Illustration courtesy of
Autodesk, Inc., Sausalito, CA.*

A CAD program is only as good as the hardware on which it runs. This chapter explains the hardware options available for your computer and describes the equipment typically used in a CAD system.

After you finish reading this chapter, you will be able to recognize your computer's major components (often called *peripherals*). You will have a basic understanding of the tasks these components perform and their usefulness to your CAD system.

The Computer Hardware

All computer systems feature one main "box," which coordinates the peripheral's activities and runs the software. The box typically measures about 2 feet wide by 8 inches high by 18 inches deep and houses the following components:

❑ The central processing unit (CPU), most commonly an Intel 80286, 80386, or 80486 chip

❑ Possibly a math (or numeric) coprocessor

❑ A hard disk

❑ One or two floppy disk drives

❑ The system memory (called *RAM*, for *random-access memory*)

❑ Several *expansion cards* that connect the computer to the disk drives, printer, plotter, and video screen

Figure 2.1 shows a typical computer system and a few of the listed components. The following sections examine each of these parts so that you can better understand each component's function.

Fig. 2.1.
A typical CAD
station.

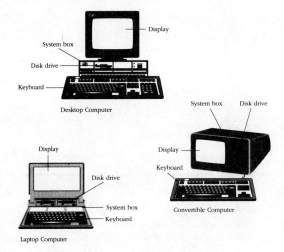

The Microprocessor (CPU)

The Microprocessor (CPU)

The computer's main processor—commonly called the *central processing unit*, or *CPU*—is located on the computer's *motherboard*. The motherboard has all the connections for the memory, expansion slots, keyboard, power supply, loudspeaker, and the CPU.

The main processor is the chip that does almost all the work in your computer. It translates instructions from your programs (requests for performing calculations, opening files, writing to the screen, managing the memory, and so on) into the hardware instructions needed to get the job done. As a program user, you do not need to understand what those instructions are—just rest assured that they work. If the software is properly written, your program will run smoothly.

For the most part, today's computers use one of three CPUs, which are designed by Intel, Motorola, and Sun. Computers that use the Intel 80286, 80386, and 80486 chips are most popular. With Release 11, AutoCAD no longer runs on a PC using the 8088 or 8086 CPU. The Motorola 68020 and 68030 CPU chips are used in Apple Macintosh, Sun, and Apollo computers. Some Sun computers use a new CPU called SPARC. The version of AutoCAD you can use depends on the type of CPU your system uses, as follows:

If your CPU is	You can use this version of AutoCAD Release 10
8088	DOS
8086	DOS
80286	DOS, OS/2
80386SX	DOS, OS/2, 386, SCO UNIX
80386	DOS, OS/2, 386, SCO UNIX
80486	DOS, OS/2, 386, SCO UNIX
68020	Mac, Sun, Apollo
68030	Mac, Sun, Apollo
SPARC	Sun

If your CPU is	You can use this version of AutoCAD Release 11
8088	None
8086	None
80286	286, OS/2
80386SX	386, OS/2, SCO UNIX
80386	382, OS/2, SCO UNIX
80486	386, OS/2, SCO UNIX
68020	Mac, Sun
68030	Mac, Sun
SPARC	Sun SPARC
VAX	DEC VAX

You can see that the computer with the 80386 or 80486 CPU offers the most options. Specific versions of AutoCAD are written for other computers, including Macintosh, Sun, Apollo, and DEC.

NOTE

There are several reasons for avoiding computers based on the Intel 80286 CPU. Intel, a developer and manufacturer of CPU chips, intends that all its future CPU designs will be compatible with the 80386, not the 80286. Operating systems such as OS/2 and Windows eventually will abandon the 80286. Although AutoCAD still supports 80286-based computers, Release 11 may be the last version to do so. The Advanced Modeling Extension will not be available with the 286 DOS version of Release 11.

The Math Coprocessor

To run AutoCAD, your computer may need one additional chip, called a *math* (or *numeric*) *coprocessor*. This chip, which is sometimes an option when you buy your system, performs the mathematical calculations AutoCAD requires. AutoCAD uses mathematical functions to locate intersections of lines, draw arcs, and calculate planes in three-dimensional space. *AutoCAD does not work without a math coprocessor.*

Other programs—mainly spreadsheet and mathematical analysis programs—also take advantage of the math coprocessor's capabilities. You probably will see this chip in many computers because it speeds up the throughput for these programs.

If your computer uses an Intel 80286 or 80386 CPU, it needs the corresponding 80287 or 80387 math coprocessor. Because Intel's 80486 CPU performs the functions of the math coprocessor, the computer does not require an additional chip. Similarly, all Macintosh computers include the math chip.

The Disk Drives

Your computer's operating system, the AutoCAD program, and your AutoCAD-based drawings all are stored in *files*. You will learn more about files in Chapter 3; for now, just remember that a computer file is a compilation of related information, reduced to code the computer can understand. When a file is in use in computer memory, the file's information is stored in memory chips as a series of tiny electronic pulses. The computer's memory, however, is only temporary; that is, when you shut off the computer, the memory's contents are lost. If you want to maintain a permanent copy of a file, therefore, you must store the file on a *disk*.

A computer disk is a flat disk covered with a magnetic medium. When you store a file on a disk (this process is called *saving* a file), the computer reads the file's contents from memory and translates the information into magnetic pulses. The data is recorded on the disk's magnetic surface via a tiny read-write head mechanism, in much the same way as information is recorded on cassette tape. Once a file is on disk, you can read it back into memory to use and modify it. You also can copy files from one disk to another.

Today's computers use two kinds of disks: *floppy disks* and *hard disks*. Generally, drawing files are stored on the hard disk. You can copy a file from the hard disk to a floppy disk to make a backup copy or to give a copy to a client.

Hard Disks

Typically, a computer's hard disk drive is built in; that is, the disk usually cannot be removed from your computer, as floppy disks can. Nevertheless, a hard disk offers a substantial advantage in data access speed and storage capacity. Hard disks have storage capacities ranging from 20M (megabytes) to 320M or more. A megabyte is equivalent to 1,048,576 bytes of information, or just a little less than one high-density (1.2M) floppy disk. Further, a typical hard disk can store or retrieve information 10 to 20 times faster than a floppy disk drive. In fact, some of the fastest hard drives can access data in as little as 15 or 18 milliseconds (*ms*). This means faster loading of drawing and data files, and faster execution of programs such as AutoCAD, which frequently access the disk.

The hard disk influences how well a computer can run AutoCAD. In fact, AutoCAD will not operate on a PC without a hard disk. The program reads and writes files many times to and from the hard disk. The AutoCAD program, its support files, and your drawing files use a great deal of space on the hard disk. AutoCAD Release 11 with the AME (Advanced Modeling Extension) option takes up about 10M of disk space. The size of an average drawing file is about 100K. A large project can take up 10M or 20M of disk space for drawings.

For best results with AutoCAD, your computer's hard disk should be large and fast. Consider buying a hard drive with a capacity of 80M or more, if you can afford it. Before you purchase a hard drive for your system, be sure to find out the unit's average access time; that is, the average amount of time the drive needs to read or write data. The difference between trying to work with an 18ms drive and an 80ms drive is incredible.

For more information on hard disks and hard-disk management, see *Using Your Hard Disk*, published by Que Corporation.

Floppy Disks

A floppy disk, or *diskette*, is a portable disk made of plastic. The storage capacity varies, as does the disk size (see fig. 2.2). Currently, 5 1/4-inch floppy disks (the most common format for PCs) are available in two capacities: a *double density* disk holds about 360K (approximately 360,000) bytes of information; a *high density* disk holds about 1.2M (1.2 million). The newer 3 1/2-inch disks hold either 720K (double density) or 1.44M (high density). Computers from Sun, Apollo, and DEC tend to use computer tapes rather than floppy disks.

A *word about mass-storage systems* . . .

Although you can use floppy disks to store backup copies of your drawings, you may eventually get frustrated with the floppy disks' slow speed. There are several alternatives available that make backups faster and more convenient. Because these alternatives hold many files, they are referred to as *mass-storage devices*.

Tape drives are the most common form of backup storage system, after floppy disks. You can install an *internal* tape drive inside the computer (this is the more convenient approach), or attach an *external* tape drive (if there isn't enough room inside the computer). Tape drives have capacities ranging from 40M to 120M. Most tape drives feature software that enables you to back up all files or selected files on your computer's hard disk. Users often set up their computer so that the backup occurs automatically after they leave for the day.

Removable hard drives are rugged, portable hard drives that can be removed from the computer. This feature makes them useful for sharing drawing files between computers, taking work home, and backing up your computer's fixed hard drive. Removable hard drives generally have capacities of 20M to 80M.

Bernoulli drives are like large floppy disks with the capacity of a hard drive (44M). They are more damage-resistant than removable hard drives. Bernoulli boxes have been around for many years; many firms have at least one.

WORM drives (short for *write-once read-many*) look like a 5 1/4-inch compact disk. A laser beam writes files to the disk, which you can read back. WORM drives are popular for their very large capacity (over 300M) and extreme durability.

Fig. 2.2.
A 5 1/4-inch and a 3 1/2-inch diskette.

A 5 1/4" disk

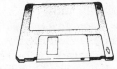

A 3 1/2" disk

Although these capacities may seem substantial (and there was a day when they were!), in modern personal computer CAD work, a large drawing can easily exceed the storage space of the lower-capacity disks. Two lines and a circle, for example, can take up 1.7K. Multiply those entities several hundred times and you can see that storage space fills up quickly as drawings become complex.

Distinguishing between a 3 1/2-inch disk and a 5 1/4-inch disk is easy, but how do you tell whether a disk is double density or high density? The 3 1/2-inch disks that hold 720K may be labeled *1M*, whereas 1.44M-capacity disks are often labeled *2M*. On both kinds of disks, the difference is shown by the letters *DD* (for *double density*) and *HD* (for *high density*) on the disk label. The difference is always reflected in the price.

Storage is not the only limitation of floppy disks; speed is a major drawback to any extensive use of floppy disks. The floppy disk is the slowest form of storage and retrieval on your system. You can read drawings from a floppy disk into AutoCAD, but your work will proceed much more quickly if you first copy the file to the hard disk and then read it into memory from there. As a result, floppy disks are used primarily for archiving purposes and for transferring information between computers.

Tech note . . .

If you have an IBM or compatible computer running DOS V3.3 or V4.0, you may think that your disks are compatible with everyone else's. Not so! Even though 360K disks (and 720K as well) may be a dying breed, there are still four standard disk formats (360K, 720K, 1.2M, and 1.44M), as mentioned previously. You also may come across some older IBM disks that hold only 160K, 180K, or 320K.

The variety of formats can pose a problem with data circulation. Many CAD offices—especially those that receive or send information to other firms—utilize every disk format. To avoid disk-compatibility problems, make sure that at least one computer has both a 5 1/4-inch and a 3 1/2-inch high-density floppy drive. This way, you will be able to read any of the four standard disk formats, because high-density floppy drives can read and write double-density disks as well as high-density disks.

Random-Access Memory (RAM)

Random-access memory (usually called *RAM*) is the area of the computer from which the program is executed. People often confuse RAM with the storage capacity of a hard disk. Perhaps the best way to explain it is that a hard disk holds your programs when they are not running and when your computer is turned off. When you want to start a program, it must be loaded from the hard disk into RAM and then executed. (Chapter 4 shows you how to start AutoCAD.) When you draw and edit with AutoCAD, your work is kept in RAM until you save it to disk. RAM is only a temporary electronic storage area, whose contents are lost when power is shut off.

Many IBM-compatible computer systems come with 1M or more of RAM. If you want to run AutoCAD Release 11 (or AutoCAD 386 Release 10), your PC should have at least 2M of RAM, and preferably 4M or more. AutoCAD uses all the memory for storing itself, the drawing file, and other files it may need. If there isn't enough room in RAM, AutoCAD automatically stores the remaining data on the hard disk, thus slowing down the program's operation. If your computer does not already have 4M or more of RAM, your AutoCAD work probably will be slow going. It's better to buy more memory than to work inefficiently because of a lack of memory.

Tech note . . .

PC-compatible computers make use of one or more of the following five types of random-access memory: *low*, *high*, *extended*, *EMS memory*, and *caching* memory. Each is useful for different reasons.

Low memory is the first 640K of RAM in which DOS allows most programs to run.

High memory is the RAM between 640K and 1M that DOS uses for its own purposes.

Extended memory is all memory beyond 1M that DOS normally cannot access; some programs (like AutoCAD 386) can access this memory.

EMS (*expanded memory specification*) memory is a special type of paged memory first designed for Lotus 1-2-3, but now used by many programs.

Caching memory is a small amount of high-speed memory. This memory (about 32K to 128K in size) is expensive, but it enables AutoCAD to run about 25 percent faster than on a comparable computer without this type of memory. If your computer uses 32K of caching memory, it is said to have a 32K *memory cache*.

If your 80386 or 80486 computer has 4M of RAM, it contains 640K of low memory, 384K of high memory, and 3M of extended memory.

Tech note (continued) . . .

AutoCAD Release 11 and AutoCAD 386 Release 10 load most of themselves into extended memory. AutoCAD Release 10 loads most of itself into low memory but can use up to 4M of extended or EMS memory for storing parts of the drawing that don't fit into low memory.

All versions of AutoCAD temporarily store themselves or parts of the drawing on the hard disk if the computer does not have enough available RAM. This is not desirable, however, because AutoCAD works more slowly. The solution is to add more RAM to the computer.

The Video Screen

The video screen (usually called the *monitor*) is an integral part of AutoCAD. The proper video screen can make a significant difference in your productivity as a CAD user. Video screens range in size from 12 to more than 21 inches; the typical monitor used with CAD measures 19 inches diagonally.

Video cards and screens can display different resolutions that affect their look. Monochrome screens (generally white, green, or amber on black) offer better resolution at lower cost than color. The following resolutions are available in monochrome:

Category	Resolution	Name
Medium	720x348	Hercules
	640x480	Monochrome VGA
High	1024x768	Full page
Ultra-high	1600x1200	Double page

Because the output is often plotted only in black, some users see no need for the extra expense of a color monitor.

Color cards and screens offer a variety of resolutions and colors that are limited only by your budget. Those colors and resolutions boil down to the following basic categories:

Category	Resolution	Name
Low	640x200	CGA
	640x350	EGA
Medium	640x480	VGA
	800x600	Super VGA
High	1024x768	Extended VGA, 8514/A
	1280x1024	
Ultra-high	1600x1200	
	2048x2048	

A *word about resolution* . . .

The quality of output from a graphics board, plotter, or printer is called *resolution*. If the device offers good resolution, circles and diagonal lines look smooth. Resolution is measured differently for each type of output device.

For graphics boards, resolution is measured according to the number of *pixels* per line and the number of horizontal lines that can be displayed on-screen. A single pixel (short for picture element) is the smallest dot the graphics board can display. The more lines and pixels, the higher the resolution and the better the display. The most common resolution, 640x480, means that the graphics board can display 640 pixels on 480 lines.

The resolution of plotters is measured in steps per inch. This indicates how short a line the plotter can accurately draw. The shorter the line, the higher the resolution. Most plotters have a resolution of 1,000 steps per inch, which is sometimes listed as 0.001".

The resolution of printers is measured in dots per inch (dpi). Printers lay down a series of dots on the paper; the closer together the printer can place the dots, therefore, the higher the resolution. Most printers have a resolution of 120 dots per inch, although many laser printers offer resolutions of 300 dots per inch or more.

Low-Resolution Graphics

IBM's *Color/Graphics Adapter*, or *CGA*, is the original graphics device for the PC. At its highest resolution (640x200), a CGA screen is limited to monochrome. With AutoCAD Release 11, the CGA graphics board is no longer directly supported. IBM's *EGA (Enhanced Graphics Adapter)* has somewhat higher resolution (640x350) and can display 16 colors simultaneously.

Hercules Computer Technology has a monochrome graphics board (also called the HGC) that continues to be popular for budget computer systems. It displays 720x348 resolution on low-cost monochrome monitors. Many graphics programs, including AutoCAD and AutoShade, typically support most of IBM's graphics boards and the Hercules board.

Medium-Resolution Graphics

The *video graphics array*, or *VGA*, has become the standard color video card in use today. Invented by IBM, VGA offers a higher resolution (640x480) with 16 colors. At lower resolution, it can display up to 256 colors at once; on a monochrome monitor, it can display 64 shades of gray.

Other manufacturers have copied the VGA and improved its capabilities. *Super VGA* boards display up to 800x600 in 16 or 256 colors, whereas *extended VGA* boards display up to 1024x768 resolution in 16 or 256 colors. Extended VGA is useful for displaying AutoCAD in high resolution and AutoShade in full color. You need a monitor capable of multiple scan rates (such as the MultiSync monitor invented by NEC) to display both the high and the regular resolution of a VGA board.

AutoCAD's user interface may not work with some older graphics boards. If the program's pop-down menus and dialogue boxes are important to you, ask the supplier whether the graphics board supports the AUI (*Advanced User Interface*) feature. Almost all newer graphics boards support the AUI.

High-Resolution Graphics

IBM's standard for high-resolution graphics is named the *8514*, after the monitor it works with. The 8514 displays 1024x768 in 16 colors; the 8514/A model features extra memory so that it can display 256 colors. Other manufacturers have copied the 8514/A to make it more easily available.

Several other standards exist for displaying graphics at 1024x768 or 1280x1024 resolution. Many high-resolution graphics boards use TIGA-340 (*TI graphics architecture*), a standard promoted by Texas Instruments. Others use DGIS (*direct graphics interface standard*), PGL (*professional graphics language*) or a proprietary method.

Some graphics boards, including IBM's 8514, use an *interlaced* display on the monitor. This lets the board designer use a lower-cost monitor for high-resolution display. Unfortunately, interlacing causes flicker, particularly on a light-colored background, that can bother the CAD operator. The same graphics board may display lower-resolution graphics in *noninterlaced* mode. When you buy a graphics board, make sure that it uses noninterlaced graphics at the resolution you plan to use.

Ultra High-Resolution Graphics

You can purchase graphics boards and monitors that display AutoCAD at 1600x1200 or higher resolution. In monochrome, such systems are cost-effective and especially popular for desktop publishing. In color, such systems are rare and extremely expensive. You may not even notice the difference between ultra-high and high resolution.

Selecting a Graphics Board

You should keep five criteria in mind when selecting a graphics board: resolution, colors, speed, extra features, and price. The competition is so intense between board manufacturers that—for AutoCAD users—differences between monitors may be measured only in terms of extra features.

Resolution and Color

Several years ago, only expensive graphics boards could provide high-resolution graphics (1024x768) or display 256 colors simultaneously. Today, the Extended VGA board provides the same resolution and number of simultaneous colors. (If you need to create special renderings that require an even wider variety of colors, you can buy a more expensive board that displays as many as 16.7 million colors.)

Speed

The graphics board's design has an effect on how fast AutoCAD can display its graphics. In the days of 8088- and 80286-based computers, the expensive graphics boards proved to be much faster than EGA or VGA graphics boards in displaying AutoCAD graphics. High-end boards had their own very fast CPU chip, whereas the EGA and VGA graphics boards relied on the computer's relatively slow CPU. This has changed in recent years. In computers that use the 80386 and 80486 CPU, the VGA graphics board is now just as fast as the high-end boards but far less expensive. For practical purposes, therefore, speed should no longer be a primary consideration when choosing a graphics board or monitor.

Extra Features

Because resolution, colors, and speed are the same for most graphics boards, today's graphics adapters are distinguished from one another by their features. The expensive graphics boards tend to include features that are an extra-cost option on Extended VGA boards. These features include display-list processing, bird's-eye view, color toggling, and instant access to frequently used commands. You may find these features useful for working in AutoCAD, or you may find that they get in the way.

> **Tech note . . .**
>
> *Display-list processing* is a technology that enables AutoCAD to do accelerated zooms and pans. The graphics board stores the *display list* (a list of the entities appearing on-screen) in EMS memory. Whenever you ask AutoCAD to zoom or pan, the graphics board intercepts the command and substitutes its own faster zoom or pan. Display-list processing has become so common that it is now considered a standard feature in graphics boards (both Extended VGA and high-end) used for AutoCAD. If your VGA board does not include display-list processing, you can purchase this feature as a separate software option.

Price

You no longer need to spend a great deal of money on a graphics board. Extended VGA graphics boards are inexpensive and match the high-end boards in resolution, colors, and speed. Color monitors, however, have not decreased in price as dramatically as graphics boards; the monitor's cost may limit how much resolution you can afford.

As you might expect, the higher the resolution, the more expensive the graphics board and monitor. The price difference between low- and medium-resolution graphics is so slight that there is no longer any reason to purchase a CGA or EGA board. (The higher-resolution boards often include the lower-resolution standards for compatibility.) On the other hand, ultra-high resolution is so much more expensive than high resolution that the extra resolution may not be cost-effective for your firm.

Input Devices

AutoCAD supports many different input devices. The most commonly used input devices for AutoCAD work are keyboards, mice, and digitizing tablets.

Each of these devices has good and bad points; all have features that make them acceptable as AutoCAD input devices. Later chapters show you how to use these devices for input into AutoCAD.

The Keyboard

The keyboard's advantage over any other input device is that every computer has one; it is not an additional piece of equipment that must be bought to work with your CAD package. Figure 2.3 shows a typical computer keyboard. Keyboards are most useful for typing commands and numbers. You can use the keyboard's cursor-movement keys to move AutoCAD's on-screen cursor, but cursor control is much easier with the aid of a mouse or digitizing tablet. This is especially true in Release 10; if you use Release 10, you will find pointing with the cursor keys a slow process.

Fig. 2.3.
A keyboard.

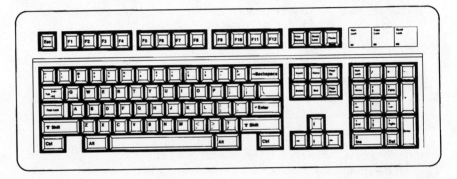

If you use AutoCAD Release 11, you can take advantage of a new feature called "command aliasing." Aliasing enables you to reduce a command to a single keystroke, allowing more productive use of the keyboard.

Keyboards are being designed for greater flexibility. Some computer systems have special keyboards that are part "normal" keyboard and part trackball or digitizing pad. When used with CAD and computer paint programs, these new keyboards combine normal keyboard input with the ease of graphic drawing.

Mice

The mouse has become the second "keyboard" of the 1990s, thanks in part to the incredible usefulness that mice have shown with Macintosh computers. The mouse is the preferred method of input in IBM operating systems such as Windows and OS/2, and in any graphics program.

The mouse was originally designed by Xerox at the Palo Alto Research Center in the early 1970s. Since then, mice have crept into almost every aspect of computer use. Some computers (most notably the Macintosh) are designed to work most quickly if a mouse, rather than the keyboard, provides the input.

The look of a mouse is pretty much standard. It looks like a bar of soap with a cord connecting it to your computer. Mice usually have one, two, or three buttons for command input (see fig. 2.4). Most mice are *mechanical* mice; a small ball on the underside allows the computer and its software to track the mouse's movements. An alternative design, called the *optical* mouse, tracks movement by light reflected from a special pad to the mouse's sensors, which are located on the mouse's underside.

Fig. 2.4.
A mouse.

Digitizing Tablets

Of all input devices, the digitizer is the one used most with AutoCAD. The digitizer not only controls the cursor (like a mouse) but also can be used for entering commands and tracing drawings.

A digitizer is a large flat pad that emulates the screen. With this pad, you use a *puck* (which looks like a mouse). As you move the puck across the surface of the digitizer, wires in the pad track the puck's movements.

Digitizers vary in size from the typical 12-inch-by-12-inch tablet (see fig. 2.5) to tablets that measure 48 inches by 60 inches. The larger digitizers are used for tracing existing plans into the computer. If you use a small digitizer, you will need to trace the paper drawing in small pieces and match the parts together later. Small tablets are more common because they require less room.

Fig. 2.5.
A 12-inch-
by-12-inch
digitizing
tablet with a
four-button
puck.

You can use a puck or a *stylus* with the digitizer. The puck is like a small mouse. Most have 4 buttons, but models are available with 12 or 16 buttons. A stylus looks like a large pen, with a button on the side and another built into the tip. The stylus is used mostly for freehand drawing.

When you register your copy of AutoCAD, Autodesk sends you a bonus package that includes a plastic overlay template. When you place the overlay on top of the digitizer, it lets you enter any AutoCAD command simply by picking the command's icon with the puck or stylus.

Tech note . . .

There is a significant difference between using a mouse and a digitizer with AutoCAD. The difference involves the way each input device controls the screen cursor.

A mouse uses *relative* movement. You move the AutoCAD cursor by moving the mouse. It doesn't matter where the mouse is positioned. If you lift the mouse and put it down in a different place on your desk, AutoCAD isn't aware of the change.

The digitizer uses *absolute* movement. Moving the puck also moves the AutoCAD cursor, but the position of the puck does matter. If you pick up the puck and put it down in a different position on the pad, AutoCAD instantly moves the cursor to the corresponding position on-screen because the pad's sensors detect the puck's new location.

This is why a mouse cannot be used for tracing drawings and why a digitizer can.

Other Input Devices

Many other input devices can be used with AutoCAD. Each type of device has its own unique advantages but also has enough disadvantages to make it less popular than the mouse, digitizing tablet, or keyboard.

Joysticks are inexpensive but have the aura of being used with computer games. A joystick is awkward for controlling the cursor.

Trackballs use less space than a mouse or tablet; moving the cursor with a track ball is a bit more difficult than with a mouse.

Touch screens are special screens that sense where your finger touches. Their resolution is too low for CAD use.

Stereoscopic screens let you see drawings with true depth but require you to wear special glasses.

Light pens were popular in AutoCAD's early days, but your arm tires from holding the pen against the screen.

Speech input is extremely fast for AutoCAD commands but slow for numerical data, such as coordinates.

Keypads are available in 20- and 300-button configurations. They let you pick commands as you would with a digitizer, but you can still use your mouse.

Many-button mice with 6 or 20 buttons let you perform more functions than the traditional two- or three-button mouse. The difficulty comes in learning the functions of the many buttons.

Sonic digitizers sense the puck's location by ultrasonic waves. Some models enable you to input three-dimensional data.

Cyberspace lets you enter a computer-generated stereoscopic environment of your design. This technology is still in its infancy.

Choosing an Input Device

Almost all input devices are compatible with AutoCAD. Most digitizers are compatible with the Summagraphics tablet, the de facto digitizing-tablet communications standard. All mice and most digitizers are compatible with the Microsoft Mouse, the de facto mouse communications standard.

Most AutoCAD users have either a mouse or a digitizing tablet as their input device. If you need to digitize paper drawings or pick commands from an overlay, you should use a digitizer. Otherwise, the mouse is the better choice because it costs far less.

The other consideration is the number of buttons on the input device. The device needs at least two buttons: a pick button and an Enter button. If a device has additional buttons, AutoCAD can use as many as 16 of them. The three-button mouse, four-button puck, and two-button stylus are the most commonly used.

Output Devices

As you work on your drawing, and once it is finished, you need to print or plot it on some form of *hard copy* (paper, vellum, or Mylar). Many different kinds of output devices can be attached to your computer and used with AutoCAD. This section describes the following output devices:

❏ Dot-matrix printers

❏ Laser printers

❏ Pen plotters

❏ Electrostatic and thermal plotters

Dot-Matrix Printers

Dot-matrix printers have many uses in computer applications. These low-cost printers print text and graphics as a series of dots; hence the name. The more dots the printer can print, the clearer your characters and pictures will be.

The two basic types of dot-matrix printers are 9- or 24-pin printers (see fig. 2.6). The number of pins in the print head determines how well circles and arcs will be printed. Those printed with a 9-pin printer tend to look jagged; circles and arcs printed with a 24-pin printer look smoother because more dots are printed closer together.

*Fig. 2.6.
A dot-matrix
printer.*

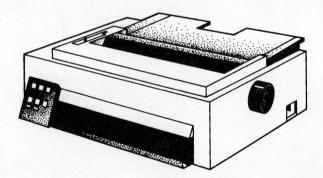

Dot-matrix printers can print in black-only or in color, and on A-, B-, or C-size paper. The resolution range is from under 72 dpi (*dots per inch*) to 360 dpi.

Laser Printers

Laser printers, like dot-matrix printers, use a series of dots to make up characters and pictures. Laser printers, however, operate at speeds that conventional dot-matrix printers cannot match. Laser printers commonly print at 300 dpi resolution (more densely than dot-matrix printers) and most are limited to A-size media, although some models have a resolution of 600 dpi or can use B-size paper. The laser printer uses a dry toner (similar to that used in photocopiers) that adheres to plain paper.

Laser printers often are used for check plots, A-size final plots, or for desktop publishing. The typical laser printer looks like the one shown in figure 2.7.

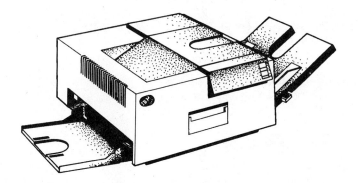

Fig. 2.7.
A laser
printer.

Pen Plotters

Pen plotters offer the highest-quality output, by using an ink pen to produce a hard copy of your AutoCAD drawing. Pen plotters offer resolutions of 1,000 steps per inch or higher, making all circles and arcs as smooth as possible, even to the most discriminating eye.

Pen plotters can be used with different pen types (felt tip, ballpoint, liquid ink, and even pencil) and sizes (0.005 inch and larger). AutoCAD maps its colors to different pens when performing a plot. This enables you to produce plots with different line widths or colors. A pen plotter does not limit you to one line weight or color for the whole plot, as do most other output devices.

Pen plotters also give you the flexibility of plotting onto different media of different sizes. All media you use with manual drafting (bond, vellum, and Mylar) are available for pen plotters. On most pen plotters designed for CAD, you can plot any sheet size up to 24 inches by 36 inches (D-size); on a few, you can plot up to 36 inches by 48 inches (E-size) and even longer, if you buy a roll-feed plotter.

Electrostatic and Thermal Plotters

Electrostatic plotters and *thermal plotters* work like laser printers. All are raster devices that are incredibly fast at producing plots. Plots that might take an hour on a pen plotter will take less than five minutes on an electrostatic or thermal plotter. This speed, however, comes at a price: electrostatic and thermal plotters are the most expensive kinds of plotters.

An electrostatic plotter applies a high voltage to specially treated paper to create an electrostatic charge. The paper passes over liquid toner, which attaches to the charged areas. A heater dries the toner to create a permanent image. For color plots, the process repeats four times.

A thermal plotter applies small charges of electricity to specially treated paper, which heats up and turns black, forming the image. Thermal plotters produce only monochrome or two-color plots.

Electrostatic and thermal plotters can plot at resolutions of 100 to 400 dpi; both can plot up to E-size images.

Other Output Devices

You can use several other types of output devices with AutoCAD; one of the following devices may suit you better than any of the output options already described:

Ink-jet printers are similar to dot-matrix printers but squirt a fine jet of ink against the paper. Ink-jet printers are the quietest output device you will find, and they are available in black-only or in color.

Thermal wax plotters melt a thin layer of wax against the medium. These plotters quickly produce color A- or B-size plots but are expensive.

Slide recorders, the highest-resolution (up to 4096x4096) output device, produce slide pictures or Polaroid prints of your drawing directly from the computer.

Silver halide printers use a process similar to camera film to produce high-resolution color A-size prints.

Laser plotters, an E-size version of the laser printer, produce fast, crisp monochrome plots but are extremely expensive.

Choosing a Plotter

The plotter you select depends on the kind of plotting you need to do. For learning AutoCAD and doing check plots, a low-cost dot-matrix printer is fine. For technical publishing or other A-size plots, a laser printer is the best choice.

For small-volume large-format plotting, a pen plotter is appropriate. For large-volume large-format plotting, an electrostatic or thermal plotter will pump out completed drawings most quickly.

AutoCAD works with almost all plotters and printers. Most dot-matrix printers are compatible with Epson. Most laser printers are compatible with HP LaserJet (also known as PCL) or PostScript. Most pen and electrostatic plotters are compatible with HP Graphics Language (HPGL). AutoCAD supports all these standards.

To help you better understand output quality, figures 2.8 to 2.10 are plots from a dot-matrix printer, a laser printer, and a pen plotter, respectively. By comparing them, you will see the difference in resolution and quality.

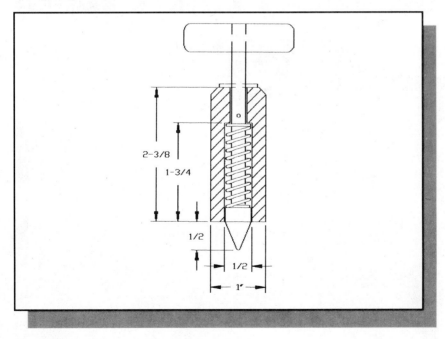

Fig. 2.8.
A plot from a
dot-matrix
printer.

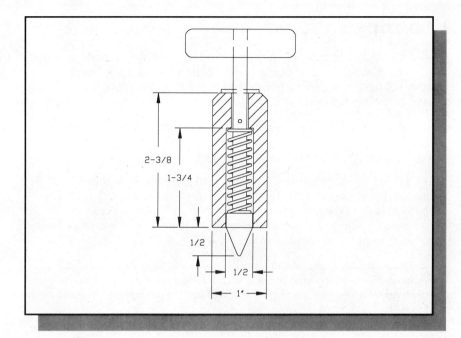

Fig. 2.9.
*A plot from a
laser printer.*

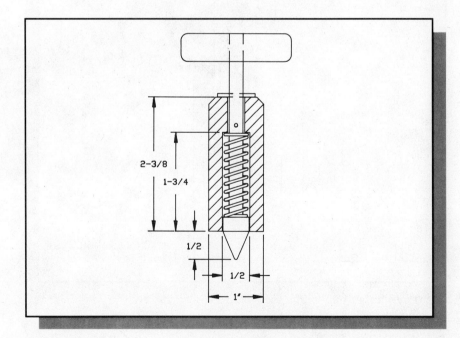

Fig. 2.10.
*A plot from a
pen plotter.*

Minimum and Recommended AutoCAD Systems

With so many hardware options available for building an AutoCAD system, you may want to consider the sample specifications in table 2.1. The "basic" system is all you need if you don't use AutoCAD much; the "recommended" system is for those who use AutoCAD all day long. (Remember that these sample specifications are for your use in comparison shopping, when purchasing or upgrading your AutoCAD system. The sample specifications are in no way an endorsement of any particular product or products).

Table 2.1
Sample Specifications for "Basic" and
"Recommended" AutoCAD Systems

Specification	Basic	Recommended
CPU	80386SX	80486
Speed	16MHz	33MHz
Math chip	80387SX	Included
Operating system	DOS V3.3	DOS V3.3
Hard disk	40M 28ms	110M 18ms
Floppy drive	1.2M	1.2M and 1.44M
RAM	4M(*)	8M
Graphics board	HGC	Extended VGA
Monitor	Monochrome	MultiSync to 1024x768
Input device	Mouse	12"x18" tablet
Output device	Dot-matrix printer	E-size pen plotter or PostScript laser printer

(*) AutoCAD Release 10 for DOS works with a minimum of 512K RAM.

Summary

This chapter explains each piece of hardware in your CAD system and its function. Armed with this knowledge, you can start taking advantage of these devices to speed up your work and produce output for your firm and your clients.

Chapter 3 explains your computer's operating system and some of its basic commands.

Illustration courtesy of
Autodesk, Inc., Sausalito, CA.

3

Operating Systems

Whether you like the thought or not, you must deal (at least occasionally) with your computer's operating system. This chapter covers operating system commands and operations that are important to today's CAD stations, and which you will use specifically with AutoCAD or any other PC-based application. If you already are comfortable using your computer's operating system, go on to the next chapter.

This chapter covers the three most common operating systems under which AutoCAD runs:

❑ MS-DOS (or PC DOS)

❑ OS/2

❑ UNIX

If your CAD station requires another operating system (such as VAX/VMS, Mac/OS, or AEGIS), the information in this chapter does not apply to you.

IBM originally provided its customers with PC DOS (which stands for *Personal Computer Disk Operating System*) as the operating system for IBM personal computers. Soon after the advent of the IBM PC, Microsoft developed MS-DOS (which stands for *Microsoft Disk Operating System*) for use with IBM-compatible computers. MS-DOS and PC DOS are essentially the same. DOS V4.0 includes an optional windowing interface, called the *DOS Shell*, which may make DOS easier for you to use.

Operating System/2, or OS/2, is a newer, DOS-compatible operating system (developed by IBM in 1987) that lets you run several programs at the same time in a process known as *multitasking*. OS/2 includes *Presentation Manager*, a windowing interface that makes OS/2 far easier to use than DOS. The original version of OS/2 required an 80286 computer. The most recent version, V2.0, requires an 80386 computer with 4M of RAM.

55

The UNIX operating system was developed in the 1960s by AT&T. UNIX is very popular on minicomputers and work stations, because it enables several users to run several programs simultaneously (the process is known as *multiuser multitasking*). UNIX is available for PCs under the name SCO UNIX (previously called SCO XENIX).

Even if your computer uses OS/2 or UNIX, read the sections about MS-DOS. The three operating systems have related functions. Of the three, MS-DOS is the easiest to learn.

About Operating Systems

Computers would be expensive paperweights if there were no programs to tell them what to do. Chapter 2 discussed hardware ranging from monitors to computers to mice. The computer, the keyboard, and the monitor are hardware. *Software* is the program (provided on floppy disks) that interacts with the hardware to perform a certain task or variety of tasks. The AutoCAD program is software.

Just as AutoCAD lets you draw with your computer, the operating system (also software) acts as the moderator between AutoCAD and the computer. If your computer could not run MS-DOS, OS/2, UNIX, or another type of operating system, you would not be able to access any of the data or programs stored on your disks. Among other things, the operating system permits you to do the following:

❑ Store and organize information
❑ Use the keyboard, mouse, or digitizing tablet to control your software's operations
❑ Transfer data and programs from one disk to another
❑ Run programs, such as AutoCAD

AutoCAD uses the operating system to read and write files to and from the hard disk, and to read input from the keyboard and mouse. In order to speed up its operation, AutoCAD actually bypasses the operating system when it draws on the graphics screen and sends a drawing to the plotter.

The operating system itself will not do certain things for you—it won't draw, do mathematical calculations, or compose music. It simply provides a foundation of basic capabilities so that you and your applications programs can interact with the computer.

If you are new to computers, you probably already have heard horrifying stories about getting hopelessly lost in an operating system, but you need to realize that the operating system will not bite you. Just keep repeating: "The operating system is good. The operating system is my friend."

Any operating system, however, shows little patience or mercy if you type the wrong thing. The following two operating system commands may look very much alike, for example, but are substantially different:

DIR C:*.DWG
DEL C:*.DWG

The first command displays a list of all the drawings stored on your computer's hard disk; the second command erases them. These kinds of commands and their dangers are discussed in the following sections. If you have some experience with an operating system, you probably are aware of the disasters that can result from issuing a command incorrectly. If you are new to computers and operating systems, keep in mind the following caveat: Don't issue a command until you have read about it first. Keep your computer's manuals handy, and seek advice from an experienced computer user before you use a command you are not familiar with.

A *word about upper- and lowercase letters* . . .

It is important to realize that when you are working with MS-DOS or OS/2 file names and commands, you can use upper- or lowercase letters. If you want the operating system to display a list of files, you can type **DIR**, **Dir**, or **dir**. Both operating systems always interpret the characters you type as uppercase.

AutoCAD works in a similar fashion. If you want to work on a drawing called SUITE, you can type **SUITE**, **Suite**, or **suite**.

UNIX, however, is different. It is *case-sensitive*, and considers a command typed in lowercase to be different from the same word typed in uppercase. To list files, you must type **ls**; **LS** or **Ls** won't work. In general, UNIX expects all commands, including AutoCAD commands, to be typed in lowercase.

About MS-DOS

You interact with almost any program, including AutoCAD, by giving it commands. MS-DOS is no exception to this rule. This section explains some commands MS-DOS recognizes, and what these commands do. Not all MS-DOS commands are covered here—only those commands you need to understand as a CAD operator. The commands are separated into the following areas of usage:

❏ Commands that control files
❏ Commands that affect the directory structure

❏ Commands that influence disks

❏ Commands that enable you to "talk" with your hardware

For complete coverage of MS- and PC DOS, see *Using DOS*, published by Que Corporation.

When DOS is ready for your commands, it displays the following characters, called the *C prompt*, on-screen:

```
C:>
```

The C: indicates that your computer is running DOS from the hard disk. The greater-than symbol (>) indicates that the operating system is ready to receive a command.

Throughout this book, the characters *C:* are used to designate the computer's hard disk drive. If your computer's hard drive has been assigned a different designator—such as D:, E:, or F:—substitute the correct letter for the C: shown in the examples.

Other operating systems display other prompts. If you are using OS/2 without Presentation Manager, you may see the following prompt:

```
[C:>]
```

If you use UNIX, you probably will see a hash mark:

```
#
```

The words "may" and "probably" are used here because all three operating systems let you change the appearance of the prompt. The prompts described here are the *default* prompts; that is, they are the prompts provided automatically by the operating system if no changes have been made.

Commands that Influence Files

The term *file* applies to anything on a disk. In simple terms, a file is a collection of related data. If you use a word processor, you store each of your documents in its own file on a disk (either the hard disk or a floppy disk). If you use a spreadsheet program, you store each worksheet in its own file. Software programs also are contained in files. AutoCAD's command routines, device drivers, and support data are stored in separate but related files. When you create an AutoCAD drawing, you store it in a file.

The MS-DOS commands covered here include DIR, COPY, RENAME, and ERASE. (These names also apply to the OS/2 commands; most of the equivalent UNIX commands, however, have different names). These commands give you control over the files on your disks. You will use these commands to create, modify, manage, and destroy your files. Some of these commands can be accessed from within AutoCAD. From AutoCAD's Main Menu, press **6** for File Utilities.

Understanding Files

Everything stored on disk is stored in either a program file or a data file. *Programs* are files that do work (like AutoCAD, a word processor, or a spreadsheet program); programs process the information stored in data files. As mentioned previously, a data file might contain a drawing, letter, or worksheet.

All files have names and are referred to by name. If, for example, you use AutoCAD to draw the floor plan of a bathroom, you might store the drawing's data in a file named BATHROOM.DWG. As this example shows, a file name can have two parts, which are separated by a period. The first part of the file name is called the *root name*, and tells you what is in the file. (If you see a file named BATHROOM, you should have a good idea of what the file contains.) DOS and OS/2 limit the root name to a maximum of eight characters.

The second part of the file name, called the *extension*, tells you what type of file you are dealing with. DOS and OS/2 limit the extension to a maximum of three characters. In the file name BATHROOM.DWG, the DWG extension tells you that the file is a data file that contains the information for a drawing. If a file has an EXE or COM extension, then it it an executable program file. The main AutoCAD program file, for example, is ACAD.EXE. (For more information on file-name extensions in AutoCAD, see Appendix G.)

Generally, you should never need to change the name of a program file. You have a great deal of freedom, however, when it comes to naming data files. When you *save* a file (that is, when you store its contents on disk), AutoCAD lets you give the file any root name you like; AutoCAD automatically supplies the extension.

Changing a File's Name (RENAME or REN)

You use the RENAME command (or REN, for short) to change the name you have given a file. Suppose that you have a drawing file called FLOOR2.DWG and that you want to change the name to indicate that it is the plan of the first, not the second, floor. To change the name to FLOOR1.DWG, type the following command at the C:> prompt:

REN FLOOR2.DWG FLOOR1.DWG

The preceding example assumes that the file resides on the computer's hard disk, named drive C. Suppose, however, that the file resides on a floppy disk. To change the file's name, insert the disk in drive A and type the following command at the C:> prompt:

REN A:FLOOR2.DWG A:FLOOR1.DWG

Although you can use the RENAME command to change the name of a specific file, you cannot use it to change a file's location or to create multiple copies of a file. You need to use the COPY command for these functions.

Copying Files (COPY)

If you need to copy a drawing file from your hard disk to a floppy disk, or vice versa, use the COPY command. COPY lets you copy a file from one disk to another disk, or from one directory to another directory on the same disk (directories are explained shortly). COPY is probably the second-most used MS-DOS command. Suppose that you want to copy the SUITE.DWG file from your hard disk (drive C) to a floppy disk in drive A. The following command does the job:

COPY C:SUITE.DWG A:

Or, if you need to copy the file from a floppy disk to the hard disk, type the command this way:

COPY A:SUITE.DWG C:

After copying the file, MS-DOS displays the following message:

```
1 File(s) copied
```

Removing Files (ERASE or DEL)

From time to time, you need to delete unneeded files to make room for active drawings on a disk. Although a 100M hard disk may seem large, the day will come when you need to erase old or unwanted files to free up space.

But be careful when you erase files. If you enter the command incorrectly, you may delete the wrong file (or all files) from the disk or directory. Although it is possible to get back erased files, MS-DOS itself cannot do the job. Instead, you will need to purchase software specifically designed for recovering lost data.

Suppose that you want to erase the floor plan drawing named FLOOR1.DWG from your hard disk, which is named drive C. Just type the following command:

DEL C:FLOOR1.DWG

If you prefer, you can use the ERASE command, which works the same way:

ERASE C:FLOOR1.DWG

If you want to remove a file from your hard disk but would like to keep a copy of it for future use, you have several options. The simplest option is to copy the file to a floppy disk before erasing the file from the hard disk. If you have a large group of files that will not fit on a single disk, you can copy them to several floppy disks. Otherwise, you may want to consider using one of the mass storage devices described in Chapter 2.

You can remove a file from a floppy disk just as easily as you can remove one from the hard disk. Suppose that the file FLOOR1.DWG resides on a floppy disk, and that you no longer have use for the file. Place the disk in drive A and enter the following command at the C:> prompt:

DEL A:FLOOR.DWG

Again, you can use the ERASE command, if you prefer:

ERASE A:FLOOR.DWG

A *word about file names and wild cards . . .*

MS-DOS, OS/2, and UNIX allow you to reduce the amount of typing needed when you enter file names. You can use the ? and * *wild-card* characters, which represent one or more undefined characters in a file name.

The ? represents a single character, whereas the * represents a group of characters. To better understand their use, consider the following example.

Suppose that your hard disk contains the following files:

FLOOR1.DWG	SPELL.DOC
FLOOR2.DWG	TEST-2.DWG
FLOOR1.BAK	TESTING.DWG
DRAWING2.DWG	TEST-2.BAK
QUARTER.WKS	DRAW.DWG

If you want to delete the files FLOOR1.DWG and FLOOR2.DWG from the disk, you can enter the following commands to erase the files individually:

DEL C:FLOOR1.DWG
DEL C:FLOOR2.DWG

A word about file names and wild cards (continued) . . .

You can delete both files at once, however, by using a wild-card character with the DEL command:

DEL C:FLOOR?.DWG

This command causes MS-DOS and OS/2 to delete every file with *FLOOR* as the first five characters of the root name, with any character as the sixth character in the root name, and with *DWG* as its extension.

Now, suppose that you enter the following command:

DEL C:*.DWG

This command tells the operating system to delete every file with the extension DWG, no matter what root name the file has. That is, the * wild-card character matches all characters. The command, therefore, eliminates the following files from your disk:

    FLOOR1.DWG
    FLOOR2.DWG
    DRAWING2.DWG
    TEST-2.DWG
    TESTING.DWG
    DRAW.DWG

Now, suppose that you want to erase all the DWG files from the disk, but you also want to get rid of the SPELL.DOC file. You can erase both types of files with one command, even though their file names and extensions are different. Enter the following command:

DEL C:*.D??

This is the same as entering **DEL C:*.D***. The command tells DOS to delete any file whose file-name extension begins with the letter *D*, regardless of what the file's root name is, and no matter which two characters appear in the extension after the *D*. The command, therefore, deletes the following files:

    FLOOR1.DWG
    FLOOR2.DWG
    DRAWING2.DWG
    SPELL.DOC
    TEST-2.DWG
    TESTING.DWG
    DRAW.DWG

A *word about file names and wild cards (continued)* . . .

Wild cards give you an easy way to manage your AutoCAD drawings. By using wild cards, you can copy or delete several files at once. The two wild-card characters work with almost any operating system command and with many AutoCAD commands.

Wild-card characters extend the power of your operating system commands. While these characters can be extremely helpful, they also can be extremely harmful to your data if you do not use them with caution. The command DEL C:*.*, for example, can erase every file on a disk! Be sure you learn more about wild cards before using them with your operating system commands.

You may want to consider the power of wild cards as you select your file names. By choosing an organized system of file names, you can more easily copy, delete, or find the appropriate files.

Tech note . . .

Many software products, including AutoCAD, will make a duplicate of your original file. This duplicate file is for backup purposes—a spare in case the original becomes lost. A duplicate is helpful also if you want to see the previous edition of the current drawing.

Suppose that you are working on your FLOOR1.DWG file. When you save the file to the hard disk, AutoCAD copies the previous version of the file (before the current changes were made) to a new file called FLOOR1.BAK. The backup file is there in case you need to "go back" to that version of your drawing. AutoCAD does this automatically whenever you save the drawing file.

These BAK files tend to accumulate, however, and you may want to delete the outdated backup files to create more room on your hard disk. You can delete all backup files by issuing the following command:

DEL C:*.BAK

Commands that Affect the Directory Structure

You can store hundreds—even thousands—of files on a large hard disk. When your hard disk is loaded with files, however, you may find it hard to determine which files relate to which program. Whether you use MS-DOS, OS/2, or UNIX, you can better organize your files by storing them in *directories*.

Understanding Directories and Subdirectories

Directories—or *subdirectories*, as they also are called—enable you to group related files together. Most of your AutoCAD program files, for example, are probably stored together in a directory (or subdirectory) called ACAD. Similarly, you can store all files related to a specific AutoCAD project in one directory. Subdirectories allow you to create a unique area for each project's related files. After placing the files in a subdirectory, you still can access them as you have before. Subdirectories are not limited to hard disks; you also can create them on floppy disks.

Figure 3.1 shows a graphical representation of a disk's directory structure. The layout of the directory structure is similar to a tree. Like a tree, a disk's directory structure is formed from the root. The *root directory* is the disk's master directory, from which all subordinate directories and subdirectories are formed. The root directory can store not only files but also other directories, which in turn can store their own files and subdirectories. This root directory/directory/subdirectory arrangement is called the *directory hierarchy*.

Fig. 3.1.
A disk's
subdirectory
structure
looks like a
tree.

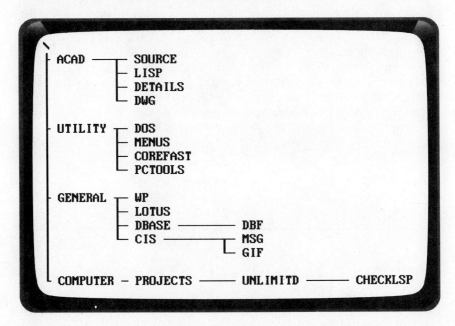

Figure 3.1 shows a sample hierarchical directory structure. The tree starts with the root directory, which is represented in the figure and in DOS commands by the backslash (\). The root directory can hold many files and directories. In the figure, the ACAD, UTILITY, GENERAL, and COMPUTER directories have been created as branches of the root directory. These four directories are called *level-one* directories because of their relationship to the root directory; that is, they are at the first level of the directory hierarchy (if you think of the root directory as being "ground zero") because no intervening directories exist between them and the root directory.

The four level-one directories also are called *parent* directories, because subordinate subdirectories have been created within them. For example, the ACAD directory is the parent directory of the SOURCE, LISP, DETAILS, and DWG subdirectories. Because of their relationship to the root directory, these four subdirectories are called *level-two* directories. That is, the parent directory ACAD intervenes between them and the root directory.

Notice that the GENERAL directory is the parent of four level-two subdirectories, two of which are in turn the parents of three level-three subdirectories. The COMPUTER directory is parent to a level-one, a level-two, and a level-three subdirectory.

Remember that all these directories can hold files and other directories. The hierarchical directory structure enables you to organize your files and programs logically on the hard disk by grouping related files into the same directory or subdirectory. Directory organization is discussed later in this chapter.

Notice how subdirectories relate to one another by location. Moving up and down branches of the tree is easy; jumping from branch to branch is harder. To get to the SOURCE directory, for example, you would have to go first to the ACAD directory. If you can visualize the directory structure in this manner, you will have an easier time getting around in your disk's directory structure. An upcoming section tells you how to move from one directory to another.

You can use operating system commands to perform the following tasks related to directory (or subdirectory) management:

❏ Create a directory

❏ Make a different directory the active directory

❏ View a directory's contents

❏ Remove an unneeded directory from the disk

Creating a Subdirectory (MKDIR or MD)

Suppose that you have a group of utility files (these could be batch files, small programs that speed up printing or file searches, and so on) that you want to add to your hard disk. Because these files are all related, you should place them together in an appropriately named subdirectory—UTILITY, for example.

Now suppose that you do not yet have a directory named UTILITY on the hard disk, and that you want to create one as a level-one directory. To create the new directory, use the MKDIR (for Make Directory) command, as follows:

MKDIR C:\UTILITY

MKDIR also has a shorthand form, MD. If you prefer to use the shorter version of the command, enter it as follows:

MD C:\UTILITY

The operating system creates a new UTILITY subdirectory as a "branch" off the root directory. If a file or subdirectory of the same name already exists, DOS displays a warning message, and you must think of a different name for the new subdirectory.

Remember that you are not limited to creating subdirectories under the root directory. Subdirectories can have other subdirectories under them. For example, to create the DOS subdirectory below the UTILITY subdirectory, as shown in figure 3.1, you would enter the following command:

MD C:\UTILITY\DOS

You also can create directories on floppy disks. If you want to create a UTILITY directory on a floppy disk, place the disk in drive A and type the following command at the C:> prompt:

MD A:\UTILITY

You can create as many subdirectories as you want (although there is a theoretical limit, based on the size of your computer's hard drive). In practical terms, however, the more directories you have, the harder it is to move between them.

A typical hard drive might have 6 to 12 directories branching off of the root directory: one directory for each major program file (one for AutoCAD, one for a word processor, one for a spreadsheet program, and so on). Each of these directories might contain several additional subdirectories to hold the data files that go with each program: one for AutoCAD's AutoLISP files, one for block libraries, one for each drawing project, and so on.

Setting the Current Subdirectory (CHDIR or CD)

Once you have created a new directory, you probably will want to "go into" it. That is, you will want to make the new directory the *current*, or active directory. When a directory is current, you can work directly within that directory; you can open, save, copy, and delete the files in the current directory without telling DOS which directory to use each time you issue a command. You save a great deal of time and keystrokes by changing to (that is, making current) the appropriate directory before you try to use that directory's files. To change the current directory, use the CHDIR (for Change Directory) command, as follows:

CHDIR C:\UTILITY

Like MKDIR, CHDIR has a shorthand form, CD. If you prefer to use the shorter version of the command, enter it as follows:

CD C:\UTILITY

To change directly back to the root directory, type **CD** at the C:> prompt.

To jump between unrelated subdirectories, you need to specify the full subdirectory *path*; that is, you must list the parent and child directories in descending order from the root directory on down to the desired destination directory. Suppose that the UTILITY subdirectory is currently active, and you want to make CHECKLSP the new current directory (refer to fig. 3.1). To do this, enter the following CHDIR command:

CD C:\COMPUTER\PROJECTS\UNLIMITED\CHECKLSP

Viewing a Directory's Contents (DIR)

Remember that a subdirectory contains related files. Suppose that ACAD is the current (active) directory. You can view a list of all the files in the current directory by typing the **DIR** command at the DOS prompt, as follows:

C:> **DIR**

```
Volume in drive C is THIS
Directory of C:\ACAD

.                 <DIR>        9-12-90     7:19p
..                <DIR>        9-12-90     7:19p
ACAD       EXE    1731825      6-29-90     4:25p
ACADL      EXP      47990      6-19-90    11:51a
ACAD       MNX     155924      6-19-90    11:50a
ACAD       DWG       4645      9-16-90    10:28p
ACAD       BAK       4645      9-16-90    10:30p
        7 File(s)  12877824 bytes free
```

The first line of the directory listing tells you the current drive's name (C) and volume label (THIS). The second line tells you the name of the current directory (ACAD).

You can safely ignore the next two lines, which are the shorthand names for the current (.) and the parent (..) subdirectories (<DIR>).

The next five lines list the names of files in the subdirectory. The file names and extensions are listed in the order that DOS finds them on the disk. Notice that DOS does not show the period between the file name and the extension.

After each extension, DOS lists the size of the file in *bytes* (total number of characters), and the date (in month-day-year format) and time that file was created or last modified and saved to the disk.

The final line totals the number of files listed (five, plus the two <DIR> files) and the number of free bytes remaining on the disk (about 12M).

You also can use the DIR command to see whether a certain drawing resides in a directory. Suppose that you want to see if any drawing files with the file-name extension DWG are in the current subdirectory. You can find out by entering the following command:

DIR *.DWG

```
Volume in drive C is THIS
Directory of C:\ACAD

.                 <DIR>       9-12-90     7:19p
..                <DIR>       9-12-90     7:19p
ACAD      DWG      4645       9-16-90    10:28p
     3 File(s)   12875776 bytes free
```

Using the * wild card reduces the directory listing to a single file, ACAD.DWG.

If there are so many files that the list scrolls off the top of the screen, reissue the DIR command and add the /P "switch," as follows:

DIR *.DWG /P

```
Volume in drive C is THIS
Directory of C:\ACAD

.                 <DIR>       9-12-90     7:19p
..                <DIR>       9-12-90     7:19p
ACAD      DWG      4645       9-16-90    10:28p
Strike any key when ready...
```

This tells DOS to *pause* the listing whenever the screen is full. To continue to the next screenful, press any key on the keyboard.

You probably will use the DIR command more than any other MS-DOS command. At any time, you can view a list of the files in the current directory. You also can use DIR to find out what files reside in any other directory besides the current directory. To view a list of the files of another directory, you can either first make that directory current (by using the CHDIR command) and then issue the DIR command, or you can leave the current directory as it is and type the following command:

DIR *[path]*

In this generic syntax, *[path]* is made up of the names of the directories (usually starting from the root directory), each separated from the next by a backslash (\). Suppose that you are in the CHECKLSP directory and you want to know what is in the SOURCE directory (refer to fig. 3.1). You can find out by issuing the following command:

DIR \ACAD\SOURCE

To get a list of subdirectory names only, type **DIR ***.

Removing a Subdirectory (RMDIR or RD)

You've learned how to create a directory, change directories, and see what is in an existing directory, but what if you want to remove an unneeded directory from the disk? You can do so in three steps.

To remove a directory, you must first delete all the files in that directory by using the **DEL *.*** command. (As a safety measure, MS-DOS and OS/2 prompt for confirmation before actually erasing all the files.)

Next, you must move up to the root directory by using the **CD** command. Finally, remove the subdirectory from the disk by using the RMDIR (for Remove Directory) command. RMDIR also has a shorthand form, RD. Here are the steps for removing the UTILITY directory you created earlier:

```
CD C:\UTILITY
DEL C:\UTILITY\*.*
Are you sure (Y/N)? Y
CD\
RD C:\UTILITY
```

Tips for Using Subdirectories

You can create a more efficient CAD station if you organize your hard drive's directory structure. By assigning well-named directories, you can easily store, locate, and retrieve drawings related to any project. As an added bonus, subdirectories overcome the eight-character file-name limitation imposed by MS-DOS and OS/2. Note that OS/2 with the HPFS (high-performance file system) option and UNIX do not impose the eight-character limit on file names.

For an example of using a logically organized directory structure to store drawings related to a project, see figure 3.2. Here the hard drive is first divided into projects by year (YR_1990). This directory contains only two project subdirectories, PARK_100 and PARK_50, which are further divided into subdirectories that hold the drawings for each building (BLDG_79, BLDG_80, etc.). The directory names leave little doubt as to where you might find the drawings for the tenants of Building 79 in Park 100.

Fig. 3.2. A logical directory structure makes it easier to keep track of your project files.

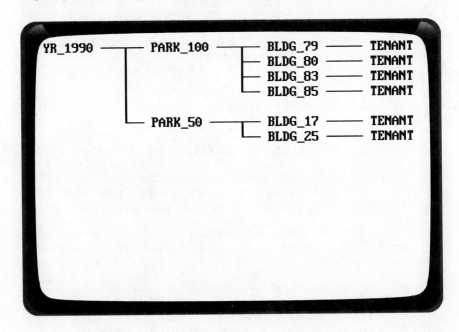

Commands that Influence Disks

When you work with disk storage, it is important to have as much control over the medium as possible. MS-DOS and OS/2 share one command for preparing a disk the first time you use it, and another for verifying the disk's reliability. These commands work with either floppy or hard disks.

Preparing a Disk To Receive Data (FORMAT)

In order for a new disk to hold data, you must first *format* the disk. When formatting a disk, the computer writes over the entire area of the disk and verifies that it can hold information. This procedure creates a magnetic structure that enables the disk to hold data.

You should remember the following points about the FORMAT command:

❑ A disk must be formatted before your computer can copy files onto it.

❑ If you format a disk that already contains data, *all the information on that disk will be destroyed by the formatting procedure*.

❑ Sometimes a disk begins to suffer from read or write errors. If you don't need the information on the disk, reformatting the disk may fix it.

❑ *Do not* format your hard disk. Hard-disk formatting should be done *only* if you are proficient in the use of your system.

To format a new floppy disk, enter the following command:

FORMAT A:

This assumes that your computer's floppy drive is named drive A. If not, substitute the correct name for the drive in the command. DOS displays the following prompt:

```
Insert new diskette for drive A:
and strike any key when ready
```

Put a new diskette in the disk drive, close the drive gate, and press Enter. The formatting process begins, and the following information appears on-screen:

```
Formatting...

Format complete

1213952 bytes total disk space
1213952 bytes available on disk
Format another (Y/N)?
```

If you don't want to format additional disks, just type **N** and then press Enter. After you format a disk, DOS displays the disk's total storage capacity (in this case, 1,213,952 bytes for a high-density floppy disk).

If DOS says that the number of bytes available on disk is somewhat smaller than number of bytes total disk space, the FORMAT command found some flaws on the disk. You can still safely use the disk. If the number of available bytes is a great deal smaller (under 900,000 bytes, for example), you may have tried to format a double-density disk meant to hold only 360K.

Important information can be lost accidentally when you reformat a disk. To reduce the chance of accidental reformats, find out which directory contains your FORMAT command program file, and then use the RENAME command to rename the FORMAT command as FORMAT!. Suppose that your FORMAT command file is stored in a level-one directory named DOS. Make that directory current (by using the CHDIR command), and then rename the file as follows:

RENAME FORMAT.COM FORMAT!.COM

From now on, you must type **FORMAT!** to format a disk, rather than just **FORMAT**. This prevents others from easily using the FORMAT command on your computer.

Checking a Disk's Reliability (CHKDSK)

You can use the CHKDSK command to verify the amount and type of data on a disk, determine the disk's (and RAM's) free space, and find out how many files are on the disk. To run the CHKDSK program on a floppy disk, place a disk in drive A and type **CHKDSK A:** at the C:> prompt. If you are checking a 1.2M floppy disk, for example, the CHKDSK command's output might look like this:

```
1213952 bytes total disk space
      0 bytes in 1 hidden files
 567296 bytes in 10 user files
 646656 bytes available on disk

 655360 bytes total memory
 528496 bytes free
```

You're already familiar with the number in the first line. The second line counts the number of *hidden files* (files the operating system doesn't let you see). The next two lines show that there are 10 files on the disk (taking up a total of 567,296 bytes) and that 646,656 bytes are still free.

The last two lines show you how much random-access memory is available on your system. Most MS-DOS computers show a total memory of 655,360 bytes. This is all that DOS recognizes, although your computer may have several megabytes of RAM. The final line shows how much memory remains in which you can run programs. The difference between the two lines is the amount of memory already used by DOS and programs that remain in memory.

Tech note . . .

If you shut off the computer while AutoCAD is operating, a number of files remain open. You can't see them and, even worse, they take up hundreds of kilobytes of disk space. Once a week, you should use the CHKDSK /F command. If CHKDSK finds these files, it will ask whether you want to recover them; answer **Y**. Finally, you need to erase the files CHKDSK finds, as follows:

CHKDSK /F
```
Convert lost chains to files (Y/N):? Y
```
DEL *.CHK

The /F (for *fix*) switch tells CHKDSK to fix the disk's directory structure. It finds any hidden (and useless) files that were left behind when the AutoCAD session was not ended properly.

When CHKDSK cleans up the disk, it renames portions of files sequentially, beginning with `FILE0001.CHK`, and places them in the root directory. Often, there will be several CHK files; they are useless. You can erase them all at once by issuing **DEL *.CHK.**

Commands that Print and Display Files

The operating system does much more than help you manage your files and directories. You can use the operating system to communicate in a basic way with some of your computer equipment. This section shows you how to send files to the printer and monitor.

Printing Files (PRINT)

You can print a file with your printer by using the PRINT command, provided that the file is in ASCII (text) format. *ASCII* format means that a file can be understood by a person. You cannot read most computer programs, and printing them results in gibberish. The AutoCAD program and the drawing files are in this "inhuman" format, which is called *binary*.

Many disks, including AutoCAD's, come with a file of information that didn't make it into the manual. This ASCII file is often called READ.ME or README.DOC. To print a file called README.DOC, make sure that the directory containing the file is current. Next, make sure that the printer is connected to the computer and turned on. Then type the following command at the C:> prompt:

PRINT README.DOC

This command tells DOS to send the file to the printer, where the file is printed on paper.

Viewing Files (TYPE)

The TYPE command is similar to the PRINT command, except that the information is sent to the monitor rather than the printer. To view the README.DOC file's contents on-screen, make sure that the directory containing the file is current, and issue the following command:

TYPE README.DOC

DOS then displays the file's contents (text) on-screen.

TIP

If a readable file contains more text than will fit on one screen, you can use the | MORE filter, which makes the TYPE command show only one screenful of information at a time (don't forget the vertical bar):

TYPE README.DOC | MORE

When you are done reading one screen of the file, press any key (the space bar usually is recommended), and the next screen of information appears.

About OS/2

Because OS/2 was derived from DOS, most of the two operating systems' commands work in the same way. You can manage subdirectories by using the MD, CD, and RD commands in OS/2, just as you can in DOS. You can use OS/2's DIR command to list files, COPY to copy files, and DEL to erase files.

What's different about OS/2 is that you probably won't type those commands to use them. You can if you want to, but you'll probably prefer using OS/2's built-in windowing environment, called *Presentation Manager* (see fig. 3.3). This environment, invented by the same Xerox research lab that invented the mouse, is similar to what you see on the Macintosh screen.

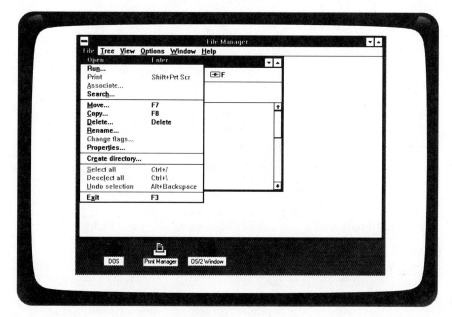

Fig. 3.3.
The OS/2
Presentation
Manager
interface lets
you run
several
programs
simultaneously,
each in its
own window.

Presentation Manager (called *PM*, for short) displays each program in its own window on-screen. This window can be any size—from the entire screen to as small as an icon. Because each program is in its own resizeable window, you can display several programs on-screen, each running simultaneously (multitasking).

To erase a file in PM, use your mouse to first pick the file name from a list appearing in a window, then pick the Files pull-down menu from the top of the window, and finally the ERASE command. The other commands you learned in this chapter operate in much the same way.

To run a program, you pick the program's name from the list of files. You no longer need to type commands or file names—you just pick them.

Because OS/2 is the successor to MS-DOS, you can run the DOS version of AutoCAD under OS/2 (but not vice versa). Because of the friendly Presentation Manager environment, AutoCAD is easier to run under OS/2 than under MS-DOS. The drawback is that OS/2 runs AutoCAD somewhat slower than MS-DOS.

For a detailed discussion of OS/2 and Presentation Manager, see *Using OS/2*, published by Que Corporation.

About UNIX

UNIX is special because it can simultaneously support several users (by means of additional screens and keyboards, known as *terminals*) and run several programs. Because it can do all this, UNIX is much more complicated than MS-DOS or OS/2. Companies that run UNIX on their computers often have one person in charge of maintaining the operating system and helping users. This person usually is called a *system administrator* or *system manager*.

UNIX comes in many flavors, known by different names on different computers. PCs have XENIX and SCO UNIX, IBM minicomputers use AIX, Hewlett-Packard minicomputers use HPUX, and the Macintosh can use A/UX. Like OS/2, UNIX can support a windowed environment (known as X Windows); like MS-DOS, however, it is more often used without one.

Since MS-DOS was derived from UNIX, some of the commands are similar. You can use commands such as md, cd, and rd to manage your directories, just as you would in MS-DOS. Most other commands are different from the DOS versions, however, and make little sense to the new user (for instance, the *ls* command lets you view a list of the file names in a directory). The symbol for the root directory is different, too—it's the slash (/) rather than the backslash used by MS-DOS and OS/2. Subdirectory names also are separated by a slash. Another difference is that upper- or lowercase names make a difference. In UNIX, you begin AutoCAD by typing **acad**, not **ACAD** or **Acad**.

UNIX needs programs that are written especially for it. You cannot run the copy of AutoCAD that works under MS-DOS or OS/2 on a computer that uses UNIX. Because of the difficult command names, running AutoCAD under UNIX can be harder than under MS-DOS or OS/2. The advantage, however, is that AutoCAD operates faster under UNIX than under either of the other two operating systems.

For a detailed discussion of UNIX, see *Using UNIX*, published by Que Corporation. If you will be using AutoCAD on a multiuser UNIX system, contact your system administrator for more information.

Summary

This chapter has shown you how to perform basic file- and directory-management operations for PC DOS, MS-DOS, OS/2, and UNIX. If your CAD station is based on another operating system, you should learn how that operating system performs the operations described in this chapter.

The information in this chapter is intended to introduce you to some of these operating systems' functions; it is in no way a complete list of the operating systems' capabilities. Hopefully, you have found that MS-DOS and OS/2 don't bite (UNIX does snarl). With a little more practice and patience, perhaps you soon will be saying, "The operating system is good. The operating system is my friend."

Part Two

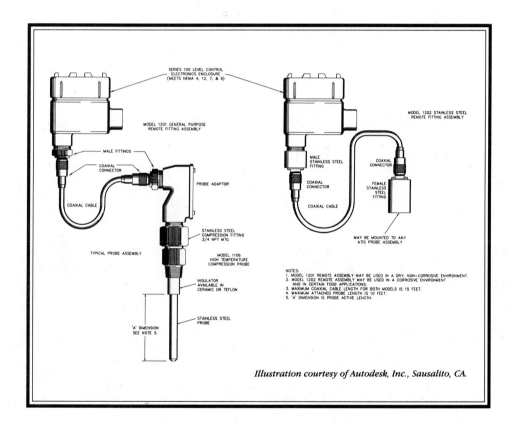

SERIES 100 LEVEL CONTROL
ELECTRONICS ENCLOSURE
(MEETS NEMA 4, 12, 7, & 9)

MODEL 1201 GENERAL PURPOSE
REMOTE FITTING ASSEMBLY

MODEL 1202 STAINLESS STEEL
REMOTE FITTING ASSEMBLY

MALE FITTINGS

COAXIAL
CONNECTOR

MALE
STAINLESS STEEL
FITTING

COAXIAL
CONNECTOR

PROBE ADAPTOR

COAXIAL
CONNECTOR

FEMALE
STAINLESS
STEEL
FITTING

COAXIAL CABLE

COAXIAL CABLE

STAINLESS STEEL
COMPRESSION FITTING
3/4 NPT MTG

MAY BE MOUNTED TO ANY
ATIS PROBE ASSEMBLY

TYPICAL PROBE ASSEMBLY

MODEL 1106
HIGH TEMPERATURE
COMPRESSION PROBE

INSULATOR
AVAILABLE IN
CERAMIC OR TEFLON

NOTES:
1. MODEL 1201 REMOTE ASSEMBLY MAY BE USED IN A DRY, NON-CORROSIVE ENVIRONMENT.
2. MODEL 1202 REMOTE ASSEMBLY MAY BE USED IN A CORROSIVE ENVIRONMENT
   AND IN CERTAIN FOOD APPLICATIONS.
3. MAXIMUM COAXIAL CABLE LENGTH FOR BOTH MODELS IS 15 FEET.
4. MAXIMUM ATTACHED PROBE LENGTH IS 10 FEET.
5. 'A' DIMENSION IS PROBE ACTIVE LENGTH.

STAINLESS STEEL
PROBE

'A' DIMENSION
SEE NOTE 5.

Illustration courtesy of Autodesk, Inc., Sausalito, CA.

Learning To Use AutoCAD

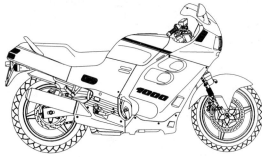

*Illustration courtesy of
Autodesk, Inc., Sausalito, CA.*

4

A Quick Start in AutoCAD

This chapter shows you how easy it is to get into and out of AutoCAD.
You'll learn how to draw lines and circles, and how to correct your
mistakes.

This quick start gives you a chance to become comfortable with the
AutoCAD environment. If you are just beginning and have never been
exposed to CAD, this short demonstration of how to draw with a
computer may be invaluable. The capabilities and complexities of the
CAD environment may seem overwhelming. As you work with AutoCAD,
however, you will be amazed at how quickly you learn and grow
comfortable with the program.

This chapter discusses the following subjects:

- ❏ Starting an AutoCAD drawing session
- ❏ The Main Menu
- ❏ The Drawing Editor
- ❏ The AutoCAD coordinate system

You also will learn about the following commands:

- ❏ Circle
- ❏ Line
- ❏ End
- ❏ Oops
- ❏ Erase
- ❏ Quit
- ❏ Help
- ❏ Undo

Once you finish reading this chapter and complete the example
presented, you should feel comfortable with starting a new AutoCAD

drawing. You also should have a basic understanding of the AutoCAD coordinate system and the different methods of specifying coordinates to AutoCAD commands. This information will prove valuable as you move on to the more complex example that begins in Chapter 5.

Starting AutoCAD

There are many ways to set up your computer so that you can access different programs. If you're using AutoCAD on your own, the following paragraphs explain how to start AutoCAD on your PC. Because the standards of your business determine how your system is set up, you may need to find out from the system manager how to access AutoCAD.

If you have not yet installed AutoCAD, install the program on your computer as described in Appendix A. You then can use the examples in this chapter to get up and running quickly on AutoCAD.

To start AutoCAD Release 11 (or AutoCAD 386 Release 10), type **ACAD386** at the DOS prompt. Doing so runs a *batch* file that sets up the DOS environment for AutoCAD and then loads AutoCAD into RAM for your use. This file, which contains all the information AutoCAD needs in order to start running, is created automatically by the Install program (see Appendix A). The batch file simplifies the process of starting AutoCAD; without it, you would have to type several lines of information.

To start AutoCAD Release 10, first go to the directory in which AutoCAD is stored. (On many IBM-compatible computer systems, this directory is called C:\ACAD.) At the DOS prompt, type **ACAD** and then press Enter. This starts the program.

On some computer systems, a menu system may already be set up. If AutoCAD is available to you from a menu system installed on your computer, an option labeled A u t o C A D should be visible. Select that option to start AutoCAD.

Once you start AutoCAD (regardless of the method), one or two preliminary screens may be displayed. Press Enter until AutoCAD displays the Main Menu.

The AutoCAD Main Menu

From AutoCAD's Main Menu, you can access each of AutoCAD's main options. These enable you to start a new drawing, continue working with an existing drawing, leave AutoCAD entirely, or perform a variety of other tasks. The menu displayed on your screen should be similar to the one shown in figure 4.1. (The Main Menu for AutoCAD Release 10 does not show Option 9.)

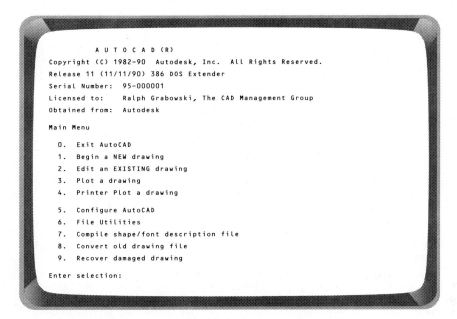

Fig. 4.1.
The Main
Menu.

At the top of the Main Menu screen, you will notice some important information:

- ❏ The AutoCAD release number
- ❏ The program's serial number
- ❏ The licensee's name (presumably yours)
- ❏ Your dealer's name

If you need to contact Autodesk, you will be asked to provide this information. (Note particularly the AutoCAD release number. If you are not using Release 10 or 11, then parts of this text may not apply to you.)

Tech note . . .

Differences between versions of AutoCAD become important if you plan to share drawings with other people who are also using AutoCAD. As AutoCAD has grown, its programmers have made changes to the way drawing files store graphics information. Because of these changes, you cannot use an older version of AutoCAD (such as Release 10) to work on drawings created with Release 11.

Tech note (continued) . . .

To avoid this compatibility problem, make sure that everyone is using the same version of AutoCAD or that you have a drawing translator program to convert new-format drawings to an older format.

Fortunately, this problem occurs only when you change from a newer version of AutoCAD to an older one. Drawing files are *upwardly compatible*, which means that files created by an older version of AutoCAD can be read by newer releases of the program. Release 11 will read drawings created in Release 10.

To select an option from the Main Menu, simply type the desired option's number at the `Enter selection:` prompt and press Enter. If you enter an invalid response at the prompt, AutoCAD tells you of your error and lets you try again.

All the Main Menu options are covered in detail later in this chapter. The first two Main Menu options enable you to exit from AutoCAD or begin a new drawing.

Option 0 — Exit AutoCAD

When you finish using AutoCAD, select Option 0, Exit AutoCAD, to get out of AutoCAD and return to the operating system.

Option 1 — Begin a New Drawing

When you want to start a new drawing, select Main Menu Option 1. An on-screen message prompts you for the name of the drawing. For this quick start, call the drawing "SAMPLE." Give your new drawing this name by typing it as follows:

`Enter NAME of drawing:` **SAMPLE**

The drawing's name is the name of the file in which AutoCAD stores information about the drawing. The file's name must follow the requirements for DOS, OS/2, UNIX, or whatever operating system you are using with AutoCAD. The DOS and OS/2 specifications follow:

❑ Drawing names can be up to eight characters long. You do not need to add an extension because AutoCAD automatically adds the DWG extension for drawing files.

❏ Drawing names can contain numbers, letters (both upper-
and lowercase), and the dollar sign ($), hyphen (-), and
underline (_) characters.

DOS does not allow spaces in a file name. To simulate a space, use a
hyphen or an underline character. As you enter the file name (or any
other information) into AutoCAD, remember that AutoCAD treats the
space bar the same as the Enter key. If you try to insert a space by
pressing the space bar, AutoCAD assumes that you have finished entering
the name and calls up the Drawing Editor.

If you want your drawings to reside in a subdirectory other than the
current one (or on another drive), you must indicate the appropriate
path, as you would in DOS. For information on subdirectories and how
your hard disk might be set up, be sure to read Chapter 3.

When AutoCAD prompts you for the name of the drawing, be sure to
include the path before the name, if necessary. For example, if you want
to store the drawing (SAMPLE) in the QUE subdirectory of the ACAD
directory, you would respond to the prompt as follows:

```
Enter NAME of drawing: \ACAD\QUE\SAMPLE
```

If the drawing name you enter already exists, AutoCAD lets you know.
Then you can either choose a new name or copy over (delete) the
existing file, effectively replacing the existing drawing with the new one
you are about to create.

The Drawing Editor

After you enter the drawing's name, AutoCAD displays the Drawing Editor
screen (see fig. 4.2), the area in which you will do all your drawing and
editing.

The Drawing Editor screen has the following parts:

❏ **Drawing area.** This is the area in which you draw. The
crosshair cursor shows where you are pointing with your
input device (such as a mouse or puck). Try moving your
input device or pressing the keyboard's arrow keys and
watch the crosshairs move across the screen. If the cursor
does not appear on-screen, press Home, and the cross
hairs should become visible.

❏ **Command Area.** At the bottom of the screen is the area in
which you type commands. AutoCAD uses this area when
it requests information from you, information that may
relate to a specific command. You should see the word
Command: at the bottom of the screen, as shown in
figure 4.2. This is called the *command prompt*. It is
AutoCAD's way of letting you know it is ready for you to
type in a command.

Fig. 4.2.
The AutoCAD
Drawing
Editor.

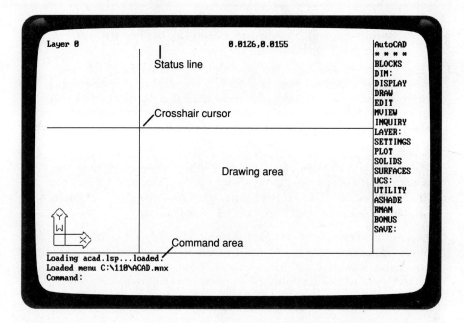

❑ **Screen menu.** You can use the screen menu (or Root
Menu, as it is sometimes called) along the right side of the
screen as another way of entering AutoCAD commands. If
you have a mouse, puck, or stylus, try moving the
crosshairs into the screen menu. One word should light
up. You can pick the commands from the screen menu
instead of typing them at the keyboard. (You can press Ins
to use these commands from the keyboard if you don't
have a mouse or a digitizer.)

❑ **Pull-down menus.** As an alternative to the command
prompt, the screen menu, and tablet menu, you can
access many (but not all) of AutoCAD's commands from
pull-down menus (see fig. 4.3). These menus are similar
to the pull-down menus used by Windows 3, OS/2
Presentation Manager, and other graphical interfaces. The
advantage of pull-down menus is that they can display
more information than the screen menu can. The
disadvantage is that many commands are not available
from the pull-down menus; almost all commands,
however, are listed in the screen menu.

❑ **Status line.** In the status line at the top of the screen,
AutoCAD displays important information about the status
of your drawing. The status line displays the current layer
name (Layer 0), the active modes (Ortho, Snap, P, and

Tablet), and the coordinate position of the crosshair cursor. The status line also hides the pull-down menus. Move the crosshairs up to the status line and notice how the status line changes to a row of words. When you "pick" any word, a menu pops down. (Picking is explained shortly.) You can get rid of the menu by picking anywhere else on the screen. You cannot access the status line or the pull-down menus by using the arrow keys.

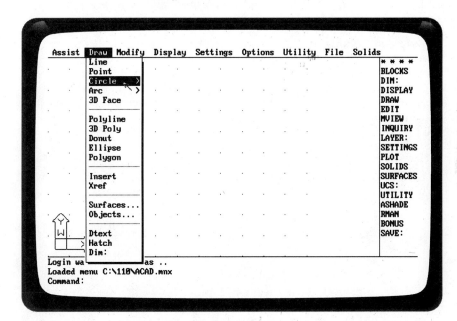

Fig. 4.3.
The Draw pull-down menu shows many, but not all, of AutoCAD's drawing commands.

NOTE

Throughout this text, you enter AutoCAD commands primarily through the keyboard, in response to the C o m m a n d : prompt and other prompts that appear at the bottom of the screen. This book uses the command area because that's the best way to learn how each command works; menus sometimes automate or reduce the number of options available with a command.

A Short Drawing Exercise

Now that you have been introduced to the Drawing Editor, your next step is to see what drawing with AutoCAD is like. At this point, you'll learn a few basic commands; later chapters explain these commands and their options in greater detail. By following this drawing exercise (from now on called the "sample drawing," or the "example"), you will begin to understand how easy it is to work with AutoCAD's Drawing Editor.

Drawing Lines (Line)

The simplest command to start with is the Line command. This command (like most AutoCAD commands) does just what its name implies: it draws a line from one point to another.

Try the Line command now. At the `Command:` prompt, type **Line** and press Enter. AutoCAD displays the `From point:` prompt to ask you where to begin drawing the line. Use the arrow keys or your input device to move the cursor around the screen and pick a point.

You can enter points in several ways, but the easiest way is by *picking*. When you pick points, you use a pointing device (such as a mouse or puck) or the keyboard's arrow keys to move the crosshairs to the desired point in the drawing. You then tell AutoCAD to accept the point as part of the drawing. You can pick points either in two- or three-dimensional drawings. The way you pick points depends on the type of input device you use, as follows:

Input Device	To Move the Cursor	To Pick a Point
Keyboard	Press cursor keys	Press Enter key
Mouse	Move mouse	Press left button
Puck	Move puck	Press first button
Stylus	Move stylus	Press tip button

Now move your input device again and notice how a line stretches from the newly picked point to the cursor. This phenomenon is called *rubber-banding*, and is AutoCAD's way of letting you preview where your next line will go.

Pick another point. You've drawn your first line in AutoCAD! Now pick several more points, anywhere on the screen. Notice how the lines connect. Now press **C** (for *close*) and press Enter; the last line connects with the first.

A word about arrow keys . . .

AutoCAD offers you several ways to move around the screen, pick points, and specify commands. The more of these options you can access, the easier your AutoCAD work will be. Most users find that a mouse or digitizing tablet gives them complete freedom of movement and choice in AutoCAD.

> ## A *word about arrow keys (continued)* . . .
>
> Even though they are not as versatile as a mouse or tablet, your keyboard's arrow keys can be used to move the crosshair cursor and to access AutoCAD's side menus. In fact, the arrow keys are often referred to as "the poor man's mouse." Simply press the appropriate arrow key to move the crosshairs in the desired direction. When you press the PgUp or PgDn keys, you increase or decrease the distance the crosshairs move when an arrow key is pressed.
>
> You will find, however, that the slow cursor movement becomes irritating. The best solution, therefore, is to buy a mouse; even the cheapest mice work with AutoCAD.

You also can draw lines by specifying exact coordinates. Before you try this, however, you need to clear the screen; that is, you need to "clean off" the lines you just drew, so that the drawing area will be blank. Clear the screen by typing **U** and pressing Enter. (You'll learn more about the U command later.) Now try the Line command again. This time, use the keyboard to type the following X,Y coordinates:

Prompt	Response	Explanation
Command:	**Line**	Starts the Line command
From point:	**1,1**	Starting point for first line
To point:	**9,1**	Ending point for first line
To point:	**10.1,6.5**	Last point, draws second line
To point:	Press Enter	Ends the Line command

After you enter this command sequence, your screen should look like the screen shown in figure 4.4. (The figure shows coordinate locations so that you understand where the numbers you typed placed the line endpoints. These numbers won't actually appear on your screen.)

Fig. 4.4.
*The Drawing
Editor after
you draw two
lines.*

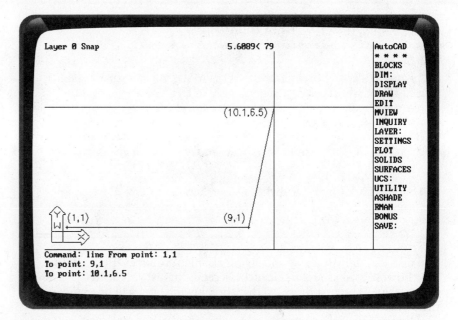

```
Layer 0 Snap                        5.6089< 79          AutoCAD
                                                        * * * *
                                                        BLOCKS
                                                        DIM:
                                                        DISPLAY
                                                        DRAW
                                                        EDIT
                                        (10.1,6.5)      MVIEW
                                                        INQUIRY
                                                        LAYER:
                                                        SETTINGS
                                                        PLOT
                                                        SOLIDS
                                                        SURFACES
                                                        UCS:
                                                        UTILITY
                                                        ASHADE
                                                        RMAN
          (1,1)                       (9,1)             BONUS
                                                        SAVE:

Command: line From point: 1,1
To point: 9,1
To point: 10.1,6.5
```

TIP

At any time, you can interrupt a command in progress by pressing
Ctrl-C. (While holding down the Ctrl key, press C.) This tells
AutoCAD to stop executing the command and to return to the
Command: prompt. (Three commands—Pedit, Layer, and Dim—
require you to press Ctrl-C twice to return to the Command:
prompt.)

Understanding AutoCAD's Coordinate Systems

You probably learned in school about several coordinate systems.
AutoCAD normally uses the Cartesian coordinate system, which often is
called the *World Coordinate System* (or *WCS*, for short). This is the same
system you used in high school; the X,Y,Z axes locate any point in three
dimensions. The origin of this coordinate system is 0,0,0 (X=0, Y=0, and
Z=0).

Because you will want to work first in two dimensions, the following
descriptions refer only to the X,Y coordinate system. Three-dimensional
drawing and the X,Y,Z coordinate system are covered in greater depth in
later chapters.

In two-dimensional drawing, you draw as if you were looking straight
down on your project from above (this bird's-eye view is called the *plan
view*). Every object you draw in AutoCAD has X,Y coordinates associated

with it. The origin of this coordinate system is at 0,0 (which should correspond to the lower left corner of the Drawing Editor screen).

The *UCS icon*, located in the lower left corner of the Drawing Editor, serves as a reminder of the X and Y directions. The icon, meant for three-dimensional drawing, is discussed in detail in Part Five.

TIP

If you find that the UCS icon gets in your way, you can turn it off with the following command:

```
Command: Ucsicon
ON/OFF/All/Noorigin/Origin <ON>: Off
```

You can turn the icon back on by entering the Ucsicon command again and typing **On** at the prompt.

Understanding Absolute and Relative Coordinates

In 2-D drawing, AutoCAD accepts coordinates in two formats: Cartesian or polar. In the Cartesian system, you identify the X,Y coordinate, such as (5,7). Type the X value, followed by a comma, then type the Y value. When you press Enter, AutoCAD accepts the point.

Cartesian coordinates also are known as *absolute coordinates* because they are all measured from the same origin (0,0). Use absolute coordinates if you need to input survey points, for example.

Polar coordinates consist of a distance and an angle. In AutoCAD, you use the format $@d<A$, where d = distance and A = angle. Suppose, for example, that you enter the following coordinates as part of a Line command:

```
To point: @10<90
```

These coordinates tell AutoCAD to draw the line 10 units long at 90 degrees from the most recently picked point.

Because AutoCAD measures polar coordinates from the most recently picked point, polar coordinates are also known as *relative coordinates*. AutoCAD calculates the angle counterclockwise from three o'clock. Thus, 90 degrees is straight up. You can change the angle orientation by using the Units command, as explained in Chapter 5.

Drawing Lines with Relative Coordinates

You also can draw lines with the Line command using relative coordinates. Repeat the preceding Line command sequence with polar coordinates, as follows:

Prompt	Response	Explanation
Command:	**Line**	Starts the Line command
From point:	**1,1**	Starting point for first line
To point:	**@8<0**	Draws a line 8 units long in the direction of 0 degrees (to the right, or due east)
To point:	**@5.61<79**	From the last point, draws a line 5.61 units long at an angle of 79 degrees from the last point
To point:	Press Enter	Ends the Line command

Your screen should look like figure 4.5, which shows the polar coordinates along both lines. (It looks exactly the same as figure 4.4.)

Fig. 4.5.
The same lines, drawn using relative coordinates.

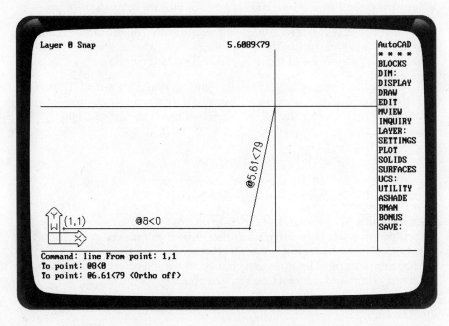

The advantage of relative coordinates is that you can draw entities by referencing points. You can draw walls by knowing their length, for example, instead of having to calculate all the absolute coordinate points.

The difference between absolute and relative coordinate entry will become clearer as you work with AutoCAD. You should remember, though, that either form of input can be used whenever you are prompted for location information.

Drawing a Circle (Circle)

As mentioned previously, a command's name usually describes the command's function. The Line command draws lines, the Circle command draws circles, and so on. AutoCAD is designed to be easy to use, as the command names suggest.

Unlike the Line command, which is easy to use, the Circle command has several variations. These variations are explained in more detail in Chapter 5. For now, you need only become familiar with AutoCAD's basic circle-drawing capability. The following command sequence, therefore, demonstrates only the Circle command's default operation. That is, you simply pick the circle's center and then specify a radius, as follows:

Prompt	Response	Explanation
Command: 3P/2P/TTR/	**Circle**	Starts the Circle command
<Center point>:	**6,3**	Places center of circle at point 6,3
Diameter/<Radius>:	**2**	Specifies a radius of 2 inches

Now your screen should look like the one shown in figure 4.6.

Saving the Drawing

AutoCAD has been storing information about the line and circle in the computer's RAM memory. If the power were to fail now, you would lose all the work you've done so far. For this reason, it is important to save your work to the hard disk every 10 or 15 minutes. To do so, type **Save** at the Command: prompt; then press Enter at the next prompt:

    File name: <SAMPLE>:

Unlike some other programs, AutoCAD does not automatically save your work to disk. It's up to you to remember to use the Save command. By frequently saving your drawing to disk, you minimize the amount of work you'll have to do over if the power fails.

Fig. 4.6.
Your first
drawing: two
lines and a
circle.

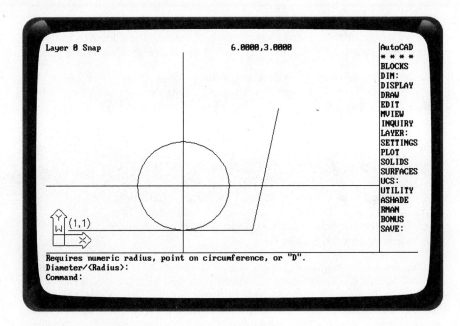

Erasing Objects (Erase)

You've now drawn some lines and a circle. What if you made a mistake? AutoCAD enables you to draw with ease, and it lets you easily change anything you've drawn. Everyone makes mistakes. In AutoCAD, you can erase your mistakes by using the Erase command. The following command sequence demonstrates this command's use:

Prompt	Response	Explanation
`Command:`	**Erase**	Starts the Erase command
`Select Objects:`	**Last**	Chooses the circle (the last object drawn)
`Select Objects:`	Press Enter	Erases the circle

Notice how the circle changed when you picked it. The change, called *highlighting*, is AutoCAD's way of letting you know that it found the circle (see fig. 4.7).

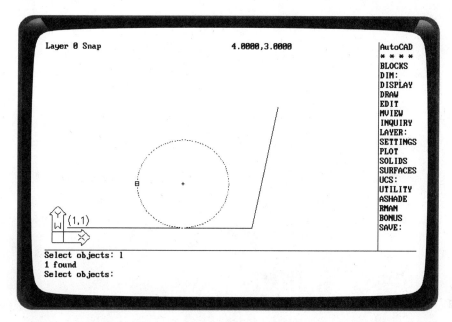

Fig. 4.7.
When you pick
an entity,
AutoCAD
highlights it.

During the Erase operation, you also may have noticed that the cursor changed shape, from the crosshairs to a small box. The box cursor, called the *pickbox*, makes it easier for you to pick an object on-screen.

Correcting Your Mistakes (Oops and U)

It may sound odd, but sometimes you can make a mistake by erasing a mistake. If you erase too much, you may lose information that you really wanted to keep in the drawing. To save you from having to redraw accidentally erased objects, AutoCAD provides two commands: Oops and U (for *Undo*). Both allow you to "step back" one or more commands and recover entities that you may have altered inadvertently.

The difference between the Oops and U commands is subtle. Oops brings back the last group of entities erased, whereas U undoes the last command you entered. The following examples clarify the differences between the commands:

Prompt	Response	Explanation
Command:	**Oops**	Puts the circle back on the screen

The U command lets you step backward through all the commands you entered, even all the way back to when you entered the Drawing Editor.

The following example shows how it works:

Prompt	Response	Explanation
Command:	U	Re-erases the circle you un-erased (undoes the Oops command)
Command:	U	Undoes the Erase command and brings back the circle
Command:	U	Undoes the Circle command, leaving only the lines
Command:	U	Undoes the Line command

If you have followed this example, you can see that using U to step back through the drawing commands leaves you with the blank screen you saw when you entered the Drawing Editor.

Finding Help (Help)

If you are working in the Drawing Editor and are not sure which command to use, AutoCAD can help. AutoCAD's built-in help system can give you general information about the program, or specific information about a command.

To initiate the help facility, type **Help** at the Command: prompt. AutoCAD responds with the following prompt:

```
Command name <RETURN for list>:
```

If you want general information about AutoCAD, press Enter in response to this prompt. AutoCAD then displays an alphabetized list of commands, like the one shown in figure 4.8. This is the first in a series of general-information screens. Press Enter again, and the second half of the alphabetized command list appears. Press Enter once more, and AutoCAD displays a screen of information on point entry and the user coordinate system. Press Enter a fourth time, and you will see a screen of information on object selection. This is the last of the general-information screens. At the bottom of this screen appears a Command: prompt. You can enter a command here, such as the Line command, to return to the Drawing Editor. For now, however, just press F1 to flip back to the drawing screen.

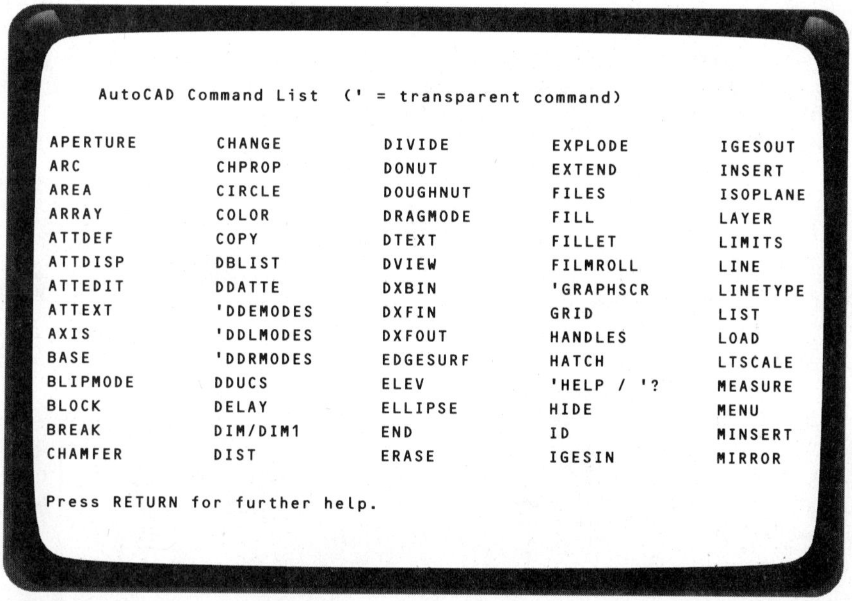

```
   AutoCAD Command List   (' = transparent command)

APERTURE      CHANGE       DIVIDE      EXPLODE     IGESOUT
ARC           CHPROP       DONUT       EXTEND      INSERT
AREA          CIRCLE       DOUGHNUT    FILES       ISOPLANE
ARRAY         COLOR        DRAGMODE    FILL        LAYER
ATTDEF        COPY         DTEXT       FILLET      LIMITS
ATTDISP       DBLIST       DVIEW       FILMROLL    LINE
ATTEDIT       DDATTE       DXBIN       'GRAPHSCR   LINETYPE
ATTEXT        'DDEMODES    DXFIN       GRID        LIST
AXIS          'DDLMODES    DXFOUT      HANDLES     LOAD
BASE          'DDRMODES    EDGESURF    HATCH       LTSCALE
BLIPMODE      DDUCS        ELEV        'HELP / '?  MEASURE
BLOCK         DELAY        ELLIPSE     HIDE        MENU
BREAK         DIM/DIM1     END         ID          MINSERT
CHAMFER       DIST         ERASE       IGESIN      MIRROR

Press RETURN for further help.
```

Fig. 4.8.
The first of AutoCAD's general-information help screens.

If you want to learn about a specific command, type **Help** at the Command: prompt and press Enter to initiate the help system. When the Command name <Return for List>: prompt appears, enter the name of the command with which you need help. AutoCAD then displays a screenful of information about that command. Suppose, for example, that you want to learn more about the Line command. Type **Line** at the prompt, press Enter, and your screen should look like the one shown in figure 4.9. To return to the Drawing Editor, press F1.

You also can get help while you are executing another command. To do this, type **'Help** (notice the apostrophe), or a question mark (**?**) at the prompt for which you need help. The apostrophe enables you to execute one command from within another command.

Exiting from the AutoCAD Drawing Editor (End or Quit)

Getting out of the AutoCAD Drawing Editor is as easy as getting into it. At the Command: prompt, you can type either **End** or **Quit** to get back to the Main Menu. The difference between the End and Quit commands is significant:

❑ The End command saves your drawing before returning you to the Main Menu. This is the command you will use most of the time to get out of the AutoCAD Drawing Editor.

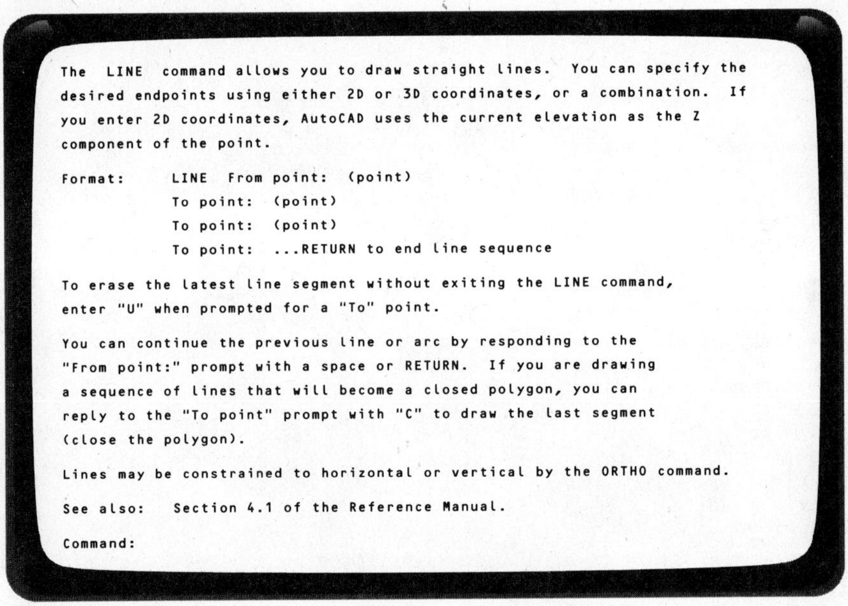

*Fig. 4.9.
Help for the
Line
command.*

```
The  LINE  command allows you to draw straight lines.  You can specify the
desired endpoints using either 2D or 3D coordinates, or a combination.  If
you enter 2D coordinates, AutoCAD uses the current elevation as the Z
component of the point.

Format:     LINE  From point: (point)
            To point:  (point)
            To point:  (point)
            To point:  ...RETURN to end line sequence

To erase the latest line segment without exiting the LINE command,
enter "U" when prompted for a "To" point.

You can continue the previous line or arc by responding to the
"From point:" prompt with a space or RETURN.  If you are drawing
a sequence of lines that will become a closed polygon, you can
reply to the "To point" prompt with "C" to draw the last segment
(close the polygon).

Lines may be constrained to horizontal or vertical by the ORTHO command.

See also:   Section 4.1 of the Reference Manual.

Command:
```

❑ The Quit command does not save your work; it simply
exits back to the Main Menu. Use Quit if you really don't
want to save your work. AutoCAD asks if you are sure you
want to exit without saving your changes. If you are sure,
type **Y** (for Yes) and press Enter. Be careful with this
command—once you say "yes," the work you have done
will be lost forever.

You have just finished your first drawing in AutoCAD. What you have
done is simple, but you have drawn with a computer. This experience
will give you confidence as you continue the path to creating complex
drawings with AutoCAD.

The Other Main Menu Options

AutoCAD has a total of 10 Main Menu options (numbered 0 through 9).
Option 0, Exit AutoCAD, and Option 1, Start a New Drawing, were
covered earlier in this chapter (before the drawing exercise). The
remaining Main Menu options are discussed briefly in the following
sections.

Option 2 — Edit an Existing Drawing

Select Main Menu Option 2 if you want to work with a drawing that
already exists. If AutoCAD cannot find the drawing file, the following
message appears:

```
**Drawing SAMPLE is not on file.
Press RETURN to continue.
```

Press Enter to try again. You may have to access the File Utility Menu
(Main Menu Option 6, described later in this chapter) to see which
drawing files are available in the current directory.

If the drawing you want to edit is in another directory or on another
drive, you must include the path or drive with the drawing's name. See
the explanation of Main Menu Option 1, earlier in this chapter, for a
description and example of this process.

When you choose to edit a drawing that already exists, AutoCAD
remembers all the settings. The drawing appears on the screen as it did
when you ended the last editing session. This is convenient: you can end
a drawing and, when you resume working, AutoCAD brings up the
drawing at the exact stage at which you stopped.

Option 3 — Plot a Drawing

There are two ways to a produce hard copy of your drawing on a pen
plotter. One way is to select Option 3 from the Main Menu. The other
way is to use the Plot command within the Drawing Editor (as described
in Chapter 8).

The only difference between the two methods is that when you choose to
plot from the Main Menu, you do not see the drawing before you plot it.
The advantage is that you don't need to wait for a large drawing to load
before plotting it. If you need to see the drawing before plotting, enter
the Drawing Editor and use the Plot command.

Option 4 — Printer Plot a Drawing

AutoCAD also can create a hard copy of your drawing on a printer that
accepts graphics information. Again, there are two ways to do this. Either
select Option 4 from the Main Menu or issue the Prplot command from
within the Drawing Editor.

Option 5 — Configure AutoCAD (A Brief Look)

Before you can use AutoCAD, you must let the program know what hardware you want to run. By choosing Option 5, Configure AutoCAD, you can set up your computer's graphics card, digitizing device, plotter, printer, and any other peripherals you will use. After you set up your equipment, you can return to the Main Menu. The configuration process is covered in greater detail in Appendix A.

If you change the graphics board, plotter, or any other peripheral, you must reconfigure AutoCAD. The software needs accurate information about each peripheral. Otherwise, the hardware may not work. If a problem should occur, check the following possible causes:

❑ Is the peripheral turned on? Some digitizers and plotters go into stand-by mode and look as if they are turned off.

❑ Is the peripheral hooked up? If you are familiar with your computer, look behind it and make sure that the cable is connected securely at the peripheral and at the computer. Always tighten the connecting screws; a loose cable can look all right but not be fully connected.

❑ Is the cable connected to the correct port? Computer ports can look similar, but perform different functions. Label all ports and connections, or have someone do it for you.

If you are not comfortable with these steps, or if they do not work, call your service representative. If your system was configured by an authorized AutoCAD dealer, the dealer should be able to correct any problems.

Option 6 — File Utilities

Use Main Menu Option 6 to access the File Utility Menu (see fig. 4.10). This menu lets you copy files, list the names of drawing files, and perform other file-related chores. Most of these functions are duplicates of the operating system's commands. For more information on operating system commands and their effects on your computer and its hard disk, refer to Chapter 3.

Briefly, the File Utility Menu offers the following options:

Option 0 (Exit) leaves the File Utility Menu and returns you to the Main Menu.

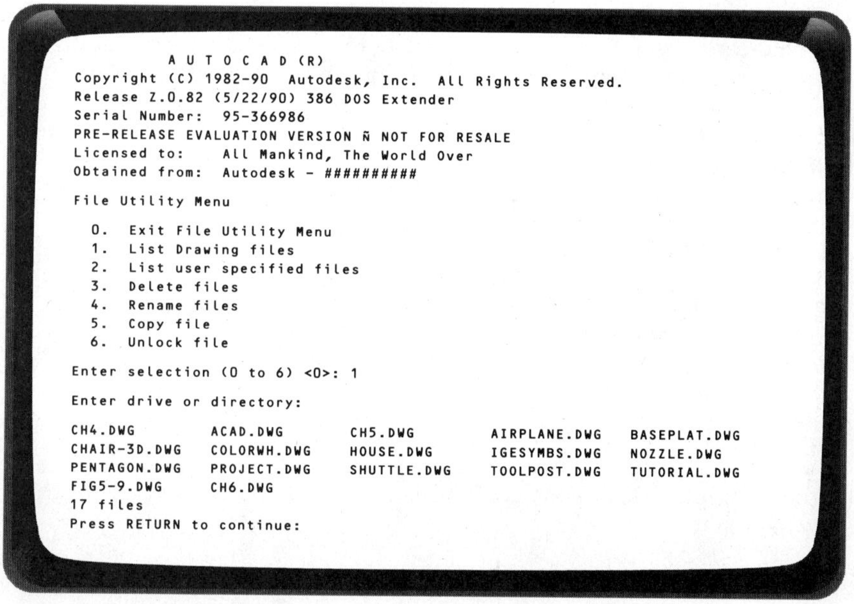

```
        A U T O C A D  (R)
Copyright (C) 1982-90  Autodesk, Inc.  All Rights Reserved.
Release Z.0.82 (5/22/90) 386 DOS Extender
Serial Number:  95-366986
PRE-RELEASE EVALUATION VERSION ñ NOT FOR RESALE
Licensed to:     All Mankind, The World Over
Obtained from:  Autodesk - ##########

File Utility Menu

   0.   Exit File Utility Menu
   1.   List Drawing files
   2.   List user specified files
   3.   Delete files
   4.   Rename files
   5.   Copy file
   6.   Unlock file

Enter selection (0 to 6) <0>: 1

Enter drive or directory:

CH4.DWG       ACAD.DWG      CH5.DWG       AIRPLANE.DWG   BASEPLAT.DWG
CHAIR-3D.DWG  COLORWH.DWG   HOUSE.DWG     IGESYMBS.DWG   NOZZLE.DWG
PENTAGON.DWG  PROJECT.DWG   SHUTTLE.DWG   TOOLPOST.DWG   TUTORIAL.DWG
FIG5-9.DWG    CH6.DWG
17 files
Press RETURN to continue:
```

Fig. 4.10.
The File Utility
Menu.

Option 1 (List drawing files) lists the drawing files in any directory you specify. If you want to know which drawing files are in the current directory, select Option 1 and press Enter at the Enter drive or directory: prompt.

You also can list the drawing files on another drive. To list files from drive A, for example, select Option 1 from the File Utility Menu and then type **A** at the Enter drive or directory: prompt:

Option 2 (List user specified files) on the File Utility Menu lets you list any file. You can use the DOS wild-card characters, **?** and *****, with path names and the drive designation. If you want to list all files that begin with *SUITE* (such as SUITE-1.DWG, SUITE-2.DWG, and SUITE-3.DWG, for example), select Option 2 from the File Utility Menu. AutoCAD then displays the following prompt:

　Enter file search specification:

To list all drawing files whose names begin with *SUITE*, type **SUITE*.DWG** in response to the prompt.

This specification tells AutoCAD to list all the files in the current subdirectory with names that start with *SUITE*, followed by any other characters, and end with the *DWG* extension.

Option 3 (Delete file) erases files from any drive or directory. You can use wild-card characters to delete more than one file at a time, but if you do, be very careful. When you use wild-card characters with the Delete files selection, you can accidentally delete files you did not intend to delete. As a safeguard, AutoCAD will ask you to confirm individually the deletion of each file. The default is N. If you press Enter to accept the default, the file remains intact. You must type **Y** to delete the file.

Option 4 (Rename file) lets you rename a file. This can be helpful if you decide to change the name of a drawing file, or if you misname a drawing. Suppose, for example, that you have a file named ROOM-2.DWG, and you want to rename it SUITE-2.DWG. Start by selecting Option 4 from the File Utility Menu. AutoCAD displays the following prompt:

```
Enter current filename:
```

At this prompt, type **ROOM-2.DWG**. AutoCAD then prompts you for the new file name:

```
Enter new filename:
```

At this prompt, type **SUITE-2.DWG**.

You also can rename files in other directories or on other drives.

Option 5 (Copy file) lets you make a copy of a file. This is handy for copying files from your hard drive to a floppy disk for backup or distribution to a client. Start by selecting Option 5 from the File Utility Menu. AutoCAD then displays the following prompt:

```
Enter name of source file:
```

AutoCAD is asking you to specify the name of the file to be copied. In this example, type **SUITE-2.DWG** and press Enter. AutoCAD then displays the following prompt:

```
Enter name of destination file:
```

Suppose that you want to copy SUITE-2.DWG to a floppy disk in drive A. To do so, enter the following response to the destination prompt:

A:SUITE-2.DWG

Remember that you must include both the file name and the extension when you specify a file for copying.

Option 6 (Unlock file) lets you unlock one or more files that have been locked by you or another user. After you select this option, AutoCAD asks for the name of the file you want to unlock. You can use wild cards if you want to unlock more than one file.

After you have worked with the File Utility options, return to the Main
Menu to continue learning about its options.

Option 7 — Compile Shape/Font Description File

Main Menu Option 7 compiles shape and font files that you may have
created outside AutoCAD. These files must be compiled before you use
them. Shapes and font descriptions are advanced AutoCAD techniques
not covered in this book. You can learn more about these aspects of
AutoCAD by reading *AutoCAD Advanced Techniques*, published by Que
Corporation.

Option 8 — Convert Old Drawing File

Main Menu Option 8 updates old file formats to the current release of
AutoCAD. The drawing-file format changed dramatically after AutoCAD
Release 2.0. Some types of entities were removed and new ones were
added.

Drawings from more recent versions of AutoCAD automatically update
the first time you load them into Release 11. Use the End command to
save the drawing in Release 11 format. As stated earlier in this chapter,
you will need a translation program to convert drawings from Release 11
to an older version. Option 8 does just the opposite: it updates very old
versions of a drawing.

If you try to edit a very old drawing in a new release of AutoCAD, and the
file is rejected because it is old, simply use Option 8 to convert the file;
then edit it.

Option 9 — Recover Damaged Drawing

Sometimes AutoCAD drawing files go bad. This can happen for several
reasons. Fortunately, it does not happen very often. When a drawing file
goes bad, AutoCAD can no longer read the file and you can no longer
work with the drawing. With AutoCAD Release 11, two features help you
recover damaged drawing files. One of these features is that the files
themselves contain *redundancy*, duplicate information about important
parts of the file. The other is *file auditing*, in which AutoCAD checks the
information to ensure that it is a valid drawing file.

When you select Option 9, AutoCAD attempts to fix or eliminate the errors it finds in the drawing file. When AutoCAD is done, you may have to redo portions of the drawing AutoCAD was unable to recover. That's a lot easier than having to redraw the entire drawing.

This option will not work on drawings created with Release 10 or earlier. You can purchase a third-party program to fix such drawings.

Summary

This chapter has introduced you to AutoCAD. You have learned about the Main Menu and its options. You also have learned the basics of entering and exiting the AutoCAD Drawing Editor and working in the AutoCAD coordinate system.

Although AutoCAD is an extremely powerful and versatile drafting tool, it is not so complex that a casual user cannot use it to create simple drawings. This chapter showed you how AutoCAD drawings are created. The following chapters demonstrate how you can put AutoCAD's commands to work for you.

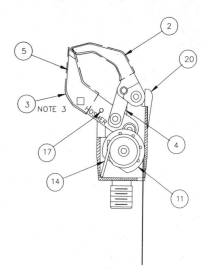

5

Drawing Basics

*Illustration courtesy of
Autodesk, Inc., Sausalito, CA.*

In this chapter you will learn how to use the basic AutoCAD drawing commands. You also will learn four different ways to input AutoCAD commands. This chapter shows you how to enter commands from the following sources:

- ❏ Keyboard
- ❏ Pull-down menu
- ❏ Screen menu
- ❏ Digitizing tablet

When you find the command-entry method that works best for you, you can go on to learn the following basic drawing commands from the examples in this chapter:

❏ Arc	❏ Point
❏ Circle	❏ Polygon
❏ Donut	❏ Setvar
❏ Ellipse	❏ Solid
❏ Line	❏ Units
❏ Pline	

These commands create many of the entities shown in figure 5.1. You use these entities to create your drawings.

Fig. 5.1.
AutoCAD
creates
drawings from
these 19 basic
entities.

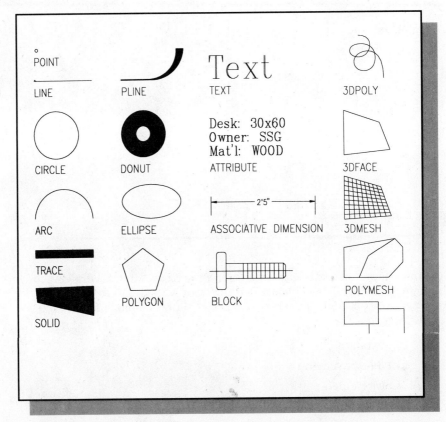

After you finish reading this chapter and have worked through the example, you should have a good understanding of how to use AutoCAD's drawing commands.

The Role of Commands

If you have drawn with a paint program, you will find drawing with AutoCAD different. In a paint program, you mostly draw freehand—usually with a mouse—and don't worry much about accuracy. Commands in a paint program are simple and offer few options; most are simply picked from a menu on the screen.

AutoCAD drawing is different because precision is of much greater importance in AutoCAD than in simple paint programs. Freehand drawing is the exception, not the rule, in AutoCAD. You can use a mouse, but you are just as likely to type in coordinate points.

AutoCAD has far more commands than any paint program. Many of the commands are used for altering what you have already drawn, or for extracting information from the drawing. While nearly all of AutoCAD's commands are available from the screen menu, you can't truly learn how a command works unless you type it in at the keyboard. The screen menu makes command entry semiautomatic, by supplying some responses to save you work. The menus can help you work more efficiently, but you will better appreciate the menus' advantages after you have learned how to use AutoCAD the "old fashioned" way—by entering commands and selecting options from the keyboard.

This is why this book shows you how to use AutoCAD by typing commands at the keyboard. Occasionally, you will learn a shortcut method by using the screen menu or one of the program's pull-down menus.

Entering Commands in AutoCAD

AutoCAD lets you enter commands in several ways. No one particular method is the best for all drawing situations. You should familiarize yourself with each method of command entry so that you can determine which one works best for you in a given situation.

Certain methods of command entry, however, work poorly or not at all with the keyboard—they require a digitizer or mouse. If you are uncertain about your system's hardware options, read Chapter 2, which discusses the most commonly used CAD-system equipment.

Entering Commands from the Keyboard

The keyboard is an integral part of every computer. If you are a touch typist, you will probably prefer the keyboard for command input. If you hunt-and-peck your way around the keyboard, you probably will want to use one of AutoCAD's other input methods.

When you use the keyboard to enter AutoCAD commands, you type in the command's full name (your keystrokes appear after the `Command:` prompt at the bottom of the screen), and then press either the Enter key or the space bar. The result of pressing either the Enter key or the space bar is the same; both keys tell AutoCAD to execute the command you just typed.

Many AutoCAD commands have subcommands. To execute the subcommand, you need to type only the capitalized portion of the subcommand—usually just a single letter—to invoke it.

A *word about making mistakes* . . .

As you saw in Chapter 4, AutoCAD is forgiving when you make drawing mistakes and also lets you correct typing errors.

If you catch a typing mistake before you press Enter, you can erase the error by using the Backspace key.

If you don't catch the error, AutoCAD will. Here is an example of how AutoCAD lets you try again after you try to enter a misspelled Line command:

```
Command: Limf
Invalid command
Command: Line
From point:
```

If, in the middle of a command, you realize that you want to do something else, type Ctrl-C (which shows up on-screen as ^C), as follows:

```
Command: Line
From point: ^C
*Cancel*
Command:
```

The Ctrl-C sequence cancels the command and returns you to the `Command:` prompt.

Shortcut Keys

In addition to Ctrl-C, AutoCAD lets you take advantage of several other shortcut keystrokes. These shortcuts vary according to the computer you are using; refer to the AutoCAD *Installation and Performance Guide* for more information. For PC-compatible computers, the shortcut keystrokes are as follows:

To:	*Press:*
Enter a command	Enter or space bar
Cancel a command	Ctrl-C
Cancel a dialogue box	Esc
Delete a command	Ctrl-D
Backspace	Backspace
Delete characters to the end of a line	Ctrl-X
Move the cursor up	↑
Move the cursor down	↓
Move the cursor left	←
Move the cursor right	→
Send the cursor to the screen menu	Ins
Return cursor to screen	Home
Speed up cursor movement	PgUp
Slow down cursor movement	PgDn
Send the cursor to the next view port	Ctrl-V
Switch the screen between text mode and graphics mode	F1
Toggle the coordinate display	Ctrl-D or F6
Toggle grid markings on and off	Ctrl-G or F7
Toggle orthographic mode on and off	Ctrl-O or F8
Toggle snap mode on and off	Ctrl-S or F9
Toggle the tablet between menu and digitizing	F10

You also can use *command aliases* to replace a command name with a single keystroke. Command aliasing is covered in detail in Chapter 13.

Selecting Commands from the Screen Menu

As you saw in Chapter 4, the AutoCAD Drawing Editor screen has a menu on the right side of the screen. This *screen menu* gives you fast access to all of AutoCAD's commands. That is, to execute a command, you simply pick it from the menu instead of typing its full name. Although you can access the screen menu's commands by pressing the keyboard's arrow keys, the menu is easier to use with a mouse or digitizing tablet.

Using the screen menu has two advantages: you can work "heads up," choosing commands without looking away from the screen, and you never make a typing mistake.

The screen menu is several layers deep, as shown in figure 5.2. The basic screen menu—that is, the one you see when you first enter the Drawing Editor—is called the *Root Menu*. From this menu you can access many other menus, including menus of editing commands, drawing commands, and display commands. The screen menu hierarchy shown in figure 5.2 is taken from Autodesk's MENUTREE sample drawing.

To access the screen menu from the keyboard, press Ins. A highlighter bar appears at the bottom of the menu. You then can use the arrow keys to move the highlighter up or down to the command you want to execute. When the desired command is highlighted, press Enter or the space bar to execute the command.

If you use a mouse or digitizer, move the pointing device to the right until the cursor is in the screen menu and a menu item is highlighted. Next, move the pointing device up or down to select a command, and then press the pick button to execute the command. The location of the pick button varies, as follows:

Input Device	Pick Button
Mouse	The left button
Puck	The first button
Stylus	The tip button

If you want to draw a line, for example, select DRAW from the Root Menu. The Root Menu is replaced by the Draw Menu, from which you can select a drawing command, such as Line.

Each screen menu offers its own list of options. The following options— which help you work more quickly—are common to most screen menus:

- ❏ **AutoCAD** always returns you to the Root Menu.
- ❏ ******** accesses special commands, such as Redraw and the object snap overrides. As an alternative, the third puck or third mouse button also accesses this menu item.

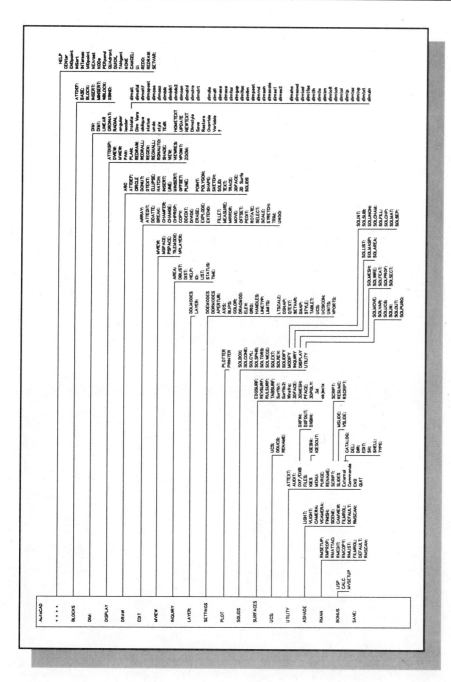

*Fig. 5.2.
AutoCAD's
screen menu
hierarchy.*

❏ **NEXT** appears at the bottom of the current screen menu if there is more than one screen of commands. The NEXT option takes you to the next page of menu commands.

❏ **PREVIOUS** returns you to the preceding menu page.

❏ **LAST** lets you backtrack through the menus.

Selecting Commands from the Pull-Down Menus

If your video card is Hercules or IBM-compatible (CGA, EGA, VGA, or 8514/A) or uses the Autodesk Device Interface (ADI) driver, you can use AutoCAD's pull-down menus. Like the screen menu, pull-down menus let you work heads-up, but display more information than the Root Menu can.

When you use the mouse, puck, or stylus to move the crosshairs to the status line at the top of the screen, the pull-down menu headings appear (see fig. 5.3). To select a particular pull-down menu, move the highlighter to the appropriate heading and pick it. The menu pops down below the heading (see fig. 5.4). You cannot access the pull-down menus from the keyboard.

Fig. 5.3.
The pull-down
menu line.

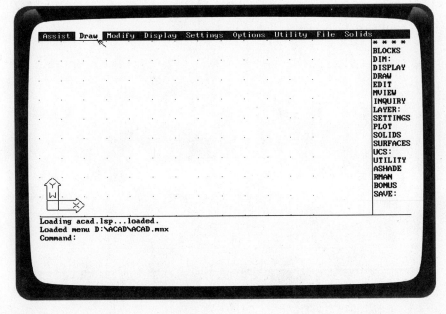

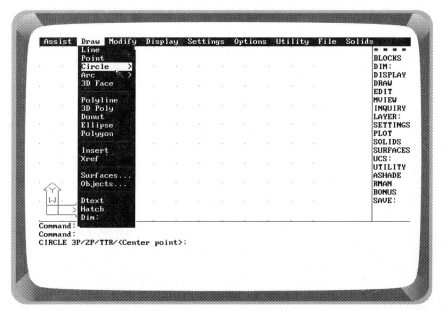

Fig. 5.4.
The Draw
pull-down
menu, with
the Circle
command
highlighted.

To make a selection from the pull-down menu, move the cursor vertically through the menu, highlight the command you want, and then press your pointing device's pick button to execute the command. The diagram of pull-down menus shown in figure 5.5 is taken from the MENUTREE drawing supplied by Autodesk.

Some commands on the pull-down menus are programmed to repeat themselves. This is convenient if, for example, you want to draw several filled circles at a time. After you finish using the Donut command, press Ctrl-C to stop the command from executing further, and to return you to the Command: prompt. Even if a command does not repeat itself automatically, you still can easily repeat a command.

A word about repeating commands . . .

AutoCAD gives you two ways of repeating a command so that you don't need to reselect it by typing or picking it.

AutoCAD will repeat the last-executed command if you press the Enter key or space bar on the keyboard (or the pick button on the mouse or puck) at the Command: prompt. Suppose, for example, that you have just finished using the Line command. To use it again, do the following:

    Command: Press Enter
    Command: LINE

Fig. 5.5.
AutoCAD's
pull-down
menu
hierarchy.

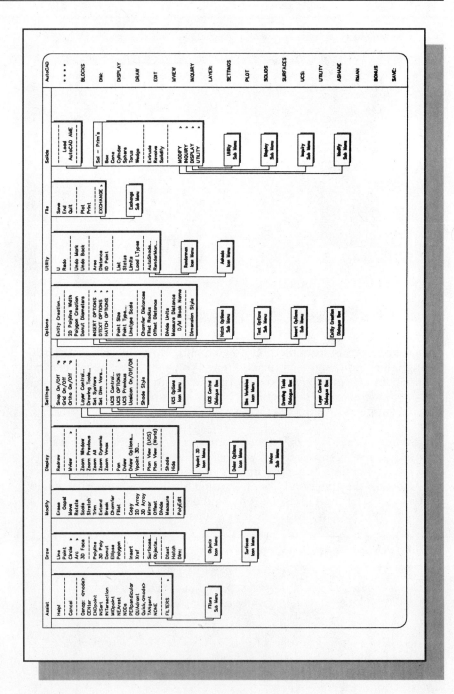

A *word about repeating commands (continued)* . . .

If you want a command to be repeated many times, use the Multiple command prior to the command to be repeated. For example, you can repeat the Circle command (described later in this chapter) as many times as necessary by typing the following at the `Command:` prompt:

> `Command:` Multiple Circle

AutoCAD then displays the normal Circle command prompts, but the command repeats automatically after each circle is finished (you do not need to press Enter or the space bar to repeat the command). To cancel the repetition, press Ctrl-C.

Some commands executed from the pull-down menus display a *dialogue box* that AutoCAD temporarily superimposes over your drawing, as shown in figure 5.6. You can interact with the dialogue box by entering values, changing settings, or picking options.

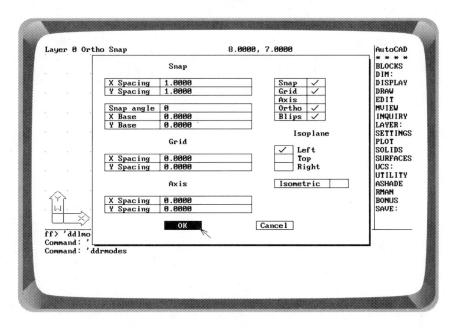

Fig. 5.6.
This dialogue box lets you set the drawing modes.

To remove the pull-down menu or dialogue box from the screen without entering a command, you can do one of the following:

❏ Press Ctrl-C.

❏ Press the Cancel button (the middle button on a three-button mouse, or the third puck button).

❏ Pick in a blank slot in the menu.

❏ Pick in an area of the screen not covered by the pull-down menu.

❏ On the dialogue box only, pick the Cancel button.

Even if you do not understand all the AutoCAD commands, practice using the pull-down menus to familiarize yourself with the commands' locations on the menus.

Selecting Commands from the Digitizing Tablet

If you've attached the AutoCAD overlay template (see fig. 5.7) to your digitizing tablet, you can use a stylus or a puck to enter commands from the digitizer. The tablet lets you issue commands in much the same way as the screen and pull-down menus; that is, you can pick the commands from the tablet overlay without typing them. The additional advantage of the digitizer overlay is that all AutoCAD commands are visible simultaneously, rather than hidden away in multiple menus.

The tablet menu contains only the most commonly used AutoCAD commands. Figure 5.7 shows a drawing (supplied by Autodesk) of the tablet menu with the different menu areas indicated. As well as selecting commands from the overlay, you can use the digitizer to control the pull-down menus and screen menu by using the MENUBAR and SCREEN MENU segments of the overlay. You also can add your own custom commands to the top portion of the overlay.

Choosing the Best Input Method for You

You may find yourself using all four methods of command input. The keyboard is best for entering numbers, and is the fastest way to enter commands if you're a touch typist.

The pull-down menus are slow for simple commands (such as Line or Circle), but extremely useful for complex commands (such as Shade or Style). Experienced AutoCAD users often use the Root Menu to supplement the pull-down menus.

If you have many customized commands or use predrawn symbols, the tablet overlay may be your best means of controlling AutoCAD. If you familiarize yourself with all methods of command input, you'll quickly discover the most efficient method for any situation.

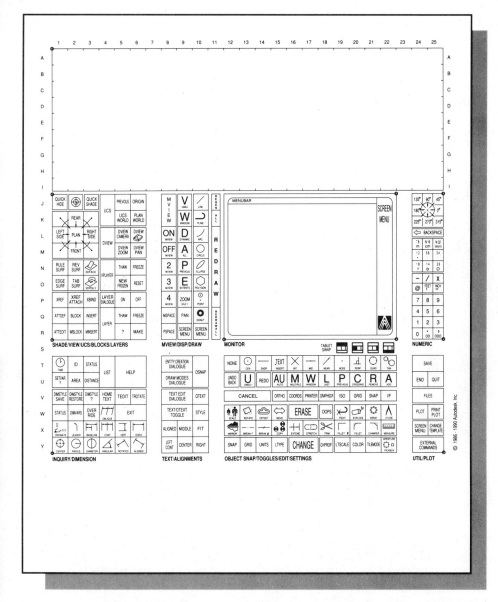

Fig. 5.7.
The AutoCAD
Release 11
digitizer
overlay,
courtesy of
Autodesk, Inc.

At the end of the puck is a clear plastic extension with wire crosshairs through the center. The digitizer tracks the location of the crosshairs as you move the puck, and tells AutoCAD exactly where you are pointing on the tablet. Place the crosshairs over the box on the overlay that corresponds to the command you want to execute, and press the pick button to execute the command.

The Sample Drawing

To learn how to create two-dimensional drawings with AutoCAD, you will create a drawing of an apartment floor plan that demonstrates all the commonly used AutoCAD commands. The example begins with simple elements, building on them to create a complex drawing.

You will start by creating a bathroom using only the AutoCAD drawing commands. In Chapter 6, you will use the editing commands to create the rest of the floor plan with a minimum of work.

Start AutoCAD and select Option 1 from the Main Menu. Name the drawing SUITE.

Learning To Use AutoCAD's Drawing Commands

The AutoCAD drawing commands form the basis for almost anything you create. Autodesk has tried to make the commands easy to use, and they generally are easy to learn. For example, most AutoCAD commands have names that describe their function: the Line command draws lines, the Circle command draws circles, and the Erase command erases them.

All AutoCAD commands have a *default response*, which is displayed in angle brackets <like this>. Default responses help speed up your work because they decrease the amount of typing required. AutoCAD commands use two kinds of default response:

❏ AutoCAD remembers how you last responded to the command, and assumes that you are likely to answer the same way. Your last response to a command usually appears in angle brackets the next time you issue the command.

❏ If you have not changed the default response to a command, the current setting appears in the angle brackets.

If the default response represents the action you want to take, simply press Enter (or the space bar) to select it.

Setting Display Format and Precision (Units)

AutoCAD can work in the same units of measurement you are accustomed to using. If you look at the status line, you see the X and Y coordinates displayed with four decimal places (for example, 2.0000,3.4321). AutoCAD also can display coordinates as fractional units (1/2") or scientific units (1E+02). Similarly, you can have AutoCAD display angles in degrees, radians, grads, or in surveyor's units (such as N45E).

You use the Units command to set the format in which measurements are displayed, and to establish the degree of precision to which AutoCAD calculates measurements and angles. This command lets you change any of the following:

❑ Unit format

❑ Unit display precision

❑ Angle format

❑ Angle display precision

❑ Angle direction

For the sample drawing, you will use architectural units of feet and inches, and decimal degrees.

Report Formats

Enter **Units** at the `Command:` prompt and press Enter. AutoCAD displays the following menu of available formats, with examples of how each is displayed:

```
Report formats:        (Examples)

   1. Scientific        1.55E+01
   2. Decimal           15.50
   3. Engineering       1'-3.50"
   4. Architectural     1'-3 1/2"
   5. Fractional        15 1/2

      Enter choice, 1 to 5 <2>:
```

Choose option 4 to use architectural units. The Decimal option (the default) can be used for metric units as well as decimal Imperial units.

Your response to AutoCAD's next question depends on which system of units you select. Since you selected 4 (Architectural), AutoCAD displays the following prompt:

```
Denominator of smallest fraction to display
(1, 2, 4, 8, 16, 32, or 64) <16>:
```

Because you will be working to the nearest inch, type **1**. (If you were to type **8**, AutoCAD would display fractions to the nearest 1/8".)

When you select option 1 (Scientific), 2 (Decimal), or 3 (Engineering), the following prompt appears:

```
Number of digits to right of decimal point (0 to 8)
<4>:
```

Angle Measurement

After you have selected the report format and precision, AutoCAD prompts you for an angle format, as follows:

```
Systems of angle measure:          (Examples)
   1. Decimal degrees              45.0000
   2. Degrees/minutes/seconds      45d0'0"
   3. Grads                        50.0000g
   4. Radians                      0.7854r
   5. Surveyor's units             N 45d0'0" E
      Enter choice, 1 to 5 <1>:
```

The example to the right of each selection shows the syntax to use when you enter an angle within AutoCAD. For this example, leave the angle system at 1 (Decimal degrees) by typing **1** in response to the prompt.

Next, AutoCAD displays the following prompt:

```
Number of fractional places for display of angles
(0 to 8) <4>:
```

You can specify a precision of up to eight decimal places. In the sample drawing, you work with a precision of one decimal place, so type **1** in response to this prompt.

If you are working with degrees/minutes/seconds (D/M/S), the number you enter determines the accuracy of the minutes and seconds:

Value Entered	Display
0	Degrees only
1 or 2	Degrees and minutes
3 or 4	D/M/S
5 to 8	D/M/S and fractional seconds with 1 to 4 decimal places

AutoCAD prompts you for the direction of zero degrees. The default is 3 o'clock—the positive X direction—with angles calculated counter-clockwise from the 3 o'clock position. At the following prompt, you can change both the zero angle and the direction in which other angles will be calculated.

```
Direction for angle 0.0000:
    East    3 o'clock  =    0
    North  12 o'clock  =   90
    West    9 o'clock  =  180
    South   6 o'clock  =  270
     Enter direction for angle 0.0000 <East>:
```

Press Enter because you are going to use AutoCAD's default of east-is-zero. (East-is-zero comes from AutoCAD's X,Y-coordinate system.)

If you want to specify an angle that is not listed, press F1 to switch to the graphics screen. Indicate the desired angle by picking two points on the screen.

 If you indicate a new zero direction by picking it on the screen, be sure to remember the direction you choose. Using a nonstandard angle as the zero direction can lead to confusion.

The final prompt controls whether the direction of angles is measured clockwise or counterclockwise:

```
Do you want angles measured clockwise? <N>:
```

Press Enter to keep AutoCAD's default of measuring angles counter-clockwise from the positive X axis. Answer **Y** if you want the angles to be measured clockwise.

Drawing Lines (Line)

As you saw in Chapter 4, AutoCAD lets you draw lines easily by using the Line command. To draw a line, you simply tell AutoCAD the line's starting and ending points. If you want to draw several connected lines, you just keep telling AutoCAD where the next end point is. The Line command also has an option called Close; by joining the last line's ending point to the beginning point of the first line, this option simplifies the process of closing a polygon.

Now, use the Line command to create the bathroom walls. Enter the following responses to AutoCAD's prompts. (Be sure to press Enter after each response.)

Prompt	Response	Explanation
Command:	**Line**	Starts the Line command
From Point:	**0,0**	Starts line at point 0,0
To Point:	**@7'0"<0**	First wall line
To Point:	**@5'0"<90**	Second wall line
To Point:	**@7'0"<180**	Third wall line
To Point:	**C**	Draws last line back to starting point

The results of this command sequence appear in figure 5.8.

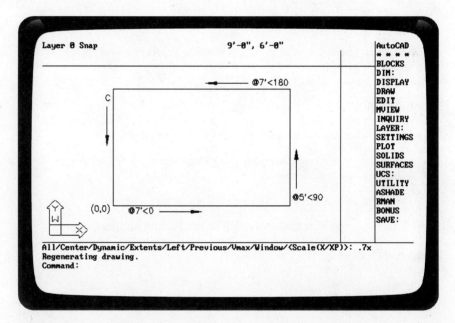

Fig. 5.8.
The walls of the bathroom, drawn by using absolute and relative coordinates.

In the previous series of keystrokes, you entered absolute and relative coordinates. The absolute coordinates are the X,Y pair (0,0); the relative coordinates begin with the @ symbol (@7'0"<0). The difference between absolute and relative points was discussed in Chapter 4.

NOTE

You don't need to type unnecessary digits in coordinates. For example, if you type a dimension without units, AutoCAD assumes that the value is inches. The line drawn as @7'0"<0 in the preceding example could have been entered as @7'<0. The angle of 0 degrees is still necessary, but the 0 inches and the " symbol are not.

If you can't see the four wall lines, type **Zoom E**, followed by **Zoom 0.8x**. These commands (which are discussed in Chapter 7) bring the entire drawing, with some breathing space around it, into view.

While you're at it, go ahead and draw the tub. The tub is simple to create. Enter the following commands and coordinates, remembering to press Enter after each response:

Prompt	Response	Explanation
`Command:`	**Line**	Starts the Line command
`From Point:`	**5',0**	Starts the tub's edge
`To Point:`	**@5'<90**	Draws it up to other wall
`To Point:`	Press Enter	Ends the Line command
`Command:`	Press Enter	Restarts the Line command
`Line From Point:`	**6'9,3**	Draws the inner tub line (3" inside the wall and tub lines)
`To Point:`	**@1'6<180**	Draws the first of four sides
`To Point:`	**@4'6<90**	Draws the second side
`To Point:`	**@1'6<0**	Draws the third side
`To Point:`	**C**	Finishes with last side

Your drawing should now contain the elements shown in figure 5.9. At this stage, all the corners of the tub are sharp (and liable to hurt you if you got in). All the inner lines are parallel to the outer lines, which normally doesn't happen with tub design. In Chapter 6, you will learn to use editing commands to make the tub look more realistic.

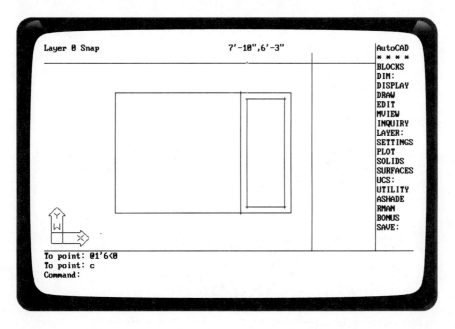

Fig. 5.9.
The bathtub, drawn using the Line command.

Now use the Line command again to draw the edges of the sink. (Later, you will use the Ellipse command to draw the sink basin.) The following command sequence walks you through the process of drawing the sink edges:

Prompt	Response	Explanation
Command:	**Line**	Starts the Line command
From Point:	**0,5'**	The beginning point of the first line of the bathroom sink
To Point:	**@1'6<270**	Draws the first line of the sink
To Point:	**@2'6<0**	Draws the second line of the sink
To Point:	**@1'6<90**	Draws the third line
To Point:	**C**	Draws the fourth line, and connects it with the beginning point of the first line

Figure 5.10 shows the bathroom to this point, with its wall, tub, and sink lines. The following sections teach you how to use other commands to "flesh out" the drawing.

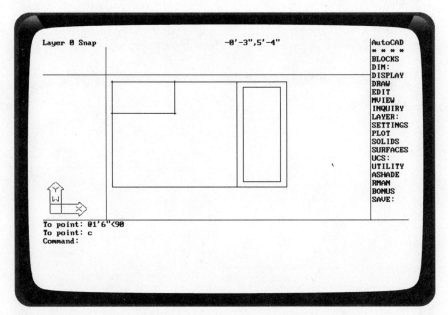

Fig. 5.10.
The bathroom
floor plan
with the sink
outline added.

Cleaning Up the Display (Redraw)

At this point, your screen may be cluttered with blip marks—the little plus signs (+) that AutoCAD puts down whenever you pick a point.

These blips are not permanent. When they clutter the display, use the Redraw command to clean them up, as follows:

    C o m m a n d : **Redraw**

The screen clears briefly; then the drawing is quickly redrawn without the blip marks.

Drawing Circles (Circle)

The following example shows you how to use the Circle command to create the bathtub drain. Later in this chapter, you will use the Donut command to draw the sink drain.

Circles can be drawn in several ways. The most common method is to specify a center point and radius. You also can specify the center point and diameter, or AutoCAD can describe a circle based on two or three points that you pick. AutoCAD also can build a circle on tangent points and a radius, which you specify (see fig. 5.11). Here, you will draw the circles by using the command's default option; that is, you pick a center point for the circle and then specify a radius.

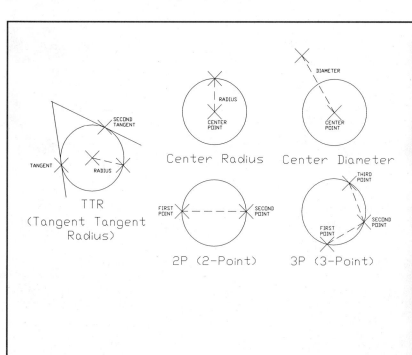

Fig. 5.11.
AutoCAD lets
you draw
circles five
different
ways.

Follow this command sequence to draw the bathtub drain:

Prompt	Response	Explanation
Command	**Circle**	Starts the Circle command
3P/2P/TTR/<Center point>:	6',1'3	Locates the center of the bathtub drain
Diameter/<Radius>:	1	Specifies a radius of 1"

Your bathroom should now look like the drawing in figure 5.12.

Fig. 5.12.
A circle forms the tub drain.

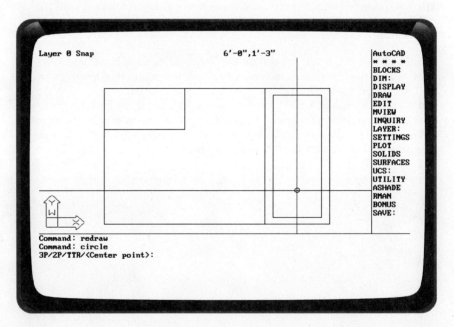

In all, AutoCAD lets you describe a circle in five ways, as follows:

Circle-Radius You can pick the circle's center point and then specify a value for the circle's radius:

```
Command: Circle
3P/2P/TTR/<Center point>: Pick center point
Diameter/<Radius>: 12
```

Center-Diameter You can pick the circle's center point and then specify a value for the circle's diameter:

```
Command: Circle
3P/2P/TTR/<Center point>: Pick center point
Diameter/<Radius>: D
Diameter: 24
```

2P (Two-Point) You can pick two points that lie on the circle's perimeter to define the circle's diameter:

```
Command: Circle
3P/2P/TTR/<Center point>: 2P
First point on diameter: Pick first point
Second point on diameter: Pick second point
```

3P (Three-Point) You can pick three points that lie on the circle's perimeter:

```
Command: Circle
3P/2P/TTR/<Center point>: 3P
First point: Pick first point
Second point: Pick second point
Third point: Pick third point
```

TTR (Tangent-Tangent-Radius) You can pick two points where the circle is tangent to an existing object (such as a line or circle) and then specify the circle's radius:

```
Command: Circle
3P/2P/TTR/<Center point>: TTR
Enter Tangent spec: Pick first point
Enter second Tangent spec: Pick second point
Radius: 12
```

Remember to save your work to disk periodically by issuing the Save command. If your system suffers a power failure, or if your computer locks up, you will lose your work unless you use the Save command, as follows:

```
Command: Save
File name <SUITE>: Press Enter
```

If you make a habit of saving your work every 10 minutes, you will lose—at most—the last 10 minutes of work should your system fail.

Drawing Ellipses (Ellipse)

Now it's time to add the outline of the bathroom sink. The following command sequence shows you one way to use AutoCAD's Ellipse command to draw an elliptical shape for the basin:

Prompt	Response	Explanation
`Command:`	**Ellipse**	Starts the Ellipse command
`<Axis endpoint1>` `/Center:`	6,4'3	Locates the starting point of the first axis
`Axis endpoint 2:`	@1'6<0	Specifies the length and direction of the first axis
`<Other axis distance>` `/Rotation:`	@6<90	Specifies the length and direction of the second axis

To create an accurate ellipse (see fig. 5.13), you first specify the length of its major axis. The length of the major axis is the distance across the widest section of the ellipse. You then specify the minor axis, which is the narrower section of the ellipse. From the two unequal axes you specify, AutoCAD creates the oval shape of an ellipse.

Fig. 5.13.
An ellipse has both a major and a minor axis.

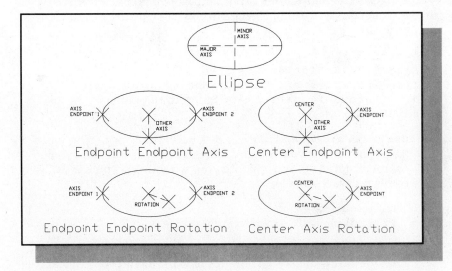

AutoCAD also enables you to create an ellipse by using the Center option to specify the center of the ellipse, and then visually picking the locations for the major and minor axes' endpoints. This method, however, produces a less accurate ellipse.

Now use the Ellipse and Line commands to draw the toilet:

Prompt	Response	Explanation
`Command:`	**Line**	Starts the Line command
`From Point:`	2'10,4'11	Specifies the starting point of the toilet tank
`To Point:`	@1'6<0	Draws the first line of the toilet tank

Prompt	Response	Explanation
To Point:	@8<270	Draws the second line of the toilet tank
To Point:	@1'6<180	Draws the third line of the toilet tank
To Point:	C	Draws the final line of the tank, and closes it with the beginning point of the first line
Command:	**Ellipse**	Starts the Ellipse command
<Axis endpoint 1> /Center:	C	Specifies the Center option
Center of ellipse:	3'9,3'8"	Specifies the center point of the toilet bowl
Axis endpoint:	@6<270	Specifies the endpoint of the major axis
<Other axis distance> /Rotation:	@6<90	Specifies the length of the minor axis

Figure 5.14 shows the bathroom with all the objects you have drawn so far, including the basin and toilet.

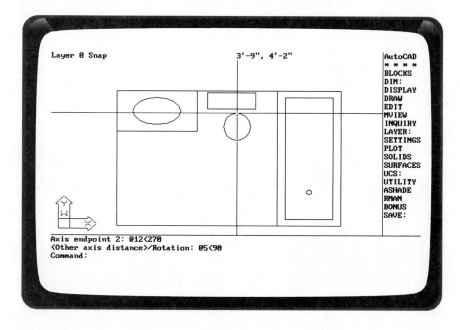

Fig. 5.14.
The toilet has been added to the bathroom drawing.

The Polyline Command (Pline)

For the next element of the bathroom, you will use a variation of the Line command, called Pline (short for *polyline* and pronounced "P-line"). Polylines are special entities in AutoCAD; that is, polylines are lines and arcs connected end-to-end to form a single entity. You can connect ordinary lines and arcs together, but they only look as though they're connected end-to-end; they actually remain separate entities.

Polylines are extremely versatile: the individual segments of a polyline can be tapered, wide, or slender arcs or lines. Some of AutoCAD's other entities—ellipses, donuts, and polygons—are created with their own commands but are actually made of polylines.

Polylines are so useful that you may find yourself using the Pline command far more often than the Line command. The Pline command can replace the Line, Solid, and Trace commands (Solid and Trace are discussed later in this text). You could use polylines to draw contour lines or arrowheads. Other AutoCAD commands create entities out of polylines.

Next, you will use the Pline command to draw the bathroom door, which is made from four lines. Because the Pline command draws four connected lines and treats them as a single entity, the door is easier to modify. If you want to move or rotate it to fit the opening (as you will in the next chapter), you can pick any piece of the door and AutoCAD selects the entire door (all four lines) as a single entity.

The initial prompt for the Pline command is similar to the prompt for the Line command. When you enter **Pline**, AutoCAD prompts you for the starting point of the polyline:

```
Command: Pline
From point:
```

When you have picked that point, the following prompts appear on-screen:

```
Current line width is 0'-0"
Arc/Close/Halfwidth/Length/Undo/Width/<Endpoint of line>:
```

By default, the Pline command draws a thin line, but you also can draw polylines that have a consistent width (1", for example) from one end to the other, or which have a tapered width. (Use the Width option to assign widths to a polyline.) In this example, you create the door by indicating the line's endpoint (the default option). You can select any of the other options from the prompt by typing the desired option's first letter. These options are discussed shortly. For now, take the following steps to create the door:

Prompt	Response	Explanation
Command:	**Pline**	Starts the Pline command
From Point:	**0,4**	Specifies the starting point of the door
.../<Endpoint of line>:	**@2'6<0**	The door's length is 2'6"
.../<Endpoint of line>:	**@1<90**	The door's width is 1"
.../<Endpoint of line>:	**@2'6<180**	Draws the third side of the door
.../<Endpoint of line>:	**C**	Closes the polyline back to the beginning

Your door should resemble the one shown in figure 5.15.

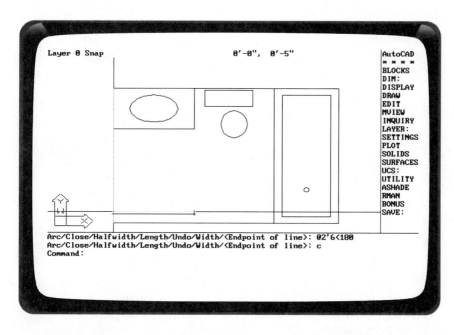

Fig. 5.15. The door is drawn as a polyline.

You can use the Pline command's six other options to draw arcs, to specify the polyline's width or half-width, to specify the length of the next segment, or to close the polygon (see fig. 5.16). These options are described in the following paragraphs.

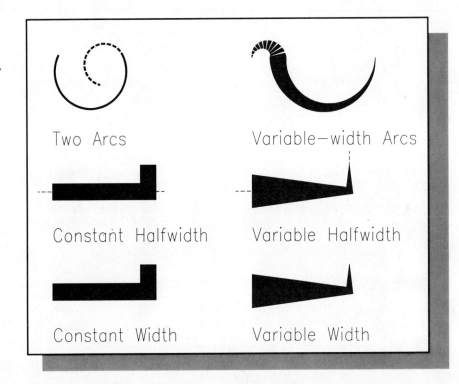

Fig. 5.16.
Polylines are
versatile.

Arc If you want to draw a polyline arc, select the Arc option by picking it from the drawing menu (or by typing **A** at the Pline prompt shown earlier, and then pressing Enter). AutoCAD displays the following prompt:

```
Angle/CEnter/CLose/Direction/Halfwidth/Line/Radius
/Second pt/Undo/Width/ <endpoint of arc>:
```

As you can see, there are many ways to draw a polyline arc. These options are described in detail in the next section during the discussion of the Arc command.

Close A polyline can be open or closed. Closing a polyline performs the same function as the Line command's C option; it draws a line or arc segment from the last point you entered to the beginning of the polyline.

Width A special property of polylines is that they can have thickness, or width. You can specify the width either as the full width or as half the width from either side of a center line. The Width option displays the following prompts:

```
Starting width <0.00>:
Ending width <0.00>:
```

If you want the line (or arc) to have uniform width, enter the same value at both prompts. If you want the line to taper from one end to the other, enter two different values.

Halfwidth Use the Halfwidth option to specify a different width on either side of a center line. AutoCAD displays the following prompts:

```
Starting half-width <0.00>:
Ending half-width <0.00>:
```

You can enter a pair of values, or pick the width (or halfwidth) on-screen.

Length The Length option continues drawing the polyline in the same direction for the length you specify. This option is useful when you want to draw a polyline that is tangent to an arc.

Undo Select the Undo option when you want to undo the last segment you drew. The effects of Undo are the same in Pline as they are in the Line command, as described in Chapter 4.

AutoCAD will not let you use the Pline Arc command to draw a full circle. The work-around is to draw two polyline arcs, each of which makes half the circle, or to use the Donut command.

In the next section, you will use the Arc command to show the door's path when it opens.

Drawing Arcs (Arc)

The Arc command is one of the most complex AutoCAD drawing commands. It has 11 options for creating arcs. The fastest way to create an arc is to start the Arc command and pick three points that don't lie on a straight line. You can use the third point to drag the arc into place.

With AutoCAD, a *highlighted* image is quickly drawn and moves as you move the cursor. The movement of this temporary entity is called *dragging*. Dragging the temporary "ghosted" image lets you check the way the entity looks before it becomes a part of the drawing.

AutoCAD lets you draw arcs 10 other ways, as shown in figure 5.17.

The methods, frequently referred to by their initials (SSE for Start-Second-End, for example), are described in the following paragraphs.

SSE (Start-Second-End) You can supply a starting point, a second point that lies somewhere along the arc, and the end point:

```
Command: Arc
Center/<Start point>: Pick starting point
```

Fig. 5.17.
AutoCAD lets
you draw arcs
in 11 different
ways.

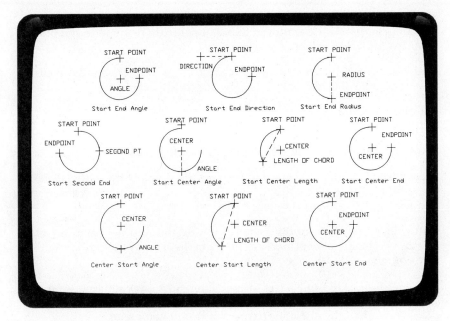

```
Center/End/<Second point>: Pick second point
End point: Pick ending point
```

SCA (Start-Center-Angle) You can supply the starting point, the arc's center point, and the angle through which the arc should pass:

```
Command: Arc
Center/<Start point>: Pick starting point
Center/End/<Second point>: C
Center: Pick center point
Angle/Length of chord/<End point>: A
Included angle: 45
```

SCL (Start-Center-Length) You can supply the starting point, the arc's center point, and the length of chord (connecting the starting and ending points):

```
Command: Arc
Center/<Start point>: Pick starting point
Center/End/<Second point>: C
Center: Pick center point
Angle/Length of chord/<End point>: L
Length of chord: 12
```

SCE (Start-Center-End) You can supply the starting point, the arc's center point, and the arc's ending point:

```
Command: Arc
Center/<Start point>: Pick starting point
Center/End/<Second point>: C
Center: Pick center point
Angle/Length of chord/<End point>: Pick end point
```

SEA (Start-End-Angle) You can supply the starting point, the ending point, and the included angle:

```
Command: Arc
Center/<Start point>: Pick starting point
Center/End/<Second point>: E
End point: Pick ending point
Angle/Direction/Radius/<Center point>: A
Included angle: 45
```

SED (Start-End-Direction) You can supply the starting point, the ending point, and a direction vector tangent to the start point:

```
Command: Arc
Center/<Start point>: Pick starting point
Center/End/<Second point>: E
End point: Pick ending point
Angle/Direction/Radius/<Center point>: D
Direction from start point: Pick direction
```

SER (Start-End-Radius) You can supply the starting point, the ending point, and the arc's radius:

```
Command: Arc
Center/<Start point>: Pick starting point
Center/End/<Second point>: E
End point: Pick ending point
Angle/Direction/Radius/<Center point>: R
Radius: Specify radius
```

CSA (Center-Start-Angle) You can supply the arc's center point, the starting point, and the included angle:

```
Command: Arc
Center/<Start point>: C
Center: Pick center point
Start point: Pick starting point
Angle/Length of chord/<End point>: A
Included angle: 45
End point: Pick ending point
Angle/Direction/Radius/<Center point>: C
Center: Pick center point
```

CSL (Center-Start-Length) You can supply the arc's center point, the starting point, and the chord length:

```
Command: Arc
Center/<Start point>: C
Center: Pick center point
Start point: Pick starting point
Angle/Length of chord/<End point>: L
Length of chord: 12
```

CSE (Center-Start-End) You can supply the arc's center point, the starting point, and the ending point:

```
Command: Arc
Center/<Start point>: C
Center: Pick center point
Start point: Pick starting point
Angle/Length of chord/<End point>: Pick ending point
```

The next example shows you how to use the Start-Center-Angle option to create an arc to indicate the bathroom door's path of travel. Arcs are ideal for indicating door swings in floor plans. Notice that the following command sequence includes a new command, INT (short for INTersection). INTersection is one of AutoCAD's *object snap* modes, which enables you to specify a point without entering its coordinates. Don't worry about learning how object snaps work just yet. For now, just follow the command sequence:

Prompt	Response	Explanation
Command:	**Arc**	Starts the Arc command
Center/<Start point>:	**Int**	Specifies the INTersection object snap
of	Pick point	Starts the arc at the intersection point of the door lines
Center/End/<Second point>:	**C**	Specifies the center point of the arc
Center:	**Int**	
of	Pick point	Specifies that the center point is located where the door and wall meet

Prompt	Response	Explanation
Angle/Length of chord /<End point>:	A	Specifies that you want to enter the arc angle
Included angle:	90	Draws the arc for a fully opening door

Your door swing should look like the one in figure 5.18.

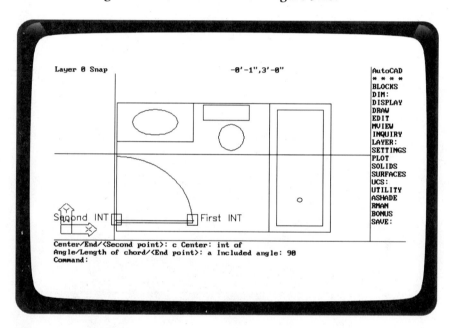

Fig. 5.18.
The door's path of travel is represented by an arc.

If you find drawing an arc too difficult, draw a circle and then use the Break command (covered in Chapter 6) to remove the portion of the circle you don't need.

Choosing What You Want: The Object Snap Overrides

AutoCAD lets you use exact locations rather than coordinates as input into a command. This capability, which is known as *object snap*, was used in the preceding example. The INTersection object snap caused AutoCAD to use the intersection of the two door lines. When you typed **Int** in the preceding example, AutoCAD located the intersection of two lines in the door and used that point as input for the Arc command.

Object snaps let you draw faster and more accurately. You don't need to know the exact X,Y coordinates; you let AutoCAD do the work of accurately finding the exact point.

Object snaps are not limited to intersections. AutoCAD has a total of 10 object snap modes (see fig. 5.19). Some you will use often, others you may rarely use, but all can be helpful. The 10 modes and the points they locate are listed in table 5.1.

Fig. 5.19.
AutoCAD's
object snap
modes.

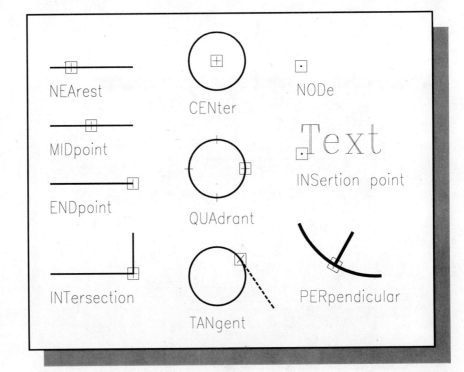

Table 5.1.
AutoCAD's Object Snap Modes

Mode	*Point located*
CENter	The center of a circle or arc
ENDpoint	The nearest end of a line, polyline, or arc
INSert	The insertion point of a block, shape, or text entity
INTersection	The point at which two lines or arcs cross or intersect
MIDpoint	The middle point of a line, polyline, or arc
NEArest	A point on the closest line, polyline arc, or circle entity
NODe	The coordinates of the closest point entity

Mode	Point located
PERpendicular	The location along a line or arc that is perpendicular (90°) to the last point you located
QUAdrant	The closest quadrant point (these points are located at 0, 90, 180, or 270 degrees) along an arc or a circle
TANgent	Allows you to locate the point along an arc or a circle that is tangent to the last point you located

To use object snap modes, you type their three-letter abbreviation (shown capitalized in table 5.1) rather than a coordinate. The ability to locate points without knowing their coordinates can come in handy. You should be familiar with and understand what all the modes do, even if you don't use some of them. You will continue to use object snap modes as you develop the sample drawing.

Drawing Regular Polygons (Polygon)

The Polygon command creates a figure with up to 1,024 sides of the same length (triangles, squares, and hexagons, but not rectangles). To create a polygon, you tell AutoCAD the number of sides to draw and whether the polygon is to be drawn inside or outside a circle with a certain radius. AutoCAD creates the polygon from a polyline.

The Polygon command is most useful when you need to draw an entity with sides that are all equal in length. In the example, you will use the Polygon command to create a unique decorator wastebasket with six sides.

Prompt	Response	Explanation
Command:	**Polygon**	Starts the Polygon command
Number of sides:	6	Indicates the number of sides
Edge/<Center of polygon>:	Pick point	Specifies the center point of the polygon
Inscribed in circle/ Circumscribed about circle I/C:	C	Draws the polygon outside a circle whose radius you will specify
Radius of circle:	3	The circle has a radius of 3"

Your wastebasket should look like the one in figure 5.20.

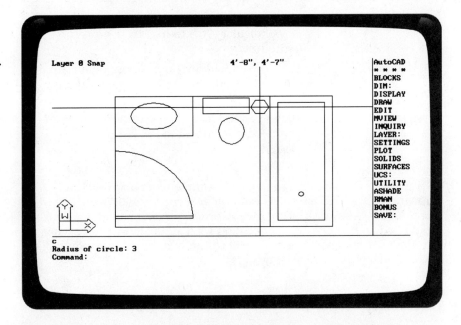

*Fig. 5.20.
The decorator
wastebasket,
made from a
polygon.*

Inscribed means that the lines making up the polygon are contained entirely within the circle upon which that polygon is based; *circumscribed* means that the lines are outside the circle. You enter either **I** or **C**, depending on where you want the polygon drawn (see fig. 5. 21). AutoCAD then displays a *ghosted* polygon (an image of what the polygon might look like) and prompts for the radius of the circle.

There is another way to have AutoCAD draw the polygon. If you want to create a polygon by first specifying the length of its sides, select the Edge option from the `Edge/<Center of polygon>:` prompt (see fig. 5.22). AutoCAD asks you for the two endpoints of the polygon side. Respond to the following prompts by picking the length of one side:

```
First endpoint of edge:
Second endpoint of edge:
```

A ghosted polygon appears after you specify the first endpoint. It can help you to select the second endpoint by showing you what the polygon will look like when you choose the second endpoint.

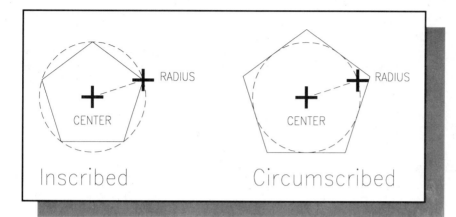

Fig. 5.21.
Examples of
inscribed and
circumscribed
polygons.

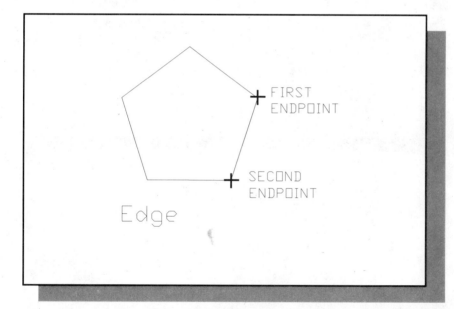

Fig. 5.22.
A polygon
drawn using
the Edge
option.

Drawing Rings and Solid Filled Circles (Donut or Doughnut)

Rings and solid filled circles (doughnuts) are another adaptation of the polyline. To draw them, use the Donut command. AutoCAD also recognizes the command's British spelling: Doughnut. Both spellings result in the same prompts and exactly the same entities are created.

Now, use Donut to draw the drain for the sink. The command sequence for Donut is as follows:

Prompt	Response	Explanation
Command:	**Donut**	Starts the Donut command
Inside diameter <0'-1">:	**1.5**	Sets the ring's inside diameter of 1.5"
Outside diameter <0'-1">:	**2**	Sets the ring's outside diameter of 2" (the outside diameter must be larger than the inside diameter)
Center of donut:	**1'3,4'3**	Indicates the center point of the drain in the sink
Center of donut:	Press Enter	Completes the Donut command

Your bathroom sink should now look like the one shown in figure 5.23.

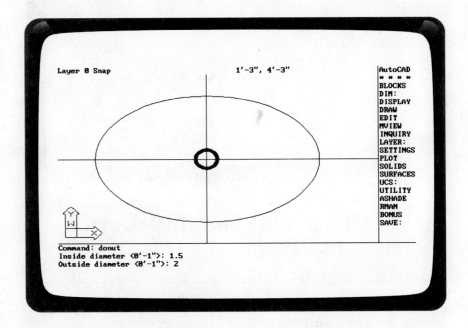

Fig. 5.23.
The Donut command draws the drain.

You don't need to use the Multiple command with Donut. You can create as many doughnuts as you want, all of the same size. You simply continue to specify a location for the center of each successive doughnut. To finish the command, press either Enter or Ctrl-C.

You can draw three kinds of donuts (see fig. 5.24):

❑ Solid-filled: set inside diameter to 0"

❑ Regular: inside diameter is greater than 0"

❑ Circle: inside diameter equals outside diameter

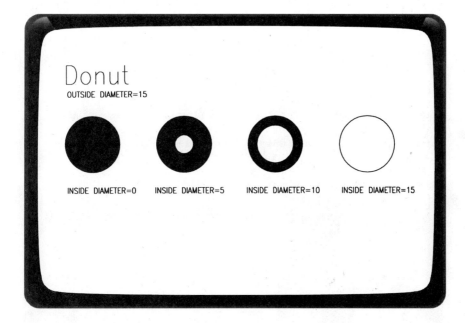

Fig. 5.24. AutoCAD lets you draw various kinds of donuts.

Creating Solid Areas (Solid)

To draw large solid rectilinear and triangular areas filled with color, use the Solid command. To demonstrate the use of the Solid command, the following example shows you how to use Solid to create a pattern of randomly placed 4-by-4-inch tiles on the bathroom floor.

When you draw solids, you indicate three or four corners of the area to be filled. AutoCAD's implementation of this command is a bit peculiar; the order in which you must indicate the corners is probably different from what you would expect. To draw a rectilinear solid, the first and third points must lie on the same edge. If you pick points in a clockwise or counterclockwise direction, AutoCAD creates a bow-tie shape.

Enter information for the Solid command as follows:

Prompt	Response	Explanation
Command:	**Solid**	Starts the Solid command
First point:	**2',2'8**	Specifies the first corner point of the tile
Second point:	**2',3'**	Locates the second point 4" above the first point
Third point:	**2'4,2'8**	The third point is 4" to the right and 4" down
Fourth point:	**2'4,3'**	The last point is 4" to the right and 4" up, completing the solid
Third point:	**Press Enter**	Completes the Solid command

Notice this last prompt. After you've drawn the first solid, AutoCAD continues to cycle through the Third point: and Fourth point: prompts to let you draw connecting solids. In this example, however, press Enter to stop the command.

Figure 5.25 shows the results of this command sequence.

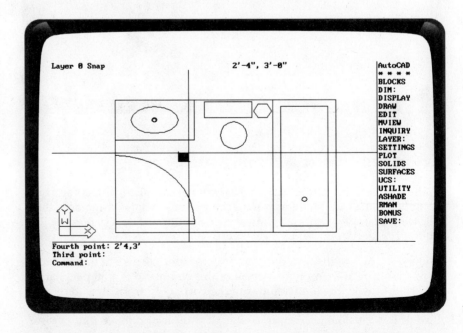

Fig. 5.25. The Solid command draws solid filled areas.

By using the Solid command, you have laid the first tile in the bathroom. Use the same command sequence to lay two other tiles, with their lower left corners at the following coordinate locations: 8",8" and 16",20".

You figure out the X,Y locations for the other three corners of each tile. Then try drawing some solids by just picking points on the screen. Once these tiles are laid, your drawing should look something like figure 5.26.

As you work with the Solid command you will start to understand how AutoCAD implements it. Remember that the first point is always connected to the third; if there is a fourth point, the second is connected to it.

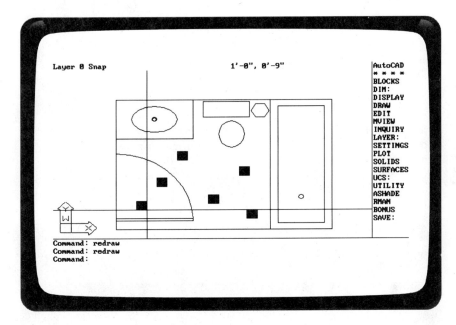

Fig. 5.26. Randomly patterned tiles made from solids.

Indicating Locations (Point)

Points can be used for many different purposes. They can be used to represent the following:

❏ The center line of structural beams

❏ Intersections of entities

❏ Problem areas with parts that fit together

❏ Crucial points within blocks

❏ Points of contact and centers of rotation for mechanical parts

Whenever you need a special entity to indicate something, use a point.

Typically, the point entity is used for temporary purposes until another entity can be laid in over it. Many programs that send information to AutoCAD use the point to show the location of information, such as the corners of a surveyed lot. Once an entity is placed over that point, the point is erased or removed from the drawing screen.

To insert point entities in a drawing, type **Point** at the `Command:` prompt and press Enter. At the `Point:` prompt, indicate the point's location. That's all there is to it—the point is inserted. Point locations may be indicated with an absolute coordinate, or relative to the most recently drawn entity. You also can indicate points by using your input device to move the cursor to the desired location on the screen, and then pressing the pick button. Points also can be drawn using the object snap modes discussed earlier in this chapter.

Now try using the Point command to lay a random pattern on the tile floor.

Prompt	Response	Explanation
Command:	**Point**	Starts the Point command
Point:	Pick point	Specifies a location for the point

Repeat the command sequence several times to create a random pattern of dots on the floor. To repeat the command, either press Enter or retype Point at the `Command:` prompt. When you are done, the floor will be littered with blips, the markers AutoCAD uses to show where you picked a point on the screen. Use the Redraw command to clean up the screen, as follows:

Command: **Redraw**

Your floor should look something like the floor in figure 5.27.

Fig. 5.27. By default, the Point command draws a small dot.

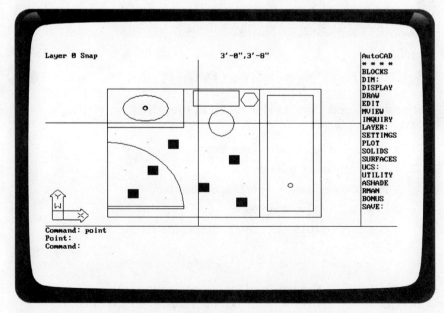

Changing the Appearance of Points

You can change the style and size of the point by using a pair of AutoCAD's system variables: PDSIZE and PDMODE. (If you are using Release 10, you need to use the Setvar—for *set system variable*—command.) AutoCAD has more than 100 system variables that give information about the current state of AutoCAD or control how AutoCAD does things (see Part Six for a complete listing of these system variables). The system variable PDSIZE changes the size of points.

The system variable PDMODE controls your points' appearance (see fig. 5.28 for all 20 possible settings). The setting of PDMODE affects all points in a drawing identically. If you change the setting, all point entities change to the new variable setting.

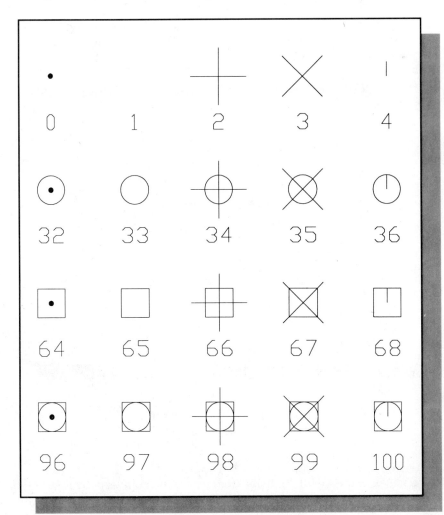

Fig. 5.28.
You can use the PDMODE system variable to change points to any of these shapes.

To change the way points look, use the Setvar command, as follows:

Prompt	Response	Explanation
`Command:`	**Setvar**	Starts the Setvar command to change a system variable
`Variable name or ?:`	**PDMODE**	Specifies that you want to change PDMODE
`New value for PDMODE<0>:`	**35**	Specifies the crossed circle mode
`Command:`	**Regen**	Regenerates the image to show the new point style

Note that you should use the Regen (for *regenerate*) command to redraw the display after changing the point style. Regen is discussed in Chapter 7. The results of this change appear in figure 15.29.

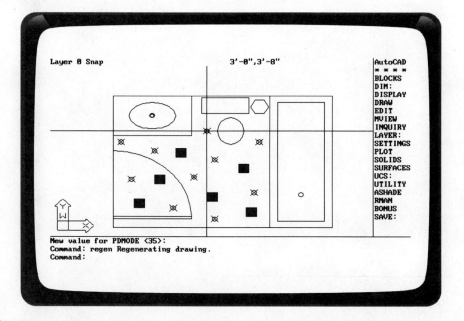

*Fig. 5.29.
Points
displayed as
crossed
circles.*

If you use AutoCAD Release 11, you do not need to type **Setvar** before you change a system variable. You can type the name of the system variable (in this case, PDMODE) directly at the `Command:` prompt.

For a dotted-circle effect (see fig. 5.30), repeat the command and try PDMODE with a value of 32. Remember to use Regen to see the new point style.

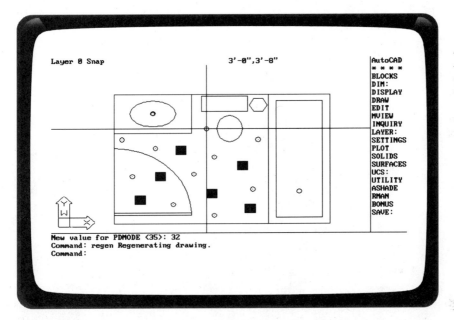

```
Layer 0 Snap                          3'-0",3'-0"              AutoCAD
                                                              * * * *
                                                              BLOCKS
                                                              DIM:
                                                              DISPLAY
                                                              DRAW
                                                              EDIT
                                                              MVIEW
                                                              INQUIRY
                                                              LAYER:
                                                              SETTINGS
                                                              PLOT
                                                              SOLIDS
                                                              SURFACES
                                                              UCS:
                                                              UTILITY
                                                              ASHADE
                                                              RMAN
                                                              BONUS
                                                              SAVE:

New value for PDMODE <35>: 32
Command: regen Regenerating drawing.
Command:
```

Fig. 5.30.
Points
displayed as
dotted circles.

Ending the Drawing Session

You have now finished the drawing example for this chapter. At this point you have two options: you can use the End command to save your drawing and exit from the Drawing Editor, or you can go on to Chapter 6 and continue building the example. By choosing the End command, you can take a break and then come back to your drawing. If you decide to continue on to Chapter 6 now, be sure to use the Save command to save the drawing to disk.

Summary

This chapter has shown you how the fairly simple drawing entities can be combined to create a complex drawing. At this point, you have used only drawing commands to create a sample drawing.

You have learned about the different ways to enter commands and how to locate points on a drawing entity by using the object snap overrides.

The work you have completed sets the stage for Chapters 6 and 9. With the information in these chapters, you will be able to complete the floor plan.

Illustration courtesy of
Autodesk, Inc., Sausalito, CA.

6

Editing Basics

In Chapter 5, you learned how to use AutoCAD to create a drawing. As you know by now, every drawing is made up of basic entities, such as lines, circles, arcs, and polylines. The real power of computer-aided design, however, is not in the drawing—you can do that part with a pencil—but in the editing.

After you draw something, you may want to change it. AutoCAD lets you change the location, size, color, and other aspects of any entity. Some editing commands enable you to create new entities from existing ones.

What sets AutoCAD apart from manual drafting is the capability to easily edit a drawing. Editing on-screen is far easier than applying the electric eraser. In fact, AutoCAD makes editing so easy that you can afford to do "what-if" scenarios with your drawings before deciding on the final version. With this ability you can examine questions about your design, such as "What if we route this steam pipe over there?" "What if we add more trees to the lawn?" "What if we try a railroad overpass rather than an underpass?" If you don't like the change, you can easily get back the original drawing.

Editing involves changing an existing entity in some way. You can lengthen or shorten it, move it to another place in the drawing, make many copies, erase them, change the color and thickness, or orient the entity in three-dimensional space. With AutoCAD, you should never have to draw anything twice. In theory, you could draw a single line and then use editing commands to create the entire drawing.

To move a building on a manually drawn site plan, the draftsperson must erase and redraw, or cut and paste. Using AutoCAD's Move command, the process takes only a few seconds. If you want to create the conceptual

151

design of a parking lot by hand, you need dozens of tracing paper overlays. If you use AutoCAD, however, you can simply use the Undo and Erase commands to get rid of a bad design, or the Layer command to separate designs from each other.

You can use AutoCAD's editing commands not only to make changes to a drawing, but to help create the drawing, as well. Commands such as Mirror and Array create multiple copies. In manual drafting, you have to draw every office of a multi-office floor plan. With CAD, you can draw just one office and then use editing commands to places copies of that office down the hallway.

This chapter discusses most of AutoCAD's editing commands. By reading and working through the examples in this chapter, you will add many commands to your collection of AutoCAD tools and develop a better understanding of the ways in which AutoCAD manipulates drawings.

The following commands are discussed in this chapter:

❏ Array   ❏ Mirror

❏ Break   ❏ Move

❏ Chamfer   ❏ Offset

❏ Copy   ❏ Rotate

❏ Divide   ❏ Scale

❏ Erase   ❏ Stretch

❏ Extend   ❏ Trim

❏ Fillet   ❏ Zoom

❏ Measure

Two other editing commands (Change and Pedit) are discussed in Chapter 9.

Continuing with the Sample Drawing

In Chapter 5, the sample drawing demonstrated AutoCAD's basic drawing commands. So far, the SUITE drawing consists of a bathroom floor plan that you laid out using several drawing commands. This chapter shows you how to add a bedroom and a kitchen to the drawing. This exercise gives you a chance to flex your CAD muscles a little and shows you how easy it is to expand a drawing with help from AutoCAD's editing commands.

If you ended your drawing to take a break, you can get the drawing back onto the screen by starting AutoCAD and choosing Option 2 (Edit an Existing Drawing), from AutoCAD's Main Menu. When the program asks for the drawing's file name, type **SUITE** and press Enter. The AutoCAD Drawing Editor appears on-screen and displays the bathroom floor plan.

Selecting AutoCAD Entities

You can use AutoCAD's editing commands to work with a single entity or a group of entities. Once you have selected one or more entities, you can execute an editing command on the selected entity or entities. Editing a single entity is easy; you just pick it. Because picking several dozen entities can be a tedious task if you pick them one at a time, AutoCAD gives you several ways to pick a group of entities. When you select a group of entities for editing, that group is called the *selection set*. A selection set can be one entity, such as a single line, or several entities that make up part of the drawing. The entire drawing can even be specified as a selection set.

A *word about entities* . . .

When you draw with AutoCAD, you work with *entities*. An entity is any object predefined by AutoCAD that you can place with a single drawing or editing command—lines, arcs, circles, and polylines, for example. You cannot create entities, but you can use AutoCAD's predefined entities to create any kind of drawn representation you like.

The simplest entity is a point; a polyline is the most complex. AutoCAD lets you add an unlimited number of entities to a drawing. The practical limits to a drawing are the computer's capacity to hold the drawing.

In AutoCAD, an entity or collection of entities is often referred to as an *object* . When you use an editing command, the first prompt usually is `Select object:`. When this prompt appears, AutoCAD is asking you to select a single entity or a group of entities. Once you select the desired entities, they are highlighted on-screen. When you execute the editing command, the command affects the highlighted entities.

When you execute an editing command, the crosshair cursor changes to a small box, called a *pickbox*, and AutoCAD displays the `Select objects:` prompt. You use the pickbox to choose the entity you want to edit. To select an entity with the pickbox, simply move the pickbox to any part of the desired entity and press Enter or your input device's pick button.

Generally, when you issue an editing command, AutoCAD responds by asking you to select the entities on which the command should operate. Whenever AutoCAD asks you to choose entities, you can build the selection set by using one of several options. These options (see table 6.1) enable you to add entities to the selection set (or remove entities from the selection set) in different ways.

Table 6.1
Options for Building Selection Sets

Option	Function
Pickbox	Use the pickbox to pick a single entity and add it to the selection set. You can change the size of the pickbox by modifying the PICKBOX system variable. (For more information on AutoCAD's system variables, see the System Variable Reference in Part Six of this text.)
Window	When you use this option, AutoCAD asks you to pick the two corners of a rectangle that surround the entities you want to edit. After you pick the second corner point, AutoCAD chooses all the entities that are completely enclosed within the window.
Crossing	The crossing window works like the Window option, except that it chooses any entity that touches or crosses the window border, as well as those entities contained within the window. You can tell that you have a crossing window by its highlighted border.
Last	This option tells AutoCAD to choose the last entity drawn and visible on-screen.
Previous	You can use the previous selection set as the current selection set. This option is helpful when you want to use several commands on the same group of entities.
Multiple	AutoCAD normally scans the database whenever you select an entity. (This process can be slow in a complex drawing.) The Multiple command makes AutoCAD scan the drawing database only once, looking for all entities in the selection set in one fell swoop.

Option	Function
Undo	The Undo option allows you to step back through the entity-selection process and remove entity groups in the reverse order that you chose them. For example, if you were to add a set of entities by using the Window option, and then decided you didn't need them, you could use the Undo option to remove those windowed entities from the selection set.
Remove	If you have selected some entities you don't want, you can use the Remove option to remove them from the selection set. Accidentally picking unwanted entities can happen with the Window and Crossing selection. When you type **R**, AutoCAD displays the `Remove objects:` prompt. You can use all the options listed here to remove entities from the selected set.
Add	If you are in Remove mode, the Add option switches back to Selection mode. The `Select objects:` prompt returns and you can resume adding entities to the selection set.
Enter	Pressing Enter causes AutoCAD to stop asking you to select objects, and continue with the editing command.
Ctrl-C	This is the quickest way to cancel the entity-selection process. Press Ctrl-C to return immediately to the `Command:` prompt. AutoCAD does not remember the selection set, which you cannot use with the next editing command.

You can use any of these options in any sequence at any time, provided that AutoCAD continues to prompt `Select objects:`. For example, you can build a selection set by picking some entities one by one and using the Window option to add others. You'll probably use most of these options.

You will use several of these selection options to build selection sets in the following examples. Now it's time to look at the basic editing commands.

The Editing Commands

As discussed at the beginning of this chapter, AutoCAD's editing commands let you make changes to your drawing. You can quickly enhance a drawing by using editing commands in conjunction with the drawing commands discussed in Chapter 5. Editing commands give you much greater drafting speed than the drawing commands alone can offer.

Although you will access most commands in this book from the keyboard, you can also pick nearly all of them from the screen menu. This menu groups commands logically (Draw, Edit, Utilities) in alphabetical order.

When you pick Edit, for example, you see all editing commands from Array to Extend. There are so many editing commands that they don't all fit on one screen menu; pick Next to see the commands from Fillet to Undo. The screen menu lets you see all (or half) the related command names at one time. This is useful if you can't remember a name.

Many of the commands also are available from the editing pull-down menu. This menu, called Modify, contains 11 of the most commonly used editing commands, from Erase to Edit Polylines. This book describes some commands that are easier to use from the pull-down menu than from the command line.

Before you start learning to use the editing commands, take a moment to make sure that the sample drawing (SUITE) is loaded into the Drawing Editor.

Copying Entities (Copy)

The Copy command makes copies of objects that already exist in the drawing. This simple but powerful command enables you to use an entity over and over again in a drawing, after drawing the entity only one time. You can use this command to create a selection set that contains the entities you want to copy. In the following command sequence, you use the Copy command to give a width (4") to the bathroom walls, copying one wall section at a time. As you enter the following commands, notice how the crosshair cursor changes to a pickbox.

Prompt	Response	Explanation
Command:	**Copy**	Starts the Copy command
Select objects: 1 selected, 1 found	Pick wall	Selects the top wall of the bathroom

Prompt	Response	Explanation
`Select objects:`	Press Enter	Ends object selection
`<Base Point or displacement>` `/Multiple:`	Pick a point on the wall	Specifies the point from which you will be copying
`Second point of displacement: @4"<90`		Specifies the point to which you are copying

This operation copies the top wall line 4 inches up (that is, in the 90° direction). Now use the Copy command to copy the other three walls 4 inches out. The three other directions are 180, 270, and 0 degrees for the left, bottom, and right walls, respectively. When you are done, the screen should look like the one in figure 6.1.

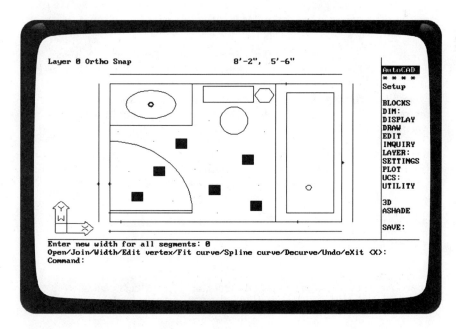

```
Layer 0 Ortho Snap                    8'-2", 5'-6"
```

```
Enter new width for all segments: 0
Open/Join/Width/Edit vertex/Fit curve/Spline curve/Decurve/Undo/eXit <X>:
Command:
```

Fig. 6.1.
The bathroom walls, after the Copy command has been used four times.

When you copy an object, AutoCAD creates a new object (the copy of the original object) and then moves the new object to a new location, which you specify. The *base point* is the spot from which the move begins. The *displacement* is the distance by which the new copy is moved from the original location. You can pick the from-point and the to-point, or AutoCAD can calculate the distance for you. If you supply coordinates at the `Base point or displacement` prompt and simply press Enter at the `Second point of displacement` prompt, AutoCAD uses the coordinates as the distance to copy objects from their original location.

You did the following three things during the Copy operation:

❏ Selected the entities to copy

❏ Picked a base point to copy from

❏ Picked the point to copy to

Most of the editing commands work this way, asking you to select a from-point and a to-point. Although this method may feel a little odd, it works easily after you practice a few times.

NOTE

The Copy command has an option (called Multiple) that lets you make multiple copies of the selection set. (Don't confuse it with two other multiples: AutoCAD's Multiple command and the Multiple option for creating a selection set.) After you've chosen the base point, the Multiple option lets you pick more than one second-point location.

Filleting Entities (Fillet)

The Fillet command rounds off the intersection of two lines. You can fillet a pair of lines, arcs, or circles, or the length of a polyline. You're not limited to filleting only similar entities; you can fillet a line and a circle, for example. The two lines must intersect at some location within the drawing, however, because AutoCAD cannot fillet parallel lines. Fillet trims or extends the two entities until the fillet fits.

If the fillet radius is zero, the two lines will meet with a sharp corner, as shown in the following example. The Fillet command is nifty for cleaning up wall intersections on floor plans (or for anything that requires sharp corners). The Fillet command sequence goes like this:

Prompt	Response	Explanation
Command:	**Fillet**	Starts the Fillet command
Polyline/Radius/ <Select two objects>:	Select the two wall lines shown in figure 6.2	Selects object to fillet

Now repeat the Fillet command to clean up the other three intersections.

The default fillet radius is set to 0, which produces a sharp corner. You can give a rounded corner to an intersection by specifying a different fillet radius. You will create fillets with rounded corners later in this chapter.

When you type **Fillet**, AutoCAD changes the crosshair cursor to a pickbox, which you then use to select the two entities to fillet. The location of the point you pick determines where the fillet will be placed; this is especially noticeable with arcs and circles.

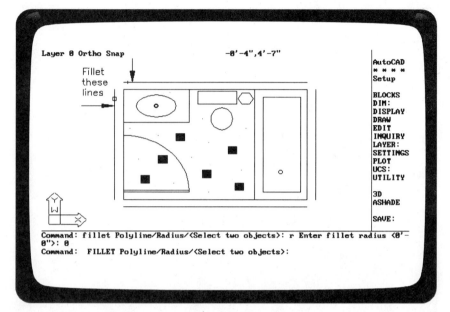

Fig. 6.2.
Selecting lines
for the Fillet
command.

It's possible (and equally correct) to produce either of two fillets (see fig. 6.3). In such an instance, AutoCAD will place a fillet on the first entity closest to the point at which you picked the second entity. The results may not be what you want. To get the results you want, undo the fillet and try again. Select the entities at different points, closer to where you want the fillet to occur.

If you want to fillet a polyline, first select the Polyline option. When you fillet a polyline, every corner (also called a *vertex*—the point at which two sections of a polyline meet) is filleted to the specified radius. You could, for example, round off the four corners of the door with a single Fillet command, because the door is made of a polyline.

AutoCAD will not create a fillet if the length of the lines (or the distance between polyline vertices) is less than or equal to the fillet radius. For example, you cannot get a one-inch radius fillet on a pair of lines one inch long. To get around this restriction, just reduce the fillet radius to 0.9999 inches.

Offsetting Entities (Offset)

The Offset command creates a copy of an existing entity and places it parallel to the original. AutoCAD places the new entity away from the original at a distance you specify. The Offset command is quicker than the Copy command for creating many parallel lines.

Fig. 6.3.
*The location
of a fillet
between two
arcs or circles
depends on
the pick
points.*

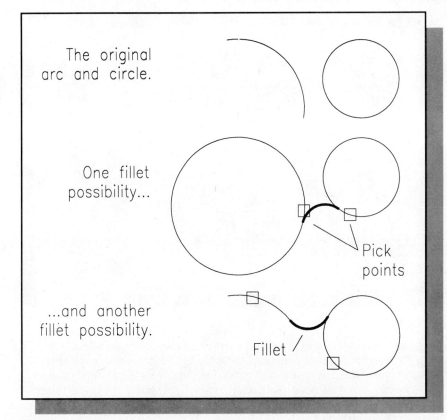

The original
arc and circle.

One fillet
possibility...

...and another
fillet possibility.

Pick
points

Fillet

You will use Offset to create new rooms and a hallway for the apartment
floor plan. A copy of the wall at the top of the screen needs to be offset
up (that is, in the 90° direction) by eight feet to form part of the kitchen.
Follow the command sequence to create the first wall then create the
other two walls on your own.

Prompt	Response	Explanation
`Command:`	**Offset**	Starts the Offset command
`Offset distance or Through <Through>:`	**8'**	Specifies the distance to offset the new line from the original line
`Select object to offset:`	Pick the top bathroom wall line	Specifies the entity to be offset

Prompt	Response	Explanation
`Side to offset:`	Choose point above the bathroom wall	Specifies the side of original entity where you want the new one to be created
`Select object to offset:`	Press Enter	Ends the Offset command

A copy of the wall near the bottom of the screen needs to be offset by 10 feet to create the second bedroom wall. The left bathroom wall (with the door) needs to be offset 3 feet to the left to form a hallway connecting the rooms. Create these two walls on your own. When you finish, your drawing should look like figure 6.4.

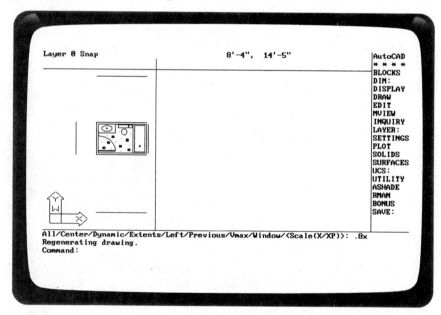

Fig. 6.4.
The Offset command creates new walls for the kitchen, bedroom, and hallway.

You can enter an offset distance by typing in the value of the distance (as described in the preceding command sequence), or you can show AutoCAD the distance by picking two points on the screen.

The T (for *Through*) option lets you reverse the process; that is, you can pick the entity before you specify the through distance. This is useful if you want to pick a distance on the screen relative to the entity.

When AutoCAD prompts you to `Select object to offset:`, you can pick only one entity at a time. After the first offset is complete, you can offset other entities to the same offset distance. AutoCAD repeats the prompt until you cancel the command or press Enter twice.

After you select the entity and specify the offset distance, AutoCAD asks you for `Side to offset:`. The side of the original entity you choose determines where the new offset entity will be placed.

A problem may occur when you try to offset complex curves, such as an ellipse, a polyline, or an arc. If you repeatedly offset to the interior of the curve, AutoCAD eventually will pass beyond the center point of the arcs and be forced to approximate the offset, which can no longer be accurate.

Seeing More of Your Drawing (Zoom)

When you offset the wall lines, the drawing grew larger. You may not see the new lines, however, because they are somewhere off the screen.

To see all the lines in the drawing, use AutoCAD's Zoom command. This command allows you to see more of the whole drawing (by zooming out) or to see more detail (by zooming in). Take the following steps to see the full drawing:

Prompt	Response	Explanation
`Command:`	**Zoom**	Starts the Zoom command

`All/Center/Dynamic/Extents/`
`Left/Previous/Vmax/Window/`
`<Scale (X/XP)>:`
	E	Specifies the Extents option; AutoCAD zooms out to display the entire drawing

Here you zoom out to see the entire drawing so that it fills the screen (this view is called the drawing's *extents*). You may still find it a bit difficult, however, to see the lines right at the edge of the screen. You can add some space around the drawing (so that your screen looks more like the one shown in figure 6.4) by zooming out a bit more:

Prompt	Response	Explanation
`Command:`	**Zoom**	Starts the Zoom command

`All/Center/Dynamic/Extents/`
`Left/Previous/Vmax/Window/`
`<Scale(X/XP)>:`
	0.8x	Zooms out farther to add space around the drawing

The Zoom command does not change your drawing in any way; it simply allows you to examine your drawing at different magnifications. Zoom's options give you a better view of the areas in which you are drawing. As you continue through the example, you may want to use Zoom to make your screen match the figures in this chapter.

This is just a brief introduction to the Zoom command. For more information, read Chapter 7.

Now that you can see the whole drawing, use the Fillet command to make the four outer wall lines meet.

Extending Entities (Extend)

The Extend command extends a line to a boundary. The boundary can be almost any other entity, provided that it is visible on-screen. You cannot extend to a block because AutoCAD doesn't know where the edges of the block lie. (Blocks are discussed in Chapter 12.)

The Extend command is useful for making lines end at a specific boundary. It is a substitute for the Fillet command, which cannot fillet two polylines.

When you type **Extend**, the following prompts appear:

```
Select boundary edge(s)...
Select objects:
```

AutoCAD is asking you to select the entities you want to use as the boundaries to which other entities will be extended. As you pick them, AutoCAD highlights the entities you choose as boundaries.

Figure 6.5 shows the first pair of wall lines to be extended, and the boundary line to which they will extend. When you select the entity you want to extend, AutoCAD immediately extends it to the closest boundary. Now, extend the two lines that make up the lower bathroom wall. Later, you will create an opening for a door in this wall.

Follow this command sequence to extend the bathroom wall:

Prompt	Response	Explanation
`Command:`	**Extend**	Starts the Extend command
`Select boundary edge(s)...` `Select objects:`	Pick the extreme left wall line, then press Enter	Specifies the entity to which you want to extend

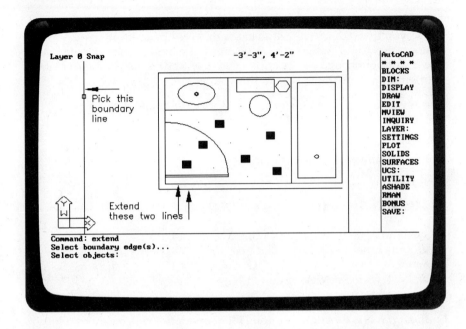

Fig. 6.5.
Extend the lower bathroom wall.

Prompt	Response	Explanation
`Select objects:` `<Select Object to extend>` `/Undo:`	Pick the bathroom's two lower wall lines	Selects the entities to be extended

Repeat the Extend command to connect the bathroom walls to the right side of the apartment (see fig. 6.6).

As mentioned earlier, you now can place a door in the newly extended bedroom wall. To prepare for this operation, make a copy of the door and its path (the arc that represents its path of travel). Use the Copy command to pick the two objects. Remember that the door's four sides count as a single entity because you created the door as a polyline. Copy them from the bathroom to any convenient place in the bedroom (see fig. 6.7). Once they are in the bedroom, you can use these two entities to practice executing the Rotate command.

Rotating Entities (Rotate)

You can use the Rotate command to rotate lines, arcs, circles, polylines, and anything else drawn on the screen. You supply AutoCAD with three pieces of information by selecting the objects you want rotated, picking a base point, and then specifying the rotation angle. The base point is the "pivot" point around which you want AutoCAD to rotate the selected objects. The rotation angle tells AutoCAD how far around you want the objects rotated from their current position. For example, supplying an angle of 90 degrees moves the objects perpendicularly; an angle of 180 degrees rotates them so that they're upside down.

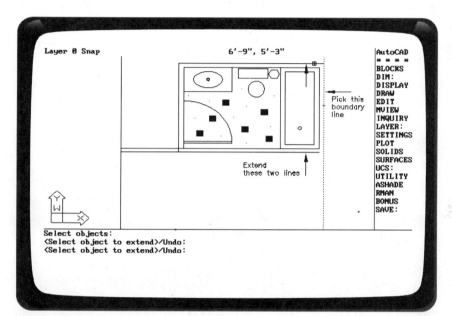

Fig. 6.6. Extending the remaining bathroom walls.

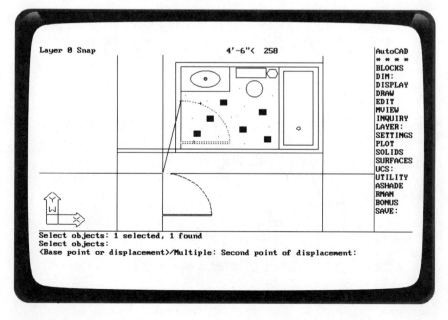

Fig. 6.7. Copy the bathroom door into the bedroom.

The Rotate command lets you draw a part in normal X,Y coordinates and then place it at any angle in the drawing. If the wing of a building goes off at 75 degrees, you can draw the wing initially at 0 degrees and then rotate it into place. If you need to do editing after the wing is in place, use the Snap Rotate command to rotate the grid and snap to match the 75-degree angle of the wing. (The use of AutoCAD's Snap and Grid commands are discussed later in this text.)

The following command sequence illustrates how the Rotate command works:

Prompt	Response	Explanation
Command:	**Rotate**	Starts the Rotate command
Select objects:	Pick the bathroom its path of travel	Specifies the selection set to be rotated
Select objects:	Press Enter	Ends the selection of objects
Base point:	Pick a corner of the door	Choose the point around which you will rotate the selected objects
<Rotation angle> /Reference:	-90	Specifies the rotation angle

When AutoCAD asks you for the base point, it needs to know the point around which the entities will rotate. A ghosted image appears on-screen to give you an idea of what the rotated entities will look like. Figure 6.8 shows the original entities and the highlighted image as you prepare to perform the rotation.

You can enter a rotation angle or work with a reference. Specify a rotation angle by entering a value at the keyboard or by using the highlighted image as a guideline.

If you choose the Reference option, AutoCAD calculates the rotation angle based on a reference you provide. If you want to continue to rotate the entity from its current angle of 45 degrees to a new angle of 27.25 degrees, you could calculate and enter the difference of –17.75 degrees. Or you could let AutoCAD do the calculation for you. You simply choose the Reference option and, at the prompt Reference angle <current>:, enter 45 (the current angle). When AutoCAD asks for New angle:, enter 27.25. With this option, AutoCAD does the work of calculating the difference.

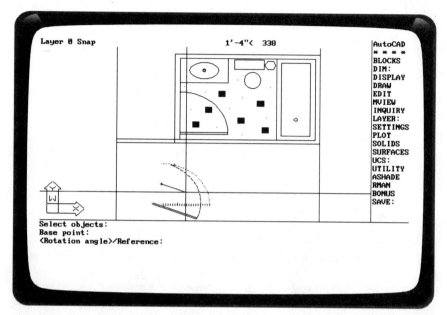

Fig. 6.8.
The Rotate
command
displays a
highlighted
image to show
what the
rotation will
look like.

If you don't know the current angle, you can pick two points that represent the angle. AutoCAD calculates the angle from the two pick points. You can use object snap modes to lock precisely onto the entity.

Moving Entities (Move)

Use the Move command to move an object to a new location. Move is similar to the Copy command, except that Move erases the original object.

Now that you have rotated the door, use the Move command to position the door in the wall. To move the door, first grab the door's corner intersection and drag the door to the desired location on the wall. Use the following command sequence to move the door:

Prompt	Response	Explanation
`Command:`	**Move**	Starts the Move command
`Select objects:`	**P**	Use the previously selected door and arc
`Select objects:`	Press Enter	Ends object selection

Prompt	Response	Explanation
`Base point or displacement:`	**INT**	Specifies the INTersection object snap override
`of`	Pick the door's upper left corner	Locks onto the desired corner of the door
`Second point of displacement:`	**NEA**	Specifies the NEArest object snap override
`of`	Pick a spot near corner of walls	Shows AutoCAD where to locate the door

Figure 6.9 shows the NEAr object snap positioning the door on the wall.

Fig. 6.9.
The
INTersection
object snap
lets you place
the door
precisely.

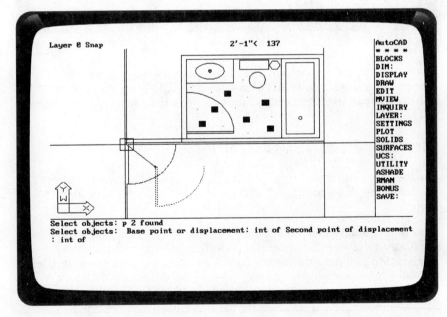

Figure 6.10 shows the new bedroom door in position.

You may want to enlarge the view to see the doorway more clearly. Use the Zoom Left command, as follows:

Prompt	Response	Explanation
`Command:`	**Zoom**	Starts the Zoom command

`All/Center/Dynamic/Extents/`
`Left/Previous/Vmax/Window/`
`<Scale (Y/XP)>:`
	L	Selects the Left option

`Lower left corner point:`	**-4',-2'**	Specifies the lower left corner of the new view
`Magnification or Height` `<14'-2'>:`	**5'**	Specifies the height of the new view

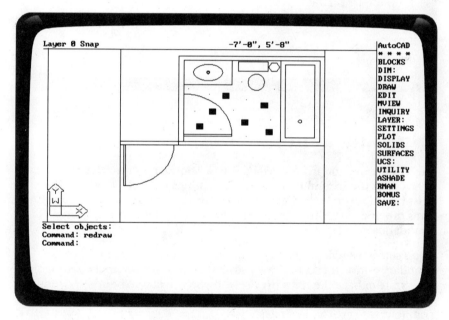

Fig. 6.10.
The bedroom has a door.

An enlarged view of the doorway appears, making it easier to edit. (The Zoom command is covered in detail in Chapter 7.)

Now, use the Line command to draw two lines that form the end caps of the wall. When you draw these short lines, first pick a point on the wall line that meets the door. You want to draw the lines directly across to the opposite wall line, so that the end caps lie perpendicular to the long wall lines, as shown in figure 6.11. To draw the end caps most easily, and to make sure that they are perpendicular to the long wall lines, use the PERpendicular object snap when you respond to the Line command's `To point:` prompt. When the object snap's aperture box appears, use it to select the second wall line, and AutoCAD automatically draws in the end cap so that it is perpendicular to the two long wall lines.

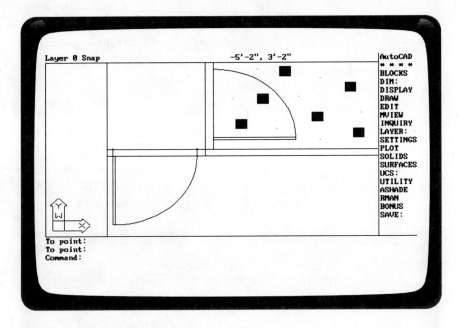

Fig. 6.11.
Two short
lines form the
wall end caps
for the door
opening.

Trimming Entities (Trim)

The Trim command trims lines back to a boundary. Trim, therefore, is the opposite of the Extend command. The entities you select as boundaries must be visible on-screen. As you select the line to be trimmed, AutoCAD trims the line from the point at which you picked it to the specified boundaries.

If you select a single boundary entity, Trim trims from the end to the boundary entity. If you've drawn several lines that overlap a crossing line, you can trim back the lines precisely. If you select two boundary entities, Trim will remove the portion between the boundaries. You also can use Trim to create arcs from circles.

Like Extend, Trim makes a square fillet of two polylines (which the Fillet command can't do) by using the Trim command twice—once to cut back each polyline to the other.

The following command sequence shows you how to use Trim to create an opening for the bedroom door.

Prompt	Response	Explanation
Command:	**Trim**	Starts the Trim command
Select cutting edge(s)... Select objects: 2 selected, 2 found	Pick the two wall end caps that form the bedroom door opening	Specifies the boundaries to which to trim the wall lines
Select objects:	Press Enter	Ends object selection
<Select object to trim:>/ Undo:	Pick the wall lines to trim	Specifies the entities to be trimmed

Figure 6.12 shows the wall lines being trimmed to create the door's opening.

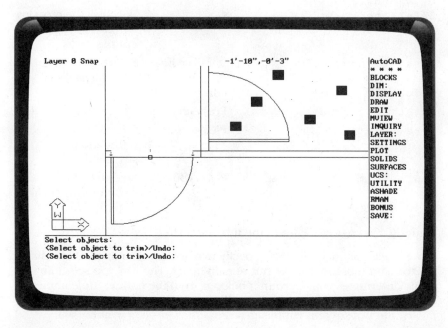

Fig. 6.12. Creating the opening for the bedroom door.

Use the Trim command to clean up the wall intersections around the bathroom door.

Stretching Parts of a Drawing (Stretch)

The Stretch command moves portions of objects without disturbing the connections between entities. You can use the command to make entities longer or shorter, or to change their alignment.

The Stretch command lets you move part of an object while connected parts remain in place. For example, you can lengthen a floor beam or move a window along a wall. The Stretch command, however, differs from all the other editing commands in one respect. That is, you must create the Stretch commands selection set by using the Crossing or Window options (although you can add and remove objects from the set by picking them).

You created the bathtub in Chapter 5. Now it is time to make the tub look more realistic. First, use the Stretch command to alter the angle of the tub's inner lines, as shown in the following command sequence. Then use Fillet to remove the tub's sharp interior corners.

Prompt	Response	Explanation
`Command:`	**Stretch**	Starts the Stretch command
`Select objects to stretch by window...`		
`Select objects:`	C	Specifies the crossing window to select entities
`First corner:` `Other corner:` `2 found`	Window lines of upper right corner of tub	Selects the objects to be altered
`Select objects:`	Press Enter	Ends object selection
`Base point:`	Pick corner	Specifies the corner of the tub to be stretched
`New point:`	@1<180	Stretches the upper right interior corner 1" to the left

Figure 6.13 shows a corner of the tub being stretched.

The Stretch command lets you specify two groups of entities: those that stretch, and those that move but remain intact. The way you select an entity determines which group it belongs in. If the entities are completely inside the selection window, they will move (similar to the Move command) but not stretch; entities that cross the Crossing window will stretch.

You can stretch only one selection set at a time. If you choose a second window or crossing, AutoCAD ignores the first selection set. Stretch uses only the most recent selection set.

Now use the Stretch command to make the other tub corner correspond to the first.

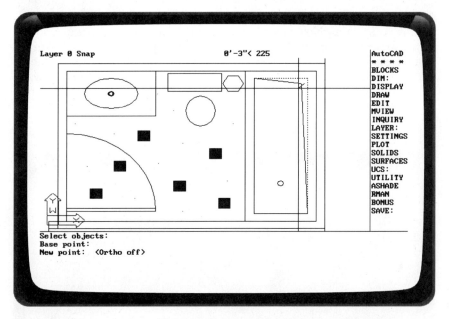

Fig. 6.13.
*Stretching the
corners of the
tub inward.*

The inner lines now look more like a bathtub, but you still have the sharp
corners. This is where the Fillet command comes in. Set the fillet radius
to 3 inches and try filleting two of the tub lines. Suddenly the sharp
corners are rounded off! Use the Fillet command to take the sharpness
out of the other corners; try specifying different radii. You can end up
with a tub like in figure 6.14 by setting the fillet radius to 3.

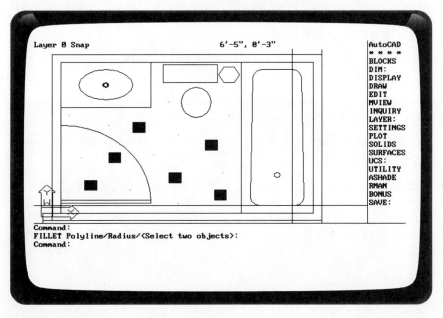

Fig. 6.14.
*The modified
bathtub, with
rounded
corners.*

So far, you've had detailed step-by-step guidance in using AutoCAD's editing commands. Now you can strike out on your own, putting your new knowledge to work. Before going on to the next section, try adding countertops in the kitchen. Locate the counter tops 20 inches from the kitchen wall lines (see fig. 6.15). To complete this exercise, you may want to use the Offset and Extend commands. Note that, initially, your counters will have some excess lines; the next section shows you how to cut out the excess lines.

Fig. 6.15.
The
countertops
roughed in
with the Offset
command.

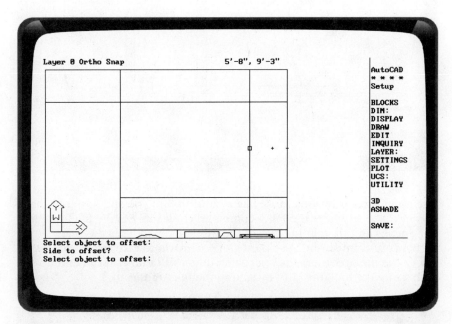

Erasing Parts of Entities (Break)

The Break command removes sections of an object. It also lets you break an entity into two parts without removing either part. You can use Break on lines, arcs, circles, and polylines.

Use the Break command to finish the basics of the kitchen counters you created earlier:

Prompt	Response	Explanation
Command:	**Break**	Starts the Break command
Select object:	Pick a line	Selects the counter line you want to break

Prompt	Response	Explanation
Enter second point (or F for first point):	F	Tells AutoCAD that you are going to pick two break points
Enter first point:	INT	Turns on the INTersection object snap
of	Pick a point	Specifies the first intersection at which you want to break the line
Enter second point:	INT	Turns on the INTersection object snap
of	Pick a point	Specifies the second intersection at which you want to break the line

Figure 6.16 shows how this sequences works when breaking out one of the excess counter lines.

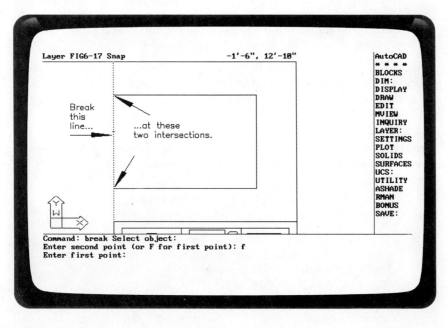

Fig. 6.16.
Breaking out an excess counter line.

AutoCAD begins by asking you to select the object you want to break (in this case, the counter line shown in fig. 6.16). After you select that line, AutoCAD asks you to do the following:

```
Enter second point (or F for first point):
```

Here you have two options. If you specify a second point, that completes the Break command. What happens is that AutoCAD uses the pick point (the point at which you selected the entity to be broken) as the first break point. The second point defines the other end of the part to break out.

The other option is to type **F** (for *first point*) to define the first break point. This is the option you used in the preceding command sequence.

If you work with the Autodesk tablet menu, two Break command selections are available on the menu:

❏ Break, which removes part of an entity

❏ Break @, which divides an entity into two parts

The tablet menu's Break @ selection is useful for creating hatching boundaries. (Hatching is covered in detail in Chapter 10.) When you use this menu selection, AutoCAD prompts for only one point, the point at which the entity will be divided.

To use Break @ from the keyboard, pick the first point and type @ for the second point. As Chapter 4 explained, you use the @ symbol for relative input. By using @, you are telling AutoCAD that you want it to use the same point again.

If you break a line, arc, or polyline, AutoCAD removes the portion of the entity between the two specified break points. If one break point lies past the end of the entity, the entity is deleted from the first break point to the endpoint nearest the second break point.

A word about breaking circles . . .

You may become frustrated when you try to use Break to break out a portion of a circle. The process is easier, however, if you remember two things:

1. AutoCAD calculates breaks on a circle counterclockwise (the same way it calculates other circular operations). The specified portion extends counter-clockwise from the first break point to the second break point.

2. Break @ cannot be used on circle entities. When you break a circle, AutoCAD changes it into an arc. But AutoCAD does not allow arcs of 360 degrees or more of rotation. Using Break @ on a circle causes AutoCAD to try to create an arc with 360 degrees of rotation, which is not possible.

After you use the Break command to break out the first unwanted sections of the countertop lines, use the command again to trim back the remaining extraneous lines. Although this is easier to do with the Trim command, doing it once or twice with Break is a good exercise.

To prepare the sample drawing for the next editing command (Mirror), you need to create the outline of a sink. First, draw a line from the MIDpoint of the counter's short end to PERpendicular to the wall line. Then you can use the Offset command to offset the line 12" above and below its current location. The following command sequence shows you how to create these lines:

Prompt	*Response*	*Explanation*
`Command:`	**Line**	Starts the Line command
`From point:`	**Mid**	From MIDpoint...
`of`	Pick a line	...of the short counter line
`To point:`	**Per**	To PERpendicular...
`of`	Pick a line	...of the right wall line
`To point:`	Press Enter	Ends the Line command
`Command:`	**Offset**	Starts the Offset command
`Offset distance or Through <Through>:`	**12**	Copies the line 12 inches
`Select object to offset:`	Pick the line	Specifies the line you just drew
`Side to offset:`	Pick a point anywhere above the line	...above and...
`Select object to offset:`	Pick original line again	
`Side to offset:`	Pick a point anywhere below the original line	...below
`Select object to offset:`	Press Enter	Ends the Offset command

The results are shown in figure 6.17.

In the upper rectangle of the sink you just created, draw the sink basin lines. These lines are offset 1/2" from three surrounding sides, and 4" from the outer wall line. After these lines have been offset, you need to trim back the excess portions of the inner sink lines. Then use Fillet with a radius of 1" to round off the inner sink lines. Add a drain, made from a circle with a 1" radius. Your drawing should now look like figure 6.18.

Fig. 6.17.
The sink area.

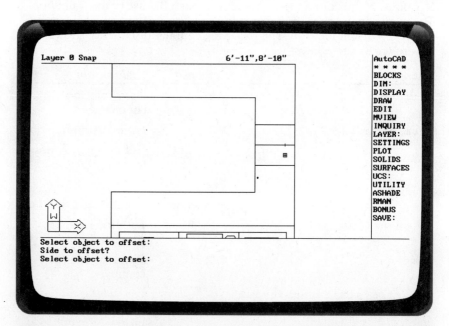

Fig. 6.18.
The Offset,
Fillet, and
Circle
commands
created this
sink.

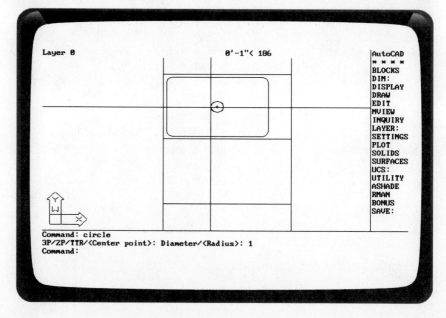

Creating Mirror Images (Mirror)

AutoCAD's powerful Mirror command produces a mirror image of objects along a *mirror line*. A mirror line is just what it sounds like—a line that shows where the mirror image reflects the original. You can specify the line at any angle to the original objects.

The Mirror command is ideal for creating symmetrical objects. Many objects are *singly* or *doubly* symmetric. For example, you can draw the upper half of the letter *E* and mirror the bottom half. Or you can draw the upper left quarter of the letter *O* and mirror it twice: to the left to create the upper half, and then to the bottom to create the full letter.

Many design parts—particularly round ones—are symmetrical. If you look carefully at the design you may find the lines of symmetry; these would be the mirror lines used by the Mirror command. There may be one mirror line or there may be a dozen. If so, you just need to draw one half (or one-twelfth) of the part and let Mirror draw the other half (or the other twelfths). If you plan ahead, mirroring can eliminate a great deal of extra drafting.

As you draw, you become aware of relationships between entities. Sometimes objects you draw are simply mirror images of each other. If you need to create symmetrical entities, Mirror greatly reduces the amount of drawing you would do otherwise.

When you enter **Mirror**, AutoCAD prompts you to specify the objects you want to mirror. In the following example, you mirror the lines, fillets, and circle that make up the sink you just created. After you select these entities, AutoCAD prompts as follows:

```
First point of mirror line:
```

Now you pick one end of the mirror line. Figure 6.19 shows the location of the mirror line (the first line you drew when creating the sink area; that is, the line between the two sink basins) used in the next example.

To mirror the sink, use the following command sequence:

Prompt	Response	Explanation
Command:	**Mirror**	Starts the Mirror command
Select objects:	**W**	Specifies a window selection box, so that only the entities inside the window are chosen

Prompt	Response	Explanation
`First corner:`	Pick a point just outside the sink's lower left corner	Starts the window
`Other corner:` `9 found`	Pick a point just outside the sink's upper right corner	Completes the window
`Select objects:`	Press Enter	Ends object selection
`First point of mirror line:` **NEA**		Tells AutoCAD to use the NEArest object snap
`of`	Pick one end of the mirror line	Specifies the start of the mirror line
`Second point:`	**NEA**	
`of`	Pick the other end of the mirror line	Specifies the end point of the mirror line
`Delete old objects?<N>:`	Press Enter	Tells AutoCAD not to delete the original entities after creating the mirror image

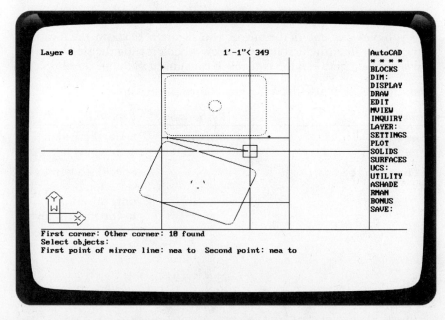

Fig. 6.19.
The Mirror command lets you mirror objects around a line.

The NEArest object snap mode lets you pick the mirror line without needing the cursor right on the line. As long as the mirror line falls within the pickbox, AutoCAD finds it. Using object snap modes greatly speeds up the drawing process because you don't need to pick the exact point. To revise an old saying, "close enough" only counts in horseshoes, hand grenades, and object snaps.

After you enter the first endpoint for the mirror line, AutoCAD displays a ghosted reflection of the entity you selected. This reflection helps you set the other endpoint for the mirror line. If you want a horizontal or vertical mirror line, you can specify a relative distance with your angle set to 0, 90, or 180 degrees.

Finally, AutoCAD asks the following:

```
Delete old objects? <N>:
```

If you want the Mirror command to create a symmetrical duplicate of the original object, press Enter to accept the default answer of No (this is what you want in the sample drawing). On the other hand, deleting the original entities may be appropriate in certain instances. In those cases, press **Y** to have AutoCAD delete the original objects. Your kitchen sink should now look like the one in figure 6.20.

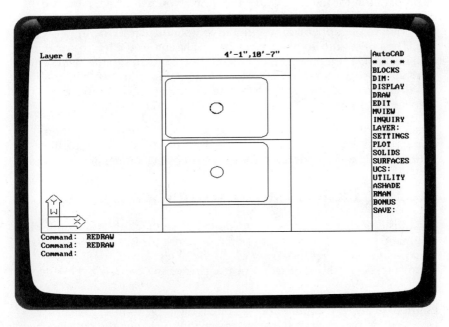

Fig. 6.20.
The upper sink is mirrored to produce the second sink.

Removing Entities (Erase)

As you learned in Chapter 4, Erase is an editing command that removes unwanted entities. AutoCAD needs to know only which objects you want to erase.

To initiate the Erase command, enter **Erase**. The prompt `Select objects:` appears and the crosshair cursor turns into a pickbox. As mentioned earlier in this chapter, AutoCAD then waits for you to create a selection set. This set contains the objects you want AutoCAD to remove from the drawing. By following the next command sequence, you erase the first line you drew when you began creating the sink (the line between the two basins):

Prompt	Response	Explanation
`Command:`	**Erase**	Starts the Erase command
`Select objects:`	Select the first-drawn sink line	Selects the entity to be erased
`Select objects:`	Press Enter	Erases the selected entity

In preparation for the next command, Scale, you will create rangetop burners for the kitchen. To draw the rangetop, draw a line from the MIDpoint of the upper counter line to PERpendicular to the upper wall line. Then offset the line 6 inches to the right and to the left to create the cooking area. Then offset the right-hand line 12 inches to the right. This gives you two 12-inch-wide areas for the stovetop's burners. The first line you drew (in the center of the left-hand burner area), will serve as a baseline for drawing the burners; you will erase this line later.

Next, place the two burners (each a circle with a 4" radius) with their centers at 2'8",12'10" and 2'8",12'. Your drawing should now look like figure 6.21. Now you are ready for the next editing command.

Scaling Parts of a Drawing (Scale)

To adjust the size of entities proportionally, use the Scale command. The command prompts for Scale are similar to those for Rotate. You need a base point as the reference from which the object grows (or shrinks). Then you specify the scale factor or use part of an object as a reference.

The Scale command can resize a single entity, a group of objects, or the entire drawing. If you have drawn a detail too large to fit in the corner of the drawing, you can use the Scale command to change the detail's size. It changes the size of the object equally in all dimensions; you cannot specify a different scale in the X, Y, and Z directions.

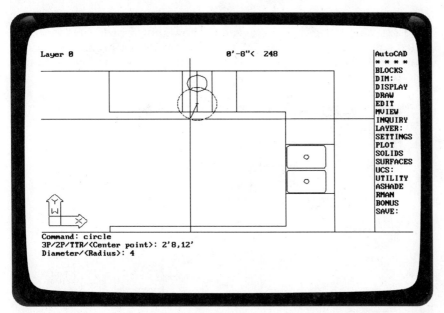

Fig. 6.21.
The Offset and
Circle
commands
create the
rangetop
burners.

A sample command sequence for Scale follows:

Prompt	Response	Explanation
`Command:`	**Scale**	Starts the Scale command
`Select objects:`	Choose the lower burner	Specifies the object to be scaled
`Select objects:`	Press Enter	Ends object selection
`Base point:`	**CEN**	Tells AutoCAD to use the center...
`of`	Pick burner	...of the burner as the base point
`<Scale factor>/Reference:`	**R**	Tells AutoCAD to compute the scale factor
`Reference length <1>:`	**8**	Specifies the current diameter (remember that the burner originally was created with a 4" radius)
`New length:`	**6**	Specifies the new diameter for the burner

After you set the base point, a ghosted image appears on the screen (see fig. 6.22). This image can be dragged to show approximate sizes for the scaled entity. At the <Scale factor>/Reference: prompt, you can enter a scale factor or choose to work with referencing (as you did in the preceding command sequence).

Fig. 6.22.
The Scale
command
changes the
size of the
lower burner.

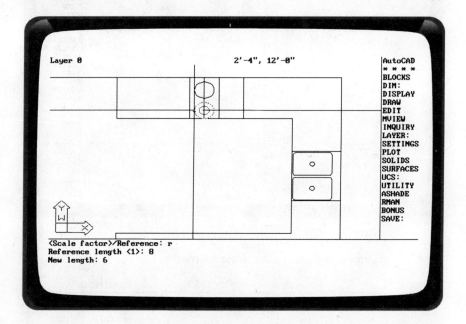

AutoCAD uses the scale factor to multiply the size of the original entity, as follows:

Factor	Effect
Larger than 1.0	Increases the size
1.0	Maintains the original size
Smaller than 1.0	Reduces the size

You cannot enter a negative number.

If you choose the Reference option, AutoCAD calculates the scale factor based on a reference you provide. Suppose, for example, that you know that the side of a polygon is 1.375 units long, but you want it to be 3.375 units long. You could work out the scale factor (2.4545455) with a calculator, but scale-factor referencing makes more sense because AutoCAD does all the work.

When you choose the Reference option, the following prompt appears:

    Reference Length <1>:

Enter the current length of the side (1.375). When AutoCAD asks `New length:`, enter the final length (3.378). You don't need to reach for your calculator.

There is a second way to use the `Reference` option. If you don't know the current length, you can use object snap to show the endpoints. At the next prompt, enter the new length.

You can create the right-hand burners quickly with the Mirror command. Use the center line as the mirror line. When done, erase the baseline you originally created for drawing the left-hand burners; you won't be needing it again (see fig. 6.23). For now, leave in the line that divides the left and right sides of the stovetop; you may want to use it as a reference later.

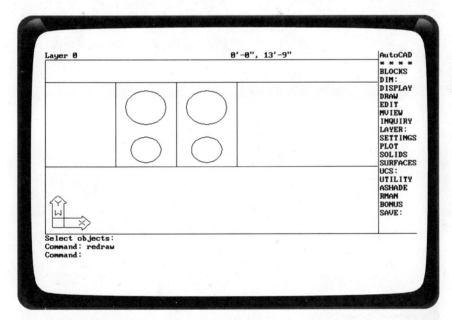

Fig. 6.23.
The left-hand burners were mirrored to create the right-hand burners.

Partitioning Entities (Divide and Measure)

When you need to divide an entity into several sections of equal length, you can use one of two commands—Divide and Measure—that place points at a specified distance along a line, arc, circle, or polyline.

Seeing the effect of these commands will be easier if you change the way AutoCAD displays points. As you may recall from the discussion of points in Chapter 5, AutoCAD can display points in 20 different ways. However, AutoCAD normally displays points as small dots, which are invisible on an entity. Change the point display to a tick mark in the following manner:

Prompt	Response	Explanation
`Command:`	**Pdmode**	Initiates the Pdmode command
`New value for PDMODE<53>:`	**4**	Sets a new value of 4
`Command:`	**Pdsize**	Starts the Pdsize command
`New value for PDSIZE<2>:`	**1**	Sets a size of 1

If you follow this sequence of commands, each point will be displayed as a short vertical line. These points will assist you during the upcoming exercise, when you create a grill on the right side of the range. Before you use the Measure command to create the grill, however, you need to create an area for the grill by offsetting the right stove line by 10 inches. Then draw a construction line from the top of the upper stove burner (use QUAdrant object snap) to the new vertical line (use PERpendicular object snap). Then offset this line 16 inches down. The result should look like figure 6.24.

Fig. 6.24. Construction lines placed for the grill.

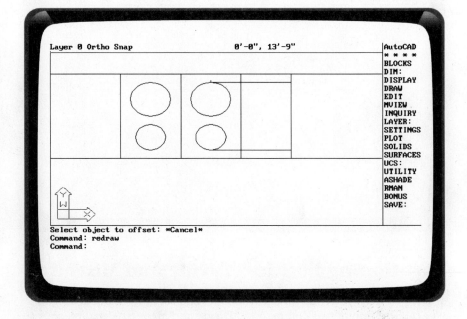

Measuring Distances along Entities (Measure)

The Measure command can be used by many disciplines. You can use it to add cross ties to railroad tracks (or pickets to a fence), to add stationing to a road's center line, or to lay out parking spaces along a curb. (The center line or curb would have to be a single, continuous polyline for Measure to work correctly.)

The Measure command places points (called *blocks*) at specified intervals along a line (or arc, or circle, or polyline). You must define the interval length that AutoCAD uses to measure the entity. Follow this command sequence to measure off the spaces in the grill's cooking surface:

Prompt	Response	Explanation
`Command:`	**Measure**	Starts the Measure command
`Select object to measure:`	Choose top line of grill	Specifies the object to be measured
`<Segment length>/Block:`	**1**	Specifies the distance between the measured points

Figure 6.25 shows the result of this command sequence, with the blocks positioned along the top construction line.

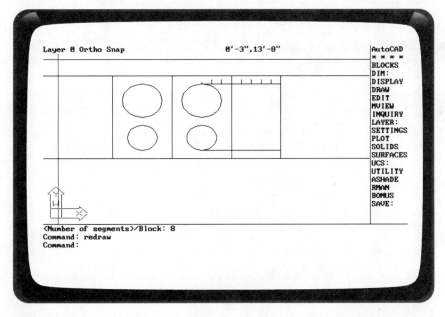

Fig. 6.25.
The Measure command places points at measured distances along an entity.

When you enter **Measure** at the `Command:` prompt, AutoCAD asks you to `Select object to measure:`. You can select only one object. After you select the entity you want to measure, you have two choices. You can specify a distance to use as the segment length, or you can choose the Block option, which that means AutoCAD will use a block instead of points. Blocks are discussed in detail in Chapter 12.

You can specify the measured length either by typing a value or by picking two points on the screen.

Don't be sad, but now you need to use the Undo command reverse what you have just drawn. Next, you will use Divide to do something similar.

Dividing Entities into Equal Parts (Divide)

The Divide command divides (with points or blocks) an entity into equal parts. Divide is subtly different from the Measure command, which places points at specified intervals. Instead of prompting you for the interval's length, Divide asks how many parts you want.

At the `Command:` prompt, enter **Divide**. After you select the object you want to divide, AutoCAD gives you two options. You can specify the number of segments, or choose Block (notifying AutoCAD that you want to divide the entity with blocks). Here you will specify eight segments, as follows:

Prompt	Response	Explanation
`Command:`	**Divide**	Starts the Divide command
`Select object to divide:`	Choose the top line of the grill	Specifies the object to be divided
`<Number of segments>/Block:`	8	Specifies the number of pieces into which to divide the entity

Like the Measure command, Divide permits you to divide only one object at a time.

Now use the Line command to finish drawing the grill. The lines extend from the NODe of the points created with the Divide command to PERpendicular to the lower line. After you draw the lines, erase the points with the Erase W command. By using the Window option, you erase only the points, and no other entities. Finally, use the Trim command to clean up the construction lines, and use Erase to remove the vertical line between the burners, which is no longer needed. Your grill should look like the one shown in figure 6.26.

Chamfering Lines (Chamfer)

AutoCAD's Chamfer command draws a bevel between two intersecting lines. It does this by trimming or extending the lines and then connecting them with an angled line segment. The two lines must intersect; AutoCAD cannot chamfer parallel lines. Because of the way the Chamfer command works, only lines and polylines can be chamfered.

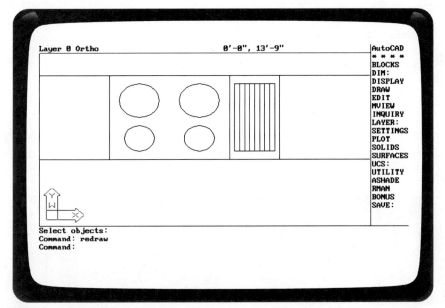

Fig. 6.26.
The nearly completed grill.

A chamfer is used by machinists to smooth the sharp edge of a metal part. AutoCAD lets you chamfer any two intersecting lines, whether they represent a metal part or not. Chamfer lets you join two lines with a third line, whereas a fillet connects two lines with an arc.

With Chamfer, you need to set the *chamfer distances* (the distances that specify where the bevel begins on the intersecting lines) before you can chamfer a corner:

Prompt	*Response*	*Explanation*
`Command:`	**Chamfer**	Starts the Chamfer command
`Polyline/Distances/` `<Select first Line>:`	**D**	Tells AutoCAD that you want to set the chamfer distances
`Enter first chamfer` `distance <0'-0">:`	**.5**	Specifies a chamfer distance of 1/2" for the first line
`Enter second chamfer` `distance <0'-1">:`	**.5**	Specifies the same chamfer distance for the second line
`Command:`	Press Enter	Restarts the Chamfer command

Prompt	Response	Explanation

`Chamfer Polyline/`
`Distances/<Select first`
`Line>:`
	Pick the top line of the grill	Specifies the first line of the pair to be chamfered

`Select second line:`	Pick the left line of the grill	Specifies the second line of the pair to be chamfered

Continue using the Chamfer command to finish beveling all four corners of the grill. The results are shown in figure 6.27.

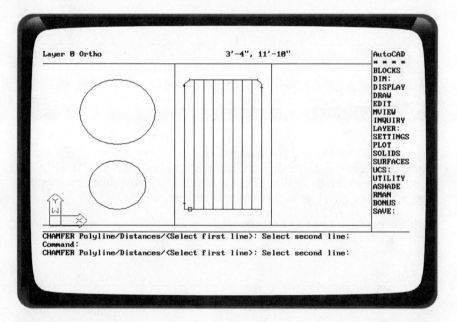

Fig. 6.27.
The Chamfer command adds bevels to the grill's corners.

When you enter **Chamfer** at the `Command:` prompt, AutoCAD displays the following prompt:

`    Polyline/Distance/<Select first line>:`

To set the chamfer distances, type **D**. AutoCAD prompts you for the two distances. The first distance you enter applies to the first entity you pick for the chamfer operation. If the first and second distances are the same, you get a 45-degree chamfer. If both the distances are 0, you get a sharp corner.

Enter **P** if you want to chamfer the entire length of a polyline. A vertex that is not large enough to be chamfered remains unchanged, as with the Fillet command. When you chamfer a polyline, the first distance applies to the first segment of the vertex.

TIP

You can use either the Fillet or the Chamfer command to clean up intersecting lines. If you find that you frequently use the Fillet command (with a radius), then set the Chamfer distances to 0,0. Using just the Chamfer command for cleaning up intersections saves you from setting the Fillet radius back to 0.

Arrays of Entities (Array)

The Array command lets you make many uniformly placed copies. Array is like the Copy Multiple command. Using an array is definitely the easiest way to produce multiple copies of entities. You can create rectangular patterns (called *rectangular arrays*) or circular patterns, called *polar arrays*.

The Array command places objects at a consistent distance from each other, although you can have different distances in the X and Y directions. The prompts displayed by the Array command depend on whether you are working with rectangular or polar arrays.

Rectangular Arrays

Rectangular arrays are based on columns and rows: *columns* are the vertical series in an array; *rows* are the horizontal series. This is similar to the way we describe a spreadsheet—by columns and rows. Also similar to a spreadsheet is the concept of a *cell*. In an array, the distance between the center lines of rows is called the *row distance*, and the distance between the center lines of columns is the *column distance*. These two distances and the entity used in the array make up a *unit cell*.

The following example shows you how to use the Array command to create a tile pattern in the hallway. The pattern is similar to the bathroom pattern, except that the new tile layout is uniform rather than random.

To create the entities to be arrayed, use the Pline command to create two 6"-by-6" tiles, as follows:

Prompt	Response	Explanation
Command:	**Pline**	Starts the Pline command
From point:	Pick point	Pick the starting point 3" from the upper left corner of the hallway
Current line-width is 0'-0" Arc/.../Width/<Endpoint of line>:	**W**	Selects the Width option
Starting width <0'0">:	**6**	Sets the starting width at 6"

Prompt	Response	Explanation
`Ending width <0'-6">:`	Press Enter	Sets the ending width at 6", making a uniform 6" polyline
`Arc/.../Width/<Endpoint of line:`	@6<0	Draws a line 6" long, producing one 6"-by-6" tile
`Arc/.../Width/<Endpoint of line>:`	Press Enter	Ends the Polyline command

Create a second tile by using the Copy command, as follows:

Prompt	Response	Explanation
`Command:`	**Copy**	Starts the Copy command
`Select objects:`	Pick tile	Specifies the tile you just drew as the object to be copied
`Select objects:`	Press Enter	Ends object selection
`<Base point or displacement>/Multiple:`	**INT**	Tells AutoCAD to use the INTersection object snap mode
`of`	Pick corner	Pick the upper left corner of the tile
`Second point of displacement:`	**INT**	
`of`	Pick corner	Pick the lower right corner of the tile

You now have two 6"-by-6" tiles (see fig. 6.28) that will form a 12" cell for the Array command.

To repeat the tile pattern down the hallway, you must make a rectangular array of the two tiles. The following command sequence shows you how:

Prompt	Response	Explanation
`Command:`	**Array**	Starts the Array command
`Select objects:`	**L**	Chooses the last polyline drawn
`Select objects:`	Pick other polyline	Chooses the first polyline drawn

Prompt	*Response*	*Explanation*
Select objects:	Press Enter	Ends object selection
Rectangular or Polar array (R/P):	R	Creates a rectangular array
Number of rows (---) <1>:	14	Indicates the number of rows in the array
Number of columns (|||) <1>:	3	Indicates the number of columns in the array
Unit cell or distance between rows (---):	-12	Specifies the distance between the center of the rows in the downward (negative) direction
Distance between columns (|||):	12	Specifies the distance between the center of the columns in leftward (positive) direction

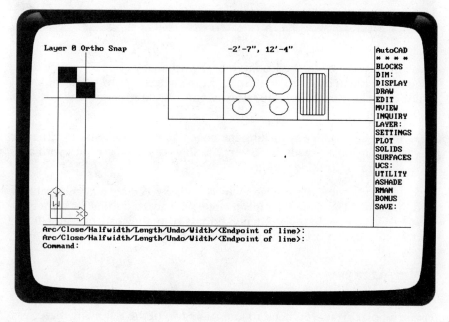

Fig. 6.28.
Two wide polylines form the unit cell of the tile-pattern array.

The graphics represent lines in the horizontal (−−−) or vertical (|||) direction. AutoCAD asks for the distance between the center of the rows and columns in the array. If you enter a positive number, AutoCAD draws the rows upward and columns to the right from the starting object. If you enter a negative number, rows are drawn downward and columns are drawn to the left from the starting object. Issue the Zoom Extents command to see the hallway, which should now look like figure 6.29.

Fig. 6.29. The Array command makes short work of drawing the tiles along the hallway.

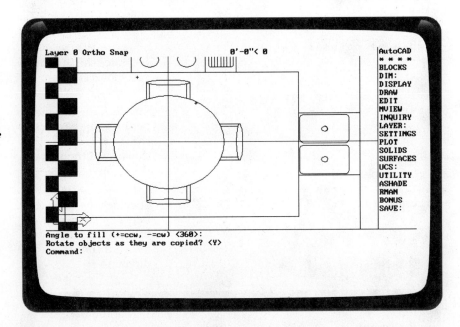

Erase the last tile by the bedroom door. Notice that you need to pick the edge of the tile in order to erase it. You can't select a polyline (or other solid) by picking in the middle because AutoCAD knows only the boundary of the polyline.

If you have difficulty picking the edge of a polyline, you can either zoom in closer (with the Zoom Window command) or pick with a very small Crossing window.

Before you try AutoCAD's polar array, you need to create a kitchen table and one chair. The table is simply a circle with an 18" radius; its center point is in the middle of the kitchen floor. Create the chair by using lines and an ellipse, and use the Trim command for clean-up (see fig. 6.30).

Polar Arrays

Polar arrays are multiple copies arranged in a uniform circular pattern. To create a polar array, you need to know any two of the following three pieces of information:

❏ How many items you want to create

❏ The center point and angle specifying the arc along which the entities should be replicated

❏ The angle between individual items

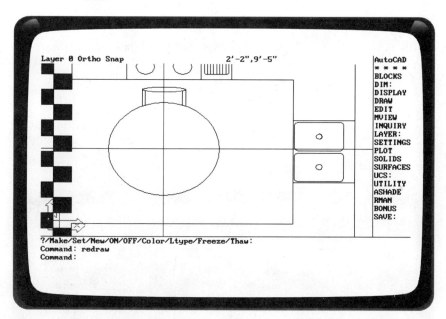

Fig. 6.30.
The kitchen table and chair are drawn from simple objects: a circle, an ellipse, and four lines.

The following command sequence shows you how to use AutoCAD's polar array feature to make three copies of the chair, and place them around the circular table:

Prompt	Response	Explanation
Command:	**Array**	Starts the Array command
Select objects:	**W**	Specifies the window object-selection option
Select objects:	Select the chair	Specifies the chair as the object to be arrayed
Select objects:	Press Enter	Ends object selection
Rectangular or Polar array (R/P):	**P**	Specifies a polar array
Center point of array:	**CEN**	Specifies the CENter of the kitchen table as the center of the array

Prompt	Response	Explanation
Number of items:	4	Places four chairs around the table (this number includes the chair already drawn)
Angle to fill (+=CCW, -=CW) <360>:	Press Enter	Spaces the copies equally around 360 degrees
Rotate objects as they are copied?<Y>:	Y	Tells AutoCAD to rotate the entities as they are copied

The results of the Array operation appear in figure 6.31.

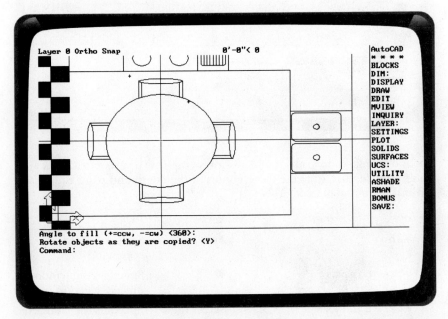

Fig. 6.31.
The Array
Polar
command
draws three of
the four chairs
and
distributes
them around
the table.

You start the polar array in the same way you start a rectangular array; just remember that the entities will be copied along an arc or a circle. When AutoCAD asks for the Number of items: to create, you must provide a whole number that represents the *total* number of objects. This can be confusing, since the first object already exists. To make three copies of the chair, you answer with 4.

WARNING

The Array command can make many objects very quickly. However, the array also can make the drawing's size swell quickly, using up more disk space and slowing down screen redraws and regenerations. For this reason, AutoCAD prompts for verification if you try to create a very large array.

If you press Enter at the `Number of items:` prompt, you tell AutoCAD you don't know how many objects you want drawn. AutoCAD asks for an `Angle between items:`, which lets it calculate the number of objects.

The `Angle to fill (+=CCW, -=CW) <360>:` prompt asks for an angle that defines the length of the arc created around the specified center point. A positive angle does counterclockwise rotation; a negative number causes a clockwise rotation, as the `(+=CCW, -=CW)` portion of the prompt reminds you. If you use a 360° angle (a circle, by default), then it doesn't matter whether you specify a positive or negative angle.

After you enter this array-definition information, AutoCAD asks `Rotate objects as they are copied? <Y>:`. If you answer **Y**, each object is rotated as it is placed around the array arc. Figure 6.32 shows the effect of answering **N**: the entities were not rotated.

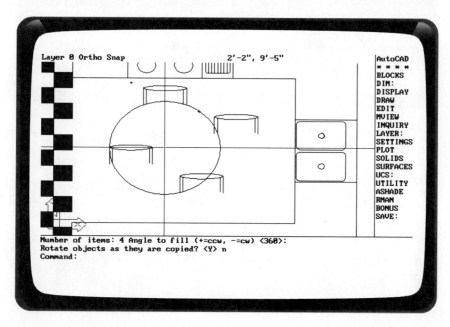

Fig. 6.32.
Sometimes it makes sense not to rotate objects in a polar array; sometimes it does.

Summary

This chapter showed you most of AutoCAD's editing commands. You used these commands to add a hallway, bedroom, and kitchen to the apartment's floor plan. Your drawing now should look like figure 6.33.

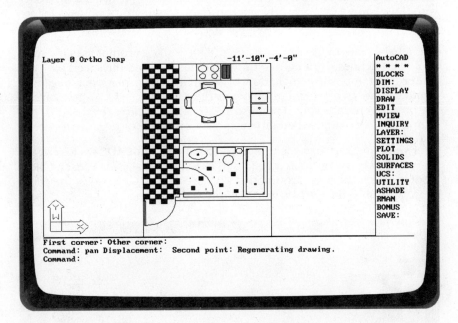

Fig. 6.33.
Most of this
apartment
floor plan was
drawn using
AutoCAD's
editing
commands.

As you work with the editing commands, you will discover that AutoCAD is truly versatile. Unlike manual drawing systems, in which you must "begin anew" whenever you have to make changes to a basic drawing, AutoCAD allows you to modify previously created entities as often as you like, with little effort, and with no erasing. You can create a basic set of drawings and, with the capabilities of the editing commands, modify the entities to suit your needs without having to start from scratch.

In the next chapter, you will learn different ways to view your drawing on-screen.

7

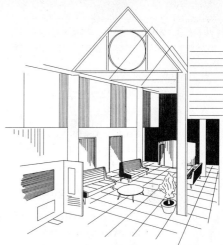

Illustration courtesy of Autodesk, Inc., Sausalito, CA.

Viewing a Drawing

So far, you have learned that AutoCAD work consists of drawing objects and then modifying them to suit your needs. As important as the act of drawing may be, however, the ability to view your drawing in detail is crucial. What good is the power of computerized drafting, after all, if you can't see the results of your efforts?

You can see your drawing on the screen or on paper. If you are not familiar with CAD, you may be more comfortable with a drawing you can hold in your hands. Chapter 8 discusses the options for producing a hard copy. After reading these two chapters, you will feel comfortable using either output method.

This chapter shows you how to look at your drawing on-screen. By letting you see your drawing in different ways, AutoCAD gives you the means to draft with greater speed, ease, and accuracy than are possible in manual drafting. AutoCAD also enables you to create slide presentations of your drawings, as you will learn later in this chapter. In the following sections you will learn about controlling the display of 2-D images only; Chapter 18 discusses the display of three-dimensional entities.

This chapter covers the following commands:

- ❑ Mslide
- ❑ Pan
- ❑ Redraw
- ❑ Regen
- ❑ View
- ❑ Vslide
- ❑ Zoom

199

CAD presents a problem that you don't have in manual drafting; that is, sometimes the CAD user cannot see the entire drawing in enough detail on the computer's screen.

You can solve this problem in two ways. One is to use an ultra-high resolution graphics board that lets you see all the drawing's details. Even the highest-resolution graphics boards available today limit you to seeing all the details on a drawing that would fit a C-size (24"-by-17") sheet. Beyond that, details cannot be resolved.

The other solution is to let the CAD package increase and decrease the drawing's magnification. When you see the entire drawing (even one as small as your SUITE drawing) on-screen, you may not see all the details. AutoCAD can enlarge the view it presents of the drawing so that you can see all the details. When the view is enlarged, however, you no longer see the entire drawing. Viewing only a small portion of the drawing enlarged on the screen may seem strange at first, but after a while you will become accustomed to working this way.

Refreshing the Screen (Redraw)

The Redraw command tells AutoCAD to refresh the screen image. When you draw and edit, AutoCAD leaves *blips* (tiny crosses at pick points) and *holes* (created when an erased entity overlies another entity). You can use the Redraw command any time you want to clean up the image on the screen:

Command: **Redraw**

The screen blinks once as AutoCAD redraws the SUITE drawing. Sometimes, such as when you turn off a layer or use the Undo command, AutoCAD automatically redraws the screen. If AutoCAD didn't do this, you wouldn't see the drawing correctly.

You can issue the Redraw command at any time, even transparently (transparent commands are discussed shortly). This transparent capability gives Redraw great flexibility because you can use it to clean up the screen whenever you want—even while AutoCAD is executing another command that "dirties" the screen.

Sometimes, however, the Redraw command does not clean up the screen correctly. At such times, you may want to regenerate the drawing completely by issuing the Regen command. (Regen is discussed in the next section.) Because Redraw is significantly faster than Regen, you should try a Redraw first.

A *word about transparent commands . . .*

AutoCAD lets you use some commands while other commands are executing. When you issue commands in this manner, the second command is called a *transparent* command, because it is invisible to the first command, and has no effect on the first command's operation. Transparent commands give you a great deal of flexibility. You can use one command to draw a certain object, and use a transparent screen-control command to change to another view while the first command sequence is still in progress.

To use one command transparently at any point during another command's execution, first type an apostrophe ('), followed by the transparent command's name. You can practice using transparent commands by issuing the Setvar command transparently while the Point command is in progress, as the following command sequence demonstrates:

```
Command: Point
Point: 'Setvar
>>Variable name or ?: PDSIZE
>>New value for PDSIZE <1.0000>: 20
Resuming Point command.
Point:
```

AutoCAD displays the double angle bracket (>>) to remind you that a transparent command is in use. The following commands can be used transparently:

❏ Ddemodes	❏ Redrawall
❏ Ddlmodes	❏ Resume
❏ Ddrmodes	❏ Setvar
❏ Graphscr	❏ Textscr
❏ Help	❏ Zoom (except All and Extents)
❏ Pan	❏ ?
❏ Redraw	❏ All system variables

You cannot use a transparent command, however, in all situations. For example, you cannot use a transparent command when one of the following commands is active:

❏ Dtext	❏ Shell
❏ Dview	❏ Sketch
❏ Pan	❏ View
❏ Plot	❏ Vpoint

A *word about transparent commands (continued)* . . .

❏ Prplot   ❏ Zoom
❏ Pspace   ❏ Any dialogue box

If you are unfamiliar with any of these commands, don't worry. They are discussed later in this text.

You cannot use a transparent command while another transparent command is in use, nor can you use the transparent version within the same command. For example, you cannot use the transparent 'Zoom command within the nontransparent Zoom command. AutoCAD will not carry out a transparent Pan or Zoom command if it would cause a regeneration of the drawing. If you try to issue a transparent command that requires the drawing to be regenerated, AutoCAD displays the following message:

```
** Requires a regen, cannot be transparent.
```

Because the Zoom All and Zoom Extents options always force a regeneration, the transparent Zoom prompt does not include them. Sometimes the transparent command does not go into effect until the next time AutoCAD redraws or regenerates the image (as is the case in the preceding Pdsize example).

The Zoom and Pan commands can be used in the middle of another command that draws a very long line. If you are zoomed into a part of the drawing, and you want to draw a line that extends beyond the current view, use the Pan command transparently to see the line's other endpoint.

To try this, execute the Line command and pick a starting point. When AutoCAD prompts for the second point, type **'Pan** instead:

```
Command: Line
From point: Pick point
To point: 'Pan
>>Displacement: Pick point
>>Second point: Pick point
Resuming LINE command.
To point: Pick point
```

AutoCAD temporarily suspends the Line command to let you pan over in the drawing. When you've picked the new view, the Line command resumes and lets you draw the other endpoint.

Zoom and Pan are discussed in detail later in this chapter.

Regenerating the Display (Regen)

The Regen command (short for *regeneration*) recalculates the drawing's data on-screen. You should use the Regen command if the image presented by Redraw does not correctly reflect your drawing. When you type **Regen** at the `Command:` prompt, AutoCAD displays the following message:

    Regenerating drawing.

AutoCAD automatically regenerates the drawing in several situations, such as when you first call up an existing drawing, or if a Zoom or Pan causes a significant change to the display. A regeneration may also occur when you freeze or thaw layers.

Because Regen goes through the drawing's entire database and redisplays the information on-screen, this command can take two to 10 times longer than Redraw. The benefit is that the regenerated image is as accurate as possible.

TIP

Some commands force AutoCAD to regenerate the drawing automatically. If you are not sure whether you want such automatic regenerations to take place, you can ask AutoCAD to warn you before it regenerates the screen image. To do so, type **Regenauto** at the `Command:` prompt. When you issue Regenauto, AutoCAD displays the prompt On/Off <On>:. Type **Off** at the prompt. This forces AutoCAD to ask for your permission before regenerating the drawing, as follows:

    About to regen, proceed? <Y>:

At this point you can answer **N** to stop the regeneration, if you want.

Magnifying the Drawing (Zoom)

An important aspect of CAD drafting is the ability to see your drawing clearly. To see this point for yourself, call up the sample drawing, SUITE. When the drawing is in the Drawing Editor, enter **Zoom .001** at the `Command:` prompt.

Where did the drawing go? It hasn't disappeared. You probably see a small rectangle near the center of the screen. This is the entire drawing! The drawing has not changed; you just told AutoCAD to make it 1,000 times smaller. You can return to the original view by entering the **Zoom** command, and then **E** (for *Extents*).

What good is a drawing this small? If you are drawing a large apartment complex with many suites, you have to zoom out in this manner if you want to see the entire building (although each suite looks very small from such a perspective). This zooming technique is similar to using a wide-angle lens on a camera to see a larger view.

To work on a bathroom, you must zoom back in to see the details. The photographic equivalent is to switch to a telephoto lens to capture a detail of the building. In either case, remember that the building itself does not change; only your view through the camera changes. The same is true of AutoCAD's Zoom command. Zoom does not affect the drawing's size or scale as some editing commands do. Zoom only changes the size of the image on the computer screen.

Because AutoCAD uses double-precision real numbers for its calculations, its zoom ratio is a trillion-to-one. That's more zoom power than some other CAD packages have and more than you'll ever need.

Chapter 6 gave you a brief introduction to AutoCAD's zoom capabilities and taught you two zoom options. But Zoom features more options, power, and flexibility than you may have guessed. Now look at the command, its options, and its use.

When you enter **Zoom** at the `Command:` prompt, AutoCAD displays the following selection of options:

```
All/Center/Dynamic/Extents/Left/Previous/Vmax/
Window/<Scale(X/XP)>:
```

The following sections examine each of these options in turn.

Zoom All

If you issue the Zoom command and then select the All option, AutoCAD displays the drawing to its *limits* or its *extents*, whichever is larger. The size of the drawing's limits is controlled by the Limits command, which is discussed in Chapter 11. The imaginary rectangular area that encloses your drawing is the extents. Practice using Zoom All, as follows:

```
Command: Zoom
All/Center/Dynamic/Extents/Left/Previous/Vmax/
Window/<Scale(X/XP)>:A
Regenerating drawing.
```

Your screen should display the SUITE drawing, as shown in figure 7.1.

When you issue Zoom All, AutoCAD can't know exactly where the extents of the drawing are. You may have drawn objects that go beyond the previous extents. To recalculate the extents, AutoCAD always regenerates the drawing during a Zoom All operation. Sometimes AutoCAD may do one or two additional redraws before displaying the new view. This is why you cannot use Zoom All as a transparent command.

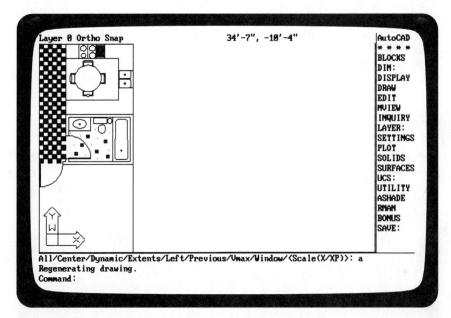

```
Layer 0 Ortho Snap              34'-7", -10'-4"        AutoCAD
                                                       * * * *
                                                       BLOCKS
                                                       DIM:
                                                       DISPLAY
                                                       DRAW
                                                       EDIT
                                                       MVIEW
                                                       INQUIRY
                                                       LAYER:
                                                       SETTINGS
                                                       PLOT
                                                       SOLIDS
                                                       SURFACES
                                                       UCS:
                                                       UTILITY
                                                       ASHADE
                                                       RMAN
                                                       BONUS
                                                       SAVE:

All/Center/Dynamic/Extents/Left/Previous/Vmax/Window/<Scale(X/XP)>: a
Regenerating drawing.
Command:
```

Fig. 7.1.
The Zoom All command displays a drawing to its limits or extents, whichever is larger.

Zoom Center

When the Zoom Center option is used, AutoCAD creates a new view of the drawing based on a new center point, which you choose. If you select Zoom Center, AutoCAD prompts for the center point of the new view. The following command sequence is an example of how you might use Zoom Center to zoom in on the bathroom sink:

Prompt	Response	Explanation
Command:	**Zoom**	Starts the Zoom command
.../<Scale(X)>:	**C**	Specifies the Center option
Center point:	**1'3,4'3**	Specifies the coordinates of the center of the new view (the bathroom sink)
Magnification or Height <23'-8">:	**1'**	Specifies the height of the new screen (that is, the new view shows a one-foot-tall section of the sink)

This sequence zooms in on the bathroom sink (see fig. 7.2). When AutoCAD displays the `Center point:` prompt, the program needs to know which part of the drawing you want to place at the center of the new view. You can respond by specifying exact coordinates (as in the preceding example), or by using your input device to pick a point on the screen. In the example, you specified the center of the sink's drain as the center of the new view.

Fig. 7.2.
The Zoom
Center
command
creates the
new view
around a
specified
point, in this
case, the
bathroom
sink's drain.

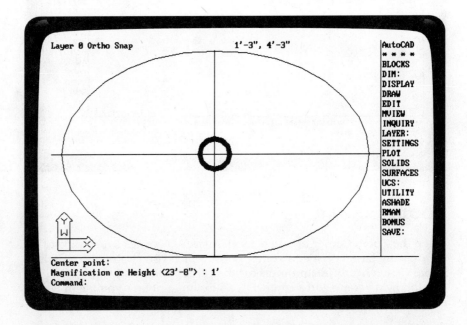

Next, AutoCAD prompts you for the magnification or the height of the new view. If you supply a number followed by an X, AutoCAD reads it as the magnification—the X stands for "times" or the magnification power. Numbers larger than 1.0 tell AutoCAD to zoom in; smaller numbers cause AutoCAD to zoom out. If you supply a number without the X, AutoCAD reads the number as the height of the new view, in the current units (feet and inches, in this case). Because the AutoCAD drawing is in full size, you're telling AutoCAD to take a one-foot-tall piece of the drawing and fit it onto the screen. Half the height you specify is displayed above the screen's center point, half is below the center point. If you had specified 2' as the new view's height, the bathroom sink would have appeared at the center of the screen, only smaller. The edges of the vanity also would have appeared.

Zoom Dynamic

When you select Zoom Dynamic, several new tools appear in the Drawing Editor (see fig. 7.3). The Zoom Dynamic screen gives you five pieces of information. Even if you do not have a color monitor, the symbols are distinct enough to be recognized easily.

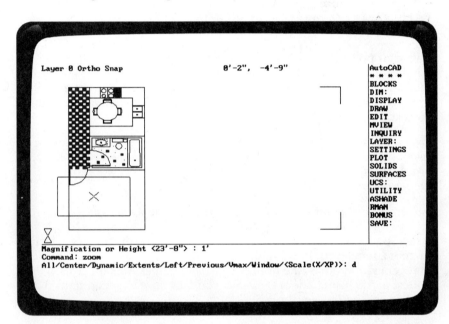

```
Layer 0 Ortho Snap                    0'-2",  -4'-9"            AutoCAD
                                                                * * * *
                                                                BLOCKS
                                                                DIM:
                                                                DISPLAY
                                                                DRAW
                                                                EDIT
                                                                MVIEW
                                                                INQUIRY
                                                                LAYER:
                                                                SETTINGS
                                                                PLOT
                                                                SOLIDS
                                                                SURFACES
                                                                UCS:
                                                                UTILITY
                                                                ASHADE
                                                                RMAN
                                                                BONUS
                                                                SAVE:

Magnification or Height <23'-8"> : 1'
Command: zoom
All/Center/Dynamic/Extents/Left/Previous/Vmax/Window/<Scale(X/XP)>: d
```

*Fig. 7.3.
The Zoom
Dynamic
screen lets you
zoom and pan
with greater
control.*

Zoom Dynamic symbol	Meaning
Large white box	Shows the drawing's extents
Dotted green box	Shows the screen's current view (in this case, around the bathroom sink)
Four red corner angles	*Regeneration limits* marking the *virtual screen* (the area you may zoom into without causing a regeneration)
White box with X or arrow	*View box* representing the area that will be drawn next on the screen (the X indicates Pan mode; the arrow means Zoom mode)
White hourglass	Warns that the view box you select will cause a regeneration

The Zoom Dynamic screen shows you important zooming information, such as the drawing's extents and the regeneration limits. Zoom Dynamic enables you to choose the location of your next display while avoiding a time-consuming regeneration. Try the Zoom Dynamic command now:

```
Command: Zoom
All/Center/Dynamic/Extents/Left/Previous/Vmax/
Window/<Scale(X/XP)>: D
```

Move your pointing device around. Notice how the view box (the one with the X) also moves. This movement is called *panning*. In panning, you display a different part of the drawing without changing the zoom factor (you will learn more about panning and the Pan command later in this chapter).

Now move the view box past the red corner markers (the regeneration limits). Notice how the hourglass symbol shows up in the lower left corner. AutoCAD is warning you that selecting this view will cause a regeneration.

Now press your pointing device's pick button. The X changes to an arrow (see fig. 7.4). Slowly move the pointing device. The box grows bigger and smaller as you move the pointing device back and forth. You are selecting different zoom levels. If the view box grows large enough to go outside the regeneration limits, the hourglass symbol comes back on. This is the trickiest part of using Zoom Dynamic; you may have to spend time practicing sizing the view box.

*Fig. 7.4.
The arrow marker indicates that Zoom Dynamic is in Zoom mode.*

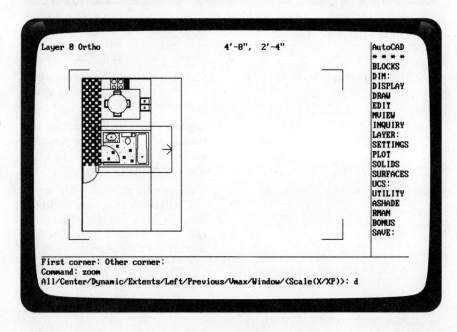

Press the pick button again. The arrow changes back to the X because you are back in Pan mode. You can keep switching between panning and zooming to change the new screen area and its size. When you have what you want, press the Enter button. AutoCAD displays the new view (see fig. 7.5).

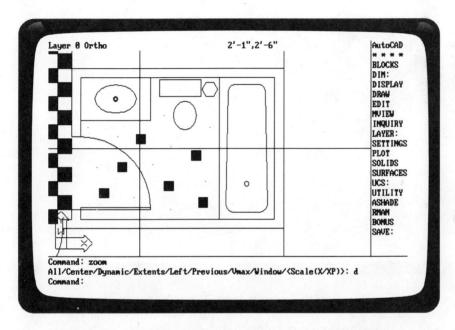

Fig. 7.5.
The new view resulting from the Zoom Dynamic exercise.

If you are not sure what your next view of the drawing should be, use Zoom Dynamic. This Zoom option gives you the complete view of the drawing and is much faster than performing the two steps of Zoom Extents (to see the full drawing) and then Zoom Window (to move back in again). Initially, Zoom Dynamic is hard to understand but once you get the feel of it, you may prefer using it to most other Zoom options.

Zoom Extents

The Zoom Extents option lets you see the entire drawing on-screen. The drawing's extents are the precise area of what you have drawn. In the sample drawing, the extents are the four outer walls. As you add to the drawing beyond the four walls, the extents grow to encompass all objects.

Try Zoom Extents now:

```
Command: Zoom
All/Center/Dynamic/Extents/Left/Previous/Vmax/
Window/<Scale(X/XP)>:E
Regenerating drawing.
```

The drawing now fills the entire screen and looks exactly like the results of the Zoom All (see fig. 7.6). Zoom Extents always causes a regeneration, for the same reasons as Zoom All.

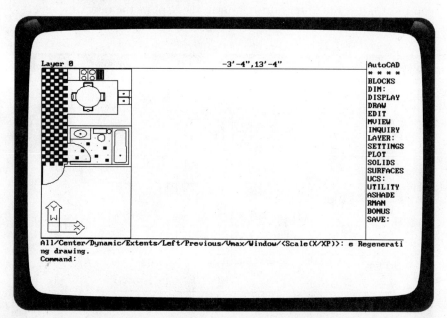

Fig. 7.6.
The view
created by
Zoom Extents
is often
similar to that
created by
Zoom All.

If you unintentionally force AutoCAD to regenerate a very large drawing (which can take a long time), you can press Ctrl-C. AutoCAD halts the regeneration and displays the following message:

    Regen aborted.

The drawback of aborting an unfinished regeneration is that you will see only as much of the drawing as AutoCAD has regenerated to that point. The advantage is that you can see entities that otherwise are hidden (because they are hidden beneath other entities).

Zoom Left

Zoom Left lets you specify a zoomed view by specifying the location of the new view's lower left corner and a view height. You can pick the lower left corner and view height on the screen, or you can supply coordinates. Just pressing Enter at the `Magnification or Height:` prompt is the same as panning to the new location specified by the coordinates of the lower left corner, as follows:

```
Command: Zoom
All/Center/Dynamic/Extents/Left/Previous/Vmax/
Window/<Scale(X/XP)>: L
Lower left corner point: 1',7'
Magnification or Height <23'-8">:  Press Enter
```

AutoCAD asks which point you want to use as the lower left corner of the new screen. Pick a point or type in a pair of coordinates, such as 1',7'. AutoCAD then prompts you for the new screen's height or a magnification factor. Press Enter to pan the screen to a new location.

Zoom Previous

Select Zoom Previous to return to the preceding view. AutoCAD remembers the previous 10 views. Try the Zoom Previous command several times in a row:

```
Command: Zoom
All/Center/Dynamic/Extents/Left/Previous/Vmax/
Window/<Scale(X/XP)>: P

Command:  Press space bar to repeat the Zoom command
All/Center/Dynamic/Extents/Left/Previous/Vmax/
Window/<Scale(X/XP)>:  P
```

This command causes AutoCAD to display the views you've been practicing with, in reverse order. Because Zoom Previous usually does not force a screen regeneration, you probably will use this Zoom option often.

Zoom Vmax

If you use AutoCAD Release 11, you also can select the Zoom Vmax option. Zoom Vmax zooms out to the drawing's *virtual screen* limits. The virtual screen is the area in which AutoCAD can zoom and pan without having to regenerate. The virtual screen frequently matches the extents or the limits of the drawing. Because it does not require a regeneration, however, Zoom Vmax is preferable to Zoom Extents or Zoom All. Try Zoom Vmax as follows:

```
Command: Zoom
All/Center/Dynamic/Extents/Left/Previous/Vmax/
Window/<Scale(X/XP)>: V
```

You now should see the same view you saw after issuing the Zoom All command (refer to fig. 7.1), but without the time-consuming regeneration. If the previous Zoom or Pan caused a regeneration, Zoom Vmax redraws the current view. You will need to use the Zoom Extents command (and endure the wait during a regen) to return to the view of the entire drawing.

Zoom Window

Zoom Window lets you zoom into an area you enclose within a rectangle (called a *window*). The Zoom window works in much the same manner as the window you use to create a selection set of entities. Zoom Window is possibly the most frequently used Zoom option. Try the Zoom Window command now:

Prompt	Response	Explanation
Command:	**Zoom**	Starts the Zoom command
All/.../Window/ <Scale(X)>:	**w**	Selects the Window option
First corner:	Pick a point at the bathroom's lower left corner	Specifies the window's first corner
Other corner:	Pick a point at the opposite corner of the bathroom	Completes the window

Notice how the window box grows out of the first point as you move your pointing device in response to the Other corner: prompt. Figure 7.7 shows you what the Zoom window looks like as it is stretched across the screen to include the desired view. When you press the pick button to pick the second corner, AutoCAD displays the windowed view of the bathroom, as shown in figure 7.8.

You may not always get the view you select with the window, because AutoCAD must display a view that fits your screen; the window you pick may be too tall or wide to fit. Generally, AutoCAD displays, in the lower left corner of the screen, the window you picked plus any surrounding material that fits on the screen.

Zoom Scale

Zoom Scale lets you to zoom in and out on the drawing while maintaining the same center point of the screen. When you use Zoom Scale, the objects at the center of the screen remain there, but their apparent size is enlarged or reduced. This type of zooming is just like zooming in or out through a stationary camera lens or a telescope. If you include an X in the scale factor, the image is magnified in relation to the current view. Try using the Zoom command and setting the scale at 2X:

```
Command: Zoom
All/Center/Dynamic/Extents/Left/Previous/Vmax/
Window/<Scale(X/XP): 2X
```

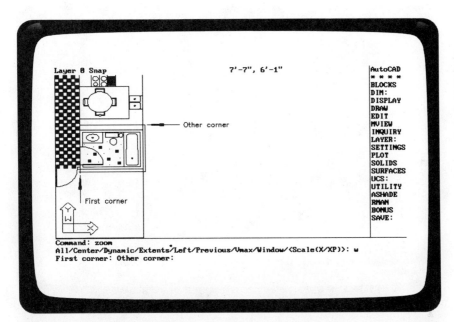

Fig. 7.7.
Zoom Window lets you pick two opposite corners of the zoomed-in view

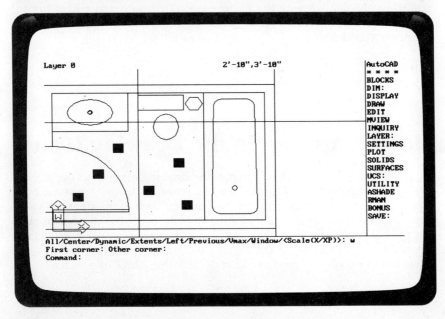

Fig. 7.8.
The view of the bathroom, created by the Zoom Window command.

AutoCAD redraws the drawing so that it is twice as large as the previous view, but with the same center point.

If you leave out the X, the magnification is relative to the current limits. Enter **Zoom 2**, and AutoCAD displays the drawing at twice the scale of the limits (see figs. 7.9 and 7.10).

Fig. 7.9.
The view of
the current
limits, as a
result of
Zoom 1.

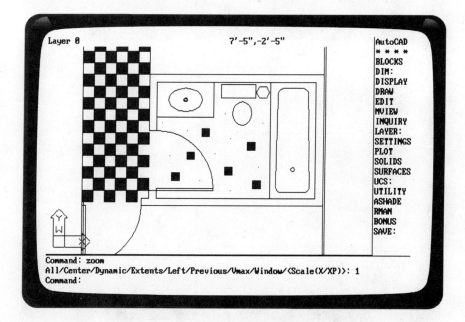

You will grow familiar with the Zoom options as you practice drawing. You probably will use the following Zoom options most frequently in your everyday drafting:

❏ Zoom Window

❏ Zoom Previous

❏ Zoom Vmax

Moving Around in the Drawing (Pan)

Suppose that you want to see a part of the drawing that lies to the right of the current screen. As you learned earlier, you can change your view by zooming out from the current view, windowing part of the drawing's right side, then zooming into that window. This is too many steps to take just to shift your view from one part of the drawing to another, especially if you don't want to change the current zoom factor. Luckily, AutoCAD offers a faster way to move around in the drawing: the Pan command.

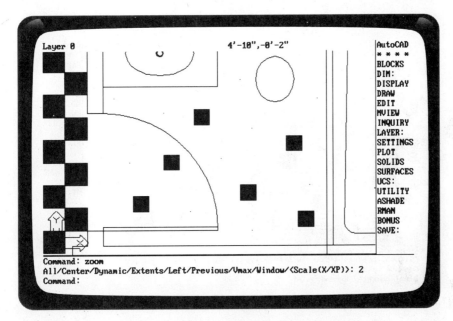

*Fig. 7.10.
The Zoom 2
command
doubles the
size of the
view.*

The Pan command lets you move around in the drawing without zooming first. If you are working in one part of the drawing and need to work in an adjacent part, you can just pan from one area to the other.

Practice using the Pan command, as follows:

Prompt	Response	Explanation
Command:	**Zoom**	Starts the Zoom command
All/.../<Scale(X/XP)>:	**2**	Zooms in to allow the Pan command to work without a regeneration
Command:	**Pan**	Starts the Pan command
Displacement:	Pick point	Pick the point on the screen
Second point:	Pick point	Pick a second point on the screen (see fig. 7.11)

Fig. 7.11.
The Pan
command
shows a
rubberband
line of the
displacement
distance.

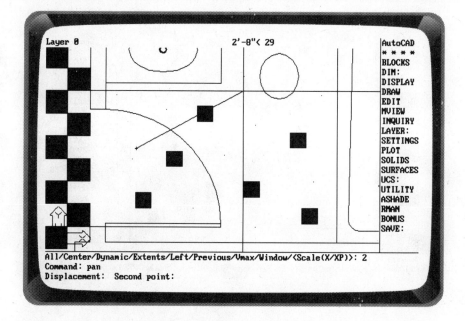

AutoCAD shifts the view on the screen by the distance between the two picked points (see fig. 7.12). The shift may not be in the direction you expect. AutoCAD does not shift the screen to the second point; rather, the shift is in the direction from the first point to the second.

Fig. 7.12.
The view after
the Pan
command.

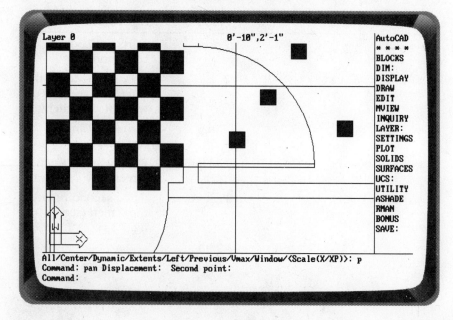

The `Displacement:` prompt can be confusing because you can answer it in two ways. The easier way is to ignore the prompt and simply pick the point that will become the new edge of the screen. When AutoCAD prompts for the second point, pick another point that represents how far you want the screen to move.

You also can execute a pan by supplying AutoCAD with a pair of coordinates (such as 1,2), and pressing the Enter key at the `Second point:` prompt. AutoCAD moves the view over 1 unit and up 2 units.

If you pan too far, you must wait for AutoCAD to regenerate the drawing. To avoid this, use the Zoom Dynamic command rather than the Pan command. The hourglass symbol on the Zoom Dynamic screen warns you if you try to pan into an area that will cause a regeneration.

Making Views (View)

Zooming and panning do not take much time if your drawing is small, but these operations can slow you down if you are working with a large drawing (even if you always manage to avoid regenerations). To speed up your work, you can use the View command to create specific views of your work areas. Then you can flip quickly between these views without guessing where they are (as is often the case when you use the Pan command), or having to use the complicated Zoom Dynamic command.

Enter **View** at the `Command:` prompt, and AutoCAD displays the following options:

        `?/Delete/Restore/Save/Window:`

The following sections discuss each option individually.

View ?

The View ? option lists all views that are currently defined in the drawing. This list is a reminder of the names you've given to the views you have already created. If you have not yet defined any views, AutoCAD reports `No matching views found.`

View Delete

If you want to remove a view reference from the list, select View Delete. Only the view's name and reference coordinates are removed; the drawing itself remains intact. You can always re-create the view later.

View Restore

Select View Restore when you want to display a named view. This restores the previously defined view to the screen. You will learn how to define and restore a view shortly.

View Save

To save the current on-screen image as a view, choose View Save. When you select this option AutoCAD asks you to give the new view a name before saving it. The name can be up to 31 characters long and can contain letters, numbers, and the dollar sign ($), hyphen (-), and underscore (_) symbols. You and AutoCAD use the name to reference the view. AutoCAD automatically remembers the view's coordinates with the name. You learn how to save, name, and restore a view later in this chapter.

View Window

View Window is a more efficient version of View Save. The View Window option lets you create a view by enclosing the desired portion of the drawing in a window. This view-saving method is faster than using Zoom Window to move into the desired area, then using View Save, and finally zooming to the area for the next view.

Try creating some views now. First, issue the Zoom Extents command to see the entire drawing (notice how AutoCAD takes the time to regenerate the entire drawing). Now save a view of the entire drawing, as follows:

```
Command: View
??/Delete/Restore/Save/Window: S
Name of view to save: All
```

You named the view *All*. You will come back to this view later. Now use the View Window command to save a windowed view of the bathroom, as follows:

Prompt	Response	Explanation
Command:	**View**	Starts the View command
??/Delete/Restore/Save/ Window:	**W**	Selects the Window option
Name of view to save:	**Bathroom**	Names the view "Bathroom"

First point:	Pick a point to the lower left of the bathroom	Specifies the window's first corner
Other point:	Pick point to the upper right of the bathroom	Completes the window

Figure 7.13 shows the windowed bathroom view as it is being created.

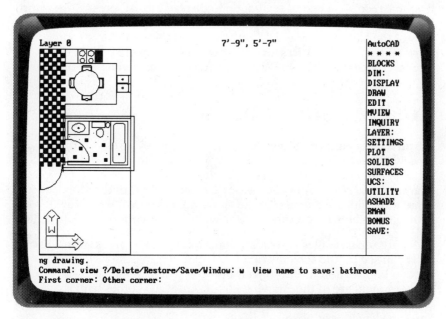

```
Layer 0                          7'-9", 5'-7"         |AutoCAD
                                                      |* * * *
                                                      |BLOCKS
                                                      |DIM:
                                                      |DISPLAY
                                                      |DRAW
                                                      |EDIT
                                                      |MVIEW
                                                      |INQUIRY
                                                      |LAYER:
                                                      |SETTINGS
                                                      |PLOT
                                                      |SOLIDS
                                                      |SURFACES
                                                      |UCS:
                                                      |UTILITY
                                                      |ASHADE
                                                      |RMAN
                                                      |BONUS
                                                      |SAVE:
ng drawing.
Command: view ?/Delete/Restore/Save/Window: w  View name to save: bathroom
First corner: Other corner:
```

Fig. 7.13.
The View
Window
command lets
you create a
named view of
a windowed
portion of the
drawing.

Pick the first corner of the window at the lower left corner of the bathroom; the other corner is the upper right corner. Finally, do a View Window of the kitchen, and save the view with the name *Kitchen*.

Type **View ?** to see the list of the three views you just saved. Press Enter at the Views to list<*>: prompt to get a list of all views:

```
Command: View
??/Delete/Restore/Save/Window: ?
View(s) to list <*>: Press Enter
```

Usually, AutoCAD switches to text mode (yours may not) and displays the following list:

```
Saved views:
View name        Space

ALL              M
BATHROOM         M
KITCHEN          M
```

AutoCAD Release 11 lists the view names in alphabetical order; older versions of AutoCAD display the names in the order they were created. Space M means that the view was created in model space, which is discussed in the chapters on three-dimensional drawing and editing.

If your screen switched to text mode to display the list, press F1 to return to the graphics screen. Next, try the **View R Bathroom** command. The view of the bathroom now fills the screen. Do the same for the kitchen view. Finally, use **View Restore** to place the view named All on the screen. Notice that this time AutoCAD does not regenerate the image.

Creating Slide Shows

As you have seen throughout this chapter, AutoCAD gives you the power to view your drawing in nearly any way you want, to make drawing creation and editing easier. AutoCAD also lets you create presentation images, called *slides*. AutoCAD slides are "snapshots" of drawing views; in some ways slides are similar to the views you create with the View command. Whereas you can edit a view, however, you cannot edit a slide.

Slides are separate files you create and save. A slide is an exact image of what you see on the screen when you create the snapshot. Slides can contain information useful to your drawing. You can look at a slide whenever you are in the Drawing Editor. AutoCAD comes with a slide called COLORWH that displays the 255 numbered colors in a color wheel. You can view it right now:

```
Command: Vslide
Slide file <SUITE>: Colorwh
```

In Release 11, a file dialogue box appears when you issue the Vslide command (see fig. 7.14). With your pointing device, pick COLORWH from the list of slide files. Then pick the OK box.

The image of the COLORWH drawing file should appear on your screen. The Vslide (View Slide) command brings up a slide of a color wheel showing the 255 color numbers that AutoCAD uses.

You cannot edit or zoom into slides: they are just pictures, not drawings. This can be an advantage if you want to give someone an image of your drawing that cannot be edited. To remove the slide from the Drawing

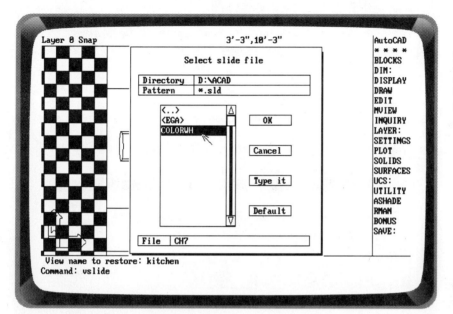

Fig. 7.14.
The dialogue
box for
viewing a slide
in Release 11.

Editor, use the Redraw command. The slide image disappears and is replaced by the SUITE drawing.

Another advantage of slides is that they display quickly on the screen. Further, you can automate the slide display through script files, so that you can present different options at a meeting or do simple animation sequences. (You will learn how to create slide shows in Chapter 13.)

You can make a slide of any drawing, or of any view of a drawing. To practice making a slide, zoom into the kitchen area of SUITE. Once you have the view you want to capture, use the Mslide (Make Slide) command, as follows:

```
Command: Mslide
Slide file<SUITE>: Kitchen
```

For the slide's file name, you can use any name up to eight characters long with the standard DOS limitations. After you enter a valid file name, AutoCAD saves the slide view as a disk file with the name KITCHEN.SLD. So that you can recognize them, all slide file names have the SLD extension.

In Release 11, the Create slide file dialogue box pops up on the screen, to enable you to name your newly created slide. Pick the file-name box at the bottom, backspace over the name SUITE, type **Kitchen**, and press Enter twice.

Go ahead and make more slides of the entire apartment (called *All*) and the bathroom (called *Bathroom*). You can use the View Restore command to recall the previously saved views, followed by the Mslide command.

You can now view your slides by using the Vslide command. For example, enter **Vslide kitchen** to display the slide of the kitchen (see fig. 7.15). Remember that slides are simply snapshots of drawings. You can view them at any time while you are working on any drawing. Your current drawing is neither changed nor removed from the Drawing Editor.

Fig. 7.15.
The slide of
the kitchen
can be
displayed any
time you are
in the
Drawing
Editor.

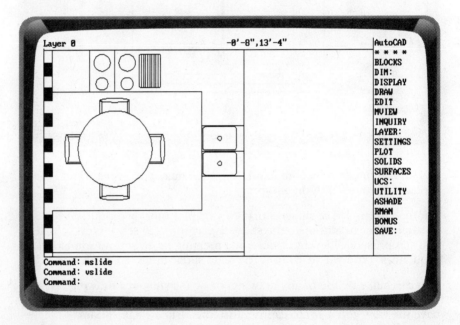

Unlike views, slides are not saved with the drawing. Rather, AutoCAD places them on the hard disk. If you are copying the drawing and want to include the slides, remember to copy the slide files, too.

Some other graphical programs can accept AutoCAD slide files. Many desktop publishing and graphics programs can read SLD files and insert the image into a document.

Creating Slide Libraries (SlideLib)

If you use AutoCAD Release 9, 10, or 11, you can combine slides into groups, called *libraries*.

A slide library is a collection of individual slides in one big file. The advantage is that you can group an entire project of similar slides into one file and reduce the risk of losing or misplacing an individual slide. This approach also reduces the amount of disk space needed to store many individual slide files. You can retrieve a specific slide at any time from this library.

After you create the slides, as was described earlier, you can combine them to form a library (you also can build a library from slides created in older versions of AutoCAD). You create a slide library by running a program outside AutoCAD at the DOS prompt, called SlideLib.Exe. You type all the information on one line, as follows:

C:\ACAD\> **SlideLib** *LibName* < *FileList*

LibName is the name you want to give to the slide library. *FileList* is the name of the file containing the list of slide names you want to add to the slide library.

You have to create a separate ASCII text file (the *FileList*) that lists the names. The fastest way to do this is to use the DOS Copy command, as follows:

C:\ACAD\> **COPY CON SLIDES**
ALL
BATHROOM
KITCHEN

After you type the list of slide file names, note that you press F6. This tells DOS that you have finished creating the file called SLIDES. Then use DOS *redirection* (<) to have SlideLib read the slide names from the ASCII file SLIDES and place them in a slide library called SUITE:

C:\ACAD\> **SlideLib SUITE < SLIDES**

Here, SUITE is the *LibName* and SLIDES is the *FileList*. The redirection symbol tells the SlideLib program to "redirect" the contents of file SLIDES into file SUITE.

AutoCAD creates the slide library on the disk, and gives the library the name SUITE.SLB. The SLB extension indicates that the file is a slide library.

After you have created the slide library file, you can view its slides from within AutoCAD. To view the slides, type the library's name followed by the original slide name (in parentheses). Follow this command sequence to recall the Bathroom slide from the SUITE slide library:

Prompt	Response	Explanation
Command:	**Vslide**	Starts the VSlide command
Slide file:	**SUITE (Bathroom)**	Calls up Bathroom slide from the SUITE library file
Command:	**Redraw**	Removes the slide image from the screen

The SlideLib program is a good start for organizing many slide files on your computer's hard disk, but it does little for slide-library management. Once the slides are in the library, SlideLib offers no means of finding out their names. Further, slides cannot be removed from the library when you no longer need them.

If you find that you frequently use slide libraries, you may want to get a copy of a third-party slide-management program.

Summary

This chapter discussed the many ways to view 2-D drawings in AutoCAD. These options range from enlarging and reducing the image, to remembering different views, to capturing screen images in disk files. As you saw, controlling the visual aspects of CAD and the drafting environment is important.

Chapter 8 shows you how to get a picture onto paper. It covers the procedures you need to follow in order to produce a hard copy of an image, either by printing or plotting.

8

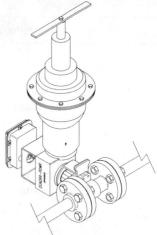

*Illustration courtesy of
Autodesk, Inc., Sausalito, CA.*

Plotting a Drawing

As you work on a CAD drawing, you eventually will want to see the image on paper. Your boss may want to see how your work is progressing, you may want to make sure that each drawing element is in its proper scale or location, or you may be ready to produce final plots for a client. This chapter shows you how to reproduce an AutoCAD drawing on paper.

The term *hard copy* describes a tangible reproduction of a screen image. A hard copy of your drawing can take many forms, including slides, videotape, prints, or plots. This chapter discusses the two most commonly used processes for getting a hard copy: plotting and printing.

This chapter discusses the following commands:

❏ Plot   ❏ Prplot

After completing this chapter, you will be able to produce any screen image on paper by using the Plot or Prplot command. You also will be familiar with considerations specific to producing hard copies of your images. These considerations range from selecting the appropriate media, pens, and colors to obtaining the proper combination of plotted linetype widths.

Plotting Considerations

Someone once said "The paperless office is as likely as the paperless bathroom." In this age of computers and electronically stored information, you might expect such a statement to be false. But the need for paper copies is greater than ever. As you will see, there are several reasons for this.

The most obvious advantage of using computers is that electronic information storage provides us with a compact, easily accessed source of information. A single floppy disk that weighs an ounce and fits in your pocket can hold nearly all the text in this book. The book itself is much bulkier.

Computers have their disadvantages, as well, and this fact extends even to CAD applications. Consider some of the disadvantages of CAD-based drawings:

❏ Unless a drawing is already on-screen when you need to view it, you must take the time to load the file.

❏ You may lose track of the scale and the relationship between objects. Plotted text may look too large, a line may look too thin, or the pieces of the drawing may be arranged incorrectly.

❏ A drawing file may contain unneeded or unwanted information, such as lines you thought had been erased.

You may not notice such conditions until it's too late. Therefore, it is important not only to have paper copies of the drawing file but also to make intermediate plots as you progress with the drawing.

You also need to take the following considerations into account when you plan to create a hard copy of a drawing file:

❏ **Configuration changes.** AutoCAD lets you quickly assign pen colors and speeds, rotation, scale factor, and other aspects of the plot. Although you can control any of these settings at the plotter, you will find it easier to let AutoCAD control the plotter for you.

❏ **Plotting time.** Unless you can afford a fast electrostatic or thermal plotter, a plot can take a long time to produce. A 100K drawing file takes 15 to 30 minutes to plot, depending on the speed of the pen plotter. When you plan project timing, you need to make allowances for plotting time.

❏ **Multiple copies.** Because today's plotters have enough memory to hold the entire plot, you can use them to make multiple copies. However, you may find it faster to use a diazo copying machine to make copies of the original plot.

Until all information is transmitted electronically, paper plots will continue to be the most important format for exchanging drawings.

As a new AutoCAD user, you need to become familiar with your drawing's appearance, both on the screen and on paper. AutoCAD's full-scale drawing approach and the relationship between drawing elements take time to grasp. To understand AutoCAD more fully, you should create a hard copy of your current work whenever it is practical to do so. As you become more familiar with CAD, you should need to plot your drawings less often. Many experienced AutoCAD users don't plot a drawing until it is substantially complete or someone wants to see it.

Time Considerations

In many offices, finished drawings are the result of a "plot, mark-up, plot" process. For this reason, *check plots* (also called *progress prints*) are needed. You can reduce the number of check plots (and save time and expense) by completing as much of the CAD drawing as possible before making a plot.

Plot times for drawings can range from two minutes to over an hour. Careful time management of the plotter and the use of out-of-house plotting services, when necessary, can be the key to meeting tight deadlines instead of missing them. Scheduling plotting jobs during lunch time, for example, turns otherwise idle time to more productive use.

Hardware Considerations

To minimize downtime and plotting problems, you should put your printer or plotter on a schedule of regular maintenance. This includes removing (and recapping) the pens after you finish plotting, using the proper plotter media, replacing worn ribbons or used toner, and periodically cleaning the moving parts. These common-sense types of maintenance will help you avoid potential problems.

Computers and monitors often are purchased without a maintenance contract. With computers, little can go wrong that isn't covered by the warranty. The situation is different with output devices, which are mechanical devices that operate at high speed. When you purchase a plotter, you probably will find the cost of a maintenance contract is money well spent.

The price of contracts varies according to the speed of response (four-hour service is more expensive than next-day service) and where the work is done (on-site repairs cost more than those done in the shop). If your firm has only one plotter, a four-hour on-site maintenance contract is cheap insurance. A service call can be very expensive if you don't have a contract.

Finally, you need to make the right choices when you select pens and media for your plotter. The many possible pen and media combinations are mind-boggling; they can be distilled down to the following:

❏ Ball point (or fiber tip) pens and bond paper, a low-cost combination that produces a lower-quality output useful for check plots

❏ Technical pens and mylar, an expensive combination that produces the highest-quality output for final presentation and archive plots

Your plotter's manufacturer can recommend the best pen and media combinations for your plotter.

To produce a hard copy of your CAD work, you need AutoCAD's plot commands and a printer or plotter. The different types of hardware that produce hard copy are discussed in Chapter 2. This chapter's examples use a common eight-pen E-size plotter and a dot-matrix A-size printer plotter.

The following sections show you how to use AutoCAD's Plot command to create a hard copy of the SUITE drawing on a pen plotter. If you have a printer plotter hooked up to your computer, skip ahead to the section on producing a drawing on a printer plotter.

Understanding AutoCAD's Plotting Options

This section discusses the Plot command and shows you how to use it to get a hard-copy reproduction of your CAD drawing.

Load the SUITE drawing into the AutoCAD Drawing Editor. Use the Zoom Window command to zoom in on the bathroom (see fig. 8.1). Make sure that the plotter is turned on, hooked up to your computer, and equipped with paper and pens. If you have a pen plotter, enter **Plot** at the Command: prompt. The following prompt appears:

```
What to plot -- Display, Extents, Limits, View, or
Window <E>:
```

AutoCAD lets you choose the part of the drawing you want to plot, as indicated by the Plot command's list of options. The following sections describe each of the options.

Plotting the Display (Plot Display)

The Display option plots the image currently on the screen. AutoCAD will not plot any part of the drawing not seen on the screen (this is called *clipping*). This option is useful if you want to plot only part of the drawing.

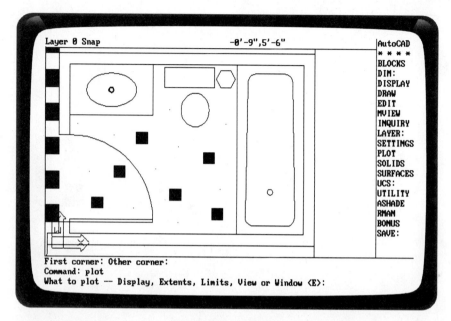

Fig. 8.1.
The Plot command can be entered in the Drawing Editor or at the Main Menu.

Before you select the Display option, make sure that the view you want is on the screen (by using Pan or Zoom, as described in Chapter 7). Then issue the Plot command, enter **D** at the prompt, and then press Enter in response to the next three prompts. (You can ignore these prompts for now; they are discussed in greater detail later.) The plotter should begin plotting. When AutoCAD is finished sending the drawing to the plotter, the following message appears:

```
Plot finished.
Press RETURN to continue:
```

Press Enter to return to the Drawing Editor. The plotter should produce a drawing of the bathroom similar to the one shown in figure 8.2.

If the plot did not work, the following problems may have occurred:

1. The plotter is not communicating with the computer. (See the proper configuration for your plotter in your computer's installation guide, or ask your dealer for help.)

2. You forgot to install the pens.

3. The plotter may be set for the wrong COM or LPT port.

Fig. 8.2.
The plot
produced by
the Plot
Display
command is
identical to
the view in the
Drawing
Editor.

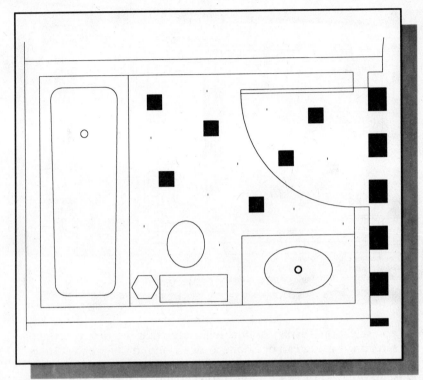

Plotting the Drawing's Extents (Plot Extents)

If you select the Extents option, the plotted image is the same as the image on the screen after you issue the Zoom Extents command. This commonly used option ensures that the entire drawing is plotted, regardless of the setting of the Limits command.

Plotting the Drawing's Limits (Plot Limits)

The Limits option plots the drawing to its limits (limits and the Limits command are discussed in Chapter 11). Because limits are no longer used much with AutoCAD, however, Limits probably is the least-used plotting option.

Plotting a View (Plot View)

If you plot a previously created view, the plot is identical to the screen image after the View Restore command is used to bring the view on-screen. View plotting makes it easy to plot predefined areas of a drawing. For example, remember that you created a view of the kitchen in Chapter 7. Try plotting the kitchen view by entering **V** at the Plot prompt, as follows:

```
Command: Plot
What to plot? Display, Extents, Limits, View, or
Window <D>: V
View Name? Kitchen
```

Press Enter four times in response to the prompts, and wait while the plotter finishes a plot of the kitchen.

Plotting a Windowed Portion of the Drawing (Plot Window)

You can plot a specified window of the current screen area. This is similar to using the Zoom Window command to zoom into a specific portion of the drawing, and then using Plot Display to plot the on-screen view created by the window. You can use your pointing device to pick the window's corners, or you can specify the window's corners by entering a pair of coordinates.

You cannot plot slide files. Also, when you return to the Drawing Editor after using the Plot or Prplot command, the Undo function resets; you cannot Undo a plot or any editing done to the drawing before the plot.

Producing a Drawing on a Plotter

Suppose now that you want to plot the entire suite. Issue the Plot command, then enter **E** for extents. AutoCAD switches to the text screen and displays the following information:

```
Plot will NOT be written to a selected file
Sizes are in Inches
Plot origin is at (0.00,0.00)
Plotting area is 43.00 wide by 33.00 high (E size)
Plot is NOT rotated 90 degrees
Pen width is 0.010
Area fill will NOT be adjusted for pen width
```

```
Hidden lines will NOT be removed
Plot will be scaled to fit available area

Do you want to change anything? <N>:
```

This information tells you what parameters AutoCAD will use when it plots the drawing. (The information on your screen may be different, depending on the type of plotter you use. This example assumes that AutoCAD is configured for the Hewlett-Packard DraftMaster plotter.) The following discussion explains each line of this prompt, and shows you how to change these settings. Because you want to look at all the options, press **Y** in response to the prompt.

Making Pen Assignments

When you press Enter, AutoCAD displays a pen-assignment table. This table shows which pen colors, plotter linetypes, and pen speed are used:

```
Entity        Pen  Line  Pen    Entity Pen  Line  Pen
Color         No.  Type  Speed  Color  No.  Type  Speed
1 (red)       1    0     36     9      1    0     36
2 (yellow)    1    0     36     10     1    0     36
3 (green)     1    0     36     11     1    0     36
4 (cyan)      1    0     36     12     1    0     36
5 (blue)      1    0     36     13     1    0     36
6 (magenta)   1    0     36     14     1    0     36
7 (white)     1    0     36     15     1    0     36
8             1    0     36

Line types    0 = continuous line
              1 = .........................
              2 = ----  ----   ----    ----
              3 = ----- ----- ----- -----
              4 = ------.  ------.  ------. ------.
              5 = ---- -        ---- -         ---- -        ---- - --
              6 = --- - -  --- - -  --- - - - --- - -

Do you want to change any of the above parameters? <N>:
```

AutoCAD assigns pens by entity color. In this example, all objects in the drawing will be drawn with the pen plotter's first pen. In the SUITE drawing, you drew everything in white (or black, if your screen shows a white background). In this case, AutoCAD instructs the plotter to use the same pen (#1) for all lines.

AutoCAD uses numbers to assign different pen widths to draw specific colors. You simply tell AutoCAD which pens are of which color, and assign the correct pen to draw lines of a specific color. You also can "twist" this pen-assignment feature to serve a different purpose. Suppose, for example, that you want some lines to be drawn wider than others. You can draw the wide lines in red (even if you don't have a color monitor). Then assign pen #1 to the color red, and made sure that the plotter has a wide pen in holder #1.

You also can use numbers to assign a *hardware linetype*. AutoCAD can generate different linetypes (see Chapter 12), as can many kinds of plotters. You probably will get better results if you use AutoCAD linetypes and leave the plotter linetype set to 0, for a continuous line.

The pen-speed setting controls how fast the pen plotter draws your drawing. Unfortunately, you don't always want it at the fastest setting (in this case, 36 inches per second). This speed is fine for draft plots with a felt-tip or roller-ball pen. You should use a slower speed (such as 16 inches per second) with high-quality technical or liquid-ink pens.

You can change the pen assignment, pen speed, and linetype by responding **Y** to the Do you want to change any of the above parameters? prompt. Then AutoCAD displays the following prompt:

```
Enter values, blank=Next value, Cn=Color n,
   S=Show current        values, X=Exit

   Layer      Pen   Line  Pen
   Color      No.   Type  Speed
   1 (red)    1     0     36     Pen number <1>:
```

If you want to leave a setting as is, press Enter. Otherwise, type a new value. AutoCAD won't let you type invalid numbers, such as a negative pen number or a pen speed that is too high. If you want to jump ahead (or back) to pen #8, type **C8.**

To see the full list of pen assignments, press **S** (for Show) at any time. To leave this area, press **X**.

You can make all values following the current one take on the same value by typing an asterisk (*) before the number. For example, to reduce the speed of all pens to 16 inches per second, type ***16** at the Pen speed <36>: prompt for pen #1.

Sending the Plot to a File

If you do not want to send the drawing directly to the plotter, AutoCAD allows you to send the file to disk, so that it can be plotted later. To send the plotting instructions to a disk file, answer **Y** to the following prompt:

```
Write the plot to a file? <N>
```

AutoCAD normally sends the plot data to the serial port, but this prompt causes AutoCAD to send the plot data to disk. This is useful if you need to use a plotter connected to another computer that isn't running AutoCAD. You can copy the file to a floppy disk and then transfer the disk to the other computer.

 If you own an electrostatic plotter or dot-matrix printer that emulates a Hewlett-Packard pen plotter (that is *HPGL-compatible*), you will want to connect it to your computer's parallel port. AutoCAD, however, expects HP plotters to be connected only to the serial port. To get around this problem, answer **Y** to the `Write the plot to a file?` prompt and supply the file name **PRN**, as follows:

```
Enter file name for plot <SUITE>: PRN
```

This command tricks AutoCAD into sending the plot data to the parallel port.

Setting Imperial or Metric Units

AutoCAD lets you work with Imperial or metric units. While plotting paper and pens with Imperial measurements are used in the United States, metric-standard sizes are used in most other countries. You can choose a unit of plotting measurement at the following prompt:

```
Size units (Inches or Millimeters) <I>:
```

This prompt merely sets the units for the following prompts, in inches or millimeters. If you are working in inches, press Enter; if you are working in metric units, type **M**.

Setting the Plot Origin

AutoCAD determines the image's location on the page according to the *origin*. The origin is the position on the page where you tell AutoCAD to place the lower left corner of the drawing. You can specify a new origin at the following prompt:

```
Plot origin in Inches <0.00,0.00>:
```

Usually you want the lower left corner of the drawing in the lower left corner of the paper. This corner of the page is indicated by the coordinates 0,0, which mean 0 inches up or to the right of the page's lower left corner. AutoCAD lets you shift the origin if you need to avoid a preprinted title block, or if you want to plot several drawings on a single sheet of paper.

As an alternative, many plotters enable you to change the origin. Move the paper or pen position with the plotter's arrow keys or joysticks, so that you can see the plotter's starting location.

Selecting the Media Size

Plotting paper comes in several standard sizes, ranging from A (the smallest, at 8 1/2-by-11 inches) to E (the largest, at 36-by-48 inches). In metric, the equivalent standards are A4 or A0. Although other standards exist, AutoCAD lists only the most commonly used paper sizes. The MAX size is the largest plot the plotter can create on a given size of paper.

You can specify which paper size to use at the following prompt:

```
Standard values for plotting size

Size      Width Height
A         10.50    8.00
B         16.00  10.00
C         21.00  16.00
D         33.00  21.00
E         43.00  33.00
MAX       44.72  35.31
Enter the Size or Width,Height (in Inches) <E>: E
```

Because the HP DraftMaster plotter can produce plots ranging from A- through E-size, AutoCAD lists the five sizes of paper commonly used with that plotter. The width and height values are nominal plotted sizes, slightly smaller than the sheet's actual size; this allows for a blank strip around the four edges. You type the letter (A though E, or MAX) that matches the paper size loaded into the plotter.

The actual maximum plotting area varies from plotter to plotter. Smaller plotters show fewer options. Dot-matrix printers, for example, may show only the A- and B-sizes.

If you cannot use any of the sizes listed, you can type a custom size as *width,height*, as follows:

```
Enter the Size or Width,Height (in Inches) <E>:
12,24
```

AutoCAD remembers the 12×24 dimension and presents it as the USER option the next time you plot.

Rotating the Plot

Because CAD-based drawings tend to have a horizontal orientation, pen plotters are set up to plot drawings that way. Occasionally, you may create a drawing that is taller than it is wide. AutoCAD lets you change the orientation with the following prompt:

```
Rotate plot 0/90/180/270 <0>:
```

Press Enter for a normal plot, or enter **90** to rotate the plot by 90 degrees. A rotation of 180 or 270 degrees turns the plot upside down.

In Release 10, the prompt asks whether you want 2-D drawings rotated by 90 degrees. Answer **N** for a horizontal plot, or **Y** for a vertical plot.

Many plotters have an option that enables them to rotate plots. Unless you need the plot rotated at an angle other than 90 degrees, you'll save time by letting AutoCAD take care of the plot rotation.

Changing the Pen Width

When AutoCAD draws solids and wide polylines (such as the hallway and bathroom tiles in the SUITE drawing), it compensates for the width of the pen. If the plotter uses a wide pen, AutoCAD tells it to use fewer, more widely spaced strokes to fill the solid region; narrow pens must use closely spaced strokes. You can tell AutoCAD the pen's width at the following prompt:

```
Pen width <0.010>:
```

Because 0.01" is the most commonly used pen width, just press Enter in response to this prompt. This option does not affect "thin" entities, such as lines and polylines with zero width.

Adjusting Area Fill Boundaries

When the plotter draws a solid-filled area, it finishes the area by drawing a line around the perimeter of the solid area (which makes the plot look neater). If the plotter uses a wide pen, the solid area will be too large. You can tell AutoCAD to compensate for the pen width at the following prompt:

```
Adjust area fill boundaries for pen width? <N>
```

AutoCAD compensates by moving the pen in (by half the pen width), thereby adjusting the area fill boundary for pen width. Because the 0.01" pen does not cause this problem, however, you can just press Enter to say "no."

Removing Hidden Lines

AutoCAD can remove hidden lines from three-dimensional drawings. Hidden lines are those that normally would be obscured by objects placed in front of them. Two-dimensional drawings do not have hidden lines (as AutoCAD defines them). Because the pen plotter has far higher resolution than that of the graphics board, AutoCAD recalculates the hidden lines before doing a plot. SUITE is a two-dimensional drawing, however, and has no hidden lines to be removed.

```
Remove hidden lines? <N>
```

Press Enter in response to the prompt. Later, when you begin working in three dimensions, you probably will want AutoCAD to take the hidden lines out of the plot, to make your drawings look more realistic.

Specifying the Scale

After creating a full-size drawing, you must tell AutoCAD how large to draw it on the paper. To do so, you must supply a scale factor at the following prompt:

```
Specify scale by entering:
Plotted Inches=Drawing Units or Fit or ? <F>:
```

Here AutoCAD gives you the following three options:

❑ **Plot to scale.** AutoCAD makes the process of producing scale drawings easy. You create the drawing full size and let AutoCAD do the work of scaling the drawing at plot time. You enter the scale as *plot=drawing* size. To get a quarter-inch scale drawing, enter **1/4=1'**; anything that is one foot long in the drawing is plotted 1/4-inch long on the paper. AutoCAD understands many scale formats. For example, the scales 1/4"=1', 1:48, and 1"=4' all mean the same thing to AutoCAD.

❑ **Plot to fit.** If you don't need the plot done to scale (as often happens with check plots), you can have AutoCAD scale the plot so that it fits the paper. Just enter **F**.

❑ **?** If you enter a question mark at the prompt, AutoCAD displays a brief help screen describing the available options for scaling your plot.

AutoCAD does not save these plotting parameters with the drawing. Rather, they are saved as the default values for the next plotting session. Therefore, you may need to change the parameters if you want to plot a different drawing during the next plotting session.

Starting the Plot

Once you've given AutoCAD all the options, it reports the area that the plot will fill on the paper:

```
Effective plotting area:    2.67 wide by 5.92 high
Position paper in plotter.
Press RETURN to continue or S to Stop for hardware setup
```

If AutoCAD determines that the plot will not fit on the paper, it warns you and asks if you want to continue plotting the drawing. If you continue, AutoCAD clips the part of the drawing that doesn't fit on the page.

To start the plot, press Enter. AutoCAD reports its progress as it converts the drawing into the plotter's graphics language by displaying the number of vectors processed:

```
Processing vector: 16
```

Drawings with many circles and a great deal of text will have many more vectors than those with mostly straight lines. An E-size plot will have more vectors than an A-size plot. For the plot parameters entered in this sample exercise, the SUITE drawing has 2,064 vectors. (Depending on the amount of experimenting you have done, however, your version of the SUITE drawing may contain more or fewer vectors.)

Tech note . . .

When AutoCAD draws objects on the screen or plotter, it draws them as *vectors*. Simply put, a vector is a line. Everything AutoCAD draws is made up of lines. Even circles and arcs are made up of many short lines. In most cases, these lines are so short that you don't notice any straight line segments; the circles and arcs look smooth and round. Wide polylines and solids are made up of many closely spaced lines.

Because plotters are vector-drawing machines, AutoCAD can very easily translate its drawing into a form of data the plotter understands.

If something goes wrong or if you change your mind about the plot, you can cancel the plot by pressing Ctrl-Break (rather than Ctrl-C) at any time. AutoCAD reports:

```
Plot canceled.
Press RETURN to continue:
```

When AutoCAD finishes transmitting plot data to the plotter, this slightly misleading message appears on-screen:

```
Plot finished.
Press RETURN to continue
```

The plot isn't finished, but AutoCAD is finished with the plot. The plotter will keep working for a while longer. Press Enter to return to the Drawing Editor.

You now have a 1/4"=1'-0" scale copy of your SUITE drawing.

Plotting from AutoCAD's Main Menu

AutoCAD lets you plot from within the Drawing Editor, as you've just seen, or from AutoCAD's Main Menu. To plot from the Main Menu, choose Option 3.

When plotting from the Main Menu, you follow nearly the same procedure you use when plotting from the Drawing Editor. The only difference arises if you want to use the Plot Window option. Because you are not in the Drawing Editor, you cannot use your pointing device to pick the window. Instead, you must supply a pair of coordinates for the window's corners.

The advantage to plotting from the Main Menu is that you save the time you otherwise would spend loading the drawing into the Drawing Editor. The disadvantage is that you cannot see the drawing before you plot it.

Producing a Drawing on a Printer Plotter (Prplot)

This section discusses the Prplot (short for *Printer Plot*) command and shows you how to use the command to get a hard-copy reproduction from a printer plotter. Prplot uses a slightly different command sequence than does the Plot command.

Load the SUITE drawing into the AutoCAD Drawing Editor. Use the Zoom Window command to zoom in on the bathroom (refer to fig. 8.1). Make sure that the printer is turned on, hooked up to your computer, and equipped with paper.

Next, enter **Prplot** at the `Command:` prompt. The following prompt appears:

```
What to plot -- Display, Extents, Limits, View, or
Window <D>:
```

Prplot and Plot give you the same options for selecting the portion of the drawing you want to print or plot. To plot the entire suite, enter **E** for extents. AutoCAD switches to the text screen and displays the following information:

```
Plot will NOT be written to a selected file
Sizes are in Inches
Plot origin is at (0.00,0.00)
Plotting area is 7.99 wide by 11.00 high (MAX size)
Plot is NOT rotated
Hidden lines will NOT be removed
Plot will be scaled to fit available area
Do you want to change anything? <N>
```

This list shows the parameters AutoCAD uses for printing the drawing. (The information listed may differ, depending on the printer for which AutoCAD is configured; for this example, AutoCAD is configured for the A-size Epson FX-80 dot-matrix printer.) Because you want to look at all the options, press **Y** at the `Do you want to change anything?` `<N>` prompt.

When you use the Prplot command, AutoCAD does not display a pen assignment table because the printer cannot plot in color.

Sending the Plot to a File

AutoCAD normally sends the printer-plot data to the parallel port. If you want to store the plot data in a file on disk, answer **Y** at the following prompt:

```
Write the plot to a file? <N>
```

This option is useful if you need to use a printer connected to another computer that isn't running AutoCAD. You can copy the file to a floppy disk and then transfer the disk to the other computer. For this example, press Enter at this prompt.

Setting Imperial or Metric Units

AutoCAD lets you specify plot parameters in imperial or metric units, at the following prompt:

```
Size units (Inches or Millimeters) <I>:
```

This prompt merely sets the units for the following prompts. Inches are the default units of plot measurement; if you want to continue plotting in inches, press Enter at this prompt. If you are working in metric, type **M**.

Setting the Plot Origin

As explained in the section on plotting, AutoCAD lets you specify the location of the drawing's lower left corner on the page. You can change the origin's location by entering a new coordinate value at the following prompt:

```
Plot origin in Inches <0.00,0.00>:
```

Usually, you want the plot to start in the lower left corner of the paper (indicated by the coordinates 0,0). AutoCAD lets you shift the origin if you need to avoid a preprinted title box or if you want to place several drawings on a single sheet of paper.

Setting the Image Size

Some printer plotters can accept different sizes of paper. Typically, however, printer plotters use standard A-size (8 1/2-by-11-inch) paper. This is reflected in the following prompt, which enables you to set the size of the image based on the size of the paper you are using:

```
Standard values for plotting size

Size        Width Height
MAX          7.99  11.00

Enter the Size or Width,Height (in Inches) <MAX>:
```

Because the Epson FX-80 accepts only A-size paper, the MAX value of 7.99" by 11.00" is listed as the only option for the image size. The width and height values are the maximum printable area (slightly smaller than the paper's actual size), to allow for a blank strip around the paper's four edges. Larger dot-matrix printers usually list other common size options.

If the size does not match your needs, you can type in a custom size in the *width,height* format, as follows:

```
Enter the Size or Width,Height (in Inches) <E>: 7,10
```

AutoCAD remembers the 7 X 10 dimension and presents it as the USER option the next time you plot.

Rotating the Image

Although AutoCAD normally plots horizontally with a pen plotter, it tends to present the vertical orientation as the default for printer plotting. To obtain a horizontal plot, rotate the orientation by 90 degrees by typing **90** at the following prompt:

```
Rotate plot 0/90/180/270 <0>:
```

Some printer plotters can plot variable line widths, but AutoCAD does not support them. Thus, the Prplot command lacks questions about pen width and adjusting area fill boundaries.

Removing Hidden Lines

As discussed in the previous section on plotting, AutoCAD can remove hidden lines from three-dimensional drawings. If you want hidden lines to be removed from the printed image, AutoCAD recalculates the hidden lines before printing. The process can take a long time. To remove hidden lines from the drawing during printing, answer **Y** at the following prompt:

```
Remove hidden lines? <N>
```

Because SUITE is a two-dimensional drawing, just press Enter at the prompt.

Specifying the Scale

Although the SUITE drawing was drawn at full size (1:1 scale), it will not fit on a small piece of paper. For this reason, you must specify a scale factor that AutoCAD will print, as follows:

```
Specify scale by entering:
Plotted Inches=Drawing Units or Fit or ? <F>: 1/4=1'
```

Here AutoCAD gives you three options: Plot to scale, Plot to fit, and the question mark (?). For more information on these options, refer back to the section on plotting.

Starting the Printer Plot

After you give AutoCAD all the options, it reports back the area the image will take up on paper, as follows:

```
Effective plotting area:     7.99 wide by 10.66 high
Position paper in printer.
Press RETURN to continue:
```

If AutoCAD senses that the image will not fit on the paper, it warns you and asks whether you want to continue printing. If you do, the part of the drawing that doesn't fit will be clipped.

To start the plot, press Enter. AutoCAD shows you its progress as it converts the drawing into the plotter's graphics language by reporting the number of vectors it has processed, as follows:

```
Processing vector: 16
```

When AutoCAD finishes transmitting the data to the printer, it displays this message:

```
Printer plot complete.
Press RETURN to continue:
```

Press Enter to return to the Drawing Editor. The printer plotter continues working after AutoCAD is done. You now have a copy of your SUITE drawing, plotted by your printer to fit the paper.

Just as when you are plotting a drawing, you can print a drawing from AutoCAD's Main Menu. To print from the Main Menu, select Option 4. The procedures are identical to the ones you follow when printing from the Drawing Editor, except that you cannot use your pointing device to pick a window if you want to use the Prplot Window command. Instead, you must create the window by typing in a pair of coordinates to specify its corners.

Improving the Plotting Process

The procedure for obtaining output from the plotter or printer is much the same. Still, there are qualitative differences that you should consider. A plotter generally produces a better-quality image than a printer can, but usually is slower than a printer. Thus, the plotter is better suited to final drawings; the printer is better suited to check plots.

Because AutoCAD translates the entity information into plotter instructions (known as a *graphics language*) faster than the plotter can use them, AutoCAD has to wait for the plotter to catch up. You can speed up the plotting process either by using a device that enables the plotter to keep up with AutoCAD, or by purchasing a faster plotter.

Buffers and Spoolers

A *hardware buffer* intercepts and stores the plot information as it moves from the computer to the plotter. The buffer has a large memory capacity and can accept data from the computer faster than the plotter can. As a result, the buffer frees the computer sooner, so that you can continue working while plotting progresses. The buffer sends the stored data to the plotter at the slower speed, while continuing to accept data from the computer at the faster speed.

A *plot server* is an intelligent stand-in disk drive dedicated to the plotter. The server contains a disk drive (either 1.2M 5 1/4" or 1.44M 3 1/2" format) and a few controls. You plot the drawing to disk and take the floppy disk to the plot server. When you insert the disk, the plot server begins reading the data on the disk and sending it to the plotter. Controls on the plot server let you choose which data file to plot. The advantage of the plot server is that it lets everyone access the plotter without the expense of a network. The disadvantage is that the plot file cannot be larger than the capacity of the floppy disk.

A *software spooler* resides in the computer's memory. Like a hardware buffer, the spooler intercepts the information the computer sends to the plotter. This information is temporarily stored on the hard disk and then sent on to the plotter. Spoolers are far faster and cheaper than hardware buffers. However, spoolers use some computer RAM (no longer a consideration with AutoCAD 386 for Release 10 or Release 11).

Faster Plotters

If you use a buffer or spooler, AutoCAD does not need to wait for the plotter to finish. Buffers and spoolers, however, don't make the plotter itself work any faster. If you want to generate plots more rapidly, you need a plotter that is faster to set up and takes less time to plot.

Pen plotters are fussy creatures. Many things can go wrong, which can increase the time it takes to get the perfect plot: pens clog or run out of ink, the paper jams or tears. To reduce these problems, you might consider replacing your pen plotter with another technology. Because electrostatic, thermal, laser, and dot-matrix plotters don't use pens, they can't run out of ink or clog up. Paper handling also is smoother with these plotters.

If you prefer the high quality of pen plots, read the plotter's manual to see whether the plotter's performance can be improved. Often the pen speed and acceleration can be increased so as to reduce plotting time. You might consider replacing (or supplementing) the plotter. Today's pen plotters are much faster than those of 5 or 10 years ago: look for a plotter with a speed of at least 24 ips (inches per second) and an acceleration of 4g (gravity) or more.

Summary

This chapter showed you how to create a hard copy of an AutoCAD drawing. You have learned the two commands to obtain plots and printed plots, ways to customize the plotting process within AutoCAD, and ways to improve your plotting efficiency.

Chapter 9 shows you new ways to edit and enhance your AutoCAD drawing, building on the skills you have learned so far in this text. Chapter 9 also shows you how to make your AutoCAD drafting easier and faster.

Part Three

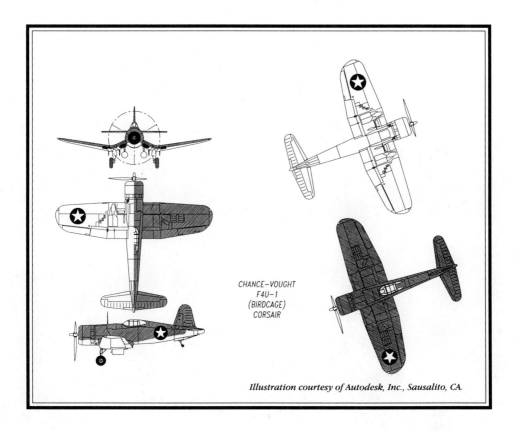

CHANCE–VOUGHT
F4U–1
(BIRDCAGE)
CORSAIR

Illustration courtesy of Autodesk, Inc., Sausalito, CA.

Moving Beyond the Basics

9

Advanced Editing Techniques

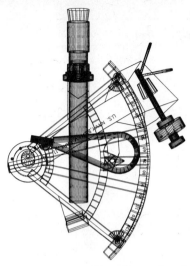

Illustration courtesy of Autodesk, Inc., Sausalito, CA.

Chapter 6 discussed most of AutoCAD's editing commands. You used the commands to manipulate objects in the SUITE drawing. The editing commands also enable you to create new entities, without having to draw them. Two powerful editing commands (Change and Pedit) are fully discussed in this chapter. Both commands have so many options that they need a chapter of their own to cover them completely.

This chapter also covers the Layer command, which is AutoCAD's most important control command. When you learn to use Layer, you can control the way your drawing is displayed and managed.

When you finish this chapter, you will know how to use the following commands:

- ❏ Change
- ❏ Chprop
- ❏ Ddemodes
- ❏ Ddlmodes
- ❏ Layer
- ❏ Pedit
- ❏ Rename

By the end of Chapter 6, you had made a number of modifications to your simple apartment floor plan. You probably were ready to start cooking breakfast in the new kitchen! In this chapter, you continue to build the sample drawing as you learn the concepts behind the Pedit, Layer, Change, Chprop and Rename commands.

Editing Polylines (Pedit)

As you learned in Chapter 5, polylines have advantages over normal line and arc entities. If you string together several lines and arcs into one polyline, you can manipulate the objects as a single entity. You can copy, offset, or move one object (even a large or complex one) more easily than you can manipulate several objects individually.

Another advantage to polylines is that they have width, and their width can be modified. Lines and arcs have no width information. By converting ordinary lines and arcs into polylines, you can give them a uniform or varying width.

Because of the special nature of polylines, AutoCAD provides the Pedit (for Polyline edit) command, which is designed specifically for editing them. Pedit is a versatile command that enables you to change polylines. You use Pedit to do the following:

- Convert a line or arc into a polyline
- Open or close a polyline
- Join two or more polylines into a single polyline
- Add segments to a polyline
- Change the width of a polyline
- Separate a polyline into segments
- Insert new vertices or remove existing ones
- Move vertices
- Fit a curve or a spline to a polyline
- Take the curves out of a polyline

There are three versions of the Pedit command. This chapter discusses the Pedit command that works with 2-D polylines. Chapter 17 covers the Pedit commands that work with 3-D polylines and 3-D polyline meshes.

Before you begin learning about the Pedit command, use the Line command to draw the outline of a queen-size bed (60 inches wide by 80 inches long). You can place the bed wherever you like in the bedroom; fig. 9.1 shows one possible location.

Converting a Line into a Polyline

Now you will learn how to turn a line into a polyline. Although you can draw objects with polylines in the first place, sometimes you draw with lines and arcs and realize later you would prefer they were polylines. The following command sequence shows you the steps to take:

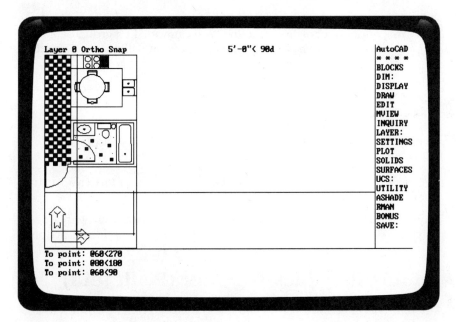

Fig. 9.1.
The four bed
lines will
illustrate the
Pedit
command.

Prompt	Response	Explanation
Command:	**Pedit**	Starts the Pedit command
Select polyline:	Pick a line on the bed	Specifies the object to be turned into a polyline
Entity selected is not a polyline. Do you want to turn it into one? <Y>:	Press Enter	Turns the line into a polyline
Close/Join/Width/ Edit vertex/Fit curve/Spline curve/Decurve/ Undo/eXit<X>:	Press Enter	Terminates the Pedit command

If the line (or arc) you choose is not a polyline, AutoCAD asks if you want to change it into one. If you type **Y** or press Enter (to tell AutoCAD that you accept the default response Y), the entity changes into a polyline and the Pedit command continues. This is a handy way to change entities into polylines.

The Pedit command works with only one entity at a time, whether that entity is a polyline or a line. You cannot edit a group of polylines together. Also remember that Pedit will not turn a circle into a polyline.

The Pedit Subcommands

When you select the polyline you want to edit, AutoCAD displays the following (rather long) prompt:

```
Close/Join/Width/Edit vertex/Fit curve/Spline
curve/Decurve/Undo/eXit<X>:
```

Each of these options is an editing command that works only with a polyline. The following examples show you how these options function.

Joining Polylines Together (Pedit Join)

The Join option enables you to add lines, arcs, and other polylines to an existing polyline. The lines and arcs automatically convert into polyline segments. The entities must touch end-to-end, otherwise the polyline will not extend through them. Join works only with an *open* polyline (whose starting and ending points don't meet).

As entities are added to the polyline, they take on the attributes of the original polyline. These include the polyline's thickness, color, and layer (layers are discussed later in this chapter). Now, use the Join option to add the three other bed lines to the newly created polyline:

Prompt	*Response*	*Explanation*
`Command:`	**Pedit**	Starts the Pedit command
`Select polyline:`	Pick the bed line that was turned into a polyline	Selects the polyline to which the remaining lines will be joined
`Close/Join/.../` `eXit<X>:`	**J**	Specifies the Join option
`Select objects:`	Pick the remaining lines and press Enter	Selects the lines to be joined to the polyline

```
3 segments added                          AutoCAD joins the
to polyline                               four objects into a
                                          single polyline

Close/Join/.../eXit<X>:                   Press Enter
                                          Terminates the Pedit
                                          command
```

AutoCAD does not highlight the entities as you pick them. Rather, it marks the selected entities with blips. After you select all the desired entities and press Enter, AutoCAD tells you how many entities have been joined to the polyline (three segments, in this example). After you finish with an option, Pedit redisplays its list of options, so that you can select another option. At the prompt, press Enter to exit from the Pedit command.

If the Pedit Join command cannot join all the objects you select, AutoCAD does not tell you which objects were left off. To find out if any of the selected objects were not joined, use the Move command to pick the original polyline. This makes AutoCAD highlight the length of the new polyline. The missed entities won't be highlighted. Press Ctrl-C to cancel the Move command.

Restart the Move command and use the ENDpoint object snap to make sure that the missed entities are touching end-to-end, as follows:

Prompt	Response	Explanation
`Command:`	**Move**	Starts the Move command
`Select objects:`	Pick missed object	Specifies the object to be moved
`Select objects:`	Press Enter	Ends object selection
`Base point or displacement:`	**END**	Specifies the ENDpoint object snap
`of:`	Pick near the missed object	Tells AutoCAD to the end of move the object by its endpoint
`Second point of displacement:`	**END**	Specifies the ENDpoint object snap
`of:`	Pick near the end of the polyline	Tells AutoCAD to move the object to the end of the polyline

Now reuse the Pedit Join command to add the nomadic entities.

Opening a Polyline (Pedit Open)

A *closed* polyline has starting and ending points that meet. When you
pick a closed polyline, the Open option appears in the Pedit prompt. The
Open enables you to open up a closed polyline by removing the
polyline's last segment (that is, the segment that end at the polyline's
starting point).

Practice using the Open option on the bed polyline, as follows:

Prompt	Response	Explanation
Command:	**Pedit**	Starts the Pedit command
Select polyline:	Pick bed	Selects the bed polyline
Open.../eXit<X>:	**O**	Specifies the Open option and removes the last segment of the polyline
Open.../eXit<X>:	Press Enter	Ends the Pedit command

The last polyline segment disappears, as shown in figure 9.2.

*Fig. 9.2.
The Pedit
Open
command
removes the
last segment
of a closed
polyline.*

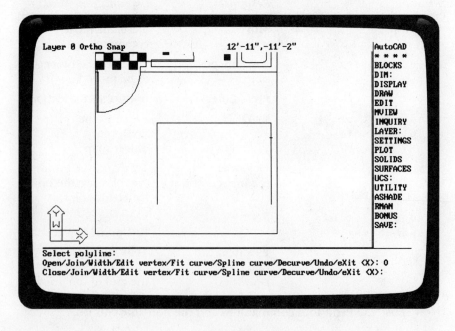

A polyline that looks closed may actually be open (see fig. 9.3). If you close a polyline with your pointing device or with coordinate values, it is actually open. An open polyline reacts differently to the Fillet, Chamfer, and Hatch commands than a closed polyline. Some commands, such as Rulesurf, will not work at all if one polyline is open and the other closed. A polyline is truly closed only when you use the Close option while drawing it, or close it with the Pedit Join command.

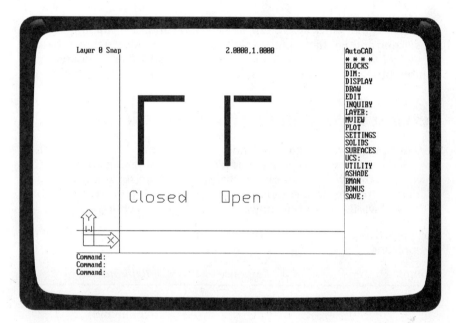

Fig. 9.3.
Although a polyline looks closed, there may be a small gap between the ends.

Closing a Polyline (Pedit Close)

When you select an open polyline, the option Close appears in the Pedit prompt. Experienced AutoCAD users generally prefer closed polylines to open ones, because closed polylines usually are easier to manipulate. If you ever create an open polyline and want to close it, you can use the Pedit command's Close option.

Now practice using the Close option on the bed:

Prompt	Response	Explanation
Command:	**Pedit**	Starts the Pedit command
Select polyline:	Pick bed	Selects the bed polyline for closing

Prompt	Response	Explanation
`Close/.../eXit<X>:`	**C**	Specifies the Close option and adds a new segment to close the polyline
`Close/.../eXit<X>:`	Press Enter	Terminates the Pedit command

The bed has four sides again. The Close option adds a segment that joins the starting and ending points of the open polyline. Although you have created a four-sided polyline, polylines can be made of an unlimited number of segments, and the segments can be either lines or arcs.

Setting a Polyline's Width (Pedit Width)

Generally, when you create a polyline, the polyline has a uniform width along its entire length. One of the advantages to using polylines, however, is that their width can be changed. You can set a polyline's width by using the Pedit command's Width option. When you use Pedit Width, the width is set uniformly along the polyline's entire length.

Now, practice using the Pedit Width command to change the width of the bed polyline:

Prompt	Response	Explanation
`Command:`	**Pedit**	Starts the Pedit command
`Select polyline:`	Pick the bed polyline	Specifies the polyline to be modified
`Open/Join/Width/...` `/eXit<X>:`	**W**	Specifies the Width option
`Enter new width for all segments:`	**4**	Makes the polyline 4" wide
`Open/Join/Width/...` `/eXit<X>:`	Press Enter	Ends the Pedit command

Figure 9.4 shows the effect of changing the polyline width to four inches. You can change the width back to a thin line by specifying a width of zero inches.

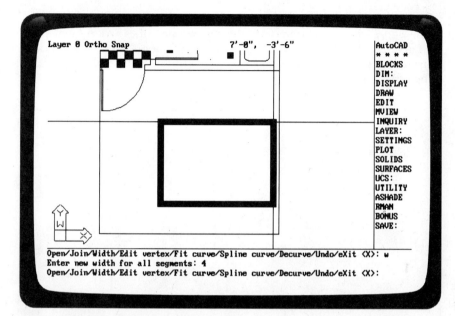

Fig. 9.4.
The Pedit
Width
command
changes the
polyline's
width
uniformly
from one end
to the other.

A polyline of zero width is drawn as thin as possible. On your monitor or printer, the polyline is drawn only one pixel wide. Ordinary lines, arcs, and circles are always drawn with a width of zero.

You can specify the polyline's width in two ways. As the preceding example described, you can type in a value (such as 6"). If you prefer, you can "show" AutoCAD the new width by picking two points near the polyline. The distance between the two points represents the polyline's new thickness. There is no limit to the maximum width of a polyline; the minimum width is zero. Negative widths are not permitted.

Later in this chapter, you will learn how to give a polyline segment a tapered width, and to use the Edit vertex option, which lets you change the width of individual segments.

Fitting a Curve (Pedit Fit curve)

The Fit curve option draws a curve that passes through each vertex of the polyline. The curve is made of simple arcs. Two arcs connect one vertex to the next: one is tangent to the first vertex, the other is tangent to the first arc and the second vertex. You have no control over how much curve fitting happens; the curve is fit to the entire polyline.

Figure 9.5 shows the effect of curve fitting different shapes of polylines. In the figure, the straight lines are the original polylines around which the curved lines are fit by the Fit curve option. When the Fit curve option is used on a polyline with many right-angle corners, the result looks like a bunch of grapes.

Fig. 9.5.
The Pedit Fit curve command has a different effect on different shapes of polylines.

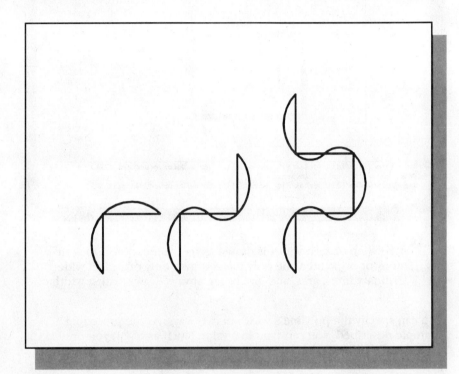

You can change the rectangular bed into a Hollywood-style circular bed by using the Fit curve option, as follows:

Prompt	Response:	Explanation
Command:	**Pedit**	Starts the Pedit command
Select polyline:	Pick the bed	Specifies the polyline to be modified
Open/.../Fit curve/.../eXit<X>:	**F**	Selects the Fit curve option, which rounds the bed
Open/.../Fit curve/.../eXit<X>:	Press Enter	Ends the Pedit command

The result of this command sequence is shown in figure 9.6.

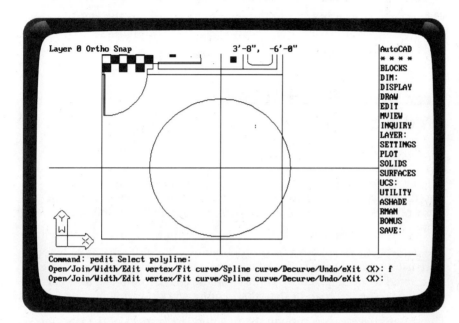

Fig. 9.6.
*The Pedit Fit
curve
command
makes the
rectangular
bed round.*

If the curve doesn't look right, you can change it by moving the polyline's vertices or by changing the curve's tangency (by using the Edit vertex option, which is discussed later).

Unfitting the Curve (Pedit Decurve)

Decurve is the opposite of the Fit curve and Spline curve options. (Splines are discussed later.) Decurve converts the curved polyline segments back to straight lines.

Practice using Decurve to straighten out the bed, as follows:

Prompt	Response	Explanation
Command:	**Pedit**	Starts the Pedit command
Select polyline:	Pick the bed	Specifies the polyline to be modified
Close/.../Decurve/Undo/ eXit<X>:	**D**	Selects the Decurve option, which returns the bed to its original shape

Prompt	Response	Explanation
`Close/.../Decurve/Undo/` `eXit<X>:`	Press Enter	Ends the Pedit command

The round bed changes back to a rectangular bed.

Creating a Spline Curve (Pedit Spline curve)

Pedit gives you another option when you want to curve a polyline. *Splines* are polylines that are curved according to a mathematical formula, called a *B-spline* curve. The "B" is short for Bezier, the mathematician who discovered the properties of this curve. Bezier curves are used in many non-CAD drawing programs, such as programs that define text fonts.

The earliest use of splines was in shipbuilding. Long thin strips of wood were used to define the shape of the ship's hull. Heavy lead weights held the curved wood in place. Since then, splines have found use in other disciplines, such as road design, that require smoothly flowing curves.

The spline curve passes though the first and last vertices of the polyline, using them as *anchor points*. As the curve passes them, the in-between vertices pull the spline toward them. The resulting curve is smoother than one created by the Fit curve option.

When you use a polyline to define a spline curve, the original polyline is used as a *frame* that defines the spline's shape. The spline changes shape as the frame changes. The shape also depends on the setting of three system variables: SPLINETYPE, SPLINESEGS, and SPLFRAME.

SPLINETYPE (which stands for *spline type*) determines whether the B-spline curve is drawn as a cubic or quadratic spline. The difference between the two types of splines is their smoothness. The cubic B-spline (when SPLINETYPE is set to a value of 6) is smoother; the quadratic B-spline (when SPLINETYPE is set to a value of 5) runs closer to the frame.

You can take the following steps to change the SPLINETYPE variable's value:

```
Command: Setvar
Variable name or ?: SPLINETYPE
New value for SPLINETYPE <6>: 5
```

SPLINESEGS (which stands for *spline segments*) controls the spline's resolution; that is, this variable determines whether the curve looks rough or smooth. AutoCAD draws the spline curve as a series of straight lines. The setting of SPLINESEGS determines how many lines are used to construct the spline curve. The default setting of 8 draws eight line segments between two frame vertices. This value is fine for vertices that are close together. If the line segments are noticeable, you can change SPLINESEGS to a higher value, as follows:

```
Command: Setvar
Variable name or ?: SPLINESEGS
New value for SPLINESEGS <8>: 20
```

A SPLINESEGS value of 0 draws no spline curve; a value of 1 draws straight segments between the frame segment's midpoints. A large number of segments makes curves look smoother, but AutoCAD needs more time and file space to generate the spline if SPLINESEGS is set very high. A value of 20 is a good compromise.

SPLFRAME (which stands for *spline frame*) determines whether the original polyline (the frame) is displayed. The default value of SPLFRAME is 0, so that the frame is not displayed unless you change the system variable's setting. If you want AutoCAD to display both the spline curve and its frame, you can change SPLFRAME's value to 1, as follows:

```
Command: Setvar
Variable name or ?: SPLFRAME
New value for SPLFRAME <0>: 1
```

Figure 9.7 shows the effect of these three system variables on splined polylines. In the figure, the same polyline is used as the frame for all the curves; notice that the spline curves utilize the frame in a much different manner than the fit curve. Notice, too, that SPLFRAME is set to a value of 1 in the figure, so that the polyline frame is displayed.

Now, convert the rectangular bed into a spline-shaped bed, as follows:

Prompt	Response	Explanation
Command:	**Pedit**	Starts the Pedit command
Select polyline:	Pick the bed	Specifies the polyline to be modified
Close/.../Spline curve/ .../eXit	S	Selects the Spline curve option and creates a spline from the original bed polyline

The results of this operation are shown in figure 9.8.

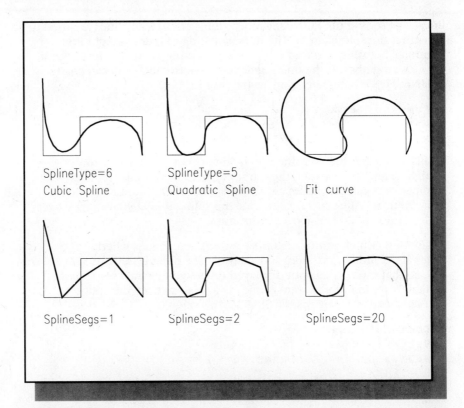

Fig. 9.7.
Spline
curves are
controlled by
three system
variables.

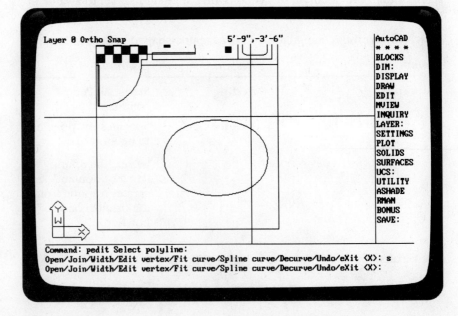

Fig. 9.8.
The Pedit
Spline-curve
command
creates Bezier
curves.

Splines can be edited like other entities. The spline (and its frame) can be moved, erased, copied, mirrored, rotated, and scaled. You can use AutoCAD's Offset command to generate a spline parallel to the original. You can use the Stretch command to stretch the polyline frame; AutoCAD then refits the spline to the new frame. The spline (not the frame) is the reference when you use the Divide, Measure, Area, Hatch, Fillet, and Chamfer commands.

 If you want to use a splined or curve-fit polyline to define an irregular curve, you may need to use trial and error to fit the curve correctly.

To edit splined polylines, you must use the Edit vertex/Move option or the Stretch command to move vertices until the curve fits. It can be helpful to turn on the frame by using the SPLFRAME system variable.

To edit a curve-fit polyline, you can use the Edit-vertex/Move option or the Tangent option. You don't need to turn the frame on because the frame's vertices fall on the fitted curve.

Changing the Last Pedit (Pedit Undo)

When you use Pedit, you can perform several editing operations in a row. The Undo option undoes the most recent one, and can continue back to the beginning of the Pedit session.

The Pedit Undo command acts the same as the Undo command you issue at the `Command:` prompt. The Pedit Undo command is more convenient, however, because you don't need to leave Pedit to do the undo. Because of this convenience, Undo enables you to test a modification. If it doesn't work, you can easily restore the polyline to its original state. Restore the bed to its rectangular shape:

```
Close/.../Undo/eXit<X>: U
Close/.../Undo/eXit<X>: Press Enter
```

You've now worked through seven Pedit options that apply to the entire length of a polyline. The Pedit command, however, has nine more suboptions hidden in the Edit vertex option. These suboptions let you edit each vertex along the polyline. Some of the suboptions even have further options (or sub-suboptions, you might say).

Editing Polyline Vertices (Edit vertex)

The Pedit command's Edit vertex option enables you to edit each vertex between polyline segments. The ability to edit individual vertices gives you finer control over the polyline's shape. Vertex editing lets you change the shape, width, and location of segments between vertices.

When you select the Edit vertex option, AutoCAD displays the following prompt:

```
Next/Previous/Break/Insert/Move/Regen/Straighten/
Tangent/Width/eXit <N>:
```

AutoCAD marks the first vertex (that is visible on-screen) with a graphical X (see fig. 9.9). The X acts as a place marker so that you know which vertex you are editing.

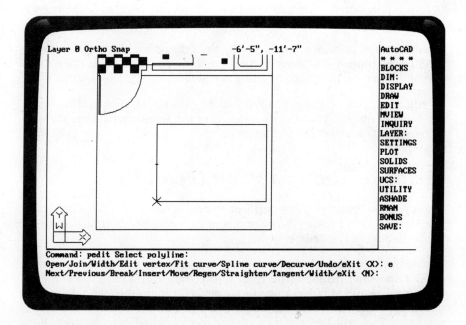

Fig. 9.9.
The Edit vertex option marks the first visible vertex with an X.

If you are editing a splined polyline, the X appears at the frame polyline's vertices (whether the frame is visible or not). This is not a consideration for curve-fit polylines, since their vertices lie on the polyline.

Moving the Place Marker (Next and Previous)

To get to the vertex you want to edit, use the Next or Previous options to move the X place marker. Next is the default option and moves the place marker *forward* to the next vertex. AutoCAD considers the forward direction as the direction in which the polyline was drawn. Watch how the X travels around the bed's vertices as you take the following steps:

```
Command: Pedit
Select polyline: Pick bed
Close/.../Edit vertex/.../eXit<X>: E
```

```
Next/Previous/.../eXit<N>: Press Enter
Next/Previous/.../eXit<N>: Press Enter
```

Press Enter until the X has moved all the way around the bed. Now make the X travel backward by typing **P** (to make the Previous option the default) and then pressing Enter four times.

Breaking a Polyline at a Vertex (Break)

The Pedit Break option breaks a polyline at a vertex. This command is different from the Break command you use at the Command: prompt, which lets you break the polyline anywhere along its length. The Pedit Break option is less flexible, because it enables you to make the break only at a single vertex (breaking the polyline into two pieces), or to break out a segment between two vertices.

When you choose the Break option, you see a new prompt with four options:

```
Next/Previous/Go/eXit <N>:
```

The first break point occurs at the vertex marked by the X when you entered the Break option. Use Next and Previous to move the X indicator to the second vertex. To complete the break, use the Go option, removing the segment(s). If you enter Go immediately after you enter Break, the polyline is broken at the first vertex.

Adding Vertices (Insert)

The Insert option adds a new vertex between two existing vertices. This option enables you to change the shape of the polyline, which is especially handy when you are creating a complex shape or if you want to fine-tune a frame for a polyline curve. AutoCAD places the new vertex between the current vertex (that is, the vertex marked by the X) and the next vertex.

To practice adding vertices to a polyline, select the Insert option and then use your pointing device to pick a point somewhere near the current vertex.

As you move the pointing device, AutoCAD ghosts a drag line from the existing vertices and the new one (see fig. 9.10). When you are satisfied with the location of the new vertex, press the pick button on the pointing device. (If you specify the location of the new vertex with the keyboard, press Enter instead.) You can also supply a coordinate location.

Fig. 9.10.
The Insert
option adds a
new vertex to
the polyline.

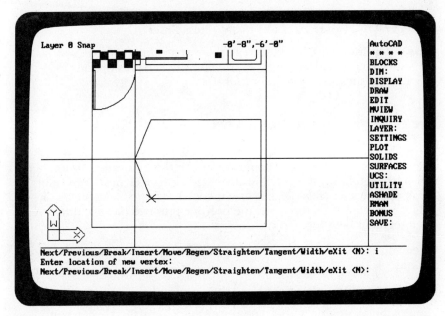

Moving Vertices (Move)

The Move option moves a vertex to a new location. To move a vertex, select the Move option, and then position the X marker on the vertex you want to move. Then use your pointing device to locate the new position for the vertex. Try using the Move option to straighten out the end of the bed. To do this, mark the vertex you add with the Insert option, and move it over so that the end of the bed once again is a straight line. As you move the pointing device to the new vertex location, AutoCAD draws a drag line (see fig. 9.11). After you pick the point where you want the vertex located, AutoCAD moves the vertex to that location and adjusts the polyline. This is useful for making curve-fit or splined curves match an irregular outline.

Removing Vertices (Straighten)

The Straighten option removes one or more vertices that reside between two other vertices. A single polyline segment fills the gap. This is handy for removing extraneous vertices, such as the one you added to the bed.

The Straighten option has the same suboptions as the Break command. The vertex marked by the X when you begin the Straighten option is the first vertex. You can move forward or backward until you reach the second vertex. Enter **G** for "go" and AutoCAD removes all vertices between the two.

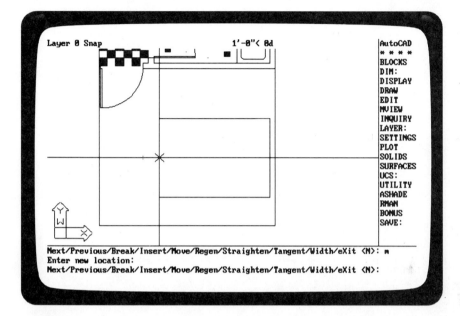

Fig. 9.11.
The Move
option lets
you relocate
a polyline
vertex.

Changing Tangency (Tangent)

The second way to adjust a curve-fit polyline is by using the Tangent option. (The other way is with the Move vertex option; Tangent does not affect splined curves.) The Tangent option overrides the polyline frame to define a new tangent direction for the curve.

You define an angle to which the curve is tangent. Then you use the Fit-curve option to obtain the curve; Tangent doesn't work after the curve-fit has been applied. Play with the Tangent option to get a feel for how it works. One possible result appears in figure 9.12.

Changing the Width of a Polyline Segment (Width)

You can use the Edit vertex Width option to change the width of individual polyline segments. (The Pedit Width command, in contrast, affects the width of the entire polyline.) The Edit vertex Width option is useful for modifying or creating *tapered* entities; that is, you can use this option to give a polyline segment different beginning and ending widths.

Take the following steps to assign a varying width to one segment of the bed:

Fig. 9.12.
The Tangent
option
adjusts curve-
fit polylines.

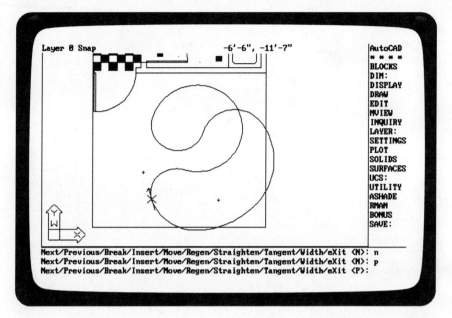

Prompt	Response	Explanation
`Next/.../Width/eXit <N>:`	**W**	Selects the Width option
`Enter starting width:`	**0**	Specifies a starting width of 0"
`Enter ending width:`	**12**	Specifies an ending width of 12"
`Next/.../Width/eXit <N>:`	**X**	Ends the Edit vertex subcommand

The change in width doesn't go into effect until you exit from the Edit vertex option. The preceding command sequence makes one of the bed's lines look like an arrow (see fig. 9.13). Return the wide segment to zero width by using the Undo option.

Redrawing a Polyline (Regen)

After an edit operation such as Move or Width, you may find that the polyline has chunks "missing." You can patch up the holes by issuing the Edit vertex Regen option.

Autodesk programmers placed this option here as a convenience so that you don't need to return to the `Command:` prompt to clean up the screen. To save time, only the polyline regenerates. To clean up blip marks and other garbage, use the Redraw command transparently.

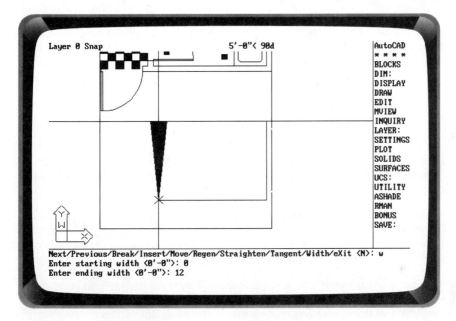

*Fig. 9.13.
The Edit
vertex Width
option can
assign
varying width
to polyline
segments.*

Leaving Edit Vertex and Pedit (eXit)

The eXit option returns you from the Edit vertex option to the main Pedit
prompt. All changes you made to the polyline are preserved, whether you
type **X** or cancel Edit vertex with Ctrl-C.

Select eXit again or press Ctrl-C a second time to return to AutoCAD's
Command: prompt. To reverse the effect of the entire Pedit session, use
AutoCAD's Undo command.

You can see how powerful the Pline and Pedit commands are. To take
advantage of their strength, you will use these two commands a great
deal. Yet, there are some aspects of polylines that Pedit cannot change.
Later in the chapter, you will learn about the Change and Chprop
commands.

Working with Layers (Layer)

In manual drafting, the draftsperson often uses a technique called
overlay drafting. In overlay drafting, transparent sheets of Mylar are
stacked, with each sheet containing a different element of the total
drawing. The bottom sheet, for example, might contain the site plan.
Other sheets are placed on top to show the structural grid, the furniture
layout, or the landscaping. Different sheets are combined to produce the
finished drawings.

AutoCAD enables you to "stack" different parts of the drawing. Instead of using sheets of Mylar, however, you use AutoCAD's built-in *layers*. Like the transparent sheets used in overlay drafting, each AutoCAD layer holds different parts of the drawing. You can turn AutoCAD's layers on and off so that the computer displays only the layers you need to see. AutoCAD's layers are more powerful than most other CAD programs' layers. In AutoCAD, the properties of entities on any layer can be changed all at once or one at a time. You can easily move objects from one layer to another.

Until now, you have drawn everything on Layer 0. This is the only layer that exists in a new AutoCAD drawing. If you want parts of your drawing to reside on other layers, you first have to create the new layers.

You use the Layer command to create new layers, or to change the color, linetype, and condition of any existing layer. You can create and modify layers two ways: from the Command: prompt or through a dialogue box. In the following sections, you will learn how to use both methods.

You can draw on only one layer at a time. The layer with which you are working is called the *current* layer. The name of the current layer is displayed in the upper left corner of the Drawing Editor screen (see fig. 9.14). Layer names can be up to 31 characters long, but only the first eight characters appear on the status line.

Fig. 9.14.
AutoCAD
displays the
first eight
characters of
the current
layer's name
on the status
line.

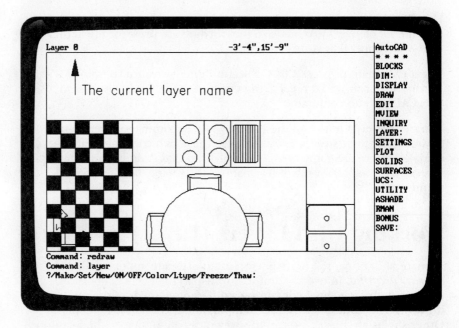

When you enter **Layer** at the `Command:` prompt, AutoCAD displays the following options:

`?/Make/Set/New/ON/OFF/Color/Ltype/Freeze/Thaw:`

Each option controls a different aspect of layers. Two options, Color and LType, affect all entities on a layer. The other eight options control the *state* of the layer or create new layers. Any layer is in the state of on, off, frozen, or thawed.

Creating a New Layer (Layer New)

The Layer command's New option creates a new layer. Create a new layer for the SUITE drawing, and name the new layer FURNITURE, as follows:

Prompt	Response	Explanation:
`Command:`	**Layer**	Starts the Layer command
`?/Make/Set/New/ON/ OFF/Color/Ltype/ Freeze/Thaw:`	**N**	Creates a new layer
`New layer name(s):`	**FURNITURE**	Names the new layer FURNITURE
`?/Make/Set/New/ON/ OFF/ Color/Ltype/ Freeze/Thaw:`	Press Enter	Ends the Layer command

When AutoCAD prompts you for a layer name, you can enter a name of up to 31 characters. The name can consist of letters, numbers, and the hyphen (-), underline (_), and dollar ($) characters. You cannot give a new layer the same name as an existing layer.

TIP

You can create more than one layer at a time by separating the new layers' names with a comma. Here's how you can create three new layers called FURNITURE, TILES, and APPLIANCES, all at the same time:

`Command:` **Layer**
`?/Make/Set/New/ON/OFF/Color/Ltype/Freeze/Thaw:` **N**
`New layer names(s):` **FURNITURE,TILES,APPLIANCES**

Every new layer always has the same default properties:

❑ The color is white

❑ The linetype is continuous

❑ The layer is turned on

Layer 0 has the same properties when you begin a new drawing. You can change these properties to suit your needs by using the Layer command's options.

Changing the Current Layer (Layer Set)

You've created the new layer but you can't draw on it yet. Layer 0 is still the current layer, as you can see by looking at the status line. The Set option tells AutoCAD to change to a different layer:

```
Command: Layer
?/Make/Set/New/.../Thaw: S
New current layer <0>: FURNITURE
?/Make/Set/New/.../Thaw: Press Enter
```

AutoCAD prompts you for the name of the layer to make current. You must enter the name of an existing layer. This layer becomes the current layer and its name appears on the status line, in this case as FURNITUR (the first eight characters of the layer name "FURNITURE").

TIP

You can use wild-card characters to reduce the amount of typing during the Layer command. Because only one FURNITURE layer exists in the SUITE drawing, you need only type **F*** when AutoCAD prompts you for the layer name.

Moving Existing Objects to a New Layer (Layer Change)

So that the new layer will have some ready-made entities, move the kitchen table and chairs to the FURNITURE layer. The Change command (which is discussed in detail later in this chapter) accomplishes the move, as follows:

Prompt	Response	Explanation
Command:	**Change**	Starts the Change command
Select objects:	**W**	Tells AutoCAD that the selection set will be selected by a window
First corner:	Pick a point to the lower left of the kitchen furniture	Specifies the window's first corner

Prompt	Response	Explanation
`Other corner:`	Pick a point to the upper right of the kitchen furniture	Specifies the window's opposite corner
`21 found`		AutoCAD finds 21 objects
`Select objects:`	Press Enter	Ends object selection
`Properties/<Change point>:`	**P**	Selects the Properties option
`Change what property (Color/LAyer/LType/ Thickness)?`	**LA**	Specifies the LAyer option
`New layer <0>:`	**FURNITURE**	New layer name for kitchen furniture
`Change what property (Color/LAyer/LType/ Thickness)?`	Press Enter	Ends the Change command

Creating a New Layer that Automatically Becomes Current (Layer Make)

The Make option combines the Set and New options into a single operation. This makes it faster to create a new layer and immediately begin drawing on that layer. Once you enter the new layer's name, Make searches for the layer name to determine whether it already exists. If the name does not exist, Make creates the new layer and makes it the current layer.

Now, practice using Make by creating a new layer (named TILES), which automatically becomes the current layer:

Prompt	Response	Explanation
`Command:`	**Layer**	Starts the Layer command
`?/Make/Set/New/.../ Thaw:`	**M**	Selects the Make option
`New current layer <FURNITURE>:`	**TILES**	Creates a new layer, named TILES, and makes it the current layer
`?/Make/Set/New/.../ Thaw:`	Press Enter	Ends the Layer command

Notice that Layer TILES appears on the status line. Using the Change command, window the tiles in the hallway and bathroom and change them to the TILES layer. You may need to use several object-selection options to get all the tiles; try Crossing, Remove, Add, and Picking.

If you mistype the layer name with the Set or Make options, you can correct the spelling by using the Rename command. Suppose that you named the new layer RILES rather than TILES. Take the following steps to correct your mistake:

```
Command: Rename
Block/Dimstyle/LAyer/LType/Style/Ucs/VIew/VPort: LA
Old layer name: RILES
New layer name: TILES
```

You cannot rename layer 0. You also can use the Ddlmodes command to rename layers. (Both Rename and Ddlmodes are covered in detail later in this chapter.) You can use this command to change the names of other named entities in AutoCAD, including views, linetypes, and text styles.

Regardless of how you set the current layer (using either the Set or Make options), all subsequent drawing occurs on the current layer. If you want to work on another layer (that already exists), use the Set option. Use the Layer Set command now to change the current layer back to 0.

Naming Layers by Convention

As you work with layers in CAD, you will find that it helps to have a consistent layer scheme for all your drawings. Although the scheme should include layer names conventional to your field of work, you don't need to include all the layers you might ever need. If you exchange drawing files with clients, you and the client should agree on a layer-naming convention.

When naming layers, you should give common layers the same first characters. By allowing the use of wild cards, the Layer command makes it easy to turn all common layers on and off together.

Two layer-naming conventions have been developed for the *A/E/C* (architectural, engineering, and construction) industry. Other disciplines have not yet adopted layer-naming conventions. One convention is based on named layers, the other on numbered layers.

Named Layers

The *CAD Layer Guidelines* were prepared by the Task Force on CAD Layer Guidelines, which is sponsored by the following organizations:

- ❏ The American Institute of Architects
- ❏ The American Consulting Engineers Council
- ❏ The American Society of Civil Engineers
- ❏ The International Facility Management Association
- ❏ The US Army Corps of Engineers
- ❏ The Naval Facility Engineering Command
- ❏ The Department of Veteran Affairs

The AIA-sponsored layer name uses four fields:

x-xxxx-xxxx-xxxxxxx

The last two fields are optional.

According to this convention, you construct a layer's name by picking an appropriate abbreviation for each field. Here are some abbreviations recommended by the task force:

Field 1   Major Group (1 character)

Abbreviation	Meaning
A	Architectural
S	Structural
M	Mechanical
P	Plumbing

Field 2   Minor Group (4 characters)

Abbreviation	Meaning
WALL	Walls
DOOR	Doors
GLAZ	Glazed openings
FLOR	Floors
SECT	Building sections

Field 3   Modifier (4 characters—optional)

Abbreviation	Meaning
IDEN	Identification
WDWK	Woodwork

Abbreviation	Meaning
APPL	Appliances
DIMS	Dimensions
PATT	Hatch patterns

Field 4   User-defined (1 to 8 characters—optional)

Abbreviation	Meaning
MFR1	Manufacturer 1
MFR2	Manufacturer 2
A	Quadrant A
01	Floor 1

For example, you could have a layer that identifies doors called **A-DOOR-IDEN**. If the drawing contains catalog information from several door manufacturers, you could devote a layer to each manufacturer's doors: **A-DOOR-IDEN-MFR1**. If you are drawing a large multi-story building, you could split the drawing up into floors (01) and quadrants (A): **A-DOOR-IDEN-MFR1-01-A**.

Layer names are available in two styles: long and short. The long form can be up to 17 characters long (not including hyphens); longer abbreviations are more meaningful. The short form takes only eight characters, which makes it suitable for display on AutoCAD's status line. The short form of the previous example is **ADOID-M2**.

A copy of the guidelines ($15) is available from the American Institute of Architects, 1735 New York Avenue NW, Washington DC 20006.

Numbered Layers

The layer system based on the Construction Specification Institute's format is used by most product literature. CSI-approved construction specs are divided into 16 categories of labor and materials (architectural, mechanical, interior finishes, and so forth). Many designers are already familiar with the 16-division protocol.

The CSI layer standard uses three fields:

    xx y z

The last field is optional.

According to this convention, you construct a layer number by picking the appropriate material definition. Following the preceding example, the existing doors to be removed would be drawn on layer 0802 (08 is the doors and windows group; 02 is the existing-to-be-removed group). A fifth number can be added for multistory projects. For example, layer 0802-3 represents existing doors to be removed on floor 3.

Here are some digits used by CSI:

Field 1   Basic Divisions (2 digits)

Digits	Meaning
00	Intra-team comments
02	Site work and civil engineering
03	Concrete work
04	Masonry work
05	Structural and ornamental steel
06	Wood and plastic work
07	Waterproofing and roofing
08	Doors and windows
09	Partitions and ceilings
10	Lockers and toilets
11	Food-service equipment
12	Furnishings
13	Special construction
14	Elevators and escalators
15	Mechanical and HVAC systems
16	Electrical engineering

Field 2 describes the actions to be taken for each division.

Field 2   Details (2 digits)

Digits	Meaning
01	Existing equipment to remain
02	Existing equipment to be removed
03	New equipment

A short form for small projects can be implemented by only using the first two digits.

A copy of the CSI layering protocol is available from Facilities Data Management, PO Box 70107, Bellevue WA 98007.

Finding Out Layer Names (Layer ?)

The ? option lists the names of all the layers in a drawing. Once you have created several layers, remembering their names can be confusing. To see the list of layers, type **Layer** at the `Command:` prompt and type **?** at the `?/.../Thaw:` prompt. AutoCAD then prompts as follows:

```
Layer name(s) to list <*>:
```

The asterisk (*) is a wild-card character that means you want all the layers listed. AutoCAD switches to the text screen and lists the three layers that now exist in the SUITE drawing, as follows:

```
Layer name        State     Color          Linetype
0                 On        7 (white)      CONTINUOUS
FURNITURE         On        7 (white)      CONTINUOUS
TILES             On        7 (white)      CONTINUOUS
Current layer: 0
?/.../Thaw:
```

Press Enter at the final prompt; the `Command:` prompt appears. Press F1 to return to the Drawing Editor.

A complex drawing can have several dozen layers, and you probably won't find it helpful seeing all their names listed. AutoCAD allows you the option of listing the names of groups of layers. If the drawing has several layers that begin with *BASE*, for example, you can list them by entering **BASE-***.

Making Layers Visible or Invisible (Layer ON and Layer OFF)

As mentioned earlier, the state of a layer affects the way it is seen on-screen. You can have all layers on, so that they all are displayed. If the drawing is complex, however, details can get lost in the maze of lines. For that reason, you should turn off unnecessary layers.

A single AutoCAD drawing can contain an entire project. By turning layers on and off before plotting, you can create the appropriate paper plans for your client. Further, you can save regeneration time by freezing unneeded layers, as explained shortly.

AutoCAD provides four options for controlling the state of layers: ON, OFF, Freeze and Thaw. Remember that all newly created layers are turned on. Once a layer is turned on, the entities on that layer are visible on-screen.

When a layer is turned off, its entities are not visible on-screen. AutoCAD recognizes that the entities still exist and that they are still part of the drawing, but does not show them.

Now, turn off the FURNITURE layer, as follows:

Prompt	Response	Explanation
Command:	**Layer**	Starts the Layer command
?/.../ON/OFF/.../ Freeze/Thaw:	**OFF**	Selects the OFF option
Layer name(s) to turn Off:	**FURNITURE**	Turns off the FURNITURE layer
?/.../ON/OFF/.../ Freeze/Thaw:	Press Enter	Ends the Layer command

The kitchen table and chairs disappeared! When you remove them from the screen, the drawing is not as cluttered. You can draw on a turned-off layer, but you won't see (nor can you edit) what you've drawn until you turn on the layer. Use the Layer ON command to make the furniture visible.

Freezing and Thawing Layers (Layer Freeze and Layer Thaw)

The Freeze option goes a step beyond OFF. When you *freeze* a layer, AutoCAD ignores that layer's entities, as if they did not exist.

Practice using the Freeze option now, as follows:

Prompt	Response	Explanation
Command:	**Layer**	Starts the Layer command
?/.../ON/OFF/.../ Freeze/Thaw:	**F**	Selects the Freeze option
Layer name(s) to Freeze:	**TILES**	Tells AutoCAD to freeze the layer named TILES
?/.../ON/OFF/.../ Freeze/Thaw:	Press Enter	Ends the Layer command

The tiles in the hallway and bathroom disappear. When you freeze one or more layers, the Regen command works faster. Frozen entities greatly reduce the time AutoCAD requires to regenerate the drawing, because AutoCAD can ignore the entities on a frozen layer. Regeneration time is reduced because AutoCAD does not need to recalculate the position and characteristics of the entities on a frozen layer. Use the Regen command now to see how much faster the SUITE drawing regenerates.

The Thaw option reverses the effect of freezing a layer. The layer goes back to its original state of ON or OFF.

Prompt	Response	Explanation
Command:	**Layer**	Starts the Layer command
?/.../ON/OFF/.../ Freeze/Thaw:	**T**	Selects the Thaw option
Layer name(s) to Thaw:	**TILES**	Tells AutoCAD to thaw the frozen layer named TILES
?/.../ON/OFF/.../ Freeze/Thaw:	Press Enter	Ends the Layer command

The tiles reappear. Now use the Regen command, and you should find that regeneration is about 50 percent slower. Table 9.1 summarizes the effects of the layer states:

Table 9.1
The effect of layer states

	ON	OFF	Freeze
Layer can be current	Yes	Yes	No
Entities visible	Yes	No	No
Draw entities on layer	Yes	Yes	No
Edit entities on layer	Yes	No	No
Change entities to layer	Yes	Yes	No
Entities regenerated	Yes	Yes	No

Assigning Layer Colors (Layer Color)

All entities drawn on a new layer are colored white, unless you assign a different color to a layer. You may want to assign colors to certain layers.

You gain two advantages by assigning different colors to your drawing's layers. First, you will find it easier to keep track of objects on-screen. For example, all furniture on the FURNITURE layer could be colored red, while all tiles on the TILES layer could be colored blue.

You realize the other advantage at plotting time. AutoCAD assigns pens by entity color. That means that you can have the red furniture drawn with a red pen, and have the tiles drawn with a wide black pen.

Change the color of the SUITE drawing's layers, as follows:

Prompt	Response	Explanation
Command:	**Layer**	Starts the Layer command
?/.../Color/Ltype/ .../Thaw:	**C**	Selects the Color option
Color:	**RED**	Specifies the color red
Layer name(s) for color 1 (red) <0>:	**FURNITURE**	Assigns the new color to the layer named FURNITURE
?/.../Color/Ltype/ .../Thaw:	**C**	Reselects the Color option
Color:	**BLUE**	Specifies the color blue
Layer name(s) for color 5 (blue) <0>:	**TILES**	Assigns the new color to the layer named TILES
?/.../Color/Ltype/ .../Thaw:	Press Enter	Ends the Layer command

The SUITE drawing regenerates in glorious color! Red furniture and blue tiles with white walls and appliances. You can change the color of individual objects by using the Change command (which is discussed in detail later in this chapter).

Some graphics boards will display the layer name on the status line in the layer's color. Unlike layer names, there are no conventions for layer colors. If you are using a monochrome monitor, AutoCAD displays colored layers in different shades of gray.

Assigning Linetypes (Layer LType)

You can assign a *linetype* to each layer. By default, AutoCAD displays entities with continuous, unbroken lines. You can use the LType option, however, if you want AutoCAD to display lines, circles, and polylines as patterns of broken lines. When you assign a linetype to a layer, all entities on the layer use that linetype. For a graphical listing of AutoCAD's built-in linetypes, see Appendix D.

In preparation for setting the linetype, use the Change command to move all kitchen appliances to the APPLIANCES layer. Use the Layer Make command to create this new layer, which should include the double sink, range, and grill.

Before you can set a new linetype, you need to *load* it into the drawing by using the Linetype command. Chapter 11 discusses the Linetype command in detail. For now, just take the following simple steps:

```
Command: Linetype
?/Create/Load/Set: L
Linetype to load: DOT
```

AutoCAD stores the linetype information in a file named ACAD.LIN. If you use Release 11, a dialogue box appears asking you to select the appropriate linetype (LIN) file. Make sure that the file name ACAD is highlighted, and pick the OK button from the dialogue box (see fig. 9.15). (In Release 10, you need to type in the file name **ACAD**.) The command continues with the following prompts:

```
Linetype DOT loaded.
?/Create/Load/Set: Press Enter
```

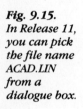

Fig. 9.15.
In Release 11,
you can pick
the file name
ACAD.LIN
from a
dialogue box.

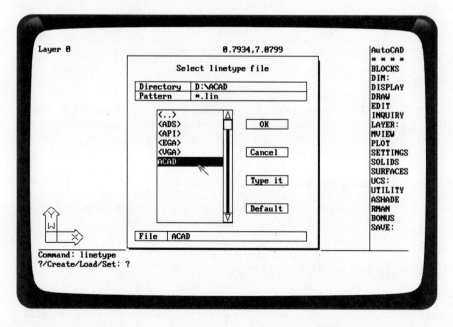

Next, select the Layer command's LType option to set the linetype for the layer named APPLIANCES:

Prompt	Response	Explanation
`Command:`	**Layer**	Starts the Layer command
`?/.../Color/Ltype/` `.../Thaw:`	**L**	Selects the Linetype option
`Linetype (or ?)` `<CONTINUOUS>:`	**DOT**	Specifies the linetype DOT

`Layer name(s) for`
`linetype DOT`
`<APPLIANCES>:`
	Press Enter	Assigns the DOT linetype to the APPLIANCES layer (in this case, you press Enter to accept the default layer name, which is APPLIANCES)

`?/.../Color/Ltype/` `.../Thaw:`	Press Enter	Ends the Layer command

AutoCAD automatically regenerates the drawing so that it can calculate where the dots lie (see fig. 9.16). The Ltype option has a sub-option, ?, that lists all the linetypes available in the drawing. As with colors, you can use the Change command to assign different linetypes to individual objects in the drawing.

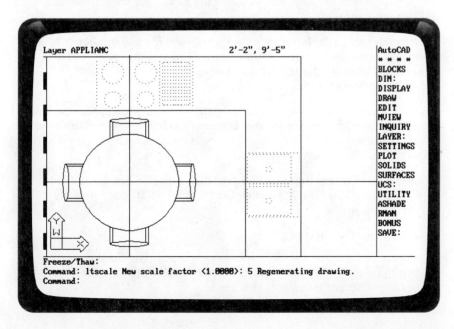

Fig. 9.16.
All objects on the APPLIANCES layer are drawn with the DOT linetype.

If you can't see the dots, use the Ltscale (Linetype scale) command to increase the spacing between dots, as follows:

```
Command: Ltscale
New scale factor <1.0000>: 5
Regenerating drawing.
```

By entering a value of 5, you increase the spacing between dots fivefold. The default spacing is based on the linetype's definition. For the DOT linetype, the dots are spaced 0.25 units apart when Ltscale is set to 1.

You have seen how powerful layers are for managing elements of your drawings. The Layer command enables you to freeze objects that you don't need to see, assign different colors to different types of objects, or give entities special linetypes to make them more distinguishable.

Layers are also important to plotting. The color of entities is the only way to determine which pen the plotter will use. Turning combinations of layers off and on before plotting creates plan sets from the electronic drawing.

Using Dialogue Boxes To Control Layers (Ddlmodes)

If your graphics board can handle the Advanced User Interface (most boards can), you can take advantage of pop-up dialogue boxes. There are many such boxes in AutoCAD. You already saw some with the Mslide and Vslide commands.

Dialogue boxes make it easier, and often faster, for you to alter the drawing's settings. If your computer cannot display AutoCAD's dialogue boxes, don't worry; all the dialogue boxes' functions are provided through other commands.

This section discusses only the Layer dialogue box. Sometimes you will find that layers are easier to control through a dialogue box. On the other hand, if you need to control many layers, it easier to use wild-card characters with the Layer command.

The command that brings up the Layer dialogue box has the unlikely name of Ddlmodes. The *Dd* stands for "dynamic dialogue," and the *l* for "layer." Try it now:

```
Command: Ddlmodes
```

The Layer dialogue box should appear on-screen. The dialogue box shown in figure 9.17 is for Release 11; the Release 10 dialogue box looks somewhat different (see fig. 9.18).

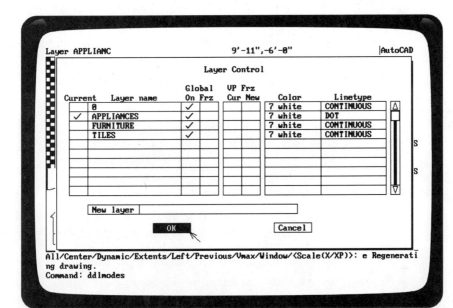

Fig. 9.17.
The Layer dialogue box for Release 11.

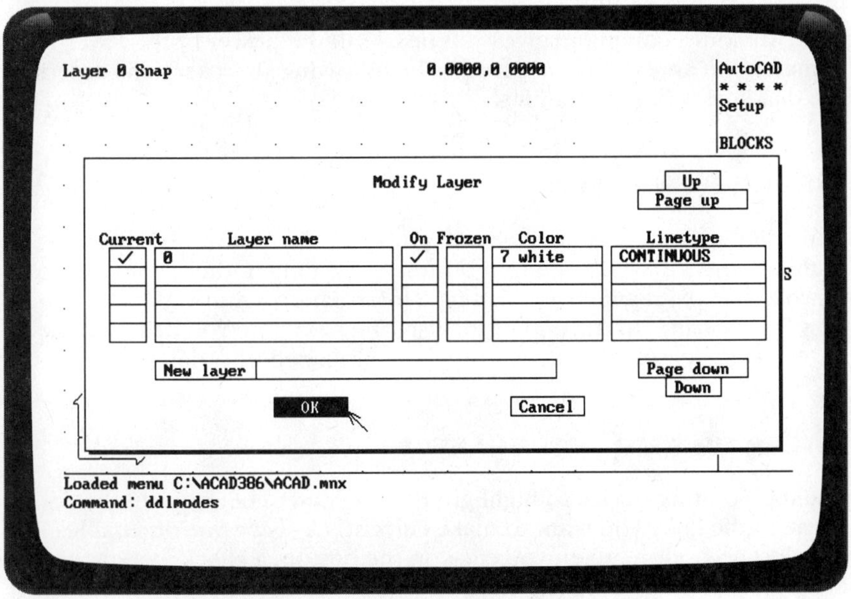

Fig. 9.18.
The Release 10 dialogue box shows only five layer names at a time.

You can bring up the Layer dialogue box in three ways:

❑ Type **Ddlmodes** at the `Command:` prompt, as you just saw.

❑ Use **'Ddlmodes** as a transparent command in the middle of another command. This lets you change layers in the middle of drawing and editing commands.

❑ Move the cursor to the top of the screen, pick Settings from the menu bar, and then pick Layer Control.... Picking is faster than typing **'Ddlmodes**; note that the command is automatically transparent.

There are several ways to leave a dialogue box:

❑ Near the bottom of the dialogue box are two rectangles (called *action buttons*) labeled `OK` and `Cancel`. After making modifications to the information in the dialogue box, pick the `OK` button to make the changes permanent.

❑ Pick the `Cancel` button to tell AutoCAD not to make any changes and return to the `Command:` prompt.

❑ Press Ctrl-C; this has the same effect as picking the `Cancel` button.

The Ddlmodes command gives you nearly all the power of the Layer command in an easier-to-use form. The following short sections describe the dialogue box's capabilities.

Adding New Layers

You add a new layer to your drawing by using the pointing device to highlight the `New Layer` input button and typing in the name. (An *input button* is a box in which you can type information.) AutoCAD adds the new layer's name to the end of the list. The next time you bring up the Layer dialogue box, the names appear in alphabetical order.

Changing the Current Layer

Use the pointing device to highlight the `Current` check button by the name of the layer you want to make current. (A *check button* enables you to select an option; when you click on the button, a check-mark appears.) When you pick the button, AutoCAD moves the check-mark symbol next to that layer. AutoCAD will not let you make a frozen layer current.

If there are more layer names than can be seen at one time, move your pointing device over to the *scroll bar* (the vertical bar at the extreme right side of the dialogue box). Pick the small box and pull it down. As you do, the layer names scroll past. Let go of the box when you see the layer name you need.

Turning Layers On and Off

Ddlmodes enables you to turn individual layers on and off quickly and easily. Move your pointing device to the `On` check button next to the layer name. When you pick the button, the status of the layer changes: if it was on, the check mark disappears to show that the layer will be turned off; if off, the check mark appears to show that the layer will be turned on when you leave the dialogue box.

This method is easier than using the Layer command to type the ON (or OFF) command and then typing the layer name(s).

Freezing and Thawing Layers

The Layer Control dialogue box lets you freeze and thaw layers much more quickly than is possible by using the Layer command. Pick the `Freeze` button next to the layer names you want frozen. A check mark shows the layer will be frozen; no check mark means the layer will be thawed when you leave the dialogue box.

Renaming a Layer

To change the name of a layer, pick the layer name. AutoCAD displays an input button that lets you edit the name (see fig. 9.19). When you are done, pick the `OK` button next to the new name.

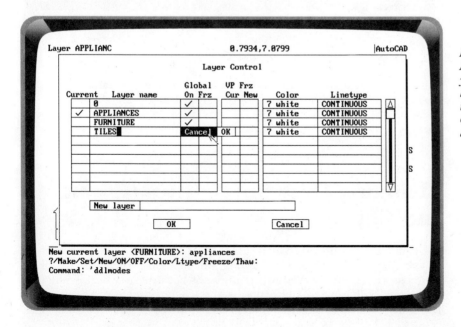

Fig. 9.19.
AutoCAD lets you edit the layer name in the Layer Control dialogue box.

Changing a Layer's Color

When you use the pointing device to pick a layer's color, AutoCAD displays a second dialogue box that illustrates the first seven available colors (see fig. 9.20). You can pick one of the colors from this box or type in the new color number.

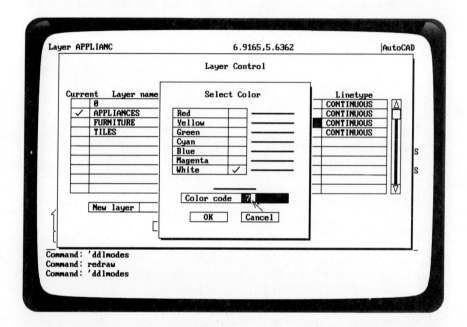

Fig. 9.20. The Select Color dialogue box lets you pick from the first seven colors or type in a color number.

Altering a Layer's Linetype

You can change a layer's linetype by picking the linetype name next to the layer name. As with the color option, AutoCAD displays another dialogue box that lets you specify the new linetype (see fig. 9.21). If the linetype has not been loaded, a warning box appears (see fig. 9.22).

Changing Drawing Entities (Change and Chprop)

The Change and Chprop (which stands for Change Property) commands let you change all entities in a drawing, one at a time. They are possibly the most frequently used editing commands because they modify the properties of all objects. Chprop is used to change an entity's properties. These include color, linetype, thickness, elevation, or layer location.

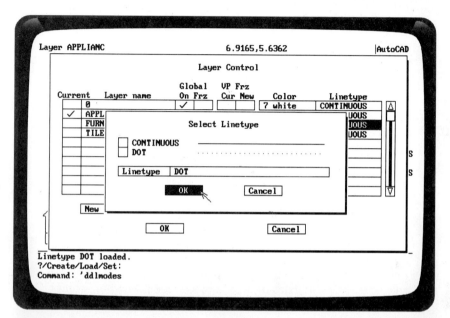

Fig. 9.21.
The Select
Linetype
dialogue box.

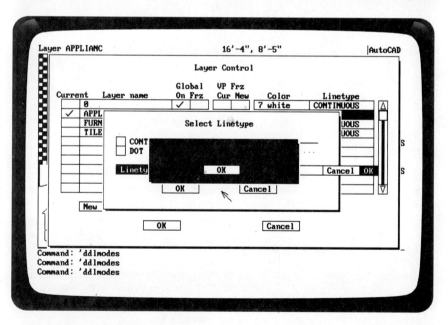

Fig. 9.22.
AutoCAD
displays a
warning box
if the linetype
does not
exist.

Change can do all that, but also can change the location of endpoints and make certain changes to circles, text, blocks, and attributes.

These changes are discussed in the following sections.

Changing an Entity's Properties

First, look at the traits Change and Chprop have in common. When you enter Change at the `Command:` prompt, AutoCAD asks you to select the entities you want to change:

Prompt	Response	Explanation
`Command:`	**Change**	Starts the Change command
`Select objects:`	Pick the sink ellipse	Selects the object to be changed
`1 selected, 1 found`		
`Select objects:`	Press Enter	Ends object selection
`Properties/<Change point>:` **P**		Selects the Properties option

After you select the objects to be changed and tell AutoCAD that you want to change specific properties of those objects, the following prompt appears:

```
Change what property (Color/Elevation/LAyer/LType/
Thickness) ?
```

The Chprop command only changes an entity's properties, so it leaves out the `Properties/<Change point>:` prompt. This makes it faster to use than the Change command. Otherwise, Chprop operates in exactly the same manner as Change.

Color, elevation, layer, linetype, and thickness are properties of nearly every entity in an AutoCAD drawing. As this prompt indicates, each property may be altered for the entities you select.

Release 11 leaves out the Elevation option in the Change and Chprop commands. You can no longer change an object's elevation with the two commands. Instead, use the Move command.

Changing Colors (Color)

Entities normally take on the color of their layer. If you select the Change command's Color option, AutoCAD asks for a new color. This lets you assign a different color to individual objects, regardless of the layer on which they reside. The objects you select will change to the new color you specify. To see this effect, continue editing the bathroom sink:

```
Change what property (Color/...): C
New color <BYLAYER>: RED
Change what property (Color/...): Press Enter
```

The sink ellipse turns red. AutoCAD gives you the option to respond four ways:

❑ You can enter the color's name: red, yellow, green, cyan, blue, magenta, or white. This works only for the first seven colors.

❑ You can enter the color's abbreviation: R, Y, G, C, B, M, or W.

❑ You can enter the color number. This lets you specify any one of AutoCAD's 255 available colors.

❑ You can make the entity's color correspond with another setting: BYLAYER or BYBLOCK. BYLAYER changes the objects to the same color as the layer they are on. If the objects are part of a block, BYBLOCK changes them to the color of the block, overriding the layer color (blocks are discussed in Chapter 12).

Typing in the color's name is easier than trying to remember the color's number, but limits you to the first seven colors. If you want to change the entity's color to the color of the layer, enter **BYLAYER** as the color name. Table 9.2 shows the correlation between color names, abbreviations, and numbers.

Table 9.2
AutoCAD's standard color names and numbers

Color Name	Abbreviation	Number	Notes
Black	*none*	0	The screen background color
Red	R	1	
Yellow	Y	2	
Green	G	3	
Cyan	C	4	Light blue
Blue	B	5	
Magenta	M	6	Pink
White	W	7	Looks black on a white background
Red hue		10	
Yellow hue		50	
Green hue		90	
Cyan hue		130	
Blue hue		170	
Magenta hue		210	
Gray hue		250	

On monitors that can display all 256 colors, the hue is determined by the first two digits of the color number; if you want orange, use color 30; 20 is a reddish-orange, while 40 is a yellowish-orange. The gray hues range from 250 (the weakest) to 255 (the brightest).

The intensity (saturation) is determined by the third digit, which can range from 0 (the brightest) through 2, 4, 6, or 8 (the dimmest). Color 178, for example, is a very dark blue.

Changing Elevation and Thickness (Elev and Thickness)

In three-dimensional drafting, you can give objects an *elevation* (the height above 0') and a *thickness*. The Change command's Elev (stands for elevation) option lets you give a two-dimensional object a location in three-dimensional space, or to change its elevation above the X,Y-plane. A positive value moves the object up in the Z direction; a negative value moves it below the X,Y-plane. The Elev option is no longer available in Release 11.

Thickness is another property of the third dimension. It is the extrusion distance of an object. A positive value extends the object up; a negative value extends the thickness downward. Thickness and elevation are discussed in greater detail in Part Five of this text.

Changing Layers (LAyer)

The LAyer option lets you move entities from one layer to another. Practice using this option by moving the bathroom sink from its current layer to layer 0, as follows:

Prompt	Response	Explanation
Command:	**Change**	Starts the Change command
Change what property (.../LAyer/...):	**LA**	Specifies the LAyer option (Note that you must to type **LA** to differentiate the LAyer option from the LType option)
New layer name <TILES>:	**0**	Relocates the sink to layer 0
Change what property (...):	Press Enter	Ends the Change command

When an entity moves to another layer, it takes on the properties of the new layer (color and linetype), unless these properties are overridden with the Change command.

TIP

If you use Release 10, you can type **LA** at the Change command's Properties/<Change point>: prompt, and skip the Change whatproperty? prompt. This shortcut was eliminated with Release 11.

Changing the Linetype (LType)

The LType (which stands for linetype) option lets you change an object's appearance. As you recall from the discussion of layers, AutoCAD can draw objects in solid lines (called *continuous*) or in broken line (as dashes or dots or a combination of the two). Drafters often use linetypes to indicate different kinds of lines. For example, a center line shows up more clearly if it is broken.

You have used the Layer command to change an object's linetype. Now practice using the Change command's LType option to change the bathroom sink's linetype, as follows:

Prompt	Response	Explanation
Command:	**Change**	Starts the Change command
Select objects:	Pick sink	Selects the bathroom sink
1 selected, 1 found		
Select objects:	Press Enter	Ends object selection
Properties/<Change point>:	**P**	Selects the Properties option
Change what property (.../LAyer/...):	**LT**	Specifies the LType option
New linetype <BYLAYER>:	**DOT**	Assigns the DOT linetype to the bathroom sink
Change what property (.../LAyer/...):	Press Enter	Ends the Change command

The sink is now made of red dots. As with color, the linetype can be set with the Layer command but overridden with the Change command. You must use BYBLOCK, however, if the entity is part of a block. It then takes on properties of the block. You can change the linetype back to that of its layer by using the BYLAYER option.

Changing End and Insertion Points (Change point)

A *change point* defines the new location for:

- ❑ The endpoint of a line, polyline, or arc
- ❑ The insertion point of text or a block
- ❑ The circumference of a circle

You use a change point to modify an entity's size or physical position within a drawing. You cannot, however, use a change point to modify an ellipse or a donut. To see the effect, pick the four counter lines that surround the bathroom sink:

```
Command: Change
Select objects: Pick the four lines
Properties/<Change point>: Pick a point nearby
```

By picking a point in the drawing (instead of typing **P**), you specify a change point. This is because the Change point option is the default. AutoCAD uses this point as the new endpoint for the entities in the selection set.

If you select several lines and apply a change point, the lines all radiate from that point. AutoCAD changes the endpoints that are closest to the change point (this does not work on splined polylines). Figure 9.23 shows the result of using Change point on the bathroom countertop.

> The change-point capabilities of the Change command were important with older versions of AutoCAD. Since version 2.5, however, many of the same functions can be done more easily with the Stretch command.

If you pick a circle, its radius changes. The change point you pick determines the new circumference of the circle.

If you apply the Change command to text or blocks, their insertion point changes to the new point. You can always use the U command to undo changes you don't want (to put the bathroom counter back in shape, for example).

Changing an Entity

The other changes the Change command can make are to individual parts of four types of entities: circle, text, block, and attribute. Using Change to modify an entity is usually faster than erasing the entity and then

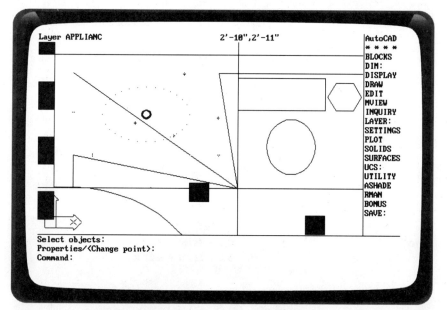

Layer APPLIANC   2'-10",2'-11"

```
AutoCAD
* * * *
BLOCKS
DIM:
DISPLAY
DRAW
EDIT
MVIEW
INQUIRY
LAYER:
SETTINGS
PLOT
SOLIDS
SURFACES
UCS:
UTILITY
ASHADE
RMAN
BONUS
SAVE:
```

```
Select objects:
Properties/<Change point>:
Command:
```

Fig. 9.23.
The Change
command
changes the
end points of
lines, arcs,
and polylines.

redrawing it. On the other hand, some editing commands are easier to use than Change. For example, you can use the Scale command to change a circle's radius, you can use the Tedit command to change text, and you can use Attedit to change attributes. Historically, the Change command preceded the others; in practice, you should use the command you find easiest.

If you press Enter at the Properties/<Change point>: prompt (instead of typing **P** or picking a point), AutoCAD displays a new series of prompts. These prompts are different for each entity and are explained in the following sections.

Changing Circles

When you press Enter at the Properties/<Change point>: prompt, AutoCAD enables you to change the radius of a circle. First, however, you must issue the Change command and select the circle that is to be modified (this is how AutoCAD "knows" to let you change the radius). Now, change the radius of the kitchen table:

Prompt	Response	Explanation
`Command:`	**Change**	Starts the Change command
`Select objects:`	Pick the kitchen table	Specifies the entity to be modified
`1 selected, 1 found` `Select objects:`	Press Enter	Ends object selection
`Properties/<Change point>:`	Press Enter	Selects the default Change point option
`Enter circle radius:`	Pick a point inside the circle	Specifies a new, smaller radius for the table

AutoCAD ghosts the new radius of the kitchen table as you move your pointing device (see fig. 9.24). Press Enter or enter a radius value and the table takes on its new size.

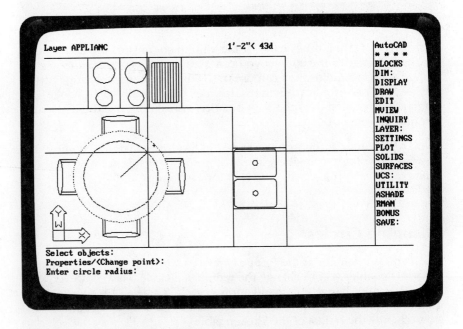

Fig. 9.24.
The Change command can resize circles.

You can use the keyboard to provide an exact radius for the circle, or you can use the change-point method to pick the new radius visually. Use the method that meets your needs better. When you are finished practicing on the kitchen table, use the Undo command to change the table back to its original size.

Changing Text

You can use the Change command to change all aspects of text, except its justification. If you select some text and then press Enter at the `Properties/<Change point>:` prompt, AutoCAD prompts you, in turn, for each of the following:

❏ A new text insertion point

❏ A new style (or font)

❏ A different height

❏ A new rotation angle

❏ A different text string

The new style must already have been defined. If the text style is defined with a fixed height, AutoCAD will not prompt you for it. Chapter 10 covers text in detail.

Changing Blocks and Attributes

If the selection set contains a block, only one property can be changed: the rotation angle. If the block contains attributes, you can change the insertion point, style, height, rotation angle, tag, prompt string, and default value of the attribute. Blocks and attributes are discussed in Chapter 12.

Modifying Entities through a Dialogue Box (Ddemodes)

The Ddemodes (which is short for Dynamic dialogue Entity MODES) command shows you the current setting of the following:

❏ Color

❏ Elevation

❏ Layer

❏ Linetype

❏ Thickness

The next entity you draw will have these attributes, no matter which layer it resides on.

Ddemodes also lets you change the settings. Obviously, these properties also can be changed with individual AutoCAD commands. The effect of using the Ddemodes command is the same as that of using the following commands:

❏ Color

❏ Elevation

❏ Layer Set

❏ Linetype Set

When you type **Ddemodes** at the `Command:` prompt, your screen should look like the one shown in figure 9.25. (Note that the text style shown will be whatever was used last.)

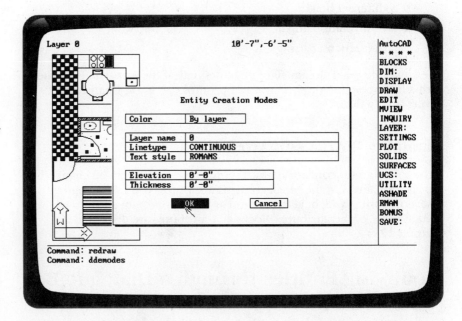

Fig. 9.25.
The
Ddemodes
command
makes it
easier to set
the properties
of entities.

If you select Color, Layer, or Linetype, a subdialogue box appears, showing you the choices. If you select Elevation or Thickness, AutoCAD expects you to type the information.

You can issue the Ddemodes command transparently, by typing **'Ddemodes** at the `Command:` prompt. The modified information does not take effect until the next command is given. Changing color or linetype through Ddemodes or through the Color or Linetype commands overrides the layer settings. This can be confusing because the color and linetype of the entities may no longer match the layer's settings.

Renaming Entity Traits (Rename)

As you know, you can assign names to several AutoCAD components: views, layers, text styles, blocks, and others. But what happens if you want to change one of the names you have been using? You can use the Rename command to change the name of any of the following objects:

❏ Blocks

❏ Dimension styles

❏ Layers

❏ Linetypes

❏ Text styles

❏ User coordinate system (UCS)

❏ Views

❏ Viewport configurations

This supposes, of course, that you already have named the component you want to rename. For example, you can create a UCS, but you do not necessarily have to give it a name. The Rename command works only on objects that already have a name. Note also that Rename cannot be used to change the name of layer 0 (it must remain layer 0) or the CONTINUOUS linetype.

When you enter **Rename** at the `Command:` prompt, AutoCAD responds with the following prompt:

```
Block/Dimstyle/LAyer/LType/Style/Ucs/VIew/VPort:
```

These options let you specify the type of object you want to rename. For example, if you want to change the name of the ELECTRICAL layer to ELECTRONICS, enter **LA** in response to the prompt. AutoCAD then asks for the existing and new layer names, as follows:

```
Old layer name: ELECTRICAL
New layer name: ELECTRONICS
```

After you select the type of object you want to rename, AutoCAD asks for the object's old name. The exact prompt varies according to the object you are renaming. If you enter a name that refers to a nonexistent object, AutoCAD generates an error message and ends the Rename command.

After you enter the object's old name, AutoCAD asks for the new name. Enter a valid AutoCAD object name; that's all there is to it. If the name you enter is currently being used for another object, AutoCAD will tell you so and will not make the change.

Summary

This chapter completes the discussion of AutoCAD's editing commands. The editing commands covered here—Pedit, Change, and Chprop—are among the most powerful in AutoCAD.

This chapter also covered the Layer and Ddlmodes commands, their features and benefits. The ability to place entities on layers gives you better control over the way your drawing presents information. If your layer convention is well-planned, some of AutoCAD's functions are accelerated.

Chapter 10 shows you how easily you can add text, hatching, and dimensioning to your drawing. You also will learn how to use AutoCAD as a sketch pad.

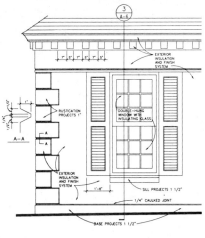

10

Advanced Drawing Techniques

Illustration courtesy of Autodesk, Inc., Sausalito, CA.

As you worked on the sample drawing, you learned how AutoCAD turns lines, arcs, and circles into objects with meaning. You used AutoCAD's editing commands to copy and embellish these objects, and you learned how to use some of AutoCAD's helpful drafting aids. You also learned how to view and plot a drawing.

So far, however, all you have is a simple picture. It lacks information. This chapter shows you how to add text, hatch patterns, and dimensions to your drawing. These elements make your drawing a more complete document.

This chapter introduces the following commands:

❏ Dim   ❏ Qtext

❏ Dim1   ❏ Sketch

❏ Dtext   ❏ Style

❏ Hatch   ❏ Text

These commands help give your drawings a finished look.

Working with Text

No drawing is complete until important information has been labeled. Rooms need to be named on floor plans. Machine shop drawings need assembly notes. The following sections show you how to add text to your drawings.

AutoCAD features powerful text facilities which let you assign fonts, enter and edit notes, and even alter the text's properties to reduce regeneration times.

AutoCAD has two commands for entering notes and labels into your drawing: Text and Dtext. The Text command is the basic method of adding text to your drawing. Dtext gives you a more flexible way to enter text.

To prepare for using these commands, load the SUITE drawing and create a new layer, which will hold the text you add to the drawing:

Prompt	Response	Explanation
Command:	**Layer**	Starts the Layer command
?/Make/.../Thaw:	**M**	Makes a new layer
New current layer <0>:	**TEXT**	Names the new layer TEXT
?/Make/.../Thaw:	Press Enter	Ends the Layer command

Entering a Line of Text (Text)

The Text command enables you to enter one line of text at a time. If you want to add more text, repeat the command. Text has four options, but only three of the options appear when you enter the command:

```
Justify/Style/<Start point>:
```

Use the Start point option to specify the starting point of the text, using left justification as the default option.

The Justify option lets you pick one of 14 text-justification options.

Style lets you specify the *style*, or text font, used for text. You can use several text styles in a drawing.

The fourth option is to press Enter at the Justify/Style/<Start point>: prompt if you want to add a second line of text precisely under the first line without respecifying the options.

Entering Text

The default method for entering text is just to pick a point on the screen. Try the Text command now by adding the title "One Bedroom Suite" to the sample drawing. Follow these steps:

Prompt	Response	Explanation
`Command:`	**TEXT**	Starts the Text command
`Justify/Style/` `<Start point>:`	**10',-4'**	Specifies the starting point for the text
`Height <0'-0">:`	**12**	Sets the text height at 12"
`Rotation angle <0.0>:`	Press Enter	Accepts the 0 rotation angle, so that the text is written horizontally
`Text:`	**One Bedroom Suite**	Specifies the text to be added to the drawing

Figure 10.1 shows the results of this command sequence. If you cannot see the text on the screen, issue the Zoom Extents command to display the entire drawing.

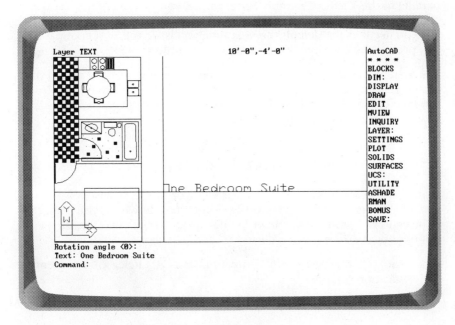

Fig. 10.1.
The Text command adds a title to the SUITE drawing.

This is the easiest way to insert a line of text into a drawing. You simply specify the point (by pointing or by entering an X,Y coordinate) at which you want the text to start. When you enter the desired text, it starts at the specified point and continues to the right (text arranged in this fashion is called *left-justified text*).

AutoCAD can insert text at any size and at any angle. The `Height` option refers to the height of the text you are currently entering. You should pick a height that can easily be read once the drawing is plotted. As a title to the sample drawing, 12 inches is a good choice (if this seems large, remember that you are creating the drawing at full size). If you plot the drawing at a scale of 1/4" =1', the text appears 1/4" tall.

The `Height <0'-0">:` prompt remembers the last height you entered, and presents it in angle brackets as the default. If you want to use the default height, just press Enter. You also can specify a new height for the next line of text.

Text on a CAD system is easy to use and generally of very high quality because of the accuracy and clarity of pen plotters. If you use a pen plotter, you can print smaller than you normally would without sacrificing legibility. When plotted, even tiny text reads quite well.

The `Rotation angle <0.0>:` prompt lets you enter text at any angle. This is helpful for entering text along sloped lines. To position text parallel to the Y-axis of a graph, for example, you would enter **90** at the prompt. AutoCAD remembers the last rotation angle you specified, and lets you use it as the default the next time you issue the Text command. If you prefer, you can specify a new angle each time you enter text.

The final prompt, `Text:`, asks for the line of text you want to add to the drawing. A single line of text can include as many as 256 characters. You can type in any character on the keyboard, as well as several other characters, which are discussed later.

Justifying Text (Text Justify)

Most text you enter into a drawing (or in a word processor) is left-justified, as demonstrated previously. Sometimes, however, you want text to be centered or fit between two points. AutoCAD gives you those options and a dozen more.

When you pick the Text Justify command, AutoCAD Release 11 presents 14 justification options:

```
Align/Fit/Center/Middle/Right/TL/TC/TR/ML/MC/MR/BL/BC/BR:
```

This selection might seem intimidating, but you can separate these options into two groups. The first group includes the justification options you use frequently (such as Align, Center and Right); the second group includes those you rarely use (all the others).

Otherwise, you can group the options into those that require two picks (Align and Fit), and those that require one pick (all the others).

NOTE Release 10 only offers the first five justification options: Align, Fit, Center, Middle, and Right.

The justification option you select determines the text's *insertion point*. This is the point in the drawing at which the text starts. It is also the point that the INSertion object snap mode picks, should you ever need to snap to the text. Figure 10.2 summarizes the justification options and their insertion points.

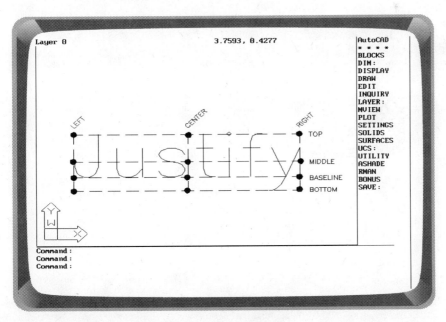

Fig. 10.2.
AutoCAD's
text-
justification
options.

Centering Text (Center and Middle)

To center the text around a specified insertion point, select the Center option and specify a center point. When you use centered justification, AutoCAD draws the text so that its baseline is centered on the pick point. Centered text is useful for titles or columnar data. Now, enter a new centered line of text to the SUITE drawing:

Prompt	Response	Explanation
`Command:`	**Text**	Starts the Text command
`Align/Fit/Center/` `Middle/.../BR:`	**C**	Selects the Center text-justification option
`Center point:`	**16'10,-6'**	Specifies the coordinates for the text's center point
`Height <1'-0">:`	**9"**	Specifies the text's height
`Rotation angle <0.0>:`	Press Enter	Accepts the default 0 rotation angle, so that the text is entered horizontally
`Text:`	**Hotel California**	Specifies the text to be added to the drawing

The results of this command sequence are shown in figure 10.3.

Fig. 10.3.
The Center option centers text on the insertion point.

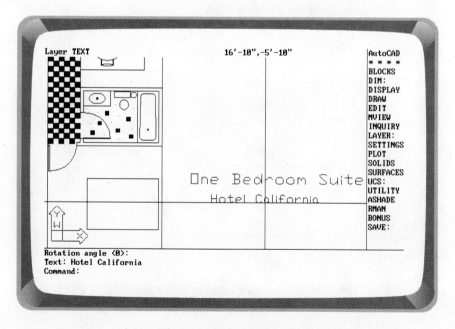

The text is centered on the point you specify. After you pick the center point, AutoCAD asks for the text's height, rotation angle, and text, as described previously. Notice that AutoCAD remembered the height (12") you specified the last time you used the Text command.

The Middle option is similar to the Center option, except that it does double centering. That is, Middle centers text to the left and right of the pick point, as well as above and below the pick point (see fig. 10.4).

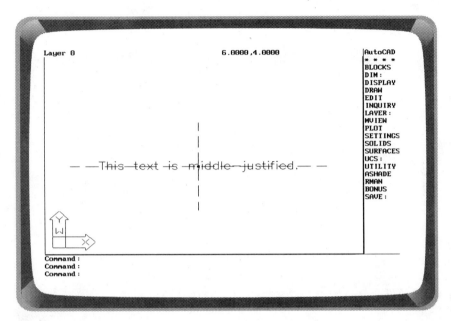

Layer 0   6.0000,4.0000

```
AutoCAD
* * * *
BLOCKS
DIM:
DISPLAY
DRAW
EDIT
INQUIRY
LAYER:
MVIEW
PLOT
SETTINGS
SOLIDS
SURFACES
UCS:
UTILITY
ASHADE
RMAN
BONUS
SAVE:
```

— —This—text—is —middle—justified.— — —

```
Command:
Command:
Command:
```

Fig. 10.4.
This text uses
middle
justification.

Aligning Text (Align and Fit)

The Align option places text between two points and adjusts the text's height so that it looks natural. This prevents the text string from appearing oddly stretched as AutoCAD makes it fit between the two points. You should use aligned justification to make text fit into a restricted space, such as a title block.

When you use the Align option, AutoCAD asks for a start and finish point and then for the text string itself:

Prompt	Response	Explanation
Command:	**Text**	Starts the Text command
Justify/Style/ <Start point>:	**J**	Selects the Justify option
Align/Fit/Center/ Middle/.../BR:	**A**	Selects aligned justification
First text line point:	**10',-7'**	Specifies the text's starting point
Second text line point:	**@15'10<0**	Specifies the text's ending point
Text:	**A Conglomerate Development**	Specifies the text to be added to the drawing

The results of this command sequence appear in figure 10.5.

Fig. 10.5.
The Align
option
stretches text
to fit between
two points.

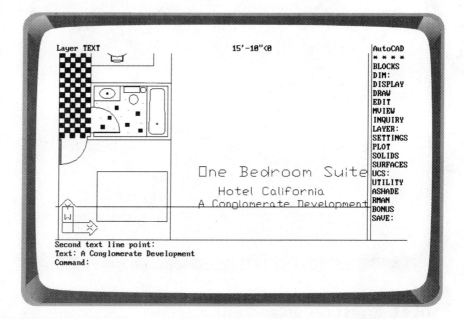

By using the Align option, you made "A Conglomerate Development" fit in the same amount of space as "One Bedroom Suite." AutoCAD doesn't ask for the height or rotation angle because they are determined by the two points you pick. If you pick the finish point to the left of the start point, you end up with upside-down text.

The Fit option is similar to Align, except that AutoCAD lets you specify the text height. AutoCAD adjusts the width of the text so that the text string fits between the two points, but this option can result in some unusually squeezed or compressed-looking text. Therefore, you should use Fit if you want all text to be the same height; use Align if you want the text to look natural regardless of its height (see fig. 10.6).

Other Justification Options

Like a word processor, AutoCAD lets you right-justify your text. You can align text to the right by using the Right option. The prompts are similar to the Center option.

Release 11 adds nine justification options that let you place text by a combination of the top, middle, bottom, left, center, and right edges. If you want to place text in the middle of the bedroom, you could use the MC (short for middle center) justification option. AutoCAD will place the text centered about the middle of the insertion point you pick. The text is centered both horizontally and vertically. All the other "two-letter" justification options work similarly, and several duplicate the one-letter justifications.

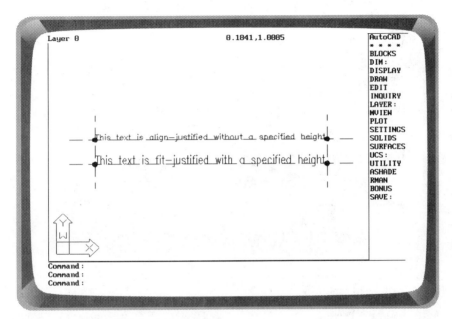

Fig. 10.6.
The Align and Fit justifications force text between two points.

Customizing Fonts (Text Style)

The Style option lets you specify the name of a customized font that AutoCAD uses for the text. AutoCAD features 22 built-in fonts, ranging from a spartan-looking font called TXT to the clean-looking RomanS (short for *Roman single-stroke*) to Old-English Gothic lettering and symbols (see fig. 10.7). So far, you've been using the TXT font, which is automatically loaded into every new AutoCAD drawing.

Before you can use a different font, you have to load it into AutoCAD by using the Style command, which is different from the Text Style option. The Style command is discussed later in this chapter.

Repeating the Text Command

Once you have entered a line of text, you can reuse the same values for the text's rotation angle and height. As mentioned, you can just press Enter to reuse the last height and angle you specified.

Fig. 10.7.
Three of
AutoCAD's
built-in fonts.

You can save those keystrokes by pressing Enter, instead of typing the Text command again:

```
Command: Press Enter
Justify/Style/<Start point>: Press Enter
Text:
```

Here's a way to speed up the text-entry process, when you need to enter several lines of text: Type the first line of the paragraph to set up the options (height and angle) for the following lines. When you finish the first line, press Enter to get back to the Command: prompt.

Now press Enter twice to repeat the Text command a second time and have AutoCAD skip over the options. Notice how AutoCAD highlights the most recently entered line of text. The highlighting helps you spot the last line's location. The new line of text will be placed immediately below it, using the same justification as before.

Using Special Characters in Text

Besides letters, numbers, characters, and spaces, you can include *control codes* in your text. Control codes are special characters that add underlining and symbols to the text. You can use the following control codes in AutoCAD:

Code	Character
%%o	Overscore
%%u	Underscore
%%d	Degree symbol
%%p	Plus/minus symbol
%%c	Diameter symbol
%%%	Percent sign
%%*nnn*	ASCII character with decimal code *nnn*

Tech note . . .

AutoCAD's text fonts normally use only the first 126 ASCII characters. You can, however, customize the text font files to go beyond ASCII 126. To access these characters, use the *%%nnn* code. For example, use %%130 to insert ASCII 130. If the code is not defined, AutoCAD inserts a question mark (?) in the text.

The following command sequence shows you how to use these special codes:

Prompt	Response	Explanation
Command:	Text	Starts the Text command
Text Justify/Style/ <Start point>:	Pick a point on the screen	Specifies the text's insertion point
Height:	6"	Sets the text height
Text:	**%%oOverscore%%o and %%uunderlined%%u text**	Use %%u and %%o to underline and overscore text
Command:	Press Enter	Repeats the Text command
Justify/Style/ <Start point>:	Press Enter	Skips option selection
Text:	**The degree symbol: 90.0%%d**	Use %%d to insert a degree symbol
Command:	Press Enter	Repeats the Text command
Justify/Style/ <Start point>:	Press Enter	Skips option selection

Prompt	Response	Explanation
Text:	The diameter symbol: 4.60"%%c	Use %%c to insert a diameter symbol
Command:	Press Enter	Repeats the Text command
Justify/Style/ <Start point>:	Press Enter	Skips option selection
Text:	The tolerance symbol: %%p0.005"	Use %%p to insert a plus/minus symbol

The text entries appear in figure 10.8.

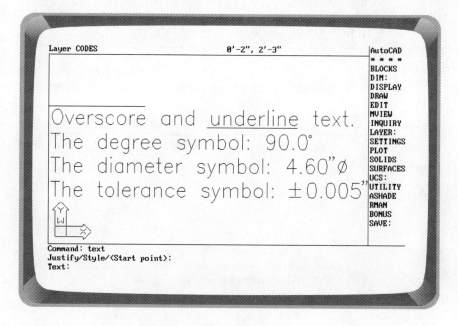

Fig. 10.8. Control codes let you add special symbols to text.

If you want to erase this text, use the Undo command repeatedly until the text is gone.

Editing Text

You can use the Change command (which was introduced in Chapter 9) to modify text. You can change the insertion point, style, height, rotation angle, and the text itself. Now, change the logo "A Conglomerate Development" to "An Environment-friendly Development," and watch AutoCAD "ghost" the changes as you work through the Change command:

Prompt	Response	Explanation
Command:	**Change**	Starts the Change command
Select objects:	Pick text	Specifies the text to be modified
1 selected, 1 found		
Select objects:	Press Enter	Ends object selection
Properties/<Change point>:	Press Enter	Skips the Change options
Enter text insertion point:	Press Enter	Maintains the same insertion point
Text style: STANDARD	Press Enter	Maintains the same text style
New style or RETURN for no change:	Press Enter	
New text <A Conglomerate Development>:	**An Environment-friendly Development**	Specifies a replacement text string

The only property that cannot be changed is the justification (Center, Align, and so on). If you want to change the justification, you must erase the text and retype it from scratch.

If you use Release 11, you also can use the Ddedit (Dynamic Dialogue EDIT) command, which makes text editing much easier. When you issue Ddedit, AutoCAD displays the following prompt:

    <Select a TEXT or ATTDEF object>/Undo:

After you pick a line of text (or an attribute), AutoCAD displays a dialogue box that contains the text (see fig. 10.9). When you pick the point you need to correct, AutoCAD places a block cursor there. You then can use the left- and right-arrow keys to move the cursor along the line of text.

You can use Ddedit to edit only one line of text (or attribute data) at a time. If you make a mess of the editing, or change your mind, you can use the Undo option.

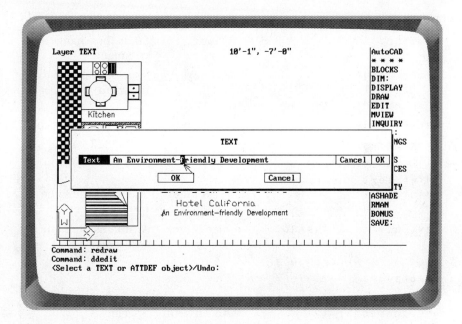

Fig. 10.9.
The Ddedit
command's
dialogue box.

Defining a Text Font (Style)

Like a desktop publishing package, AutoCAD can use many different fonts. As mentioned previously, AutoCAD features 22 built-in fonts, but many more are available from third-party suppliers.

If you want to use a different text font, you need to use AutoCAD's Style command to load the desired font into the drawing. The Style command lets you customize the font into a particular style. When you ask AutoCAD to load a font into a drawing, the program prompts for the following information:

- ❏ The style name for this font customization
- ❏ The name of the font
- ❏ The text height
- ❏ The width factor
- ❏ The slant angle
- ❏ How the text should be oriented: backward, upside down, or vertically

You generally will press Enter in response to most of these questions. The following command sequence shows how the Style command works:

Prompt	Response	Explanation
`Command:`	**Style**	Starts the Style command
`Text style name (or ?)`	**LARGE**	Specifies a name for the customized font
`Select Font File <TXT>:`	Pick Romans and OK	Specifies the file containing the font definition (In Release 10, you must type in the file name "Romans" when you are prompted `Font file <TXT>:`.)
`Height <0'-0">:`	**0**	Sets a text height of 0
`Width factor <1.00>:`	**.85**	Sets a value by which AutoCAD will compress (or stretch) the letters
`Obliquing angle <0.0>:`	**15**	Sets a slant value in degrees
`Backwards? <N>`	Press Enter	Tells AutoCAD not to draw the letters backwards
`Upside-down? <N>`	Press Enter	Tells AutoCAD not to draw the letters upside-down
`Vertical? <N>`	Press Enter	Tells AutoCAD not to draw the letters vertically

You have just created a customized text style, called Large, and made it the current text style. Large is a modified version of the RomanS text font. By modifying AutoCAD's built-in text fonts, you can create many different styles. The Standard style (using the TXT font) is always present when you create a new drawing.

You can give your customized fonts any name you like; the font name can contain up to 31 characters.

If you enter **?** (instead of giving a style name), AutoCAD lists the style names already loaded into the drawing. The list looks like this:

```
Style name (or ?) <Large>: ?
Text styles:

Style name: LARGE Font files: romans
    Height: 0.0000 Width factor: 0.85        Obliquing angle: 0
```

```
Generation: Normal

Style name: STANDARD     Font files: txt
   Height: 0.0000 Width factor: 1.00      Obliquing angle: 0
   Generation: Normal

Current text style: LARGE
```

The `Font file` is the name of the font file used to create the style. Font files are stored on the hard disk with an SHX extension. This file contains the information that defines what each character looks like. Appendix E lists the names and sample text of the fonts included with AutoCAD. For this example, you are currently using a file called ROMANS.SHX.

The Height option lets you set two kinds of heights: variable or fixed. If you enter a height of 0, AutoCAD asks you for a text height each time you use the Text command. If you enter a height (such as 6"), AutoCAD does not ask for a height during the Text command and always prints the Large text at a height of 6".

Text entry can go much more quickly if you first load three styles in your drawing, each with a fixed height. For example, you might load a customized "Large" font with a height of 24", a "Medium" font with a height of 12", and a "Small" font with a height of 6". At 1/4"=1' scale, these fonts plot out as 2", 1", and 1/2" text. By standardizing the height, you save yourself from repeatedly answering the height prompt in the Text command.

The Width factor option lets you compress or stretch the width of all characters in this style. The default of 1 means that the characters are not modified. You can squeeze more text (without making the text look squeezed) into a fixed space by using a width factor of 0.85.

You can give the characters a slanted look by setting the obliquing angle between -15 and 15 degrees (see fig. 10.10). All text entered with this style will have that slant. If you enter an obliquing angle of more than 15 degrees, AutoCAD uses 15 degrees as the angle. The default of 0 degrees leaves the text upright.

The Style command's final three options—Backwards, Upside-down, and Vertical—make the text print in those directions. Most of the AutoCAD-supplied fonts can use these options, but a few, like the map and musical symbols, do not. Most users generally do not need these options, but they are available if you want to use them.

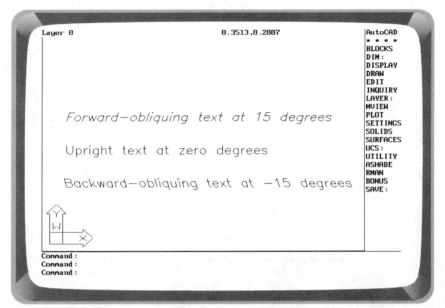

Fig. 10.10.
AutoCAD lets
you slant text
up to 15
degrees.

Defining Fonts from a Pull-down Menu

If your system can use AutoCAD's pull-down menus, you have an easier
way to load fonts than by using the Style command. Pick the Options pull-
down menu, the DTEXT OPTIONS selection, then Text Font. (If you use
Release 10, pick Options and then Fonts.) AutoCAD displays an *icon
menu* of the available font styles (see fig. 10.11).

The icon menu displays an icon, or a graphical representation, of each
available text style. When you select a style (by picking the box next to the
icon), AutoCAD automatically loads the font file and names the style for
you. You just need to answer the Style command's prompts, starting with
text height.

To prepare for the next section, pick Roman Simplex, give the style a
height of 0, a width factor of 0.85, and press Enter at the remaining four
prompts. The newly selected text font affects only text you add from now
on. To change existing text to the new font (or style), either use the
Change command or redefine the style with the Style command. If you
want to see more fonts, pick the Next box. To exit from the icon menu,
pick Exit.

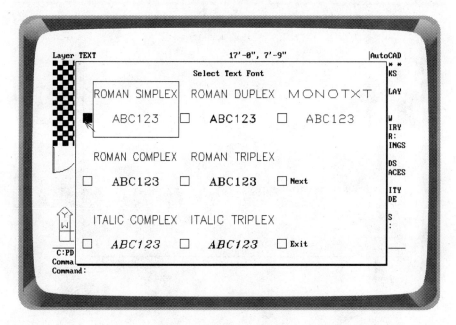

Fig. 10.11.
The Select
Text Font icon
menu.

Dynamically Adding Text (Dtext)

The Dtext (Dynamic text) command enables you to enter several lines of text at once, without needing to repeat the Text command. The lines of text can be sequential (as in a paragraph) or scattered about the drawing. You also can use Dtext to do crude editing of previous lines of text without issuing the Change command.

Dtext has the same options as the Text command:

```
Justify/Style/<Start point>:
```

These options operate in exactly the same manner as the Text command's options.

On-screen you will notice that Dtext acts differently than the Text command when you add text to the drawing (see fig. 10.12). When you start typing the text, a small white box appears in the Drawing Editor at the text's insertion point. The box functions as a cursor, to show you where the text will be placed. AutoCAD displays the text on the screen as you type. Although this lets you see that the text is placed correctly, it works correctly only with left-justified text. Text of any other justification (centered, right, and so on) displays left-justified until you finish using the Dtext command. Then AutoCAD erases the text and reprints it at the correct justification.

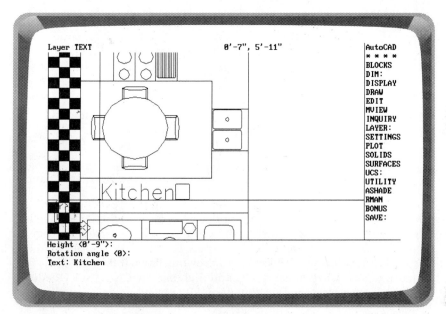

Fig. 10.12.
The Dtext
command
displays a box
cursor and the
text as you
type.

Now, use the Dtext command to name the suite's bathroom, bedroom, and kitchen, as follows:

Prompt	Response	Explanation
`Command:`	**Dtext**	Starts the Dtext command
`Justify/Style/<start point>:`	**J**	Selects the Justify option
`Align/Fit/Center/.../BR:`	**C**	Selects the Center option
`Center point:`	Pick the center of the bathroom	Specifies the text's insertion point
`Height <0'0">:`	**9"**	Sets the text height to 9"
`Rotation angle <0>:`	Press Enter	Accepts the default response of 0, telling AutoCAD to display the text horizontally
`Text:`	**Bathroom**	Specifies the text to be added to the drawing

Prompt	Response	Explanation
Text:	Move the cursor to the bedroom, pick a point, and type **Bedroom**	The Dtext command repeats, enabling you to enter another line of text without specifying new text options
Text:	Move the cursor to the kitchen, pick a point, and type **Kitchen**	The Dtext command repeats again
Text:	Press Enter	Ends the Dtext command

Dtext lets you edit incorrect text more easily than the Text command does. As you enter text, you might notice an error. Use the Backspace key to go back over the text to correct the error. As you backspace to reach the error, you erase the text you just typed. If your error is more than one line back, Dtext lets you backspace to previous lines. If the mistake is too far back, it is easier to finish typing and then use the Change or Ddedit commands to correct the line containing the error.

Hiding Text (Qtext)

As you already have learned, the more complex a drawing becomes, the more time AutoCAD requires to regenerate the drawing. Text is a complex object in many AutoCAD drawings. Fonts such as TXT and RomanS are simple and regenerate quickly. Complex fonts like RomanT and Gothic take much longer. Chapter 9 showed you how to decrease drawing regeneration time by using the Layer Freeze command on layers you don't need to see. This lets AutoCAD bypass entities on frozen layers when regenerating the drawing. If you find that text takes a long time to regenerate, you can freeze the layer that contains the text, but you will no longer be able to see the text's location. AutoCAD provides an alternative, called *quick text*, that shows the text's location (by drawing rectangles that outline each line of text) without actually displaying the text.

Whichever text style you choose, you can use the Qtext command to reduce the time needed for text to be regenerated, thereby saving time when the rest of the drawing must be regenerated.

The Qtext command draws a rectangular box where the text string normally is displayed. The text is still in the drawing database, but it is not regenerated on the screen—only the box is displayed. This box is the same height and a similar width to the text that normally would occupy that location in the drawing. Qtext's only value is on or off. Practice using Qtext now:

```
Command: Qtext
ON/OFF <off>: ON
Command: Regen
```

You must specify ON if you want boxes to be drawn (see fig. 10.13) and OFF if you want the text to be displayed normally. Qtext affects every piece of text in the drawing. After you use the Qtext command, you must use the Regen command to display the text in its new format.

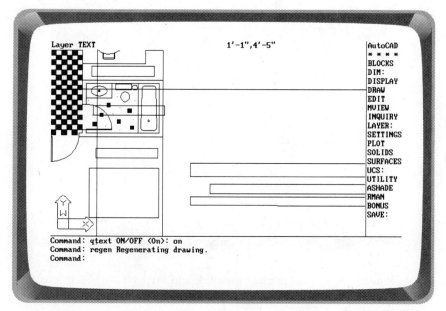

Fig. 10.13.
The Qtext command replaces text with boxes to reduce regeneration time.

Be aware that Qtext's outline rectangles are only approximations of the text's length. A rectangle may be longer (or shorter) than the actual length of a line of text.

TIP

Qtext's boxes can become annoying after a while, especially when you cannot remember what the text is supposed to say. If you want to avoid using Qtext altogether (many AutoCAD users do avoid using it), you can have text applying to different parts of the drawing on different layers. For example, place title block's text on its own layer, which you can then freeze when you do not need to see it.

Adding Hatching to a Drawing

Hatch patterns indicate material types on a drawing. The pattern can be anything from a brick wall to a cross-section of a steel part to marshlands (see fig. 10.14). Manual drafters often have trouble drawing even-looking hatch lines. AutoCAD makes hatching easy by doing it for you. With the Hatch command, you can use any one of AutoCAD's 53 built-in patterns, or you can design your own. See Appendix C for the complete list of AutoCAD's built-in hatch patterns.

Fig. 10.14.
Some of
AutoCAD's
built-in hatch
patterns.

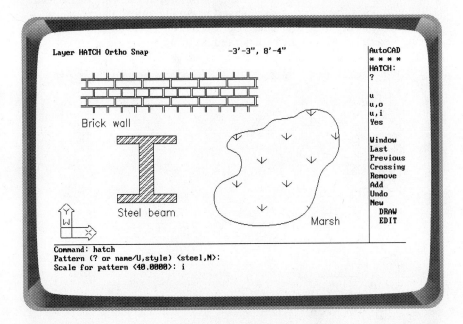

Before you try using the Hatch command, add lines to the bed to create the effect of sheets. (Hint: the folded-back sheet was drawn with the Mirror command.)

Hatching Areas (Hatch)

The Hatch command adds a pattern of lines to an enclosed area. When you type **Hatch** at the `Command:` prompt, AutoCAD presents the following options:

```
Pattern (? or name/U,style):
```

The Pattern option lets you enter the name of a predefined pattern.

The ? option lists the names of patterns included in the hatch pattern file ACAD.PAT.

U lets you define a hatch pattern on the fly.

You also can press Enter to skip the hatch questions.

To prepare for the next section, you need to draw a boundary to contain the hatching. To make the job simpler, turn on the INTersection object snap (object snap is discussed in detail in Chapter 11), as follows:

Prompt	Response	Explanation
`Command:`	**Osnap**	Starts the Osnap command
`Object snap modes:`	**INT**	Specifies the INTersection object snap override
`Command:`	**Pline**	Starts the Pline command
`From point:`	Pick a corner of the bedspread	Specifies the polyline's starting point
`Current line-width is 0.0000` `Arc/.../<Endpoint of line>:`	Pick next corner of the bedspread	
`Arc/.../<Endpoint of line>:`	Continue to pick corners in order	
`Arc/.../<Endpoint of line>:`		
`Arc/.../<Endpoint of line>:`		
`Arc/.../<Endpoint of line>:`		
`Arc/.../<Endpoint of line>:`	**C**	Closes the polyline
`Command:`	**Osnap**	Turns off object snap
`Object snap modes: off`		

Using Predefined Patterns

To use a predefined pattern, type its name at the prompt. You can give the bedspread a pinstripe pattern by following these steps:

Prompt	Response	Explanation
`Command:`	**Hatch**	Starts the Hatch command
`Pattern (? or name/` `U,style):`	**PLASTI**	Specifies the name of the predefined hatch pattern to be added to the drawing

Prompt	Response	Explanation
`Scale for pattern <1.0>:`	**48**	Sets the pattern's scale (a scale of 1 is normal size)
`Angle for pattern <0>:`	Press Enter	Accepts the default response of 0, which adds the pattern at its normal angle of rotation
`Select objects:`	**L**	Selects the last entity drawn, which is the polyline outline of the bedspread
`1 found`		
`Select objects:`	Press Enter	Ends the Hatch command

The bedspread now has a pinstripe pattern (see fig. 10.15). When the hatch pattern is drawn, it may be too large or too small for the area you are trying to hatch. You can correct the problem by using the Undo command (to erase the hatching) and then assigning a different scale to the hatch pattern. To do this, just reissue the Hatch command and enter a different value at the `Scale for pattern <1.0>:` prompt. A larger number increases the spacing between hatch lines; a smaller number decreases the spacing.

Fig. 10.15.
Hatching gives
the bedspread
a pinstripe
pattern.

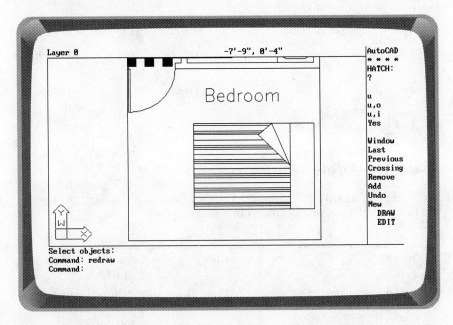

Large areas of hatch patterns drawn at a small scale take up a lot of room in the drawing file, consuming disk space and making regeneration times very long. To avoid these problems, you can place the hatching on its own layer, and keep the layer frozen when not needed. Otherwise, you should try to hatch sample patches over the large area.

If the hatch boundary is complex, you may want to trace the boundary with a polyline drawn on a separate layer. Use the polyline as the boundary for the hatching (which is drawn on yet another layer), and then turn off the polyline layer.

Hatch patterns are drawn in reference to the X axis. If you want the hatching rotated to a different angle, enter the rotation angle at the `Angle for pattern <0>:` prompt.

Using Hatching Styles (Hatch Style)

When you select the objects you want hatched, you should be aware of the rules AutoCAD applies to hatching. The first rule is that the entities you pick must form a closed boundary. Circles and closed polylines are great for this. If you use lines and arcs, be sure they all connect end-to-end; otherwise the hatching will "leak" out and cover most of the drawing.

The second thing to remember is that you must select all the boundaries that delineate the hatched area. Because you may find it tricky dealing with areas internal to a hatching boundary, the Hatch command offers the Style option. AutoCAD provides three styles of hatching (see fig. 10.16):

❏ **Normal** hatches every other selected hatch boundary, working from the outside in.

❏ **Outermost** hatches only the outermost selected boundary.

❏ **Ignore** hatches everything inside the outermost hatch boundary.

You specify the hatching style as part of the pattern name. For example, to specify the outermost style with the Plasti pattern, you would type the following:

```
Command: Hatch
Pattern (? or name/U, style): Plasti, O
```

This command sequence tells AutoCAD to hatch the outermost areas with the Plasti pattern.

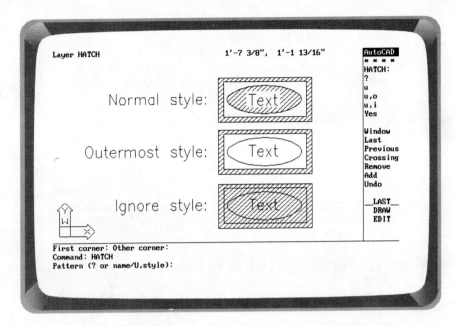

Fig. 10.16.
The Hatch
Style
command lets
you control
hatching in
three ways.

The Normal and Outermost styles hatch around text, solids, and attributes if they are part of the hatch boundary selection set; Ignore hatches over text, solids, and attributes.

If you are working with blocks, AutoCAD selects an entire block and hatches according to the individual entities contained in that block. For proper hatching of a block, you may need to hatch areas before creating the block. (Blocks are discussed in more detail in Chapter 12.)

Getting a Listing of Pattern Names (Hatch ?)

Remember that AutoCAD has 53 built-in hatch patterns, and you can design patterns of your own. If you use hatch patterns often, you may find it difficult to remember the names of all the patterns. If you are unsure of the pattern names, you can either look in Appendix C of this book or use the Hatch command's ? option, as follows:

```
Command: Hatch
Pattern (? or name/U,style): ?
Pattern(s) to list <*>: Press Enter
```

AutoCAD lists all the hatch patterns contained in the ACAD.PAT file (see fig. 10.17).

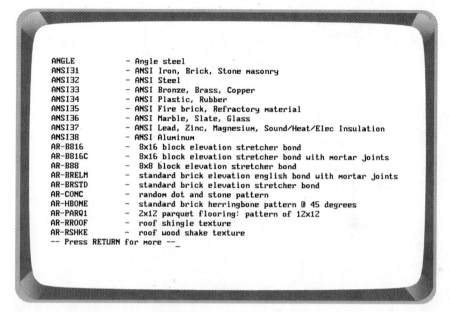

```
ANGLE          - Angle steel
ANSI31         - ANSI Iron, Brick, Stone masonry
ANSI32         - ANSI Steel
ANSI33         - ANSI Bronze, Brass, Copper
ANSI34         - ANSI Plastic, Rubber
ANSI35         - ANSI Fire brick, Refractory material
ANSI36         - ANSI Marble, Slate, Glass
ANSI37         - ANSI Lead, Zinc, Magnesium, Sound/Heat/Elec Insulation
ANSI38         - ANSI Aluminum
AR-B816        - 8x16 block elevation stretcher bond
AR-B816C       - 8x16 block elevation stretcher bond with mortar joints
AR-B88         - 8x8 block elevation stretcher bond
AR-BRELM       - standard brick elevation english bond with mortar joints
AR-BRSTD       - standard brick elevation stretcher bond
AR-CONC        - random dot and stone pattern
AR-HBONE       - standard brick herringbone pattern @ 45 degrees
AR-PARQ1       - 2x12 parquet flooring: pattern of 12x12
AR-RROOF       - roof shingle texture
AR-RSHKE       - roof wood shake texture
-- Press RETURN for more --_
```

*Fig. 10.17.
The Hatch ?
command lists
the hatch
patterns in the
ACAD.PAT file.*

If you want to use one of the patterns, re-enter the Hatch command and then enter the desired pattern's name at the Pattern (? or name/ U,style) prompt.

Creating A Pattern on the Fly (Hatch U, style)

To create a simple hatch pattern out of straight lines, select U,style (the U stands for *user-defined*). AutoCAD asks for the angle of lines (relative to the X axis), the spacing between lines, and whether you want the area to be double-hatched.

Practice creating a user-specified hatch pattern now:

Prompt	Response	Explanation
Command:	**Hatch**	Starts the Hatch command
Pattern (? or name/ U,style):	**U,O**	Specifies a user-defined pattern that does an outermost hatch
Angle for crosshatch lines <0>:	**45**	Specifies a hatching angle of 45 degrees

Prompt	Response	Explanation
`Spacing between lines <1.0000>:`	2	Sets a spacing of 2" between the hatch lines
`Double hatch area? <N>:`	Press Enter	Tells AutoCAD not to cross-hatch the area
`Select objects:`	Pick the bathroom walls	Specifies the area to be hatched

You may need to zoom in before picking the bathroom walls. The result of this command sequence appears in figure 10.18.

Fig. 10.18. Hatching the bathroom walls with a custom-made pattern.

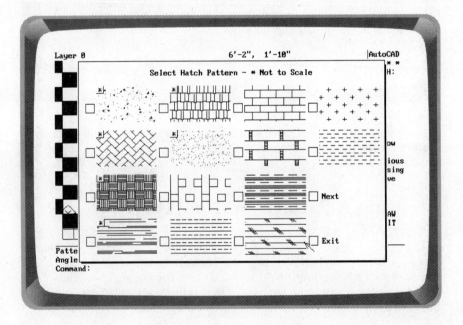

You can specify hatching style (Normal, Outermost, or Ignore) when you select the U option. If the hatching leaks out, create a new layer and trace around the walls with a single polyline, using the Close option to seal it shut.

Using the Hatch Icon Menu

The Hatch Options pull-down menu simplifies your use of the Hatch command by showing you each available hatch pattern. To see and select a pattern, pick the Options menu, choose HATCH OPTIONS, and finally Hatch Patterns. When you do, you will see a series of screens like the one shown in figure 10.19. Use your pointing device to pick the box next to the pattern you want.

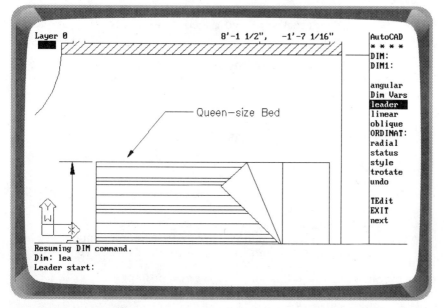

Fig. 10.19.
The Hatch
icon menu
shows
AutoCAD's
hatch
patterns.

Dimensioning

Even though you can create extremely accurate drawings with AutoCAD,
any drawing's dimensions need to be noted. If dimensions are added to
the drawing, its users can see critical information such as lengths, widths,
angles, clearances, and tolerances without measuring them. AutoCAD's
dimensioning mode gives you a fast, accurate system of calculating and
annotating this information.

In manual drafting, dimensioning is typically the last step in the drawing
process. Because you are working in AutoCAD's unique drawing
environment, however, you can add dimensioning to your drawing at any
time. Because dimensions are like any other entity within a drawing, they
can be stretched, erased, copied, and changed as the drawing develops.
You can make the dimensions fit your own style of annotation.

The next few pages show you how to use dimensions and how to
customize them to suit your needs. The two commands that put you into
dimensioning mode are Dim and Dim1. Dim puts AutoCAD into
dimension mode until you exit from it; when dimension mode is active,
the Command: prompt is replaced by the Dim: prompt. Dim1 lets you
execute a single dimensioning command and then returns you to the
Command: prompt.

These are not the only commands involved in dimensioning.
AutoCAD has 19 dimensioning subcommands and several variables

associated with dimensioning. The large number of options can seem intimidating until you realize that you need only a few of them, at least when you are starting out.

The following sections teach you how to use AutoCAD's dimensioning subcommands. At the end of this chapter, you will see how AutoCAD's system variables can change the way dimensioning works for you.

Entering Dimensioning Mode (Dim and Dim1)

AutoCAD separates dimensioning from all other operations, and gives you a separate set of subcommands and system variables that work only when you are adding dimensions to your drawing. Drawing and editing commands cannot be used when you are in dimensioning mode, nor can the dimensioning subcommands be used from the Command: prompt.

As mentioned already, the familiar Command: prompt changes to Dim: when you enter dimensioning mode. The new prompt lets you know which mode is active and which commands you can use. When you want to leave dimensioning mode and work with other commands, press Ctrl-C or type **EXIT** at the Dim: prompt. Either method returns you to AutoCAD's Command: prompt.

AutoCAD's dimensioning subcommands can be divided into six groups, as follows:

Type of Dimension	Related Dimensioning Subcommands
Linear	HORizontal, VERtical, ALIgned, ROTated, BASeline, CONtinue
Circular	RADius, DIAmeter
Angular	ANGular
Ordinate	Ordinate
Associative	HOMetext, NEWtext, UPDate, OBLique, OVErride, REStore, SAVe, TEDit, TROtate, VARiables
Utilities	CENter, EXIt, LEAder, REDraw, STAtus, STYle, UNDo

Many subcommands do exactly what their names imply. You use HORizontal for horizontal dimensioning, VERtical for vertical dimensioning, and RADius for indicating the radius of circles. You can type in the full subcommand name or its three-letter abbreviation (denoted by the capital letters). In the following examples, you will use each type of dimensioning on the SUITE drawing.

The Fundamentals of Dimensioning

Each type of AutoCAD dimension consists of (at least) dimension text, dimension lines, arrows, and extension lines (see fig. 10.20).

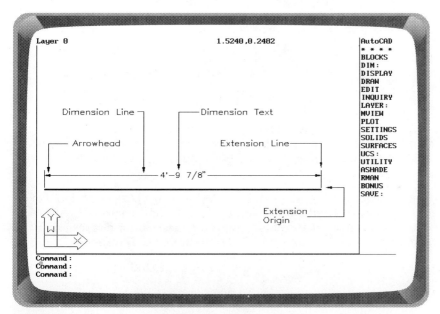

Fig. 10.20. A dimension entity consists of dimension lines, arrows, text, and extension lines.

AutoCAD makes use of two types of dimensions: *normal* and *associative*. AutoCAD draws normal dimensions as individual entities. That is, in a normal dimension, the dimension text is text, and the dimension lines are lines. Normal dimensions are left over from older versions of AutoCAD.

Associative dimensioning—now AutoCAD's default method of creating dimensions—groups each dimension's text, lines, and arrows together into a single entity. You will find it easier to edit this type of entity because the dimension acts as a single object; AutoCAD modifies the dimension text to reflect the change, and automatically redraws the dimension.

With these fundamentals out of the way, you can look at the types of dimensioning available in AutoCAD. First, though, you need to create a new layer in the SUITE drawing on which you can place the dimensions:

```
Command: Layer
?/Make/.../Thaw: M
New current layer <O>: DIM
?/Make/.../Thaw: Press Enter
```

Next, you need to set the scale of dimensions. Scale is discussed in greater detail later in this chapter; for now, just issue the following commands:

```
Command: Dimscale
New value for DIMSCALE <1.0000>: 48
```

Now enter the world of dimensioning by issuing the Dim command.

Single Linear Dimensioning (HORizontal, VERtical, ALIgned, and ROTated)

Linear dimensioning is the most basic type of dimensioning. In linear dimensioning, you measure the distance (vertical, horizontal, or at an angle) from one point to a second point. AutoCAD provides six types of linear dimensioning.

You can start by dimensioning the bed. (You may first want to zoom in on the bedroom, using the transparent 'Zoom Window command.) After you enter HORizontal (or any of the three other basic linear dimensioning commands: VERtical, ALIgned, or ROTated), AutoCAD responds:

```
First extension line origin or RETURN to select:
```

You have two options here: pick a point or press Enter.

Picking an Extension Point

If you specify a point, AutoCAD uses it as the origin for the first extension line. For accurate dimensions, it helps to turn on object snap. You can snap to the endpoint or intersection of lines, the center of a circle, and even the insertion point of text.

After you pick (or supply the coordinates for) the first extension line origin, AutoCAD carries on:

```
First extension line origin or RETURN to select: INT
of Pick lower-left corner of the bed
Second extension line origin: INT
of Pick lower-right corner of bed
Dimension line location: Pick a point below the bed
Dimension text <6'-8">: Press Enter
```

If enough room exists, the dimension text is centered between the extension lines. Otherwise, the text is placed outside the extension lines. You should end up with a dimension as shown in figure 10.21. This sort of dimensioning is called *semi-automatic*. You decide where you want the dimension to go, and AutoCAD measures and draws the dimension for you.

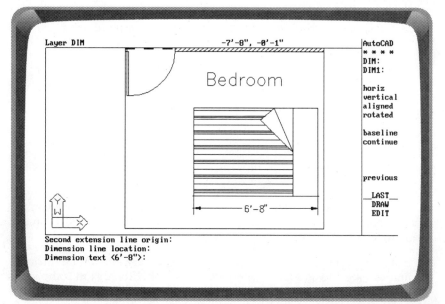

*Fig. 10.21.
The bed is
dimensioned
with the
Dim HOR
command.*

At the `Dimension text:` prompt, AutoCAD gives you an opportunity
to override the dimension it calculated (based on the distance between
the two extension lines). If you draw full-size and accurately, the default
value should be correct: simply press Enter and AutoCAD prints the text
as shown.

You also can type in a value. This value can be any text, including words.
The text is centered within the dimension line or, if there is not enough
room between the extension lines, to the side of the line.

TIP

You can use transparent commands within the `Dim:` environment,
such as 'Zoom W and 'Pan.

Picking Other Entities

If you press Enter at the `First extension line origin or
RETURN to select` prompt, AutoCAD responds as follows:

    Select line, arc, or circle:

This prompt provides a fast alternative to dimensioning a single object.
AutoCAD asks you to pick a line, an arc, or a circle. For lines and arcs,
AutoCAD uses their endpoints for the first and second extension lines.

If you pick a circle, the diameter of the circle is dimensioned. How it's dimensioned depends on the type of dimensioning you are using, as follows:

❏ HORizontal: at 0 degrees

❏ VERtical: at 90 degrees

❏ ROTated: at an angle you define

❏ ALIgned: at the point you where picked the circle

VERtical calculates a vertical dimension, the Y-axis distance between two points. VER uses the same prompts as HOR to define a dimension. Try using VER to dimension the foot of the bed.

HOR and VER calculate only horizontal and vertical distances. It doesn't matter what angle the object is at. To place a dimension at the same angle as an angled object, use the ALIgned subcommand.

ALI places the dimension line parallel to an imaginary line drawn through the first and second extension-line pick points. The dimension is the true distance from the first point to the second point. The prompts are the same as for the HOR and VER subcommands.

The tub's insides are drawn at an angle to show how ALI works. Figure 10.22 shows the difference between dimensioning the inside with VER and ALI.

Fig. 10.22.
The Dim ALI
subcommand
measures the
true distance
of angled lines
on the left side
of the tub,
while VER
measures the
true vertical
distance on
the right side
of the tub.

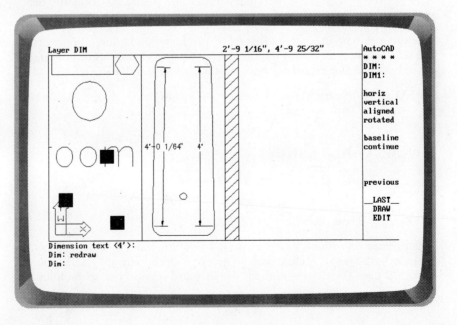

Practice using VER and ALI to measure the angled lines in the tub:

Prompt	Response	Explanation
`Command:`	**Dim**	Starts the Dim command
`Dim:`	**VER**	Starts vertical dimensioning
`First extension line origin or RETURN to select:`	**END**	Tells AutoCAD to use the ENDpoint object snap override
`of`	Pick the top end of the left inner tub line	Specifies the origin of the first extension line
`Second extension line origin:`	**END**	Tells AutoCAD to use the ENDpoint object snap override
`of`	Pick the bottom end of the same tub line	Specifies the origin of the second extension line
`Dimension text <4'-0 1/64">`	Press Enter	Accepts the default response, which is the vertical length of the line, as calculated by AutoCAD
`Dim:`	**ALI**	Starts aligned dimensioning
`First extension line origin or RETURN to select:`	**END**	Tells AutoCAD to use the ENDpoint object snap override
`of`	Pick the top end of the the right inner tub line	Specifies the origin of the first extension line

Prompt	Response	Explanation
`Second extension line origin:`	**END**	Tells AutoCAD to use the ENDpoint object snap override
`of`	Pick the bottom end of the same tub line	Specifies the origin of the second extension line
`Dimension text <4'>:`	Press Enter	Accepts the default response, which is the length of the angled line as calculated by AutoCAD

The ROTated subcommand lets you set a rotation angle for the dimensioning. This option is useful if you want to dimension an object that is not horizontal or vertical, and you do not want to align the dimension (see fig. 10.23).

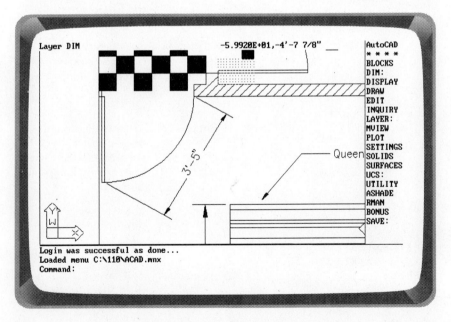

Fig. 10.23. The ROT subcommand dimensions the path of the bedroom door.

When you enter the ROT command, AutoCAD first displays the following prompt:

`Dimension line angle <0.0>:`

Enter the angle at which you want the dimension line to appear. With ROT, the dimension is measured between the extension line origins at the angle you define.

Practice using ROT to dimension the bedroom door's swing arc, as follows:

Prompt	Response	Explanation
Command:	**Dim**	Starts the Dim command
Dim:	**ROT**	Starts rotated dimensioning
Dimension line angle:	**60**	Sets the dimensioning at an angle of 60 degrees from the X axis
First extension line origin or RETURN to select:	Press Enter	Switches to entity dimensioning
Select line, arc, or circle:	Pick the bedroom door swing arc	Specifies the entity to be dimensioned
Dimension line location:	Pick a point below the arc	Tells AutoCAD to place the dimension below the arch
Dimension text <3'5">:	Press Enter	Accepts the length of the arc, as calculated by AutoCAD

Multiple Linear Dimensioning (BASeline and CONtinue)

The BASeline and CONtinue subcommands let you draw more than one dimension at a time. After you draw one linear dimension, you can use the BASeline command to draw subsequent linear dimensions (all moving in the same direction) that start at the first extension line of the first dimension. BASeline makes all its measurements from this first point to any subsequent extension points you choose.

CONtinue uses the second extension line of the previous dimension as the first extension line of the next dimension. This lets you draw a chain of dimensions, one right after the other.

Practice using the BAS and CON dimensioning subcommands on the right wall of the apartment. Because BAS and CON take reference points from the previous dimensions, you can use them only after another dimension has been entered. Use VER to set the initial dimension; then use BAS and CON to finish the dimensioning. After practicing with BAS (see fig. 10.24), use the UNDo command twice and then practice using CON (see fig. 10.25).

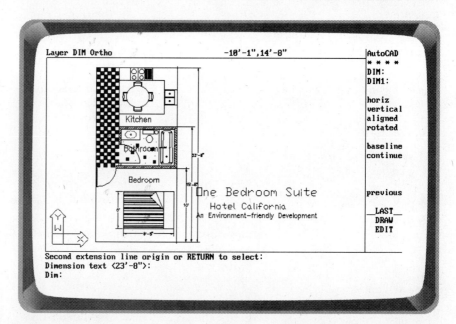

Fig. 10.24.
The Dim
BASeline
subcommand
draws all
linear
dimensions
from a
common
baseline.

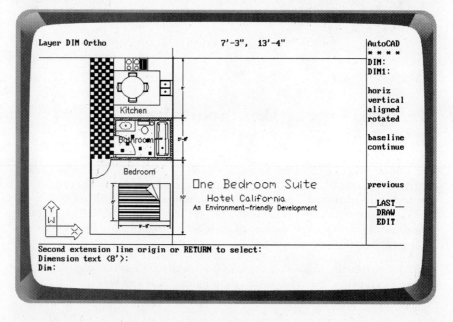

Fig. 10.25.
The Dim
CONtinue
subcommand
uses the
previous
dimension's
second
extension line
as the first
extension line
for the next
dimension.

In Release 10, BAS or CON only work immediately after you have drawn a dimension. In Release 11, you can begin a BAS or CON Dim by selecting any existing dimension.

When you select the second extension line origin and AutoCAD displays the `Dimension text <#>:` prompt, you should press Enter to accept the text. You should not press the space bar. If you use the space bar to accept the text, the dimension line appears with no text on it.

Circular Dimensioning (RADius and DIAmeter)

The RADius and DIAmeter subcommands draw dimensions for circle (and arc) radii and diameters. Both commands share common prompts.

Practice using RADius on one of the stove's burners:

Prompt	Response	Explanation
`Dim:`	**RAD**	Starts the Radius subcommand
`Select arc or circle:`	Pick a stove burner	Selects a circle to be dimensioned
`Dimension text <0'-4">:`	Press Enter	Accepts the default dimension text
`Enter leader length for text:`	Pick a point and press Enter	Positions the leader (the arrow that points from the object to the dimension)

Pick the circle or arc you want dimensioned. Be careful: the location of the dimension arrow is determined according to location of the point you pick (see fig. 10.26). As in linear dimensioning, you have the opportunity to override the calculated dimension text. AutoCAD automatically indicates radii with an R and diameters with the diameter symbol.

The DIAmeter subcommand works in much the same way as the RADius subcommand. Practice using DIA on the kitchen table. You should get a diameter of 3', as shown in figure 10.26.

Fig. 10.26.
AutoCAD adds
the radius and
diameter
dimensions;
ANG measures
angles.

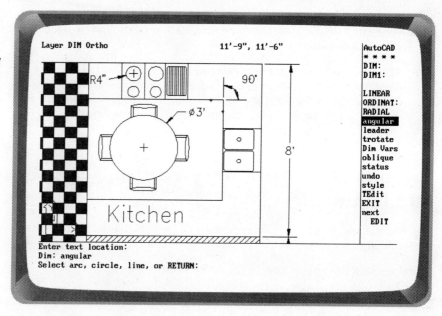

Angular Dimensioning (ANGular)

In angular dimensioning, an angle is measured between two objects. The ANGular subcommand draws the dimension as an arc with an angle between the two lines. The lines do not have to physically intersect for angular dimensioning to work, but they cannot be parallel. AutoCAD considers two lines that meet end-to-end at 180 degrees to be parallel, and will not let you dimension them with the ANGular subcommand.

Use the ANG subcommand to measure the angle of two of the kitchen counter lines:

Prompt	Response	Explanation
Dim:	**ANG**	Starts the ANGular subcommand
Select arc, circle, line, or RETURN:	Pick the upper counter line	Specifies the first line that creates the angle to be dimensioned
Second line:	Pick the right counter line	Specifies the second line that creates the angle to be dimensioned

Prompt	Response	Explanation
`Enter dimension line arc location:`	Pick the point where you want the dimension's arc to be inserted	Specifies the location of the dimension arc
`Dimension text <90>:`	Press Enter	Accepts the default value, which is the degree of the angle as measured by AutoCAD
`Enter text location:`	Pick the point where you want the dimension's text to be inserted	Specifies the location of the dimension text

The resulting dimension is shown in figure 10.26.

The dimension arc generated by the ANG command passes through the point you specify at the `Enter dimension line arc location:` prompt. The arc ends at the two lines you selected to define the angle.

If there isn't enough room for the arc and arrows, AutoCAD displays the message `Arrows don't fit, will be moved outside`. The arrows and arc are placed outside the angle.

Ordinate Dimensioning (ORDinate)

11

ORDinates show coordinates, rather than dimensions. Ordinate dimensions are used by machinists who use lathes and milling machines. These machines determine where to cut from an origin point. Thus, all dimensions need to be relative to the origin. AutoCAD measures the X or Y coordinate of the point you pick:

Prompt	Response	Explanation
`Dim:`	**ORD**	
`Select Feature:`	Pick object	
`Enter leader endpoint (Horizontal/Vertical /Xtype/Ytype):`	**X**	
`Enter leader endpoint:`	Pick point	
`Dimension text <1.25>:`	Press Enter	

When you enter **X**, AutoCAD measures the X coordinate at the picked point and uses it as the origin from which to measure. When you pick the second point, AutoCAD measures the relative coordinate. AutoCAD then draws a leader line and the coordinate value (see fig. 10.27).

Fig. 10.27.
The Dim Ord
command
does ordinate
dimensioning.

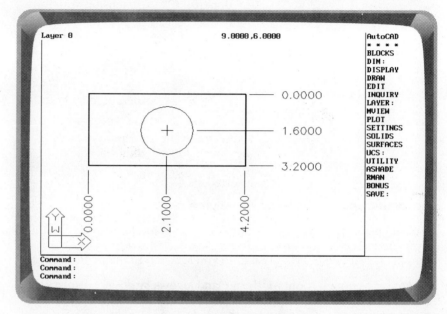

Associative Dimensioning Commands

Associative dimensions are extremely versatile because they change as parts of the drawing change. AutoCAD automatically uses associative dimensions unless you tell it otherwise. The dimensions you entered earlier are all associative.

You can see how associative dimensioning works by using the Stretch command to make the bed longer. Issue the Stretch command and window the head of the bed. Move your pointing device to stretch the head of the bed toward the wall. When you press Enter, AutoCAD automatically updates the length dimension. Because AutoCAD treats all the parts of an associative dimension as a single entity, this type of dimension is a bit more difficult to modify than normal dimensions. AutoCAD provides 10 specialized subcommands to help you deal with associative dimensions.

Modifying Associative Dimensions (HOMetext, NEWtext, and UPDate)

The HOMetext, NEWtext, and UPDate commands affect the way dimension text, arrows, and extension lines appear in associative dimensions.

If the dimension text is in the wrong place, you can easily move it by using the Stretch Crossing command (as discussed in Chapter 6). After you've moved the text, you may want to put it back where it was. The HOMetext command returns the dimension text to its "home" location (usually the center of the dimension line).

The NEWtext subcommand enables you to change the value of the dimension text. After you type in the new text, you are prompted to pick the dimensions that should be modified. The old text is changed to match the new text.

The UPDate command redraws all associative dimensions to reflect the current settings of the dimension variables. These variables change the type of arrow, text style, and other features of a typical dimension all at once. Dimension variables control all aspects of dimensions and are discussed later in this chapter.

Editing Associative Dimensions (OBLique, TEDit, and TROtate)

If you use AutoCAD Release 11, you have access to three more commands that enable you to fine-tune associative dimensions. These commands are OBLique, TEDit, and TROtate.

OBLique lets you set the angle at which extension lines are drawn. Normally, they are drawn at right angles to the dimension line. Angled extension lines are useful when they might otherwise disappear under the lines being measured.

TEDit lets you change the location and angle of associative dimension text, but only one dimension at a time. You can change the text's justification, angle, and location by dynamically dragging the text. The dimension lines and extension lines maintain their current position; you can move only the dimension text itself when you use TEDit.

TROtate sets the angle of the dimension text. You use it after you have dimensioned objects; the command works on a selection set of text.

Associative Dimension Settings (VARiables, SAVe, REStore, and OVErride)

Release 11 users also have access to a series of dimensioning subcommands that can change the settings used with associative dimensions. These subcommands are VARiables, SAVe, REStore, and OVErride.

You can find out the current setting of any dimension variable by using the VARiables subcommand. You can list the variable by name (DIN, for example) or by picking the dimension. If you enter a tilde (~) before the name (as in ~DIN), the command shows the difference between the current setting and the default setting.

SAVe saves your customized dimension settings by name as a Style. REStore reads in the customized setting. If you enter a ? after either of these subcommands, AutoCAD lists the current styles; the ~ shows the differences between the current style and the named style.

OVErride lets you override one or more dimension settings connected with a dimension. If you would like the override to become permanent, AutoCAD can update the Style setting at your request.

Dimension Utility Commands

The dimension utility subcommands are extra features that make dimensioning easier. The subcommands let you clean the screen (with a redraw) or change text styles without exiting from the Dim: environment.

Cleaning Up the Screen (REDraw)

REDraw redraws the screen in the same manner as AutoCAD's regular Redraw command. AutoCAD includes REDraw as part of the dimensioning subcommands so that you do not need to leave the Dim: environment to clean up the screen.

Marking Center Points (CENter)

CENter places a mark at the center of a circle or an arc. The mark can be a cross or a dash, depending on the value of the DIMCEN system variable.

Changing the Text Font (STYle)

STYle changes the text font for dimension text. This lets you use a
different font for dimension text within the Dim environment. For more
information on fonts and font styles, refer to the discussion of the Style
command earlier in this chapter.

Creating Leader Lines (LEAder)

The LEAder subcommand lets you place dimension notes (sometimes
known as *callouts* or *leader lines*) in a drawing (see fig. 10.28). To create
a leader line, enter **Leader** at the Dim: prompt. AutoCAD responds with
the following prompt:

    Leader start:

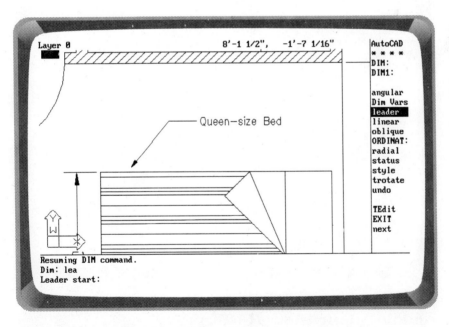

*Fig. 10.28.
The Dim LEA
command lets
you add notes
with arrows to
your drawing.*

At the Leader start: prompt, specify the point in the drawing at
which you want the leader arrow to appear. Use your pointing device to
select the point. At the next prompt, To point:, specify the vertex for
the leader line. You can continue specifying vertices until the leader line
gets to where you need it. When you are satisfied with the leader line,
press Enter without specifying a point. AutoCAD then prompts as follows:

```
Dimension text <current>:
```

Enter the text to be displayed at the end of the leader line. You are
limited to one line of text, although the Text (or Dtext) command can be
used to add more lines of text. AutoCAD uses the last specified dimension
as a default for this text.

Listing Dimension Variables (STAtus)

The STAtus subcommand displays a list of dimensioning variables and
their current value (see fig. 10.29). The variables control the "look" of a
dimension. When used effectively, they can make the process of
dimensioning very easy. The dimensioning variables are discussed in
detail later in this chapter.

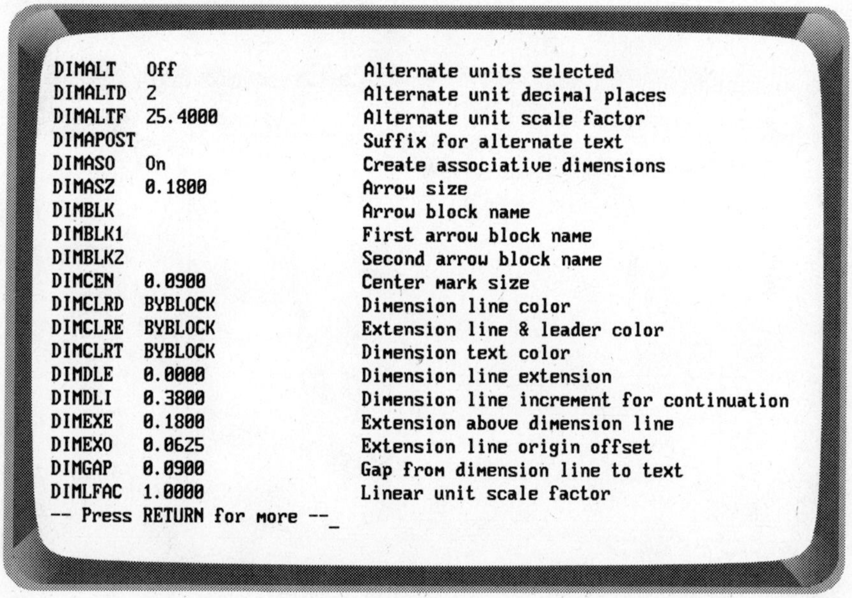

Fig. 10.29.
The Dim STA
command lists
the current
status of all
dimensioning
variables.

```
DIMALT     Off              Alternate units selected
DIMALTD    2                Alternate unit decimal places
DIMALTF    25.4000          Alternate unit scale factor
DIMAPOST                    Suffix for alternate text
DIMASO     On               Create associative dimensions
DIMASZ     0.1800           Arrow size
DIMBLK                      Arrow block name
DIMBLK1                     First arrow block name
DIMBLK2                     Second arrow block name
DIMCEN     0.0900           Center mark size
DIMCLRD    BYBLOCK          Dimension line color
DIMCLRE    BYBLOCK          Extension line & leader color
DIMCLRT    BYBLOCK          Dimension text color
DIMDLE     0.0000           Dimension line extension
DIMDLI     0.3800           Dimension line increment for continuation
DIMEXE     0.1800           Extension above dimension line
DIMEXO     0.0625           Extension line origin offset
DIMGAP     0.0900           Gap from dimension line to text
DIMLFAC    1.0000           Linear unit scale factor
-- Press RETURN for more --_
```

Undoing Dimensions (UNDo)

UNDo, in dimension mode, works like the Undo command you issue at
the Command: prompt. UNDo enables you to undo dimensions by
stepping back through the dimensioning commands you have issued
during the current dimensioning session. If you use dimensioning
subcommands and then use Undo back at the Command: prompt, you
undo the results of the entire dimensioning session.

Leaving the Dim Command (EXIt)

When you issue the EXIt subcommand, AutoCAD leaves dimensioning mode and returns you to the familiar `Command:` prompt. You also can exit from dimensioning mode by pressing Ctrl-C at any time during the dimensioning session.

Controlling Dimensions

AutoCAD uses system variables to control the look of dimensions. You can change any system variable in two ways. The more common method is to enter the variable's name at the `Dim:` prompt. The second method is to use the Setvar command at the `Command:` prompt. (In Release 11, system variables can be entered at the `Command:` prompt without Setvar.) In either case, AutoCAD displays the variable's current setting and prompts you to modify the variable.

The system variables that govern dimensioning can be separated into the following general categories according to what the variables affect:

❏ The dimension in general

❏ Dimension text and lines

❏ Arrow heads

❏ Extension lines

❏ Tolerances and limits

❏ Alternative dimensions

To list all the dimension variables and their values, use the STAtus command, as described previously. The list includes a brief description of each variable and is similar to the list produced when you enter **Setvar DIM*** at the `Command:` prompt.

System variables store information about the current state of the drawing or information that applies to all entities in the drawing. System variables can have a numeric value, or a value such as ON or OFF. Some system variables contain a name as their value. For example, the system variable DIMASO can have a value of ON or OFF. If the variable's value is ON, AutoCAD draws all dimensions as associative; if the value is OFF, AutoCAD draws normal dimensions. You can change the value of DIMASO as follows:

```
Command: Setvar
Variable name or ? DIMASO
New value for DIMASO <1>: 0
```

In AutoCAD, the value 1 means ON; the value 0 means OFF. If you change
the value of DIMASO as shown here, any dimension you draw from now
on will not be associative. If you end the editing session, AutoCAD
remembers the value of DIMASO (and all other system variables) for the
next session. You can make your dimensions associative again by
returning the value of DIMASO to ON (that is, by changing its value to 1).
Part Six contains a reference to AutoCAD's system variables, which
describes each variable's definition and values.

After you change the value of a dimensioning variable, use the
UPDate dimensioning subcommand to redraw any associative
dimensions you want updated. When you enter **UPD** at the `Dim:`
prompt, you are prompted to `Select objects:`. AutoCAD then
updates the dimensions you select.

System Variables that Affect Dimensioning in General

Four of AutoCAD's system variables affect all dimensioning operations.
These variables are

- ❑ DIMASO
- ❑ DIMCEN
- ❑ DIMLFAC
- ❑ DIMSCALE

DIMASO

If DIMASO is on, AutoCAD makes all dimensions associative; if it is off,
the dimensions are normal. You can change an associative dimension to a
normal one by using the Explode command (discussed in Chapter 12).
You cannot, however, make a normal dimension associative.

AutoCAD automatically places associative dimensions on a special layer,
called DEFPOINTS. AutoCAD creates this layer to hold the points that
define the dimension's endpoints. You should never edit the DEFPOINTS
layer; it is turned off by default.

DIMCEN

DIMCEN (CENter marker) controls the size of the marker used to denote
the center of an arc or circle. You use the CEN, RAD, and DIA
dimensioning subcommands to place these markers in a drawing. The
value used for this variable is the distance from the center of the mark

along one of the line segments that make up the mark. The default is 0.09. If a value of 0 is used, no center mark appears; if the value is negative, only a center line (no cross mark) is used.

DIMLFAC

You should change the value of the DIMLFAC (Linear FACtor) variable if you are drawing in anything other than full scale. The default value for DIMLFAC is 1, indicating a scale factor of 1, or full scale (where one drawing unit equals one object unit). If you are drawing in half scale, you should set this variable to 2. AutoCAD multiplies the calculated dimension values by the value of this variable. Angular dimensions are not affected.

DIMSCALE

DIMSCALE is an overall scale factor. Use this variable if you are working with a drawing that is large or very small. DIMSCALE scales the entire dimension by the same amount and should equal the plot scale. The default value is 1. Entering a value larger than 1 results in a dimension that is multiplied by that factor; the same is true if you enter a value of less than 1. All dimensions are scaled.

System Variables That Affect Dimension Text and Lines

Most of AutoCAD's system variables affect dimension text or dimension lines. These dimensioning elements are controlled by the following system variables:

- ❑ DIMSOXD
- ❑ DIMTIX
- ❑ DIMTAD
- ❑ DIMTXT
- ❑ DIMTVP
- ❑ DIMTIH
- ❑ DIMTOH
- ❑ DIMTOFL
- ❑ DIMPOST
- ❑ DIMRND
- ❑ DIMSHO
- ❑ DIMDLI
- ❑ DIMCLRD
- ❑ DIMCLRE
- ❑ DIMCLRT
- ❑ DIMGAP
- ❑ DIMZIN

The following sections describe the functions of each of these system variables.

DIMSOXD

Normally, AutoCAD draws dimension lines between two extension lines. If there is not enough space between the lines for the dimension, dimension line, and arrows, AutoCAD places them outside the extension lines. When set ON, DIMSOXD (Suppress Outside-eXtension line Dimensions) forces AutoCAD to place the dimension text, lines, and arrows between the extension lines. If AutoCAD calculates that not enough room is available between the extension lines, the dimension is not displayed.

DIMTIX

If DIMTIX (Text Inside eXtension lines) is set ON, dimension text can appear only between extension lines. If AutoCAD calculates that not enough room is available, the dimension text is not displayed. The dimension lines and arrows, however, may appear outside the extension lines while the text is inside.

DIMTAD

DIMTAD (Text Above Dimension line) controls whether the dimension text is placed above the dimension line. If DIMTAD is set to OFF (the default), the dimension text is centered in relation to the dimension line, as dictated by the relationship between DIMTVP (the variable controlling vertical placement of the dimension text) and DIMTXT (the variable controlling dimension-text height).

DIMTVP

If DIMTAD is set OFF, DIMTVP (Text Vertical Placement) controls the placement of dimension text in relation to the dimension line. This is done through the formula DIMTVP – DIMTXT. Thus, the default setting of 0 for DIMTVP results in an offset of 0 units above or below the dimension line, so that the dimension text is centered vertically within the dimension line. As you change DIMTVP, the dimension text's position changes. A positive value for DIMTVP causes the dimension text to move above the dimension line; a negative value causes it to move below the line.

If DIMTVP has an absolute value of less than 1, the dimension-text line will be split automatically (as needed) to fit within the required dimensioning area (see fig. 10.30).

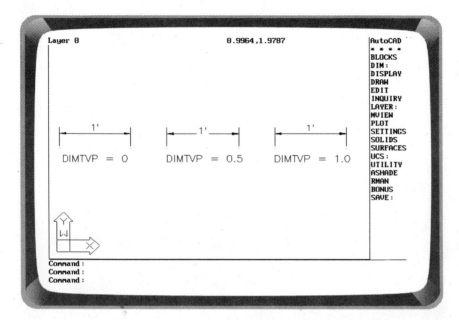

Fig. 10.30. The variable DIMTVP positions dimensioning text in relation to the dimension line.

DIMTXT

DIMTXT (TeXT) is used to specify the height of the dimension text. The default is 0.18 units, but you can change the text height as needed. A negative value has no practical value. If the current text style has a height other than 0, then the dimension text ignores the size specified by DIMTXT and takes on the size specified by the Style command.

DIMTIH

DIMTIH (Text Inside Horizontal) controls the orientation of text that appears between extension lines. When DIMTIH is set ON (the default), all text between the extension lines is drawn horizontally. If set OFF, the dimension text is aligned parallel to the dimension line. For example, if DIMTIH is on, and the dimension line is at a 45-degree angle to the X axis, then the dimension text still appears parallel to the X axis. If DIMTIH is off, then the dimension text appears at a 45-degree angle, in line with the dimension line (see fig. 10.31).

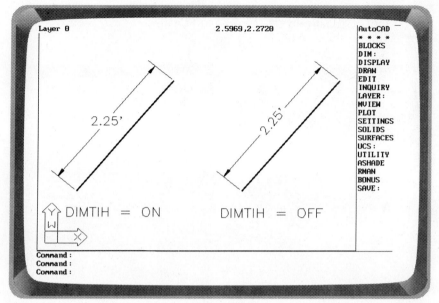

Fig. 10.31.
The variable
DIMTIH
determines
whether text is
aligned with
the dimension
line.

DIMTOH

DIMTOH (Text Outside Horizontal) is similar in function to DIMTIH, but controls all dimension text appearing outside the extension lines. When DIMTOH is set ON (the default), all text outside the extension lines is drawn horizontally. If DIMTOH is set OFF, the dimension text is aligned parallel to the dimension line.

DIMTOFL

Normally, the dimension line is located where the dimension text appears. You can override this location of the dimension line by setting the DIMTOFL (Text Outside Force Line) system variable. If set ON, DIMTOFL causes the dimension line to appear between the extension lines (if it will fit), even if the text is placed outside the extension lines. The default for DIMTOFL is OFF.

DIMPOST

Use DIMPOST (POSTfix) to add a default suffix to dimension text. For example, if you want to add the characters *approx.* to the end of each dimension, you could do so by setting DIMPOST to *approx.* The setting of DIMPOST has no effect on angular dimensions. To get rid of the suffix, set DIMPOST to no characters.

DIMZIN

DIMZIN (Zero INches suppression) affects dimension text only if you are working with architectural units and the calculated dimension has 0 inches. When DIMZIN is turned off, any dimension with 0 inches is displayed without the inches. For instance, the dimension 12'0" appears simply as 12'. If DIMZIN is ON, the dimension appears as 12'0".

DIMSHO

If, when you edit dimensions, the DIMSHO (SHOw new DIMension) variable is on and the dimensions are associative, the dimension-text values are updated as the dimension changes. The change in the entity's length is echoed in the dimension text as the highlighted entity is dragged. If DIMSHO is off (the default), the dimension text is updated only after the change is complete.

DIMDLI

AutoCAD uses the DIMDLI (Dimension Line Increment) system variable to control the incrementing factor for successive uses of BASeline and CONtinuous, two of the linear-dimensioning commands. DIMDLI prevents two closely placed dimensions from overwriting each other. This variable's value represents units and has a default of 0.38.

DIMGAP

DIMGAP (DIMension line GAP) specifies the gap distance between dimension lines and the text. The default value is 0.09 units.

DIMCLRD, DIMCLRE, and DIMCLRT

DIMCLRD (CoLoR of Dimension), DIMCLRE (CoLoR of Extension) and DIMCLRT (CoLoR of Text) hold the name (or number) of the colors you want to assign to the various elements of your dimensions. The default value is BYBLOCK.

System Variables That Affect Dimension Arrows

AutoCAD gives you complete control over the size and appearance of the arrows within a dimension. You can even replace the arrows with library blocks, which are discussed in Chapter 12.

Dimension lines can be tipped with any of the following entities:

❏ Arrows

❏ Tick marks

❏ Dots

❏ A user-defined block

The following system variables control the use of arrows within AutoCAD:

❏ DIMASZ   ❏ DIMSAH

❏ DIMTSZ   ❏ DIMBLK1

❏ DIMDLE   ❏ DIMBLK2

❏ DIMBLK

The following sections cover each of these system variables.

DIMASZ

The DIMASZ (Arrow SiZe) variable holds the scaling factor for arrow size. The variable's value is multiplied by the size of the arrow or block (whichever is used) to calculate a display size. The default value is a scale factor of 0.18.

DIMTSZ

DIMTSZ (Tick SiZe) controls whether arrows or tick marks are used at the ends of dimension lines. If DIMTSZ is set to 0 (the default), arrows are used; if set to a number other than 0, tick marks are used and scaled according to the value of DIMTSZ (see fig. 10.32).

DIMDLE

If you are using tick marks (that is, when DIMTSZ is set to a value other than 0), you can use the DIMDLE (Dimension Line Extension) variable to extend the dimension line past the extension lines. This helps make the dimension look clearer, and copies the style of some manual drafters. DIMDLE holds the number of units by which you want to extend the dimension line. The default value is 0.

DIMBLK

If you need an indicator other than the arrows or tick marks, you can create a block and indicate its name with DIMBLK (BLocK). Blocks are covered in greater detail in Chapter 12. You draw the block for the right side of a horizontal dimension, and it is rotated 180 degrees for the left side. The block must be available when it is needed for the dimensioning operation, or AutoCAD defaults to either arrows or internally generated tick marks.

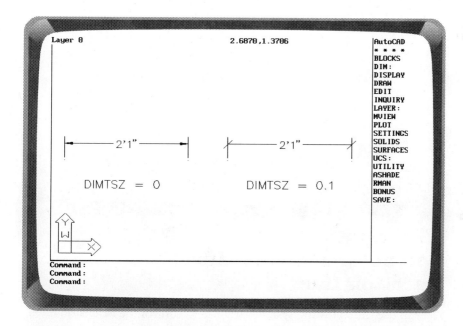

Fig. 10.32.
The variable
DIMTSZ
controls the
tick size.

If you set DIMBLK to DOT, and no block with that name is available, AutoCAD provides a dot marker for use by the dimensioning commands (see fig. 10.33). Set DIMBLK to a blank character (nothing) to return to the regular arrow.

DIMSAH, DIMBLK1, and DIMBLK2

If you are using library blocks rather than arrows, you can use a different block at each end of the dimension line. To do this, set DIMSAH (Separate Arrow Heads) ON and specify (in DIMBLK1 and DIMBLK2, or in DIMBLK) the names of the block or blocks. If DIMSAH is set ON and DIMBLK1 and DIMBLK2 define blocks to be used at the first and second extensions, respectively, the block name stored in DIMBLK is ignored; only DIMBLK1 and DIMBLK2 are used.

Fig. 10.33.
The variable
DIMBLK lets
you replace
the dimension
line's
arrowheads
with other
symbols, such
as dots.

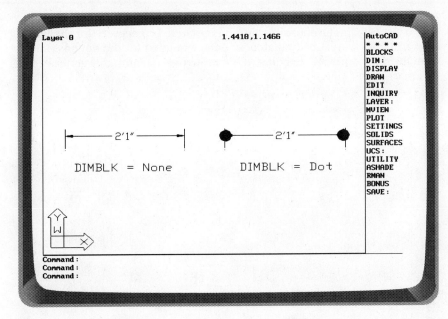

System Variables that Affect Extension Lines

You can use the following system variables to control the extension lines created by AutoCAD during linear and angular dimensioning:

❏ DIMEXO

❏ DIMEXE

❏ DIMSE1

❏ DIMSE2

The following sections discuss these system variables.

DIMEXO

When AutoCAD creates an extension line, the distance from the extension line's origin to the beginning of the extension line is controlled by the DIMEXO (EXtension line Offset) system variable. This variable represents the number of units in the gap between your pick point and the beginning of the line. This keeps the extension line from touching the object you are measuring. The default is 0.0625; if the value is set to 0, the line touches the pick point.

DIMEXE

The distance the extension line extends beyond the dimension line is controlled by DIMEXE (EXtension line Extension). If you set DIMEXE to 0 units, the extension line meets the dimension line. The default value for DIMEXE is 0.18. A negative value is not allowed.

DIMSE1 and DIMSE2

You can suppress display of either of the extension lines by changing the settings of DIMSE1 (Suppress Extension line 1) and DIMSE2 (Suppress Extension line 2). If DIMSE1 is set ON, the first extension line is not displayed. Setting DIMSE2 ON suppresses the display of the second extension line. The default for both variables is OFF, which means that the extension lines are visible.

System Variables that Affect Tolerances and Limits

AutoCAD lets you display both regular dimensions and dimensions that use tolerances or limits. The following five variables affect the display of this information:

- ❏ DIMTOL
- ❏ DIMLIM
- ❏ DIMTP
- ❏ DIMTM
- ❏ DIMRND

The following sections discuss these system variables.

DIMTOL and DIMLIM

If the value of DIMTOL (TOLerances) is ON (normally it is OFF), tolerances are displayed with each dimension. DIMLIM (Limits) works the same way for limits; if set ON, limits are displayed. If you are displaying limits (that is, if DIMLIM is set ON), the values in DIMTP and DIMTM are used as the limits.

DIMTP and DIMTM

DIMTP (Tolerance Plus) and DIMTM (Tolerance Minus) are the upper and lower tolerance ranges. DIMTP contains the "plus" portion of the tolerance; DIMTM the "minus" portion. If both DIMTP and DIMTM are set to the same value, the tolerance appears as a single number preceded by a plus-or-minus sign (±). DIMTM is assumed to be a negative number; the negative value of whatever you enter is used for the tolerance display. Thus, if you enter a negative value, it is negated and a positive value is displayed.

Remember that any dimension-text suffix specified in DIMPOST is attached to the end of any displayed tolerances or limits.

DIMRND

DIMRND (RouNDed) sets a rounding value for all dimensions. If DIMRND is set to 0.5, for example, all dimensions are rounded to the nearest half unit. The default is no rounding.

System Variables that Affect Alternative Dimensions

AutoCAD can be set to use two measurement systems simultaneously during dimensioning—typically, to provide measurements in English and metric units. If you want to use the two systems simultaneously, you must change the values of the following system variables:

- ❏ DIMALTF
- ❏ DIMALT
- ❏ DIMALTD
- ❏ DIMAPOST

Alternative dimensioning has no effect on angular dimensions.

DIMALTF

DIMALTF (ALTernate scale Factor) is the conversion factor to be used in calculating the alternative dimension. For instance, if the primary dimensions are provided in inches, and the alternative unit of measure is to be centimeters, DIMALTF should be set to 2.54 (the number of centimeters in an inch). Conversely, if the primary dimension unit is centimeters and the alternative is inches, DIMALTF should be set to 0.3937 (the number of inches in a centimeter). After accounting for the global scaling factor in DIMLFAC, AutoCAD multiplies the calculated dimension by the value in DIMALTF.

DIMALT

The value of DIMALT (ALTernative units) determines whether the alternative dimensions are displayed. The default is OFF, but if DIMALT is set ON, alternative dimensions are used in addition to the default dimensions.

DIMALTD

DIMALTD (ALTernative unit Decimal places) is used to specify the number of decimal places to be used in the alternative dimension values. The default value is 2.

DIMAPOST

DIMAPOST (Alternative POSTfix) adds a default suffix to alternative dimension text. In the previous example (of centimeters used as the alternative dimension unit), setting DIMAPOST to *cm* would be helpful. To get rid of the suffix, set DIMAPOST to nothing.

Using AutoCAD as a Sketch Pad (Sketch)

The Sketch command lets you use AutoCAD for freehand drawing. The command is useful if you want to trace a drawing into AutoCAD (using a digitizing pad). Sketching can give the drawing the look you want (using a mouse or digitizer) if hatch patterns and other AutoCAD drawing commands are not enough. Because sketched entities are made of lines (or polylines), they are part of the drawing and can be dimensioned and edited like other entities.

To enter Sketch mode, issue the Sketch command at the `Command:` prompt. AutoCAD displays the following prompt:

```
Record increment <0'-0">:
```

The freehand sketch you create is actually made up of many short segments. When AutoCAD asks for a record increment, it wants to know how far the pointing device travels from the previous segment before it draws the new segment. The smaller the increment, the better the resolution.

If you do use small increments in your freehand sketching, remember that AutoCAD must use more disk space to record the shorter segments because a larger number of segments are required to create the drawing. If you are working on an A-size drawing, a record increment of 1/10" is a good starting point. You can always increase or decrease the increment. For larger drawings, set a larger increment.

NOTE Sketching in AutoCAD is based on line or polyline segments, as determined by the system variable SKPOLY. When SKPOLY is set to 1, AutoCAD treats the sketch as polyline segments; with SKPOLY set to 0, the sketch is made of line segments. If you want to do a great deal of sketching, draw with polyline segments (by setting the value of SKPOLY to 1). A polyline sketch requires less memory and is easier to edit.

After you specify the record increment, AutoCAD displays the following list of options:

```
Sketch. Pen eXit Quit Record Erase Connect .
```

To enter options at the prompt, just type the first letter (except for the period and eXit); you do not have to press Enter.

Making the Pointing Device Imitate a Pen (Pen)

AutoCAD uses the analogy of a pen plotter for the Sketch command; that is, you draw by using your pointing device as a "pen." To make the pointing device imitate a pen, select the Pen option.

Your pointing device's pick button also controls the pen. Sketch some lines; the pen is "down." When you press the pick button, you can move the pen without drawing; the pen is "up." If you sketch too fast, AutoCAD beeps. Stop drawing to let AutoCAD catch up with you.

When you enter Sketch mode, AutoCAD reconfigures the first seven buttons of your pointing device, as shown in table 10.1. You cannot reassign these buttons.

Table 10.1
The Button Assignments during the Sketch Command

Button	Command	Meaning
0 (Pick)	P	Pen up and down
1	.	Draw line
2	R	Record sketch
3	X	Record sketch and exit
4	Q	Disregard sketch and exit
5	E	Erase sketch
6	C	Connect to last sketch

Recording the Sketch (Record and eXit)

In Sketch mode, the segments you draw are retained in memory until you exit from Sketch mode (by selecting the eXit option) or record the sketch to disk (by selecting the Record option). This is similar to periodically saving your drawing to disk as you work on it.

Erasing Sketch Lines (Erase and Quit)

The Sketch command has limited erasing capabilities. Press **E** to use the Erase option. The cursor blinks as you move across the segments on the screen. To erase in Sketch, you must backtrack your work from the last segment drawn. You cannot erase lines that have been recorded until you leave Sketch mode; then you must use the Erase command. Press **P** to stop erasing. If you have second thoughts and decide not to erase a line, press **E**.

If you do not want to record what you have drawn, you can select the Quit option. AutoCAD returns you to the Command: prompt; the segments you have sketched are not recorded.

Connecting Sketches Together (Connect and .)

The Connect option enables you to connect the current sketch to the previous sketch after you lift the pen. Place the crosshair cursor on the end of the last line you sketched, and type **C**. AutoCAD connects to that segment, and you can continue sketching.

If you enter a period (.), AutoCAD draws a segment from the endpoint of the last segment to the cursor's current location. Then the pen returns to the up position.

 Snap and Ortho modes affect the way Sketch draws. In Ortho mode, you get only horizontal and vertical lines. In Snap mode, all endpoints are locked onto the grid, no matter what your record increment may be. (For more information on Ortho and Snap modes, see Chapter 11.) If your sketches are choppy, check the status of these modes.

Figure 10.34 shows a logo created with the Sketch command (with increment set to 1"). The scribbling was mirrored, then enclosed in an ellipse. The PEdit command changed the ellipse's width to 1".

Fig. 10.34.
The logo was
designed with
AutoCAD's
Sketch
command.

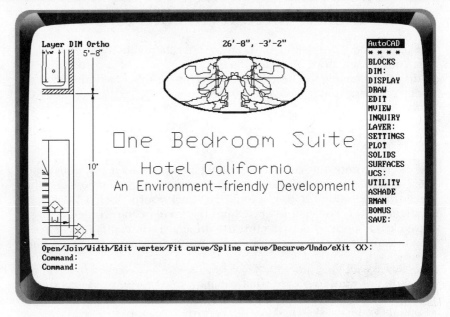

Summary

This chapter has shown you AutoCAD commands that make your drawing come alive. Adding text explains the drawing, while hatching and dimensioning are the final steps of producing a drawing. Sketching lets you do freehand drawing.

This chapter also showed you how to use AutoCAD's dimensioning variables to customize the Dim and Dim1 commands. The variables make dimensions look the way you want them to.

In the next chapter you will learn how to set up the drawing environment and how to get information from AutoCAD.

Part Four

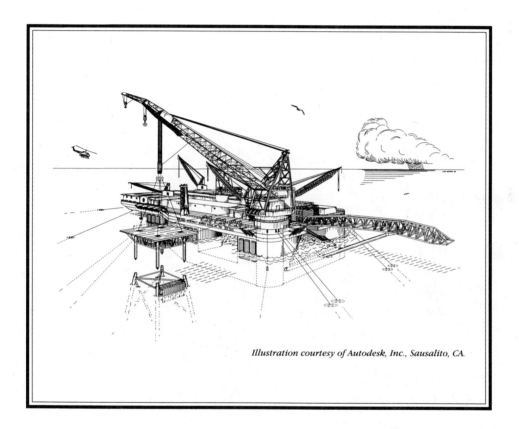

Illustration courtesy of Autodesk, Inc., Sausalito, CA.

Customizing the AutoCAD
Environment

11

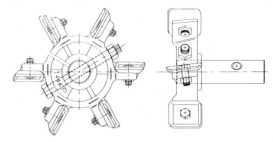

*Illustration courtesy of
Autodesk, Inc., Sausalito, CA.*

Setting Up the
Drawing Environment

In Parts Two and Three, you learned about AutoCAD's drawing, editing,
viewing, and plotting commands. These commands form the basis of your
work in AutoCAD's Drawing Editor.

This chapter teaches you a number of shortcuts that can make your
AutoCAD work easier. The shortcuts include handy commands that
enable you to pick certain points on entities, and keyboard toggles that
change the coordinate display or print a record of your work.

This chapter introduces the following commands:

- ❏ Axis
- ❏ Grid
- ❏ Isoplane
- ❏ Limits
- ❏ Ortho
- ❏ Osnap
- ❏ Snap

In addition to these commands, you will learn how to use the coordinate
and printer toggles (^Q and ^D, respectively). Although these toggles
are not actual AutoCAD commands (like Line), you do type them at the
Command: prompt.

This chapter also introduces two commands that change the characteristics
of entities:

- ❏ Color
- ❏ Linetype

You also will learn to use commands that retrieve information from the drawing database. Finally, you will learn to run operating system commands from within AutoCAD, and how to use AutoCAD commands that emulate certain operating system commands. These commands include:

❏ Area	❏ Id
❏ Catalog	❏ List
❏ Dblist	❏ Purge
❏ Del	❏ Sh
❏ Dir	❏ Shell
❏ Dist	❏ Status
❏ Edit	❏ Time
❏ Files	❏ Type

The following sections examine the commands that speed up the drawing and editing process within AutoCAD. These commands—called *mode commands*—aid you in your AutoCAD drawing, just as T-squares and protractors would aid you in manual drafting.

Setting the Drawing's Size (Limits)

A drawing's *limits* are the boundaries that define the drawing area. You generally can ignore the limits because AutoCAD uses the limits only for the Grid and Zoom All commands. The Grid command uses the limits setting to determine the area within which to draw the grid. Zoom All uses the drawing's limits (or extents, whichever is larger) as the outermost boundaries of the view it presents.

To set the drawing's limits, use the Limits command, as follows:

Prompt	Response	Explanation
`Command:`	**Limits**	Starts the Limits command
`ON/OFF/<Lower left corner>` `<0'-0",0'-0">:`	**-4',-11'**	Sets the location of the drawing's new lower left corner
`Upper right corner` `<1'-0",0'-9">:`	**27',14'**	Sets the location of the drawing's new upper right corner

You can answer the two prompts by specifying absolute coordinates or by picking points on the screen.

Using AutoCAD's Mode Commands

You used several of AutoCAD's mode commands as you worked on the sample drawing in previous chapters. Whenever you used INT (to grab the intersection of two lines), or the PER function (to locate a point perpendicular to the point you are drawing), you used a subset of AutoCAD's Object Snap mode, called *object snap override*. These commands simplify your work in the Drawing Editor.

This section discusses several AutoCAD mode commands—Snap, Grid, Ortho, Osnap, Isoplane, and Axis—and shows you how to toggle these commands from the keyboard.

Setting the Snap Mode (Snap)

Earlier in this text, you learned to use the Units command. The Units command causes coordinates, distances, and angles to be displayed to the number of decimal places you choose. Even with the drawing's units set, you still can draw at any coordinate. AutoCAD's Snap mode goes one step further by limiting the cursor's on-screen position to the value you set. In effect, snap ensures that your drawing is accurate, by setting the drawing resolution. For example, if you set snap to 1", you can move the cursor only in increments of one inch. If snap is 1/16", you can move the cursor only in increments of 1/16". You can override the snap setting, however, by typing in a coordinate.

Now, set the snap spacing in the SUITE drawing, as follows:

```
Command: Snap
Snap spacing or ON/OFF/Aspect/Rotate/Style <0'-0">: 1'
```

You have set snap to 1'. Move your pointing device and notice how the crosshair cursor jumps, instead of moving smoothly. The Snap command has five options, which are discussed in the following sections.

Setting the Snap Increment (Snap Spacing)

At the Snap command's prompt, you can enter a value to set the snap spacing, or increment. If you set snap to 1', then you can move the cursor only in one-foot increments.

TIP

If you zoom in too close with snap turned on, you may find that the cursor no longer moves. That's because the snap increment is greater than the screen width. To correct this problem, turn snap off or zoom out a bit.

Toggling Snap (Snap ON and Snap OFF)

You toggle snap by using the Snap command's ON and OFF options. When you turn snap on, the word `Snap` appears on the status line. (Some graphics boards display only the letter `S`.) You also can toggle snap by pressing Ctrl-B or F9, or you can use your pointing device to pick the Snap On/Off option from the Settings pull-down menu.

Setting the Aspect Ratio (Snap Aspect)

You can set the snap spacing differently for the X and Y directions. If you set snap to an aspect value of 2' and 4', for example, you can easily draw a reflected ceiling pattern.

The following command sequence shows you how to set up such an aspect ratio:

Prompt	Response	Explanation
`Command:`	**Snap**	Starts the Snap command
`Snap spacing or ON/OFF/Aspect/Rotate/ Style <1'-0">:`	**A**	Selects the Aspect option
`Horizontal spacing <1'-0">:`	**2'**	Specifies a 2' snap increment in the X direction
`Vertical spacing <1'-0">:`	**4'**	Specifies a 4' snap increment in the Y direction

Now when you move the cursor around, it jumps horizontally in two-foot increments and vertically in four-foot increments.

Rotating the Snap (Snap Rotate)

The Rotate option enables you to rotate the snap. This option gives you the opportunity to change the base point or starting position of the snap. There are many times when you may want the snap to begin, say, at the inside intersection of a wall. If angles are your style, the Rotate option enables you to change the snap to any point on the compass. This makes it easier to work on drawings that use angles other than right angles, such as the angled wing of a building.

Prompt	Response	Explanation
Command:	**Snap**	Starts the Snap command
Snap spacing or ON/OFF/Aspect/ Rotate/Style <A>:	R	Selects the Rotate option
Base point <0'-0",0'-">:	Press Enter	Keeps the base point at the origin (0,0)
Rotation angle <0>:	**30**	Changes the snap rotation to 30 degrees from the X axis

The results of this command sequence are shown in figure 11.1.

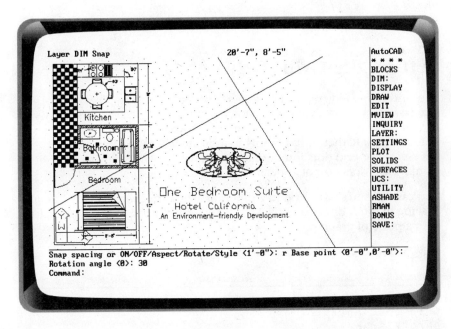

*Fig. 11.1.
The Snap
Rotate
command
rotates the
grid.*

Selecting the Grid Style (Snap Style)

The Style option sets one of two grid styles: standard (which you see now) and isometric, which aids in isometric drawing. You will learn about isometric drawing and the isometric grid style later in this chapter. For now, set the Snap settings back to normal, as follows:

Prompt	Response	Explanation
Command:	**Snap**	Starts the Snap command
Snap spacing or ON/OFF/Aspect/ Rotate/Style/<A>:	**R**	Selects the Rotate option
Base point <0'-0",0'-0">:	Press Enter	
Rotation angle <30>:	**0**	
Command:	Press Enter	
Snap spacing or ON/OFF/Aspect/ Rotate/Style/<A>:	**1'**	

Setting the Grid (Grid)

The Grid command creates a pattern of dots on the screen. These uniformly spaced dots are a drawing aid that you can use in much the same way you use the lines on a sheet of graph paper. AutoCAD's grid, however, does not use lines. Rather, it has points to indicate where the lines would intersect. The grid dots interfere less with the drawing than a grid of lines would. Grid dots do not appear on the plotted drawing.

You can set AutoCAD's grid to a different size whenever you like. The grid spacing in the X direction can even differ from the Y direction. Try that with a piece of graph paper!

Now, practice using the Grid command, as follows:

Prompt	Response	Explanation
Command: Grid spacing(X) or ON/OFF/Snap/Aspect	**Grid**	Starts the Grid command
<0'-0">:	**ON**	Selects the ON option to turn on the grid dots
Command:	Press Enter	Repeats the Grid command
Grid spacing(X) or ON/OFF/Snap/Aspect <0'-0">:	**1'**	Sets the grid spacing to one-foot intervals

A grid of dots covers the sample drawing (see fig. 11.2). Notice that the Grid command's prompt gives you six options. As the following sections explain, these options enable you to set the amount of space between the grid's dots, toggle the grid on and off, and modify the grid's aspect ratio.

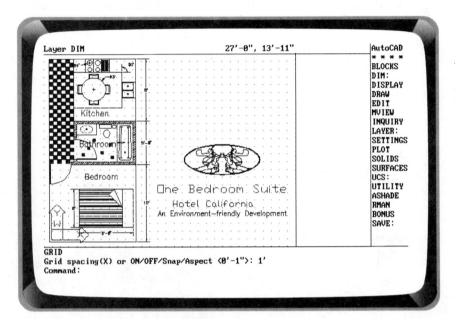

Fig. 11.2.
The grid acts
as a drawing
aid.

Setting the Grid Spacing

You can set the space between the grid's dots to any value you find useful. For the sample drawing, a value of 1' is useful. You need to be aware, however, of the effects of using certain grid settings. A value of 0 makes the grid conform to the snap spacing; this is the same as using the Grid command's Snap option.

AutoCAD cannot display the grid if the dots are spaced too close together. If you set the grid so that it is too fine, AutoCAD displays the error message Grid too dense to display. If you zoom in far enough, the grid does appear. If the grid spacing is just large enough for AutoCAD to display, it may take a long time to display and obscure the drawing like a snow storm. If this happens, you can press Ctrl-C to halt the grid; then select a wider spacing.

Many experienced AutoCAD users like to set the grid larger than the value of the snap. This lets you work accurately, without a grid so closely spaced that it gets in the way.

Toggling the Grid

Use the Grid command's ON and OFF options to turn the grid on and off (this switching on and off is called *toggling*). When you turn the grid off, AutoCAD automatically redraws the screen to clean away the grid dots. The grid automatically turns on when you set the grid spacing.

You also can use one of the following shortcuts to toggle the grid on or off quickly:

- ❏ Press F7. This lets you toggle the grid any time, within any command.
- ❏ Press Ctrl-G (short for *grid*). This has the same effect as pressing F7.
- ❏ Use your pointing device to pick the Grid On/Off option from the Settings pull-down menu. If you prefer to use the screen menu, pick SETTINGS, then GRID:, then ON or OFF.

Changing the Grid's Aspect Ratio

You can use the Aspect option to have AutoCAD display the grid with different spacings in the X and Y directions. This uneven spacing is useful for drawing where the X axis is greatly exaggerated, such as in highway cross-section design.

Uses for the Grid Command

The grid has several uses within the Drawing Editor. Its most important use is as a drawing aid that enables you to visualize equal spacings. The grid also gives you a sense of the drawing's size because the grid's limits match the drawing's limits.

The grid, along with the Snap command, is helpful for creating modular designs. If you are creating a drawing from a series of modules, for example, and the modules are based on a one-foot spacing, you can fit the modules more accurately if you first set the grid to a spacing of 1'.

The Snap and Grid settings are separate, and you can give them different values. You can set your grid for one spacing and set a smaller value for Snap. The grid display is only for reference, but Snap restrains the crosshair at the specified increments.

Using Ortho Mode (Ortho)

AutoCAD's Ortho mode lets you draw lines that are exactly perpendicular or parallel to one another. The command is helpful when you need to draw lines that are strictly horizontal or vertical, as you have done in the SUITE drawing.

The Ortho command is simply a toggle (on or off); it has no other features. You can toggle Ortho mode by using the Ortho command, by pressing Ctrl-O (short for *ortho*) or by pressing F8. You also can use your pointing device to pick the Ortho On/Off option from the Settings pull-down menu.

When you activate Ortho mode, the word Ortho appears on the status line. If you use the Ctrl-O or F8 keys, <Ortho on> appears in the Command: prompt area. The message <Ortho off> appears when you turn Ortho mode off.

You can draw only horizontally or vertically when Ortho mode is active, regardless of the cursor's on-screen position. The rubber-band line, which usually travels from the first point you picked to the crosshairs, is drawn as a straight horizontal or vertical line only—not as a diagonal line.

AutoCAD determines the direction in which you are drawing by the change in the cursor's X value compared with the change in the cursor's Y value. If you are drawing horizontally, the change in X is greater than the change in Y; conversely, the change in Y is greater than in X if you are drawing vertically.

If the grid is on while you work with ORTHO, the crosshairs lock onto the grid and can move only up, down, or directly sideways from one grid dot to the next. Believe it or not, this restricted movement actually can speed up your drawing. Using Ortho mode can save you a great deal of time when you need to draw parallel and orthogonal lines. Experiment with Ortho mode, as follows:

Prompt	Response	Explanation
Command:	**Ortho**	Starts the Ortho Command
ON/OFF<off>:	**On**	Turns on Ortho mode
Command:	**Line**	Starts the Line command
From point:	Pick a point	Specifies the line's starting point
To point:	Move the cursor around screen	

As you move the cursor with your pointing device, notice how the rubberband line appears only at 12 o'clock, 3 o'clock, 6 o'clock, and 9 o'clock. Press Ctrl-C to cancel the Line command.

Although Ortho mode mainly affects lines, polylines, and traces, it also restricts the drawing of arcs. Further, because it restricts movement to orthogonal directions, Ortho affects editing commands such as Copy, Move, Stretch, and Change.

Locking onto Objects (Osnap)

Chapter 5 discussed AutoCAD's object snap overrides, which let you pick construction points during a command. With the Osnap command, you can choose one (or more) object snap settings before you use a drawing or editing command. This saves you from repeatedly specifying the desired object snap override during the command.

The Osnap command is used like this:

Prompt	Response	Explanation
Command:	**Osnap**	Starts the Osnap command
Object snap modes:	**INT**	Specifies the INTersection object snap override

This sequence turns on the INTersection object snap until you turn it off again (AutoCAD calls this a *running* object snap). The object snap settings include NEArest, ENDpoint, MIDpoint, CENter, NODe, QUAdrant, INTersection, INSert, PERpendicular, and TANgent. You can use the Osnap command to turn on more than one object snap at a time. Three other modes, QUIck, OFF, and NONe, work only with the Osnap command. QUIck mode forces AutoCAD to choose the first entity that matches the Osnap request. NONe and OFF turn off object snap.

Creating Isometric Drawings (Isoplane)

Many disciplines use isometric drawing to show an object in "three dimensions." An isometric view shows three sides of an object at once (see fig. 11.3). AutoCAD's Isoplane command helps you create isometric drawings. This command sets the isometric plane on which you are drawing. An *isoplane* is the top, left, or right side of the isometric view.

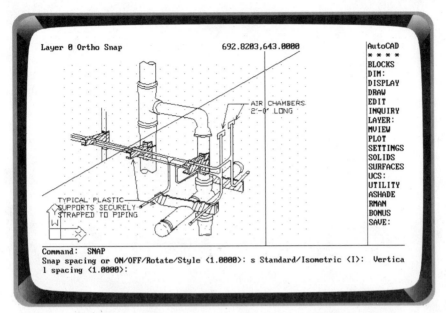

*Fig. 11.3.
The isometric
view shows
the top, left,
and front
sides of an
object.*

Practice changing the active isoplane, as follows:

Prompt	Response	Explanation
Command:	**Isoplane**	Starts the Isoplane command
Left/Top/Right/<Toggle>:	Press Enter	Toggles to the next isoplane

AutoCAD permits the use of three isometric planes:

❏ The Left isometric plane is the plane defined by the 90- and 150-degree axis pair.

❏ The Top isometric plane is the plane defined by the 30- and 150-degree axis pair.

❏ The Right isometric plane is the plane defined by the 90- and 30-degree axis pair.

The Toggle option lets you use the Enter key to move from one isoplane to the next. To toggle isoplane from the keyboard, press Ctrl-E.

The Snap command's Style option sets the isometric grid pattern (see fig. 11.4). Along with the Isoplane toggling, the two commands make isometric drawing easy.

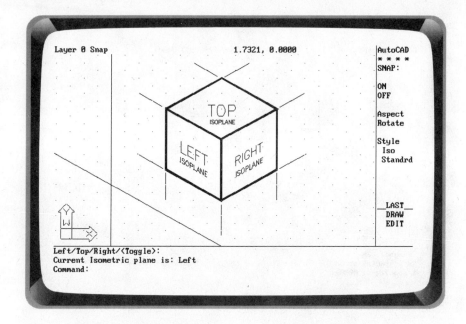

Fig. 11.4.
The Snap
Style and
Isoplane
commands
help you
create
isometric
drawings.

Setting Up Temporary Ruler Lines (Axis)

The Axis command places ruler lines along the right and bottom edges of the drawing screen. You can space the tick marks at any increment you like. If you find that AutoCAD's grid gets in the way of your drawing and editing, try using the axis instead, as shown in figure 11.5.

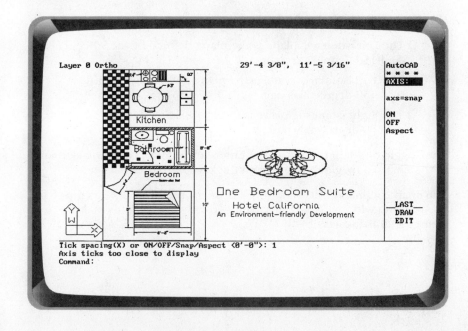

Fig. 11.5.
The Axis
command
places ruler
lines along
the edges of
the drawing
area.

The following command sequence demonstrates the Axis command:

Prompt	Response	Explanation
`Command:`	**Axis**	Starts the Axis command
Tick spacing (X) or ON/OFF		
`/Snap/Aspect <0'-0">:`	12	Specifies an axis spacing of 12"

The four options are the same as the Grid command's. You can turn the axis markings on or off, select a spacing, set the spacing equal to the snap increment, and set different X and Y tick spacings. The Snap Rotate command's setting determines the slant of the axis markings.

Modifying the Drawing's Settings (Ddrmodes)

The Ddrmodes (Dynamic dialogue DRawing MODES) command enables you to view and modify the current drawing settings. When you type **Ddrmodes** at the `Command:` prompt, AutoCAD displays a dialogue box similar to the one in figure 11.6.

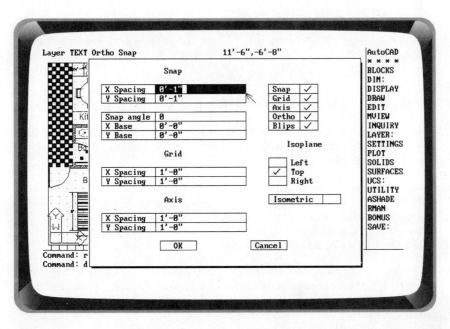

Fig. 11.6.
The Ddrmodes command lets you set the drawing modes.

As you can tell from figure 11.6, Ddrmodes affects several settings, including the following:

❏ Axis settings

❏ Grid spacings

❏ Isoplane settings

❏ Snap angle

❏ Snap spacing

The Ddrmodes command bundles together all the functions of the following commands into one screen:

❏ Axis

❏ Blipmode

❏ Grid

❏ Isoplane

❏ Ortho

❏ Snap

When you set the snap X spacing, AutoCAD automatically sets the Y spacing to the same value.

You may find it easier to use Ddrmodes than each of the individual commands, especially because many of the commands are interdependent; that is, one command's setting can affect other commands.

Toggling the Coordinate Display (Ctrl-D)

You can toggle AutoCAD's coordinate display by pressing Ctrl-D. Use this toggle to change the coordinate readout on the status line from static display to dynamic display.

When set to *static* display, AutoCAD shows the crosshair's coordinates only when you use the pick button to respond to an AutoCAD command. The *dynamic* display constantly displays the crosshair's position as it moves across the screen. The relative format *distance < angle* displays when the rubber-band cursor is on-screen.

If you like, you can press Ctrl-D to turn off dynamic coordinate display. There is no practical reason, however, for leaving dynamic coordinate display off. This toggle is a holdover from early versions of AutoCAD, when computers were so slow that constantly updating the coordinate display significantly slowed them down.

Echoing Information to the Printer (Ctrl-Q)

Press Ctrl-Q to turn on printer echo. This switch sends all AutoCAD text prompts—and all the information that you type—to the printer. Printer echo is useful if information listed on the screen (such as layers) is too long to be written by hand, or if you need to pinpoint a problem in a command sequence (a process called *debugging*).

Because the printer is usually slower than the screen, you may find that AutoCAD runs hesitantly when printer echo is on. Press Ctrl-Q a second time to turn off printer echoing.

Changing Entity Traits

Remember that the Layer command lets you assign a color to all objects on a layer. The color also applies to objects that are moved to that layer. Two other commands change the look of objects, regardless of the layer setting. These commands are Color and Linetype.

Overriding Layer Color (Color)

AutoCAD's Color command lets you override the default layer color for an entity. You can use this command to assign a specified color to any entity you draw. When you enter the Color command at the `Command:` prompt, AutoCAD displays the following prompt:

```
New entity color <BYLAYER>:
```

To change the color of all objects you draw from now on, enter the name or number of the desired color. The color you select overrides the layer color setting. You can switch back to the layer's color by entering BYLAYER.

If you want to change the color of objects after you've drawn them, use the Change command. To change previously drawn objects to the current layer color, use the Change command to change their color to BYLAYER. (Change is discussed in Chapter 9.)

Overriding Layer Linetype (Linetype)

The Linetype command lets you override the linetype set for the layer. When you type **Linetype** at the `Command:` prompt, AutoCAD displays the following prompt:

```
?/Create/Load/Set:
```

The Linetype command presents you with four options, which are discussed in the following sections.

Listing Linetypes (Linetype ?)

If you need to see a list of available linetypes, select the ? option. Then, at the `File to list <ACAD>:` prompt, type the name of the file that contains the linetype. In most cases, you will use the ACAD.LIN file. AutoCAD displays the list of linetypes and then returns you to the Linetype prompt.

For a complete graphical listing of AutoCAD's built-in linetypes, see Appendix D.

Creating a Linetype (Linetype Create)

Select Create if you want to create a linetype while working within a drawing. Once you create the linetype, you can use it within the drawing. The following command sequence shows you how:

Prompt	Response	Explanation
`Command:`	**Linetype**	Starts the Linetype command
`?/Create/Load/Set:`	**C**	Selects the Create option
`Name of linetype to create:`	**DOTS**	Names the new linetype DOTS
`Create or append linetype file:`	**SUITE**	In Release 11, a `Create or append linetype file` dialogue box appears (see fig. 11.7). Move the cursor to the file name ACAD, click on it, backspace over it, type in **SUITE**, and press Enter. Pick the `OK` button.
`Descriptive text:`	**Dotted linetype**	Description of the linetype
`Enter pattern (on next line)` `A,`	**1,0**	Defines linetype as a dash of length 1 and a space
`New definition written to file.`		

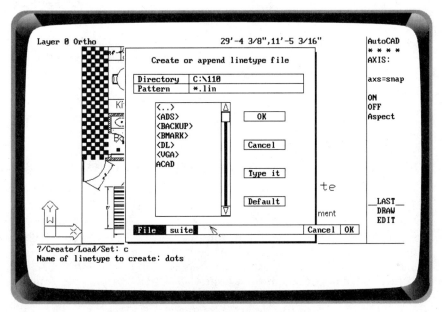

*Fig. 11.7.
The "Create
or append
linetype file"
dialogue
box.*

Loading a Linetype (Linetype Load)

Before you can use a linetype, you must load it into the drawing. To load
a linetype, select the Load option from the Linetype command prompt, as
follows:

Prompt	Response	Explanation
Command:	**Linetype**	Starts the Linetype command
?/Create/Load/Set:	**L**	Selects the Load option
Linetype(s) to load:	**DOTS**	Specifies the newly created DOTS linetype as the linetype to be loaded
Select linetype file:	**SUITE**	Specifies the new SUITE.LIN file as the file containing the linetype's information

Linetype DOTS loaded.

All linetype definitions are stored in LIN files on disk. AutoCAD prompts
you for the file that contains the desired linetype. The default filename is
ACAD.LIN. You do not have to specify a file extension, however, because
AutoCAD assumes that the extension is LIN.

Setting the Linetype (Linetype Set)

Once you've loaded the linetype, you can set it. Use the Linetype Set option to set the linetype with which you will work. This option lets you override the default layer linetype, and use the specified linetype for all the entities you draw.

Now set the DOTS linetype as the current linetype in your drawing:

```
Command: Linetype
?/Create/Load/Set: S
New entity linetype (or ?) <BYLAYER>: DOTS
?/Create/Load/Set: Press Enter
```

All lines you draw from now on will take on the DOTS linetype. The line may look solid to you; if so, the resolution of your graphics board is too low, you are zoomed out too far, or the value of Ltscale is too low. If you want to change the linetype, type the name of the linetype you want. To return to the layer's default linetype setting, respond by typing **BYLAYER**. To return to solidly drawn lines, use the CONTINUOUS linetype. You can use the Change command to change previously drawn entities to the current layer setting, or to a different linetype.

TIP

Polylines do not always handle broken linetypes well. The problem is that AutoCAD fits the linetype between the polyline's vertices. If the vertices are close together, the linetype may never have a chance to break. You can avoid this problem by using your plotter's hardware linetypes, if it has such a feature.

Be careful about changing entities. When you first learn AutoCAD, you can become confused quickly if you start overriding layer settings. You can expect a dashed linetype on the DASHED layer, for example, but if you use the Linetype command to set DASHDOT as the current linetype, you will be drawing with a dash-dot linetype.

A word about consistent linetypes at any scale . . .

Text and linetypes suffer when you draw at full scale. When the drawing is plotted, both need to be large enough to be legible, but small enough so as not to overpower the drawing. To overcome the problem, use AutoCAD's Ltscale command to set the lines and spaces of linetypes to a reasonable value.

The Ltscale you use depends on the scale you plan to use when you plot the drawing. In any new drawing, Ltscale equals 1.0 as the default. If you plan to plot at full scale (1=1), then the default Ltscale setting is fine. If your plot will be at a smaller scale (such as 1=48), then you need to increase the size of the linetype by increasing the value of Ltscale (48, in this example).

A word about consistent linetypes at any scale (continued) . . .

To change the linetype scale, enter **Ltscale** at the `Command:` prompt. AutoCAD responds with the following prompt:

`New scale factor <1.0000>: 48`

The new scale factor is the inverse of the drawing scale. For the sample drawing, which you plot at 1/4"= 1' (or 1:48), the Ltscale should be 48. For a large-scale map of 1:50,000, the scale factor is 50000.

After you set Ltscale, use the Regen command to redisplay the linetypes at the new scale.

Getting Information from AutoCAD

AutoCAD stores a great deal of information about the drawing. The information is stored in the drawing *database*. Most of the information is available to you in a variety of forms.

The following sections show you how to extract information from AutoCAD's database. The methods described here are fairly simple; the more advanced techniques of data extraction are beyond the scope of this book.

Identifying Points (Id)

The Id command returns the position information of a specified point in the drawing. Practice using the Id command as follows:

Prompt	Response	Explanation
`Command:`	**Id**	Starts the Id command
`Point:`	Pick the lower right corner of the bathroom sink counter	Specifies the point whose coordinates you want

AutoCAD displays the following information about the picked point:

`X = 2'-6"    Y = 3'-6"    Z = 0'-0"`

If you use your pointing device to select a point in your drawing, AutoCAD displays the point's three-dimensional coordinates. Typically, the Z coordinate is equal to the current elevation for the plane on which the point is located (usually the current UCS). However, if you use an Osnap mode to snap to a point on a three-dimensional object, the Z coordinate will be the true elevation for the selected point.

If, instead of picking a point, you enter the point's X,Y,Z coordinates, AutoCAD places a blip on-screen to indicate the point's position. Note that this is different from points created with the Point command. Id does not draw a point; it simply indicates the location of a specified set of coordinates.

Id is a quick and effective method of resetting AutoCAD's "last-known point" variable. Why is this important? Because most people draw objects relative to other objects. So, if you want to insert a door 1' 6" from a corner, it makes sense to insert the door relative to the intersection of the walls. The Id command can set the wall intersection as the last-known point and thus locate the door.

Reporting Distances (Dist)

The Dist command reports the distance between two points you pick on the drawing. You can use the command, for example, to check the clearance between a corner of the bed and the bedroom door's arc, as follows:

Prompt	Response	Explanation
Command:	**Dist**	Starts the Dist command
First point:	**INT**	Selects the INTersection object snap override
of	Pick the corner of the bed that is nearest to the door	Specifies the of first point
Second point:	**PER**	Selects the PERpendicular object snap override
to	Pick the door swing arc	Specifies the second point

AutoCAD then reports the following information (remember that your information may be different, depending on where you drew your bed):

```
Distance=2'3" Angle in X-Y Plane=138, Angle from X-Y Plane=(
Delta X=-1'-8", Delta Y=1'-6", Delta Z=0'-0"
```

Calculating Area (Area)

The Area command finds the area of an object. AutoCAD maintains a running total of the area at all times; holes can be subtracted to find a net area.

You can find the area of the one-bedroom apartment. When you type
Area at the `Command:` prompt, AutoCAD displays the following prompt:

```
<First point>/Entity/Add/Subtract:
```

These four options are discussed in the following sections.

Finding the Gross Area (Area First point)

The First point option lets you enter points clockwise or counterclockwise. To close the polygon that encloses the area, you do not have
to indicate the first point again because AutoCAD retains it as the original
starting point. AutoCAD automatically closes the area back to your
starting point.

To practice using this option, select First point and then pick the four
outside corners of the apartment floor plan. (Hint: This is easier if you
use the INTersection object snap.) AutoCAD displays the following
information (again, your information may be different, if you have
experimented with the sample drawing):

```
Area = 36352 square in. (252.44 square ft.),
Perimeter = 68'-8"
```

Finding the Area of an Entity (Area Entity)

The Entity option calculates the area of a circle or closed polyline.
Practice using this option on the kitchen table, as follows:

```
Command: Area
<First point>/Entity/Add/Subtract: E
Select circle or polyline: Pick kitchen table
```

AutoCAD displays the following information about the table:

```
Area = 1018 square in. (7.07 square ft.),
Circumference = 9'-5"
```

When you choose the circle, its circumference and area are displayed. If
you choose a polyline, AutoCAD displays the length of the perimeter and
the area. Pick the bed's polyline: you should get a perimeter of 23' 4" and
an area of 4800 square inches.

Finding the Net Area (Area Add and Area Subtract)

With the `Add` and `Subtract` options, you can add and subtract areas
from the results of earlier calculations. AutoCAD keeps a running total of
the area, based on the entities you select.

You can use the Area command to find out the net square footage of the apartment. To do so, follow this command sequence:

Prompt	Response	Explanation
Command:	**Osnap**	Starts the object snap command
Object snap modes	**INT**	Selects the INTersection object snap override
Command:	**Area**	Starts the Area command
<First point>/Entity/ Add/Subtract:	**A**	Selects Add mode
<First point>/Entity/ Subtract:	Pick point	First corner of apartment
<First point>/Entity/ Subtract:	Pick point	Second corner of apartment
<First point>/Entity/ Subtract:	Pick point	Third corner of apartment
<First point>/Entity/ Subtract:	Pick point	Fourth corner of apartment
<First point>/Entity/ Subtract:	**S**	Select Subtract mode
<First point>/Entity/ Add:	Pick point	First corner of kitchen counter

Continue subtracting from the floor area by making seven more picks around the kitchen cupboards and the bathroom walls. This results in an exact calculation of available floor space in the apartment, rather than total square feet of area.

Listing Entity Information (List and Dblist)

When you need information about entities in your drawing, use the List and Dblist (short for DataBase LIST) commands.

Use the List command to get information about specific entities within the drawing. Type **List**, pick an entity, and all the information AutoCAD knows about it appears on the text screen. When the list is finished, press F1 to return to the graphics screen.

If you want the information to be sent to your printer, press Ctrl-Q first. Try the List command now:

```
Command: Ctrl-Q
<Printer echo on>
Command: List
Select object: Pick kitchen table
Select object: Press Enter
```

AutoCAD switches to the text screen and displays the layer, color, linetype, center point (in X, Y, Z), radius, circumference, and radius, as follows:

```
       CIRCLE          Layer: FURNITURE
                       Space: Model Space
                       Color: BYLAYER     Linetype: Continuous
       center point, X=  2'-2"    Y=  9'-5"    Z=  0'-0"
       radius          1'-6"
circumference     9'-5 1/8"
       area       1017.88 sq in (7.0686 sq ft)

Command:
```

AutoCAD Release 11 also displays the space (model or paper) the entity is in.

After the printer is done, press Ctrl-Q again. You may feel a bit overwhelmed when you use the List command on a complex polyline. AutoCAD reports details of every vertex, information that can run several pages. Press Ctrl-S to pause the display; press Ctrl-S again to continue it. To see this effect, try the List command again, this time picking the bathroom sink. Make sure that printer echo is off. If the listing goes on too long, you can press Ctrl-C to cancel it.

TIP

The List command can tell you about objects in the drawing that might be puzzling you. For example, it can tell you which layer contains a specific object, or what linetype an object should have (if Ltscale is set too small).

Dblist reports on every entity in the drawing, including entities on frozen layers, in the order that you drew them. Dblist uses the same format as List when displaying the information. The fact that Dblist lists the entire drawing (a process that takes seven minutes for the SUITE drawing) makes it too cumbersome to be effective.

Getting the Status of AutoCAD (Status)

The Status command provides information about your drawing and AutoCAD. Status reports the following information:

❏ Layer settings

❏ Toggle settings

❏ Drawing extents

❏ Drawing limits

❏ Disk space available

❏ I/O page space available

To use the command, type **Status** at the Command: prompt and press Enter. Figure 11.8 shows the report AutoCAD Release 11 generates based on the sample drawing. Yours may be different, but the figure should give you an idea of the output provided.

TIP

A line near the bottom of the Status screen reads Amount of program in physical memory/Total (virtual) program size: 100%. As long as the number remains at 100%, AutoCAD is keeping all of itself and the drawing in memory. If the number dips below 100%, the least-used parts of AutoCAD and the drawing are being stored on disk, in a process called *paging*. When paging is used, unused parts of the program and drawing file are temporarily copied to the disk, to free RAM space for necessary program and drawing data. When the paged data is needed, it is read back into RAM, and other portions of the program and drawing are moved to the disk.

Paging slows AutoCAD down. If this happens consistently, you should consider adding more memory to the computer to improve AutoCAD's performance.

Keeping Track of Time (Time)

The computer's clock keeps track of the current time and date. AutoCAD uses this clock to maintain time information about your drawing.

When you type **Time** at the Command: prompt, AutoCAD returns several pieces of information. The display on your screen should resemble the following:

```
Current time:              12 Oct 1991 at 16:25:03.180
Drawing created:           03 Oct 1991 at 13:59:51.000
Drawing last updated:      12 Oct 1991 at 12:38:20.770
Time in drawing editor:    0 days 07:46:46.990
Elapsed timer:             0 days 07:46:46.990
Timer on.
Display/ON/OFF/Reset:
```

The Time display contains the following information:

Drawing created is the date and time the current drawing was created. The time is set to 0 when you execute Main Menu Option 1 (Begin NEW Drawing) or use the Wblock command (which is discussed in Chapter 13).

Drawing last updated is the time you last updated the current file. This time is updated whenever you use the Save or End commands.

Time in drawing editor is the total amount of time you have spent in all drawing sessions in the Drawing Editor with this drawing. When you end a session by using the Quit command, the time in the Drawing Editor is not recorded. The time naturally includes time you spend at coffee breaks with the drawing loaded in AutoCAD.

Elapsed timer is the amount of time you spend in the Drawing Editor during the current session, provided that you have not reset the timer.

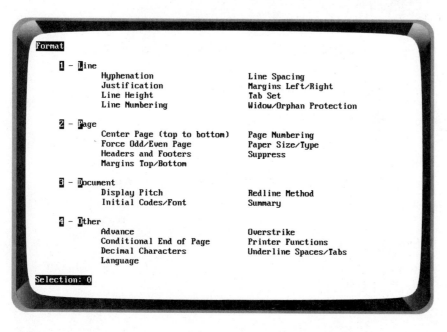

Fig. 11.8.
The Status command reports on the status of AutoCAD and the current drawing.

The Time command has four options, which only affect the elapsed timer. The timer can be used like a stopwatch. The Reset option resets the elapsed timer to 0 and turns it on. If you want to see the display again (updated for the elapsed time), choose the Display option. OFF turns off the elapsed timer. ON turns the timer on, if it is off.

Because AutoCAD uses the computer's clock, you must make sure that the computer's date and time are set correctly.

Removing Unwanted Baggage (Purge)

After you work with a drawing for some time, it can become cluttered. The drawing may contain layers, for example, that you've created but no longer need. The Purge command lets you remove unwanted named objects from a drawing. This reduces the size of the drawing file, reducing the time it takes to load the drawing into AutoCAD.

You can use the Purge command to remove the following objects from a drawing:

- ❏ Layers
- ❏ Blocks
- ❏ Linetypes
- ❏ Shapes
- ❏ Text styles

In Release 11, the Purge command also removes unused dimension styles.

The commands for certain named objects (such as viewports, views, and UCSs) have their own built-in deletion capabilities. You cannot use Purge to delete these objects from a drawing.

Now practice using Purge. End your drawing and return to the Drawing Editor, then follow this command sequence:

Prompt	Response	Explanation
`Command:`	**Purge**	Starts the Purge command

`Purge unused Blocks/`
`Dimstyles/LAyers/LTypes/`
`SHapes/STyles/All:`
	A	Selects the All option

Prompt	Response	Explanation
`No unreferenced blocks found.`		Purge finds no unreferenced blocks
`No unreferenced layers found.`		Purge finds no unreferenced layers
`Purge linetype DOTS? <N>:`	**Y**	Purge finds one unreferenced linetype (DOTS)
`Purge text style LARGE? <N>:`	**Y**	Purge finds one unreferenced text style (LARGE)

`No unreferenced dimension styles found.`

With this purging, the SUITE drawing file shrinks by about 50K. AutoCAD lets you specify the type of objects you want to delete. In most cases, you will use the `All` option to clear out everything you do not need. You can use Purge only as the first command when you enter the Drawing Editor, before you issue any drawing or editing commands. Purge removes only named objects that are not used in the drawing. This occurs when you create a block, for example, but never insert it, or when you create a layer but never draw anything on it.

Purge checks through the database just once. To be sure that all extraneous objects actually are deleted, you may need to execute several purges, saving your drawing, and then exiting and restarting AutoCAD between the purges.

The Wblock command can be more effective than Purge. (Wblock is discussed in Chapter 13.) When you use Wblock on the entire drawing, you create the undocumented side effect of eliminating all unnecessary data from the drawing. Here's how you use Wblock:

```
Command: Wblock
Create drawing file: SUITE
The specified file already exists.
Do you want to replace it? OK
Block name: *
```

The asterisk (*) tells AutoCAD that you want to use Wblock on the entire drawing. Unlike Purge, Wblock can be used any time you are in the Drawing Editor. Remember to Quit (not End) and reload the drawing to take advantage of its cleaner, leaner size. This purging reduces the SUITE drawing another 602 bytes.

Accessing the Operating System

AutoCAD lets you use the features of the operating system whenever you like, without exiting from AutoCAD. If you use MS-DOS, AutoCAD's Shell command is an important feature that lets you run other programs without leaving AutoCAD. For multitasking operating systems, like OS/2 and Mac OS, the Shell command is unnecessary.

Performing AutoCAD File Operations (Files)

You may need to perform basic file-management operations, such as deleting or renaming a file, while working in AutoCAD. You can perform these tasks (and others) by issuing AutoCAD's Files command.

When you type **Files** at the Command: prompt, you are taken immediately to AutoCAD's File Utility menu (described in detail in Chapter 4). From this menu you can do the following tasks:

❑ List drawing files
❑ List other files
❑ Delete files
❑ Rename files
❑ Copy files

If you need help using the File Utility menu, refer to Chapter 4.

Accessing DOS (Shell and Sh)

If you want to access DOS while you are working in AutoCAD, you can do so by using AutoCAD's Shell commands. These commands let you exit from the Drawing Editor temporarily so that you can execute DOS commands. You do not have to reload AutoCAD when you exit from the Shell.

Shell lets you execute almost any DOS command. The exceptions are memory-resident programs, DOS environment statements, and commands that affect the status of the hard disk (such as CHKDSK).

When you type **Shell** at the Command: prompt, AutoCAD displays this prompt:

```
OS command:
```

Here you have two choices. If you enter a DOS command, it is executed and you are returned to the Command: prompt.

If you simply press Enter at the OS command: prompt, you can execute several DOS commands. You then can return to AutoCAD's Command: prompt by typing **EXIT** at the DOS prompt.

The Sh command is similar in function to the Shell command, but because it frees up less memory, Sh is faster than Shell. If you receive an error message indicating that there is not enough memory available, try the Shell command instead. If you receive the message again, you are trying to execute a command or program that takes too much memory to function. You must exit from AutoCAD to run the other program or command.

AutoCAD 386 for Release 10 frees up less memory (about 220K less) than the DOS version does. Programs that you could run with Shell in the DOS version Release 10 DOS (programs such as dBASE III) may no longer work in 386 Release 10. If this is a problem for you, try using a third-party program that makes more memory available.

AutoCAD Release 11 includes a memory-management program, called ShRoom, that frees up almost all memory during the Shell command. To use it, type **ShRoom** (instead of ACAD) at the DOS prompt. ShRoom then loads AutoCAD automatically.

Other DOS Operations

A few AutoCAD commands parallel DOS commands. These special commands are executed by a customized version of the Shell command.

Listing Files (Catalog and Dir)

AutoCAD's Catalog and Dir commands list the contents of disk directories. When you type **Catalog**, AutoCAD displays the following prompt:

    File specification:

Catalog is the equivalent of Shell Dir /W.

When you type **Dir**, AutoCAD displays the following prompt:

    File specification:

If you press Enter, AutoCAD lists all files in the current subdirectory. If you enter the name of a subdirectory, the files in that subdirectory will be listed. Or you can use DOS wild-card characters (* and ?) to list selected files:

```
File specification: *.DWG
```

This command lists all the drawing files in the current subdirectory.

Deleting Files (Del)

Like the DOS DEL command, the AutoCAD Del command deletes files. When you type **Del** at the `Command:` prompt, AutoCAD responds as follows:

```
File to delete:
```

At this prompt, specify the name of the file (or path and file) you want to delete.

If you respond with *.*, you are asking DOS to delete all files. Be sure that you really want to do this.

Using EDLIN (Edit)

The AutoCAD Edit command executes EDLIN, DOS' rudimentary line editor. When you type **Edit** at the `Command:` prompt, AutoCAD prompts as follows:

```
File to edit:
```

Specify the full name of the file; do not use wild-card characters. The use of EDLIN is beyond the scope of this book; for more information on EDLIN, see *Using DOS*, published by Que Corporation.

Viewing the Contents of Text Files (Type)

You use the Type command when you want to view the contents of a text (or ASCII) file. When you enter **Type** at the `Command:` prompt, AutoCAD responds:

```
File to list:
```

Enter the full name of the file; no wild cards are allowed. This command invokes the DOS TYPE command.

Summary

This chapter has shown you AutoCAD commands that speed up your work by providing tools similar to those used in manual drafting. To make the tools easier to use, AutoCAD often provides keyboard toggles that give you the flexibility of turning on and off the tools in the middle of any command.

You also have learned how to use the AutoCAD commands that give you information about entities and the current drawing's status. Used properly, these commands can help you make more efficient use of the time you spend working in AutoCAD. They relieve you of the guesswork associated with keeping track of time, calculating areas of odd-sided figures, and monitoring your drawing's status.

Chapter 12 shows you how to create libraries of objects and symbols that you use repeatedly in your drawings.

12

*Illustration courtesy of
Autodesk, Inc., Sausalito, CA.*

Creating a
Symbol Library

This chapter shows you how to create, manipulate, and attach information to blocks. A *block* is a group of entities collected together as a single object. The block can be a *symbol* that you use often in drawing, such as the symbol that represents a door, window, tree, shrub, nut, or bolt. A collection of symbols (or blocks) is called a *symbol library*. The block is drawn and edited as a single entity. This may sound similar to a polyline, but a block can be made of any AutoCAD entities, including polylines. A block's contents can range from a single point to an entire drawing.

In this chapter, you learn how to create a block, insert it into a drawing, and save the block to disk. Then you learn how to add attribute information to the block and extract the information from the drawing for use in a report. Finally, you learn about a special block called an Xref, which lets you view other drawings without making them part of the current drawing.

This chapter shows you how to use the following commands:

❏ Attdef	❏ Explode
❏ Attdisp	❏ Insert
❏ Attedit	❏ Minsert
❏ Attext	❏ Wblock
❏ Block	❏ Xbind
❏ Ddatte	❏ Xref

The Advantages of Using Blocks

Experienced AutoCAD users routinely employ blocks and symbol libraries. You gain the following four advantages by using blocks in your AutoCAD drawings.

❏ **Reduced file size.** By using blocks rather than the Copy command, you hold down the size of your drawing files. AutoCAD merely keeps track of where the copies of the block are located in the drawing. This technique is more efficient than keeping multiple copies of the same information in the drawing. When blocks are used efficiently, even hundreds of copies take up very little space in the drawing, because each copy is patterned after the original definition.

❏ **Shared blocks.** You can store a copy of a block on disk, for use in your other drawings or for other people to use in their drawings. If your office has a standard set of details, one person needs to draw them only once, then share them with everyone else. (Such a collection of standardized blocks is often referred to as a *symbol library*.)

❏ **Ease of modification.** If you decide to change the symbol for a light switch, all you need to do is redefine the block definition for a light switch. AutoCAD automatically updates all the light switches (that are based on that block) in your drawing to reflect the change. Because you use a block, you don't have to change each light switch symbol, one by one.

❏ **Ease of information extraction.** A block can contain information about itself. These pieces of information are called *attributes*. Attributes can be extracted and sent to another program, such as a spreadsheet or database program, for analysis.

Creating Library Parts (Block)

In AutoCAD, a block is a single object that is composed of many entities. You can draw these entities as you normally would, using AutoCAD's drawing and editing commands. You then can use the newly created block to represent a symbol in your drawing. This symbol can be anything, from a square to an electrical outlet to a drawing of a sports car. You get the most benefit from blocks that you use often in your drawing.

Once you have drawn the objects that make up the block, you use the Block command to compile the objects into a block. The Wblock command, which is described later in this chapter, is used to write the block to disk, making it accessible to all your other drawings.

Figure 12.1 shows the blocks you will create for the sample SUITE drawing. The sample blocks are electrical symbols. Take a few minutes to create the symbols in the Drawing Editor. Set the layer to 0 and set Snap to 1". Zoom into a blank area of the SUITE drawing. You can draw all these simple symbols by using the Line and Circle commands; some also need the Text and Arc commands. Do not include the descriptive text beside each symbol; the text is added to the figure to tell you what the symbols represent. You may find the Copy, Mirror, and Array Polar commands helpful. The 1-foot grid shows you the scale. The symbol for the double outlet has a deliberate error, which you will fix later in the chapter.

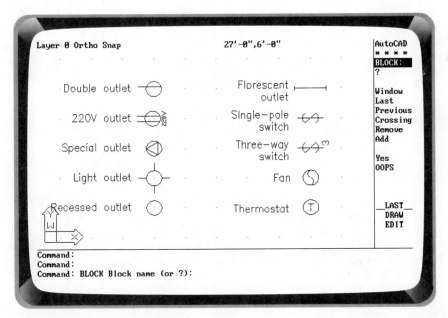

Fig. 12.1.
These residential electrical symbols can be inserted as blocks.

After you draw the symbols, you can create your first block. To create the block of the double outlet, use the following command sequence:

Prompt	*Response*	*Explanation*
Command:	**Block**	Starts the Block command
Block name (or ?):	**OUTLET**	Names the block "OUTLET"
Insertion base point:	**QUA**	Tells AutoCAD to use the QUAdrant object snap
of	Pick circle near left side	Specifies the circle's left side as the insertion base point
Select objects:	**W**	Tells AutoCAD you want to select the symbol (the circle and line) with a window
First corner:	Pick a point to the lower left of the symbol	Specifies the window's first corner
Other corner:	Pick a point to the upper right of the symbol	Specifies the window's last corner
2 found Select objects:	Press Enter	Ends object selection and the Block command

When you press Enter, the symbol disappears! That's because AutoCAD assumes that the spot at which you initially draw the block is not where you want to insert it. You can bring back the entities that make up the block (not the block itself) by using the Oops command. Try it now; then use the U command to remove the symbol again and restore its new block definition.

You also can use the Undo command to reverse the block-creation process.

You've created your first block. Although the double outlet symbol has disappeared from the drawing screen, the circle and line that make up the symbol are stored as a block definition in the drawing's database. Later, AutoCAD will use this object as the template when you want to create copies of the outlet, to insert into the drawing.

You can use any name you like when you name a block, up to 31 characters in length. If you want to store the block on disk, however, you will hit the eight-character limit imposed by DOS. For this reason, you should limit your block names to eight characters.

You can see a list of the drawing's blocks by entering a question mark (?) at the Block prompt, as follows:

```
Command: Block
Block name (or ?): ?
Block(s) to list <*>: Press Enter
```

AutoCAD then switches to text mode and displays the following information (the information on your screen may be different from this example, depending on how much experimenting you have done on your sample drawing):

```
Defined blocks.
    OUTLET
User      External     Dependent  Unnamed
Blocks    References   Blocks     Blocks
  1          0            0         12
```

A complete list of the blocks currently in your drawing scrolls up the text screen. As the screen shows, you can use four kinds of blocks in AutoCAD. *User blocks* are blocks that you create; so far, you have created just one block, called OUTLET. *External references* are blocks that exist in other drawings, and which you bring into the current drawing by using the Xref command. (Xref is covered in detail later in this chapter.) *Dependent blocks* are blocks that are bound to the current drawing with the Xbind command. (Xbind also is covered later in this chapter.) *Unnamed blocks* are the hatch and associative dimension blocks generated by AutoCAD when you use the Hatch and Dim commands. The sample drawing contains 12 unnamed blocks. To return to the graphics screen, press F1.

If you enter the name of an existing block (OUTLET, for example) at the `Block name (or ?):` prompt, AutoCAD displays the following message:

```
Block OUTLET already exists.
Redefine it? <N>:
```

AutoCAD is asking whether you want to redefine (or replace) the existing block with a new one. If you choose to do this, the old block is replaced by the new one, and every occurrence of that block in the drawing changes to match the new block. By using this feature of AutoCAD, you can easily update each occurrence of a symbol after changing the block itself only once.

The Block command's `Insertion base point:` prompt asks you to choose a point of reference. AutoCAD uses this reference point when inserting the block into the drawing. When you insert the block, the block's insertion base point falls at the point you pick on the drawing. When you create the block, make sure that you select a reference point that will be convenient for future insertions. The block's center or lower left corner are commonly used points.

After you identify the insertion base point, AutoCAD prompts you to select objects. AutoCAD also lets you combine blocks to form another block, called a *nested block*. To create a nested block, include the desired block (or blocks) within the selection set of the new block you are creating.

Points To Consider When Creating a Block

When you create a block, you need to be aware that layer, color, and linetype can have an effect on the block. In its discussion of the Change command, Chapter 9 introduced two key words for resetting colors and linetypes: BYLAYER and BYBLOCK. Remember that blocks are made up of individual entities, and those entities can have layers, colors, and linetypes associated with them. These associations can lead to complications when you try to merge entities with different layers, colors, and linetypes into a single block. Here are two rules for creating happy blocks:

1. When you create a block, you probably want it to take on the properties of the layer onto which it will be inserted. For this to happen, the block's entities must be on Layer 0 when you use the Block command. A block created on Layer 0 can be inserted on any other layer and will adopt the characteristics of that layer.

    If the block was created from entities on any other layer, it keeps the characteristics of that layer. If the block's entities reside on several layers, the block's pieces are spread across those layers. If the block was created on a layer that no longer exists, AutoCAD recreates that layer when you insert the block.

2. If you want a block's entities to take on the properties of the layer on which they are inserted, set entity properties to BYLAYER before you create the block. If the entities within the block have been assigned specific colors or linetypes, these will always be used rather than the default layer properties.

3. To make it easy to insert a block at any scale, draw the block to *unit size*. To make it easy to scale a block, draw the symbol to *unit size*. When drawn to unit size, the symbol is one foot (or one inch) in size. Suppose that you drew the

electrical symbols so that they all were 1' wide. When it comes time to scale, you just supply the new size; AutoCAD scales the block for you. For example, if you want the double outlet box to be drawn 2' across, you specify a scale factor of 2. If the block should be 6", use a scale factor of 0.5.

Of course, you may want the block to retain the layer, color, and linetype traits of the original entities. In that case, feel free to ignore these rules.

Inserting Symbols into a Drawing (Insert)

Now that you have created your first symbol library, the next step is to use it in your drawing. This is done with the help of the Insert command, which copies the block definition to a specified point in the drawing.

Before you use the Insert command, turn off the TILES, TEXT, HATCH, and DIM layers to unclutter the screen. Make a new current layer, called ELECTRICAL. The insertion process is easier if you turn Snap mode on and Ortho mode off. Next, use Zoom Window to get a close-up view of the bedroom.

Now, insert the outlet symbol (or block) against the bedroom wall, by using the following command sequence:

Prompt	Response	Explanation
`Command:`	**Insert**	Starts the Insert command
`Block name (or ?):`	**OUTLET**	Specifies the block to be inserted into the drawing
`Insertion point:`	**NEA**	Tells AutoCAD to use the NEArest object snap
`to`	Pick a point against the bedroom wall	Specifies the block's location in the drawing
`X scale factor <1>/Corner/XYZ:`	**0.5**	Sets the X-scale factor to 0.5
`Y scale factor (default=X):`	Press Enter	Makes the Y-scale factor the same as the X-scale factor
`Rotation angle <0>:`	**270**	Rotates the block by 270 degrees before inserting it into the drawing

The double outlet symbol is drawn against the upper bedroom wall. Practice using Insert again, by placing a second double outlet against the lower bedroom wall. You will use this outlet symbol later. When you are done, your bedroom should resemble the one in figure 12.2.

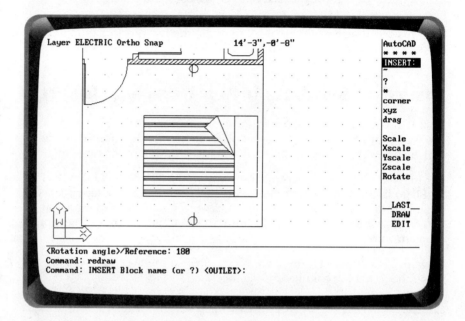

Fig. 12.2. The Insert command adds the double outlet symbol to the drawing.

You can insert a block in two ways. You just learned one method, which maintains the symbol as a block (a group of entities that act as a single object).

If you want to modify a block after you insert it, you can insert the block with its entities separated, or *exploded*. To explode a block when you insert it into the drawing, type an asterisk (*) followed by the block's name at the Block name (or ?): prompt, as follows:

```
Command: Insert
Block name (or ?): *OUTLET
```

The symbol is inserted as a group of individual entities (a circle and a line). An upcoming section discusses exploded blocks in detail and explains the use of the Explode command.

The Insert command lets you make two modifications to the block. One change is the scale, which can be different in the X and Y directions. The Insert command gives you the following three scale options:

```
X scale factor <1>/Corner/XYZ:
```

The default value for the X-scale factor, 1, inserts the block at the 1:1 scale (the scale at which the block was originally drawn).

After you enter the X-scale factor (and if you did not use the XYZ option), you are prompted for the Y-scale factor:

```
Y scale factor <default=X>:
```

You can enter a Y-scale factor that is different from the X-scale factor. If you want both factors to be the same, press Enter. Figure 12.3 shows the effect of using different values for the X- and Y-scale factors.

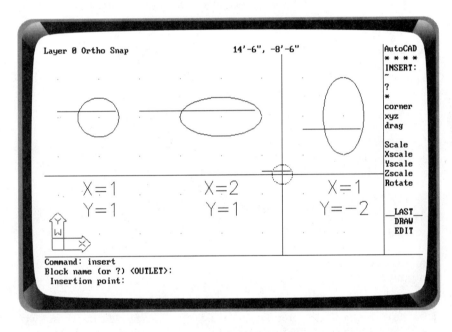

Fig. 12.3.
The Insert command lets you specify different X- and Y-scale factors.

You can insert both two- and three-dimensional blocks with different X, Y, and Z scales. Scaling is useful if you want to use a single standard block to meet a variety of situations. If you select the XYZ option, the following prompts appear:

```
X scale factor <1>/Corner:
Y scale factor <default=X>:
Z scale factor <default=X>:
```

You can supply numeric values or pick points in the drawing.

AutoCAD also accepts negative scale values. A negative value mirrors the block. One of the blocks shown in figure 12.3 was inserted with an X factor of 1 and a Y factor of –2. As you can see, it not only stretched the block but also mirrored it.

If you insert a block with different X-, Y-, and Z-scale factors, you cannot explode that block later.

You can rotate a block as it is inserted into the drawing. If you want to insert the block at the same orientation at which it was created, accept the default angle of 0 at the following prompt:

```
Rotation angle <0>:
```

If you want to rotate the block around the insertion point, type the desired angle of rotation at the prompt, or use your pointing device to pick an angle. AutoCAD ghosts the rotation as you move the crosshairs.

Breaking Blocks Apart (Explode)

Within the AutoCAD drawing environment, several types of entities are composed of smaller individual pieces. They include the following:

❏ Blocks

❏ Associative dimensions

❏ Hatch patterns

❏ Polylines

❏ Meshes

Normally, you can treat such compound entities only as a whole. There may be times, however, when you want to work with the individual entities that make up a compound entity. You can gain access to the compound entity's "pieces" by using the Explode command to break the compound entity apart.

Explode separates a compound entity into its original components. To show how the Explode command works, you will explode one of the two double outlets in the bedroom, so that you can modify the symbol later:

```
Command: Explode
Select block reference, polyline, dimension, or mesh: Pick
the double outlet
```

You can explode only one entity at a time. When you select it, the block blinks once to indicate that AutoCAD has exploded it into separate pieces.

Explode is particularly useful for working with blocks. Sometimes you need to modify and redefine a block. The easiest way to do this is to insert the block, use Explode, make your modifications, and then redefine the block. When you explode a block, all entities are moved back to the layer on which they originally were created (when the block was defined). In this case, the exploded outlet is moved back to layer 0.

As you may remember, associative dimensions also are compound entities. When these dimensions are exploded, they revert to the lines, arcs, and text entities that make up the dimension.

You can use Explode to clean up and edit hatch patterns. When a hatch pattern is exploded, all the entities are moved to Layer 0, regardless of the layer on which the pattern was created. You then can edit the basic line segments that make up the pattern.

When a polyline (including ellipses, polygons, and doughnuts) is exploded, any information specifying width for the segments is lost. Line segments and arc segments become lines and arcs with zero width.

Meshes, which are discussed in this text's chapters on 3-D, also can be exploded. When a mesh is exploded, it becomes a series of individual three-dimensional faces. You then can edit the 3-D entities by using the 3-D editing techniques discussed in Part Five.

When you explode blocks or other compound entities, you can greatly enlarge the drawing's size, taking up more room on the hard disk. If you explode a complex mesh that is defined in the database as one entity, you can add hundreds of entities to the database.

The Explode command ungroups compound entities one level at a time. If you explode a block made of polylines, the polylines remain intact. You need to use the Explode command again if you want to explode the polylines. If you explode one step too far, you can use the Undo command to put the entity back together again.

Updating a Symbol

If you decide to change a symbol's design, you can update the drawing file with a single command. Remember that the double outlet symbol was incorrectly drawn with a single line. The symbol actually needs two lines. You've exploded the double outlet block; now add the missing line as shown in figure 12.4. (This is easy to do if you use the Mirror command. To define the mirror line, snap to the circle with CENter and QUAdrant.) Redefine the OUTLET block by first creating the new OUTLET block, then using the Insert command to update all OUTLET blocks. Because you should create the block on Layer 0, first change the current layer to 0.

Prompt	Response	Explanation
Command:	**Block**	Starts the block command
Block name (or ?):	**OUTLET**	Names the block OUTLET
Block OUTLET already exists.		AutoCAD displays this warning so that you don't accidentally eliminate the existing OUTLET block

Prompt	Response	Explanation
`Redefine it <N>:`	**Y**	Tells AutoCAD that you want to redefine the OUTLET block
`Insertion base point:`	**QUA**	Specifies the QUAdrant object snap
`of`	Pick the circle near its left side	Specifies the block's insertion base point
`Select objects:`	Pick the entities that make up the symbol	Specifies the objects from which the block should be defined
`Select objects:`	Press Enter	Ends object selection
`Block OUTLET redefined`		AutoCAD redefines the outlet block
`Regenerating drawing.`		AutoCAD regenerates the drawing to show the newly redefined blocks
`Command:`	**Insert**	Starts the Insert command
`Block name (or ?):`	**OUTLET**	Specifies the OUTLET block as the block to be inserted
`Insertion point:`	Pick a point on the wall	Insert block where the previous outlet block was redefined
`X scale factor <1>/Corner/XYZ:`	**0.5**	Specifies an X scale of 0.5
`Y scale factor (default=X):`	Press Enter	Sets the Y scale the same as the X scale
`Rotation angle <0>:`	Press Enter	Outlet has been redefined as rotated by 270 degrees
`All the OUTLET blocks are updated.`		AutoCAD updates all blocks

The results of this command sequence appear in figure 12.4.

The alternative method is to use the Insert command to replace one block with a different one. The different block can be another block in the drawing or a block residing on disk (covered in greater detail later in this chapter), as in the following command sequence:

Prompt	Response	Explanation
Command:	**Insert**	Starts the Insert command
Block name (or ?):	**OUTLET= DIFF-OUT**	Redefines all outlet blocks with a different block called DIFF-OUT
Insertion point:	Pick a point	The remaining prompts are the same as previously discussed
X scale factor <1>/Corner/XYZ:	Press Enter	
Y scale factor (default=X):	Press Enter	
Rotation angle <0>:	Press Enter	
Block OUTLET redefined		AutoCAD reports that the outlet block is redefined
Regenerating drawing.		AutoCAD then regenerates the drawing to display the new blocks

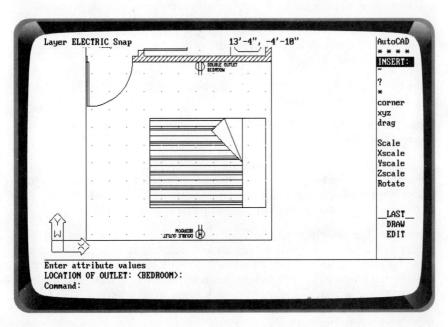

Fig. 12.4.
The SUITE drawing with updated double outlet symbols.

Writing Blocks to a File (Wblock)

After you create blocks in one drawing, you can use the Wblock (short for Write BLOCK) command to save the blocks to disk for insertion into other drawings. Wblock writes blocks to the hard disk; once a block has been saved to the disk, you can use the Insert command to insert the block into other drawings. If Insert cannot find the block in the drawing, it automatically looks on the disk.

You can write the entire SUITE drawing to disk by using Wblock, as follows:

```
Command: Wblock
File name: SUITE-B
Block name: *
```

At the File name: prompt, enter the name of the disk file that will hold the block. To keep the confusion down, it's useful to use the block's name for the file. In this example, the block file is named SUITE-B so that it doesn't overwrite the original SUITE drawing file. This is the reason for keeping the block names down to eight characters. AutoCAD adds the extension DWG to the file name you specify.

As you may suspect, AutoCAD simply creates a new drawing file that will hold the block definition. There is no difference between a block file and a drawing file, other than how they were created.

The Block name: prompt asks you for the name of the block to write to the file. There are four ways to respond to this prompt. One is to type in the block's name.

If the block and the file have the same name, you can type an equal sign (=) rather than repeating the name.

If you have not yet created the block, press Enter; AutoCAD then prompts you to create the block.

As mentioned in the discussion of the Purge command, Wblock also can remove layers, blocks, styles, and other unused objects from the drawing. If you enter an asterisk (*) rather than a file name in response to the Block name: prompt, the entire drawing is written to disk.

Sometimes the definition of the block written to disk gets changed and differs with a block in another drawing but named the same. To bring these two definitions for the same block into agreement you must update the internal block definition in your current drawing. You do this by putting an equal sign (=) after the block name to be inserted. This tells AutoCAD to ignore the internal block definition and go out to the disk and locate a new definition.

You can now add the SUITE-B drawing to the original SUITE drawing, as follows:

Prompt	Response	Explanation
Command:	**Insert**	Starts the Insert command
Block name (or ?):	**SUITE-B**	Specifies the block that was saved to disk
Duplicate definition ignored		Ignoring any block definition in the new drawing that has the same name as one in the old drawing, AutoCAD uses the old drawing's definition
Insertion point:	Pick a point adjacent to the left edge of the original	Specifies the block's insertion point
X scale factor <1>/Corner/XYZ:	**–1**	Mirrors the block
Y scale factor (default=X):	**1**	Tells AutoCAD not to mirror the block about the Y axis
Rotation angle <0>:	Press Enter	Tells AutoCAD not to rotate the block upon insertion, and completes the Insert command

You now have two floor plans next to each other, the second being a mirror image of the first (see fig. 12.5). The entire floor plan is a single block. If you want to make changes to it, use the Explode command to change it from a single entity into its parts.

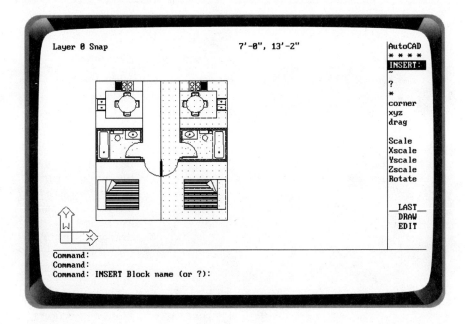

Fig. 12.5.
The block
SUITE-B
inserted as a
mirrored
floor-plan
drawing.

Specifying a New Insertion Point (Base)

When you insert one drawing into another, the insertion point of the inserted drawing is (0,0) by default. If the two drawings have different origins, you can use the Base command to redefine the insertion point to match the first drawing, as follows:

Prompt	Response	Explanation
`Command:`	**Base**	Starts the Base command

`Base point`
`<0'-0",0'-0",`
`0'-0">:`
	–3'-7",–10'-3"	Specifies a new base point

When this drawing is inserted into another drawing, the point defined by the Base command (–3'7",–10'13") is used as the insertion point; the origin (0,0) is not used.

Inserting More than One Block (Minsert)

To insert a block into an array, you can use the Array command. If you want the array of blocks to be a single block itself, use the Minsert command (short for Multiple Insert). This command enables you to insert the block in a rectangular array of rows and columns, which lets you insert a block many times very quickly.

To practice using the Minsert command, you will first use Wblock to write the two suites to disk. Then you will use Minsert to insert a series of suites along an imaginary hallway.

First use the Wblock command, as follows:

```
Command: Wblock
File name: SUITE-B
The specified file already exists.
Do you want to replace it? Y
Block name: *
```

You have replaced the drawing file SUITE-B with a new one of both floor plans. Now use it with the Minsert command to quickly draw six more suites, as follows:

Prompt	Response	Explanation
Command:	**Minsert**	Starts the Minsert command
Block name (or ?)	**SUITE-B**	Inserts the SUITE-B drawing
Insertion point:	Pick a point adjacent to the right edge of the original floor plan	Specifies the block's insertion point
X scale factor <1>/Corner/XYZ:	Press Enter	
Y scale factor (default=X):	Press Enter	
Rotation angle <0>:	Press Enter	
Number of rows (---) <1>:	Press Enter	Specifies one row
Number of columns (|||) <1>:	3	Specifies three columns
Distance between columns(|||):	21'-4"	Specifies a width of two suites

Minsert inserts three more pairs of suites (see fig. 12.6). As you can see, Minsert presents a combination of Insert and Array prompts. When AutoCAD performs a Minsert, the full array becomes a block whose pieces cannot be manipulated as individual block entities. If you try to pick one of the newly added floor plans (with the Copy command, for instance) you will find that AutoCAD highlights all six. If you redefine the block, all the symbols in the array are updated.

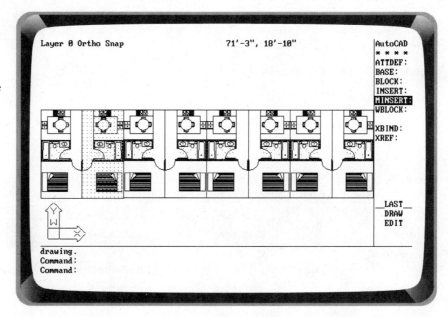

Fig. 12.6.
The Minsert
command
adds six copies
of the SUITE-B
drawing.

Adding Information to Blocks

The first part of this chapter showed you how to create, insert, and manipulate blocks. Now you will learn how to store information about a block. This information—called *attributes*—is stored with the block and is inserted with the block into a drawing.

Attributes can be predefined (when you first create the block) or you can add the information when the block is inserted. AutoCAD even lets you include questions (that you define) within the attributes. When you insert a block into a drawing, AutoCAD asks these questions and adds your responses to the block.

You can extract this attribute information from the drawing and use it to build a bill-of-materials list or to quote a proposal. Attributes can be used to detail the materials, part numbers, and costs of a specific item in the drawing. This information then can be extracted to gather project costs and inventories. The extraction procedure, which is discussed later in this chapter, provides a file that can be imported into a spreadsheet, database, or word processing program.

Take the following three steps when you want to add attributes to a drawing:

1. Use the Attdef command to define the attribute.

2. Use the Block command to bind the attribute to the symbol.

3. Use the Insert command to add the block and its attributes to the drawing.

Defining Attribute Information (Attdef)

The Attdef (ATTribute DEFinition) command sets up a framework for defining a block's attributes. When you issue the Attdef command, AutoCAD prompts you for information and then uses that information to set up the attributes. To make attribute extraction easier later, the definition created by Attdef can be used as a *template*.

The following example shows you how to attach attributes to the double outlet block. When you enter **Attdef** at the `Command:` prompt, AutoCAD responds with the following prompt:

```
Attribute modes--Invisible:N Constant:N Verify:N Preset:N
Enter (ICVP) to change, RETURN when done:
```

You can determine an attribute's appearance, or *attribute mode*. AutoCAD features the following four modes:

Invisible (I) mode controls the visibility of attributes. When a block is inserted into a drawing, you can see visible attributes as text; you cannot see invisible attributes. Invisible mode is helpful if you have lots of information to store with the block but don't want it cluttering the drawing.

Constant (C) mode forces the attribute to have the same value at all times. An example of a constant attribute value for the double outlet is its description, "DOUBLE OUTLET."

AutoCAD allows a mixture of constant and variable attributes in any given block. If a block's attributes are not constant, AutoCAD prompts you for attribute information when you insert the block. A variable attribute might be a location, such as "BEDROOM." You also can edit the attributes after the block has been inserted.

Verify (V) mode tells AutoCAD to prompt for verification that the attribute's value is correct.

Preset (P) mode enables you to assign variable attributes without being prompted for a value when the block is inserted. By editing the attributes, you can enter the values after the attributes have been inserted into your drawing. Use Preset mode if you do not anticipate knowing the attribute information for your blocks when you insert them. You also can use this mode to limit the number of attribute prompts to which you respond when inserting the block.

You set the mode(s) for the attribute by first identifying the type of mode you want to use. Select the desired mode by typing the mode's first letter: **I** for Invisible, **C** for Constant, **V** for Verify, and **P** for Preset.

Defining the First Attribute (Constant)

The first attribute you want to assign for the double outlet symbol is its name, "DOUBLE OUTLET." This is a constant attribute, which you will leave visible for now:

```
Enter (ICVP) to change, RETURN when done: C
Attribute modes--Invisible:N Constant:N Verify:N Preset:N
Enter (ICVP) to change, RETURN when done: Press Enter
```

After you set the attribute mode, AutoCAD displays the following prompt:

```
Attribute tag: DESCRIPTION
```

The *attribute tag* is a one-word label for the attribute you are defining. Because the first attribute describes the block, you can call the tag "DESCRIPTION." AutoCAD requires that you assign a different attribute tag to each attribute associated with a block, but you can type in any text you like (as long as it is a single word), as in the following examples:

```
Attribute tag: Cost
Attribute tag: Material
```

Different blocks may have the same attribute tags for their attributes, and you can have more than one attribute per block. These tags are used in the attribute-extraction process.

After you specify an attribute tag, AutoCAD prompts you for the value to assign to the attribute. In this case, you specify "DOUBLE OUTLET" as the value of the "DESCRIPTION" attribute tag:

```
Attribute value: DOUBLE OUTLET
```

The constant value "DOUBLE OUTLET" describes the block.

Next, AutoCAD needs to know how you want to display the attribute text. The location, height, and rotation angle are gathered through prompts similar to those used by the Text command:

```
Justify/Style/<Start point>: Pick point beside the outlet
symbol in the bedroom
Height <0'-2">: 2"
Rotation angle <0>: Press Enter
```

Here you need to decide where you want the attribute text to appear. In some cases, the text should be inside the block; in other cases, it is better to have the text appear next to the block. The double outlet block is too small to contain text, so you can pick a point next to the outlet. AutoCAD inserts the text at the point you pick.

Defining the Next Attribute (Variable)

After you define the first Description attribute, press Enter to execute the Attdef command again. The next attribute you will define is the outlet's location in the suite.

Prompt	Response	Explanation
Command:	Press Enter	Starts the Attdef command
Attribute modes-- Invisible:N Constant:Y Verify:N Preset:N Enter (ICVP) to change, RETURN when done:	C	Specifies the Constant option
Attribute modes-- Invisible:N Constant:N Verify:N Preset:N Enter (ICVP) to change, RETURN when done:	Press Enter	Ends mode selection
Attribute tag:	**LOCATION**	Specifies the tag name LOCATION
Attribute prompt:	**LOCATION OF OUTLET:**	Specifies the prompt AutoCAD will display when prompting for the block's location
Default attribute value:	**BEDROOM**	Sets the default value as BEDROOM
Justify/Style/ <Start point>:	Press Enter	Adds the new attribute below the previously defined attribute

The Constant mode is set to Y from the previous attribute definition. Toggle it to N by entering **C** at the Enter (ICVP) to change, RETURN when done: prompt.

With Constant mode set to N, AutoCAD prompts you for two different pieces of information. The Attribute prompt: prompt lets you define your own prompt that will appear when the block is inserted. In this example, you tell AutoCAD to prompt for the location of the outlet by displaying the prompt LOCATION OF OUTLET:.

AutoCAD limits the display of the variable attribute prompts to 24 characters, so choose the wording of the prompt carefully.

The second prompt, `Default attribute value:`, is a value you can supply that acts as a sample response, or is the most likely response. Here, you use "BEDROOM" because most of the double outlets are located in the bedroom.

If you press Enter when you get to the `Justify/Style/<Start point>:` prompt, the attribute will be placed directly below the previous one—much like the Text command—and be given the same text properties as the previous attribute.

After you have defined the two attributes for the OUTLET block, use the Block command to re-create the block symbol. First, explode the outlet symbol (next to the attribute text) with the Explode command. When you select the entities to be included in the block, include the attributes you just created and the existing outlet block next to the text. This procedure attaches the attributes to the block:

Prompt	Response	Explanation
`Command:`	**Explode**	Starts the Explode command
`Select block reference, polyline, dimension, or mesh:`	Pick block	Pick the upper outlet block in the bedroom
`Command:`	**Block**	Starts the Block command
`Block name (or ?):`	**OUTLET**	Names the block "OUTLET"
`Insertion base point:`	Pick the center of the circle	Specifies the block's insertion point
`Select objects:`	**W**	Turns on Window selection mode
`First corner:`	Pick point	Window the outlet symbol . . .
`Other corner:`	Pick point	and the two pieces of attribute text
`5 found` `Select objects:`	Press Enter	End object selection

Your double outlet block should now appear like the one in figure 12.7.

You have created your first block with attribute information. Next, you will learn how to insert blocks with attributes, as well as how to edit attribute information.

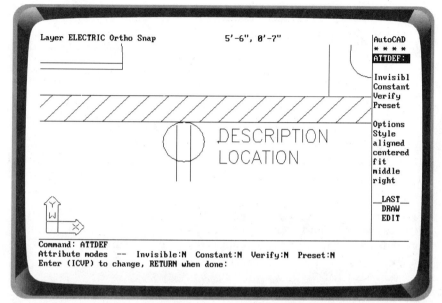

Fig. 12.7.
*You add
attributes to a
block with the
Attdef and
Block
commands.*

Inserting Blocks that Contain Attributes

Although this chapter already has discussed the process of inserting
blocks into drawings, you should learn how the Insert command differs
when the block contains attributes.

When you insert a block with attributes, AutoCAD responds in one of two
ways. If all the attributes have a constant value, the block and attributes
are inserted as before. If the block has variable attributes, AutoCAD
prompts you for their value before inserting the block and attribute text.

Erase both bedroom outlets and reinsert the blocks by following this
command sequence:

Prompt	Response	Explanation
Command:	**Insert**	Starts the Insert command
Block name (or ?):	**OUTLET**	Specifies the block to be inserted
Insertion Point:	Pick a point against the bedroom's upper wall	Specifies the block's position in the drawing
X scale factor <1>/Corner/XYZ:	**0.5**	Sets the block's X-scale factor to .5

Prompt	Response	Explanation
Y scale factor <default=X>:	Press Enter	Sets the Y-scale factor to 0.5
Rotation angle <0>:	Press Enter	Tells AutoCAD not to rotate the block when inserting it into the drawing
LOCATION OF OUTLET: <Bedroom>	Press Enter	Accepts the default response to the attribute prompt

Figure 12.8 shows the inserted block and the attribute values it displays: DOUBLE OUTLET and BEDROOM. If you insert the block at angles other than 0 degrees, the attribute text appears at the same angle.

Fig. 12.8.
The OUTLET block entered with attributes.

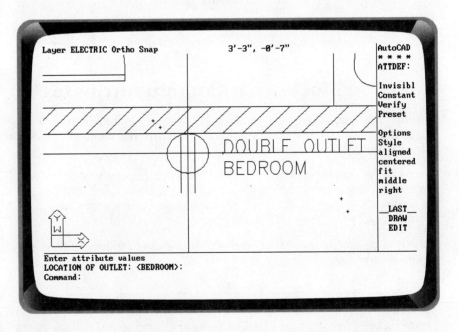

Editing a Block's Attributes (Attedit)

After you've inserted blocks with attributes, you can go back and use the Attedit command (short for ATTribute EDIT) to edit the attributes. The Change command also edits attribute values.

With Attedit, you can edit attribute values individually or by tag. If you edit by tag, the attribute tag is used as a reference. If several blocks have the same attribute tag, they all undergo the same change (this process is called *global editing*). You can edit either visible or invisible attributes.

When you enter **Attedit** at the Command: prompt, AutoCAD responds:

```
Edit attributes one at a time? <Y>:
```

If you answer **Y** (for yes), you want to edit the attributes individually; answer **N** for global editing. For this example, press Enter to accept the default response, Y.

Editing Individual Attributes

If you choose to edit attributes individually, you are restricted to editing only visible attributes. You can change the location, angle, height, and other properties of the text, as well as the attribute value. (Global editing gives you access to invisible attributes, but you can change only the attribute's value.)

The Attedit command continues with the following prompts:

```
Block name specification <*>: OUTLET
Attribute tag specification <*>: Press Enter
Attribute value specification <*>: Press Enter
```

The default response for each prompt is an asterisk (*), the wild card that tells AutoCAD that you want to edit all block names, tags, and values. If you want to limit your editing to selected attributes, enter the names of specific blocks, tags, and values.

You can enter more than one name by separating them with commas. You can use the question-mark wild card (?) to represent single similar characters.

For now, just respond to these three prompts as shown. The following prompt then appears:

```
Select attributes:
```

At this prompt, pick each attribute you want to edit (in this case, pick the "BEDROOM" text). AutoCAD does not acknowledge your selection. After you have selected all the attributes you want to edit, press Enter; AutoCAD tells you how many attributes have been selected (in this case, `1 attributes selected`).

Now the editing process begins. AutoCAD highlights the first attribute selected, places an X-marker on the screen at the attribute's text-insertion point, and displays the following prompt (see fig. 12.9):

```
Value/Position/Height/Angle/Style/Layer/Color/Next<N>:
```

Fig. 12.9.
The Attedit
command
marks the
attribute
being edited
with an X.

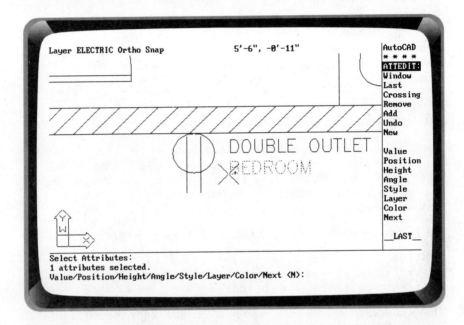

AutoCAD lets you change seven of the attribute's traits, or move on to the next attribute in the selection set.

Select the Value option if you want to change the attribute's original value. This assumes, of course, that you have not set the attribute mode as Constant. If you choose to change the value, AutoCAD displays this prompt:

```
Change or Replace? <R>:
```

If you type a **C**, indicating that you are changing the value, AutoCAD displays the following prompts:

```
String to change:
New string:
```

Type the string you want to change, press Enter, and then type the correction. You need to type only the letters that will be changed. Because the Change option is case-sensitive, be sure to enter the proper mix of upper- and lowercase characters. AutoCAD searches the original attribute value for the first occurrence of the character sequence to be changed, replacing just that portion with the new string. If AutoCAD can't find the string you want to change, it issues an error message and returns to the attribute-editing prompt.

If you type **R** (for Replace), AutoCAD displays this prompt:

```
New attribute value:
```

Type the new value and press Enter. The entire attribute value is replaced by the new value.

The Position option prompts you for a new location for the attribute:

```
Enter text insertion point:
```

The Height option enables you to change the height of the attribute text. Specify the new text height when the following prompt appears:

```
New height <0'-2">:
```

Use the Angle option to change the rotation angle of the text. Specify the new rotation angle when the following prompt appears:

```
New rotation angle <0>:
```

The Style option enables you to change the text font or style used. (Styles are discussed with the Text command in Chapter 10.) Specify the new style at the following prompt:

```
Text style: ROMANS
New style or RETURN for no change:
```

The Layer option lets you change the layer on which the attribute resides. (Refer to Chapter 9 for a discussion of layers.) Specify the name of an existing layer at the following prompt:

```
New layer <ELECTRICAL>:
```

Use the Color option if you want to change an attribute's color. Simply specify the new color (by name or number) at the following prompt:

```
New color <7 (white)>:
```

If you set the color to BYLAYER, the attributes assume the color assigned to the layer on which they reside. When you change the color, the attributes stay that color until you specifically change them later.

When you have finished editing an attribute, select the Next option. AutoCAD then moves the X-marker to the next attribute. Press Ctrl-C to cancel the Attedit command.

Global Attribute Editing

If you want to change only the value of a group of attributes, you should edit the attributes globally. AutoCAD first prompts you for the following information:

```
Global edit of attribute values.
Edit only attributes visible on screen? <Y>:
```

Type **Y** (the default) if you want to edit only the attributes that appear on-screen. If you type **N**, AutoCAD switches to the text screen and informs you that the drawing will be regenerated after you finish editing.

Then, whether you are editing all attributes or only those that are visible, AutoCAD displays a series of prompts similar to those for editing individual attributes.

When AutoCAD asks you for the `String to change:`, enter the string you want to change, then press Enter. Because you are performing a global edit, the string should be common to all attributes.

Finally, AutoCAD prompts for the `New string:`, which is the replacement value for the search string just entered. Because both search and replacement strings are case-sensitive, be sure to enter the proper mix of upper- and lowercase characters.

Now, to find the first occurrence of the character sequence to be changed, AutoCAD searches the original attribute values of each specified attribute. Then the old attribute value is replaced with the new string.

Overriding the Default Display Settings (Attdisp)

The visibility of attributes is controlled by the Invisible attribute mode. To override the visibility setting for all attributes, enter **Attdisp** at the `Command:` prompt. AutoCAD displays the following prompt:

```
Normal/ON/OFF <Normal>:
```

The prompt gives you three choices.

The Normal option defaults to the visibility setting with which the attributes were created. If you created the attributes as invisible, Normal makes them invisible; conversely, if you created the attributes as visible, Normal makes the attributes visible.

ON overrides the display settings and turns on all attributes, making them all visible.

OFF overrides the display settings and turns off the visibility of all attributes, making them invisible.

Any change to Attdisp causes a regeneration of the entire AutoCAD drawing. If your drawing is large and contains many entities, you probably will not want to change Attdisp unless it is absolutely necessary.

Editing Attributes through a Dialogue Box (Ddatte)

The Ddatte command (short for Dynamic Dialogue ATTribute Edit) brings up a dialogue box that enables you to modify attributes. Ddatte can be easier to use than the Attedit command.

When you issue this command, you are prompted `Select Block:`. After you choose the block whose attributes you want to modify, AutoCAD displays a dialogue box that allows you to edit the block's variable attributes (see fig. 12.10).

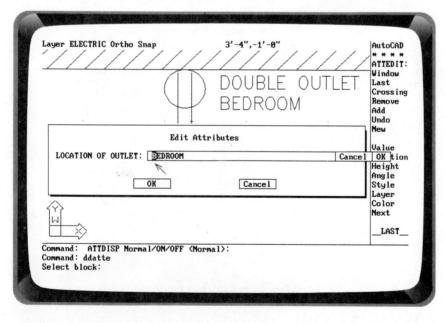

Fig. 12.10. The Ddatte dialogue box lets you edit a block's variable attributes.

In preparation for extracting attribute information from the SUITE drawing, make blocks of the remaining nine electrical symbols and assign attributes to them. Table 12.1 lists their names and attribute values. All prompts have the variable attribute LOCATION and the constant attribute DESCRIPTION. The description can be the same as the symbol's name. Figure 12.11 shows where to locate some of the symbols.

Fig. 12.11.
Blocks with
attributes
inserted in the
bathroom and
hallway.

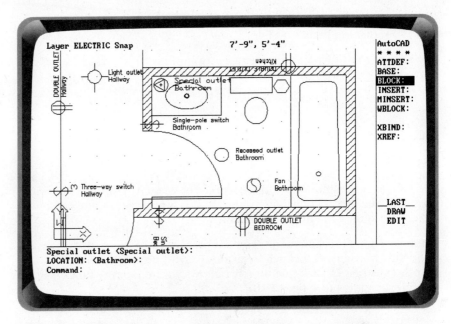

Table 12.1
Names and attributes for electrical symbols

Symbol name	Block name	Location
Lighting outlet	LIGHT	Hallway
Recessed outlet	RECESSED	Bathroom
Fluorescent light	FLUORESC	Kitchen
Double outlet	OUTLET	Bedroom
Special outlet	SP-OUT	Bathroom
220V outlet	220V-OUT	Kitchen
Single-pole switch	SWITCH	Kitchen
Three-way switch	3-SWITCH	Hallway
Thermostat	THERMOS	Bedroom
Fan	FAN	Kitchen

Extracting Attribute Information (Attext)

By assigning attributes to your blocks, you can store information with a drawing. In a procedure called *attribute extraction* (one of the most powerful aspects of a CAD program), you can pull out the information for many uses. The Attext (short for ATTribute EXTract) command places attributes in a disk file according to a format that you specify.

The file you extract from the AutoCAD database can be formatted in one of three ways:

- ❏ Comma-Delimited Format, or CDF
- ❏ Space-Delimited Format, or SDF (compatible with dBASE)
- ❏ Drawing eXchange Format, or DXF, a variation on AutoCAD's drawing interchange format

The CDF format is output as an ASCII file in which each field is separated by a comma, and each line contains information about just one block. A *field* is a piece of information. The attribute information for part of the sample drawing would look like this in a CDF file:

```
OUTLET,BEDROOM
SINGLE-POLE SWITCH,BATHROOM
THREE-WAY SWITCH,HALLWAY
```

The SDF format can be read by database programs such as dBASE. Each field takes up a specific number of spaces. In SDF format, the sample drawing's attributes might look like this:

```
OUTLET                 BEDROOM
SINGLE-POLE SWITCH     BATHROOM
THREE-WAY SWITCH       HALLWAY
```

When you choose to extract information in CDF or SDF format, AutoCAD requires you to specify a *template file* that it uses as a guide for formatting the extracted attributes. Template files are beyond the scope of this book; for more information on template files, see the *AutoCAD Reference Manual*.

AutoCAD normally uses the highly structured DXF file format to communicate drawing information to other programs. The DXF format file contains the attribute data, plus all information about the block (such as its insertion point and rotation angle):

```
   0
INSERT
   8
ELECTRICAL
62
        7
66
        1
   2
OUTLET
```

When you enter **Attext** at the Command: prompt. AutoCAD responds with the following prompt:

```
CDF, SDF or DXF Attribute extract (or Entities)? <C>:
```

To indicate the type of extract file you want to create, just type the appropriate first letter. Or, you can select entities on the screen to limit what is sent to the extract file. If you select entities (by entering E), AutoCAD asks you to create a selection set of the entities, after which you will see the Attext prompt again.

If you choose the CDF or SDF file formats, the following prompt appears:

```
Template file <SUITE>:
```

As described previously, specify the name of the file to be used as the pattern for creating the extract file. The file must have an extension of TXT. For more information on attribute extraction, see *AutoCAD Advanced Techniques*, published by Que Corporation. The attribute information is output in a file with the extension DXX.

Attribute extraction is a process that you may never use, or you may use often. When the process is automated, attribute extraction (together with a spreadsheet or database program) makes it very easy to find how many outlets and how much wiring is in the SUITE drawing.

Using External References (Xref)

When you work with a drawing, you sometimes need to refer to information stored in another drawing. Before AutoCAD Release 11, you could only superimpose the other drawing by inserting it as a block. This increased the size of the original drawing by the size of the inserted drawing.

With Release 11, you can use *external references* to view another drawing without exiting from the current drawing session. An externally referenced drawing is one that you can see but not touch; it is visible on-screen, but it is not part of the current drawing.

Here are some examples of how reference drawings are used:

❏ **Drawing border.** A simple use of reference files is the border and title block used in most construction drawings. Because the border and block usually are the same for every drawing, there is no need to store them with each drawing. By attaching the border as a reference drawing, you can see it with every drawing while saving disk space.

❏ **Master drawing.** A mechanical assembly drawing references many parts details. Any time a detail drawing is updated, the master assembly drawing is automatically updated.

❏ **Drawing coordination.** Suppose that the designers in your office are doing the drawings for a new road intersection. Different engineers in the office are working on the site grading plan, the lighting and signal plan, and the landscaping plan. All computers are linked together via a network, and all engineers can reference their work with the original site plan and check each other's progress.

Referenced drawings can reference other drawings (called *nested reference drawings*). Your hard disk's capacity is the only limit to the number of nested drawings you can use at one time.

You reference another drawing by using the Xref command. When you issue Xref at the `Command:` prompt, AutoCAD displays the following prompt:

```
?/Bind/Detach/Path/Reload/<Attach?:
```

The command gives you six options, which are discussed in the following sections.

Referencing Another Drawing (Xref Attach)

The default option, Attach, adds a referenced drawing to the current drawing. Suppose that you are working on the master floor plan for a hotel, and you want to reference the SUITE drawing from within the current drawing. The following command sequence brings SUITE into the current drawing as a reference file:

```
Command: Xref
?/Bind/Detach/Path/Reload/<Attach>: A
Xref to attach: SUITE
```

You enter the name of the AutoCAD drawing SUITE in this case. AutoCAD then makes two checks. First, AutoCAD determines whether a block named SUITE already exists in the current drawing; if so, AutoCAD stops the command. AutoCAD then checks to see if SUITE has already been attached to the drawing; if so, AutoCAD reports as follows:

```
Xref SUITE has already been loaded. Use Xref Reload
to update its definition.
```

If all is well, AutoCAD prompts for the insertion point, scale, and rotation angle, just as if you were inserting a block. If all your drawings are drawn full size, then scaling is not a problem.

Named objects in the attached drawing, like layers, blocks, and text styles, get new names. If the SUITE drawing has a block called OUTLET, AutoCAD renames it SUITE|OUTLET to let you know that the block belongs to a referenced drawing.

Listing Referenced Drawings (Xref ?)

Select the ? option if you want to see a list of the drawings referenced by the current drawing. The following prompt appears:

```
Xref(s) to list <*>:
```

AutoCAD lists each externally referenced drawing's name and the subdirectory in which it is located.

Updating the Referenced Drawing (Xref Reload)

If someone else is working on a referenced drawing, you may want to see an updated version of that drawing from time to time. The Reload option brings in the current version of a referenced drawing. When you select Reload, AutoCAD displays the following prompt:

```
Xref(s) to reload:
```

You can respond with a single name or with an asterisk (*) to update all referenced drawings.

Updating a Referenced Drawing's Path (Xref Path)

When AutoCAD attaches a referenced drawing, it also remembers the subdirectory in which the drawing resides. When you load a master drawing or use the Reload or Bind option, AutoCAD finds the referenced drawing by its path name. If the path changes, you need to use the Path option to inform AutoCAD of the change, as follows:

```
Edit path for which Xref(s): SUITE
Xref name: SUITE
Old path: C:\ACAD\SUITE
New path:
```

You can supply the new path or press Enter to leave the path unchanged. When AutoCAD finds the referenced drawing in its new subdirectory, AutoCAD reloads the file.

Detaching a Referenced Drawing (Xref Detach)

An externally referenced drawing remains attached until you detach it; the drawing does not detach when you end or quit the drawing. If you no longer need to refer to an attached drawing, you can remove it by using the Detach option. When you select Detach, the following prompt appears:

```
Xref(s) to detach:
```

Enter a drawing name, or an asterisk (*) to detach all attached files. You cannot detach a nested reference file if its master file is not detached.

Permanently Attaching a Referenced Drawing (Xref Bind and Xbind)

At times, you may need to collect all referenced drawings into a single file. This may happen if your client requests the complete AutoCAD drawing at the end of the project. The Xref Bind option adds all referenced drawings to the current (or *master*) drawing. When you select Bind, the following prompt appears:

```
Xref(s) to bind:
```

You can enter the name of one referenced drawing at the prompt, or you can enter an asterisk (*) to bind all referenced drawings into the current drawing. AutoCAD also binds all nested reference drawings. If the current drawing contains many externally referenced drawings, AutoCAD displays the message Scanning....

Named objects change their name during the binding process. The OUTLET block, for example, changes from SUITE|OUTLET to SUITE0OUTLET. If there already is a block with that name, AutoCAD increments the middle number until it finds an unused name (such as SUITE1OUTLET, SUITE2OUTLET, and so on).

The renamed objects are subject to AutoCAD's 31-character name limitation. If the bound object's name exceeds 31 characters, AutoCAD stops and undoes the Bind command. You can avoid this problem by limiting block names to 8 characters (which ensures compatibility with the Wblock command, as well).

This size limit can be a problem with layer names, which tend to be long. If you allow for the three-character 0 marker and an eight-character drawing file name, you should keep layer names to under 20 characters.

The Xref Bind option binds all the reference drawings. If you want to bind only part of a referenced drawing (such as the OUTLET block in the SUITE drawing), use the Xbind command instead:

```
Command: Xbind
Block/Dimstyle/LAyer/LType/Style: B
Block name: OUTLET
```

AutoCAD searches all referenced drawings for the OUTLET block until it finds it in SUITE. The block is added to the current drawing and renamed SUITE0OUTLET. This is more convenient if the OUTLET block hasn't been saved to disk with the Wblock command.

Summary

This chapter showed you how to produce your own symbol library. The usefulness of the Block command, coupled with attributes, is limited only by your imagination.

You also discovered that blocks are useful for saving space in a drawing or getting information about symbols that have been inserted. This information can be extracted to a database or word processor for inclusion in project cost estimates or facilities management.

Next you will learn how to automate parts of the drawing and editing process through the use of script files and menu macros.

13

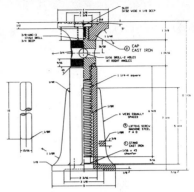

*Illustration courtesy of
Autodesk, Inc., Sausalito, CA.*

Customizing Basics

You've seen that computer-aided design is more powerful than manual drafting because CAD lets you edit your work with ease. More importantly, by using commands such as Array, Block, Copy, and Mirror, you never need to draw anything twice. But perhaps AutoCAD's most powerful feature is the freedom it gives you to automate and customize your drawing work.

In this chapter, you learn how to let AutoCAD do work for you, by making use of the following features:

❏ Command aliases

❏ Script files

❏ Menu macros

These features enable you to customize AutoCAD for the way you work, making your CAD system more productive.

To take advantage of these features, you need to use a text editor. A memory-resident pop-up editor, such as PC Tools Notebook or SideKick, is ideal. PC Tools Notebook displays spaces as small dots and carriage returns as arrows, which is handy for writing script files (you'll need to turn on the Control Codes option).

Using Command Aliases

When you use an AutoCAD command, you normally have to type in the full name. If you're not a touch typist, or if you get lost in the screen menu system, typing can be frustrating. Some commands are even tough to spell.

To get around this problem, you can use AutoCAD Release 11's *command aliasing* feature to redefine command names. When you redefine a command name, you simply give it a new name, or *alias*. AutoCAD lets you use one-, two-, or three-letter aliases. The program even comes with the following built-in aliases, some of which you have already used:

Alias	Command
A	Arc
C	Circle
CP	Copy
DV	Dview
E	Erase
L	Line
LA	Layer
M	Move
MS	Mspace
P	Pan
PS	Pspace
PL	Pline
R	Redraw
Z	Zoom

To use an alias, you type it at the `Command:` prompt just as you would its full command name. Try the alias for the Line command, as follows:

```
Command: L
LINE From point:
```

AutoCAD displays the command's full name and continues with the Line command's prompt.

AutoCAD looks in a file called ACAD.PGP for the aliases (PGP stands for ProGram Parameters). This file contains instructions that tell AutoCAD to use external commands (see Chapter 11) and command aliases. A few lines from the ACAD.PGP file look like this:

```
SHELL,,        127000,*OS Command:,0
TYPE,TYPE,     30000,File to list:,0

A,    *ARC
C,    *CIRCLE
L,    *LINE
```

You can define a new alias for any AutoCAD command. To redefine a command name, load the text editor and load the ACAD.PGP file. Take a few minutes to read through the file. You should be able to move through the file by using your cursor-control keys and the PgUp and PgDn keys.

Now, suppose that you want to create an alias for the Insert command. The alias can be the single-letter abbreviation *I*. To add an alias for the Insert command, type in the following line right after the E (for Erase) alias:

I, *INSERT

Notice that all alias definitions take the following syntax:

Alias name, **Full command name*

In this generic form, *Alias name* is the abbreviation you want to assign to the command name. *Full command name* is the name you want to abbreviate.

The alias name can be any abbreviation that you find convenient: *I* is a logical choice for the Insert command. The abbreviation is followed by the command name, which must be proceeded by an asterisk: ***INSERT**. Save the ACAD.PGP file, exit from the text editor, and return to the AutoCAD Drawing Editor. Try the I command now:

```
Command: I
INSERT Block name (or ?): Press Ctrl-C
```

The Insert command starts; press Ctrl-C to cancel the command.

If you use the Shell command to edit the ACAD.PGP file, the changes won't go into effect until the next time the Drawing Editor is loaded. To get around this restriction, issue the Plot command and then press Ctrl-C at the following prompt:

```
Do you want to make any changes? <N> Press Ctrl-C
Press RETURN to continue: Press Enter
```

When the Drawing Editor reloads, it rereads the ACAD.PGP file. This technique is faster than ending the drawing and then reloading the Drawing Editor.

Each alias uses a small amount of memory, so don't define too many aliases if your computer has only a small amount of memory.

Using Command Scripts

AutoCAD lets you automate command sequences in several different ways. Any sequence of commands you use frequently is a likely candidate for automation. Simple command sequences can be automated easily, while more complex sequences can take a long time to develop and get working properly.

You can use any of the following AutoCAD capabilities to automate a command sequence:

❏ Command scripts
❏ Menu macros
❏ AutoLISP functions
❏ ADS (AutoCAD Development System) programs

The remainder of this chapter shows you how to use command scripts and menu macros. The next chapter covers AutoLISP. ADS is meant for professional programmers and is beyond the scope of this book.

If you perform some AutoCAD operation repeatedly, it's a likely candidate for a script or menu macro. A *script* is a sequence of commands that you enter once and save as a special file (this is the most basic form of programming). AutoCAD reads the list of commands from the file and automatically performs them. You can use a script repeatedly, without needing to retype the individual commands. If you've ever written a DOS batch file, you've already used a form of scripting.

Consider the following potential uses for script files:

❏ **Drawing setup.** If you want to make a drawing conform to your company's or client's drawing standards, you can run a script file to set the snap, grid, layers, and make other settings.

❏ **Layer conversion.** If a set of drawings you receive from a client doesn't match your layer standards, you can use a script file that automatically renames the layers.

❏ **Plotter configuration.** If you plot to several different kinds of plotters, you can use a script file to automatically reconfigure AutoCAD for the right plotter.

A script has one advantage over the other three programming methods, in that it can run outside the Drawing Editor. Menu macros, AutoLISP, and ADS work only within the Drawing Editor. Thus, only a script file can reconfigure a plotter.

A script file contains the exact keystrokes that you would type at the Command: prompt. For example, the first lines you drew in the SUITE drawing were the bathroom walls (see Chapter 5). You used the following commands to create the walls:

```
Command: Line
From Point: 0,0
To Point: @7'<0
To Point: @5'<90
To Point: @7'<180
To Point: C
```

In a script file, the commands look like this:

Line
0,0
@7'<0
@5'<90
@7'<180
C

As you can see, the script file is an exact copy of your entries at the
Command: and Line prompts.

In a script file, a blank space represents the pressing of the Enter
key. Sometimes, you need to press Enter two or three times to end a
command. In such cases, you need to place two or three space
characters after the command in the script file to represent multiple
presses of the Enter key. The problem is that spaces are invisible,
which makes it hard to be sure that you have entered the correct
number of spaces. Worse, some text editors strip out extra spaces at
the end of a line of text. You should try to use a text editor that
shows spaces and avoid using an editor that strips the spaces out.
Such an editor makes it easier to write a script that works.

Running a Simple Script File (Script)

To create and run the sample script file shown previously, load your text
editor and type in the six lines of text exactly as shown. Make sure that
the file ends with a blank line at the end; the extra blank line acts as the
Enter key to end the C (for Close) option. Save the file with the name
LINES.SCR. The SCR extension tells AutoCAD that this is a script file.

If you use a word processor to write script files, make sure that you
save the files in ASCII text format. Otherwise, AutoCAD will not
understand the script (or macro) file. In WordStar, use
nondocument mode; in WordPerfect, save the files as DOS Text; in
PC Tools Notebook, save the files in ASCII format. This rule also
applies to the ACAD.PGP file, menu macros, and AutoLISP functions.

If you are using a word processor, you don't need to exit from
AutoCAD every time you need to edit an SCR or MNU file. (Menu
files are discussed later in this chapter.) Instead, use the AutoCAD
Shell command to exit from AutoCAD temporarily, and then type the
word processor's name at the OS Command: prompt (in this
example, *WP* is used to start WordPerfect):

Command: **Shell**
OS Command: **WP**

When you finish using the word processor, AutoCAD automatically
returns.

A word about creating ASCII files quickly . . .

The quickest way to create an ASCII file is to not use a text editor at all. Instead, you can use the DOS COPY command to copy the text into a file.

For the preceding example, follow these steps:

Prompt	Response	Explanation
`Command:`	**SH**	Starts the Shell command
`OS command:`	**COPY CON LINES.SCR**	Uses the Copy command to type text into a file called LINES.SCR
	Line **0,0** **@7'<0** **@5'<90** **@7'<180** **C**	Enters the commands, with a space at the end of each line
	Press F6	Saves the new file and returns you to AutoCAD
`Command:`	**Script**	Starts the Script command
`Script file` `<LINES>:`	Press Enter	Runs the script file LINES.SCR

Load AutoCAD and start a new drawing called LINES (you won't be able to see the new lines if you draw them in the SUITE drawing). Use the Units command to set architectural units. Then, at the `Command:` prompt, enter the Script command. If you use AutoCAD Release 10, the following prompt appears:

```
Command: Script
Script file <LINES>: Press Enter
```

If you use Release 11, a dialogue box appears when you enter the Script command. You can use this box to select the script file you want to run; in this case, pick the LINES script name from the dialogue box (see fig. 13.1). AutoCAD supplies the drawing name as the default script file name.

When you press Enter, the following lines flash by in the command area:

```
Command: LINE
From Point: 0,0
To Point: @7'<0
To Point: @5'<90
To Point: @7'<180
To Point: C
Command:
```

The script LINES.SCR draws the four lines faster than you can blink. Remember from Chapter 5 that this sequence of commands draws a box that is larger than the default Drawing Editor window, so you may not be able to see the lines the script file just created. If not, issue Zoom Extents to see all four lines. After zooming, erase the lines and execute the LINES script again. The bathroom walls appear as if by magic. Then press F1 if you want to see the text of the script.

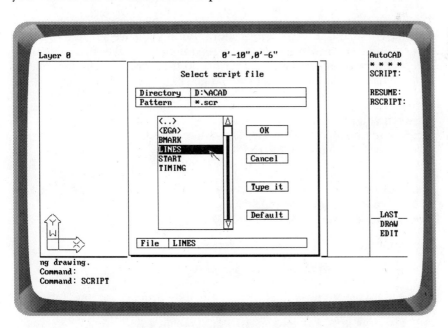

Fig. 13.1.
AutoCAD
Release 11 lets
you select the
desired script
file from a
dialogue box.

Using a Script File To Redefine Layer Names

Naturally, you wouldn't go to all this trouble just to draw four lines. The simple example demonstrates the power and speed of script files. Now try a more advanced example. This time, change the layer names in the

SUITE drawing to those advocated by the AIA's Layer Guidelines Committee. You have created the following layers in the SUITE drawing:

SUITE Layers	AIA Equivalent
0	0
APPLIANCES	A-EQPM-FIXD
DIM	A-PFLR-DIMS
ELECTRICAL	E-FLOR-FIXT
FURNITURE	A-FURN
TILES	A-FLOR-PATT

Your own version of the SUITE drawing may contain other layers, depending on the kinds of experiments you have done on your own. If you do have other layers, don't worry; they won't be affected by the script file you are about to create.

To change layer names in one or two drawings, it is easier to use the Rename command than to write a script. But if you have a dozen or several hundred drawings that all use the same set of layer names, you will save time by letting AutoCAD scripts do the work for you. Remember that the name of layer 0 cannot be changed.

Before you write a script file, you need to be familiar with the command's syntax. If you make a mistake in the script file, AutoCAD stops when it receives an unexpected response. To rename the APPLIANCES layer, you would use the Rename command, as follows:

```
Command: Rename
Block/Dimstyle/LAyer/LType/Style/Ucs/View/VPort: LA
Old layer name: APPLIANCES
New layer name: A-EQPM-FIXD
```

In a script file, the same command sequence looks like this:

Rename LA APPLIANCES A-EQPM-FIXD

Notice that you can have the entire command sequence on one line, with spaces separating responses. Go into your text editor, start a new file called LAYERS.SCR, and type in the following lines:

Rename LA APPLIANCES A-EQPM-FIXD
Rename LA DIM A-PFLR-DIMS
Rename LA ELECTRICAL E-FLOR-FIXT
Rename LA FURNITURE A-FURN
Rename LA TILES A-FLOR-PATT

A *word about scrambled screens* . . .

When you return to AutoCAD from a memory-resident text editor, the graphics screen may look scrambled. The technical reason for this problem is that AutoCAD bypasses the graphics board's BIOS, so the memory-resident program doesn't know which graphics mode to use when resetting the screen. You can avoid this problem by pressing F1 to switch to AutoCAD's text screen before pressing the text editor's hot key. If you forget to make the switch and get a scrambled screen, use the Regen command to clean up the graphics display.

If you are using a graphics board that is not compatible with an EGA or a VGA graphics board, you must flip to the text screen before you start the memory-resident text editor. Otherwise, you will not see the text editor. If you do get a blank screen, you must exit from the text editor "blind."

None of this applies if you are using a dual-monitor system, which displays graphics on one screen and text on a separate screen.

Now go back into AutoCAD and load the SUITE drawing. First, list the layer names to see the old names (see fig. 13.2). Then run the script file, and list the layers to see that the names have changed. Your Layer Control dialogue box should now look like the one in figure 13.3. AutoCAD Release 11 lists names in alphabetical order, so the new layer names are listed in a different order than the previous layer names.

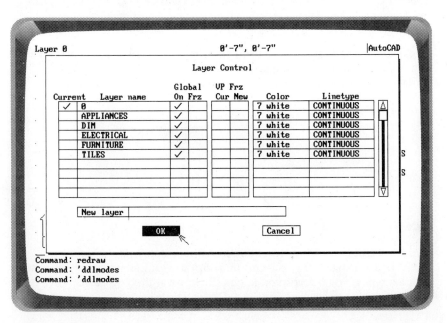

Fig. 13.2.
The SUITE drawing's original layer names.

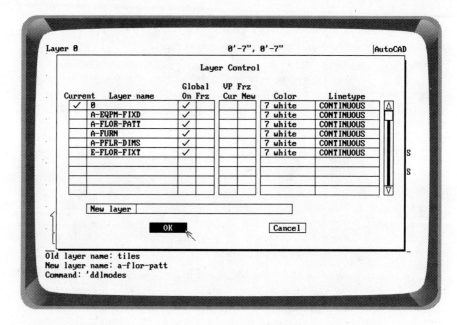

Fig. 13.3.
The layers
have been
renamed by
the script file.

You've changed the layer names to the AIA designations. (Layer
DEFPOINTS is where AutoCAD stores information for associative
dimensions; don't rename that layer.) Now use the Quit command so that
you don't preserve the changes for the following sections.

Using AutoCAD's Script-Specific Commands

Five AutoCAD commands are used specifically in script files. You can add
any of these commands to a script file, or you can issue them at the
Command: prompt:

❑ Resume

❑ Delay

❑ Textscr

❑ Graphscr

❑ Rscript

Resume

While a script is running, you can interrupt it at any time by pressing
Ctrl-C or Backspace. If you want the script to resume execution from the
point at which you interrupted it, type **Resume** at the Command: prompt.

Delay

You can use the Delay command to pause a script's execution for a specified amount of time. The delay is measured in units of 1/1000th of a second. If you add the command **Delay 1000** to a script file, for example, the script pauses for one second. The longest a script can pause is 33 seconds (actually, exactly 32.767 seconds).

Textscr and Graphscr

Some commands make AutoCAD switch to the text screen. The next command, however, may not automatically force AutoCAD to flip back to the graphics screen. The Graphscr command forces AutoCAD to return to the graphics screen; similarly, Textscr changes to the text screen. You can include Graphscr and Textscr in your script files to ensure that AutoCAD is in the correct display mode when the script ends.

Rscript

If you want the script to repeat over and over, use the Rscript (Repeat SCRIPT) command as the last line in the script file. You then can interrupt the script by pressing Backspace.

Preparing a Slide Show

If you've prepared a series of slides (with the Mslide command), you can create a script file that tells AutoCAD to display the slides over and over again. The following script shows the slide files called KITCHEN.SLD and BEDROOM.SLD:

```
Vslide KITCHEN
Delay 5000
Vslide BEDROOM
Delay 5000
Rscript
```

This script loads the KITCHEN.SLD and BEDROOM.SLD slide files and displays each slide for five seconds (5000/1000ths of a second), and then repeats with the Rscript command. You can interrupt the script at any time by pressing Backspace.

AutoCAD lets you *preload* slides to eliminate the delay associated with loading the slide files from disk. If you precede a slide's name with an asterisk in the script, AutoCAD loads the slide but does not display it until the next Vslide command. Here is the previous script, after being modified to allow preloading:

> **Vslide KITCHEN**
> **Vslide *BEDROOM**
> **Delay 5000**
> **Vslide**
> **Delay 5000**
> **Rscript**

During the five seconds that the kitchen is being displayed, AutoCAD loads the bedroom slide but doesn't display it until the next Vslide command.

TIP

You can make the current script file run another script by including the second script file's name at the end of the current script file.

Starting AutoCAD with a Script

AutoCAD can automatically load a drawing—with direction from a script file, naturally—when it starts up. When you start AutoCAD at the DOS C : \> prompt, you can include the name of a drawing and the name of a script file.

To practice starting AutoCAD with a script, quit the LINES drawing, exit from AutoCAD, load your text editor and type in the following:

2 ZOOM E ZOOM .9X

The **2** loads an existing drawing at the Main Menu. Be sure to type two blank spaces between the **2** and the **ZOOM E** (the second space accepts the default drawing file name). Also make sure that you put a blank line at the end of the file. Save the file with the name START.SCR.

Now go to the AutoCAD subdirectory (in this example, \ACAD), and type the following command at the DOS prompt:

C : \ A C A D > **ACAD SUITE START**

AutoCAD begins running, the Main Menu flashes by, the SUITE drawing loads, and the program automatically issues the Zoom Extents and Zoom 0.9X commands, all without human intervention. This script lets you start AutoCAD in the morning and go off for your coffee while DOS loads AutoCAD and AutoCAD loads SUITE. Such a script can be quite handy if you want to load a very large drawing that takes a long time to regenerate on the screen.

The START.SCR script file can be used with any drawing and any version of AutoCAD.

Using Menu Macros (Menu)

If you've written a macro in WordPerfect or Lotus 1-2-3, then you are already familiar with macros. If you've picked a name from AutoCAD's screen menu or on menu bar, then you have already used an AutoCAD macro—perhaps without even knowing it.

Menu macros let you combine many commands into a single pick from the screen menu. Unlike script files, you can combine many macros into a single menu macro file. You can use macros, for example, to eliminate redundant keystrokes, automate drawing and editing procedures, and reduce drawing errors.

AutoCAD's macros are called "menu macros" because they can be accessed only from a menu; they cannot be run from the keyboard. You can access a menu macro from the screen menu, from the pull-down menus, and from the digitizer overlay. This chapter discusses menu macros that run from the screen menu; for a discussion of the other two options, see *AutoCAD Advanced Techniques*, published by Que Corporation.

Creating and Running a Menu Macro

This section shows you how to write macros that eliminate redundant keystrokes. First, you will run the LINES.SCR file as a menu macro to see the difference between a script and a menu macro.

Load your text editor and type in the following text exactly as shown, complete with the strange-looking characters:

> **[Bathroom] ^ c ^ cLine;0,0;@7'<0;+**
> **@5'<90;@7'<180;C;**

When you are finished, save the file with the name LINES.MNU. The MNU extension tells AutoCAD that this is a menu file.

This menu macro does exactly the same thing as the LINES.SCR script file; that is, it draws the four walls of the bathroom. It may seem like more work than a script file, but as you will see later, menu macros are more flexible than scripts.

The characters [ ], ^c, ;, and + have the following meanings in a menu macro:

❏ **[Bathroom]** is the macro's name. The square brackets ([and]) tell AutoCAD that this is the macro's name. This part of the macro is not executed and is similar to a *comment line* in other programming languages.

Because a macro file can contain many menu macros, you should give it a descriptive name. Without a name, you probably won't remember what the macro does two months from now. The name can be any length, but AutoCAD has room to display only the first eight characters on the screen menu. If you don't give the macro a name, AutoCAD displays the first eight characters of the code (^c^cLine, in this case).

❑ ^c^c cancels any previous command. This is equivalent to pressing Ctrl-C twice. Most commands can be canceled with one Ctrl-C; some, like Pedit and Dim, need to be canceled with two executions of the Ctrl-C sequence.

❑ **Line;** executes the Line command. The semicolon (;) is the macro equivalent of pressing Enter or the space bar. Because menu macros let you use the semicolon, they are easier to debug than script files, which use the invisible space character to represent the pressing of the Enter key.

❑ **0,0;@7'<0;+** are the coordinates for the first line. Notice that a semicolon separates the coordinates. The plus sign (+) is a *continuation marker*, which tells AutoCAD that the macro continues on the next line. If you leave out the plus sign, AutoCAD stops executing the macro at the end of the first line.

Compare the menu macro with the script file and with the commands you would typically enter at the Command: prompt:

AutoCAD Prompt	Script file	Menu Macro
Command: **Line**	**Line**	**[Bathroom]** ^c^cLine;
From Point: **0,0**	**0,0**	**0,0;**
To Point: **@7'<0**	**@7'<0**	**@7'<0;+**
To Point: **@5'<90**	**@5'<90**	**@5'<90;**
To Point: **@7'<180**	**@7'<180**	**@7'<180;**
To Point: **C**	**C**	**C;**

Now you are ready to go back into AutoCAD and start with a new LINES drawing (remember that you quit the last one). Once you are in the Drawing Editor, load the menu macro as follows:

```
Command: Menu
Menu to load or . for none <SUITE>: LINES
Compiling menu C:\ACAD\LINES.mnu...
```

If you use AutoCAD Release 11, the Select menu file dialogue box appears when you issue the Menu command (see fig. 13.4). Pick LINES and then pick the OK button.

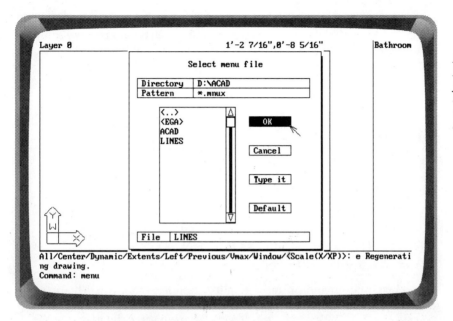

Fig. 13.4.
Release 11 lets
you select the
desired menu
macro from a
dialogue box.

The screen menu disappears and is replaced by a single word, "Bath-room" (without the square brackets). AutoCAD *compiles* menu files so that they run (and load the next time) faster.

Move the crosshair cursor over to the screen menu and pick the new Bathroom option. AutoCAD immediately draws the four bathroom wall lines, as before. (Again, you may need to issue the Zoom Extents command to see the lines.)

Pausing for User Input (\)

Menu macros are more powerful than script files because macros can pause for input. When the macro pauses, you can pick points or enter values, then let the macro continue. The backslash symbol (\) tells AutoCAD to halt the macro until you've responded in some way. Don't confuse the backslash symbol with the forward slash (/), which won't work.

In Chapter 12, you inserted blocks that represented electrical symbols. The Insert command, as you will recall, has several options that you often ignore by pressing Enter, such as the X- and Y-scale factors. Writing a menu macro with the \ symbol lets you use the Insert command but do less work.

Now, write a menu macro that runs the Insert command for you, and which pauses so that you can respond to the Insert command's prompts. Load the text editor and the LINES.MNU file. Add the following line after the [Bathroom] macro:

[Insert] ^ c ^ cInsert;\\;;

Compare the macro with the Insert command sequence:

AutoCAD Prompt	*Menu Macro*
`Command:` **Insert**	**[Insert]** **^ c ^ cInsert;**
`Block name (or ?):` Supply block name	\
`Insertion point:` Pick point	\
`X scale factor <1>/Corner/XYZ:` Press Enter	;
`Y scale factor (default=X):` Press Enter	;
`Rotation angle <0>:` Supply angle	\

Three Insert command prompts require attention from you. The first is the `Block name:` prompt; the backslash makes AutoCAD pause until you supply the block name. Another backslash pauses the macro at the `Insertion point:` prompt to let you specify the insertion point.

When you inserted the electrical symbols, you ignored the two scale-factor prompts by pressing Enter. In the macro, you supply a semicolon for the same effect. The semicolons cause AutoCAD to pass up those prompts without your pressing Enter. The final backslash makes AutoCAD pause for the rotation angle.

After you type in the Insert macro and save the LINES.MNU file, reload the SUITE drawing.

The screen menu now shows two words: Bathroom and Insert. With your pointing device, pick Insert. AutoCAD displays the Insert prompt in the command area. Supply the following responses as AutoCAD pauses the macro for your input:

```
Command: Insert
Block name (or ?): OUTLET
Insertion point: Pick point
Rotation angle <0>: Press Enter
```

AutoCAD inserts the OUTLET block at the point you picked. You can see the advantage of using macros by comparing the keystrokes required by the macro and those required when you run the Insert command yourself from the `Command:` prompt. If you insert this block by typing in commands at the keyboard, you must type 17 keystrokes (12, if you use **I**, the command alias for Insert) and a screen pick. The macro, on the other hand, requires seven keystrokes and two picks. If you insert many blocks, the savings in keystrokes rapidly add up, making you more productive and less finger-weary.

When you want the original AutoCAD screen menu back, use the Menu command, as follows:

```
Command: Menu

Menu to load or . for none <SUITE>: ACAD
```

If you use AutoCAD Release 11, enter the Menu command and then pick ACAD and the OK button from the dialogue box.

Summary

This chapter has shown you simple techniques you can use to customize AutoCAD. Command aliases reduce the number of keystrokes you must type by letting you type one or two characters rather than the command's full name. Script files let you automate repetitive tasks, such as loading drawings or changing layer names. Menu macros work in a similar manner, but also can pause for user input. All three help you work more productively.

Chapter 14 shows you how to write simple programs in the AutoLISP programming language.

14

An AutoLISP Primer

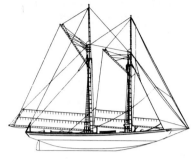

Illustration courtesy of
Autodesk, Inc., Sausalito, CA.

This chapter introduces you to the AutoLISP programming language and to the basic concepts involved in using it. Even if you don't want to be a programmer, you can benefit greatly from understanding the basics of AutoLISP. A few keystrokes in AutoLISP can save you hours and hours of work. A few lines of AutoLISP can make a tedious task fun.

This chapter introduces you to the following:

- ❏ What AutoLISP is and how to use it
- ❏ How to use a prewritten AutoLISP program
- ❏ How to enter AutoLISP at the keyboard
- ❏ How to add AutoLISP to menu macros
- ❏ How to write AutoLISP routines
- ❏ Basic AutoLISP syntax and definitions
- ❏ Some bonus AutoLISP routines useful to your work

What Is AutoLISP?

AutoLISP is often called LISP, for short; LISP is an acronym for LISt Processing. It is one of the oldest programming languages, first developed in the late 1950s. Like English, LISP has developed many dialects. AutoLISP is based on another programming language called XLISP (short for eXperimental LISP), written by David Betz as a public-domain language. XLISP was patterned after yet another dialect, called Common LISP.

If you learn one version of LISP (such as AutoLISP), you will find any dialect of LISP familiar. Each dialect has capabilities that make it suitable for a specific purpose. AutoLISP has unique features that let it work with AutoCAD.

Autodesk chose LISP as AutoCAD's programming language because LISP is very good at dealing with lists of numbers. The three-dimensional coordinates of a point, for example, are a list. LISP was designed to make it easy to manipulate lists of numbers.

AutoLISP is included free with AutoCAD. AutoLISP is important because it can have a tremendous effect on your productivity and enjoyment of AutoCAD. You need no programming skill to put it to work.

Several AutoLISP programs are included with AutoCAD. Also, many free or economical AutoLISP routines are available in AutoCAD-specialty magazines and on CompuServe's Autodesk Forum.

If you enjoy programming, you can write your own AutoLISP programs. Learning AutoLISP is not particularly difficult. It requires some study, practice, and an understanding of programming concepts. Fortunately, you can use AutoLISP at many levels of expertise. You can dabble in it or devote your life to it. AutoLISP programs range from a single line to missives longer than this chapter.

You may be intimidated by the idea that AutoLISP is a programming language, but you shouldn't be. A program is simply a set of instructions that the computer processes. The script files and menu macros you learned in the last chapter were examples of rudimentary programming. AutoLISP is a more powerful way to have AutoCAD do your work for you.

What AutoLISP Does for AutoCAD

AutoLISP can carry out changes, create new images, and record information about your AutoCAD drawing. In addition to everything a menu macro can do, here is a list of some powerful jobs AutoLISP can do:

❏ **Change objects.** AutoLISP can directly access the drawing database. It can change characteristics of objects that even the Change and Pedit commands cannot affect.

❏ **Extend existing commands.** AutoLISP can enhance AutoCAD's commands. Some commands are limited in function: Explode, for example, can only explode one object at a time, which is a serious limitation if you want to change several hundred polylines into lines.

❏ **Create new drawings.** AutoLISP can draw *parametrically*. This feature enables you to create new drawings (of bolts, for example) based only on the length of what you are drawing; the program determines all the other parameters.

❑ **Create and import databases.** AutoLISP can write
information to disk file about your drawing, and this
information can be used by other programs. Similarly,
AutoLISP can read files to import paragraphs of text,
model numbers, and other data stored in files outside
AutoCAD.

You can put AutoLISP to work customizing AutoCAD and develop
routines to do almost anything. Just as for menu macros, there is one
major limitation to AutoLISP: it only works inside the Drawing Editor.

As mentioned earlier, you can interact with AutoLISP on four levels:

❑ Loading and running prewritten AutoLISP programs

❑ Trying AutoLISP at the `Command:` prompt

❑ Adding AutoLISP to a menu macro

❑ Writing an AutoLISP program

Getting Your Hands on AutoLISP

You can try an AutoLISP routine right now, without knowing an atom
about programming. AutoLISP file names always end in LSP. Whenever
you load a LISP file, be sure that you use the proper drive and directory
path in your command; otherwise, you receive a loading error. AutoCAD
comes with several useful AutoLISP programs, including the following:

❑ **ASCTEXT.LSP** inserts (into AutoCAD drawings) ASCII text
files that you have created with a word processor. The text
can be left-, center-, middle-, or right-justified. You can
preset the distance between lines, adjust the number of
lines of text to read, and define columns. Later, you will
see how to use this program.

❑ **DLINE.LSP** Draws double lines and arcs. It also
automatically cleans up intersections. It is useful for
drawing walls.

❑ **3D.LSP** Draws nine 3-D objects: box, cone, dish, dome,
mesh, pyramid, sphere, torus, and wedge.

❑ **XPLODE.LSP** Enables you to explode as many objects as
you wish. (AutoCAD's Explode command limits you to
exploding one object at a time.)

Earlier in this book, you saw how to add text to your drawing with the
Text and Dtext commands. These commands can be cumbersome if you
have much text to type in or if you need to insert columns of text.
ASCTEXT.LSP (short for ASCII text) gives you an alternative.

You can type the full text with a word processor, then save it in an ASCII-format file (also called *nondocument mode* by WordStar and *DOS text* by WordPerfect). When you are in the AutoCAD Drawing Editor, you can use the ASCTEXT program to read the file into the drawing. This saves you the work of typing it in line-by-line with the Text command.

Just like text styles and linetypes, AutoLISP functions must be loaded into AutoCAD before you can use them in the drawing. Start a new drawing in AutoCAD and type the following at the `Command:` prompt:

```
Command: (LOAD "ASCTEXT")
C:ASCTEXT
```

You asked AutoCAD to load the AutoLISP file called "ASCTEXT". The parentheses tell AutoCAD that you are using AutoLISP's Load function. Otherwise, AutoCAD would think that you were using the Load command, which is used for loading shapes.

Now that ASCTEXT is loaded, you can use it to insert text into the drawing. AutoCAD has several ASCII files you can practice with. A file that comes with every version of AutoCAD and isn't too large is ACAD.LIN, the linetype pattern file. Insert the full text of the file into the drawing as follows:

```
Command: ASCTEXT
File to read (including extension): ACAD.LIN
Start point or Center/Middle/Right/TL/TC/TR/ML/MC/
MR/BL/BC/BR: Pick point
Height <0.2000>: 0.5
Rotation angle <0>: Press Enter
Change text options? <N>: Y
Distance between lines/<Auto>: Press Enter
First line to read/<1>: Press Enter
Number of lines to read/<All>: Press Enter
Underscore each line? <N>: Press Enter
Overscore each line? <N>: Press Enter
Change text case? Upper/Lower/<N>: Press Enter
Set up columns? <N>: Press Enter
```

The text is inserted into the drawing. More importantly, you used an AutoLISP program without knowing how to program.

Definitions

You will find it easier to understand AutoLISP if you are familiar with some terms. The following is a short list of definitions. For the complete AutoLISP command reference, see the *AutoLISP Programmer's Reference* included with your copy of AutoCAD.

Data can be formatted in different ways as *data types*. Some data types used by AutoLISP are as follows:

❑ *Real:* a number with decimal precision. For example, 7.017 is a real number; 7 is not.

❑ *Integer:* a number without decimal precision. For example, 7 is an integer; 7.017 is not (it's a real number).

❑ *String:* a collection of numeric and alphabetic characters— in other words, ordinary text. In AutoLISP, strings must be enclosed in quotation marks. For example, "7.017" is a string but 7.017 is not (it's a number). "Seven" is a string and Seven is not (it's a variable name).

❑ *Atom:* the smallest element AutoLISP recognizes as a unit. An atom can be a single number, a symbol, a variable, or a string.

❑ *Symbols:* a collection of characters that AutoLISP uses to store variables. A stored value is represented by a symbol. Seven is a symbol; "Seven" is not (it's a string).

❑ *Lists:* AutoLISP evaluates a list of symbols, integers, real numbers, and strings, one at a time. The organization of these lists and their relationships to each other determine the order of the actions AutoLISP takes to execute a routine. The boundary of the list is denoted (or *delimited*) by opening and closing parentheses.

❑ *Nil* and *null:* generally denote that nothing exists, or that a symbol represents nothing. In programming (as in mathematics) the value of 0 is not nothing. Nil is the value returned by AutoLISP when a symbol represents nothing. Null is a built-in function of AutoLISP; it tests to see whether a symbol represents nil.

AutoLISP recognizes other types of data that you won't need right away. You can find more information about them by looking at the type *function* in the *AutoLISP Programmer's Reference*.

LISPing at the Keyboard

The easiest way to get your hands on AutoLISP is at the Command: prompt. Try adding these two numbers:

```
Command: (+ 3 5)
8
```

You used AutoLISP to ask AutoCAD to add 3 and 5, and it responded with 8. You have written your first AutoLISP program! A program is also called a *routine* or a *function*; the three words are used interchangeably.

If you have never used a Hewlett-Packard calculator, the convention of (+ 3 5) may look strange to you. This convention is called *prefix notation*; think of it as "add three and five." Everything in AutoLISP works this way: first you tell it the operation (addition), then tell it the operands (3 and 5).

Also, everything in AutoLISP is enclosed in parentheses. This tells AutoLISP where the routine starts and ends. If you leave out a bracket (producing an `unbalanced parentheses` error) in long AutoLISP programs, you can get frustrated trying to find where it should go.

Here are the other functions you learned in elementary school:

```
Command: (- 5 3)
2
Command: (* 2 3)
6
Command: (/ 360 5)
72
```

AutoLISP uses the asterisk (*) as the symbol for multiplication and the slash (/) for division.

As was mentioned earlier in this chapter, AutoLISP's unique aspect as a programming language is that it deals easily with lists of numbers. For example, you can add several numbers at once, as follows:

```
Command: (+ 3 5 2 3 360 5)
383
```

Here AutoLISP first adds together 3 and 5; then it adds each following integer in order (2, 3, and so on).

From high school algebra, you may remember that you can give a variable a value. AutoLISP is no different; it enables you to save the results of a calculation in a variable. Because AutoLISP evaluates a line from the inside out, in the following routine the division problem is evaluated first and then the results are assigned to the variable ANGLE.

```
Command: (SETQ ANGLE (/ 360 5))
72
```

Here the SETQ (short for SET eQual) function stores the result of (/ 360 5) in the variable named ANGLE. Want to see the result?

```
Command: !ANGLE
72
```

The exclamation point (!) tells AutoCAD to show you the value of the variable ANGLE (here, 72).

NOTE

You can use almost any variable name you like, but it helps to use one that describes the value it is holding. The variable name must contain alphabetical letters: ANGLE1 is okay but 123 is not. The name can be up to 100 characters long, but for technical reasons the optimal length is 8 characters. The variable name cannot be a name already used by another function. For the complete list of names already in use, type **!ATOMLIST** at the `Command:` prompt.

WARNING

One function name that is often used accidentally as a variable name is T. T has special meaning in AutoLISP. It usually means that the result of some action is true. You can name a variable TT, or something similar.

You can string several calculations together. Unfortunately, AutoLISP's prefix notation makes this look confusing. Here is how you might try to calculate two-thirds of 360 degrees:

```
Command: (* (/ 2 3) 360)
0
```

Why is the answer zero? You have run into a problem with integers. When you divide two integers, you might not get an accurate answer because AutoLISP returns the nearest integer. Specifically, dividing 2 into 3 is 0. Dividing 4 into 3 returns 1.

The solution is to make one of the operands a real number. This forces AutoLISP to return a real answer. Add a decimal point and zero to one number, as follows:

```
Command: (/ 2.0 3)
0.666667
```

A zero *should* follow the decimal point, as in 2.0. On the other hand, a zero *must* precede a decimal point, as in 0.2. If you leave out the zero, AutoLISP complains with the rather mysterious error message, `Invalid dotted pair`, which has nothing to do with dotted pairs (explained later in this chapter). Now try that calculation again:

```
Command: (* (/ 2.0 3) 360)
240.0
```

AutoLISP first calculates the innermost terms (/ 2.0 3) to arrive at 0.666667 and then multiplies 0.666667 * 360. If you find *nested* calculations difficult, you can do them one-by-one, as follows:

```
Command: (SETQ TT (/ 2.0 3))
0.666667
Command: (SETQ ANGLE (* TT 360))
240.0
```

Assign a variable (TT) to the results of the first calculation. Then use the variable in the second calculation.

The Built-in Calculator

You can go one step further in using AutoLISP at the `Command:` prompt. You also can use AutoLISP in the middle of a command. This is extremely useful since it enables you to calculate two numbers without having to reach for a calculator. Try it now with the Arc command. Draw an arc that sweeps one-fifth of the way around a circle, or 1/5 of 360 degrees:

```
Command: ARC
Center/<Start point>: Pick point
Center/End/<Second point: C
Angle/Length of chord/<End point>: A
Included angle: (/ 360 5)
```

AutoCAD draws an arc of 72 degrees. The alternative is to do the calculation first and then supply the variable name, as follows:

```
Command: (SETQ ANGLE (/ 360 5))
72
Command: ARC
Center/<Start point>: Pick point
Center/End/<Second point: C
Angle/Length of chord/<End point>: A
Included angle: !ANGLE
```

Again, AutoCAD draws a 72-degree arc.

Adding LISP to Menu Macros

Typing in AutoLISP at the `Command:` is fine for "on the fly" work. Unless you intend to leave AutoCAD on indefinitely, you need a way to store the routines for repeated use. To ease into programming, you will convert the menu macro from the preceding chapter into a LISP routine.

As you may recall, you wrote a macro that reduced the number of keystrokes it takes to insert a block:

[Insert] ^ c ^ cInsert;\\ ;;\

We had compared the macro with the Insert command sequence. Here is one way to rewrite the macro in AutoLISP:

[Insert] ^ C ^ C(COMMAND "INSERT" PAUSE PAUSE "" "" PAUSE)

You can see that the macro and the AutoLISP version share some
similarities and some differences. The following table compares how the
command keystrokes, the menu macro, and the AutoLISP functions
relate:

AutoCAD Prompt	Response	Menu Macro	AutoLISP
`Command:`	**INSERT**	^c^cInsert;	(COMMAND "INSERT"
`Block name (or ?):`	Supply block name	\	PAUSE
`Insertion point:`	Pick point	\	PAUSE
`X scale factor <1>/ Corner/XYZ:`	Press Enter	;	""
`Y scale factor (default=X):`	Press Enter	;	""
`Rotation angle <0>:`	Supply angle	\	PAUSE)

The COMMAND function lets you use AutoCAD commands in the
AutoLISP program, as in (COMMAND "INSERT"). The PAUSE is equivalent
to the backslash in a menu macro: it waits for you to respond. The double
quotation marks ("") with nothing between them are AutoLISP's way of
pressing the Enter key.

The advantage of using AutoLISP in a menu macro is that it makes the
macro easier to read. Many backslashes and semicolons are not very
informative.

Writing an AutoLISP Routine

You have dabbled in AutoLISP, typed in some math at the `Command:`
prompt, and written a line of LISP in a menu macro. Now you can try
writing an AutoLISP program that stands on its own.

Rewrite the Insert macro with a few new functions that test your
knowledge of variable names. Load your text editor (either outside of
AutoCAD or using the Shell command), and then check your AutoCAD
directory for a file named ACAD.LSP. If that file exists, then load it and
add the following six lines of text to the *end* of the file. If you don't
already have a file called ACAD.LSP, then create one and type in the
following:

```
(DEFUN C:INS ()
(SETQ BLOCK (GETSTRING "Block name: "))
(SETQ INSPT (GETPOINT "Insertion point: "))
(SETQ ANGLE (GETANGLE "Rotation angle: "))
(COMMAND "INSERT" BLOCK INSPT "" "" ANGLE)
)
```

NOTE

You could have given this program any file name, but the name ACAD.LSP has special meaning. Whenever AutoCAD loads the Drawing Editor, it looks for a file called ACAD.LSP. If AutoCAD can find it, ACAD.LSP is also loaded into memory. This saves you the step of loading the LISP routine before you can run it (as happens with the ASCTEXT.LSP program).

You have used four new AutoLISP functions:

❑ **DEFUN C:** enables you to create a new AutoLISP function that operates like an AutoCAD command, as in (DEFUN C:INS). The C: tells AutoCAD you are creating a new command; don't confuse it with the DOS C: drive designation.

❑ **GETSTRING** reads a word you type in at the keyboard. (SETQ BLOCK (GETSTRING "Block name: ") reads in the name of the block and saves it in the variable called BLOCK.

❑ **GETPOINT** reads the coordinates of a point you pick on the screen or type in at the keyboard. (SETQ INSPT (GETPOINT "Insertion point: ") reads the coordinates of the insertion point (either from values you type in at the keyboard or from a point picked on the screen by your pointing device) and saves the coordinates in the variable INSPT).

❑ **GETANGLE** reads an angle. (SETQ ANGLE (GETANGLE "Rotation angle: ") reads the rotation angle of the block and saves the value in variable ANGLE.

This AutoLISP program is different from the menu macro. It first asks for information about how to insert a block. Then it starts the Insert command and supplies the values stored in the variables (BLOCK, INSPT, and ANGLE) to the Insert command.

This is an important idea in programming: you always work with variables, not with the actual values. If your needs for the program change, it is easier to have the computer update the variables than for you to retype the program to reflect the changes.

Load the SUITE drawing into the AutoCAD Drawing Editor and try out the "Ins" command:

```
Command: INS
Block name: OUTLET
Insertion point: Pick point
Rotation angle: 90
```

The OUTLET block is inserted. The prompts you typed mimic the Insert command. This may seem to you an awkward (and time-consuming) way to avoid two Insert command prompts. This example not only models how AutoLISP can be used but also shows why menu macros are better for automating simple tasks.

Tech note. . .

Programmers have many conventions for writing programs (also called *code*). These conventions make it easier for them to understand the program and for the computer to run the program.

```
(defun C:INS (/ BLOCK INSPT ANGLE)
(setq BLOCK (getstring "Block name: "))
(setq INSPT (getpoint "Insertion point: "))
(setq ANGLE (getangle "Rotation angle: "))
(command "INSERT" BLOCK INSPT "" "" ANGLE)
)
```

You followed three programming conventions in modifying the program. One convention states that function names are lowercase (defun, setq, and getstring, for example) and variable names are uppercase (BLOCK, INSPT, and ANGLE). This makes it easier to read the code and spot the variable names you invented.

The second convention is indentation. By indenting the portion of the program between the beginning (defun and the closing parenthesis, you can see the body of the code more clearly. This becomes important in long programs with many functions. Technically, parts of the code that repeat (such as while, if-then, and repeat loops) are indented also.

You also changed the variables from *global* to *local* by placing them inside the parentheses, following the slash sign: c:INS (/ BLOCK INSPT ANGLE). A local variable loses its value when the program stops running. The benefit is that local variables take up less memory, a particular concern in large programs. The drawback is that the program is more difficult to debug with local variables.

If you want to make your code look really professional, you can also do the following:

Tech note (continued)...

❏ Add comments

❏ Turn off CMDECHO

❏ Combine the `setq` statements into one

❏ Quiet the last line with (`prin1`)

```
; Ins.Lsp
; My first AutoLISP program
; From Using AutoCAD, 3rd Edition


(defun C:INS (/ CVAR BLOCK INSPT ANGLE)
; First, save the CMDECHO setting and
;  turn command-line echo off.
 (setq CVAR (getvar "CMDECHO")
  (setvar "CMDECHO" 0)
;Then, prompt the user for input values.
  (setq
    BLOCK (getstring "Block name: ")
    INSPT (getpoint "Insertion point: ")
    ANGLE (getangle "Rotation angle: ")
    )
;Now insert the block.
  (command "INSERT" BLOCK INSPT "" "" ANGLE)
;Clean up by turning command echo on again
    (setvar "CMDECHO" CVAR)
  )
(prin1)
```

AutoLISP ignores any information placed after a semicolon; this enables you to write comments or notes to yourself inside the code. Adding comments to the code helps you remember what the program does, months after writing it.

The system variable CMDECHO determines whether you see the AutoLISP code zipping by in the command-prompt area. By turning it off **(setvar "CMDECHO" 0)**, you have a *quiet* program that doesn't look as messy.

If you change any system variable at the beginning of an AutoLISP program, you need to return it to its original value at the end of the

Tech note (continued)...

program. But just turning it back on at the end of the program is not good enough. What if it wasn't on to begin with? That's why you save the value at the beginning of the program with **(setq CVAR (getvar "CMDECHO))**. The getvar function gets the value of the system variable CMDECHO and setq saves it in variable CVAR.

At the end of the program, **(setvar "CMDECHO" CVAR)** sets CMDECHO back to the value of CVAR, rather than back to 1.

Placing all setq statements in one list saves memory and takes less time to type in. Notice the second level of indentation to make the setq section clearer.

When a LISP routine finishes, it has to say so—usually with the disquieting word, nil. You can suppress the nil statement by including the function **(prin1)** at the very end.

Special Characters

In AutoLISP, certain characters can be used only for a specific purpose. For example, the following characters are math functions:

Character	Meaning
=	Equal in value
+	Addition
–	Subtraction
>	Greater than
<	Less than
*	Multiplication
/	Division
/=	Is not equal
~	Not
>=	Greater than or equal
<=	Less than or equal

They work exactly as they did in your math courses. Other special characters include the following:

( ) . " ' ;

The parentheses delimit lists for AutoLISP.

WARNING

If the program doesn't have *balanced* parentheses (an equal number of opening and closing parentheses), AutoLISP lets you know that there is a problem:

```
1>
```

AutoLISP is telling you that the program is missing one closing parenthesis. The solution is to type one in, as follows:

```
1> )
```

You will get the 1> error message also if you omit (or have one too many) quotation marks ("). AutoLISP considers everything between a pair of quotation marks as a string; if there is no closing quotation mark, AutoLISP thinks that the string continues to the end of the program. The solution is to type a quotation mark and a closing parenthesis, like this:

```
1> ")
```

Then edit the LISP code to correct the number of quotation marks.

Sometimes you may get the error message extra right paren. This means that AutoLISP has found that the program has too many closing parentheses.

In either case, your program has a *bug*. To fix the problem, you need to go back into the text editor and find the missing (or extra) parenthesis or quotation marks.

Periods are used for decimal points and to create *dotted pairs*. Real numbers must have a decimal: AutoLISP will complain about .7, whereas 0.7 is correct. If you divide two integers, such as (/ 7 5), you will get an incorrect result (namely, 1) unless you make one a real number (to get the real result, 1.4). Dotted pairs are used in the AutoCAD drawing database as *association lists*, allowing your program to retrieve information about an entity in the drawing. This is an advanced use of AutoLISP.

The apostrophe (') can be used in place of the built-in function quote. The quote forces AutoLISP to view the characters that follow exactly as they appear, instead of evaluating them as a variable.

Quotation marks (") denote a string, as discussed earlier.

Semicolons (;) enable you to add comments to your program. AutoLISP ignores comments when it processes the program. They remind you what the program does.

Parentheses, apostrophes, quotation marks, a space, and an end-of-line character will all terminate a symbol name or numeric constant in AutoLISP.

Within strings, backslashes (\) are used to tell AutoLISP that a special control character follows. Two of those control characters are a second backslash (\\) and a character that causes AutoLISP to print a new line to the screen (\n). The *n* must be lowercase; otherwise, AutoLISP will not recognize it as the new-line character. You will see how each of them is used in the examples later in this chapter.

Useful AutoLISP Programs

As noted earlier, AutoCAD comes with several AutoLISP programs that can help you work more efficiently. The following text contains two additional programs; notice how the code follows the programming conventions mentioned earlier.

A Multiple Trim Command

The Trim command lets you trim only one entity at a time. Here is an enhanced Trim command (MTRIM.LSP) that enables you to trim many objects at once:

```
(defun c:MTRIM (/ CVAR CUTEDG SS SIDE LEN I)
  (setq CVAR (getvar "CMDECHO"))
  (setvar "CMDECHO" 0)
  (prompt "Select cutting edges...")
  (setq CUTEDG (ssget))
  (prompt "Select objects to trim: ")
  (setq
    SS (ssget)
    LEN (sslength SS)
     I -1
    SIDE (getpoint "Pick side to trim: ")
  )
  (command "TRIM" CUTEDG "")
  (repeat LEN
    (setq I (1+ I))
    (command (list (ssname SS I) SIDE))
  )
  (command "")
  (setvar "CMDECHO" CVAR)
  (princ "\nMTrim is done.")
  (prin1)
)
```

Type in the program with a text editor and save it in ACAD.LSP. Bring up AutoCAD with a drawing and type the following:

```
Command: MTRIM
Select cutting edges...
Select objects: Pick edges
Select objects to trim: Select objects
Pick side to trim: Pick point
MTrim is done.
```

The program asks you to pick the objects it should use as the cutting line. Then it prompts for the objects you want to trim. You can pick them one-by-one, or you can use the Window and Crossing selection boxes to pick a whole bunch of objects. Finally, Mtrim needs to know which side of the cutting line to trim. It then trims all the lines at once. This is far faster than using AutoCAD's Trim command, which forces you to pick the trimmed lines one at a time.

Let's look at how the program works.

(defun c:MTRIM (/ CVAR CUTEDG SS SIDE LEN I)
(setq CVAR (getvar "CMDECHO")
(setvar "CMDECHO" 0)

The function is called Mtrim. Variables are made local. Command echo setting is saved and turned off.

(prompt "Select cutting edges...")
(setq CUTEDG (ssget))

The program prompts you for the entities you want to use as the cut lines and saves them as a list in variable CUTEDG.

(prompt "Select objects to trim: ")
(setq
  SS (ssget)
  LEN (sslength SS)
  I –1

Mtrim then prompts you to pick the objects you want trimmed. You can pick them one by one, or use any selection method (such as window or crossing). The objects are stored as a list in variable SS. The Sslength function counts the number of entities and stores them in variable LEN. Variable I is an index counter (set to –1) for use later.

SIDE (getpoint "Pick side to trim: "

You pick the side of the cut line you want the objects trimmed. The point location is stored in variable SIDE.

)
(command "TRIM" CUTEDG "")

Mtrim starts the AutoCAD Trim command and supplies (with CUTEDG) the entities that will act as the cut line.

```
(repeat LEN
(setq I (1+ I))
(command (list (ssname SS I) SIDE))
)
```

Mtrim goes into a *loop*, repeatedly using the Trim command's trimming function to trim the objects stored in SS. The repeat function repeats the two lines of code until I equals LEN. You can see that the value of I is increased by 1 with **(setq I (1+ I)**. The line **(command (list (ssname SS I) SIDE))** extracts the next object in the list held by SS and re-executes the Trim command to trim the next object.

(command "")

When all the objects in list SS have been trimmed (that is, when I equals LEN), the Trim command is terminated with **(command "")**.

```
(princ "\nMTrim is finished.")
(setvar "CMDECHO" CVAR)
(prin1)
)
```

The \n in "\nMTrim..." is the new-line character—it forces AutoLISP to print the sentence "MTrim is finished" on its own line in the command-prompt area. Mtrim then reports that it is finished, resets the value of CMDECHO, and quietly ends with **(prin1)**.

Freeze a Layer by Picking

The FRLAYER.LSP program makes it easier to freeze a layer. You simply pick an entity on that layer and FRLAYER freezes the layer.

```
(defun FRLAYER (/ SS1 E# ENT NAMES LYR)
  (prompt "\nSelect objects on layers to be frozen: ")
  (setq
    SS1 (ssget)
    E# (sslength SS1)
  )
  (if (> E# 0)
    (progn
    (setq
      ENT (ssname SS1 (setq E# (1- E#)))
      ENT (entget ENT)
      NAMES (cdr (assoc 8 ENT))
      E# (1- E#))
    )
    )
```

```
        (while (> E# –1)
          (setq
            ENT (ssname SS1 E#)
            ENT (entget ENT)
            LYR (cdr (assoc 8 ENT))
            NAMES (strcat NAMES "," LYR)
            E# (1– E#)
            )
          )
        (command "LAYER" "F" NAMES "")
        (princ)
        )
```

The program uses some advanced AutoLISP concepts, such as entity access, which let the program determine which layer the entity lies on.

```
    (defun FRLAYER (/ SS1 E# ENT NAMES LYR)
```

The FRLAYER.LSP program begins by defining its name and making the variables local.

```
    (prompt "\nSelect objects on layers to be frozen: ")
    (setq
      SS1 (ssget)
      E# (sslength SS1)
      )
```

The program prompts you to pick an object on the screen. The object lies on the layer you want frozen. You can pick one or more objects. The objects are stored in variable SS1; the number of objects are stored in E#.

```
    (if (> E# 0)
    (progn
```

FRLAYER checks to make sure that at least one object was picked by checking whether the value of E# is greater than 0. If it is, the program gets the first layer name in the list:

```
    (setq
    ENT (ssname SS1 (setq E# (1– E#)))
```

The first object you picked is extracted from the list and stored in ENT; the value of E# is decreased by one.

```
    ENT (entget ENT)
    NAMES (cdr (assoc 8 ENT))
```

The program retrieves the object's layer name in two steps. First, the entity information is extracted from the object and stored back in ENT. Second, the layer name is extracted from the entity information and stored in NAMES.

(while (> E# –1)

With the first layer name stored in NAMES, the program begins a loop that keeps repeating while E# is still larger than –1.

```
(setq
  ENT (ssname SS1 E#)
  ENT (entget ENT)
  LYR (cdr (assoc 8 ENT))
  NAMES (strcat NAMES "," LYR)
   E# (1– E#)
  )
```

The process of extracting the layer names from each picked object is similar to the preceding code. The list of layer names is stored in the variable NAMES, with a command separating each name.

(command "LAYER" "F" NAMES "")

Now use the Command function to execute the LAYER Freeze command, supplying it with the list of layer names to be frozen.

(princ)

And end the program quietly.

Try the program by typing it into the ACAD.LSP file. Bring up the SUITE drawing and run the FRLAYER.LSP program:

```
Command: FRLAYER
Select objects on layers to be frozen:   Pick object
```

Pick a tile and all the tiles disappear as the TILES layer is frozen. You need to use the Layer command to thaw the layer.

Summary

This chapter introduced you to the concepts behind AutoLISP and provided an elementary review of the way AutoLISP works. You were also shown the important uses of AutoLISP in prewritten routines, at the Command: prompt, in menu macros, and in the ACAD.LSP file.

This has been a brief look at some of AutoLISP's functions. Entire books have been written on AutoLISP; you can imagine the complexity and flexibility of the language. If you want to learn more about AutoLISP, you will find more detailed discussions of these topics in *AutoCAD Advanced Techniques*, published by Que Corporation.

With a solid background in 2-D drawing and an introduction to customizing AutoCAD, you are now ready for the next section: 3-D design and drafting.

Part Five

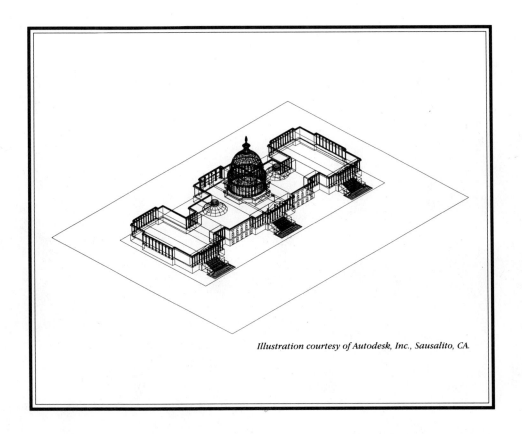

Illustration courtesy of Autodesk, Inc., Sausalito, CA.

Drawing in Three Dimensions

*Illustration courtesy of
Autodesk, Inc., Sausalito, CA.*

15

Understanding the Third Dimension

This chapter introduces you to the most exciting part of AutoCAD: three-dimensional drafting. Traditionally, drafters have drawn in two dimensions. Computer-aided three-dimensional drafting is a major evolution in the way drawings are prepared.

This chapter discusses the applications of three-dimensional drafting, and demonstrates some basic commands that can help you visualize AutoCAD's use of the third dimension. After completing this chapter, you should understand the usefulness of 3-D, be able to enter elements with X, Y, and Z coordinates, and be able to view a three-dimensional environment.

This chapter discusses the following 3-D features:

❏ Chprop Thickness

❏ Vpoint

❏ Hide

❏ Shade

So far, this book has discussed only two-dimensional drafting. As you have seen, AutoCAD lets you draw in two dimensions in much the same way you draw on a drafting board and paper. Three-dimensional computer drafting is like building a model out of toothpicks. The term *three-dimensional drafting* describes the process of drawing objects in space.

AutoCAD uses three different methods of displaying three-dimensional models. The one you see most often is called *wireframe modeling* because it looks like an object framed with wires. Wireframe objects have no sides and no inside—you can only work with the edges. Most 3-D drawing and editing work is done with wireframe representation since it can be quickly displayed on the computer screen. The drawback to wireframe models is that you can see through them, making it difficult to visualize the exact shape of the model.

Surface modeling adds sides to the wireframe objects. This enables you to easily see what the 3-D model looks like by eliminating the hidden portions of the model. Surface modeling is used by the Hide and Shade commands, described later in this chapter.

Solids modeling adds an inside to the model. This enables you to perform analysis on the model, such as finding its center of gravity or where the stress points are. Solids modeling is used by commands in the Advanced Modeling Extension.

If you are uncomfortable with the idea of drawing in 3-D, remember that you won't be stuck in the third dimension. You can design in 3-D and then make 2-D views and plots from the drawing if you like. You need to realize that you do not *have* to draw in three dimensions. In fact, many people who draft on the computer will not even consider the third dimension.

Three-dimensional AutoCAD objects are just like toothpicks, with beginning and ending points in space. Just as our world and its objects exist in three dimensions, AutoCAD drawings can be based in three dimensions. Whereas a two-dimensional drawing shows only the length and width of an object, a three-dimensional drawing shows the object's length, width, and height. In computer-aided drafting, these values are indicated by the object's *X, Y, and Z coordinates*. Three-dimensional coordinates are explained in detail shortly.

The Advantages of Drawing in Three Dimensions

Unless your drafting work is deliberately two-dimensional, there are several good reasons for drawing in three dimensions. The product of your drafting is most likely a three-dimensional object, whether it is a simple bolt or a complex chemical plant.

Until the last decade, all drafting work was by necessity two-dimensional. Since drafters did not have the tools to design in three dimensions, they developed cumbersome ways to depict 3-D objects in a 2-D environment. The traditional top-side-front views, isometric views, and even the simulated perspective views (one-point and two-point) were used to painstakingly translate a 3-D idea into a 2-D design. When the builder received the 2-D drawings, he had to convert the drawings back into the 3-D object.

Having used 2-D drafting methods for several centuries, it has become second nature to drafters. But now that CAD has the ability to draw in three dimensions, it is no longer necessary to manually develop the 2-D views. The 3-D idea can be drawn as a 3-D object in AutoCAD.

The problem is that paper drawings are still the most common way to transmit the design from drafter to builder. Here AutoCAD can help in generating the 2-D views of the 3-D drawing. In some cases, however, the 3-D design can produce the 3-D object without undergoing the 2-D translation. If AutoCAD is linked to NC (numerical control) software, the 3-D drawing can produce the instructions used to create the part on a lathe or milling machine.

With three-dimensional drafting you can draw objects as they actually appear and then check them for interference and find distances between the objects. It is easier to see if two pipes go through each other (or find the clearance between them) if you can view them in three dimensions.

If a project is drawn in three dimensions, it can be *rendered* (that is, made to look more realistic) with the Shade command, with AutoShade, or with Autodesk 3-D Studio. The drawing can even be *animated* (made to move) with AutoFlix or Autodesk Animator. These programs are discussed in Chapter 20.

Coordinate Systems

One of the most confusing aspects of three-dimensional drafting is understanding how the computer needs the information entered. Until now, you have been drawing with no regard for the entities' Z coordinates.

As you learn more about three-dimensional drafting, you will discover that AutoCAD uses 3-D coordinates for all entities in a drawing. In the preceding chapters, as you entered coordinates (either by typing them in as X and Y coordinates, as relative coordinates, or by picking a point), AutoCAD was silently adding a Z coordinate value of 0.

Drawing in two dimensions is easy. Because you use a "flat" computer screen, however, drawing in three dimensions is a challenge. This is especially true if you are working on odd angles, such as roof planes. AutoCAD has some tools to help you draw in three dimensions.

Understanding the Z Axis

While the X and Y axes limit you to drawing in two dimensions, the Z axis enables you to draw in three dimensions. So far in this book, you have specified coordinate pairs to indicate a point, such as 4,6. You could have also entered coordinate triplets—such as 4,6,0—to indicate that the point should lie in the X,Y plane.

The third coordinate indicates the distance in the Z direction, just as the first two indicate distance in the X and Y directions. If the Z coordinate is negative, then the point lies below the X,Y plane.

To draw a line in three dimensions, you can enter coordinates in three different ways: Cartesian, cylindrical, and spherical. Of the three, only Cartesian coordinates work with Release 10, as follows:

Command: **Line**
From point: **4,6,0**
To point: **1,2,3**
To point: Press Enter

Here you have drawn a line in three-dimensional space. Fig. 15.1 shows a viewpoint that emphasizes the three-dimensional quality of this line.

Fig. 15.1.
View of line
from an
altered
viewpoint.

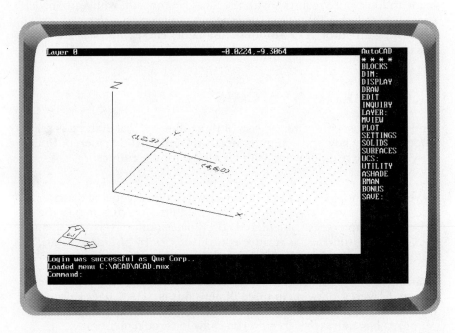

In addition to the Cartesian (x,y,z) method of entering points in three dimensions, AutoCAD Release 11 adds two more methods: cylindrical and spherical coordinates.

Cylindrical coordinates are a variation on polar coordinates (for example, 1<233). In addition to the distance (1 units, in this example) and the angle (233 degrees from the X-axis), cylindrical coordinates enable you to include the Z distance. For example:

```
Command: Line
From point: 4,6,0
To point: 2.2361<63,3
To point: Press Enter
```

You have drawn the same line as earlier but this time using cylindrical coordinates. The coordinates 2.2361<63,3 specify a point 2.2361 units from the origin (0,0,0) along a line 233 degrees from the X axis and 3 units up in the positive Z direction.

Spherical coordinates use a distance and two angles. The distance is along two angles: the first angle is from the X axis, while the second angle is up from the X,Y plane. For example:

```
Command: Line
From point: 4,6,0
To point: 3.7417<63<53
To point: Press Enter
```

This time you have drawn the same line using spherical coordinates. The coordinates 3.7417<63<53 specify a point 3.7417 units from the origin (0,0,0) along a line 233 degrees from the X axis and 31 degrees up from the X,Y-plane direction.

The Right-Hand Rule

You can better understand the direction of the positive X,Y, and Z axes by learning the *right-hand rule*. This rule shows you the positive direction of an axis. All you need is your right hand (literally!) and the positive direction of two axes.

To determine the positive direction of the Z axis, place your right hand near the screen, and do the following:

❑ Point your thumb in the direction of the positive X axis (that is, to the right).

❑ Point your index finger in the direction of the positive Y axis (that is, pointing up).

❏ Curl the other fingers toward your palm, then point the middle finger out, so that it is pointing away from the screen and directly at you: the positive Z axis points straight out from the screen.

These directions hold true only when you are working in plan view. AutoCAD lets you change your orientation at any time; when the view point is upside-down and backward, the right-hand rule becomes very helpful. You can use your hand to find the *positive rotation* for an axis. Positive rotation refers to the rotation AutoCAD uses when drawing or editing entities (such as drawing a circle or when you are using the Rotate command). Aim your right thumb along the axis in the positive direction. Close your fingers into a fist. Your fingers curl in the direction of the positive rotation along that axis.

Now point your thumb away from the computer screen, toward you. Your fingers curl in the counterclockwise direction—the direction in which AutoCAD measures angles and draws circles and arcs.

The World Coordinate System (WCS)

As you draw in two and three dimensions, you draw in a unique *world* or space. Every object is drawn with coordinates relative to the origin (0,0,0), which is fixed in space. AutoCAD's name for this system is the *World Coordinate System* (called WCS for short). When you work in the world coordinate system, you place each entity in an absolute location. You began by drawing the bathroom walls as a line from 0,0 to 0,7; that line will always be between those two coordinates, no matter which angle you view the line from.

Although the WCS is the reference for all objects in a drawing, you will soon notice that you cannot draw all three-dimensional entities in the WCS. The WCS is great for walls and table tops, but not for more complex objects, such as 3-D fillets and angled shower heads.

To draw complex 3-D parts, you need a flexible coordinate system, which enables you to position entities just as quickly and easily as if you were using the WCS. You need a system that lets you specify a different origin (and orientation) of the X,Y,Z axes. A different origin means the location of 0,0,0 changes; a different orientation changes the direction of the X,Y,Z axes. In short, you need a *user-defined* coordinate system.

The User Coordinate System

The *User Coordinate System* (called UCS, for short) is an X,Y,Z-coordinate reference placed anywhere in the WCS. You specify the direction of the UCS axes and the location of its origin. A UCS enables you to draw and edit three-dimensional entities with greater ease, because you can use the UCS to reorient the drafting plane so that you are always working in plan view. This is a capability you never needed for two-dimensional drafting.

You can define an unlimited number of user coordinate systems for each drawing. You can assign a different UCS to the side, front, and back elevations (even straight down on the plan view). The UCS command's power comes into play when you are working with inclined planes (such as a roof). A UCS is temporary; you define it when you need help in drawing and editing. You can discard it when you no longer need it, or you can save the UCS by name (so that you can reuse it later).

The Simplest Way to Draw in 3-D

You can use AutoCAD to draw three-dimensional objects in two ways. One system is left over from the elementary version of 3-D (still called *2 1/2-D*) that was first added to AutoCAD several years ago. This system limits you to drawing *extrusions*; that is, 3-D objects can only have straight lines in space (you can draw a well but not a wheel; see fig. 15.2). Its simplicity makes it suitable for certain applications.

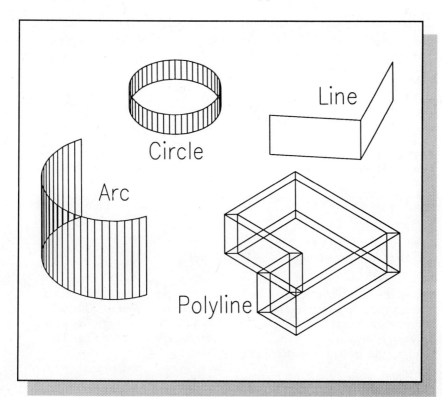

Fig. 15.2. Earlier versions of AutoCAD limited you to drawing 3-D by extrusions.

The other method, which was introduced with Release 10, enables you to draw any object in any orientation. This drawing method is more flexible, but also is harder to learn than the drawing method described previously. For that reason, you will first learn the simpler method of drawing in 3-D, and then learn more complex methods in Chapter 16.

Giving Objects Thickness (Chprop)

You can make objects in your drawing look three-dimensional by giving them a *thickness*. In AutoCAD, the term "thickness" indicates how tall an object is. You can think of thickness as the extrusion distance. If an object has positive thickness, the object's height extends up from the floor level; if the object has negative thickness, then the object's height extends downward from the floor level. Before changing any thickness in the sample drawing, freeze the layer HATCH and make layer 0 the current layer.

Now, use the Chprop command to give thickness (that is, height) to the bathroom walls in the SUITE drawing, in effect making them three-dimensional. You change the walls—which now have no height—into eight-foot-tall walls, as follows:

Prompt	Response	Explanation
Command:	**Chprop**	Starts the Chprop command
Select objects:	Pick the bathroom wall polyline	
Select objects:	Press Enter	
Change what property (Color/LAyer/LType/Thickness):	**T**	Select the Thickness option
New thickness (0'-0"):	**8'**	Make the walls 8 feet tall
Change what property (Color/LAyer/LType/Thickness):	Press Enter	

You have taken walls that had no height and made them eight feet tall! You'll notice, however, that the drawing looks no different. This is because you are still looking straight down on the drawing (that is, the drawing is displayed in *plan* view). To see the tall walls, you need to change your perspective on the drawing.

Changing the Viewpoint (Vpoint)

AutoCAD's Vpoint command (which stands for Viewpoint) lets you look at a drawing in three dimensions. The Vpoint command displays the drawing from a reference point in space. When you begin a new drawing, AutoCAD automatically displays the drawing from a viewpoint of 0,0,1 (X=0, Y=0, Z=1). That is, you see the drawing as though you are located one unit above the drawing's X,Y origin. This means you are looking straight down on the X,Y plane.

WARNING   Do not confuse the Vpoint command with the Vports command. Vports (discussed in Chapter 18) creates multiple views of a drawing.

Use the Vpoint command now to view the drawing in 3-D, as follows:

Prompt	Response	Explanation
Command:	**Vpoint**	Begins the Vpoint command
Rotate/<View point> (0'-0",0'-0",0'-1'):	**1,1,1**	Creates a three-dimensional view of the drawing

The result of this command sequence is shown in figure 15.3.

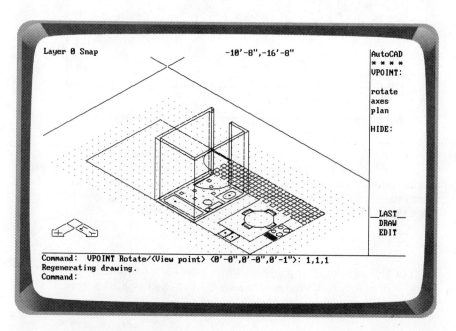

Fig. 15.3.
The Vpoint command displays a three-dimensional view of the drawing.

You can most easily understand how viewpoints work by practicing with the Vpoint command. Try the Vpoint command with several different X,Y,Z coordinates, such as 1,2,3 and –1,–1,–1. The coordinates are *unitless*. That means that it doesn't matter whether you enter 1',2',3' or 1",2",3"—you will see exactly the same view from the same distance. If you want to change your viewing distance, use the Zoom command. To view the object from below, use a negative Z coordinate, such as 1,1,–1. The command is easy to use, and if you get confused, just reissue the command and specify the coordinates 0,0,1, to return the drawing to plan view.

You can get a better orientation of the view by using the Vpoint icon menu, which is shown in figure 15.4.

Fig. 15.4.
The Vpoint
icon menu
enables you to
change
viewpoints
quickly.

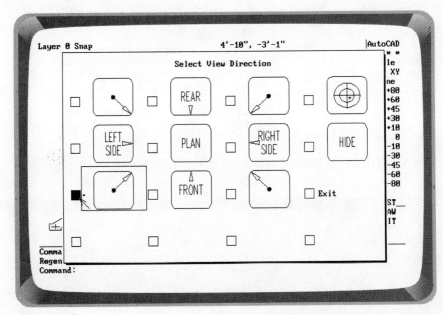

To get the icon menu, pick Display and Viewpoint 3D. . . from the screen or pull-down menus. If you want to use the `Select View Direction` menu to change your view of the drawing, you must make two selections from the menu:

❑ First, select the desired view direction. For example, pick the left-front view from the icon menu.

❑ Next, pick the angle from which you want to view the drawing. From the screen menu, pick +30 (for 30 degrees in the positive direction).

After you make these choices from the menu, the SUITE drawing appears as shown in figure 15.5. This view is from the opposite direction of the one shown in figure 15.3. To return to the plan view, issue Vpoint with the coordinates 0,0,1. Vpoint is discussed in greater detail in Chapter 17.

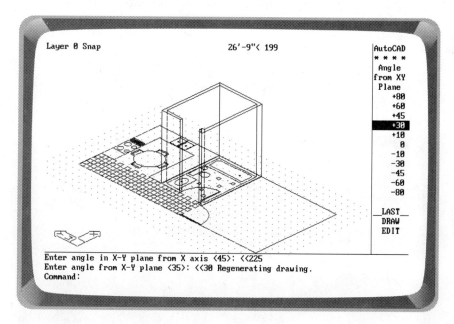

Fig. 15.5.
The SUITE
drawing
viewed from
the opposite
direction.

Making the 3-D View More Realistic (Hide and Shade)

AutoCAD draws *wireframe* objects. That is, the program only draws the outlines of objects. This is why you can see right through the bathroom walls in the SUITE drawing. Look at this simple illustration and you can easily understand how complicated 3-D drawings can become. AutoCAD provides two commands that help you make your 3-D drawings look more realistic.

The Hide command removes all lines that are hidden behind other objects. Freeze the TEXT and DIMENSION layers, and then try using the Hide command on the SUITE drawing:

```
Command: Hide
Regenerating drawing.
Removing hidden lines: 225
```

The screen goes blank as AutoCAD checks each line, determining whether it lies in front of or behind other objects. If a line lies behind another object in the drawing, that line should be hidden from view. Such lines are called *hidden lines*, and they should be removed from view for the drawing to look as realistic as possible. AutoCAD reports every time it finds another 25 hidden lines. After you use the Hide command on the SUITE drawing, your screen should look something like figure 15.6. You now can see only the parts of the bathroom that are visible through the open door; all other lines (except text) are hidden behind the bathroom walls.

You can plot hidden-line views by typing **Y** at the `Remove hidden lines?` prompt in the Plot and Prplot commands. See Chapter 19 for more details.

Fig. 15.6.
The Hide command removes lines hidden by other objects.

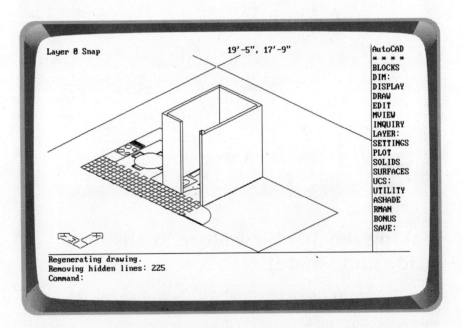

The Shade command *shades* in the area between the lines. This helps make objects look solid. Try the Shade command on the SUITE drawing, as follows:

```
Command: Shade
Regenerating drawing.
10% done.
Shading complete.
```

Once again the screen goes blank. AutoCAD lets you keep track of the Shade command's progress in ten-percent increments. After a short while, you screen should look like figure 15.7. Because you drew the SUITE drawing in only one color, you won't be able to appreciate how

the Shade command really benefits from the use of color. If you would
like to see an example, end the drawing session, load the drawing SITE-
3D, and then use the Shade command.

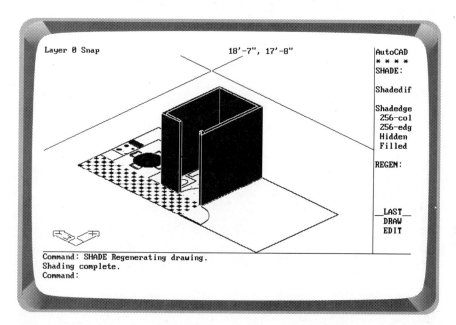

Fig. 15.7.
The Shade
command
makes
wireframe
objects look
solid.

You can continue working with the hidden-line view, but you will notice
that AutoCAD does not respect the rights of hidden lines. The hidden
portion of lines reappear as you edit the drawing, and it begins to look
more like a regular wireframe drawing. (You cannot edit or plot a shaded
drawing. If you try to pick a shaded entity, AutoCAD reports 0 found.)
After you use the Hide or Shade command, use the Regen command to
return to the normal wireframe view.

Summary

This chapter has started you on your voyage into the third dimension.
You have learned the concepts of and considerations for the different
coordinate systems, and you have been introduced to some three-
dimensional drafting techniques.

It is important to realize the potential of your CAD system's 3-D
capabilities. As you experiment, you will quickly come to realize just what
an exciting adventure AutoCAD provides.

The following chapters build on this foundation. Chapter 16 introduces more of AutoCAD's powerful 3-D drafting commands. Chapter 17 covers procedures needed as you modify your 3-D work. Finally, Chapter 18 describes the many ways in which AutoCAD enables you to view your three-dimensional work.

16

Using AutoCAD's 3-D Drawing Tools

*Illustration courtesy of
Autodesk, Inc., Sausalito, CA.*

In the last chapter, you learned how to draw simple 3-D objects: walls and cylinders. You also saw how to control the 3-D drawing environment.

This chapter will build on that foundation by showing you AutoCAD's powerful 3-D drafting tools. You will learn the importance of the user coordinate system and point filters. You also will learn how to draw complex 3-D entities with relative ease.

The following commands and features are discussed in this chapter:

- ❏ EDGESURF
- ❏ PFACE
- ❏ REVSURF
- ❏ RULESURF
- ❏ TABSURF
- ❏ 3DFACE
- ❏ 3DMESH
- ❏ 3-D Objects
- ❏ 3DPOLY

This chapter continues turning the sample SUITE drawing into a three-dimensional project. Because the scope of creating a three-dimensional project can be extensive, some of these commands are demonstrated on a limited portion of the drawing.

After reading this chapter, you will have a good understanding of some of the more involved 3-D commands. With these under your belt, you should be able to design anything you can imagine.

Adding Elevation (Elev)

In AutoCAD, the Elev command (short for ELEVation) sets the elevation and thickness of entities. *Elevation* is the object's distance up (or down) the Z axis. So far, you have not had to think about how far above (or below) the Z axis you have drawn objects. When you draw in 2-D, everything is drawn with a elevation of zero; that is, Z=0.

Consider a table top as an example. In fig. 16.1, the floor has zero elevation. The table top has an elevation of 3 feet. The table top also has a thickness of 3 inches (in the negative Z direction), given the table top's bottom side an elevation of 2' 9".

Fig. 16.1.
The table top has an elevation of 3 feet and a thickness of 3 inches.

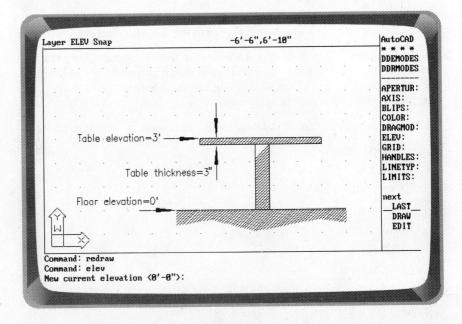

Now use the Elev command to give the kitchen table a center post and top, both with elevation and thickness. The following command sequence demonstrates the use of the Elev command to draw the center post:

Prompt	Response	Explanation
Command:	**Elev**	Starts the Elev command
New current elevation <0' - 0">:	**0**	Specifies the elevation at 0 (floor level)
New current thickness <0' - 0">:	**2'9**	Sets the thickness to 2'9" up from the floor.

The Elev command does not change the elevation or thickness of existing objects. Instead, it affects all objects you draw from now on. You need to reissue the Elev command each time you want to draw at a different elevation or thickness. Later in this chapter you will learn how to get around this inconvenience.

Draw the post by issuing the Circle command, as follows:

```
Command: Circle
3P/2P/TTR/<Center point>: CEN
of Pick kitchen table
Diameter/<Radius>: 3
```

A circle with thickness is a *cylinder*. AutoCAD draws the cylinder 2' 9" tall, with a 3" radius. You just draw the circle; AutoCAD automatically makes it a cylinder. With the viewpoint set to 1,1,1 you should see the cylinder rising out of the circle on the floor.

To draw the table top, you need to first change the elevation and thickness again. Because the bottom of the table sits on top of the post, the new elevation equals the old thickness:

```
Command: Elev
New current elevation <0'-0">: 2'9
New current thickness <2'-9">: 3
```

Now draw the table top, again using the Circle command:

```
Command: Circle
3P/2P/TTR/<Center point>: .XY
of CEN
of Pick table circle
(need Z): 2'9"
Diameter/<Radius>: .XY
of QUA
of Pick circle again
(need Z): 3'
```

You should end up with a 3-D kitchen table, as shown in fig. 16.2. This command sequence has some new command modifiers, namely .XY. These *point filters* are explained later in the next section.

Fig. 16.2.
The finished
kitchen table.

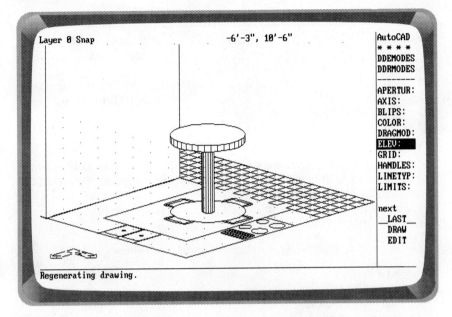

You can more easily visualize a 3-D drawing if you turn on the drawing grid. Set the limits to match the base area of your drawing (the floor plan, in the case of the SUITE drawing). Note that the grid takes the same Z coordinate as the current elevation setting.

Point Filters

A *point filter* enables you to grab a specific coordinate (such as the X coordinate) of an entity. At the `Command:` prompt, a point filter looks like **.XY** (more later). Point filters are similar to the object snap modes. Object snaps grab a specific point on an entity (its midpoint or insertion point), but point filters grab a coordinate. Point filters can work with or without object snap commands, and can act transparently.

Filters are helpful when you need to place points in relation to the current view point. Earlier in this chapter, you used point filters to draw a circle whose center and radius were equal to another circle located at floor level (via .XY), but whose elevation was 2'9".

The point filters are not limited to three-dimensional work. In fact, you can use them in many ways, such as when you are lining up text or drawing perfect boxes. You can fix a 2-D error in the sample SUITE drawing. In the bathroom, you may have been annoyed that the toilet bowl seemed off-center in relation to the tank. The following command sequence uses object snaps and point filters to center the bowl. Work through the sequence even if the image on your screen does not match the figure.

Think of how you would move the bowl by using the editing tools you have already learned about. You could construct several temporary construction lines and use object snap commands to move it over. Or, you could use the Dist command to get the change in the X coordinate (called *delta-X*) to move the bowl a specific value. Of the many ways to make the change, the following procedure is the easiest:

Prompt	Response	Explanation
Command:	**Move**	Starts the Move command
Select objects:	Pick the toilet bowl	
Select objects:	Press Enter	
Base point or displacement:	**QUA**	Snaps to the upper QUAdrant of the ellipse
of	Pick the upper edge of the ellipse, near the tank	
Second point of displacement:	**.X**	Grabs the X coordinate
of	**MID**	Snaps to the MIDpoint of the tank
of	**Pick**	Picks the horizontal line of the tank
(need YZ)	Press F8	Turns Ortho mode on

With Ortho on, drag the crosshair cursor to the left and pick any point (see fig. 16.3). By using the .X filter and MIDpoint snap, you limit AutoCAD to moving the bowl in the X direction, and filter out the unneeded coordinates.

When you respond with a filter to an AutoCAD prompt, the filter asks AutoCAD to supply some—but not all—of the coordinates. For example, if you want to draw a line from three feet above an intersection of two existing lines, you can do the following:

```
Command: Line
From point: Int
of: .xy
(need Z) 3'
```

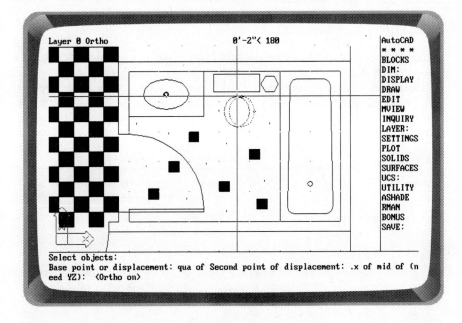

*Fig. 16.3.
Object snaps
and point
filters
eliminate the
need for
construction
lines.*

Instead of typing in the three-dimensional coordinate, you need only type in the height (3"). By using the point filter .XY, you asked AutoCAD to retrieve the X,Y coordinate for you. The object snap Intersection command will get the exact coordinates of the intersecting lines.

AutoCAD provides seven point filters, one for each combination of the three coordinates, as the following table shows:

Filter	Meaning
.X	AutoCAD grabs the X value; you are prompted to supply the Y and Z values.
.Y	AutoCAD grabs the Y value; you are prompted to supply the X and Z values.
.Z	AutoCAD grabs the Z value; you are prompted to supply the X and Y values.
.XY	AutoCAD grabs the X and Y values; you are prompted to supply the Z value.
.XZ	AutoCAD grabs the X and Z values; you are prompted to supply the Y value.
.YZ	AutoCAD grabs the Y and Z values; you are prompted to supply the X value.
.XYZ	AutoCAD grabs the X, Y, and Z values. This has the same effect as not using any point filter at all.

Defining a User Coordinate System (UCS)

The UCS command enables you to create, change, and save user coordinate systems by name. The UCS command gives you the following options:

```
Origin/ZAxis/3point/Entity/View/X/Y/Z/Prev/Restore/Save/Del/
?/<World>:
```

The Origin option defines a new UCS by locating its origin at a new position (the orientation of the X, Y, and Z axes does not change rotate):

```
Origin point <0'-0",0'-0",0'-0">:
```

The Origin option is convenient for creating a parallel UCS to the current WCS without redefining the axes' orientation.

The ZAxis option defines a new UCS with a different origin and a new Z axis:

```
Origin point <0'-0",0'-0",0'-0">:
Point on positive portion of Z axis
<0'-0",0'-0",0'-1">:
```

You define the new origin and pick a point that indicates the direction (from the origin) of the new positive Z axis. AutoCAD determines the positive direction of the other two axes. You can use the right-hand rule to help determine the new X,Y plane.

Using the Zaxis option may confuse you until you are better acquainted with AutoCAD. Defining a UCS exactly where you want it is easier than trying to figure out where the UCS is, such as with the 3point option.

The 3point option defines a new UCS by three points: the origin, the positive X axis, and the positive Y axis:

```
Origin point <0'-0",0'-0",0'-0">:
Point on positive portion of the X axis
<0'-1",0'-0",0'-0">:
Point on positive-Y portion of the UCS X-Y plane
<0'-1",0'-1",0'-0">:
```

Be sure that the three points do not form a straight line, otherwise AutoCAD cannot detrmine the UCS.

The Entity option defines a new UCS by using an existing entity:

```
Select object to align UCS:
```

AutoCAD makes the X,Y plane of the new UCS parallel to the X,Y plane in existence when the entity was drawn. The Z direction is the same direction followed by the entity.

Table 16.1 lists how the origin and X axis are determined by the Entity option. Remember that the Y axis is perpendicular to the X axis and passes through the origin. The Z axis is perpendicular to both the X and Y axes and passes through the origin point. You can visualize these axes more easily by using the right-hand rule.

Table 16.1.
The properties of entities used to create a UCS

Entity	UCS Origin	X Axis
Arc	Center of arc	Through the endpoint of the arc closest to the pick point
Circle	Center of circle	Through the point nearest the pick point on the circle
Dimension	Insertion point	Parallel to the UCS of the dimension
Line	Endpoint nearest to the pick point	Through other endpoint
Point	The point	Derived arbitrarily
2-D Polyline	Start point	From origin to next vertex
Solid	First point	On line between first and second points
Trace	First point	Along center of trace
3-D Face	First point	From first two points and Y-positive side from first and fourth points
Shape, Block, Attribute, Text	Insertion point	Axis defined by rotation

The View option defines a new UCS whose Z axis is parallel to the direction of the current view. This is an easy way to define a UCS: you set up your view point and then define the UCS according to how you are looking at the drawing. Working with the Vpoint command, determine how you want to see the drawing and then define the UCS by using the UCS command's View option.

Choose either the X, Y, or Z option to rotate the current UCS around a given axis. The following prompt appears if you select the X option:

```
Rotation angle about X axis <0>:
```

When AutoCAD prompts you for the rotation around the indicated axis, you can specify the rotation angle by typing it or by picking the angle on-screen. The angle is referenced from the current X axis. Use the right-hand rule to determine the positive direction for rotation around the given axis.

Previous takes you back to the last UCS in which you worked, much like the Zoom Previous command. This option is useful when you work temporarily in one UCS and then return to the current UCS. Define the new UCS, do your work, and then select the Previous option to return to the original UCS.

The Save option saves the UCS with a name, much like saving a View by name. AutoCAD prompts you for the name of the UCS:

```
?/Desired UCS name:
```

Give the UCS a name. The name can be 31 characters long and contain letters, numbers, the dollar sign ($), hyphen (-), and underscore (_).

The ? suboption lists the saved UCS and the coordinates for the origin and X, Y, and Z axes relative to the current UCS. For example, if you have a UCS saved by the name LEFT, the ? option responds as follows:

```
UCS name(s) to list <*>: Press Enter
Current UCS: LEFT
Saved coordinate systems:
LEFT
Origin = <0'-0",0'-0",0'-0">,
X Axis = <0'-1",0'-0",0'-0">
Y Axis = <0'-0",0'-1",0'-0">,
Z Axis = <0'-0",0'-0",0'-1">
```

If you want to use a UCS more than once, save it in the drawing with the Save option and select Restore to return to it.

The Delete option deletes any saved coordinate system. You are prompted:

```
UCS name(s) to delete:
```

You can use wild-card characters to delete more than one UCS at a time. Use ? to represent one character and * to represent all characters. Alternatively, you can list the names with commas (but no spaces) between the names.

Select the World option to return to the World Coordinate System.

Trying Out the UCS

You can define a UCS that will display the left side of the sample SUITE drawing in elevation by following this command sequence:

Prompt	Response	Explanation
`Command:`	**UCS**	Starts the UCS command

`Origin/ZAxis/3point/`
`Entity/View/X/Y/Z/Prev/`
`Restore/Save/`
`Del/?/<World>:`
	ZA	Chooses the Z axis option

`Origin point <0,0,0>`	Press Enter	
`Point on positive portion` `of the Z axis <0,0,1>`	**–1,0,0**	Using the right-hand rule, you define the Z axis to be in the direction of the negative X axis of the WCS
`Command:`	**UCS**	
`Origin/.../Save/Del/?` `/<World>:`	**S**	Saves the UCS
`?/Name of UCS:`	**LEFTSIDE**	For the "left side" of the drawing

Now that you understand the fundamentals of the UCS command, you must be thinking that there should be an easier way to define and restore a given UCS. There is—you can use a dialogue box.

Using a Dialogue Box To Modify User Coordinate Systems (Dducs)

The Dducs command brings up the UCS dialogue box, which lets you do everything the UCS command does. The box lists the user coordinate systems on file. When you type **Dducs**, the dialogue box appears on-screen, as shown in fig. 16.4. You also can access the dialogue box by picking Settings and UCS Control... from the screen menu.

To make a change, move the arrow to the appropriate box and pick it. You will be prompted for new information. When you select the `Define New Current UCS`, another dialogue box appears (see fig. 16.5). Here you find all the options for defining a new user coordinate system.

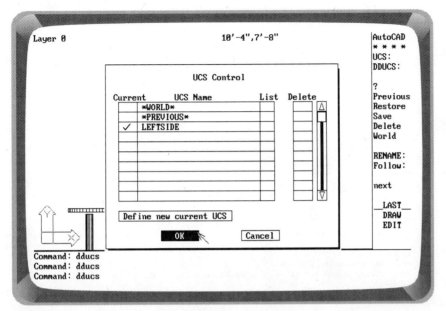

Fig. 16.4.
The Dducs dialogue box enables you to control user-defined coordinate systems.

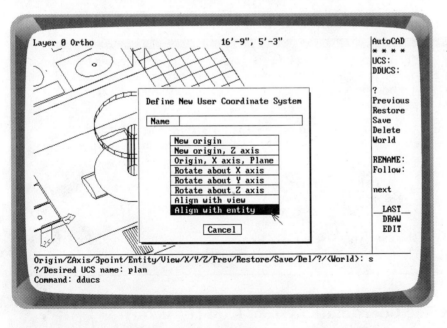

Fig. 16.5.
This dialogue box helps you define a new UCS.

AutoCAD's normal viewing angle is 90 degrees, but you still can draw and edit when the viewing angle isn't exactly 90 degrees. If you attempt to view the drawing from an angle of 0 degrees, the UCS icon changes to a broken pencil (see fig. 16.6). The new icon reminds you that you cannot draw until you change to a UCS not perpendicular to the viewing plane.

Fig. 16.6.
The broken
pencil icon (in
the lower left
corner) is a
reminder that
you cannot
draw or edit
in this view
plane.

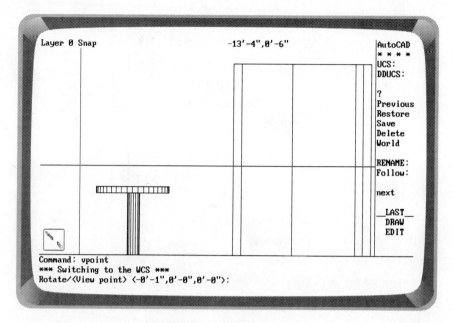

A word about entering WCS coordinates in a UCS . . .

There may be times when you want to enter coordinates based on the WCS, while you work in a UCS. One option is to set the UCS temporarily to World, enter the coordinates, and then set the UCS to Previous.

A better method is to place an asterisk (*) before the X-axis' coordinate. For example, at a `To point:` prompt, the following responses are based in the WCS:

```
To line: *5,6,13
To line: @*6<180
To line: @*-6,0,0
```

The last two coordinates designate a six-unit offset parallel to the World's X axis in the negative direction.

The Coordinate System Icon (Ucsicon)

All this time you've seen the coordinate system icon in the lower left corner of the Drawing Editor. You can turn the icon off and on and relocate it by using the Ucsicon command:

```
Command: Ucsicon
ON/OFF/All/Noorigin/ORigin <ON>:
```

If the icon gets in your way (as may be the case when you are working strictly in two dimensions), use the OFF option. The ON option turns the icon back on. The command's default setting is ON, which leaves the icon on unless you change it.

When you work with viewports, the Ucsicon options only affect the icon displayed in the active viewport (viewports are discussed later in Chapter 18). If you select the All option first, any subsequent Ucsicon option affects the icon in all viewports.

Select the ORigin option when you want AutoCAD to locate the icon at the origin of the UCS. This lets you always see where the origin is. If the origin is not visible on the screen, neither is the icon. You can return the icon to its default location (always visible at the lower left corner) with the Noorigin option.

Three-Dimensional Faces (3DFace)

The 3Dface command is the three-dimensional equivalent of the Solid. It draws flat planes in three-dimensional space. If you need to draw a three-dimensional face that isn't a flat plane, you should use the Edgesurf command (discussed later in this chapter).

The area of a three-dimensional face is not filled in, as it is with Solid. Any entities located behind the plane—or pass through the plane—are removed by the Hide command. You execute the 3Dface command a bit differently from the Solid command: you enter points clockwise or counter-clockwise, rather than crossing over.

You can try the 3Dface command now. When you drew the bathroom's walls in 3-D, you left out the lentil over the doorway. Switch to the LEFTSIDE UCS if you are not there already:

```
Command: UCS R LEFTSIDE
```

Now prepare the SUITE drawing as follows:

```
Command: VPOINT –1,–0.8,1
Command: ZOOM W
Command: HIDE
```

After the Hide command, the view of the drawing should be similar to figure 16.7, a close up of the bathroom door opening. The 3Dface command works as follows:

Prompt	Response	Explanation
Command:	**3DFACE**	Starts the 3Dface command.
First point:	**INT**	Specifies Intersection object snap.
of	Pick the first corner of the 3Dface, as shown in fig. 16.7.	Picks the first corner.
Second point:	**INT**	
of	Pick corner	Second corner.
Third point:	**@1'5<270**	Third corner.
Fourth point:	**@2'6<0**	Fourth corner.
Third point:	Press Enter	End the 3Dface command.

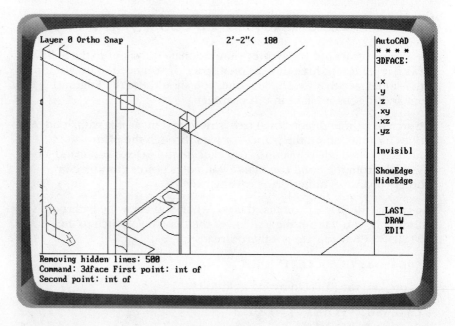

Fig. 16.7. Preparing SUITE for drawing the bathroom door's lentil with the 3Dface command.

After it is drawn, a three-dimensional face looks much like a polyline, or a line with an elevation. The faces can be three- or four-sided; to enter a three-sided face, press Enter when prompted, Fourth point:.

Entering the locations of the corners of a three-dimensional face is trickier than entering the points of a polyline or solid. It is much easier with a good viewpoint and liberal use of object snaps and point filters. If you don't get it quite right, the corner (or corners) of a three-dimensional face can be stretched with the Stretch command. This makes it easy to modify the three-dimensional face.

You have drawn the inner lentil wall; now use the Copy command to draw the outer lentil, as follows:

Command	Response	Explanation
Command:	**COPY**	Starts the Copy command
Select objects:	**L**	Select the last-drawn object 1 found
Select objects:	Press Enter	
<Base point or /Multiple:	**0,0,0**	Make a relative copy
Second point of displacement:	**0,0,4**	Copy the lentil four inches in the Z direction.

In this UCS, the Z axis is pointing out of the screen. That's why you move the lentil four inches in the positive Z direction, even though it appears to be moving in the negative X direction in the WCS.

When you want to copy (or move) an object by a known distance, give the origin (0,0,0) to the Base point prompt. Then you need only to supply the Second point prompt with the distance (0,0,4 in the preceding example). This is more accurate than picking the points on the screen and faster than calculating the actual coordinates.

Now hide the view to see what it looks like (see fig. 16.8):

```
Command: HIDE
Regenerating drawing.
Removing hidden lines: 525
```

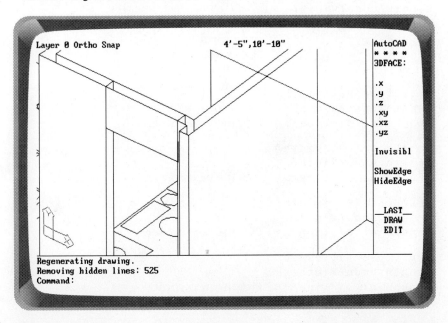

Fig. 16.8. *The Copy command draws the second lentil wall.*

Prepare for raising the counters by performing the following steps:

```
Command: UCS W
Command: Vpoint 0,0,0
Command: View R Kitchen
Command: Layer
?/Make/Set/New/ON/OFF/Color/Ltype/Freeze/Thaw: New
New layer name(s): K-counters
?/Make/Set/New/ON/OFF/Color/Ltype/Freeze/Thaw: Press
Return
```

Now use the Settings pull-down menu to make K-counters the current layer. Set the elevation to 0 and the current thickness to 3'.

Prompt	Response	Explanation
Command:	**OSNAP**	Turns on Osnap.
Object snap modes:	**INT**	Selects Intersection.
Command:	**Pline**	Begins Pline.
From point:	Use the snap Intersection command to pick the top left corner of the counter (see fig. 16.9).	Picks the first point.
Current line-width is 0'-0" Arc/Close/Halfwidth/ Length/Undo/Width/ <Endpoint of line>:	Pick the next corner in a clockwise direction.	
Arc/Close/Halfwidth/ Length/Undo/Width/ <Endpoint of line>:	Pick the next corner.	
Arc/Close/Halfwidth/ Length/Undo/Width/ <Endpoint of line>:	Pick the next corner.	
Arc/Close/Halfwidth/ Length/Undo/Width/ <Endpoint of line>:	Pick the next corner.	
Arc/Close/Halfwidth/ Length/Undo/Width/ <Endpoint of line>:	Pick the next corner.	

Prompt	Response	Explanation

`Arc/Close/Halfwidth/`
`Length/Undo/Width/`
`<Endpoint of line>:`
	Pick the next corner.	

`Arc/Close/Halfwidth/`
`Length/Undo/Width/`
`<Endpoint of line>:`
	Pick the next corner.	

`Arc/Close/Halfwidth/`
`Length/Undo/Width/`
`<Endpoint of line>:`
	Pick the next corner.	

`Arc/Close/Halfwidth/`
`Length/Undo/Width/`
`<Endpoint of line>:`
	Pick the corner you started from to close the polyline.	

`Arc/Close/Halfwidth/`
`Length/Undo/Width/`
`<Endpoint of line>:`
	Press Enter.	Ends Pline.

`Command:`	**OSNAP**	
`Object snap modes:`	**OFF**	

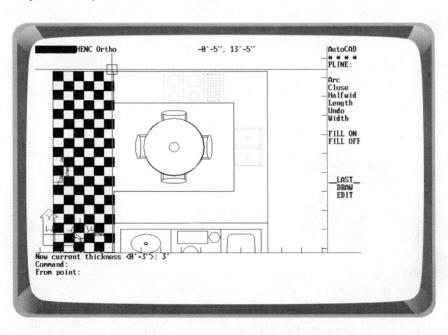

Fig. 16.9.
The first point for the Pline command.

When done, change the viewpoint and perform a hide (see fig. 16.10):

```
Command: VPOINT 1,1,1
Command: HIDE
```

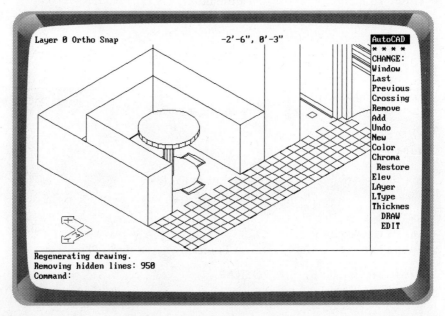

Fig. 16.10. Raising the counters shows there is no top.

You can return to the previous viewpoint with the Zoom Previous command. It remembers the previous ten Zoom and Vpoint views.

The hidden-line view shows a problem: no counter top. And where did the stove and sink go? There is no counter because you gave the lines thickness; there is nothing between them (you may have noticed the hollow bathroom walls). The stove and sink are still at floor level; they are hidden by the counter walls.

You can correct these two problems by moving the stove and sink up (in the Z direction) by three feet:

```
Command: MOVE
Select objects: Select the stove and sink by windowing
Base point: 0,0,0
Second point: 0,0,3'
Command: HIDE
```

Now you add the counter top with the 3Dface command. Use INTersection object snap again, as follows:

```
Command: OSNAP
Object snap modes: INT
```

Draw three 3-D faces, picking the corners of the counter walls. When you are done, use the Hide command to see the results (see fig. 16.11).

```
Command: 3DFACE
Command: OSNAP
Object snap modes: OFF
```

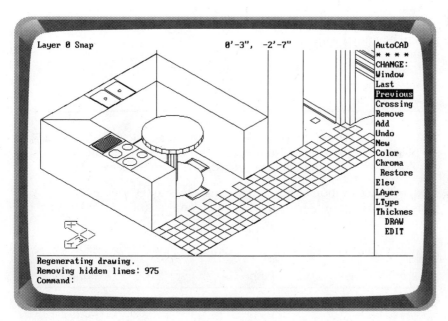

Layer 0 Snap   0'-3", -2'-7"   AutoCAD
                                                      * * * *
                                                      CHANGE:
                                                      Window
                                                      Last
                                                      Previous
                                                      Crossing
                                                      Remove
                                                      Add
                                                      Undo
                                                      New
                                                      Color
                                                      Chroma
                                                       Restore
                                                      Elev
                                                      LAyer
                                                      LType
                                                      Thicknes
                                                       DRAW
                                                       EDIT

Regenerating drawing.
Removing hidden lines: 975
Command:

Fig. 16.11. The counter tops are drawn with 3D faces.

Three-Dimensional Polylines (3DPoly)

The Pline command's advantages and applications were discussed in Chapter 5. This polyline will not allow you to enter three-dimensional coordinates. Instead, you need to use its step-brother, the 3Dpoly command.

Other than drawing in space, the 3Dpoly command has less options than Pline and is less powerful. Table 16.2 shows the differences and similarities between the two commands and what they are capable of doing.

Three-dimensional polylines (3Dpoly) can be edited with the Pedit command.

Table 16.2
Comparison of the Pline and 3Dpoly commands.

Drafting Task	Pline	3Dpoly
Draw in two dimensions	Yes	Yes
Draw in three dimensions	No	Yes
Undo the current segment	Yes	Yes
Can close the polyline	Yes	Yes
Can be edited with Pedit	Yes	Yes
Draws arcs	Yes	No
Has the Length option	Yes	No
Modify the width of the segment	Yes	No
Draw a segment at half width	Yes	No

To try out the 3Dpoly command, you will draw a basic dish drying rack. To prepare for drawing a dish drying rack, change back to the WCS. Use the Zoom Window command to get a view next to the sink area.

First, set the elevation to 3'1" and the thickness to 0 with the Elev command. Then turn Orthographic mode on. Use the Pline command to draw a 12" by 18" rectangle (see fig. 16.12). You will draw one plate holder with the 3Dpoly command, and use the Array command to have AutoCAD draw the others for you, as follows:

Prompt	Response	Explanation
Command:	**3DPOLY**	Starts the 3Dpoly command
From point:	Pick a point on the left side of the new rectangle, near the top.	
Close/Undo/ <Endpoint of line>:	**@3<0**	Draws the first segment of the plate holder
<Endpoint of line>:	**.XY**	Picks the x,y start point of the second segment using the...
of	**END**	...end of the first segment (using ENDpoint object snap).
of	Click on the end of the line.	

Prompt	Response	Explanation
`(need Z):`	**3'3**	Height of plate holder.
`<Endpoint of line>:`	**@3<0**	Draws third segment of the plate holder by...
`<Endpoint of line>:`	**.XY**	...picking the x,y start point of...
`of`	**END**	...the end of the third segment.
`of`	Click on end of line.	
`(need Z):`	**3'1**	Height of plate holder.
`<Endpoint of line>:`	**@6<0**	Draws the last segment
`<Endpoint of line>:`	Press Enter	Ends the 3Dpoly command.

Draw the other nine plate holders with the Array command:

```
Command: ARRAY
Select objects: Click on the line you just drew, and then press
Enter.
Rectangular or Polar array (R/P): R
Number of rows (--) <1>: 10
Number of columns (|||) <1>: 1
Unit cell or distance between rows (--): -1.5
```

Three-Dimensional Objects

You have seen how to draw some objects in three dimensions. AutoCAD has an icon menu that enables you to easily draw three-dimensional objects.

So that your sample SUITE drawing doesn't get too cluttered, first make a new layer (call it Torus) and freeze all the others. Pick the Draw pull-down menu, and then the Objects... menu item. AutoCAD displays the 3D Objects icon menu (see fig. 16.13). From this menu, AutoCAD helps you draw the following entities:

❏ Box

❏ Wedge

❏ Pyramid

❏ Dome

❏ Dish

❏ Cone

❏ Sphere

❏ Torus

Fig. 16.12.
The finished
plate holder.

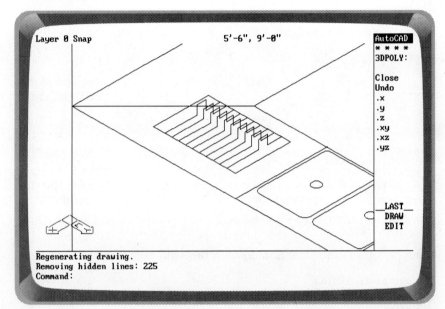

Fig. 16.13.
The 3D Objects
icon menu
makes it easy
to draw basic
3-D objects.

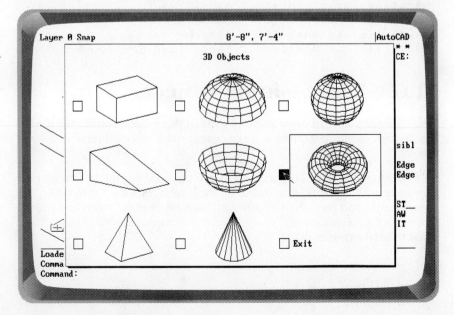

When you select an icon pick-box the first time, AutoCAD loads the
AutoLISP routine (called 3D.LSP) that prompts you and then draws the
object.

Try drawing a torus. Pick the pick-box next to the doughnut shape.
AutoCAD responds as follows:

```
Please wait...Loading 3D Objects
Center of torus: 0',3'
Diameter/<Radius> of torus: @4'<180
Diameter/<Radius> of tube: 1'
Segments around tube circumference <16>: Press Enter
Segments around torus circumference <16>: Press Enter
```

The more segments you specify, the smoother the torus will look. The
drawback is that it will take AutoCAD longer to draw, hide, and shade it.

Now try drawing a second interlocking torus, as shown in figure 16.14.

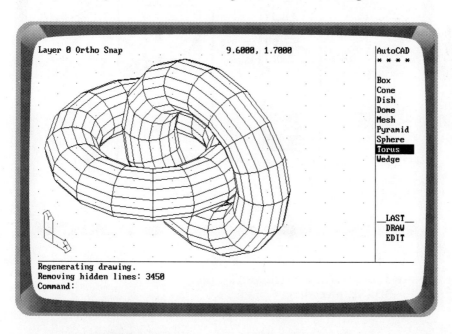

Fig. 16.14.
*The
interlocking
tori were
drawn by
changing the
UCS.*

```
Command: VPOINT 1,0,0
Command: UCS V
Command: TORUS
Center of torus: 0,0
Diameter/<radius> of torus: 4'
Diameter/<Radius> of tube: 1'
Segments around tube circumference: Press Enter
Segments around torus circumference: Press Enter
Command: VPOINT 1,1,1
Command: ZOOM E
Command: HIDE
```

You can restart the Torus command by picking Torus from the side screen menu or by typing in the LISP command **TORUS** directly, as shown above. You may need to use the Move command to correctly position the second torus.

Three-Dimensional Surfaces

The commands described in this section use other objects to create three-dimensional surfaces, or *meshes*. There are six surfacing commands (see fig. 16.15).

Fig. 16.15. AutoCAD's meshing commands enable you to draw complex surfaces.

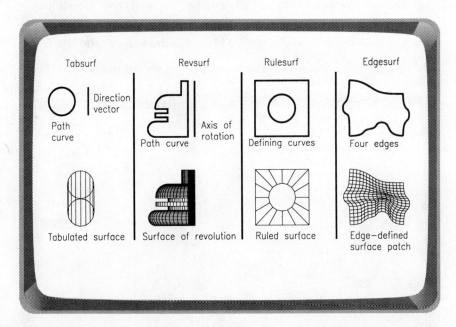

- ❏ 3Dmesh is best suited for LISP programming (such as 3D.LSP, preceding)
- ❏ Revsurf rotates a 2-D object around an axis
- ❏ Rulesurf draws a ruled surface between closed or open boundaries.
- ❏ Edgesurf draws a meshed surface between boundaries
- ❏ Tabsurf uses a boundary and a direction vector
- ❏ Pface draws arbitrary 3-D polygons

These surfaces are created from 3-D faces and can be edited with the Pedit command, covered in Chapter 17.

Specifying the Mesh Density (Surftab1 and Surftab2)

Before you start drawing meshes, you need to know more about their composition. Meshes are made up of a matrix of M x N vertices:

❑ M is the number of vertices in the column direction

❑ N is the number the row direction

The larger the number of vertices, the denser the mesh (see fig. 16.16). However, a fine mesh takes a long time to draw, hide, and shade. The M and N directions are determined differently for each surface (discussed with each command). The values of M and N are controlled by two system variables, Surftab1 and Surftab2. The default value for both is 6. This low value tends to produce coarse-looking meshes; a better value is 20.

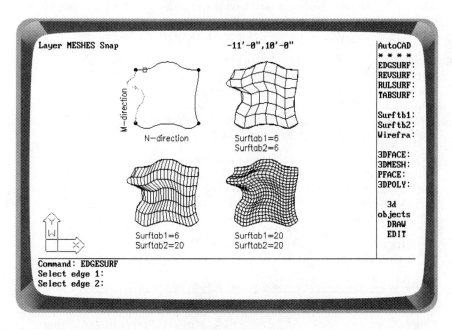

Fig. 16.16. The system variables Surftab1 and Surftab2 control the density of 3-D meshes.

System variable Surftab1 controls the density of the mesh produced by the Rulesurf and Tabsurf commands:

```
Command: SURFTAB1
New value for SURFTAB1 <6>: 20
```

Surftab1 and Surftab2 control the density of the mesh produced by the 3Dmesh, Edgesurf and Revsurf commands:

```
Command: SURFTAB2
New value for SURFTAB2 <6>: 20
```

The vertices of 3-D faces and rat's-nest meshes are defined by the user.

To construct a surface, all the surface commands (except 3Dmesh and Pface) need boundaries. The boundaries include points, lines, arcs, circles, and open or closed polylines.

General Polygon Meshes (3Dmesh and Pface)

When you use the 3Dmesh and Pface commands, you create a mesh by indicating all vertices in the mesh. 3Dmesh draws four-sided planes in space; Pface, available only in Release 11, draws multi-sided planes.

For the other surface meshes, AutoCAD automatically calculates the vertices for you; you merely specify the density. Because of the complexity of entering the information for three-dimensional meshes, 3Dmesh and Pface are best suited to LISP programming for creating objects that do not conform to the other surface commands. For example, you would use 3-D meshes to draw 3-D terrain maps.

To use the 3Dmesh command, you specify the mesh size in terms of M columns and N rows (a maximum of 256 each). AutoCAD then prompts you for the coordinates of the M×N vertices. AutoCAD assumes that you input vertices from the top of the first column "down," then move to the second column progressing "down" until all columns have been filled.

To enter a mesh in which M=5 and N=3, the syntax of the 3Dmesh command sequence is as follows:

Prompt	Response	Explanation
Command:	**3DMESH**	Starts the 3Dmesh command
Mesh M size:	**5**	Mesh will have five columns.
Mesh N size:	**3**	Mesh will have three rows.
Vertex (0,0):	**5',4'**	Pick points
Vertex (0,1):	**5',2'**	
Vertex (0,2):	**6',3'**	
Vertex (1,0):	**6',4'**	
Vertex (1,1):	**7',3'**	
Vertex (1,2):	**8',4'**	

Prompt	Response	Explanation
Vertex (2,0):	8',5'	
Vertex (2,1):	9',5'	
Vertex (2,2):	9',4'	
Vertex (3,0):	9',3'	
Vertex (3,1):	9',1'	
Vertex (3,2):	8',1'	
Vertex (4,0):	8',2'	
Vertex (4,1):	7',2'	
Vertex (4,2):	7',1'	

You can see how drawing a large mesh quickly gets tedious with the 3Dmesh command. All meshes created with the 3Dmesh command are open in the M and N directions. To close the mesh, use the Pedit command's Mclose and Nclose options (see Chapter 17).

The Pface command is used to create *arbitrary topology*, a poly-sided mesh, such as a Boolean solid. Pface gets rid of the annoying lines between vertices, saving disk space and improving redraw time.

When you use the Pface (short for Poly FACE) command, you specify the coordinates of each vertex, as with the 3Dface command. Unlike 3-D faces, however, Pface has no limit to the number of vertices, and you don't need to specify the M,N values (since poly faces are completely arbitrary).

Like 3-D faces, poly faces are meant to be used by third-party applications and AutoLISP routines.

Tabulated Surfaces (Tabsurf)

The Tabsurf command creates a tabulated surface (see fig. 16.8). It projects any shape in any direction in space. The Elev command is similar, but is limited to projecting the shape in the Z direction. The tabulated surface is defined by two entities:

- ❏ A curve path that defines the shape of the surface
- ❏ A direction vector that controls the surface direction and distance

When you enter TABSURF, the following prompts are displayed:

```
Select path curve:
Select direction vector:
```

The path curve is the entity that defines the surface. This entity can be a line, an arc, a circle, or a polyline; it cannot be a point.

The direction vector (a line or an open polyline) indicates the direction and length in which the shape should be extruded. The extrusion's direction depends on the end you select on the line or polyline.

 You normally draw the curve path in the X,Y plane and the direction vector in the Z direction. If, instead, the path and the direction vector reside on the same UCS, the surface will "smear" across the UCS.

Ruled Surfaces (Rulesurf)

The Rulesurf command creates a ruled surface between two entities, such as curves, lines, points, arcs, circles, or polylines. If one of the boundaries is open (a line segment or an arc, for example), the second boundary must also be open. Conversely, if the first boundary is closed (a circle or an ellipse), the second boundary must also be closed. You can use points as a second boundary for either open or closed boundaries to create a cone, for example.

When you enter **RULESURF**, AutoCAD displays the following prompts:

```
Select first defining curve:
Select second defining curve:
```

You can select any AutoCAD entity for the first defining curve. To start the mesh, Rulesurf uses the endpoint closest to the point at which you selected the entity. You select the second defining curve by selecting a point on a second entity. Figure 16.8 shows a ruled surface between two closed polylines. A closed boundary surface, such as a circle, starts at 0 degrees. A polyline surface starts at the first vertex.

Hiding the Edges of Three-Dimensional Faces

Sometimes you may want to make one (or all) of the edges of a three-dimensional face invisible. This is especially true for 3-D faces set next to each other, such as ruled surfaces and 3-D meshes.

To hide an edge, type **I** (for `invisible`) before you pick the starting point of the edge. This edge (and this edge only) will be hidden when you select the next edge's starting point. The invisible mode must be selected before any object snap modes, filters, or typed coordinates.

To edit a 3-D face with hidden edges, change the system variable Splframe to 1 (Splframe, which stands for SPLineFRAME, was discussed in Chapter 9). Then use the Regen command to see the edges.

Surfaces of Revolution (Revsurf)

The Revsurf command rotates a profile around an axis (see fig. 16.8). A profile is a cross-section view of the surface; this is the curve path. The axis is a line anywhere in space.

The Revsurf command prompts as follows:

```
Select path curve:
Select axis of revolution:
Start angle <0>:
Included angle (+=ccw, -=cw) <360>:
```

The path curve is the N direction of the mesh. If the path curve is either a circle or a closed polyline, the revolved surface will be closed in the N direction. The M direction is direction of rotation created by Revsurf.

The Start angle: prompt enables you to begin the surface at any angle, while the Included angle (+=ccw, -=cw) <360>: prompt enables you to specify how far the entities rotate about the axis. Pressing Enter at both prompts rotates the surface all the way around.

To produce a "cut-away" view of the inside of the revolved surface, use a starting angle of zero degrees and an included angle of 270 degrees. This leaves a gap of 90 degrees, letting you see inside.

The direction of revolution is determined by which end of the axis you pick and the Right-Hand Rule. Extend your right thumb along the axis, pointing away to the end furthest from the pick point. Your fingers will curl in the direction of revolution.

Edge-Defined Surface Patches (Edgesurf)

The Edgesurf command constructs a polygon mesh bounded on four sides (see fig. 16.8). The boundaries can be lines, arcs, or open polylines.

The four defining curves (or edges) must connect end-to-end, forming a topographically-rectangular closed path. The path is a general-space curve that defines the space between the curves. This type of mesh is called a "Coon's surface patch" after the professor who defined the meshing algorithm.

After you enter **EDGESURF** at the `Command:` prompt, AutoCAD prompts you to pick each of the four edges:

```
Select edge 1:
Select edge 2:
Select edge 3:
Select edge 4:
```

The edges may be selected in any order, but be aware that the M direction is defined by the first entity you select (see fig. 16.9). The N direction is the next connected edge. Edgesurf is harder to use than the other meshing commands but is the best way to define surfaces, such as the hood of a car.

Summary

This chapter illustrates the practical application of the concepts discussed in Chapter 15.

With their flexibility and power, these commands offer you the ability to construct almost any 3-D object. With these commands, and the tools discussed here, you can now draft in three dimensions. The next step is to edit the drawing.

Chapter 17 covers the commands you need to modify your work. It also demonstrates the differences between editing two-dimensional or three-dimensional entities with the same command.

17

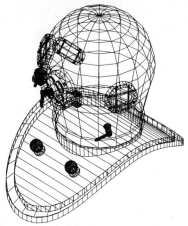

Illustration courtesy of
Autodesk, Inc., Sausalito, CA.

Editing a 3-D Drawing

In this chapter you learn some of the commands that modify three-dimensional entities. This chapter builds on the foundation laid in Chapter 16, which showed you how to convert a 2-D drawing to a drawing with 3-D entities.

This chapter also complements some of the commands discussed in Chapters 6 and 9; many editing commands work differently with 3-D entities. The editing commands in this chapter are grouped into the following four categories:

1. Commands that will not function on some 3-D entities:

    ❑ Change

2. Commands that need entities parallel with the current UCS:

    ❑ Break
    ❑ Chamfer
    ❑ Extend
    ❑ Fillet
    ❑ Offset
    ❑ Trim

3. Commands that affect 3-D entities:

    ❑ Chprop
    ❑ Explode
    ❑ Pedit

4. Commands that provide information about 3-D entities:

❑ Area

❑ Dist

❑ List

After reading this chapter and practicing with these commands, you should have a firm grasp of how to edit three-dimensional entities.

Editing Commands Restricted to Entities in the Current UCS

You learned some of the basic editing commands in Chapters 4 and 6. These commands are limited in their capabilities: they might not edit a 3-D object the way you expect them to. The following sections discuss a few of these commands and their limitations.

Changing an Entity's Elevation and Thickness (Change)

In AutoCAD Release 10, the Change command's Elevation option enables you to change the elevation of objects. This option is no longer available in AutoCAD Release 11—use the Move command instead.

If you want to change the elevation of several objects, they must all have the same elevation (or Z value). If the objects selected have different Z coordinates, AutoCAD will display the following message:

```
Cannot change elevation of entities with different
Z coordinates.
```

The Change command's Thickness option will not modify the thickness of a 3-D face, 3-D polyline, or polygon mesh because they already are three-dimensional entities.

Commands that Need Entities Parallel with the Current UCS

When you execute some of the editing commands discussed in Chapters 5 and 6, you will find that the selected objects must be in the current UCS. That is, the commands will work only if the entities' "extrusion" direction is parallel to the current Z axis. These are the commands:

❏ Break

❏ Chamfer

❏ Extend

❏ Fillet

❏ Offset

❏ Trim

When you execute any of these commands on an object that does not lie in the current UCS, you will see the following message:

```
Entity not parallel with UCS
```

Before issuing any of these commands, it is best to alter your current viewpoint so that you are looking "down" at the entity. This way, you will be editing the entity as it lies in the active UCS. You also will receive this error if the current UCS is parallel with the world coordinate system.

Editing Commands for Three-Dimensional Entities

This section discusses editing commands that have a specific effect on 3-D entities. These are the commands you execute to modify a 3-D object directly.

Changing the Properties of Entities (Chprop)

The Chprop command enables you to modify an object's properties; its Thickness option applies to 3-D entities. With the Chprop Thickness command, you can give an object an extrusion in the entity's Z-coordinate (refer to Chapter 15).

Editing Polylines (Pedit)

The Pedit command can modify 2-D polylines, 3-D polylines, and 3-D meshes. When you select the entity you want to edit, AutoCAD determines which type of polyline (two- or three-dimensional) you picked. If you select a 2-D polyline, you see this prompt:

```
Close/Join/Width/Edit vertex/Fit curve/Spline
curve/Decurve/Undo/eXit <X>:
```

If you use Pedit on a mesh, the prompt changes to this:

```
Edit vertex/Smooth surface/Desmooth/Mclose/Nclose/Undo/eXit <N>
```

After you read the following discussions on editing three-dimensional polylines and meshes, you will better understand the Pedit command and the way it applies to both types of entities.

Editing Three-Dimensional Polylines

Two- and three-dimensional polylines are edited in much the same way, but you are limited to how much you can edit a 3-D polyline. You cannot edit the width (3-D polylines do not have width), nor can you add new entities with Join. You can, however, open or close the polyline, create a spline, and straighten and edit the vertices.

To use the Pedit command, enter **PEDIT** at the Command: prompt; then select a 3-D polyline. The following prompt appears:

```
Close/Edit vertex/Spline curve/Decurve/Undo/eXit <X>:
```

These options work just as they do with a 2-D polyline. Note that the Join, Width, and Fit Curve options are missing. You can use Pedit on 3-D polylines to do the following:

- ❑ Open or close the polyline
- ❑ Remove vertices from a polyline
- ❑ Separate a polyline into segments
- ❑ Insert new vertices
- ❑ Move vertices
- ❑ Fit a 3-D spline curve to the polyline

When you pick the Edit vertex option, you get the following prompt:

```
Next/Previous/Break/Insert/Move/Regen/Straighten/eXit <N:
```

These, too, are exactly the same as the 2-D polyline Pedit.

Editing Three-Dimensional Meshes

When you use Pedit to modify a polygon mesh, you can do the following:

- ❑ Open or close the mesh in the M or N direction
- ❑ Move vertices
- ❑ Fit a smooth surface into the vertices

Pedit prompts you as follows:

```
Edit vertex/Smooth
surface/Desmooth/Mclose/Nclose/Undo/eXit<X>:
```

If the three-dimensional mesh is closed in the M direction, you will see the Mopen option rather than Mclose. If the mesh is closed in the N direction, the Nopen option replaces Nclose. These open and close options on the Pedit option prompt act as toggles. The toggle displayed depends on the current state of the entity.

The Smooth-surface option allows you to fit one of three types of smooth surface onto the mesh. The surface type is determined by the system variable SURFTYPE, similar to SPLINETYPE discussed in Chapter 5:

- ❏ 5: Quadratic B-spline
- ❏ 6: Cubic B-spline
- ❏ 8: Bezier surface

The Bezier surface is the smoothest type of surface—it has the fewest "peaks" and "valley" (see fig. 17.1).

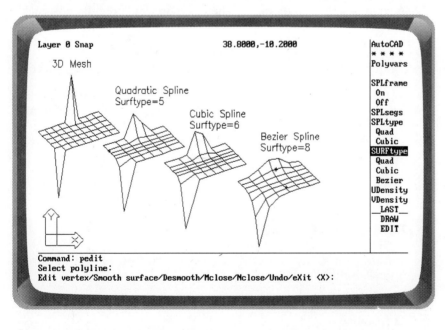

Fig. 17.1.
The SURFTYPE system variable controls the type of smoothness applied to a 3-D mesh.

After you have used the Smooth option, you can use the Desmooth option to return the 3-D mesh to its original condition.

When you choose Edit vertex, an X marker appears on the first visible vertex of the 3-D mesh, and you are prompted as follows:

```
Vertex (0,0). Next/Previous/Left/Right/Up/Down/Move/Regen/
eXit<X>:
```

The current vertex's location appears in the Vertex (m,n) area. As you use the Next and Previous options, you move through the vertices in order.

You move the X marker in the N direction with the Left and Right options.

The Up and Down options move the marker along the M direction of the mesh.

When the X marker is at the correct vertex, you can move the vertex with the Move option. When AutoCAD displays Enter new location:, enter or pick the new coordinate in three dimensions.

The Undo option allows you to undo the Pedit operations.

The Exit option ends the command and returns you to AutoCAD's Command: prompt.

You can edit three-dimensional meshes also by breaking them into individual lines and then modifying them. To break a three-dimensional mesh into lines, use the Explode command.

Breaking Apart 3-D Polylines and Meshes (Explode)

The Explode command can break a three-dimensional polyline or mesh into individual entities. If you choose a 3-D polyline, they are turned into lines. If you explode a 3-D mesh, it turns into a collection of 3-D faces. In either case, the resulting entities are placed on the same layer and have the same color and line type as the original object.

Inquiry Commands Affected by Three-Dimensional Entities

The following AutoCAD commands display information about your three-dimensional entities:

❏ List
❏ Distance
❏ Area

Finding Out about an Object (List)

The List command gives you every piece of information AutoCAD knows about an object. The command displays the following information about a three-dimensional entity:

- ❑ Its X-, Y-, and Z-location relative to the current UCS
- ❑ The X-, Y-, and Z-coordinates
- ❑ The extrusion direction in UCS coordinates (if different from the Z-axis)
- ❑ The three-dimensional length
- ❑ The angle in the current X,Z-plane
- ❑ The change (called *delta*) in the X-, Y-, and Z-directions

List also does the following:

- ❑ Labels 3-D polylines as Space
- ❑ Labels 3-D meshes as Mesh
- ❑ Displays the M✕N-size of a polygon mesh
- ❑ States whether a mesh is open or closed
- ❑ States whether the object is in Model Space or in Paper Space (Release 11 only)

Finding the Distance (Dist)

When you use the Dist command, you must consider the Z-coordinate. If no Z-coordinate is given, AutoCAD assumes the current elevation. Dist can create problems if you are grabbing entities with Osnap commands. For example, if you use Endpoint in the Dist command, you can easily get odd values if the entities' elevations are different.

To guard against potential problems, watch not only the `Distance` `returned`, but also the `Delta X,` `Delta Y` and `Delta Z` values.

Finding the Area (Area)

With the Area command, you can enter either two-dimensional (x,y) or three-dimensional (x,y,z) points. The points must lie in a plane parallel to the X,Y-plane of the current UCS.

When using Area, you must also give careful consideration to closed 2-D polylines or 2-D circles. This is important because the extrusion direction must lie in the Z-axis of the current UCS.

Summary

This chapter discussed the effect of editing commands on 3-D objects. Many of these commands were introduced in Chapters 5 and 6. Some of these editing commands do not function normally on some 3-D entities, some affect 3-D entities, and several inquiry commands provide additional information about 3-D objects.

The 3-D drafting lessons continue in the following chapter. Chapter 18 shows you how to generate specific views and plots of your three-dimensional model.

18

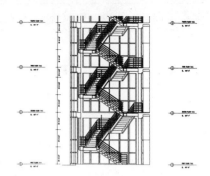

*Illustration courtesy of
Autodesk, Inc., Sausalito, CA.*

Viewing a 3-D
Drawing

Chapter 16 introduced you to some of the ways to view a 3-D drawing.
You learned how to change the viewpoint and how to remove hidden
lines. This chapter expands on the Hide, Shade, and Vpoint commands.

You will also learn about four advanced 3-D viewing commands that can
help with your 2-D work:

- ❏ Dview
- ❏ Redrawall
- ❏ Regenall
- ❏ Vports

This chapter builds on previous discussions of 3-D drafting and editing
and gives you a better understanding of AutoCAD's viewing options. You
first learn more about the 3-D viewing commands you used earlier, then
go on to the advanced commands.

Displaying Three-Dimensional Work

This section of the chapter discusses in greater detail some of the viewing
commands you learned in Chapter 16:

- ❏ Hide
- ❏ Shade
- ❏ Vpoint

Controlling the Viewpoint (Vpoint)

When you draw a CAD image in two dimensions, you view the drawing from a point directly "above" the X,Y axis. When you draw in three dimensions, you need a different *viewpoint* (the point from which you view the drawing). AutoCAD gives you several ways to change the viewpoint. One way is to use the Vpoint (short for ViewPOINT) command, as follows:

```
Command: VPOINT
Rotate/<View point> (0'-0",0'-0",0'-1"):
```

You can specify a 3-D view in three different ways. Until now, you have been typing in coordinates to see the sample SUITE drawing from different views. For example, Vpoint 1,0,0 shows the right side of the apartment suite, while 1,1,1 shows a bird's-eye view from the upper-right corner. These coordinates refer to the current UCS, not to world coordinates. If you want to use WCS coordinates, type an * before the X-coordinate, as in *1,1,1.

The second method, the Rotate option, enables you to indicate the viewpoint by entering two angles (the first in relation to the current X-axis, the second in relation to the current X-Y plane (see fig. 18.1). This is the option AutoCAD uses when you select Viewpoint from the screen menus. Both angles start at the origin, with positive angles going counterclockwise. This is the same as spherical coordinates but lacks a viewing distance (you move closer and further away with the Zoom command).

*Fig. 18.1.
You can
specify the 3-D
view point by
angles relative
to the X axis
and X,Y plane.*

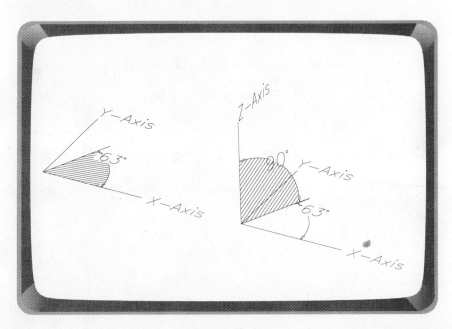

To change your viewpoint with the Rotate option, load the sample SUITE drawing and follow these steps:

Prompt	Response	Explanation
`Command:`	**Vpoint**	Starts the Vpoint command
`Rotate/<View point>` `<0''-0",0'-0".0'-1">:`	**R**	Select the Rotate option
`Enter angle in X-Y plane` `from X axis <0>:`	**–120**	Indicates new view in relation to X axis
`Enter angle from X-Y` `plane <0>:`	**45**	Indicates new view in relation to X-Y construction plane along Z axis.

The *current construction plane* is the current X-Y plane. Everything you enter is in relation to the current construction plane. The Z axis is perpendicular to the current X-Y plane.

After you enter the appropriate information, AutoCAD calculates the proper view and regenerates the drawing. Figure 18.2 shows the screen after the viewpoint has been changed.

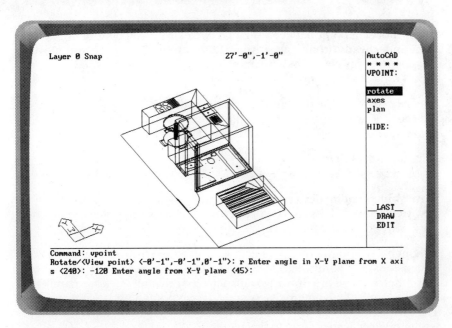

Fig. 18.2.
The view –120 degrees from east and 45 degrees up.

The third way to specify a viewpoint is to press Enter at the `Rotate/<View point>:` prompt. AutoCAD clears the screen and displays a compass and axes tripod (see fig. 18.3). The compass is a two-dimensional representation of the globe: the center is the north pole, the inner circle is the equator, and the outer circle is the south pole.

Fig. 18.3.
The compass and axes tripod help you visualize the new view point.

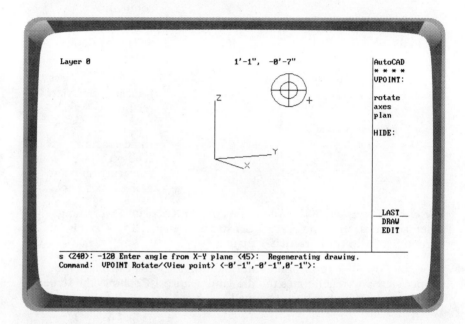

If you choose a point between the two circles, you will be looking up from underneath (from a negative position on the Z axis). As you move the pointing device, a cross moves across the compass and the axes tripod rotates accordingly.

The tripod shows the direction of the positive X, Y, and Z axes. To indicate a new viewpoint, pick a point in the compass. AutoCAD will regenerate the drawing based on the view you select. Try it now:

    Command: **VPOINT**
    Rotate/<View point> (0'-0",0'-0",0'-1"): Press Enter

Move your pointing device to any spot and pick it (or press Enter). The new viewpoint will regenerate. To return to the previous viewpoint, use the Zoom Previous command.

Although the Vpoint command enables you to see the drawing in three dimensions, it is somewhat deceiving because the image is *isometric*. In an isometric view, the drawing is displayed so that all lines are parallel. Autodesk calls the isometric view created by Vpoint a *parallel projection*. The image only seems three-dimensional; what's missing is *perspective*, where objects farther away look smaller.

Another disadvantage to the Vpoint command is that you make views by trial and error before you come up with the view you want. The Dview command, covered later in this chapter, solves both of these problems. Because the Dview command is more flexible it can be more difficult to learn and use. Thus, Vpoint has the advantage of being easier to use.

Removing Hidden Lines (Hide)

Working in three dimensions can be confusing, especially with the SUITE drawing, which has so many lines (refer to fig. 18.2). In previous chapters you cleared up some of the confusion by using the Hide command to remove hidden lines from the drawing. You simply typed Hide and pressed Enter. AutoCAD did all the time-consuming work.

The terms *hidden lines* and *hidden faces* describe entities that lie "behind" other objects. Whether an entity lies behind another depends only on your viewpoint. The Hide command will not process any entity that is made up only of text. Blocks that contain attributes are drawn without regard to their "visibility."

 Because AutoCAD still calculates entities on turned-off layers during the Hide command, it is always best to freeze a layer. Although entities on a turned-off layer are not plotted or drawn on-screen, they obscure other entities during hidden-line removal and cause confusion. To overcome this problem, always freeze layers you don't need.

Hide considers the following entities opaque:

- ❏ Circles
- ❏ Solids
- ❏ Traces
- ❏ Wide polylines
- ❏ 3-D faces
- ❏ Polygon meshes
- ❏ Extruded circles, solids, traces, and wide polylines

AutoCAD treats these as solid objects (with sides, top, and bottom). Thus, you could draw the kitchen table with an extruded circle and not have to draw a separate top. This solidity can be a drawback if you want to draw a hole. If you had drawn the kitchen table with two polyline arcs, it would have looked hollow or transparent.

AutoCAD can also display the hidden lines in another color, instead of making them invisible. Create a new layer with the name HIDDEN0 (hidden-zero) and give it the color red:

Command: **LAYER M HIDDEN0 C R HIDDEN0**

Now use the Hide command on the SUITE drawing. All hidden lines of entities drawn on layer 0 are displayed in red, rather than hidden—in a black-and-white reproduction, red entities appear gray (see fig. 18.4). You can color hidden entities on other layers by creating new layers with the prefix HIDDEN. If you have the layers WALL, DOOR, and FURNITURE, you would create HIDDENWALL, HIDDENDOOR, and HIDDENFURNITURE.

Fig. 18.4.
The HIDDEN-layer name prefix lets AutoCAD display hidden lines in other colors.

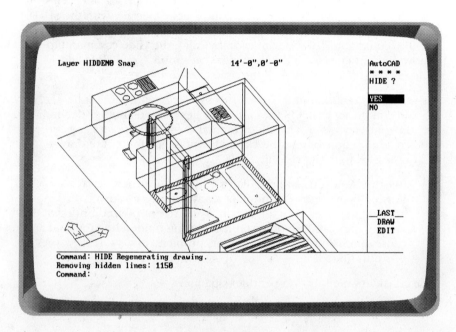

You may notice that as the SUITE drawing becomes more complicated, removing hidden lines takes longer; you should restrict your use of the Hide command because of this time-consuming process.

You can reduce the calculation time in three ways:

❑ Freeze all layers with unnecessary drawing information

❑ Zoom in to a small part of the drawing and perform a Regen first

❑ Use a faster computer: a 33MHz 486 makes hidden-line removal a trivial process

❑ After the hidden lines have been removed, preserve the view with a slide. Use the Mslide command to save the view and Vslide to recall it.

For some applications, showing how planes and surfaces are located in relation to each other in three dimensions is invaluable. Should their location be incorrect, the Hide command will quickly show it. Without question, this command (along with the Shade command) can be a powerful presentation tool.

Rendering Screen Images (Shade)

The Shade command produces a shaded view of your drawing. It can produce one of four kinds of shadings, depending on the setting of the SHADEDGE system variable and the capabilities of your graphics board:

- ❏ 0: Faces and edges are shaded.
- ❏ 1: Faces are shaded; edges are drawn in the background color.
- ❏ 2: Faces are drawn in the background color (similar to hidden-line removal).
- ❏ 3: Faces are drawn in their color with edges highlighted with the background color. (This is the default value for SHADEDGE.)

All settings result in a view similar to the Hide command, showing the hidden lines removed (see fig. 18.5). The difference is that the faces are filled in with color. Not only do shadings look more realistic, but AutoCAD can calculate a shaded image faster with the Shade command than a hidden-line view with the Hide command.

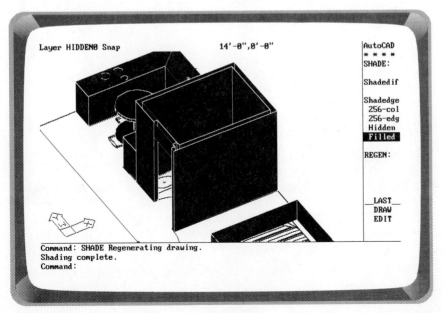

Fig. 18.5.
The Shade command shades faces and edges in color.

The first two settings require a graphics board capable of displaying 256 colors. IBM's 8514/A graphics board and many boards using an ADI driver can display 256 colors. The result is similar to using AutoShade's Fast Shade option. The difference is that there is only one light source, located at your viewpoint. This ensures fast, simple shadings that are always realistic.

You can adjust the shading contrast with the system variable SHADEDIF (short for SHADE DIFfusion). SHADEDIF is a percentage value between 0, for total ambient light (no contrast), and 100, for total diffuse reflection (high contrast). The default value of 70 gives good contrast with some ambient light.

Normally, you cannot plot or printer-plot the shaded image. To get around this, save the image with the MSlide command or with screen-capture software.

You cannot select entities in a shaded image.

Use the Regen command to return to the normal wireframe view; the Undo command will not work.

Advanced 3-D Viewing Commands

The last set of 3-D viewing commands can make working with 3-D models much easier. They are as follows:

- ❏ Dview
- ❏ Vports
- ❏ Regenall
- ❏ Redrawall

Dview is similar to but far more flexible than the Vpoint command. Vports enables you to see more than one view at a time.

Dynamically Changing Your Viewpoint (Dview)

The Dview (short for Dynamic VIEW) command enables you to see the drawing in perspective and to change the viewpoint *dynamically*; you watch the view change on-screen while you move your pointing device. This is much easier than trying to interpret what the Vpoint command's axes tripod represents.

The Dview command enables you to change the view as follows:

❏ Change the view distance and field of view

❏ Twist the view

❏ Create a perspective hidden-line view

❏ Remove objects in the front and back of the view

You may notice that the Vpoint command does not enable you to look behind things. You could get very close to the outside walls of the bathroom with the Zoom command, but you could never go inside the bathroom. With Dview, you can set a *clipping* distance which removes objects that get in your view.

Selecting the Entities to View

After typing **Dview** at the Command: prompt, you indicate the entities you want to see. The Select objects: prompt gives you two choices. One option is for you to select a set of objects from the drawing. If the drawing is small, you can use Crossing mode to select all objects. If the drawing is large, select a few entities you need to work with.

When using Dview, choose your entities carefully—AutoCAD displays only the entities you selected. If you select too many entities, you will slow down the Dview command; if you select too few entities, you will have difficulty seeing the changes to the viewpoint. Whether you pick too many or too few, you can always cancel the command and try again.

The second option is that you can simply press Enter without selecting any entities: you are telling AutoCAD to use all the drawing entities. Since dynamically changing the view of a large drawing is extremely slow, AutoCAD simplifies the display with a house graphic (see fig. 18.6). The house has a chimney, window, and open door so that you can orient yourself in the new view.

If you don't like the house graphics, you can create your own. Draw the 3-D graphic you prefer as a 1-by-1-by-1 block named DVIEWBLOCK. The block could be a simplified version of the drawing you are working on, scaled down to unit size. If AutoCAD cannot find the block with this name in the drawing, it uses the house instead.

The advantages of using the 3-D graphic are that the dynamic viewing time is greatly reduced *and* you see all entities in your drawing once you decide on the new viewpoint.

Manipulating the View

Once you select the objects (or decide to use the house graphic), you will be able to manipulate the view of the display. You can do this by adjusting the target (what you're looking at) and the camera (the direction from which you look). You do this from the Dview prompt:

```
Command: DVIEW
Select objects: Press Enter
CAmera/TArget/Distance/POints/PAn/Zoom/TWist/CLip/Hide/Off/Undo/<eXit:
```

The prompt repeats whenever you make a selection until you exit Dview.

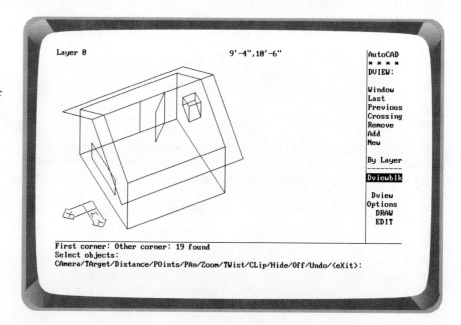

Fig. 18.6.
*AutoCAD
substitutes a
house graphic
to make the
Dview
command
faster.*

Dview is an involved command. Because several options make similar
changes to the drawing, they are grouped together in the following
sections.

Dview's Camera, Target, and Points Options

The Camera, Target, and Points options deal with the *target* and the
camera. The target is the point you look at, and the camera is the point
you look from; between them lies your line of sight, the *view direction*.
The Camera option places the camera, the Target option places the
target, and the Point option places both the camera and target.

The Camera option enables you to change your location while
maintaining a fixed target. In other words, select Camera when you want
to view the same object from several positions. Try changing the camera's
view, as follows:

```
CAmera/TArget/POints/.../<eXit>: CA
Enter angle from X-Y plane <53.30>:
Enter angle in X-Y plane from X axis <63.43>:
```

The *slider bars* at the top and right sides of the screen show the view angle relative to the X-Y plane of the current UCS (see fig. 18.7). You can type in a new angle at the keyboard or use your pointing device to move the slider bars. As you move the slider bar, the status line (at the top center of the screen) reports the currently picked angle.

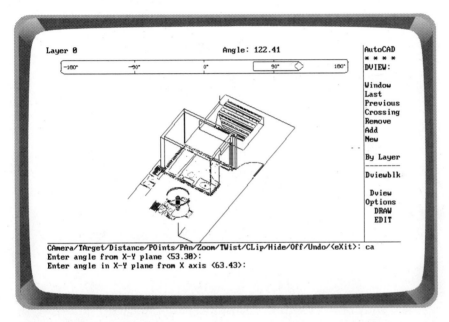

Fig. 18.7.
The slider bars (top) enable you to dynamically change the camera view.

The slider bar on the right goes from 90 degrees to –90 degrees, which has the following meaning:

- ❑ 90 degrees: you are looking straight down
- ❑ 0 degrees: you are looking straight on
- ❑ –90 degrees: you are looking straight up

The slider bar at the top of the screen goes from –180 degrees to 180 degrees:

- ❑ –180 degrees: you are looking from the left
- ❑ –90 degrees: you are looking from the front
- ❑ 0 degrees: you are looking from the right
- ❑ 90 degrees: you are looking from the back
- ❑ 180 degrees: you are looking from the left, again

The Target option enables you to move your view to different points without changing the camera location. With Target, you can look around a room while remaining in the same spot, as follows:

```
CAmera/TArget/POints/.../<eXit>: TA
```

`Enter angle from X-Y plane <53.30>:` Move right slider bar with pointing device

`Enter angle in X-Y plane from X axis <63.43>:` Move upper slider bar with pointing device

See fig. 18.8 for the results of this command.

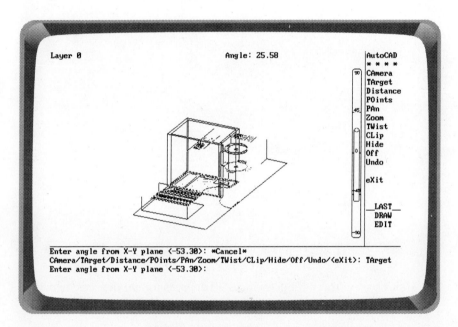

Fig. 18.8.
The Target
option moves
your view
around the
suite.

To change the camera and target locations at the same time, select the Points option. This option enables you to specify new X,Y,Z coordinates for the camera and target. You can use object snap and point filters to locate the new view. You might find Points to be the easiest of the three options:

Prompt	Response	Explanation
`CAmera/TArget/POints/.../ <eXit>:`	**PO**	Select Point option
`Enter target point:`	**CEN**	Use CENter object snap to pick the...
`of`		...kitchen table kitchen circle table top

Prompt	Response	Explanation
`Enter camera point:`	**.XY**	Use .XY point filter the select only the x and y coordinates...
`of`	**INT**	...of the intersection of the lines
`of`	Pick lower left corner of bedroom	...making up the bedroom walls.
`(need Z)`	**25'**	Finally, specify a view height distance of 25'

Your (dynamic) view should now look like figure 18.9.

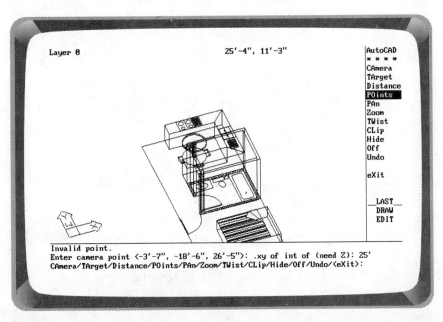

Fig. 18.9.
The Dview Point option enables you to pick the target and camera points.

Dview's Distance, Zoom, Pan, and Twist Options

Once you select the camera and target points, the Distance, Zoom, Pan, and Twist options change the view. Each option changes the view in a different way.

The Distance option allows you to move the camera along the line of sight (the line between the camera and the target). This is similar to walking closer to or farther away from what you want to take a picture of.

This option changes the camera location while retaining the current line of sight. Because the change is relative to the target, you define a new camera-to-target distance:

```
CAmera/.../Distance/PAn/Zoom/TWist/.../<eXit>: D
New camera/target distance <33'1">: 132'
```

The slider bar shows the new distance relative to the distance you began with (see fig. 18.10). It ranges from 0x to 16x, as follows:

- ❏ 0x: You are at the target point
- ❏ 1x: You are back at the starting point
- ❏ 16x: You are 16 times farther away

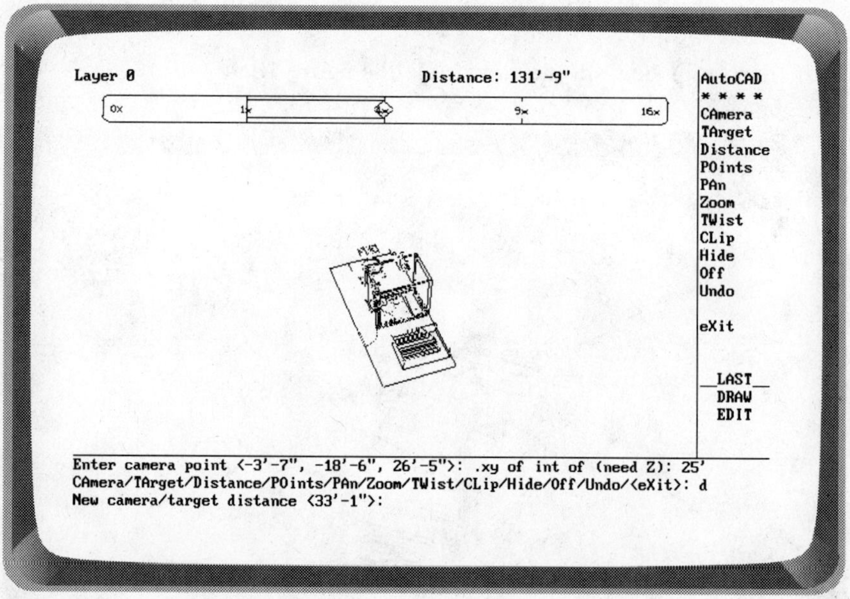

Fig. 18.10.
The slider bar
enables you to
dynamically
change the
camera's
viewing
distance from
the target.

As with the Camera and Target options, you can type in a new value or move the slider bars until the view is just right (see fig. 18.11).

The Distance feature turns on perspective; to remind you of this, the UCS icon changes to a cube seen in perspective. You can turn off perspective mode with the Off option, discussed later in this chapter.

Dview's Pan option is similar to AutoCAD's Pan command. The Pan option shifts the drawing without changing the zoom factor. With the Pan option, however, you see the panning in *real-time*; you see the changes occur after you pick the displacement base point. If you are working with objects that are only partially on-screen, you can use Pan to move them on-screen. You can move the SUITE drawing up the screen, as follows:

```
CAmera/...Distance/PAn/Zoom/TWist/.../<eXit>: PA
Displacement base point: Pick point
Second point: Pick point
```

See figure 18.12 for the results of this command.

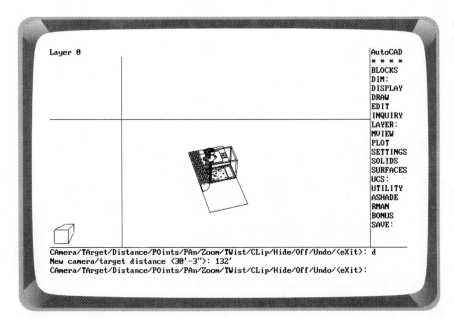

Fig. 18.11.
The SUITE drawing in perspective. The UCS icon changes to a cube to remind you that you are in perspective-view mode.

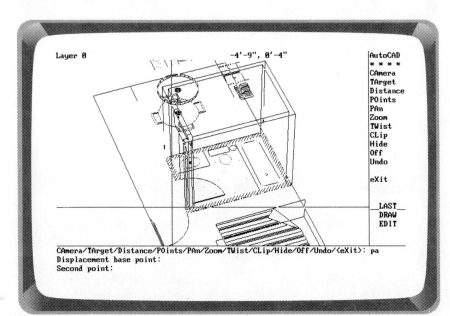

Fig. 18.12.
The Dview Pan command enables you to pan in real time.

WARNING

In perspective mode, you must use your pointing device to select the new pan view; you cannot type in a displacement at the keyboard.

The function of the Zoom option depends on whether perspective is on or off. In perspective, you use Zoom to adjust the length of the camera "lens," as follows:

❏ 0.5x = 25mm: You see more but are farther away with this wide-angle lens

❏ 1x = 50mm: The standard lens size, similar to a 1x enlargement

❏ 2x = 100mm: You see less but are closer to the target with this telephoto lens

Try the Zoom option in perspective mode now (see fig. 18.13):

```
CAmera/.../Distance/PAn/Zoom/TWist/.../<eXit>: Z
Adjust lens length <50.000mm>: 200
```

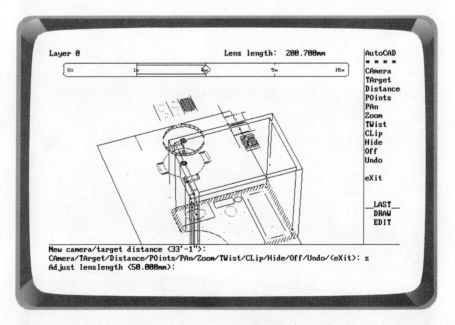

Fig. 18.13.
The Zoom
option enables
you to change
your camera's
lenses.

If the view is in perspective mode, the effect of the Zoom option is similar to the Zoom Center command: AutoCAD magnifies the drawing while retaining the current center point of the screen.

The Twist option allows you to tilt the view around the line of sight. Only the view is tilted; the camera and target remain the same. The line of sight is the axis of tilt (or twist). The angle you indicate is positive in the counterclockwise direction about the line. Try twisting the view, as follows (see fig. 18.14):

```
CAmera/.../Distance/PAn/Zoom/TWist/.../<eXit>: TW
New view to twist <0.00> 330
```

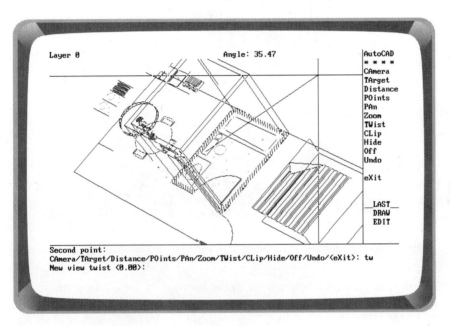

Fig. 18.14.
Results of the
Twist
command.

Dview's Hide and Clip Options

The Hide and Clip options enable you to remove parts of entities to make the view clearer.

The Hide option removes hidden lines in the current view, just like the Hide command. The difference is that Dview's Hide enables you to get a perspective hidden-line view. Do a hidden-line view now (see fig. 18.15):

```
CAmera/.../CLip/Hide/.../<eXit>: H
Removing hidden lines: 1425
```

All of the advantages, disadvantages, and options of the Hide command discussed earlier apply to the Hide option. To return the hidden lines, exit to the Command: prompt and issue the Regen command.

The Clip option enables you to add *clipping planes* to a drawing. Of all the Dview command's options, this one is the most involved. When you select this option, you are given the following options:

```
CAmera/.../CLip/Hide/.../<eXit>: CL
Back/Front/<Off>:
```

Fig. 18.15.
Hide removes
hidden lines,
even in
perspective
mode.

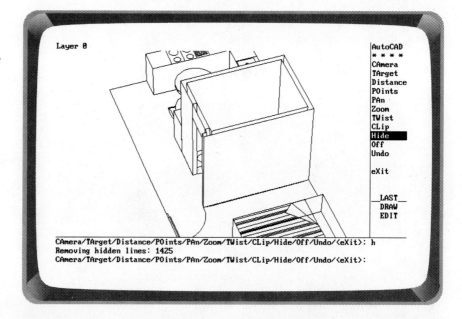

The Back and Front options refer to the location of the clipping plane. The back clipping plane cuts off whatever is behind it; the front clipping plane cuts off whatever is in front of it. Clipping planes can be applied anywhere between the camera and target; they are perpendicular to the line of sight.

Clipping is most useful in complex 3-D drawings when you find objects getting in the way of your editing and drawing. You can use Clip to isolate any part of your drawing.

To see its effect, try turning on the back and front clipping planes:

Prompt	Response	Explanation
`Back/Front/<Off>:`	**B**	Select Back clipping plane option
`ON/OFF/<Distance from target>:<7'-7">:`	**2'**	Set the clipping distance to 2 feet from the target
`Back/Front/<Off>:`	**F**	Select Front clipping plane option
`ON/OFF/<Distance from target>:<132'-0>:`	**9'**	Set the clipping distance to 9 feet

See figure 18.16 for the results of using the Clip command.

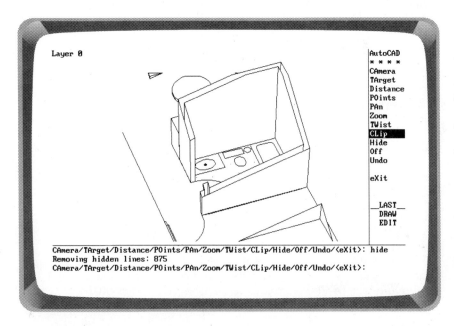

Fig. 18.16.
The Front and Back clipping planes remove entities parallel to the current view plane.

When you are working in perspective, the front clipping plane is turned on automatically and is located at the camera. Anything behind the camera is not seen when you are in perspective. As you move the distance of the camera closer into the drawing, objects begin to disappear. The clipping plane eliminates any possible strange projections of these entities during perspective.

By selecting the Off option, you disable the front and back clipping planes. Choose this option to return the Dview command to the default setting for Clip.

Dview's Off, Undo, and Exit Options

If you choose the Off option, you tell AutoCAD to turn off perspective mode. It is automatically turned on when you select the Distance option. This command has no effect if perspective mode is not on.

The Undo option allows you to undo the last Dview selection and any changes you may have made. It is wonderful for experimenting with Dview.

The Exit option returns you to the Command: prompt with all Dview options intact (including the clipping, hidden-lines removed, perspective mode, and viewpoint). You can get back to orthographic wireframe mode with the Plan command.

Seeing More than One View (Viewports or Vports)

The Viewports (or Vports) command lets you divide the screen into as many as 16 screens or *viewports* (AutoCAD Release 10 for DOS is limited to 4 viewports). You can work in any of the screens; the changes you make in one screen are reflected in the others. If you erase a door from an elevation view of your three-dimensional model, the door will disappear from the other viewports also.

These windows are called *viewports* because they are ports through which you see your drawing. To understand this command, think of it as giving you the ability to set up the four standard views of a drawing: front, side, top, and isometric. In AutoCAD, each view (or *window*) is isolated from the others. But AutoCAD does not limit you to the four standard views; each window can show any view from any angle, with hidden lines removed or shading. You can use viewports on 2-D and 3-D drawings.

Within each viewport, you can define independently the following:

❏ The grid and snap modes, and spacing
❏ Fast zoom mode, controlled with the system variable VIEWRES
❏ The coordinate system icon
❏ The three-dimensional view, selected by the Vpoint or Dview commands
❏ Perspective mode, via Dview
❏ The front and back clipping planes (also from Dview)
❏ The removal of hidden lines (with Hide) or the shading of faces (via Shade)

The Vports Options

The Vports command and its prompts look like this:

```
Command: VPORTS
Save/Restore/Delete/Join/SIngle/?/2/<3>/4:
```

The Save option enables you to save the viewport configuration by name so that you can return to it later. (You also can end your work session without saving the configuration.) To see a list of saved configurations, press **?**. To return to a saved configuration, use the Restore option. This is similar to the way the View command works; however, View works only with single-screen views.

The Delete option deletes a saved configuration, like the View command's Delete option.

The 2, 3, and 4 options enable you to choose the number of viewports you want to use. Press **2** for two viewports; the screen can be divided either horizontally or vertically (the default). Try it now on the SUITE drawing, as follows:

```
Save/.../2/<3>/4: 2
Horizontal/<Vertical>: V
```

The screen splits in two, with an identical view of the suite in each. The viewport with the heavier border (on the right side) is the *current viewport*; any command you execute is effective only in that viewport. Try the Vpoint command and turn off the grid (see fig. 18.17):

```
Command: Vpoint 1,1,1
Command: GRID OFF
```

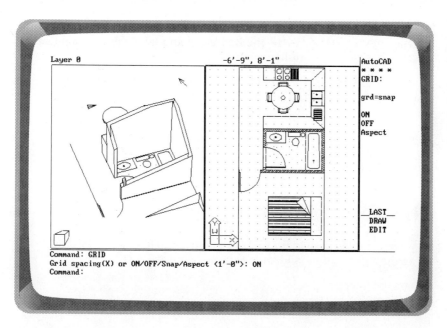

Fig. 18.17.
The Vports 2 V command splits the screen into two vertical viewports.

To access the other viewport, move the pointing device over. You notice that the crosshair cursor changes to an arrow cursor. When you pick anywhere on the viewport, the arrow changes to the crosshair. The arrow cursor reminds you that the viewport is *inactive*. You can also press Ctrl-V to move from viewport to viewport.

If you want three viewports, press **3** (the default option). AutoCAD then displays the following prompt:

```
Command: Vports
Save/.../2/<3>/4: 3
Horizontal/Vertical/Above/Below/Left/<Right>:
```

The Horizontal and Vertical options split the screen into thirds in the appropriate direction. The other options allow for one large and two small viewports. You specify the larger viewport's location in relation to the two smaller viewports.

Select the Join option to join two adjacent on-screen viewports into one viewport. You must define the viewport that will become the view in the new, combined viewport. The Single option returns you to the default configuration.

Redrawing All the Viewports (Redrawall and Regenall)

The Redraw and Regen commands work in the current viewport only. Because of this, AutoCAD has the Redrawall and Regenall commands that update all viewports simultaneously.

To redraw the images seen in all the viewports, use the Redrawall command. The command has the same effect as using Redraw in each viewport simultaneously.

To regen the images seen in all the viewports, use the Regenall command. The command has the same effect as using Regen in each viewport, one at a time.

Tips for Using 3-D Views

Viewing complex drawings in 3-D can be tricky. Here are several tips for using the Vports command and for controlling the 3-D screen.

Tips for the Vports Command

The Vports command is useful when you are working with a complex drawing. With 3-D drawings, viewports are extremely useful for showing an object from several angles at one time.

With 2-D drawings, you can show several zoomed-in views at one time. Save one viewport for the overall view of the entire drawing.

Viewports are transparent to most AutoCAD commands. You can draw a line from a point in one viewport to a point in another viewport.

Begin the Line command, as follows:

```
Command: LINE
```

```
From point: Pick a point in one viewport
```

```
To point: Move the cursor to the second viewport. Pick it once to
           select the viewport (the cursor changes to a crosshair).
           Pick a second time to place the other endpoint. AutoCAD
           cleverly places the line in the intended location. This
           seems amazing, but remember: no matter how many
           viewports are on the screen, you are still working on only
           one drawing.
```

You can also create viewports while using AutoCAD commands. Vports is a transparent command with 'VPORTS. To carry on with the example, suppose that you need another viewport in order to place the line's third endpoint:

```
To point: 'VPORTS
Save/Restore/Delete/Join/SIngle/?/2/<3>/4:
```

When you enter the Vports command preceded by an apostrophe, AutoCAD lets you create a new viewport. When you finish, you are back at the To point: prompt to finish placing the endpoint.

By using one of AutoCAD's system variables, you can cause a plan view to be generated whenever you change the current UCS. Turn on the system variable UCSFOLLOW by changing the value to 1:

```
Command: UCSFOLLOW
New value for UCSFOLLOW: <0> 1
```

When this variable is set to one, a plan view is generated whenever the UCS is altered. This feature can be set separately for each viewport you have on-screen. If you have multiple viewports, you might set up one of them to display the plan view whenever you modify your UCS.

Some commands cannot move between viewports. The following commands prohibit you from working in multiple viewports until the command is completed:

❑ Dview

❑ Grid

❑ Pan

❏ Snap
❏ Vpoint
❏ Zoom

You cannot, of course, start another Vpoint command within the first one.

AutoCAD treats each viewport as if it were the only image on the monitor. This means that Pan, Zoom, Vslide, and other commands act only on the current viewport. Only the Regenall and Redrawall commands affect all the viewports.

Tips for Better Screen Control of 3-D Work

Now that you have been exposed to many of the commands that influence the display, you should consider how you can use these commands. Think about the viewing commands discussed in Chapter 9 as well as those discussed earlier in this chapter. You have substantial control over the display when you use all the available options.

The following list includes some of the methods you can use to take full advantage of your display:

❏ Use multiple viewports whenever possible, especially in 3-D drawings. Figure 18.18 has 10 viewports.
❏ With multiple viewports, use the Pan and Zoom Previous commands to move the image. This enables you to keep an enlarged view at all times in one specific port and aids in adding detail.
❏ The saying "less is more" is especially true when you work with three-dimensional drawings. Because processing is faster with fewer faces, lines, and other entities, choose the number of entities carefully. More importantly, be selective about what you display. Having a "tight" zoom on a specific area will reduce the selection time needed.
❏ Because a three-dimensional model typically has more entities than a standard two-dimensional drawing, create and use views. You should use named views and named user coordinates often. The practice shortens the time needed to get the correct display.
❏ Slides can be used with good effect in viewports. (Refer to Chapter 9 for information about slides.) If you have four slides representing four options on one specific design, why not put them all on the screen simultaneously? With the Vports and Vslide commands, you can.

The items in this list are examples from my experience. Experiment a little: you certainly will find other ways to get the views you need.

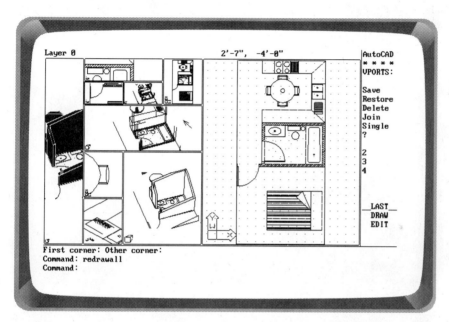

*3.18.
liberal

orts
vorking
-D
ngs.*

Summary

This chapter has shown you different ways to look at a three-dimensional drawing. It has covered commands for controlling the on-screen image and commands for displaying 3-D work.

You should now have a firm grasp of three-dimensional drafting, editing, and viewing. As you can see, it truly is an exciting extension of the way CAD drawings were once put together. The future looks bright as the features of three-dimensional work, such as ways to view your three-dimensional drawing, are developed and improved.

In Chapter 19 you will learn about optional Autodesk programs that enable you to perform rendering, solids modeling, and animation. These make your AutoCAD drawing look more realistic and add movement.

19

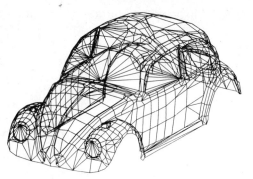

Illustration courtesy of Autodesk, Inc., Sausalito, CA.

Plotting a 3-D Drawing

In Chapter 8 you learned how to use a plotter. In this chapter, you learn some of the tricks in plotting three-dimensional drawings.

You can plot a 3-D drawing with what you learned in Chapter 8, but the result may not be what you want. There are two ways to make a 3-D plot look good: hidden-line removal and multiple-view plotting. You will work with the following commands:

- ❏ Mspace
- ❏ Mview
- ❏ Plot
- ❏ Pspace
- ❏ Vplayer
- ❏ Zoom XP

and system variables:

- ❏ MAXACTVP
- ❏ TILEMODE

Plotting with Hidden Lines Removed

You may have tried to do 3-D plots by using the Hide command followed by the Plot command. Unfortunately, this does not remove hidden lines from your plot. Instead, you need to use the Hide option in the Plot command.

551

There is a reason for having two Hide commands. Since the screen resolution is lower than the resolution of the plot, AutoCAD uses a different *algorithm* to calculate which parts of entities are hidden and need to be removed. Because the drawing is plotted at a higher resolution, hidden lines need to be removed more accurately, and this can take longer than removing hidden lines from the display.

To turn on the Plot (or Prplot) command's hide option, follow these commands:

```
Command: Plot
What to plot -- Display, Extents, Limits, View, or
Window <D>: V
```

Select the View option to plot from a saved view. If you select any other option, the 3-D view plotted is the view (including perspective views) most recently saved in the current viewport.

When you plot a perspective view, the drawing is no longer to scale. Objects further back are relatively smaller than the objects up front. For this reason, AutoCAD does not prompt you for a scale factor. Instead, it gives the following message:

```
**Plot of perspective view has been scaled to fit
available area.**
```

AutoCAD will plot the extents of the perspective view to fit the paper (see fig. 19.1). You can control the size of the plot by making the plotting size larger or smaller than the actual paper size. If the plotting size exceeds the paper size, AutoCAD will complain but will go ahead with the plot. The parts of the drawing that don't fit on the paper are *clipped* (not plotted at all).

Unless you use paper space (discussed in the next section), you cannot plot all viewports visible on the screen. Also, you cannot plot a shaded image. You can make a copy of your drawing by using screen-capture software or by photographing the screen with a camera.

```
Do you want to change anything? <N> Y
Do you want to change any of these parameters? <N> N
```

Continue responding with the default values to questions until you get to:

```
Remove hidden lines: <N> Y
```

Answer **YES** to have AutoCAD remove hidden lines from the plot (see fig. 19.2). Just as with the Hide command, it can take a long time for AutoCAD to calculate which lines to remove. The plotter will not begin plotting until AutoCAD has finished its work.

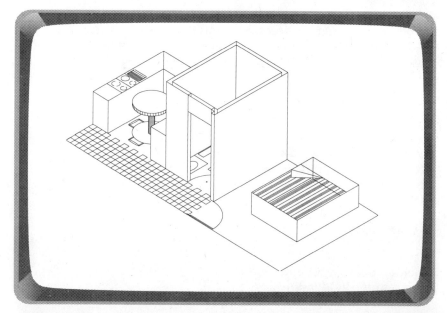

Fig. 19.1.
AutoCAD plots
perspective
views to fit the
paper.

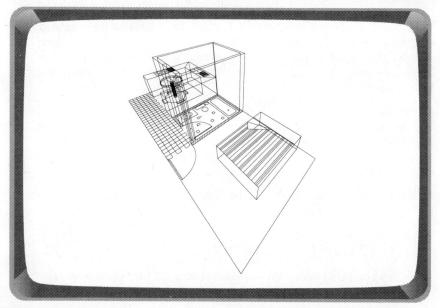

Fig. 19.2.
The drawing
plotted with
hidden-line
removal.

Because plotting with hidden lines can be very time consuming, use the Plot to File option when plotting. AutoCAD will go through the normal plotting prompts and then create a new file with the "plotted" version of your drawing; this file will have your old file name with the PLT extension. Then plot the PLT file with a plot spooler program. This way, if the plotter's pen clogs or something else goes wrong during your plot, you will not have to start completely over.

AutoCAD remembers the previous plot parameters between drawing sessions. But plotting can become tedious if you need to constantly switch between plotting drawings with hidden lines removed and without hidden lines removed. A quick solution is to write two script files: one that turns hidden-line removal on and one that turns it off.

The script file that turns on the hidden-line removal looks like this:

PLOT
Extents
Yes,make-changes
No,don't-make-pen-changes
No,don't-plot-to-file
Inches
0,0
D-size-paper
0
0.01
No,don't-adjust-fill-boundaries
Yes,remove-hidden-lines
Fit-plot

Create this file with your text editor; name the script file HIDEPLOT.SCR. There are two blank lines at the end of the script to start the plot and return to the drawing editor. In Release 10, replace the **0** in the ninth line with **No,don't-rotate-plot**. Create a second script file that turns hidden-line removal off by changing the second-last line to **No,don't-remove-hidden-lines**.

AutoCAD reads only the first character of non-numeric responses. This lets you include descriptive text in the script file, such as **Yes,remove-hidden-lines**. You must use a space-filler between words, such as a comma or dash, because AutoCAD considers the next character after a space as the response to the next prompt.

To use this script file, make sure that you are in the Drawing Editor. At the `Command:` prompt, type in the Script command, as follows:

```
Command: Script
Script file <SUITE>:  HIDEPLOT
```

You can write other script files to change tedious plot parameters such as paper size and pen assignments.

Plotting Multiple Viewports

Until now, you have done all your work in *model space*. In the process of drawing and editing the one-bedroom apartment suite, you have created an electronic model in 3-D space.

In Release 11, Autodesk added *paper space* to make it easier to plot multiple views of 2-D and 3-D drawings on a single sheet of paper. Create your drawings in full-size in model scale, and then switch to paper space to arrange views and add notes just before plotting.

Paper space has one very important function: it enables you to treat viewports like any other object in your drawing. The following tasks are easy to perform in paper space:

❏ Move and resize viewports

❏ Freeze and thaw layers in separate viewports

❏ Edit the viewport with AutoCAD's editing commands

❏ Plot all displayed viewports

In paper space, as well as model space, you can do the following:

❏ Display a different viewpoint in each viewport, including separately shaded and hidden-line views

❏ Set snap, grid, and UCS icon differently in each viewport

AutoCAD has three commands that get you in and out of paper space:

❏ Tilemode

❏ Pspace

❏ Mspace

Once in paper space, AutoCAD has three commands that enable you to create and modify viewports:

❏ Mview

❏ Vplayer

❏ Maxactvp

The Zoom command also has a paper space option. In the following pages, you will learn how to take the SUITE drawing into paper space, arrange views, and then plot them.

Entering Paper Space for the First Time (TILEMODE)

If you are familiar with Macintosh, OS/2, or another windowing interface, you know that you can have several programs displayed on the screen at the same time. Each program appears in its own *window*. The windows can be any size and can overlap.

With AutoCAD's Vports command, you can create viewports (or windows) of nearly any size, but you cannot overlap them. These special viewports are known as *tiled* viewports.

Tiled viewports are a result of the limitation of AutoCAD's model space. In paper space, AutoCAD can have overlapping viewports, just like on the Macintosh or with OS/2. In model space, however, viewports cannot overlap. AutoCAD has a system variable, called TILEMODE, that must be turned off before you can switch to paper space:

Command: **TILEMODE**
New value for TILEMODE <1>: **0**
Enter Paper space. Use MVIEW to insert Model space viewport:

Changing the value of TILEMODE to 0 turns it off and automatically switches the Drawing Editor to paper space. The screen goes blank, a P appears on the status line, and the UCS icon is replaced by a drafting triangle icon (see fig. 19.3).

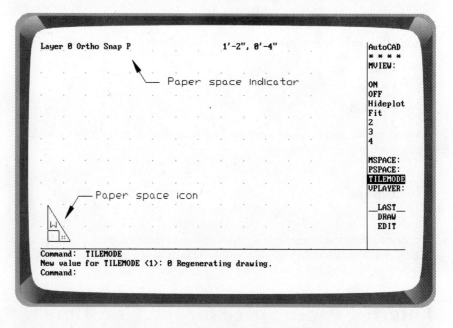

Fig. 19.3.
Turning off
TILEMODE
turns on paper
space.

You will bring back views of the SUITE drawing with the Mview command. To prepare for the Mview command, first draw the outline of a D-size sheet of paper (if you prefer, you can use any other convenient size, such as A-size).

An architectural D-size sheet of plotter paper is 36" long by 24" wide. You will draw a border line that represents the unplottable edges: usually 0.6" in on three sides and 1.5" in on the fourth. This makes the border dimensions 33.9" by 22.8". Use the Pline command to draw the border on a new layer named D-SIZE:

```
Command: LAYER M D-SIZE
Command: Pline
From point: 0,0
...<Endpoint of line>: 33.9,0
...<Endpoint of line>: 33.9,22.8
...<Endpoint of line>: 0,22.8
...<Endpoint of line>: C
Command: Zoom E
```

The border polyline represents the drawing limits as far as the plotter is concerned. Within the border, you will place four views of the kitchen with the Mview command.

Creating Views in Paper Space (Mview)

The Mview (short for Make VIEW) command enables you to create viewports while in paper space. The command prompt is as follows:

```
Command: Mview
ON/OFF/Hideplot/Fit/2/3/4/Restore/<First Point>: 4
Fit/<first point>: F
```

AutoCAD creates four viewports of equal size, three of which show the same zoomed-in view of the SUITE drawing (see fig. 19.4). This isn't quite what you want. The detail (it's of the bathroom door) looks as large as it does because of its actual size relative to the D-size paper. To change the view each viewport displays, switch back to model space with the Mspace command.

Move the cursor around. Notice how it remains a crosshair cursor no matter which viewport you are over. This means that you can work with any paper-space viewport. This is different from model space viewports in which you have to pick a viewport before you can use it. You will have the opportunity to experiment more with paper space later in this chapter.

Switching Back to Model Space (Mspace)

The Mspace command switches you back to model space, as follows:

```
Command: Mspace
```

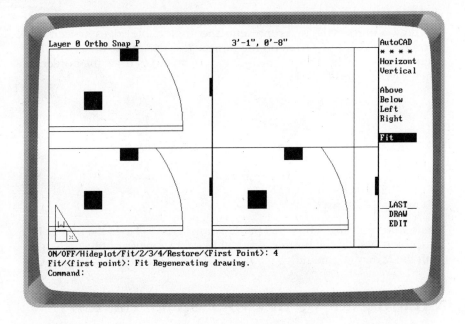

Fig. 19.4.
The Mview
command
creates
viewports in
paper space.

When you pick the upper left viewport, the arrow cursor changes to the crosshair cursor. If you don't see the entire SUITE drawing in this viewport, use the Zoom Extents command:

Command: **Zoom E**

You can use this as the *key* drawing that shows the overall plan. Move to the lower left viewport. Change the view point, as follows:

Command: **Vpoint –1,–1,1**

You now have an isometric view. Move the cursor to the lower right viewport and pick it. Zoom in to the kitchen plan view:

Command: **Zoom W**

Finally, pick the upper right viewport and zoom in on the bathroom. You now have the key plan, the isometric plan, the bathroom plan, and the kitchen plan (see fig. 19.5). But there is still one blank viewport. You can make it visible with the system variable MAXACTVP.

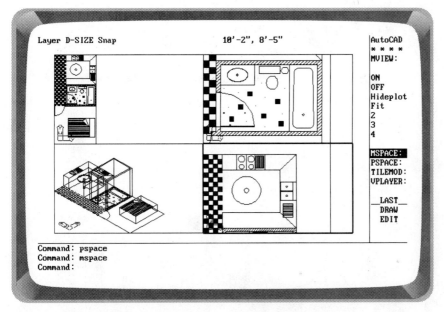

Fig. 19.5.
Back in model space, you can change the view with the Zoom and Vpoint commands.

Changing the Maximum Active Viewports (MAXACTVP)

Paper space displays, by default, the contents of 15 viewports at one time. If you have created more than 15 viewports, their outlines—but not their contents—are displayed. Model space can display up to 16 viewports simultaneously.

AutoCAD has a system variable, MAXACTVP (short for MAXimum ACTive ViewPorts), that determines the maximum number of *active* viewports. An active viewport displays the contents of the viewport; an inactive viewport doesn't. You can define up to 32,676 viewports in one drawing but only display the contents of up to 15 at a time. MAXACTVP does not affect plottable viewports in paper space. Change the MAXACTVP system variable as follows:

```
Command: MAXACTVP
New value for MAXACTVP <16>: 2
Command: Regenall
```

Now you can see the contents of one paper-space viewport (see fig. 19.6). The default setting of 16 means that AutoCAD would have been limited to 15 viewports. The "missing" viewport is paper space itself. Now turn on the blank viewports:

Command: **MAXACTVP**
New value for MAXACTVP <2>: **16**
Command: **Regenall**

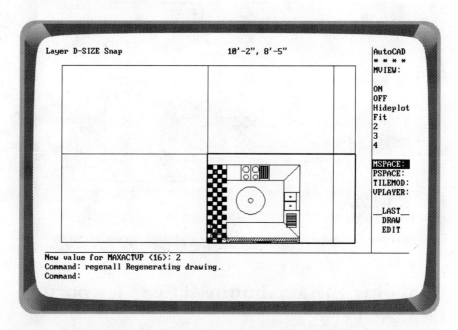

Fig. 19.6.
The system
variable
MAXACTVP
limits the
maximum
number of
active
viewports.

There are advantages to limiting the number of viewports displayed: it reduces redraw and regen time, memory requirements, and screen clutter.

Zooming Relative to Paper Space (Zoom XP)

The Zoom command's XP option enables you to zoom a viewport relative to paper space. The XP option also enables you to change the scale of a detail drawing without affecting the scale of the other viewports.

Move to the upper right viewport and pick it. Now use the Zoom XP command to draw the view at one-tenth scale (1:10), as follows:

Command: **Zoom E**
Command: **Pan** (to center the floor plan in the viewport)
Command: **Zoom**
All/.../<Scale(X/XP)>: **0.1XP**

The view in the viewport is redrawn about the bathroom. It is, in fact, drawn at one-tenth the size of paper scale. The viewport takes up one-quarter of the D-size sheet: that makes the viewport measure about 8 1/2" across. Using a 0.1XP zoom factor makes the view of the bathroom 10 times that, about 85 inches across (see fig. 19.7).

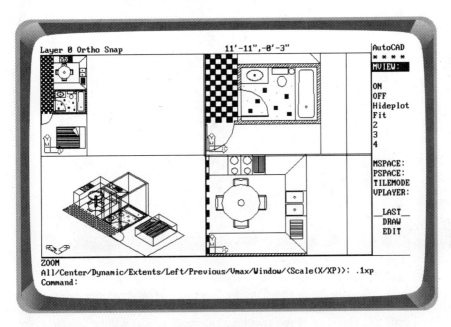

Fig. 19.7.
The Zoom XP command scales objects relative to paper space.

If you want, you can now plot or printer/plot the drawing with its four views. Make sure that you are in paper space, and then use the Plot (or Prplot) command. If you have access to a plotter that accepts D-size paper, you can simply use the Plot command's Fit option (see fig. 19.8).

WARNING

If you plot now from model space, AutoCAD plots only the current viewport. You must be in paper space before issuing the Plot command to have all four viewports plotted.

Switching Back to Paper Space (Pspace)

The Pspace command switches you from model space to paper space. Return to paper space, as follows:

Command: **Pspace**

AutoCAD reminds you that you are in paper space with the drawing triangle icon in the lower left corner of the screen and the P on the status line. This time in paper space, you will try editing the viewports with the Stretch, Copy, and Erase commands.

Fig. 19.8.
Using the Plot
command's
Fit option.

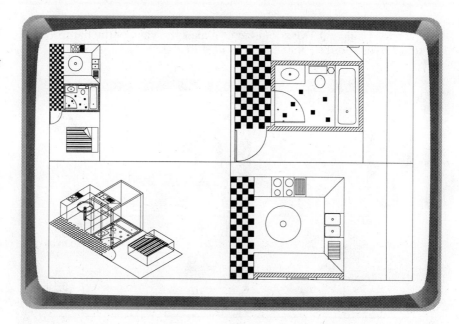

You can change the shape of a viewport with the Stretch command. When AutoCAD asks you to Select objects:, pick the viewport you want to stretch. AutoCAD highlights only the viewport's outline to remind you that only the visibility of the contents of the viewport will be affected. To edit the contents of the viewport, switch back to model space.

You can try the Move command to change the location of viewports, or the Scale command to change the size of a viewport. Figure 19.9 shows resized and moved (even overlapping) viewports. If you have unnecessary viewports, you can erase them. Use the Undo command to bring the viewport back again.

There are several commands that AutoCAD will not allow you to use in paper space:

❏ Dview

❏ Plan

❏ Transparent 'Zoom, 'Pan, and 'View

❏ Vpoint

You cannot use the UCSFOLLOW system variable in paper space since AutoCAD always displays the plan view of the current UCS. You cannot use commands like Rotate and Fillet to rotate or fillet viewports.

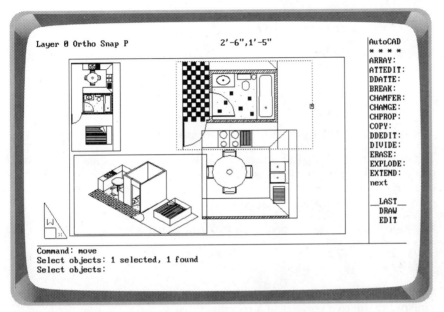

Fig. 19.9.
You can scale,
move, and
stretch
viewports
while in paper
space.

Managing Paper Space Viewports (Mview)

The Mview command has several more options than you have used so far. When you type **Mview** at the Command: prompt, it responds as follows:

Command: **Mview**
ON/OFF/Hideplot/Fit/2/3/4/Restore/<First Point>:

The Mview command works only in paper space. If you type **Mview** while in model space, AutoCAD answers Switching to paper space. Mview has nine options, which are discussed below.

Automatically Create New Viewports (Fit, 2, 3, 4, Restore)

The Fit, 2, 3, and 4 options automatically create and size additional viewports. These options mimic the Vports command's view-creation options by creating tiled viewports.

The Fit option creates a single viewport that fits the current screen. The 2, 3, and 4 options create more than one viewport. When you select two viewports, AutoCAD asks the following:

```
ON/.../Fit/2/3/4/.../<First Point>: 2
Horizontal/<Vertical>:
```

You can split the screen in half vertically (the default) or horizontally, to create two viewports.

If you select three viewports, you have more options:

```
ON/.../Fit/2/3/4/.../<First Point>: 3
Horizontal/Vertical/Above/Below/Left/<Right>:
```

The horizontal and vertical options split the screen into equal thirds. The other four options—Above, Below, Left, and Right—split the screen into one large viewport and two smaller ones. The default option, Right, places the larger viewport to the right of two smaller ports.

The four-viewport option gives you two additional options:

```
ON/.../Fit/2/3/4/.../<First Point>: 4
Fit/<First point>:
```

The Fit option splits the screen into four viewports of equal size. Or, you can specify the two corners of a rectangle that AutoCAD will fit the four viewports into:

```
Fit/<FirstPoint>: Pick one corner
Second Point: Pick other corner
```

The Restore option converts a named viewport into a paper-space viewport:

```
ON/.../Restore/<First Point>: R
?/Name of window configuration to insert: ?
```

Entering the question mark (?) makes AutoCAD list the names of saved viewports. If you had several viewports active before you went into paper space, AutoCAD lists them by number. You can supply the name or number of one of the viewports listed.

Manually Creating New Viewports (First Point)

You can create viewports of any size, wherever you like. At the Mview command's prompt, pick two points:

```
ON/.../<First Point>: Pick point
Second point: Pick point
```

AutoCAD ghosts a rectangle to show you the size of the viewport as you move the second point around. Once you are satisfied with its size, pick the second point.

With this manual method, you can quickly create many viewports, overlapping or not.

Creating a Hidden-Line Viewport (Hideplot)

The Hideplot option tells AutoCAD to remove hidden lines at plot time:

```
ON/.../Hideplot/.../<First Point>: H
ON/OFF: ON
Select objects: Pick viewport
```

Pick the lower left viewport that shows the isometric plan. Notice that AutoCAD lets you pick several viewports for hidden-line plotting. AutoCAD does not remove hidden lines at this time; rather it waits until you use the Plot command. You do not need to specify "Remove hidden lines?" during the plot command. If you want a hidden-line view now, switch to model space and use the Hide command on the viewport.

The Hideplot option of Mview only works if you start the Plot command while in paper space.

As AutoCAD plots each viewport (see fig. 19.10), it reports the viewport number, its plotted size, and whether hidden lines are being removed:

```
Plotting viewport 5
Effective plotting area: 2.29 wide by 2.24 high
Processing vector: 544
Plotting viewport 4
Effective plotting area: 3.20 wide by 1.99 high
Removing hidden lines: 1075
Processing vector: 1360
```

Controlling Viewports (On and Off)

The On and Off options turn the display of viewports on and off. AutoCAD regenerates the entire screen every time you resize or move a viewport. Although the MAXACTVP system variable limits the number of active viewports, the Off option enables you to turn off viewports selectively.

The On option makes a viewport active again by displaying its contents. A newly turned-on viewport remains blank if AutoCAD has reached its limit of active viewports. In this case, you need to turn off another viewport.

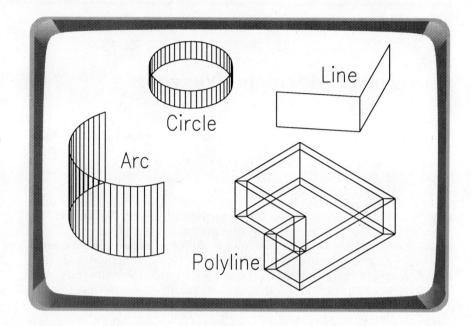

Fig. 19.10.
The Mview
command's
Hideplot
option
removes
hidden lines
at plotting
time of
specific
viewports.

If you turn off all viewports, you will not be able to return to model space with the Mspace command. AutoCAD needs at least one active viewport to return to model space via Mspace. The solution is to turn system variable TILEMODES back on.

Managing Layers in Paper Space (Vplayer)

The Vplayer (short for View Port LAYER) command enables you to control the visibility of layers within paper-space viewports. The Layer command controls layers *globally*. If you freeze a layer with the Layer command, the layer is turned off in all viewports, whether in model or paper space. With Vplayer, you can freeze a layer in one viewport but leave it thawed in other viewports. The Vplayer command has the following six options:

```
Command: Vplayer
?/Freeze/Thaw/Reset/Newfrz/Vpvisdflt:
```

Toggling Frozen Layers (Freeze and Thaw)

The Freeze and Thaw options enable you to freeze (and thaw) layers in individual viewports. Use the Freeze option to freeze the TILES layer in the upper left viewport:

```
?/Freeze/Thaw/.../Vpvisdflt: F
Layer(s) to Freeze: TILES
All/Select/<Current>: S
Select objects: Pick viewport
```

You can freeze the TILES layer in all viewports (with the All suboption) or select specific viewports with the Select suboption (see fig. 19.11). Using the All suboption is similar to using the Layer Freeze command in model space.

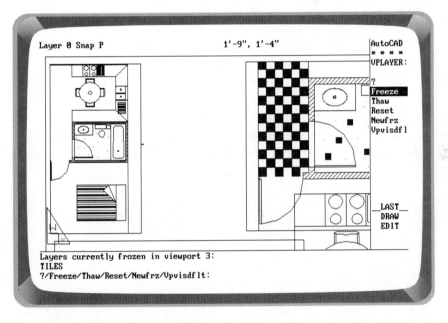

Fig. 19.11.
The Vplayer Freeze command enables you to freeze the TILES layer in one viewport and leave it visible in others.

If a layer is frozen by the Layer command, you cannot thaw it with the Vplayer command.

Create New Layers (Newfrz)

The Newfrz (short for NEW FRoZen) option enables you to create new layers. Since the idea of the Vplayer command is independent layer visibility, the new layer normally is created frozen in all viewports. The Newfrz command is useful for specifying which layers are to be frozen and which are thawed when a new viewport is created.

```
?/.../Reset/Newfrz/Vpvisdflt: N
New viewport frozen layer name(s):
```

You can then use the Thaw option to make the new layer visible in specific viewports.

Default Layer Visibility (Vpvisdflt and Reset)

The Vpvisdflt (short for View Port VISibility DeFauLT) option enables you to create a set of default visibility settings for layers. This is especially useful if you create a new viewport but don't want it to be affected by the Vplayer Freeze and Thaw commands used on the other viewports.

With the Vpvisdflt option you can specify which layers are frozen and which are thawed in a new viewport. For example, you may want the TILES layer (which is visible in three of four viewports) to be invisible in any new viewport you create. The Vpvisdflt option is used as follows:

```
?/.../Reset/Newfrz/Vpvisdflt: V
Layer name(s) to change default visibility: TILES
Change default viewport visibility to Frozen/<Thawed>: F
```

You have set the default visibility of the TILES layer to frozen. When AutoCAD asks you for the names of layers, you can supply several names, each separated by a comma, or you can use wild cards to specify groups of layer names.

If you changed the visibility of several layers in a viewport, you can change them back to the default setting with the Reset option:

```
?/.../Reset/Newfrz/Vpvisdflt: R
Layer(s) to Reset: *
All/Select/<Current>: S
Select objects: Pick viewports
```

Resetting layer settings takes place in two stages. First you specify which layers to reset (use the asterisk to reset all layers). Then you pick which viewports to reset the layers in (all or some).

Listing Frozen Layers (?)

The ? option lists the names of layers frozen by the Vplayer command. It does not list layers frozen by the Layer command, because Vplayer Thaw cannot thaw them. The list of frozen layers is specific to a single viewport, as follows:

```
?/.../Vpvisdflt: ?
Select a viewport: Pick viewport
Layers currently frozen in viewport 1: TILES
?/.../Vpvisdflt: Press Enter
```

You can use the Vplayer command in model space. AutoCAD temporarily switches to paper space to let you select the viewport.

Summary

In this chapter, you learned how to create hidden-line plots and multiple-view plots. AutoCAD's paper space makes it easy for you to plot multiple views on a single sheet of paper.

This brings to an end the tutorial on AutoCAD's drawing, editing, viewing, plotting, and customization commands. The next chapter introduces you to some of the other Autodesk programs that help you add solids modeling, rendering, and animation to your AutoCAD drawings.

20

Illustration courtesy of Autodesk, Inc., Sausalito, CA.

Rendering and Animating

So far in this book, you have learned how to draw with AutoCAD's 2-D and 3-D drawing and editing commands. For the most part, you have created *wireframe* drawings. You can see through a wireframe drawing of an object; the entities have edges but no sides and no inside. Although AutoCAD is a powerful program, it is limited in its capability to make wireframe objects appear more realistic.

When AutoCAD removes hidden lines, it determines which parts of entities lie behind others and removes the hidden parts from view. The process makes objects appear to be solid, even though they are not. By removing hidden lines from view, you make your drawing appear more realistic, but AutoCAD does not permit you to edit a hidden-line drawing. Further, AutoCAD can make mistakes when hiding lines in complex drawings, particularly at the intersection of two meshes. Even though AutoCAD does feature a simple shading capability, objects shaded in AutoCAD are somewhat less than realistic in appearance.

AutoCAD cannot *animate* objects; that is, AutoCAD cannot move an object or move the viewpoint in real time.

For these reasons, Autodesk has developed supplemental programs that model, render, and animate AutoCAD drawings. This chapter discusses these programs in the following three categories:

Solids modeling:

❏ Amelite
❏ Advanced Modeling Extension

571

Shading and rendering:

❏ AutoSolid

❏ RenderMan

Animation:

❏ AutoFlix

❏ Autodesk Animator

❏ Autodesk 3D Studio

This chapter introduces you to these programs, briefly describes how they work with AutoCAD, and lists the hardware you need to run them.

Solids Modeling

A program that can perform *solids modeling* enables you to create objects that have a solid inside. To the computer, the solid is a known volume with specific properties. A solid model is useful to anyone who needs to analyze an object's physical properties. Unlike a drawing that is created as a wireframe or with shaded surfaces, a solid model accurately displays complex intersections and can take on *material properties*. By adding material properties to a model, you can analyze the characteristics of the represented object, such as its mass, weight, and center of gravity.

You create a solid model in AutoCAD by joining basic objects, or *primitives*. These primitives are the 3-D objects you encountered in Chapter 16: the box, cylinder, sphere, torus, wedge, and cone (see fig. 20.1).

When you use two primitives to create a more complex object, you can add, subtract, or intersect the primitives. These operations are called *Boolean operations*. Adding a sphere on top of an upside-down cone makes a shape like an ice cream cone. Subtracting a cylinder from a box makes a round hole in the box. Intersecting a cone with a wedge slices off part of the cone (see fig. 20.2).

An alternative construction method is to draw the object's profile in AutoCAD and then use the Solrev (short for SOLid REVolution) command to revolve the profile, creating a solid object (much like the Revsurf command, which was discussed in Chapter 17). Other commands help create the object: Solfill (short for SOLid FILLet) and Solcham (SOLid CHAMfer) add rounded and angled edges.

AutoCAD Release 11 can use one of two solids-modeling options:

❏ Amelite, which is included with Release 11

❏ Advanced Modeling Extension (AME), which is an extra-cost option

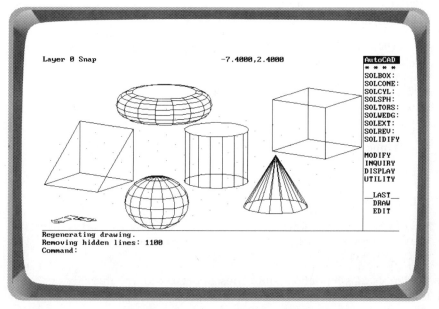

Fig. 20.1.
The solid-model primitives in AutoCAD.

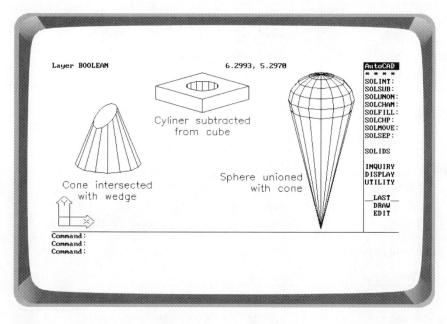

Fig. 20.2.
Complex solid objects are created by adding and subtracting primitives.

Both Amelite and AME are *EXP* programs that run in expanded memory. For this reason, they are not available for AutoCAD Release 10.

Using AutoCAD's Sol Commands (Amelite)

AutoCAD Release 11 includes a simple solids-modeling function called Amelite, which enables you to create and manipulate solid objects. You cannot use Amelite to perform advanced solids-modeling operations, such as analysis and Boolean operations. (If you want to perform these operations, you must purchase the optional Advanced Modeling Extension).

To run Amelite, you first need to load it into memory, as follows:

```
Command: (Xload "AMELITE")
"Amelite"
Command:
```

Xload is an AutoLISP function that loads EXP files into extended memory. You can unload Amelite from memory by entering the **(Xunload "AMELITE")** command.

Amelite's solids-modeling commands all begin with the three letters, *Sol*. The commands can be broken into four categories, as follows:

Object-drawing commands:

Command	Function
Solbox	Draws a solid box in 3-D
Solcone	Draws a solid cone
Solcyl	Draws a solid cylinder
Solsphere	Draws a solid sphere
Soltorus	Draws a solid torus or donut
Solwedge	Draws a solid wedge

Object-creation commands:

Command	Function
Solext	Creates an extruded solid
Solrev	Creates a revolved solid
Solidify	Converts AutoCAD objects into solids

Inquiry commands:

Command	Function
Sollist	Lists information about the object
Solarea	Calculates the object's surface area
Solvar	Sets control variables

Utility commands:

Command	Function
Solmat	Assigns a material to an object
Solwire	Displays the object as a wireframe
Solmesh	Displays the object with Pface meshes
Solpurge	Removes unused objects

When you begin drawing with solid primitives in Amelite, they look just like the 3-D wireframe objects you draw with AutoCAD's drawing and editing commands. Objects drawn in Amelite are different from objects drawn in AutoCAD, however, because you must add a polymesh before you can hide or shade an Amelite object.

Advanced Modeling Extension (AME)

If you purchase the optional Advanced Modeling Extension ($495) with AutoCAD Release 11, you can do everything that Amelite does, plus perform Boolean operations, analysis, and feature extraction.

The attraction of solids modeling is that it enables you to analyze the objects you design. Once you've created the model, you assign a material specification to it. The ACAD.MAT file contains the specifications for the following materials:

❏ Aluminum

❏ Brass

❏ Bronze

❏ Copper

❏ Glass

❏ High-strength low-alloy steel

❏ Lead

❏ Mild steel

❏ Monel 400

❏ Austenic stainless steel

You can add other materials if you provide AME with the following data about the materials:

❏ Density in kg/m^3

❏ Young's modulus of linear elasticity in GN/m^2

❏ Poisson's ratio

❏ Yield strength in MN/m²

❏ Tensile strength limit in MN/m²

❏ Thermal conductivity in watts per meter degree Kelvin

❏ Coefficient of linear expansion/10⁶ per degree Kelvin.

❏ Specific heat in KJ/kg-degree Kelvin.

Once you apply a property to the material, AME can tell you the following mass properties of the object:

❏ Mass in grams or kilograms

❏ Centroid coordinates in X,Y,Z space

❏ Moments of inertia about the X, Y, and Z axes

❏ Products of inertia

❏ Radii of gyration

❏ Principal moments about the centroid

Once you've designed and analyzed your new product, AME can help you plot drawings of it. AME can take sections of a solid object at the current UCS X,Y-plane, or create a profile of a solid object's outline (with or without hidden lines removed) at the current UCS. The result in both cases is a 2-D object that can be plotted on paper.

Both AME and Amelite have the same hardware requirements as AutoCAD Release 11. If you plan to do solids modeling of complex parts, you may want to install at least 6M to 8M of RAM in your computer.

Application Programming Interface (API)

As much as AME lets you do with solids modeling, there is far more to the subject. Autodesk includes with AME two tools that let you write programs that work with AME. The tools are the basic solids-modeling commands and a programmer's tool kit called the Application Programming Interface (API).

Third-party developers write solids-modeling software that can communicate with the AME through the API. Autodesk includes the API tools with AME; however, you need to have an understanding of the C programming language if you want to use API.

Autodesk anticipates that third-party programmers will come up with *parametric* modeling software that lets you design new objects based on a variable set of parameters (such as changed dimensions or material properties). Developers are working on programs that analyze the solid models for stress, thermodynamics, and vibration.

Shading and Rendering

Solids modeling is only one way to enhance your three-dimensional AutoCAD drawings. Another is to add shading and rendering (that is, adding surfaces and realistic colors) to your drawings by using Autodesk's AutoShade and RenderMan programs.

AutoShade

AutoShade ($500) is a *post-processor* program: it must read files created by AutoCAD before it can render them. You create rendered images with AutoShade in two steps. The first step is to load an AutoLISP file (called ASHADE2.LSP) in AutoCAD, as follows:

```
Command: (Load "ASHADE2")
ASHADE
```

The AutoLISP file lets you position camera and light symbols around the 3-D object. The camera is positioned at the location of your viewpoint of the 3-D model, while the light symbols are the location of the lights that illuminate the model. Once you are satisfied with the arrangement, you can create one or more scenes, each with one camera and any number of lights. Finally, you use an AutoLISP command to create a disk file that AutoShade can read. The file (called a *filmroll file*) contains a representation of the model along with the locations of the cameras and lights. You must exit from AutoCAD to run AutoShade.

The second step is to load AutoShade. After you've loaded the filmroll file into AutoShade, you can create four kinds of renderings:

❏ Fast Shade lets you see, very quickly, what the rendered image looks like. When you use Fast Shade, however, errors may appear in complex renderings (see fig. 20.3).

❏ Full Shade takes longer but creates an accurate rendering (see fig. 20.4).

❏ Smooth Shade smooths the facets caused by AutoCAD's straight-line modeling, creating a more realistic rendering.

A fourth style of rendering is done through an Autodesk program called RenderMan, which is discussed later in this chapter.

If you don't like the view or the lighting, you can move the camera and the target point, or change the field of view or the type of lighting. You can assign properties to objects—based on their AutoCAD color—to make them look more metallic or more plastic.

Fig. 20.3.
Fast-shaded images may contain some errors.

Fig. 20.4.
Fully shaded images take time to render but are accurately interpreted.

You can ask AutoShade to create disk files that can be read by other rendering programs and AutoCAD. Targa-compatible paint programs, for example, can read AutoShade's TGA-format files. AutoCAD can read DXB files, and PostScript laser printers can read PS and EPS. AutoShade can redisplay RND files without recalculating the image (this works in a fashion similar to AutoCAD's slide files).

Autodesk RenderMan

Autodesk RenderMan is a program included with the 386-compatible version of AutoShade Version 2.0 ($1,000). Created by Pixar, RenderMan creates photorealistic images of objects. It does this by calculating what an object looks like as light falls on the object and is reflected off it, and as it casts shadows. RenderMan technology was used to create *Tin Toy*, the first computer-generated animation to win an Academy Award.

The Autodesk version of RenderMan is an EXP file that runs in extended memory with AutoShade. The RenderMan program begins a series of calculations that can take a few minutes or all night to complete. Like AutoShade, RenderMan can do either a fast rendering or a good rendering.

RenderMan uses *shader* (SLO) files to determine an object's appearance. While in AutoCAD, you assign surface properties and finishes. RenderMan reads this information and assigns a look to every object. RenderMan features 70 built-in SLO files that define the look of glass, cloth carpet, eroded granite, dented metal, and fog objects.

 AutoShade Version 2.0 has the same hardware requirements as AutoCAD Release 11. If your system does not have a large hard disk, you should consider adding one because a single high-resolution graphics file can take up a great deal of disk space. A Targa or similar graphics board that can display up to 16.7 million colors (referred to as *true color*) makes the image look like a photograph. RenderMan supports the Weitek coprocessor chip, which lets the software do its calculations twice as fast as many other types of coprocessors. If you want to generate hard copies of your AutoShade or RenderMan files, you might consider purchasing a 4000-line slide recorder or a silver-halide color printer.

Animation

With AutoCAD, AME, and AutoShade, you work with three-dimensional objects. When you *animate* your three-dimensional drawings, you add the fourth dimension: movement over time.

By animating your drawings, you can see how mechanical parts move in relation to each other, or you can create a walk-through of your architectural project that lets your clients see what their new building looks like. Autodesk offers three animation programs that match complexity with price.

AutoFlix

AutoFlix is a simple, low-cost animation tool. It is included free with AutoShade or can be borrowed from another user.

AutoFlix includes AutoLISP programs that set up the camera and object paths. The camera (or object) moves along these paths to create the animation effect. AutoFlix can create *walk-through* animations, in which the camera (your viewpoint) moves through and past 3-D objects in an AutoCAD drawing. Or, you can create a *kinematic* animation, in which objects move independently. AutoLISP automatically generates a series of scenes, one for each camera position, in an FLM file.

The FLM file is run through AutoShade, which creates a shaded image of each scene. The scenes are converted into AutoFlix's file format (FLX). Finally, you load AutoFlix and play the FLX file to show the animation. The result is not high quality, but is good enough to let you experiment with animation (see fig. 20.5). AutoFlix uses *dithering* to simulate more colors at the expense of lowered resolution. The fastest speed is about 10 frames per second, about one-third the speed needed for smooth animation.

Fig. 20.5.
AutoFlix
produces
crude
animations
useful for low-
cost experi-
mentation.

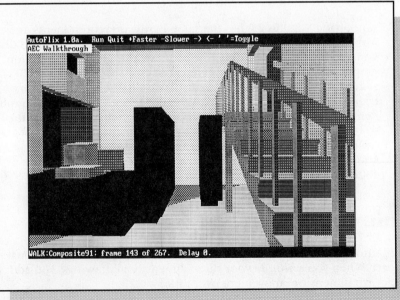

AutoFlix displays only on EGA-compatible graphics boards and all VGA boards. Its sound capabilities make use of the computer's built-in speaker only.

AutoFlix can read AutoCAD slide files and ASCII text files, which you can splice into the animation. AutoFlix can also read AutoShade RND files. AutoFlix's own file format, however, cannot be read by other programs. A variety of optical and sound effects let one movie scene fade or dissolve into another. Once you've decided you like animation, or have a need for it, you can make the move to Autodesk Animator.

Autodesk Animator

Autodesk Animator ($300) is a paint program that also creates animations. The effect is better than AutoFlix because Animator displays 256 colors and can run animations at speeds as high as 70 frames per second. Animator was written for Autodesk by the Yost Group.

There are two ways to create an animation with Animator. One is to use the AutoLISP routines provided by AutoFlix. You create the 3-D drawing in AutoCAD, add the camera path, and run the resulting FLM file through AutoShade. The movie is then converted to FLI format and displayed by Animator.

The other method is to use Animator's tools to move and transform objects over time. You specify the number of frames over which the motion should occur, and Animator automatically does the work.

Either way, you can use Animator for dozens of different projects. You might use Animator to do the following:

- ❑ Animate presentations of otherwise dry business data
- ❑ Produce children's educational movies
- ❑ Publish an electronic magazine, complete with full-color pictures and ads
- ❑ Walk your clients through a project
- ❑ Show how a complex object's parts move together

The software package includes a public-domain playback program.

Animator requires a VGA graphics board. Because animation files can be large, you might consider adding a very large hard drive to your system, if you do not already have one. Several third-party products can capture the animation to videotape and synchronize digital sound with the movie.

Animator can read files from several programs, including AutoShade RND, CompuServe GIF, and PCX files created by paint programs.

Animator is a complex program that provides hundreds of tools for creating images and animations. It does have two drawbacks, however: low resolution and lack of true 3-D display. Both of these limitations are overcome in Autodesk 3D Studio, which is discussed later in this chapter.

Autodesk Animator Clips

It can take time to develop a good-looking graphic or animation. For this reason, Autodesk has developed a series of *clip-art* images called Autodesk Animator Clips ($50). Clip-art is a predrawn image: you clip out the art and stick it into your project.

Autodesk currently offers four Animator Clips packages:

❏ Animals and fantasy

❏ Business communication

❏ Man-made ImageCels

❏ Natural ImageCels

Each package contains dozens of still and animated drawings. The Business communication package includes animations of a fax machine, a filing cabinet, and a chalkboard. Still images include a legal pad, an office scene, and a cityscape.

Autodesk 3D Studio

The 3D Studio program ($3,000) is Autodesk's most ambitious program. It combines the accurate 2-D and 3-D drafting of AutoCAD, the high-quality rendering of RenderMan, the flexible animation capabilities of Animator. Autodesk 3D Studio is written by the Yost Group for Autodesk.

The software consists of a core program that loads the other modules as EXP files. The program includes the following modules:

❏ A 2-D shaper, which draws two-dimensional objects much like the objects you produce in AutoCAD (see fig. 20.6)

❏ A 3-D lofter that creates models by running the 2-D objects along a path

❏ A 3-D editor that arranges the objects, lights, and cameras so that you can draw 3-D objects and assign material properties (see fig. 20.7)

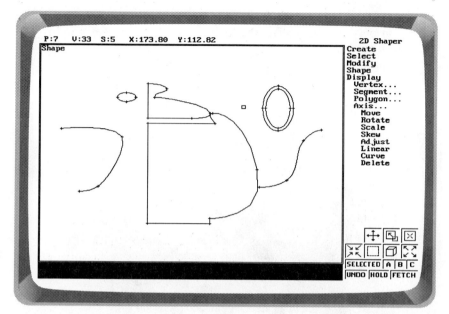

Fig. 20.6.
Autodesk 3D Studio's 2-D drafting module draws shapes with Bezier curves.

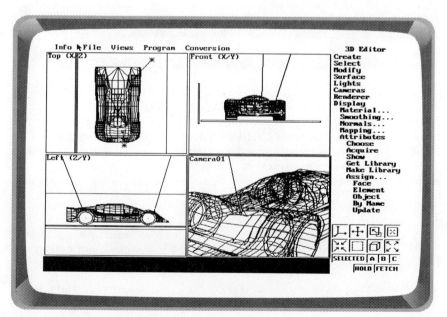

Fig. 20.7.
The 3-D Editor arranges lights, cameras, and properties.

❑ A materials editor that creates and edits material properties, which affect the look of objects when they are rendered

❑ A keyframer, which creates animations (see fig. 20.8)

❑ A renderer, which displays the scene in flat, Gouraud, or Phong smooth shading

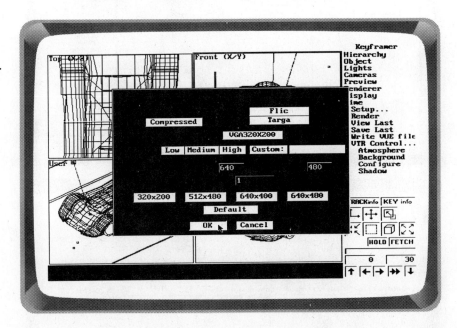

Fig. 20.8.
The keyframer creates animation sequences.

Autodesk 3D Studio can create exceptionally realistic animations. Objects are made of Bezier curves, which you saw in Chapter 5. Bezier curves are smooth curves that can be adjusted with control points. By using Bezier curves, you can easily modify an existing curve without redrawing it. For editing, 3D Studio features most of AutoCAD's commands, including multiple viewports.

The 3D Studio program's hardware requirements are similar to those of the RenderMan program. For best results, consider buying a large hard drive, a WORM drive to store long animations, a 24-bit graphics board for photorealistic images, a Weitek chip for faster calculations, and a stop-frame VCR for recording to videotape.

Autodesk 3D Studio reads AutoCAD DXF files, and outputs FLI and GIF files for Animator, TGA files for Targa paint programs, and PS for PostScript printers.

Summary

This chapter introduced you to a number of graphics programs that work with AutoCAD. If your field of work requires solids modeling, detailed renderings, or animation, you should consider buying one of the Autodesk products covered in this chapter.

These programs add capabilities that may one day be included with AutoCAD. For example, the shading and solids-modeling capabilities built into AutoCAD Release 11 were previously available only as separate programs (AutoShade and AutoSolid).

The remainder of this book is a reference section. In the following pages you can find an alphabetized summary of all AutoCAD Release 11 commands and system variables, a list of AutoCAD users' groups, a troubleshooting guide, a glossary of CAD terms, and several useful appendixes.

Part Six

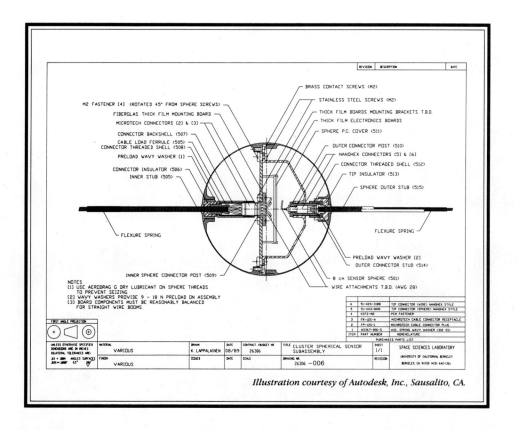

Reference

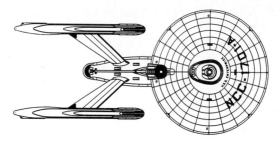

Illustration courtesy of
Autodesk, Inc., Sausalito, CA.

AutoCAD Command Reference

This command reference is an alphabetical listing of commands found in AutoCAD Releases 10 and 11. This guide is useful for reminding new and experienced AutoCAD users of AutoCAD's command syntax.

All command descriptions include reference to the following:

- ❏ Command syntax
- ❏ Shortcut and toggle keys
- ❏ Side-screen and pull-down menu locations
- ❏ Tablet overlay location and icon
- ❏ Tips, errors, and warnings
- ❏ Related system variables

These aids help you locate the commands quickly.

Some commands in Release 11 have command aliases defined in the ACAD.PGP file. These aliases enable you to execute a command by typing in the first character or two. The following commands have aliases in the ACAD.PGP file:

Alias	Command
A	Arc
C	Circle
CP	Copy
DV	Dview
E	Erase
L	Line
LA	Layer
M	Move
MS	Mspace

Alias	Command
P	Pan
PS	Pspace
PL	Pline
R	Redraw
Z	Zoom

All dimensioning subcommands are grouped together following the Dim1 command. For example, the Leader command is listed after Dim Horizontal rather than after the Layer command.

Several commands are transparent. They can be used during another command when you precede the command name with an apostrophe. The following are transparent commands:

'Ddemodes
'Ddlmodes
'Ddrmodes
'Grapgscr
'Help or ' ?
'Pan
'Redraw
'Redrawall
'Resume
'Setvar
'Textscr
'View
'Zoom (except Zoom All and Extents)

Aperture

Controls the size of the aperture box in object snap modes

Syntax
```
Command: Aperture
Object snap target height (1-50 pixels) <default>:
```

Screen Menu
SETTINGS–APERTUR:

Pull–Down Menu
None

Template Coordinates

Y 22

Description

The Aperture command enables you to change the size of the box cursor used by the Osnap command to select entities. A small aperture locates points quickly but requires precision when you line up the box cursor to select an entity; a large aperture is slower and less precise in dense drawings but makes lining up the box cursor easier.

Because the aperture is always a square box, you need to specify only the height; the width equals the height. The aperture height is specified in pixels, each pixel being a resolution dot on your video monitor. The default aperture height is 10 pixels (for out-of-the-box AutoCAD) or the last setting you used for the aperture.

The aperture value is saved in the APERTURE system variable in the ACAD.CFG configuration file. When the aperture size is set, it does not change for different drawings.

Hints

You may want to experiment with the size of the aperture. If the aperture is too small, it will be difficult for you to determine whether entities pass through it. If it is too large, too many entities will pass through, and you may select the wrong one. In any case, the aperture should be larger than the pickbox.

You can set an aperture larger than 50 pixels with the system variable APERTURE.

Error Messages

`Value must be between 1 and 50.` You specified a number outside the valid aperture size range. Choose a number between 1 and 50.

`Requires an integer value.` You did not use a whole number (for instance, you entered a number such as 2.2), or you gave a nonnumeric response. Try again with a whole number between 1 and 50.

Related System Variables

APERTURE
PICKBOX

Arc

Draws an arc segment

Syntax

```
Command: Arc
Center/<Start point>:
Center/End/<Second point>:
End point:
```

Alias

A

Screen Menu

DRAW–ARC

Pull–Down Menu

Draw–Arc

Template Coordinates

L 10

Description

This command enables you to draw an arc segment. At each prompt you can enter a point to define an arc, or you can begin by selecting the center point. If you choose to specify the center point first, you will see the following prompts in turn:

```
Center:
Start point:
Angle/Length of chord/<End point>:
```

If you start the arc by first indicating a start point and then specifying the center point, you will see a similar series of prompts (without the `Start point:` prompt).

If you choose to enter the end point for the arc, you will see the following prompts:

```
End point:
Angle/Direction/Radius/<Center point>:
```

Possible Responses

Response	Meaning
A	Indicate the included angle for the arc. Available only if you specified the center for the arc.
C	Specify the center point for the arc.
D	Specify the arc by the tangent direction from the start point. Available only if you specified the end point for the arc.
E	Specify the end point for the arc.
L	Specify the arc by entering the length of the chord for the arc. Available only if you specified the center for the arc.
R	Enter a radius for the arc.
Return	Set start point (as reply to `Start point:` prompt) and direction as end of last line or arc.

Hints

You may find it easier to draw an arc by first drawing a circle and then using the Break command to erase the part of the circle you don't need.

AutoCAD does not recognize a straight line as an arc of infinite radius. If you attempt to enter points that lie in a straight line, AutoCAD responds with an error message.

You cannot draw a circle by drawing an arc of 360 degrees.

Error Messages

`2D point or option keyword required.` You gave a nonnumeric response to a prompt that requires a point be picked on-screen or entered numerically.

`Point or option keyword required.` You gave a nonnumeric response to a prompt that requires a point be picked on-screen or entered numerically.

`*Invalid*` You entered points that lie in a line. Try again, but provide a different set of points for the arc.

Related System Variables

LASTANGLE

Area

Calculates the area of a figure

Syntax

```
Command: Area
<First Point>/Entity/Add/Subtract:
Next point:
```

Screen Menu

INQUIRY–AREA

Pull–Down Menu

None

Template Coordinates

U 2

Description

This command computes the area and perimeter, circumference, or length of an entity or a series of points you specify. The value of the area is stored in the system variable AREA; the perimeter is stored in the system variable PERIMETER. The Add and Subtract options enable you to add or subtract areas from a running total of measured areas.

You can enter points clockwise or counterclockwise. AutoCAD automatically closes the area; you do not have to reenter the first point.

Use the Entity option to compute the area of a circle or polyline.

If you select a point or an entity, the area and perimeter values are reset to zero before computation. If you select Add or Subtract, AutoCAD modifies the previous values by the new area and perimeter values.

The Add option sets add mode and switches between adding areas and subtracting areas. If you want to add and subtract areas, enter add mode first. The prompt changes to the following:

```
<First Point>/Entity/Subtract:
```

The Subtract option sets subtract mode, as follows:

```
<First Point>/Entity/Add:
```

This command returns one of the following responses, depending on what you select for the computation. In each response, x.xxxx represents the computed values:

```
Area=x.xxxx, Perimeter=x.xxxx
Area=x.xxxx, Circumference=x.xxxx
Area=x.xxxx, Length=x.xxxx
```

Possible Responses

Response	Meaning
A	Add mode
S	Subtract mode
E	Compute area of circle or polyline

Hints

If you choose to compute the area of an open polyline, AutoCAD returns an area as if the polyline were closed with a length equal to the actual polyline length.

Enter points in an organized fashion (clockwise or counterclockwise) or the results may be meaningless.

Error Messages

`Entity selected is not a circle or 2D/3D polyline.` You chose to compute the area of an entity but did not select a circle or a polyline. Try again, but select a proper entity.

`Point or option keyword required.` You have entered a point coordinate that is invalid or a keyword that AutoCAD cannot understand. Try again.

Related System Variables

AREA
PERIMETER

Array

Makes multiple copies of entities, placing them within a user-defined circular or rectangular pattern

Syntax (for rectangular array)

```
Command: Array
Select objects:
Rectangular or Polar array (R/P): R
Number of rows (--) <default>:
Number of columns (|||) <default>:
Unit cell or distance between rows (--):
Distance between columns (|||):
```

Syntax (for polar array)

```
Command: Array
Select objects:
Rectangular or Polar (R/P): P
Center point of array:
Number of items:
Angle to fill (+=CCW, -=CW) <default>:
Angle between items:
Rotate objects as they are copied? <default>:
```

Screen Menu

EDIT–ARRAY:

Pull–Down Menu

Modify–2D Array

Template Coordinates

W 21

Description

Rectangular arrays are based on horizontal rows and vertical columns. The unit cell refers to the vertical and horizontal distances between entities. If you indicate opposite corners of the array at the Unit cell: prompt, AutoCAD skips the prompt for column distances.

You can specify up to 32,767 rows or columns.

Polar arrays are based on a center point.

The Center point of array: determines the point around which all entities are copied.

The Number of items: option identifies the number of copies you want.

The Angle to fill: option is the number of degrees you want these copies to fill. This can be a number or a second point defining the angle. The angle is counterclockwise, unless it is entered as a negative angle.

The Angle between items: prompt identifies the angle that separates the entities in the array.

The last prompt asks whether the objects are to be rotated. AutoCAD will rotate the objects in accordance with the polar array.

You must provide information for at least two of these three prompts: Number of items:, Angle to fill:, and Angle between items:. If you do not want to give information at a prompt, press Enter; the next prompt will appear.

Possible Responses

Response	Meaning
P	Polar (circular) array
R	Rectangular array
C	Circular (undocumented)

Hints

Using Array to create even a single row or column of entities is quicker than using Copy Multiple.

To create a rotated array, use the Rotate option of the Snap command, and rotate your snap grid. Alternatively, you can use the undocumented Circular option. Its prompt sequence is different from the polar option and may be easier to use.

If you mistakenly create an array that is too large, use U to undo the entire array.

Error Messages

If you set up a large array, AutoCAD asks whether you really want to make so many copies of the selection set. You can use Ctrl-C to stop.

`Array expansion terminated.` You canceled the Array command by pressing Ctrl-C while AutoCAD was filling out the array. The portion of the array already expanded remains in your drawing.

`Invalid option keyword.` You have not selected either R or P as prompted.

`Requires an integer value.` When prompted for the number of rows or columns, you entered a value that is not a whole number, is out of bounds, or is nonnumeric. Enter a whole number less than 32,767.

`Value must be positive and nonzero.` When prompted for the number of rows or columns, you entered a negative or zero value. Enter a whole number between 1 and 32,767.

`Requires number or two 2D corner points.` When specifying the unit cell or distance between two rows, you entered a nonnumeric response. Try again, providing a numeric distance or selecting two on-screen points that define the size of the unit cell.

`Requires numeric distance or two points.` When specifying the distance between columns, you entered a nonnumeric response. Try again, providing either numeric distance or picking two on-screen points that define the distance between two columns.

`Yes or No, please.` You responded incorrectly when asked whether the objects should be rotated as they are copied.

Related System Variables

None

Attdef

(Short for ATTribute DEFine) Creates an attribute definition that controls aspects of textual information you assign to a block

Syntax

```
Command: Attdef
Attribute modes--Invisible:N Constant:N Verify:N Preset:N
Enter (ICVP) to change, RETURN when done:
Attribute tag:
Attribute prompt:
Default Attribute value:
Justify/Style/<Start point>:
Height <default>:
Rotation angle:
```

If you are working with Constant attributes, the following prompt will appear (instead of `Default attribute value:`):

```
Attribute value:
```

Screen Menu

BLOCKS–ATTDEF

Pull–Down Menu

None

Template Coordinates

Q 1

Description

Attributes are text entities used with blocks.

Attribute modes are settings that control the attribute. Four modes are available: Invisible, Constant, Verify, and Preset. These modes are set for each attribute you assign to a block and may be different for each attribute in the block.

Invisible mode controls the visibility of the attributes when the block is inserted in the drawing.

Constant mode gives attributes a fixed (unchangeable) value.

Verify mode prompts you for the value you entered for the attribute so that you can verify the value.

Preset mode enables you to have variable attributes without being prompted for the value upon insertion of the block.

Attribute tag: is the label for the attribute you are defining. All attributes associated with a single block must have different tags. However, different blocks may have the same tags for their attributes.

Attribute prompt: depends on the setting for Constant mode. If the attribute is constant, a prompt is not needed; the attributes do not change when the block is inserted. If the attributes are variable, the prompt is used when the blocks are inserted. You create this prompt, which appears at the command area to indicate what information the attribute needs. Spaces are accepted as spaces. Be sure to state clearly the information in the prompt so that other operators will understand and be able to use your library parts.

Attribute value: is the actual piece of information in the attribute. If your attributes are set constant, this information remains the same whenever you insert this particular block.

The remaining prompts are the same as the Text command prompts.

Possible Responses

Response	Meaning
I	Control visibility
C	Control accessibility
V	Control verification
P	Control preset mode
A	Align attribute text between two points
C	Center attribute text horizontally
F	Fit attribute text between two points
M	Center attribute text horizontally and vertically
R	Right-justify attribute text
S	Select attribute text style

Hints

Attribute commands are not grouped on a single screen menu. They usually appear as one of the first few items on a menu.

Attribute tags cannot contain blanks.

Error Messages

`Tag cannot be null.` When prompted for an attribute tag, you pressed Enter with no input. You must enter an attribute tag.

`Point or option keyword required.` When prompted to specify the start point for the attribute, you entered a letter that did not correspond to the option keywords displayed. Try again.

`Value must be positive and nonzero.` When prompted to enter the text height, you specified a height that is out of range. Enter a height greater than zero.

`Requires numeric distance or second point.` When prompted to enter the text height, you entered a nonnumeric value. Enter a numeric distance representing the height, or select two on-screen points defining the text height.

`Requires numeric angle or second point.` When asked to enter a rotation angle, you entered a nonnumeric character. Try again.

Related System Variables

AFLAGS
ATTREQ
ATTDIA

Attdisp

(Short for ATTribute DISPlay) Overrides the default display visibility setting for all attributes

Syntax

`Command: **Attdisp**`
`Normal/ON/OFF <default>:`

Screen Menu

DISPLAY–ATTDISP:

Pull–Down Menu

None

Template Coordinates

None

Description

Attdisp controls an attribute's display visibility. `<default>` is the Attdisp current setting: Normal, On, or Off.

Normal defaults to the display settings at which the attributes were created.

On overrides the display settings and turns on all attributes, making them visible.

Off overrides the display settings and turns off all attributes, making them invisible.

Possible Responses

Response	Meaning
ON	Make all attributes visible
OFF	Make all attributes invisible
N	Normal visibility (user-defined)

Hints

When editing attributes, you may want to display them even though some are set to be invisible.

When indicating On or Off, type as much of the word as possible; the letter O is insufficient and will cause an error message. However, you can abbreviate Off as Of.

Error Messages

`Ambiguous response, please clarify...` When prompted to enter a new setting, you entered the letter O. This response can mean either On or Off; you need to spell out as much of the word as necessary to remove any ambiguity.

`Invalid option keyword.` When asked to clarify your option setting, you entered a letter that does not correspond to a valid option keyword. Try again.

Related System Variables

ATTMODE

Attedit

(Short for ATTribute EDIT) Enables you to edit attributes one at a time or all attributes at once. Attribute text must first have been inserted into a drawing.

Syntax (for editing one attribute at a time)

```
Command: Attedit
Edit attributes one at a time?: Y
Block name specification <default>:
Attribute tag specification <default>:
Attribute value specification <default>:
Select Attributes:
```

Syntax (for editing all attributes at once)

```
Command: Attedit
Edit attributes one at a time? N
Edit only attributes visible on screen? <default>:
Block name specification <default>:
Attribute tag specification <default>:
Attribute value specification <default>:
Select Attributes:
```

Screen Menu

EDIT–ATTEDIT:

Pull–Down Menu

None

Template Coordinates

R 1

Description

At the Edit attributes one at a time? prompt, tell AutoCAD whether you will edit one by one or globally. If you answer Yes (for one-by-one editing), you are restricted to visible attributes. If you answer No (for global editing), you have more options.

If you answer No at the Edit attributes one at a time? prompt, you will edit globally. You can edit all attributes, visible or invisible. Specify the attributes you want to edit by indicating tag, value, or block name. When you edit globally, you can change only the value of the attribute. To change more than the value, you must edit attributes one by one.

Prompts at each attribute allow you to change the location, angle, height, and other properties as well as the value. You can further limit the attributes edited by selecting certain block names, tags, or values for the attributes.

To edit attributes one by one, you need to specify block names, attribute tags, and attribute values. Use a comma to separate two or more names. You may use wild-card characters in the names—the asterisk (*) for many characters and the question mark (?) for a single character. Only the attributes you specify will be edited.

After you select the attributes to be edited, AutoCAD enables you to edit them in reverse order; the last attribute selected is the first attribute you edit. This attribute is marked with an X, and the following prompt appears:

```
Value/Position/Height/Angle/Style/Layer/Color/Next <default>
```

Value enables you to change the value that was set when you originally inserted the block, provided that the value is not constant. AutoCAD displays the following prompt:

```
Change or Replace?
```

If you select Change, the following prompt appears:

```
String to change:
New string:
```

Type the string you want to change, press Enter, and then type only the letters that need to be changed.

If you select Replace, AutoCAD produces the following prompt:

```
New attribute value:
```

Type the new value, and press Enter.

Position enables you to specify a new location for the attribute.

Height enables you to change the height of the attribute text.

Angle enables you to change the angle of the text's baseline.

Style refers to the text font or style used.

Layer enables you to change the layer on which the attribute resides.

Color enables you to change the color for the attributes.

When you finish with one attribute, AutoCAD moves the X to the next attribute to be edited. The same series of prompts is displayed for each attribute.

Hints

The Attedit command terminates when you type **Next** after editing the last attribute you selected. Also, you can stop the Attedit command from executing by pressing Ctrl-C.

Error Messages

`Yes or No, please.` You entered an invalid character when prompted for a Yes or No response. Try again, using either **Y** or **N**.

`0 attributes selected. *Invalid*` When prompted to select attributes, you did not specify any. After this error, AutoCAD returns to the `Command:` prompt. Try again.

`*Invalid selection*`

`Expects a point or Window/Last/Crossing/BOX.` When prompted to select attributes, you entered an invalid character. Try again.

Related System Variables

None

Attext

(Short for ATTribute EXTract) Enables you to extract attribute
information from a drawing for use outside the drawing

Syntax

```
Command: Attext
CDF, SDF or DXF Attribute extract (or Entities)? <default>
Template file:
Extract file name <default>:
```

Screen Menu

UTILITY–ATTEXT:

Pull–Down Menu

None

Template Coordinates

None

Description

This command enables you to extract attribute information for use
outside the drawing in one of three formats. Indicate the form you
want the extracted file to take: CDF (comma-delimited format), SDF
(space-delimited format), or DXF (AutoCAD's own drawing exchange
format).

Specify a template file that indicates how the data in the extract file is
to be structured. Information contained in the template file may
include which attributes to extract, what information about the blocks
containing those attributes should be incorporated, and how the
extracted information should appear in the file. The default extension
for the template file is TXT. (See the AutoCAD reference manual for
information about creating a template file.)

Enter the extract file name for the extracted information. If you accept
the default by pressing Enter, the extract file is given the same name as
your drawing.

Possible Responses

Response	Meaning
CDF	Comma-delimited format

Response	Meaning
SDF	SDF format
DXF	DXF format
E	Select particular entities

Hints

If you type **E** to select particular entities, Attext prompts you to select the objects whose attributes will be extracted. After you respond to this prompt, the CDF, SDF, or DXF prompt will redisplay without the Entities option.

To send the attribute extract directly to the screen, type **CON:**.

To send the extract file to a printer, make sure that your printer is connected and ready to print and then type **PRN:**.

Error Messages

`Invalid option keyword.` You entered a character that does not correspond to any currently offered option. Check the available options, and try again.

`Invalid file name.` You entered a file name that is not allowed. Check your spelling, and try again.

`Can't open file.` You entered a template file name that AutoCAD cannot find on the disk. Check your spelling, and try again.

`** Invalid field specification:` Your template file has an error in it. Check the contents of this file, and try again.

Related System Variables

None

Audit

Determines the validity of a drawing file

Syntax

```
Command: Audit
Fix any errors detected? <default>:
0 Blocks audited
Pass 1 0 entities audited
Pass 2 0 entities audited
Total errors found 0 fixed 0
```

Screen Menu

UTILITY–AUDIT:

Pull–Down Menu

None

Template Coordinates

None

Description

Drawing files created by AutoCAD Release 11 contain redundant information. This duplicate information is used by the Audit command to repair corrupted drawing files.

When you use Audit, it saves a report of its findings in a disk file with the name of the drawing and the extension ADT.

Possible Responses

Response	Meaning
Y	Attempt to repair errors in drawing file
N	Report errors but do not repair file

Hints

Use the Audit command if AutoCAD complains it cannot read a portion of the drawing file. If AutoCAD cannot read part of the DWG file, it fails, keeping you from using the Audit command. Drawing audit (recovery) will have to be executed from the Main Menu.

Error Messages

None

Related System Variables

None

Axis

Sets up an axis of tick marks on the bottom and right side of the drawing area

Syntax

```
Command: Axis
Tick spacing(X) or ON/OFF/Snap/Aspect <default>:
```

Screen Menu

SETTINGS–AXIS:

Pull–Down Menu

Settings–Drawing Tools...

Template Coordinates

None

Description

Tick spacing is the default. Type a value at the prompt to set the spacing for both X- and Y-axis ruler lines.

On turns on the axis after the spacing is set; Off turns off the axis.

Snap sets the axis to current snap value.

Aspect allows different X and Y values for spacing.

Possible Responses

Response	Meaning
ON	Turn on axis
OFF	Turn off axis
S	Set axis to current snap value
A	Establish different tick aspects for X and Y axes
number	Set tick spacing to this number
numberX	Set tick spacing to multiple of snap spacing

Hints

Tick marks make it easier to line up the crosshairs at grid points.

If you use the Snap option or specify a tick spacing of zero, the axis will adjust automatically if the Snap resolution is changed.

The Aspect option, which sets different spacings for horizontal and vertical axis ticks, is not available when the Snap style is isometric.

To display the axes, a single viewport configuration must be active.

Error Messages

`Requires a distance, numberX, or option keyword.` You entered an improper response to the Axis prompt. Check your spelling, and try again.

`Ambiguous response, please clarify...` When prompted to enter a new setting, you entered the letter O. Because this response can mean either On or Off, you need to spell out as much of the word as necessary to remove ambiguity.

```
Requires a distance (or numberX).
```
When prompted for
horizontal or vertical spacing, you entered a nonnumeric response. Try
again.

Related System Variables

AXISMODE
AXISUNIT

Base

Creates the insertion point when you want to insert one drawing into
another or use the Block command to create a block from objects in the
current drawing

Syntax

```
Command: Base
Base point <default>:
```

Screen Menu

BLOCKS–BASE:

Pull–Down Menu

None

Template Coordinates

None

Description

Base is closely related to library blocks. You use the Base command to
set an insertion (base) point for the current drawing. This three-
dimensional coordinate is stored with the drawing and is used if you
insert the current drawing into another drawing.

The base point defaults to three-dimensional coordinates 0,0,0 in the
World Coordinate System. If you change the current elevation, the
default Z coordinate will match this elevation. The <default> option
indicates, in three-dimensional coordinates, the default (current) base
point setting.

Hints

Use this command to change the insertion point of a library block once
it has been defined. Load the block as a drawing, and then do the
change.

Error Messages

Invalid point. You specified an invalid base point or entered a nonnumeric character when prompted for a base point. Check your entry, and try again.

Related System Variables

INSBASE

Blipmode

Toggles blip markers on and off

Syntax

Command: **Blipmode**
ON/OFF <default>:

Screen Menu

SETTINGS–BLIPS:

Pull–Down Menu

None

Template Coordinates

None

Description

Blips are the small + marker symbols that AutoCAD inserts to record the location whenever you select a point or entity. Blips appear on the screen as visual aids; they do not appear on drawings.

The <ON> option is the default Blipmode setting.

Possible Responses

Response	Meaning
ON	Turn on marker blips
OFF	Turn off marker blips

Hints

Blips serve only as markers; they do not affect the operation of AutoCAD.

Your screen will look less cluttered if you work with Blipmode off.

Because blips are not entities, they cannot be erased with Erase.

You can clear your screen of blips by using the command Redraw.

Error Messages

`Invalid option keyword.` You have not selected either On or Off as prompted. Try again.

`Ambiguous response, please clarify...` When prompted to enter a new setting, you entered the letter O. Because this response can mean either On or Off, you need to spell out as much of the word as necessary to remove ambiguity.

Related System Variables

BLIPMODE

Block

Creates an object from existing entities

Syntax

```
Command: Block
Block name (or ?):
Insertion base point:
Select objects:
```

Screen Menu

BLOCKS–BLOCK:

Pull–Down Menu

None

Template Coordinates

Q 2

Description

Blocks are library parts created from objects existing in AutoCAD. The Block command enables you to create new blocks from parts of existing drawings.

To list all the blocks you created in a drawing, enter a question mark (?) at the first prompt. AutoCAD will switch to the text screen, and you will see a complete list of the blocks currently in the drawing. After this list is finished, the `Command:` prompt is returned to the screen.

The block name can be 31 characters long and contain letters, numbers, the dollar sign ($), the hyphen (-), and the underscore (_). AutoCAD automatically converts letters to uppercase.

If the block exists, AutoCAD prompts the following:

```
Block already exists.
Redefine it? <N>
```

When you redefine a block, be sure not to redefine it to itself; that is, do not take an inserted block and redefine the block to its current name. To redefine a block, either redraw the entire block, or use Explode.

`Insertion base point:` is the reference point AutoCAD uses when inserting the library part back into the drawing. After you identify the insertion base point, AutoCAD prompts you to select the objects that comprise the block.

Possible Responses

Response	Meaning
?	List names of defined blocks

Hints

Use Wblock to write the block to disk if you want to use it in a different drawing.

You can use entire files as blocks in other drawings.

To add a copy of the block to the drawing, use the Insert command. AutoCAD first searches the drawing for the block and then searches the hard drive.

Although a block name may be 31 characters long, you may want to limit it to 8 characters if you want to store it on disk.

Use the Rename command to rename blocks.

When naming blocks, keep in mind the potential for using wild cards. You may want to use common prefixes in order to group related blocks into categories.

Error Messages

`Invalid point.` When asked to select the insertion base point, you specified an invalid location. Check your entry, and try again.

`*Invalid selection*`

`Expects a point or Window/Last/Crossing/BOX/Add/ Remove/Multiple/ Previous/Undo/AUto/SIngle.` When prompted to select objects, you entered an option keyword AutoCAD does not understand. Try again.

Related System Variables

None

Break

Removes parts of an entity or separates an entity into segments

Syntax

```
Command: Break
Select object:
Enter second point (or F for first point): F
Enter first point:
Enter second point:
```

Screen Menu

EDIT–BREAK:

Pull–Down Menu

Modify–Break

Template Coordinates

X 13 (Break F)
X 14 (Break @)

Description

On the tablet menu, two Break commands are available: Break F and Break @. Break F removes parts of an entity, and Break @ separates the entity without removing a part.

If you use Break F or enter **Break** at the `Command:` prompt, AutoCAD assumes that the point at which you select an object is the first break point unless you choose the F option. If you do this, you will be instructed to choose the first point and then the second, and the break will occur between the two points selected.

Break affects different entities differently, as follows:

❑ Lines: the segment between the two points is removed.

❑ Arcs: the segment between the two points is removed.

❑ Circles: the segment counterclockwise from the first point to the second is removed.

❑ Polylines: the segment between the two points is removed. If the polyline has a nonzero width, the ends are cut square. If you fit a curve to the polyline and then break the fitted polyline, the fitting information becomes permanent, and you cannot later decurve the polyline.

Other types of entities cannot be broken.

If you are using Break @, AutoCAD will prompt you for a first point. That first point is where the entity will be divided.

Possible Responses

Response	Meaning
F	Specify first point

Hints

The easiest way to select objects for breaking is by picking, although you can select objects with any object selection method.

When you enter a second point to remove one end of an object, the second point can be beyond the end of that object.

Break cannot be used to break blocks, solids, three-dimensional lines, or three-dimensional faces.

When breaking circles, select the first and second points in counterclockwise order.

Error Messages

`*Invalid selection*`

`Expects a point or Window/Last/Crossing/BOX.` When prompted to select an object, you entered an option keyword AutoCAD does not understand. Try again.

`2D point or option keyword required.` You did not specify a break point correctly. Try again.

`Need a line, 2D polyline, trace, circle, or arc.` When prompted to select an object, you selected an entity that cannot be broken. Try again.

Related System Variables

None

Cancel

Cancels the current command

Syntax

```
Command: Ctrl-C
*Cancel*
```

Toggle Key

Ctrl-C

Screen Menu

**** – CANCEL:

Pull–Down Menu
Assist–Cancel

Template Coordinates
V 12
V 14

Description
Pressing Ctrl-C cancels the current command and returns you to the
`Command:` prompt.

Hints
Some commands, such as Pedit and Dim, may require that you press
Ctrl-C twice to return to the `Command:` prompt.

Error Messages
None

Related System Variables
None

Chamfer

Squares or bevels an intersection. Trims or extends two lines until
specified distances are met and then connects the lines with a line
segment, squaring or beveling the corner where the lines intersect.

Syntax
```
Command: Chamfer
Polyline/Distances/<Select first line>:
Select second line:
```

Screen Menu
EDIT–CHAMFER:

Pull–Down Menu
Modify–Chamfer (to use Chamfer command)

Pull–Down Menu
Options–Chamfer Distances (to set Chamfer distances)

Template Coordinates
X 21

Description

Chamfering trims or extends two lines so that they intersect. Then it trims the lines a distance you specify with an option of this command and connects them with a new connecting line.

The default chamfer distance is 0. To set these distances to the correct value, press **D** at the chamfer prompt. You will see the following prompts:

```
Enter first chamfer distance <default>:
Enter second chamfer distance <default>:
```

The first distance is applied to the first line you select; the second, to the second line selected. After specifying the distances, repeat the Chamfer command and select the lines.

If you press **P** at the chamfer prompt, AutoCAD will prompt for the polyline you want to chamfer. Select the entity, and AutoCAD will chamfer every vertex possible. After completion of the Chamfer command, you are informed of how many lines (in the polyline) AutoCAD could chamfer, along with how many were too short.

AutoCAD will not chamfer parallel or divergent lines.

Possible Responses

Response	Meaning
D	Set distances
P	Chamfer polyline

Hints

Generally, a chamfer will be at a 45-degree angle to the base angle (equal distances).

You can use this command to adjust two lines so that they end at the same point, by specifying both chamfer distances as zero. In this case the two lines are extended without a chamfer being drawn.

Error Messages

```
Lines diverge
```

Invalid You chose to chamfer two lines AutoCAD cannot use. Select two lines that are not divergent.

```
Lines are parallel
```

Invalid You chose to chamfer two lines AutoCAD cannot use. Select two lines that are not parallel.

If you are viewing from a direction oblique to the X, Y plane of the

current User Coordinate System, you will receive a message warning
that the results may be unpredictable. At this point you may want to
alter your viewing direction.

```
Chamfer requires 2 lines.
```

`*Invalid*` You did not specify two lines to be chamfered. Try again.

Related System Variables
CHAMFERA
CHAMFERB

Change

Modifies entities

Syntax
```
Command: Change
Select objects:
Properties/<Change point>:
Change what property (Color/LAyer/LType/Thickness)?
```

Screen Menu
CHANGE:

Pull–Down Menu
None

Template Coordinates
Y 16
Y 17

Description
You can change entities in two ways: by indicating a change point or
by changing the properties. A change point will modify the physical
entity. Properties that can be changed include color, elevation, layer,
linetype, and thickness.

The effect of using a change point differs slightly among entities:

❑ Line: the end of the line closest to the change point will
move to the change point. Several lines may be included
in the selection set.

❑ Circle: the radius is changed so that the circumference
passes through the change point.

❏ Text: the location of the text is changed when you move the insertion point to the change point. If you press Enter at the `Properties/<Change point>:` prompt, AutoCAD will prompt for a new text style, text height, rotation angle, and text string. You can change nearly all aspects of text. An exception is when text is defined with a fixed height; then you cannot change the height of that particular font.

❏ Block: you can provide a new insertion point by indicating a change point.

If you select `Properties`, AutoCAD displays the following prompt:

`Change what property (Color/Elev/LAyer/LType/Thickness)?`

Color changes the color of an entity. If you have overridden the layer color and want the entity to default to the layer color, type **BYLAYER**. This entry tells AutoCAD to set colors by layer. You will be prompted with the following:

`New color <BYLAYER>:`

If the current color is BYBLOCK, the entities are set to the color of the block in which they reside. You also can use this setting to override the layer color setting. Type the color, by number or by name, that you want the entity to have:

Number	Name
1	Red
2	Yellow
3	Green
4	Cyan
5	Blue
6	Magenta
7	White

The Elev option is not available in Release 11. Elev stands for elevation and will change the location of the entities with respect to the Z axis.

Layer changes the layer on which an entity resides. If the destination layer is off, the entity will disappear from the screen when you are finished with Change. If the entity's color and linetype are set BYLAYER, the entity will acquire the settings for the new layer.

Ltype changes the linetype of the entities. The comments listed under the Linetype command apply here. If you change the linetype of an entity, you are overriding the layer setting unless you are changing the linetype to BYLAYER.

Thickness modifies the thickness of the entities.

Possible Responses

Response	Meaning
P	Change properties
C	Change color
E	Change elevation
LA	Change layer
LT	Change linetype
T	Change thickness

Hints

You can change several properties at once by pressing Enter at the `Change what property?` prompt. This action allows multiple changes you request to take place.

You can no longer use the Change command to change elevations in Release 11.

Error Messages

`*Invalid selection*`
`Expects a point or Window/Last/Crossing/BOX/Add/ Remove/Multiple/ Previous/Undo/AUto/SIngle.` When prompted to select objects, you entered an option keyword AutoCAD does not understand.

`Try again. n selected, n found, (n not parallel with UCS).` When prompted to select objects, you selected at least some entities that do not have an extrusion direction parallel to the Z axis of the current UCS. Either reselect the objects, or use the Chprop command, which does not have this limitation.

`Point or option keyword required.` You selected an option keyword AutoCAD does not understand. Review the possible responses, and try again.

`Invalid option keyword.` When you chose to change properties, you entered an invalid keyword to the `Change what property?` prompt. Review the possible responses, and try again.

Related System Variables

None

Chprop

(Short for CHange PROPerty) Modifies properties of entities

Syntax

```
Command: Chprop
Select objects:
Change what property (Color/LAyer/LType/
Thickness)?:
```

Screen Menu

EDIT–CHPROP:

Pull–Down Menu

None

Template Coordinates

Y 18

Description

Chprop is a subset of the Change command, changing only a few of the properties of entities. See the description for the Change command.

Possible Responses

Response	Meaning
C	Change color
LA	Change layer
LT	Change linetype
T	Change thickness

Hints

Chprop modifies entity properties without limiting changes to entities with extrusion directions parallel to the Z axis of the current UCS.

Error Messages

```
*Invalid selection*
```

```
Expects a point or Window/Last/Crossing/BOX/Add/
Remove/Multiple/ Previous/Undo/AUto/SIngle.
```
When prompted to select objects, you entered an option keyword AutoCAD does not understand. Try again.

```
Invalid option keyword.
```
You entered an invalid keyword. Review the possible responses and try again.

Related System Variables

None

Circle

Draws a circle

Syntax

```
Command: Circle
3P/2P/TTR/<Center point>:
Diameter/<Radius>:
```

Alias

C

Screen Menu

DRAW–CIRCLE

Pull–Down Menu

Draw–Circle

Template Coordinates

M 10

Description

3P prompts you for three points. The circle is drawn with its circumference lying on the three points. You will see a rubberband circle after entering the second point.

2P prompts you for two points. The two points define the circle's location and its diameter, which equals the distance between the two points. You will see a rubberband circle after entering the first point.

TTR is short for tangent-tangent-radius. The entities to which you want the circle to be tangent must be on-screen.

Perhaps the easiest way to create a circle is to specify a center point for the circle and then respond to the following prompt:

```
Diameter/<Radius>:
```

Indicate whether the second point you specify is the diameter or the radius. In either case, you will see a rubberband circle on the screen to assist you in placing the circle.

Possible Responses

Response	Meaning
2P	Specify two end points of diameter
3P	Specify three points on circumference
D	Enter diameter rather than radius
TTR	Specify two tangent points and radius

Hints

You can indicate the radius by designating a point on the circle circumference.

Error Messages

`Point or option keyword required.` You entered an option keyword AutoCAD does not understand. Try again.

`Requires a TAN object-snap and selection of Circle, Arc, or Line.` After selecting the TTR method of specifying a circle, you entered an invalid tangent specification. Try again.

`Circle does not exist.` After selecting the TTR method of specifying a circle, you provided tangent points and a radius that do not allow a circle to be created. Try again, changing either the tangent points or the radius.

`*Requires numeric radius, point on circumference, or "D".` After selecting a center point for your circle, you entered a nonnumeric value, with which AutoCAD cannot work. Check your entry, and try again.

`Value must be positive and nonzero.` You specified an illegal diameter or radius. Try again, using a number greater than zero.

Related System Variables

None

Color or Colour

Sets the color of an entity independent of the layer or block color

Syntax

```
Command: Color
New entity color <BYLAYER>:
```

Screen Menu

SETTINGS–COLOR:

Pull–Down Menu

Settings–Drawing Tools...

Template Coordinates

Y 20

Description

You can respond to the prompt by typing the name (for standard colors) or the number of the color you want to draw with, by pressing Enter to accept the current setting, or by typing **BYLAYER** or **BYBLOCK**.

You can specify colors from 1 to 255 by number, but only the first seven by name:

Number	Name
1	**Red**
2	**Yellow**
3	**Green**
4	**Cyan**
5	**Blue**
6	**Magenta**
7	**White**

To see what the remaining colors (8 through 255) look like, bring up the CHROMA.SLD slide file, supplied with AutoCAD.

BYLAYER causes the color of entities to default to the layer color setting. The entities will be the color assigned to the layer on which they reside.

BYBLOCK causes the color of the entities to default to the color set for the block definition. The color of the block is determined when you create the block.

Possible Responses

Response	Meaning
number	Entity color number
name	Entity color name
BYBLOCK	Floating entity color
BYLAYER	Match layer's color

Hints

Use the Color command to set the color of objects independently of the layer setting.

The Plot command enables you to assign the first 15 colors to your plotter's pen numbers.

Error Messages

A color number or standard color name is required. You entered a color not recognized by AutoCAD. Check your spelling, and try again.

Related System Variables

CECOLOR

Coordinates

Changes the coordinate readout on the status line from static to dynamic

Syntax

```
Command: Press Ctrl-D
<Coords On>
```

Toggle Key

Ctrl-D or F6

Screen Menu

None

Pull–Down Menu

None

Template Coordinates

V 16

Description

Pressing Ctrl-D changes the coordinate display to a continuous X,Y readout. Pressing Ctrl-D a second time changes it to a continuous distance-angle readout. Pressing Ctrl-D a third time changes the display to static again.

Hints

There is no Coordinate command; rather, you press Ctrl-D or function key F6 to toggle the coordinate display. Ctrl-D and the F6 function key are transparent commands. They can be used during any other command.

Error Messages

None

Related System Variables

COORDS

Copy

Make copies of objects

Syntax

```
Command: Copy
Select objects:
<Base point or displacement>/Multiple:
Second point or displacement:
```

Alias

CP

Screen Menu

EDIT–COPY

Pull–Down Menu

Modify–Copy

Template Coordinates

X 15

Description

Copy makes another copy of an object. Then you can change each copy without affecting the original or other copies.

Base point provides a reference point for acting on your selection set. Displacement enables you to enter a displacement for X, Y, and Z coordinates. If you indicate a base point or displacement, you will be prompted as follows:

```
Second point of displacement:
```

With base point, indicate a second point; with displacement, press Enter.

Multiple enables you to make multiple copies at one time. If you indicate Multiple, you will be prompted as follows:

```
Base point:
```

AutoCAD still needs a reference. With Multiple, you may want the base point to be on the object you are copying. Doing so will make the copying easier to calculate. You then are prompted:

```
Second point of displacement:
Second point of displacement:
Second point of displacement:
```

AutoCAD enables you to place copies as many times as necessary. When you finish copying the object, press Enter.

Possible Responses

Response	Meaning
M	Make multiple copies

Hints

The Multiple option enables you to make multiple copies of an entity without respecifying the entity.

Use Copy when you want to place copies of entities in an irregular pattern; use Array when you want to make multiple copies in a rectangular or circular pattern.

Error Messages

```
*Invalid selection*
```

```
Expects a point or Window/Last/Crossing/BOX/Add/
Remove/Multiple/ Previous/Undo/AUto/SIngle.
```
When prompted to select objects, you entered an option keyword AutoCAD does not understand. Try again.

```
Point or option keyword required.
```
When prompted for a base point or displacement, you entered an option keyword AutoCAD does not understand. Check your entry, and try again.

Related System Variables

None

Dblist

(Short for DataBase LISTing) Lists information about all entities in the drawing

Syntax

```
Command: Dblist
```

Screen Menu

    INQUIRY–DBLIST:

Pull–Down Menu

    None

Template Coordinates

    None

Description

When this command is executed, AutoCAD switches to the text screen and lists the database information on the screen. You can pause the listing with Ctrl-S; press any key to resume. Use Ctrl-C to cancel the listing and Ctrl-Q to echo the listing to your printer.

Hints

For drawings with many entities, Dblist takes a long time to execute because it scrolls through the entire database. Use Ctrl-C if you decide to cancel.

Error Messages

    None

Related System Variables

    None

Ddatte

(Short for Dynamic Dialog ATTribute Editor) Allows attribute editing by means of a dialogue box

Syntax

```
Command: Ddatte
Select block:
```

Screen Menu

    EDIT–DDATTE:

Pull–Down Menu

    None

Template Coordinates

    None

Description

The dialogue box enables you to alter the defaults in any order you choose.

Hints

Limit attribute prompts to fewer than 24 characters with the Ddatte dialogue box; additional characters will be truncated.

You can edit only text string values, one block at a time.

Ddatte works only with the Advanced User Interface.

Error Messages

`*Invalid selection*`

`Expects a point or Window/Last/Crossing/BOX.` When prompted to select a block, you entered a character or value at the keyboard. Pick a block on-screen.

`Entity is not a block.` You selected an entity Ddatte cannot use. Check your selection, and try again.

`Block has no attributes.` You selected a block that has no attributes to edit.

Related System Variables

ATTDIA

Ddedit

(Short for Dynamic Dialog EDITor) Enables you to edit a line of text in a dialogue box

Syntax

```
Command: Ddedit
<Select a TEXT or ATTDEF object/Undo:
```

Screen Menu

None

Pull–Down Menu

None

Template Coordinates

V 8
V 9

Description

The Ddedit command is a line editor that enables you to edit a single line of text. You can use the pointing device or the keyboard's arrow keys to move the block cursor to where you want to perform the edit.

When you have finished the editing, pick the OK box; to cancel changes, pick the Cancel box.

You can use the Undo option to reverse the editing changes.

Hints

The Ddedit command is easier than the Change command to use for editing misspelled words in a line of text.

Error Messages

`Command has been completely undone.` You used the Undo option once too often. All editing changes already have been undone.

Related System Variables

None

'Ddemodes

(Short for Dynamic Dialog Entity creation MODES) Allows you to change entity properties by means of a dialogue box

Syntax

`Command:` **'Ddemodes**

Screen Menu

SETTINGS–DDEMODES

Pull–Down Menu

Options–Entity Creation...

Template Coordinates

T 8
T 9

Description

You can use Ddemodes as a transparent command within another AutoCAD command by preceding it with an apostrophe: **'Ddemodes**.

Ddmodes lets you establish five entity properties: layer, color, linetype, elevation, and thickness. The values you set with Ddemodes may not take effect until you type the next AutoCAD command.

Hints

Ddemodes works only with the Advanced User Interface.

Error Messages

None

Related System Variables

CECOLOR
CELTYPE
CLAYER

'Ddlmodes

(Short for Dynamic Dialog Layer MODES) Changes layer properties by means of a dialogue box

Syntax

Command: **'Ddlmodes**

Screen Menu

LAYER:–DDLMODES

Pull–Down Menu

Settings–Layer Control...

Template Coordinates

P 4

Description

You can use Ddlmodes as a transparent command within another AutoCAD command by preceding it with an apostrophe: **'Ddlmodes**.

Ddlmodes displays a dialogue box with all the Layer command capabilities. In addition, it enables you to rename any layer used in the drawing.

Field lengths in the dialogue box limit how many characters of the layer and linetype names are displayed.

Hints

As with other dialogue box commands, Ddlmodes relies on features of the Advanced User Interface and works only on systems supporting AUI.

Error Messages

None

Related System Variables

CLAYER

'Ddrmodes

(Short for Dynamic Dialog dRawing MODES) Sets drawing aids by means of a dialogue box

Syntax

Command: **'Ddrmodes**

Screen Menu

SETTINGS–DDRMODES

Pull–Down Menu

Settings–Drawing Tools...

Template Coordinates

U 8
U 9

Description

You can use Ddrmodes as a transparent command within another AutoCAD command by preceding it with an apostrophe: **'Ddrmodes**.

Ddrmodes enables you to set the following drawing aids from within a dialogue box: snap, grid, axis, ortho, blipmode, and isoplane.

Hints

This command relies on features of the Advanced User Interface and works only with graphics boards supporting AUI.

If you want to use this dialogue box to establish different spacings for X and Y, set the X value first and then the Y value; otherwise, the Y spacing is set equal to X.

Changing snap, grid, or axis spacing with this box does not turn the corresponding mode on or off. To change modes, use the toggle buttons.

Error Messages

None

Related System Variables

AXISMODE
AXISUNIT
BLIPMODE
COORDS
GRIDMODE
GRIDUNIT
ORTHOMODE
SNAPANG
SNAPBASE
SNAPMODE
SNAPUNIT

Dducs

(Short for Dynamic Dialog User Coordinate System) Controls User
Coordinate System by means of a dialogue box

Syntax

Command: **Dducs**

Screen Menu

UCS–DDUCS:

Pull–Down Menu

Settings–UCS Control...

Template Coordinates

J 4
K 4

Description

The Dducs command provides the same functions as the Ucs command. You
also can use Dducs to name or rename existing coordinate systems. You
accomplish the naming or renaming by entering the new name in
the UCS Name field.

Although it was developed primarily for three-dimensional use, you can use Dducs to create coordinate systems for two-dimensional drawings.

Hints

This command relies on features of the Advanced User Interface and works only on graphics boards supporting AUI.

Error Messages

None

Related System Variables

UCSNAME
UCSORG
UCSXDIR
UCSYDIR
WORLDUCS

Delay

Delays execution of the next command; used in scripts

Syntax

```
Command: Delay
Delay time in milliseconds:
```

Screen Menu

None

Pull–Down Menu

None

Template Coordinates

None

Description

Delay enables you to pause in a script file. Delay is useful when you are designing a slide presentation and want the display to pause between slides.

Delay time is input in milliseconds. If you want a delay of about a second, type **1000** at the `Delay time in milliseconds:` prompt.

Hints

The maximum delay is 32,767 milliseconds, or approximately 33 seconds.

Negative or zero values result in no delay at all.

Error Messages

`Requires an integer value.` You entered a value that is not a whole number or is greater than 32,767. Enter another delay value that is an integer between 1 and 32,767.

Related System Variables

None

Dim

(Short for DIMensions) Switches to dimensioning mode

Syntax

```
Command: Dim
Dim:
```

Screen Menu

DIM:–DIM:

Pull–Down Menu

Draw–Dim:

Template Coordinates

None

Description

Dim places AutoCAD in dimensioning mode so that you can use dimensioning commands. After you enter the Dim command, the `Command:` prompt is replaced with the `Dim:` prompt, indicating that AutoCAD is in dimensioning mode.

AutoCAD Release 11 has 27 dimensioning subcommands. You can type either the full name or just the first three letters, as follows:

Aligned
Angular
Baseline
Center
Continue

Diameter
Exit
Hometext
Horizontal
Leader
Newtext
Oblique
Ordinate
Override
Radius
Redraw
Restore
Rotated
Save
Status
Style
Tedit
Trotate
Undo
Update
Variables
Vertical

In this Command Reference section, these dimensioning commands are listed alphabetically following this command. For detailed information about each dimensioning command, see the appropriate command description.

To return to the `Command:` prompt, type **Exit** at the `Dim:` prompt or press Ctrl-C.

Hints

After you enter the Dim command, you cannot use other AutoCAD commands (except transparent commands) until you return to the `Command:` prompt.

Error Messages

`Unknown command. Type EXIT to return to COMMAND prompt.` You entered a nondimensioning command (such as Move, Line, or Plot) at the `Dim:` prompt. Type **Exit** or press Ctrl-C to return to the `Command:` prompt.

`Unknown command. Type ? for list of commands.` You entered a dimension subcommand at the `Command:` prompt. Type **Dim** to get to the `Dim:` prompt.

Related System Variables

See individual Dim subcommands.

Dim1

(Short for DIMension once) Sets dimensioning mode for one dimensioning command

Syntax

```
Command: Dim1
Dim:
```

Screen Menu

DIM:–DIM1:

Pull–Down Menu

None

Template Coordinates

None

Description

Dim1 allows you to enter a single dimension command and then returns you to the `Command:` prompt.

Hints

To remain in dimensioning mode for more than one command, use the Dim command.

Error Messages

`Unknown command. Type EXIT to return to COMMAND prompt.` You entered a nondimensioning command (such as Move, Line, or Plot) at the `Dim:` prompt. Type **Exit** or press Ctrl-C to return to the `Command:` prompt.

`Unknown command. Type ? for list of commands.` You entered a dimension subcommand at the `Command:` prompt. First enter the Dim1 command.

Related System Variables

See individual Dim subcommands.

Dim: Aligned

Places the dimension line parallel to a selected entity or to two points

Syntax

```
Dim: Ali
First extension line origin or RETURN to select:
Press Enter
Select line, arc, or circle:
Dimension line location:
Dimension text <default>:
```

Screen Menu

DIM:–LINEAR–aligned

Pull–Down Menu

Draw–Dim:

Template Coordinates

Y 6

Description

This subcommand enables you to align a dimension with an entity or along a line you select. You can pick points to locate dimension lines, or you can select an entity. To select an entity, you must point to it.

To use this command, specify the location for the extension lines by picking the extension lines on the screen or by entering numeric coordinates. If you press Enter at the first Aligned prompt, you will have an opportunity to select an entity to dimension.

`<default>` is the length of the entity or the length between the extension lines you specified. It is the default dimension text.

Hints

Only the first three letters of the command are required for AutoCAD to initiate this command.

Error Messages

`Ambiguous response, please clarify...` You did not enter enough letters to let AutoCAD know you want to use this command. Enter at least **Ali** to remove the ambiguity. Pressing Ctrl-C at this point aborts the command and exits the dimensioning subsystem.

`*Invalid*` You provided an invalid `response.` The entity selected is not a line, arc, or circle. You chose to dimension an entity but did not select one that can be dimensioned with this command.

Choose again, ensuring that the selected entity is a line, an arc, or a circle.

Related System Variables

None

Dim: Angular

Dimensions the angle between two lines

Syntax

```
Dim: Ang
Select arc, circle, line or RETURN:
Second line:
Enter dimension line arc location:
Dimension text <default>:
Enter text location:
```

Screen Menu

DIM–angular

Pull–Down Menu

Draw–Dim:

Template Coordinates

Y 4

Description

The dimension line is an arc showing the angle between two lines.

The <default> option is the angle between the two lines you specified. It is the default dimension text.

If you press Enter at the Enter text location: prompt, AutoCAD places the text within the dimensional arc. Otherwise, the text will be entered at the location you indicate. If the text does not fit, AutoCAD prompts you to enter a new text location.

If the dimensional arc line cannot be drawn between the two lines, an extension line is drawn from the center point of the dimensional arc to an intersection with the arc itself. This extension line is, as the name suggests, simply an extension of one of the lines you chose with the Angular command.

Hints

Angular works with nonparallel lines only. Trying to dimension parallel lines with this command results in an error message.

Error Messages

`Lines are parallel *Invalid*.` You selected two lines that are parallel. Parallel lines cannot be given an angular dimension. Try the command again, choosing two lines that are not parallel.

`Entity selected is not a line.` You chose an entity that is not a line. Choose again, ensuring that the selected entity is a line.

Related System Variables

None

Dim: Baseline

Enables you to use the last dimension as the base point for the next dimension

Syntax

```
Dim: Bas
Select base dimension:
Second extension line origin or RETURN to select:
Dimension text <default>:
```

Screen Menu

DIM:–LINEAR–baseline

Pull–Down Menu

Draw–Dim:

Template Coordinates

X 3

Description

Because AutoCAD uses the first extension line origin of the last dimension you input as the base point, it prompts you for the second extension line origin without prompting you for the first origin.

The `<default>` option is the measured value of the newly computed dimension. It is the default dimension text offered by AutoCAD.

Hints

Baseline repeats the last entered linear-dimensioning subcommand (Horizontal, Vertical, Rotated, or Aligned) so that all dimensions originate at the same place.

Baseline cannot be used after any other dimensioning commands, such as Angular.

Error Messages

`No dimension to continue.` You used Baseline as the first command on entering the dimensioning subsystem or after a dimensioning command that cannot be continued with Baseline. Because Baseline is intended to continue a previous dimensioning command, use it only after you use another valid dimensioning command.

`*Invalid*` When prompted to enter the second extension line origin, you entered a nonnumeric character or an invalid coordinate. Check your entry and try again, or select an on-screen point.

Related System Variables

DIMDLI

Dim: Center

Marks the center of a circle or arc

Syntax

```
Dim: Cen
Select arc or circle:
```

Screen Menu

DIM:–RADIAL–center

Pull–Down Menu

Draw–Dim:

Template Coordinates

Y 1

Description

This subcommand places a cross (+) at the center of the arc or circle you select. The size of the center mark is determined by the dimension variable Dimcen. The smaller the value, the smaller the center mark.

If you assign a negative value to Dimcen, the center mark will be the same size as the absolute value of Dimcen, but AutoCAD will add extension lines that extend from close to the end of the center mark to just past the circumference of the circle.

Hints

When you are erasing center marks (using Erase), remember that either two or six objects make up a center mark: the horizontal portion and the vertical portion and the extensions (if Dimcen is negative). Make sure that you select all these lines for complete erasure.

Error Messages

`Ambiguous response, please clarify...` You have not entered enough letters to let AutoCAD know that you want to use this command. Enter at least **Cen** to remove the ambiguity. Pressing Ctrl-C at this point aborts the command and exits the dimensioning subsystem.

`Invalid point.` When prompted to select an arc or circle, you entered an invalid point. Try again.

`Object selected is not a circle or arc.` When prompted to select an arc or circle, you chose a different type of entity. Make sure that the object you select is really an arc or circle.

Related System Variables

DIMCEN

Dim: Continue

Enables you to use the previous dimension as a reference for the next dimension

Syntax

```
Dim: Con
Select continued dimension:
Second extension line origin or RETURN to select:
Dimension text <default>:
```

Screen Menu

DIM:–LINEAR–continue

Pull–Down Menu

Draw–Dim:

Template Coordinates

X 4

Description

Continue is similar to Baseline, but Continue uses the second extension-line origin of the last dimension as the first extension-line origin of the current dimension. This keeps the dimension lines the same distance from the extension lines, when possible.

This subcommand repeats linear dimensioning subcommands such as Horizontal, Vertical, Rotated, or Aligned. It cannot be used to continue other dimensioning subcommands.

Use Continue to dimension several linear points on the same line.

The <default> option is the measured value of the newly computed dimension. It is the default dimension text offered by AutoCAD.

Hints

The distance between the dimension lines is determined by the Dimdli variable.

If you dimension an entity, exit the dimensioning subsystem, return to the dimensioning subsystem, and then use Continue, AutoCAD will not function as you would expect. Instead, Continue uses the first extension line of the last dimensioning command as the first extension line of the continuation; in this way, it is the same as Baseline. The difference is that the dimension text is not offset from the previous dimension text; the dimension text overwrites the previous dimension text.

Error Messages

Ambiguous response, please clarify... You did not enter enough letters to let AutoCAD know that you want to use this command. Enter at least **Con** to remove the ambiguity. Pressing Ctrl-C at this point aborts the command and exits the dimensioning subsystem.

No dimension to continue. You used Continue as the first command when entering the dimensioning subsystem or after a dimensioning command that cannot be continued. Because Continue is intended to continue a previous dimensioning command, use it only after using another valid dimensioning command.

Invalid When prompted to enter the second extension line origin, you entered a nonnumeric character or an invalid coordinate. Check your entry and try again, or select an on-screen point.

Related System Variables

DIMDLI

Dim: Diameter

Dimensions the diameter of circles and arcs

Syntax

```
Dim: Dia
Select arc or circle:
Dimension text <default>:
Enter leader length for text:
```

Screen Menu

DIM:–RADIAL–diameter

Pull–Down Menu

Draw–Dim:

Template Coordinates

Y 3

Description

The point at which you select the arc or circle determines where the dimension appears, because AutoCAD uses this point as the diameter end point. AutoCAD locates the second end point automatically and draws a line between the two points.

If there is not enough room to insert the dimension text, AutoCAD notifies you and asks you to enter the leader length for the text.

Hints

If the diameter of the arc or circle is less than four arrow lengths, the diameter line will not be drawn; however, an arrow will be appended to the text leader.

Error Messages

`Object selected is not a circle or arc.` When prompted to select an object, you selected one that is not a circle or arc. Try again.

`Block references not permitted.` When prompted to select entities, you chose a block. Select again.

Related System Variables

DIMCEN

Dim: Exit

Returns you to the `Command:` prompt

Syntax

```
Dim: Exi
Command:
```

Screen Menu

DIM:–EXIT

Pull–Down Menu

Draw–Dim:

Template Coordinates

W 5

W 6

Description

Use Exit when you finish working in the dimensioning subsystem and want to return to the `Command:` prompt.

Hints

You also can press Ctrl-C several times to return to the `Command:` prompt.

Error Messages

None

Related System Variables

None

Dim: Hometext

Returns associative dimension text to its default (or home) position

Syntax

`Dim:` **Hom**
`Select objects:`

Screen Menu

DIM:–next–HOMETEXT

Pull–Down Menu

Draw–Dim:

Template Coordinates

V4

Description

AutoCAD places associative dimension text in a default location. This is its home position. If dimensioning text has been positioned somewhere else, Hometext returns it to its default location.

Hints

Hometext is useful if you used Stretch on a dimension entity and want to cancel its effect.

Error Messages

None

Related System Variables

DIMASO

Dim: Horizontal

Dimensions horizontally

Syntax

```
Dim: Hor
First extension line origin or RETURN to select:
Second extension line origin:
Dimension line location:
Dimension text <default>:
```

Screen Menu

DIM:–LINEAR–horiz

Pull–Down Menu

Draw–Dim:

Template Coordinates

X 6

Description

You can specify the origins for the extension lines manually, or you can press Enter to dimension an entity automatically. The only entities you can dimension with this subcommand are lines, arcs, and circles.

Hints

The last two prompts allow you to use the derived dimension text or enter your own.

Horizontal has the same result as the Dim: Rotated subcommand with an angle of zero.

Error Messages

`*Invalid*` You entered a response that AutoCAD cannot understand. Try again.

`Entity selected is not a line, arc, or circle.` You chose to dimension an entity but did not select a valid entity. Select either an arc, a line, or a circle.

Related System Variables
> None

Dim: Leader

Enables you to add notes in a drawing

Syntax
> `Dim:` **Lea**
> `Leader start:`
> `To point:`
> `To point:` Press Enter
> `Dimension text <default>:`

Screen Menu
> DIM:–leader

Pull–Down Menu
> Draw–Dim:

Template Coordinates
> X 2

Description
> Leader enables you to add a note connected by an arrow to the entity
> the note describes. You specify the location of the leader by picking
> points that define the line segments making up the leader line. When
> you finish entering end points, press Enter. AutoCAD prompts you for
> the text you want inserted. The default text is the last dimension text
> entered.

Hints
> Respond to the To point: prompts as you would for the Line
> command. You can undo Leader segments if you want.
>
> You can enter only one line of text using the Leader option.
>
> The Leader subcommand is useful for dimensioning crowded areas of
> the drawing.

Error Messages
> `*Invalid*` You have not specified a valid point for the leader. Try
> again.

Related System Variables

None

Dim: Newtext

Enables you to change the text in associative dimensions

Syntax

```
Dim: New
Enter new dimension text:
Select objects:
```

Screen Menu

DIM:–next–NEWTEXT

Pull–Down Menu

Draw–Dim:

Template Coordinates

None

Description

This subcommand allows you to change the text within a dimensioning string. It substitutes new dimension text for associative dimensions you select.

Hints

If you use angle brackets <> as a prefix or suffix when you enter the new text, AutoCAD substitutes the dimension measurement in place of the brackets. You can enter other descriptive text, letting AutoCAD automatically substitute the actual dimension in place of the angle brackets.

Press Enter to remove text you added to the measured value.

Generally, your text style should be horizontal when you are executing any of the dimension commands because AutoCAD writes dimension text horizontally unless you change dimension variables.

Error Messages

`Unknown command. Type ? for list of commands.` The command you entered is invalid. You may have entered **Newtext** without first entering **Dim** or **Dim1.** Enter one of these commands first, and then enter **Newtext** at the `Dim:` prompt. Otherwise, check the spelling and retype the command, or press **?** to see a list of valid commands.

`Unknown command: ">_____ <".` `Type EXIT to return to` `COMMAND prompt.` You typed the angle brackets in reverse order when entering dimension text.

If the alarm sounds, you entered too much text.

Related System Variables

None

Dim:Oblique

Tilts the extension lines of associative dimensions

Syntax

`Dim:` **Obl**
`Select objects:`

Screen Menu

DIM:–Oblique

Pull–Down Menu

Draw–Dim:

Template Coordinates

W 4

Description

AutoCAD normally draws extension lines perpendicular to the dimension line. The Oblique subcommand changes the angle of the extension line.

Hints

Oblique can make extension lines more visible in a crowded drawing by changing them from linear to angled.

Error Messages

None

Related System Variables

None

Dim: Ordinate

Adds the X or Y coordinate as a dimension

Syntax

```
Dim: Ord
Select feature:
Leader endpoint (Xdatum/Ydatum):
Dimension text <default>:
```

Screen Menu

DIM:–ORDINAT:

Pull–Down Menu

Draw–Dim:

Template Coordinates

X 1

Description

The Ordinate subcommand dimensions the coordinates of points. After picking the point, AutoCAD draws a leader line and automatically supplies the X or Y coordinate. AutoCAD does not do X,Y coordinate dimensioning.

The X option forces AutoCAD to supply the X coordinate.

The Y option forces AutoCAD to supply the Y coordinate.

If you do not specify the X or Y options, AutoCAD determines which coordinate to use by measuring the distance between the pick point and the end of the leader. If the Y distance is less, then the Y coordinate is used; if the X distance is less, it is used.

Hints

Ordinate dimensioning does not measure distances or angles. Rather, it inserts the actual coordinate position of the picked point.

Error Messages

`*Invalid*` You did not supply an X or Y or pick a point in response to the Leader end point prompt. Try again.

Related System Variables

None

Dim: Override

Changes the settings of dimension variables for selected dimensions

Syntax

```
Dim: Ove
Dimension variable to override:
Current value <default> New value:
Dimension variable to override: Press Enter
Select objects:
```

Screen Menu

DIM:–next–Override

Pull–Down Menu

Draw–Dim:

Template Coordinates

W 3

Description

The Override subcommand enables you to make changes to a dimension by overriding the dimension variables controlling the look of the dimension. You can specify more than one dimension variable to change.

If a dimension you select references a dimensioning style, AutoCAD asks the following:

```
Modify dimension style? <N>:
```

An **N** answer leaves the style unchanged but detaches the dimension from its style. Answering **Y** makes it easy to update or change a dimensioning style.

Hints

Use the Override subcommand to make custom changes to dimensions or to update dimension style libraries easily.

Error Messages

None

Related System Variables

DIMSTYLE

Dim: Radius

Dimensions the radius of circles and arcs

Syntax

```
Dim: Rad
Select arc or circle:
Dimension text <default>:
Enter leader length for text:
```

Screen Menu

DIM:–RADIAL–radius

Pull–Down Menu

Draw–Dim:

Template Coordinates

Y 2

Description

This option draws a radius dimension from the center of an arc or circle to the point you select on the perimeter.

If the text you enter does not fit within the arc or circle you selected, you will be prompted for the length of a leader line from the entity to the text. You can use a positive number or a negative number for leader length. If the length is positive, the leader is drawn to the right of the point where you selected the entity; if negative, to the left.

Hints

If you need to modify the dimension, you can stretch, change, or explode it.

You can enter your own text or accept the default. Default text begins with an R, indicating a radius dimension.

Error Messages

`Invalid point.` When prompted to select an arc or circle, you responded incorrectly. Select an arc or circle.

`Object selected is not a circle or arc *Invalid*.` You selected an entity other than an arc or circle. Select an arc or circle.

`*Invalid*` You entered an invalid response for the leader length for text. Try again.

Related System Variables
DIMCEN

Dim: Redraw

Refreshes the current viewport

Syntax
`Dim:` **Red**

or

`Dim:` **'Redraw**
`Resuming DIM command.`

Screen Menu
None

Pull–Down Menu
None

Template Coordinates
L 11
P 11

Description
This command can be used from the `Command:` prompt or from the `Dim:` prompt. It functions the same way in both contexts.

Hints
Redraw reduces screen clutter by erasing any point-selection blips.

You can use the transparent 'Redraw command during a dimension subcommand.

Error Messages
None

Related System Variables
None

Dim: Restore

Sets a named dimension style

Syntax

```
Dim: Res
Current dimension style: *UNNAMED
?/Enter dimension style or RETURN to select
dimension:
```

Screen Menu

DIM:–next–Restore

Pull–Down Menu

Draw–Dim:

Template Coordinates

V 2

Description

If you have saved one or more dimension styles (see the Dim:Save subcommand), you can recall a style with the Restore subcommand. The new style affects all new associative dimensions but not those created prior to using the Restore subcommand.

*UNNAMED is AutoCAD's default name for the current dimensioning style before you assign it a name.

? displays a list of dimension styles. It prompts you with `Dimension style to list <default>:`. Press Enter to list all styles available.

If you press Enter at the Enter dimension prompt, AutoCAD asks you to Select dimension. This lets you load a dimension style simply by picking the dimension with that style.

Hints

If you have several dimensioning styles in one drawing, it is easier to keep them separate by placing each style on a different layer.

Error Messages

`No matching dimension styles found.` You asked for a list of styles in response to the Dimension style to list prompt, but no styles had been saved.

`No style found.` You have to save a style with the Dim:Save command before you can restore it.

Related System Variables

DIMSTYLE

Dim: Rotated

Sets a rotation angle for linear dimensions

Syntax

```
Dim: Rot
Dimension line angle <default>:
First extension line origin or RETURN to select:
Second extension line origin:
Dimension line location:
Dimension text <default>:
```

Screen Menu

DIM:–LINEAR–rotated

Pull–Down Menu

Draw–Dim:

Template Coordinates

Y 5

Description

This command draws linear (similar to horizontal, vertical, and aligned) dimensions rotated to an angle you specify. You can indicate the angle for the dimension line by specifying it explicitly or by dragging the entity.

If the part you are dimensioning is not horizontal or vertical, and you cannot align the dimension, use the Rotated linear dimension.

Hints

This is the only linear-dimensioning subcommand that prompts you for an angle.

Using the Rotated subcommand with an angle of zero is equivalent to the Horizontal subcommand; both draw a horizontal dimensioning line.

Error Messages

`Unknown command. Type ? for list of commands.` You entered the **Rot**ated command without first entering **Dim** or **Dim1**. Enter a Dim command and then the Rotated command.

`Invalid point.` Your response to one of the extension-line origin prompts or the dimension-line prompt was invalid. Select a point on-screen, or enter coordinates.

Invalid When prompted for a dimension-line angle, you responded inappropriately. Try again, providing either a numeric value or a second point that defines the angle.

Invalid When prompted for the first extension-line origin, you entered an invalid response. Select a point on-screen, or enter two or three coordinates.

Invalid dimension line location. When prompted for the dimension-line location, you entered an invalid response. Select a point on-screen, or enter two coordinates.

Related System Variables

None

Dim: Save

Saves a customized set of dimension variables by name

Syntax

```
Dim: Sav
?/Name for new dimensioning style:
```

Screen Menu

DIM:–next–Save

Pull–Down Menu

Draw–Dim:

Template Coordinates

V 1

Description

AutoCAD enables you to adjust many aspects of a dimension: the style of arrowhead, the color of the extension and dimension lines, and whether tolerance limits or alternate dimensions are applied. AutoCAD saves these in dimension variables. If you have customized the look of dimensions, you can have AutoCAD save the style by name with the Dim:Save subcommand.

To recall a named style, use the Restore subcommand.

Hints

Using the Save subcommand is easier than setting each of the 23 dimension variables individually.

You can save as many dimension styles as you want. Use the Restore subcommand to set a new named style.

Error Messages

None

Related System Variables

DIMSTYLE

Dim: Status

Lists the current settings of all dimension variables

Syntax

Dim: **Sta**

Screen Menu

DIM:–status

Pull–Down Menu

Draw–Dim:

Template Coordinates

W 1

Description

Values displayed for dimensioning variables are expressed in units established with the most recent Units command.

More variables exist than will fit on the screen at one time. Press Enter to see the rest of the list.

Hints

The Dim: Status subcommand is different from the Status command you enter at the command prompt. Dim: Status shows only the current status of all dimensioning variables.

Error Messages

None

Related System Variables

None

Dim: Style

Changes the dimensioning text font

Syntax

```
DIM: Sty
New text style <default>:
```

Screen Menu

DIM:–style

Pull–Down Menu

Options–Dimension Style

Template Coordinate

V 3

Description

Dimension text uses the current text style unless you change it by using the Style subcommand.

Hints

After you use Dim: Style to change dimensioning text style, the style will remain the same until you change it again.

Error Messages

`Invalid text style name.` The name you entered does not conform to naming conventions. Check your typing and try again.

`Existing style.` You entered the name of an existing style.

`New style.` The style name you entered does not refer to a style you established previously.

Related System Variables

TEXTSTYLE

Dim: Tedit

(Short for Text EDIT) Enables you to change the position and angle of text in an associative dimension

Syntax

```
Dim: Ted
Select dimension:
Enter text location (Left/Right/Home/ANgle):
```

Screen Menu

DIM:–TEdit

Pull–Down Menu

Draw–Dim:

Template Coordinates

V 5

Description

The Tedit subcommand enables you to move dimensioning text. The command has five options:

The Left option moves the text to the dimension's left side.

The Right option moves the text to the dimension's right side.

The Home option returns the text to the default (or home—usually centered) position.

The Angle option calls up the `Text angle:` prompt and enables you to rotate the dimension text.

You also can use the pointing device to drag the text into a new location anywhere on the drawing screen. Dragging does not work with the Angle option.

Hints

Tedit enables you to relocate dimension text if AutoCAD's automatic placement puts the text in an awkward location, such as over another line.

Error Messages

`Selected entity is not a dimension.` The object you picked in response to the `Select dimension` prompt is not an associative dimension. Try picking again.

Related System Variables

DIMTIH
DIMTIX

Dim: Trotate

(Short for Text ROTATE) Changes the orientation of text in an associative dimension

Syntax
```
Dim: Tro
Enter new text angle:
Select objects:
```

Screen Menu
DIM:–Trotate

Pull–Down Menu
Draw–Dim:

Template Coordinates
V 6

Description
This subcommand is similar to Tedit's Angle option, except that Trotate lets you change the text angle of more than one dimension at a time.

At the Enter new text angle: prompt, enter the new angle. You can then use all the usual selection techniques to select the group of dimensions whose text you want rotated to the new angle.

Hints
Use Trotate to change the angle of a large group of dimension texts; use Tedit to change the angle of single dimensions.

Error Messages
`Selected entity is not a dimension.` The object you picked in response to the `Select dimension` prompt is not an associative dimension. Try picking again.

Related System Variables:
DIMTIH
DIMTOH

Dim: Undo

Undoes the last dimensioning operation

Syntax

> `Dim:` **Und**

Screen Menu

> None

Pull–Down Menu

> None

Template Coordinates

> None

Description

> This command undoes the previous dimensioning command. By using it repeatedly, you can step back through the entire dimensioning session.

Hints

> To undo the effect of the last dimensioning command, type **Und** at the `Dim:` prompt.

> To cancel the entire dimensioning session, exit dimensioning mode (by typing **Exi** or pressing Ctrl-C), and type **Undo** at the AutoCAD `Command:` prompt.

Error Messages

> `Command has been completely undone.` Any effects of the command you undid have been reversed.

Related System Variables

> None

Dim: Update

Updates associative dimensions to current settings

Syntax

> `Dim:` **Upd**
> `Select objects:`

Screen Menu

> DIM:–next–UPDATE

Pull–Down Menu

Draw–Dim:

Template Coordinates

None

Description

Update causes AutoCAD to change associative dimensions to reflect the current setting of dimension variables, text style, and units. This is done only to the associative dimensions you select.

Hints

Only associative dimensions are updated with this subcommand.

Error Messages

```
Expects a point or Window/Last/Crossing/BOX/Add/
Remove/Multiple/ Previous/Undo/AUto/SIngle.
```
When prompted to select objects, you entered an option keyword AutoCAD does not understand. Try again.

Related System Variables

DIMASO

Dim: Variables

Lists the settings of dimension variables of a specified style

Syntax

```
Dim: Var
Current dimensioning style: Name
?/Enter dimensioning style name or RETURN to select dimensio
Select dimension:
Status of NAME:
```

Screen Menu

DIM:–next–Variables

Pull–Down Menu

Settings–Set Dim Vars...

Template Coordinates

W 2

Description

The Variables subcommand lists the current dimensioning style's variables without allowing you to change the value of any variable.

NAME is the name of the current dimension style.

Hints

None

Error Messages

No style found. You picked a dimension which references no style. Pick another dimension or create a style with the Dim: Save subcommand.

Related System Variables

DIMSTYLE

Dim: Vertical

Dimensions vertical distances

Syntax

```
DIM: Ver
First extension line origin or RETURN to select:
Second extension line origin:
Dimension line location:
Dimension text <default>:
```

Screen Menu

DIM:–LINEAR–vertical

Pull–Down Menu

Draw–Dim:

Template Coordinates

X 5

Description

Vertical is used to generate vertical dimensions, whether or not the object being dimensioned is vertical.

Hints

You can press Enter in response to the `First extension line origin or RETURN to select:` prompt to select an object. The vertical dimension of the selected entity will be used to derive the dimension. Alternatively, in response to the first prompt, you can pick a point to be used as the dimension origin.

Error Messages

`Unknown command. Type ? for list of commands.` You entered the Ver subcommand without first entering the Dim or Dim1 command. Enter a Dim command and then the Ver command.

`Invalid option keyword.` When prompted to select an option, you entered a response that does not correspond to a valid option keyword. Try again, selecting an option indicated in the prompt.

`*Invalid*` When prompted for the first extension-line origin, you entered an invalid response. Select a point on-screen, or enter two or three coordinates.

`*Invalid* Select line, arc, or circle:` When prompted for the first extension-line origin, you entered an invalid response. Select a line, arc, or circle.

`*Invalid* dimension line location:` When prompted for the dimension-line location, you entered an invalid response. Select a point on-screen, or enter two coordinates.

Related System Variables

None

Dist

(Short for DISTance) Calculates the distance between two points

Syntax

```
Command: Dist
First point:
Second point:
```

Screen Menu

INQUIRY–DIST:

Pull–Down Menu

None

Template Coordinates

U 3

Description

Dist returns the angle in the X,Y plane; the angle from the X,Y plane for a line drawn between the two points; and the change in X, Y, and Z values for both points. These values are expressed in current drawing units.

Dist calculates the three-dimensional distance between two points. With three-dimensional points, the current elevation is used if you omit the Z coordinates.

Dist returns the following values: distance, angle on X,Y plane, angle from the X,Y plane, and delta values for X, Y, and Z.

Hints

Once you have used Dist, you can use Setvar to recall the DISTANCE system variable setting.

Use Dist to calculate line lengths.

Error Messages

`Requires numeric distance or two points.` When prompted to insert a point, you entered a nonnumeric character. Check your entry, and try again.

Related System Variables

DISTANCE

Divide

Divides an entity into equal parts

Syntax

```
Command: Divide
Select object to divide:
<Number of segments>/Block:
```

Screen Menu

EDIT–DIVIDE:

Pull–Down Menu

Modify–Divide (to use Divide command)

Pull–Down Menu

Options–Divide Units (to set Divide distance)

Pull–Down Menu

Options–D/M Block Name

Template Coordinates

W 22

Description

If you type the number of segments, point entities will be used to mark the divisions. If you select Block, you will be prompted for the name of the block to use in place of the points.

If you type **B** in response to the `<Number of segments>/Block:` prompt, the following prompts appear:

```
Block name to insert:
Align block with object?
Number of segments:
```

If you answer No to the second prompt, the Block is inserted with a rotation angle of zero.

Possible Responses

Response	Meaning
B	Use specified block as a division marker

Hints

You can use blocks with Divide to evenly space the blocks along a line, arc, or circle. Otherwise, AutoCAD divides the entity with points. Use Pdmode and Pdsize to make the point visible.

Error Messages

`Cannot divide that entity.` When prompted to select an entity, you chose one that cannot be divided. You may select only a line, arc, circle, or polyline. Try again.

`Cannot find block.` You entered the name of a block AutoCAD cannot locate. Check your spelling, and include a library name if necessary.

`Invalid block name.` You did not provide a block name in a valid format. Check your spelling, and try again.

`Yes or No, please.` You entered an invalid character when prompted for a Yes or No response. Try again, using either **Y** or **N**.

`Requires an integer value.` When prompted for the number of segments, you entered a decimal number, a number greater than 32,767, or a nonnumeric character. Check your entry, and try again.

`Value must be between 2 and 32767.` You cannot specify a number of segments outside this range. Try again.

Related System Variables

None

Donut or Doughnut

Inserts a solid-filled or unfilled ring in your drawing

Syntax

```
Command: Donut
Inside diameter <default>:
Outside diameter <default>:
Center of doughnut:
Center of doughnut: Ctrl-C
```

Screen Menu

DRAW–DONUT:

Pull–Down Menu

Draw–Donut (to use Donut command)

Pull–Down Menu

Options–Donut Diameters (to set Donut diameters)

Template Coordinates

Q 10

Description

Inside diameter defines the inside diameter of the doughnut (that is, the doughnut hole). For solid-filled circles, set the inside diameter to zero.

Outside diameter defines the outside diameter for the doughnut.

Center of doughnut: continues the command to allow you to enter as many doughnuts as you need with a single command. If you undo the command, all doughnuts drawn with this command are undone.

To exit the Donut command, press Enter at the Center of doughnut: prompt.

Hints

If you enter an outside diameter smaller than the inside diameter, AutoCAD accepts your input but assigns the values to the logical diameters. This means that the smaller value is assigned to the inside diameter; the outside diameter is always the larger.

You can edit doughnuts with Pedit and other editing commands that work on polylines. The doughnut is drawn as two polyline arcs.

Error Messages

`Value must be positive.` You specified a negative diameter. Try again.

`Requires numeric distance or two points.` You provided nonnumeric input when prompted to enter a diameter. Check your entry, and try again.

`Invalid 2D point.` As a location for the center of a doughnut, you entered an invalid location. Check your entry, and try again.

Related System Variables

None

Dragmode

Toggles visibility of the ghosted image during dragging

Syntax

```
Command: Dragmode
ON/OFF/Auto <default>:
```

Screen Menu

SETTINGS–DRAGMOD:

Pull–Down Menu

None

Template Coordinates

None

Description

The On option permits dragging when appropriate. The Off option disables all dragging. With the Auto option, all commands that support dragging will drag.

When working with complex objects, it may be less time-consuming to turn Dragmode off until you finish.

Possible Responses

Response	Meaning
ON	Turn on dragmode
OFf	Turn off dragmode
A	Use auto mode

Hints

When an entity is dragged, only part of it is redrawn immediately. When you are satisfied with the new location, press the pick button to redraw the whole entity.

Error Messages

`Ambiguous response, please clarify...` When prompted to enter a new setting, you entered the letter O. Since this letter can mean either On or Off, you need to spell out as much of the word as necessary to remove ambiguity.

`Invalid option keyword.` You entered a letter that does not correspond to a valid option keyword. Try again.

Related System Variables

DRAGMODE
DRAG1
DRAG2

Dtext

(Short for Dynamic TEXT) Interactive text insertion

Syntax

```
Command: Dtext
Justify/Style/<Start point>: J
Align/Fit/Center/Middle/Right/TL/TC/TR/ML/MC/MR/BL/
BC/BR:
Height <default>:
Rotation angle <default>:
Text:
```

Screen Menu

DRAW–DTEXT:

Pull–Down Menu

Draw–Dtext (to use Dtext command)

Pull–Down Menu

Options–Dtext Options... (to set Dtext options)

Template Coordinates

W 8
W 9

Description

The Dtext command draws text on the screen as you type it. Dtext lets you edit with the Backspace key.

When using the Align, Center, Fit, Middle, or Right options, you must finish typing your text and press Enter before AutoCAD will adjust the text (see the Text command).

Possible Responses

Response	Meaning
A	Align text between two points
BL	Bottom left
BC	Bottom center
BR	Bottom right
C	Center text horizontally
F	Fit text between two points
J	Specify justification options
M	Center text horizontally and vertically
ML	Middle left
MC	Middle center
MR	Middle right
R	Right-justify text
S	Select text style
TL	Top left
TC	Top center
TR	Top right

Hints

With Dtext, the final Text: prompt is issued repeatedly until you exit the command by pressing Enter.

If you use Dtext with another text alignment, the text appears left-justified first and is then redrawn correctly (that is, realigned) when you exit the command.

Use Dtext when you need to place text in many different locations. At the Text: prompt, pick the new text location with your pointing device.

Error Messages

`Point or option keyword required.` When prompted to specify the start point for the text, you entered a letter that did not correspond to the option keywords displayed. Try again.

`Value must be positive and nonzero.` When prompted to enter the text height, you specified a height that is out of range. Enter a height greater than zero.

`Requires numeric distance or second point.` When prompted to enter the text height, you entered a nonnumeric value. Enter a numeric distance representing the height, or select two on-screen points defining the text height.

`Requires numeric angle or second point.` When asked to enter a rotation angle, you entered a nonnumeric character. Try again.

Related System Variables

TEXTSIZE
TEXTSTYLE

Dview

(Short for Dynamic VIEW) Dynamically defines parallel or perspective views

Syntax

```
Command: Dview
Select objects:
CAmera/TArget/Distance/POints/PAn/Zoom/TWist/CLip/
Hide/Undo/<eXit>:
```

Alias

DV

Screen Menu

DISPLAY–DVIEW:

Pull–Down Menu

Display–Dview

Pull–Down Menu

Display – Dview Options...

Template Coordinates

L 4
M 6

Description

Dview allows you to dynamically change your view of the drawing. You are asked to first create a selection set of objects that are dynamically displayed during the command. After that you see the Dview prompt, at which point you can select how you want to modify your view.

Dview works on the principle of a target (what you are looking at, typically your selection set) and a camera (your eye).

The Camera option (template coordinate L 5) allows you to change the angle, from the X, Y plane and within the X, Y plane, at which you view the selected objects. You can do this by using the on-screen slider bars or by typing the new angle. The camera is rotated around the target.

Target is the opposite of Camera. It allows you to change your target. The target is rotated around the camera when you enter numeric coordinates or use the slider bars.

The Distance command changes the distance between the camera and the target. This option turns on perspective view.

By using the Points command, you can change the location of both camera and target using X, Y, Z coordinates. The target point is specified first; the default target is located in the center of the viewport on the current UCS X, Y plane.

Pan (template coordinate M6) is like standard Pan, only dynamic. You effectively change the location, within your field of vision, of what you are viewing. Do this by specifying a displacement base point and then moving the crosshairs until the view is satisfactory.

The Zoom option (template coordinate M5) allows you to adjust the camera's lens length if perspective is on. If perspective is off, you have a standard zoom center. The default camera length is approximately 50mm long—or what you would see through a normal lens on a 35mm camera. This option is similar to the regular Zoom command but is limited to entering only a zoom factor. You can do this numerically or with the slider bar at the top of the screen.

With Twist you can tilt or twist the view around the line of sight. (This command uses a camera-target setup to define the line of sight.)

Clip allows you to define clipping planes. This is how you define cutaways in your drawing. AutoCAD blanks whatever is in front of the front clipping plane or whatever is behind the back clipping plane. You receive the following prompt:

```
Back/Front/<Off>:
```

Back blocks objects behind the back clipping plane. The following prompt appears:

```
ON/OFF/distance from target <default>:
```

Front blocks objects between you (the camera) and the front clipping plane. The following prompt appears:

```
ON/OFF/Eye/distance from target<default>:
```

If you select Eye, AutoCAD positions the clipping plane at the camera.

Off turns off perspective view; use Distance to turn on perspective.

The Hide option removes hidden lines from the currently selected entities. This is similar to the regular Hide command but affects only the entities in the selection set. Typically, this is used after you set the clipping planes.

With Undo you can undo the last Dview option executed. If you use more than one option, you can step back through the whole command.

Exit ends the Dview command and regenerates the drawing with the modified view.

Possible Responses

Response	Meaning
CA	Select camera angle
CL	Set clipping planes
D	Set distance, turn on perspective
H	Remove hidden lines
OFF	Turn off perspective
PA	Pan drawing
PO	Specify camera and target points
TA	Rotate target point
TW	Twist view
U	Undo
X	Exit
Z	Zoom

Hints

To change the viewing direction, move the camera, the target, or both.

Slider-bar icons appear at the top and side of the screen to help you dynamically change the view.

To see an approximation of your drawing with clipping planes in place, use the Hide option.

F1, which switches between text and graphics screens, will not work while you are using Dview.

Error Messages

`Ambiguous response, please clarify...` When prompted to enter an option keyword, you did not enter enough letters to let AutoCAD know what you wanted. You need to spell out as much of the word as necessary to remove ambiguity.

`Invalid option keyword.` You entered a letter that does not correspond to a valid option keyword. Try again.

`Requires numeric angle or point.` You entered a nonnumeric character when prompted for an angle. Check your entry, and try again.

`Angle must be in range ___ to ___.` You entered an angle outside the valid range for the prompt. Check your entry, and try again.

`Value must be positive and nonzero.` You entered a negative, zero, or nonnumeric response to a prompt that requires positive, nonzero responses. Try again.

`Invalid point.` You entered a point AutoCAD does not understand. Try again.

`Requires numeric angle or point pick.` When working with TWist, you entered a nonnumeric character. Check your entry, and try again.

`Requires numeric distance, point, or option keyword.` When entering a clipping plane, you entered an illegal character. Check your entry, and try again.

Related System Variables

BACKZ
FRONTZ
LENSLENGTH
TARGET
VIEWCTR

VIEWDIR
VIEWMODE
VIEWSIZE
VIEWTWIST
WORLDVIEW

Dxbin

(Short for Drawing eXchange Binary INput) Loads binary drawing exchange files, such as those produced by AutoShade program and the ADI plotter, into the current drawing

Syntax

```
Command: Dxbin
DXB file <default>:
```

Screen Menu

UTILITY–DXF/DXB–DXBIN:

Pull–Down Menu

File–EXCHANGE...–DXB In

Template Coordinates

None

Description

DXB is the extension used to indicate files saved in AutoCAD's binary drawing exchange format. It is used by other Autodesk programs, such as CAD/camera (now discontinued) and AutoShade.

For a more detailed description of this file format, see the AutoCAD Reference Manual.

Hints

Do not type the .DXB extension as part of the file name you specify. AutoCAD assumes this extension and inserts it automatically.

Error Messages

`Can't open file.` The file name you specified cannot be located by AutoCAD. Check the spelling and try again.

Related System Variables

None

Dxfin

(Short for Drawing eXchange Format INput) Loads ASCII or binary drawing files into AutoCAD

Syntax

```
Command: Dxfin
File name <default>:
```

Screen Menu

Utility–DXF/DXB–DXFIN:

Pull–Down Menu

File–EXCHANGE...–DXF In

Template Coordinates

None

Description

DXF files are created by AutoCAD (with the Dxfout command), by third-party applications, and by other CAD packages.

To import a DXF file into AutoCAD, you must begin with an empty drawing. Select `Create new drawing` in the Main Menu and respond with **Filename=**. Once in the Drawing Editor, type **Dxfin** and the name of the file to be loaded.

Hints

Use an empty or new drawing to load an entire DXF file to ensure that any layering, blocks, linetypes, text styles, named views, and coordinate systems are generated correctly. You can import a DXF file into a drawing set up with layers, linetypes, and so on, but you must have used the Entities option with the Dxfout command.

Error Messages

`Can't open file.` AutoCAD cannot locate the file you specified. Check your spelling, and try again.

`*Invalid* An error was discovered while loading a drawing.` The drawing is discarded; no loading takes place. Typically this happens if blocks are referenced in an entities-only or binary DXF file when corresponding blocks are not available in the current drawing.

`Not a new drawing--only ENTITIES section will be input.` You specified a file that was saved with Dxfout for entities only. This message is informational only.

Related System Variables

None

Dxfout

(Short for Drawing eXchange Format OUTput) Writes the current drawing file to a drawing interchange file or a binary file

Syntax

```
Command: Dxfout
File name <default>:
Enter decimal places of accuracy (0 to 16)/
Entities/Binary <default>:
```

Screen Menu

Utility–DXF/DXB–DXFOUT:

Pull–Down Menu

File–EXCHANGE...–DXF Out

Template Coordinates

None

Description

Enter the name of the file to contain the drawing information. The Enter decimal places of accuracy prompt defines the accuracy of the stored information. The greater the number of decimal places you specify, the more memory needed for the file. You can indicate specific Entities to be written, or you can specify a Binary file to export a compact binary (rather than ASCII) description of the drawing.

If you choose to save entities, Dxfout will prompt you to select the entities you want in the DXF file. Then you will again be prompted for numeric accuracy.

Possible Responses

Response	Meaning
E	Select specific entities
B	Specify binary file

Hints

If you specify a file name, omit the .DXF extension; AutoCAD inserts it automatically. Caution: if a file with the same name already exists, it will be overwritten without warning.

If you do not specify a file name, it will default to the name for the current drawing.

Error Messages

`Requires an integer value or an option keyword.` You entered an invalid value or option when asked to enter the number of decimal places. Check your entry, and try again.

Related System Variables

None

Edgesurf

(Short for EDGE-constrained SURFace) Constructs a Coons surface patch, a polygon mesh bounded on four sides

Syntax

```
Command: Edgesurf
Select edge 1:
Select edge 2:
Select edge 3:
Select edge 4:
```

Screen Menu

SURFACES–EDGSURF:

Pull–Down Menu

Draw–Surfaces...

Template Coordinates

O 1

Description

Edgesurf creates a mesh pattern using four edges you specify. Edges can be two-dimensional or three-dimensional lines, arcs, or open polylines and must connect end to end. Closed polylines cannot be used.

After picking the final edge, AutoCAD uses the system variables SURFTAB1 and SURFTAB2 to determine how many divisions are in the M and N directions, respectively. The M direction is determined by the first edge you indicate; the N direction, by the two entities connected to the first edge.

Hints

Select edges by pointing to them. You can select the edges in any order. The first one you select determines the mesh's M direction.

A polyline is a single edge, regardless of the number of vertices.

Error Messages

`Entity not usable to define surface patch.` When prompted to select an edge, you chose an entity that cannot be used as such. Try again.

`Invalid point.` When prompted to select an edge, you entered an invalid point or a nonnumeric character. Check your entry, and try again.

`Edge n does not touch another edge.` AutoCAD is not able to create the desired mesh because the edges you specified do not intersect (or would not intersect if extended). Use different edges.

Related System Variables

SURFTAB1
SURFTAB2

Elev

(Short for ELEVation) Sets the height of the current X,Y construction plane in the Z axis

Syntax

```
Command: Elev
New current elevation <default>:
New current thickness <default>:
```

Screen Menu

SETTINGS–ELEV:

Pull–Down Menu

Options–Entity Creation...

Template Coordinates

None

Description

This command sets the elevation of objects. It may adversely affect the entry of Z coordinates.

Hints

The Elev and Thickness commands make it easy to draw extruded entities.

The X,Y plane can be moved up and down the Z axis (elevation), and subsequently drawn entities can extrude above or below the construction plane (thickness).

Error Messages

Requires numeric distance or two points. When asked to enter a new elevation or thickness, you entered a nonnumeric character. Check your entry, and try again.

Related System Variables

ELEVATION
THICKNESS

Ellipse

Draws ellipses

Syntax

```
Command: Ellipse
<Axis endpoint 1>/Center:
Axis endpoint 2:
<Other axis distance>/Rotation:

or

Command: Ellipse
<Axis endpoint 1>/Center: C
Center of ellipse:
Axis endpoint:
<Other axis distance>/Rotation:
```

Screen Menu

DRAW–ELLIPSE:

Pull–Down Menu

Draw–Ellipse

Template Coordinates

N 10

Description

There are two ways to create ellipses with AutoCAD:

❏ Specify two axis endpoints. To draw the ellipses, AutoCAD uses the major and minor axes. AutoCAD uses the axes distances to set up the ellipse. The default prompts ask you to indicate one axis and then the endpoint for the other axis. After you indicate the first axis, AutoCAD prompts you for the endpoint of the second axis. AutoCAD is looking for a distance to apply to the second axis. If the distance is shorter than half of the first axis, the first axis is the major axis. If the distance is longer, the first axis is the minor axis.

❏ Enter the center of the ellipse. AutoCAD prompts you for a point to define one of the axes and then prompts you for the endpoint of the second axis.

Regardless of the method you use to establish an ellipse, the last prompt line has another selection—Rotation. Using the first axis as the major axis, AutoCAD rotates the ellipse around that axis.

Possible Responses

Response	Meaning
C	Specify center
R	Rotate ellipse around first axis

Hints

The Ellipse command actually draws an ellipse by drawing a polyline of short arc segments. Thus, the ellipse may not be accurate for high-precision work.

Error Messages

`2D point or option keyword required.` When prompted to enter the first axis endpoint, you entered an invalid point or a non-numeric character. Check your entry, and try again.

`Invalid 2D point.` When asked to enter the second axis endpoint, the center of the ellipse, or an axis endpoint after specifying the center of the ellipse, you entered an invalid point or a nonnumeric character. Check your entry, and try again.

`Requires numeric distance, second point, or option keyword.` When prompted for the other axis distance, you entered a nonnumeric character that could not be recognized as a valid option keyword. Check your entry, and try again.

`Value must be positive and nonzero.` When asked to enter the other axis distance, you entered a negative number or a zero. Enter a value greater than zero.

Requires numeric angle or second point. When asked to enter a rotation value, you entered something AutoCAD cannot use, such as a nonnumeric character. Check your entry, and try again.

Invalid You entered values from which AutoCAD cannot make an ellipse. This typically happens when you specify two axis endpoints at the same location. Change your parameters, and try again.

Related System Variables

None

End

Saves your drawing and returns you to the Main Menu

Syntax

Command: **End**

Screen Menu

UTILITY–END

Pull–Down Menu

File–End

Template Coordinates

U 24

Description

End saves your file, exits the Drawing Editor, and returns you to the Main Menu. This is in contrast with Save, which saves your file and leaves you in the Drawing Editor. (See also the Quit command.)

AutoCAD uses a temporary name for the drawing file while the drawing is being edited. When you type **End**, AutoCAD renames the file as you specify. If you specify a name AutoCAD cannot use for some reason, End will try another name, such as DWG.$$$ or 8EF.$AC. Your drawing will be saved, and messages will inform you of the file name.

Hints

Your drawing files will generally be smaller if you use Save and Quit (rather than End) to exit the Drawing Editor.

Error Messages

None

Related System Variables
None

Erase

Removes entities from the drawing

Syntax
```
Command: Erase
Select objects:
```

Alias
E

Screen Menu
EDIT–ERASE:

Pull–Down Menu
Modify–Erase

Template Coordinates
W 16–17

Description
After you create a selection set of objects, AutoCAD erases them from the drawing.

Hints
You can use any selection method to select objects.

To erase the last object drawn, type **L** (for Erase Last) in response to the Select objects: prompt. You can continue pressing **L** to erase previously drawn objects.

Use Oops or U to restore anything you wish you hadn't erased.

Error Messages
```
*Invalid selection*
```

```
Expects a point or Window/Last/Crossing/BOX/Add/
Remove/Multiple/ Previous/Undo/AUto/SIngle.
```
When prompted to select objects, you entered an option keyword AutoCAD does not understand. Try again.

Related System Variables

None

Explode

Separates a block, polyline, hatch pattern, mesh, or associative dimension into its original entities

Syntax

```
Command: Explode
Select block reference, polyline, dimension or mesh:
Exploding this polyline has lost tangent information.
The UNDO command will restore it.
```

Screen Menu

EDIT–EXPLODE:

Pull–Down Menu

None

Template Coordinates

W 20

Description

Select the block, polyline, associative dimension, mesh, or hatch pattern you want to break apart. The selected object will be highlighted on the screen. Once exploded, any color or layer assignments are set to color white and layer 0.

When you need to modify a block, you must explode the block, modify it, and then redefine the block. Each exploded part must be edited separately. You might need to use the Explode command several times on nested blocks.

If you explode a polyline that was previously fit to a curve, the original uncurved polyline is lost, and the exploded version matches the curve-fitted polyline.

Hints

You cannot explode a block inserted with Minsert, a mirrored block, or a block with different X and Y scales.

Error Messages

```
*Invalid selection*
Expects a point or Last.
```
When prompted to select an entity,

you entered a response AutoCAD cannot understand, such as an invalid point or a nonnumeric character. Check your entry, and try again.

`X, Y, and Z scale factors must be equal.` You tried to explode a block that had its scale factors changed when inserted. These blocks cannot be exploded. Select another entity to explode.

Related System Variables

None

Extend

Extends entities to a boundary

Syntax

```
Command: Extend
Select boundary edge(s)...
Select objects:
<Select object to extend>/Undo
```

Screen Menu

EDIT–EXTEND:

Pull–Down Menu

Modify–Extend

Template Coordinates

X 16

Description

The boundary and the entity (or entities) to be extended must be visible on the screen. The first two prompts request the boundaries to which you will extend. When all boundaries have been selected, press Enter. Respond to the second prompt and you will be prompted to select the object to extend. Point to the part of the entity you want to extend.

Entities can be selected as boundaries and as entities to be extended.

The Undo option reverses the extend operation, returning the entity to its previous length.

Hints

Use this command to extend entities to already-established boundaries such as walls, ceilings, or floors.

Error Messages

`*Invalid selection*`
`Expects a point or Window/Last/Crossing/BOX/Add/`
`Remove/Multiple/ Previous/Undo/AUto/SIngle.` When
prompted to select objects, you entered an option keyword AutoCAD
does not understand. Try again.

`Cannot extend a closed polyline.` You selected an invalid
entity as the object to extend. Select again.

`Entity does not intersect an edge.` The entity you selected
to extend, if extended, will not intersect any of the boundary edges
you previously specified. Select a different entity to extend.

`Cannot EXTEND this entity.` You are trying to extend an entity
that cannot be extended, such as a block or text. Select again.

`Entity not parallel with UCS.` You are trying to extend
entities whose extrusion direction is not parallel to the current UCS.
Select again.

`No edge in that direction.` You selected an entity that cannot
extend toward the desired boundary. Select again.

`No edges selected.` After selecting an edge to use as a boundary,
and upon attempting to go to the next prompt, AutoCAD discovered
that none of the entities you selected can really be used as a boundary.
Try the command again, selecting a valid boundary edge.

Related System Variables

None

Files

Allows you to accomplish some disk file-related operations while in
AutoCAD

Syntax

`Command:` **Files**

Screen Menu

UTILITY–FILES:

Pull–Down Menu

None

Template Coordinates

V 24–25

Description

Displays the AutoCAD File Utility Menu, which provides options that let you list, delete, rename, and copy files:

```
0.  Exit File Utility Menu
1.  List drawing files
2.  List user specified files
3.  Delete files
4.  Rename files
5.  Copy file
6.  Unlock file
```

Hints

This menu is the same whether you invoke it with the Files command or from the Main Menu.

Error Messages

None

Related System Variables

ACADPREFIX
DWGNAME
DWGPREFIX
TEMPPREFIX

Fill

Controls the visibility of solid fill in polylines, traces, and solids

Syntax

```
Command: Fill
ON/OFF <default>:
```

Screen Menu

None

Pull–Down Menu

None

Template Coordinates

None

Description

If Fill is on, the objects are filled; if Fill is off, only the outline of the polyline, trace, and solid appear on the screen.

Possible Responses

Response	Meaning
ON	Fills solids and wide polylines
OFF	Outlines solids and wide polylines

Hints

You can save on regeneration and redraw time by turning fill off.

The FILLMODE system variable must be set to On for fills to be drawn during plotting. To save plotting time, you may want to turn FILLMODE off when generating test plots.

Error Messages

`Invalid option keyword.` When asked to clarify your option setting, you entered a letter that does not correspond to a valid option keyword. Try again.

`Ambiguous response, please clarify...` When prompted to enter a new setting, you entered the letter O. Since this can mean either On or Off, you need to spell out as much of the word as necessary to remove ambiguity.

Related System Variables

FILLMODE

Fillet

Rounds the intersection of two entities. It trims or extends the entities and places a fillet of user-specified radius between them.

Syntax

```
Command: Fillet
Polyline/Radius/<Select two objects>:
```

Screen Menu

EDIT–next–FILLET:

Pull–Down Menu

Modify Fillet

Pull–Down Menu

Options–Fillet Radius

Template Coordinates

X 19
X 20

Description

Fillet rounds off two intersecting entities, two entities that would intersect if extended, or each vertex of a polyline. It trims or extends the entities, as required, so that an arc of a defined radius connects the entities.

When you select the Polyline option, AutoCAD prompts for the two-dimensional polyline to fillet. All segments that are long enough will be filleted. When AutoCAD has completed filleting a polyline, you are notified of how many segments were filleted.

The default radius for the fillet arc is zero; filleted entities with this radius have a sharp corner, the same as using Chamfer with chamfer distances of zero.

To change the fillet radius, type **R** at the prompt. AutoCAD prompts for the new radius:

```
Enter fillet radius <default>:
```

After you enter the radius, AutoCAD returns the `Command:` prompt to the screen. The radius you entered remains until you change it.

Possible Responses

Response	Meaning
P	Fillet polyline
R	Set fillet radius

Hints

Fillet works better in plan view than in oblique views.

If the fillet is not drawn, your objects may be spaced too far apart to be joined.

Using Fillet with a radius of zero results in a square corner. A shortcut is to use the "Fillet 0" icon on the AutoCAD template.

Error Messages

`Requires numeric distance or two points.` When specifying the fillet radius, you entered an invalid response. Enter a distance or select two points on-screen that define the distance for the radius.

`Value must be positive.` You attempted to enter a negative fillet radius. Try again, ensuring that your response is zero or greater.

`Fillet requires 2 lines, arcs, or circles.`
`*Invalid*` You did not select two objects to be filleted. Try again.

`*Invalid selection*`
`Expects a point or Window/Last/Crossing/BOX/`
`Polyline/Radius.` You entered an invalid character as an option keyword. Check your entry, and try again.

`Entity selected is not a 2D polyline.` You selected to fillet a polyline but then selected an entity that is not a two-dimensional polyline. Select again.

If you type the Fillet command with a viewing direction that is oblique to the X,Y plane for the current UCS, a message displays to warn that the results may be unpredictable.

Related System Variables
FILLETRAD

Filmroll

Generates an FLM file used for rendering by AutoShade

Syntax
```
Command: Filmroll
Enter filmroll file name <default>:
Creating the filmroll file
Processing face: xx
Filmroll file created
```

Screen Menu
ASHADE–ACTION–FLMROLL:

Pull–Down Menu
Utility–Load AShade...

Pull–Down Menu
File–EXCHANGE...–Filmroll

Template Coordinates
C 9

Description

Filmroll converts the current drawing into an FLM file that can be used with AutoShade. The current drawing file name is the default provided; AutoCAD automatically appends an extension of .FLM to the file name.

Hints

You must convert an AutoCAD drawing into a shade file before using it in AutoShade.

When entering a file name, do not type the .FLM file extension. AutoCAD appends it automatically.

Error Messages

`Invalid file name.` You provided a file name that AutoCAD cannot use. Check your entry, and try again.

Related System Variables

None

'Graphscr

Switches a single-screen AutoCAD system from the text screen to the graphics screen

Syntax

`Command:` **'Graphscr**

Screen Menu

None

Pull–Down Menu

None

Template Coordinates

V 18

Description

You can use Graphscr as a transparent command within another AutoCAD command by preceding it with an apostrophe: **'GRAPHSCR**.

Graphscr causes display of the graphics screen of the Drawing Editor on single-screen systems. On dual-screen systems, Grphscr is ignored.

See also Textscr.

Hints

You can toggle between graphics and text screens by using the F1 function key.

Error Messages

None

Related System Variables

None

Grid

Sets up a rectangular array of reference points within the drawing limits

Syntax

```
Command: Grid
Grid spacing(X) or ON/OFF/Snap/Aspect <default>:
```

Toggle Key

Ctrl-G or F7

Screen Menu

SETTINGS–GRID

Pull–Down Menu

Settings–Drawing Tools...

Pull–Down Menu

Settings–Grid On/Off ⌃O

Template Coordinates

V 20
Y 13

Description

A grid within AutoCAD is used to set up reference points on the screen to aid in drawing. The reference points are not entities.

If you enter a numeric value, this becomes the X- and Y-spacing value for the grid. Using any option except Off results in the grid becoming visible—being turned on. When you enter a value and press Enter, the grid automatically turns on at your setting.

When the grid is set up, you can toggle it on and off. The On option toggles the grid on; the Off option toggles it off. If the grid spacing is set to 0.0, the grid setting equals the snap setting.

Aspect is used to set different X and Y values for the grid. You are prompted separately for the X value and then for the Y value. Remember to respond to both prompts.

Because the points on a grid are not drawing entities, you cannot reference them physically.

Possible Responses

Response	Meaning
ON	Turn on grid
OFF	Turn off grid
S	Default grid to snap setting
A	Change X,Y values
number	Set X,Y values
numberX	Set spacing to multiple of snap spacing

Hints

Since the grid displays only within the drawing limits, you can use this option to show your drawing limits.

Many users find it handy to set their grid values to 10X—10 times the snap value.

Error Messages

`Requires a distance, numberX, or option keyword.` You entered a response AutoCAD does not understand. Try again.

`Ambiguous response, please clarify...` When prompted to enter a new setting, you entered the letter O. Since this can mean either On or Off, you need to spell out as much of the word as necessary to remove ambiguity.

`Requires a distance (or numberX).` When setting the grid aspect, you entered a nonnumeric character. Check your entry, and try again.

`Value must be positive.` When entering a value, you entered a negative number. Grid values must be positive; try again.

`Grid too dense to display` You set the grid spacing too close to view at the current zoom factor. Zoom in, or try again.

Related System Variables

GRIDMODE
GRIDUNIT

Handles

Controls the unique identifiers for entities

Syntax

```
Command: Handles
Handles are disabled.
ON/DESTROY:
Handles are enabled. Next handle: 4A
```

Screen Menu

SETTINGS–HANDLES:

Pull–Down Menu

None

Template Coordinates

None

Description

AutoCAD uses a handle to identify each entity in a drawing. On is the default. A handle is defined for all entities.

The Destroy command destroys all entity handles in the drawing. Because this option is potentially dangerous, AutoCAD switches to the text screen and displays the following special message:

```
* * * * *    W A R N I N G    * * * * *
Completing this command will destroy ALL
database handle information in the drawing.
Once destroyed, links into the drawing from
external database files cannot be made.


If you really want to destroy the database
handle information, please confirm this by
entering 'I AGREE' to proceed or 'NO'
to abort the command.
Proceed with handle destruction <NO>:
```

In order to destroy the handles, you must enter the phrase shown (one of six different phrases—such as GO AHEAD, UNHANDLE THAT DATABASE, and PRETTY PLEASE—appears each time you use this command). All database handles are then removed, and you are informed of this fact.

If you enter **No** (or any other characters), the destruction process is aborted.

4A is the name of the next handle. This value (in hexadecimal notation) will vary, depending on the number of entities in the drawing.

Possible Responses

Response	Meaning
ON	Assign handles to all entities
DESTROY	Discard all entity handles

Hints

Exercise caution when destroying handles.

Error Messages

`Invalid option keyword.` When asked to clarify your option setting, you entered a letter that does not correspond to a valid option keyword. Try again.

Related System Variables

HANDLES

Hatch

Performs hatching

Syntax

```
Command: Hatch
Pattern (? or name/U,style) <default>:
Scale for pattern <default>:
Angle for pattern <default>:
Select objects:
```

Screen Menu

DRAW–HATCH:

Pull–Down Menu

Draw–Hatch

Pull–Down Menu

Options–Hatch Options...

Template Coordinates

None

Description

Type a question mark (?) to display a list of hatch patterns available with AutoCAD.

When you want to change the hatching style, type the name of the pattern followed by a comma and the first letter of the style type: **N** for normal, **O** for outermost, or **I** for ignore. The default style is normal.

The U, style option enables you to describe your own pattern. You are prompted for the angle of the lines, the spacing between lines, and whether you want the area double-hatched:

```
Angle for crosshatch lines <default>:
Spacing between lines <default>:
Double hatch area? <default>:
```

If you are working with a large or small drawing, you will want to change the Scale of the hatch pattern. You may have to experiment to determine which scale is best.

The Angle option enables you to rotate the crosshatch pattern. All hatch patterns are created with reference to the X axis. If you want to hatch a rotated object and you want the pattern to align with the object, enter the rotation angle here.

Possible Responses

Response	Meaning
name	Use hatch pattern name from library file
U	Use simple, user-defined hatch pattern
?	List names of available hatch patterns

name and U can be followed by a comma and a hatch style from the following list:

I   Ignore style
N   Use normal style
O   Hatch outermost portion only
?   List available style types

Hints

Hatch patterns are unnamed blocks that you can scale and rotate as you would other blocks. They require special attention when you are setting up boundaries since Hatch has trouble recognizing the interior boundaries of entities. Consider using Break to create boundaries for hatching.

Use Ctrl-C to stop a pattern fill-in process. Use Undo to undo hatching.

Error Messages

```
Unknown pattern name.
```
Invalid You entered a pattern name AutoCAD cannot locate.
Check your entry, and try again. You can use the ? option to see what
hatch patterns are available.

```
Improper line style. Must be:

 N=Normal (invert in odd areas)
 O=Fill outermost areas
 I=Fill through internal structure
```

Invalid You specified an invalid fill style. You can specify only one
of those shown. Try again.

```
Value must be positive and nonzero.
```
You entered a
negative scale for the hatch pattern. Enter a positive number.

```
Requires numeric value.
```
You entered a nonnumeric response
when prompted for the pattern scale. Check your entry, and try again.

```
Requires numeric angle or two points.
```
You entered a
nonnumeric response when prompted for the pattern rotation angle.
Check your response, and try again.

```
*Invalid*
```

```
You did not select any objects to be hatched.
```
Try the
command again, selecting the objects to be considered in the hatching.

Related System Variables

SNAPBASE
SNAPANG

'Help or '?

Provides on-line documentation

Syntax

```
Command: '?
Command name (Enter for list):
```

Screen Menu

**** – HELP

Pull–Down Menu

Assist–Help!

Template Coordinates

T 5
U 6

Description

If you enter the name of a command, you will receive the documentation for it. If you press Enter, you will receive a listing of all the commands currently available in AutoCAD, as well as some general information. To use Help within a command, the apostrophe ('Help or '?) is required.

When you first enter the Drawing Editor, the Help command is activated whenever you press Enter without typing anything else.

Hints

When Help has displayed all the information it has on your topic, it returns you to the `Command:` prompt.

Error Messages

`No help found for _____.` You entered a command for which AutoCAD can locate no help. Check your entry for spelling, and try again.

Related System Variables

None

Hide

Removes lines that are hidden by three-dimensional surfaces or extruded shapes

Syntax

```
Command: Hide
Regenerating drawing.
Removing hidden lines: nnn
```

Screen Menu

DISPLAY–VPOINT:–HIDE:

Pull–Down Menu

Display–Hide

Template Coordinates

J 1

Description

You can benefit from seeing what your 3-D drawing looks like when lines not normally visible are removed. Hide removes lines from view on the screen without removing them from the drawing database.

Hints

With complex drawings, removing hidden lines can take a very long time.

Error Messages

None

Related System Variables

None

Id

(Short for IDentification) Returns the coordinates of a point

Syntax
```
Command: Id
Point:
```

Screen Menu

INQUIRY–ID:

Pull–Down Menu

Utility–ID Point

Template Coordinates

T 2

Description

This command allows you to determine the exact coordinate of a point. There need not be an entity at the point you select. You can use object snap modes to snap onto parts of entities to define specific points.

When prompted for a point, selected any point desired. You are then shown the three-dimensional coordinates for the point.

Hints

To make it easier to pick a point accurately, you might want to use an Axis ruler or set up a grid with the Grid command.

Error Messages

`Invalid point.` You entered an invalid point specification. Try again.

Related System Variables

LASTPOINT

Igesin

(Short for IGES INput) Loads IGS files in Initial Graphics Exchange Standard (IGES) file format

Syntax

```
Command: Igesin
File name <default>:
```

Screen Menu

UTILITY–IGES–IGESIN

Pull–Down Menu

File–EXCHANGE...–IGES In

Template Coordinates

None

Description

This command allows you to load a drawing that was saved in IGES format. Many CAD systems support this file type to promote cross-sharing of drawing files.

The default file name displayed is the same as the current drawing name. Enter the name of the IGES file to import. If you do not specify a file extension, AutoCAD automatically uses the extension .IGS.

You can use the Igesin command only within a new drawing.

Hints

Drawings imported with Igesin typically require editing.

Igesin can be a time-consuming command. The file loading and translation will take a great deal more time than loading a native AutoCAD drawing.

Error Messages

`IGES input may be done only in a new drawing.`

`*Invalid*` This error message is self-explanatory. Return to the Main Menu (use Quit or End), and start a new drawing. Then try Igesin again.

`Invalid file name.` You have entered a file name that is not valid. File names must conform to DOS standards. Check your entry, and try again.

When a serious error occurs while importing a drawing, input is stopped and an error message reports where the error was found. AutoCAD saves the resulting partial drawing.

Related System Variables

None

Igesout

(Short for IGES OUTput) Converts the current drawing to Initial Graphics Exchange Standard (IGES) format

Syntax

`Command:` **IgesoutT**
`File name <default>:`

Screen Menu

UTILITY–IGES–IGESOUT

Pull–Down Menu

File–EXCHANGE...–IGES Out

Template Coordinates

None

Description

This command is used to save the current drawing in a file format (IGES) that can be used by other CAD packages. For complete compatibility, you must check the specifications for the other software.

The default file name shown (`<default>`) is the same as the current drawing name. You can replace this with any file name you want. There is no need to use an extension; AutoCAD automatically appends an .IGS extension.

Hints

Drawings exported with Igesout lose attribute definitions and solid fills. There are also problems with three-dimensional representation.

Error Messages

`Invalid file name.` You entered a file name that is not valid. File names must conform to DOS standards. Check your entry, and try again.

Related System Variables

None

Insert

Inserts previously defined block

Syntax

```
Command: Insert
Block name (or ?) <default>:
Insertion point:
X scale factor <default> / Corner / XYZ:
Y scale factor (default=X):
Rotation angle <default>:
```

Screen Menu

BLOCKS–INSERT:

Pull–Down Menu

Draw–Insert

Pull–Down Menu

Options–Insert Options...

Template Coordinates

Q 3

Description

At the `Block name (or ?):` prompt, type the name of the block you want to insert. Use the question mark to see a list of the currently defined blocks. This list will not include blocks saved as separate drawing files on disk or within libraries. The default block name is shown only if you have previously inserted blocks within the current editing session.

`Insertion point:` prompts you for the location of the block. This is the point that will be aligned with the insertion base point you defined when you created the block. Notice that when this prompt is visible, a ghosted version of the block can be dragged to various locations on-screen.

At the `X scale factor <default>/Corner/XYZ:` prompt, you can enter a number or a point, or you can press Enter if you want the block inserted at the scale drawn. If you enter a point, you can show AutoCAD the X and Y scales at the same time. The default value for the scale factor is one; this value causes the block to be inserted at the scale used when it was drawn.

At the `Y scale factor (default=X):` prompt, you can enter a Y-scale factor different from the X factor. If you want the X-scale factor to be the same as the Y-scale factor, press Enter. This prompt is not displayed if, at the X-scale factor prompt, you entered a point on-screen.

Negative scale values are acceptable. A negative X value mirrors the block around the Y axis; a negative Y value mirrors the block around the X axis.

With the `Rotation angle <default>:` prompt, the block is rotated around the insertion point at the given angle. If you accept the default angle of zero, the block is inserted at the orientation created. Angle input is applied counterclockwise.

After each of these prompts has been answered, AutoCAD gives you a chance to respond to any attribute prompts attached to the block.

Possible Responses

Response	Meaning
name	Load block file name
name=filename	Create block name from file filename
*name	Retain individual part entities
?	List names of defined blocks
C	Specify corner of scale
XYZ	Readies Insert for X, Y, and Z scales
~	Display Select Drawing File dialogue box

Hints

You can remove blocks you inserted by using Undo or Erase Last command.

If you want to insert another drawing, type the tilde character (~) at the Block name or ? prompt. AutoCAD Release 11 displays a dialogue box that lets you select the file name by picking it.

Error Messages

`Can't open file.` You provided a block name AutoCAD cannot locate. Check your entry, and try again.

`Point or option keyword required.` When asked to pick an insertion point, you failed to do so. Pick a valid point, or use an option keyword to help you pick a point.

`Value must be nonzero.` When asked to specify a scale factor, you entered a zero value. Try again, ensuring that the value is nonzero.

`Requires numeric scale factor, 2D corner point, or option keyword.` When asked to specify an X-scale factor, you entered a response AutoCAD does not understand. Check your entry, and try again.

`Requires numeric angle.` When prompted for the Y-scale factor, you input a nonnumeric character. Check your input, and try again.

`Requires numeric angle or second point.` When prompted for a rotation angle, you entered an invalid angle or point. Check your entry, and try again.

Related System Variables

ATTDIA
ATTREQ
EXPERT
INSBASE

Isoplane

(Short for ISOmetric PLANE) Changes the orientation of the crosshairs when you are working in isometric modes

Syntax

```
Command: Isoplane
Left/Top/Right/<Toggle>:
Current Isometric plane is:
```

Toggle Key

Ctrl-E

Screen Menu

None

Pull–Down Menu

Settings–Drawing Tools...

Template Coordinates

None

Description

The Isoplane command is a toggle; to change among the three settings, press Enter at the prompt. AutoCAD informs you of the current isometric plane.

Possible Responses

Response	Meaning: Plane (grid axes)
L	Left plane (90 and 150 degrees)
R	Right plane (30 and 150 degrees)
T	Top plane (90 and 30 degrees)
Enter	Toggle to next plane

Hints

Isometric planes have grid axes in pairs of 90 and 150 degrees, 30 and 150 degrees, or 90 and 30 degrees. These planes can be changed using the Isoplane command, the Isoplane toggle key, the SNAPISOPAIR system variable, or through AutoLISP.

Error Messages

`Invalid option keyword.` You made an invalid response. Check your entry, and try again.

Related System Variables

SNAPISOPAIR

Layer

Create and modify layers

Syntax

```
Command: Layer
?/Make/Set/New/ON/OFF/Color/Ltype/Freeze/Thaw:
```

Alias

LA

Screen Menu

LAYER:–LAYER:

Pull–Down Menu

Settings–Layer Control...

Template Coordinates

P 4
R 6

Description

Layered drawings are like acetate sheets, stacked or superimposed to compose a single image. Layers help you control the complexity of your drawing; you can freeze layers when a drawing becomes too complex.

The Layer command lets you create new layers, change layers, and make layers visible or invisible.

Each layer has a name, color, and linetype. Each entity is associated with the layer on which it was drawn.

The ? option gives you a listing of layers and their status.

The New option creates new layers. AutoCAD prompts you for the layer names. To enter more than one layer name at a time, type the name followed by a comma and the next name; no spaces are allowed. Do not end your list with a comma.

Set identifies the layer on which you want to draw.

The Make option is a combination of Set and New. When you use Make, you are prompted for the layer you want to be the current layer. AutoCAD searches for the layer name. If the layer name is not found, AutoCAD creates a new layer with that name and sets that layer. Check your spelling with this option carefully; AutoCAD can be unforgiving and will create a new layer if you inadvertently misspell the name of an already existing layer.

The On option turns on layers. When you create a new layer, it defaults to On.

The Off option turns off layers. When layers are off, you cannot see the entities, if any, that exist on those layers.

The Color option allows you to set the layer color. AutoCAD is capable of producing 255 colors. You will not see all 255 colors if your graphics card is not capable of producing that many colors. The following colors are standard and can be referred to by number, name, or abbreviation:

Number	Name	Abbreviation
1	Red	R
2	Yellow	Y
3	Green	G
4	Cyan	C
5	Blue	B
6	Magenta	M
7	White	W

The default color for new layers is white. Setting the color also defines the color of the entities that reside on a given layer.

With Ltype you can set the linetype for the layer. The default is the solid linetype. If you enter a question mark as a linetype, you will see a list of the currently available linetypes. Linetypes cannot be used until they have been loaded with the Linetype command.

The Freeze command freezes layers. This is a timesaving option because when you freeze a layer, AutoCAD ignores the entities on that layer, which reduces the time required for a regeneration.

The Thaw command allows you to access frozen layers. AutoCAD automatically turns on thawed layers.

Possible Responses

Response	Meaning
?	List defined layers
C	Set current layer to a specific color
F	Freeze layers
L	Set current layers to a specific linetype
M	Make a layer (create, if necessary, and set to that layer)
N	Create new layers
OFF	Turn off layers
ON	Turn on layers
S	Set current layer
T	Thaw layers

Hints

When you are naming layers, consider using wild cards. You can perform certain operations on more than one layer at a time by using wild cards when you are prompted for a layer name or by listing more than one layer. Separate layer names with commas and no spaces. (You cannot use wild cards with the Make, Set, or New options.)

Error Messages

`_____` is an invalid layer name. You ended your list of layers (when using New) with a comma. All other layers were created, but AutoCAD was expecting one more name (because of the comma). Thus, you get this message; it is more an informational message than a critical error.

`Cannot find layer _____`. You entered a layer name that is nonexistent in the current drawing. Use the question mark (?) to list the defined layers. Check your entry, and try again.

`Invalid layer name`. When using the Make option, you entered more than one layer name. Check your entry, and try again.

`Layer _____ not found`. You specified a nonexistent layer name in response to a prompt. Try again.

`A color number or standard color name is required`. When prompted for a layer color, you entered a color name AutoCAD does not recognize. Check your entry, and try again.

`Invalid color number`. When prompted for a layer color, you specified a color number AutoCAD cannot recognize. Try again.

`Linetype _____ not found. Use LINETYPE command to load it`. You specified a linetype not currently loaded. Exit the Layer command and use Linetype to load the linetype, or check the spelling of your entry, and try again.

`Ambiguous response, please clarify...` When attempting to enter a new setting, you entered the letter O. Since this can mean either On or Off, you need to spell out as much of the word as necessary to remove any ambiguity.

`Really want layer _____ (the CURRENT) layer) off? <N>` You indicated that you want to turn off the current layer. AutoCAD wants to confirm this. Answer appropriately.

`Yes or No, please`. You entered an invalid character when prompted for a Yes or No response. Try again, using **Y** or **N**.

Related System Variables

CLAYER

Limits

Controls the limits of the grid display and the Zoom All display

Syntax

```
Command: Limits
Reset Model space limits:
ON/OFF/<Lower left corner> <0,0>:
Upper right corner <12,9>:
```

Screen Menu

SETTINGS–LIMITS:

Pull–Down Menu

Utility–Limits

Template Coordinates

None

Description

The limit of your drawing is always rectangular, and the limits are defined by two points that define the rectangle. AutoCAD uses the limits only to determine the extents to draw the grid pattern and the Zoom All view.

The ON option turns on the limits.

The OFF option turns off the limits.

<Lower left corner> is the lower left corner of your drawing area. The default (0,0) is the standard setting for Limits. Press Enter to accept 0,0 as the lower-left corner, or enter a point by either digitizing or typing the X and Y values.

The Upper right corner: option sets the upper right corner of your drawing. Remember that the X (horizontal) value comes first, followed by the Y (vertical) value.

To see the new drawing size, use Zoom All.

Possible Responses

Response	Meaning
ON	Turn on the limits
OFF	Turn off the limits

Hints

Use the Limits command to control the grid extents. Doing so can help make 3-D drawings clearer.

Error Messages

`2D point or option keyword required.` You entered a character at the Limits prompt that AutoCAD cannot recognize. Check your entry, and try again.

`Ambiguous response, please clarify...` You entered the letter O at the Limits prompt. Since this can mean On or Off, you need to spell out as much of the word as necessary to remove ambiguity.

`Invalid 2D point.` When prompted for the upper right corner, you entered an invalid point. Try again.

Related System Variables

LIMCHECK
LIMMIN
LIMMAX

Line

Draws a straight line

Syntax

```
Command: Line
From point:
To point:
To point:
```

Alias

L

Screen Menu

DRAW–LINE:

Pull–Down Menu

Draw–Line

Template Coordinates

J 10

Description

This command lets you draw the most basic of entities in AutoCAD: a line.

`From point:` prompts you for the beginning of the first line segment. You can enter this point by using any of the methods available for entering points. Press Enter to inform AutoCAD that you wish to continue from where you last stopped drawing entities.

`To point:` You are being prompted for the end of the current line segment. The point you enter at this prompt is used as the beginning for the next line segment. If you press Enter without entering a point, you end the Line command.

Type **U** at the To point: prompt to undo the last line segment you drew. If you remain in the Line command while you undo the segment, AutoCAD allows you to pick up the line segments at the previous point entered.

Type **C** at the To point: prompt to close the sequence of lines (draw a line from the end of the last-defined line segment to the point used at the beginning of the Line command). You must have two or more line segments to close the Line command.

Possible Responses

Response	Meaning
Enter	Start at end of previous line or arc (as reply to From point:)
C	Close polygon (as reply to To point:)
U	Undo segment (as reply to To point:)

Hints

You can continue undoing while you are in the Line command if you have not exited by pressing Enter, space bar, or Ctrl-C.

You can continue from the end of the last line by pressing Enter in response to the From point: prompt.

Error Messages

`Invalid point.` You have not specified a valid point when prompted for the starting point of the line.

`No line or arc to continue.` When prompted for a starting point for your line, you pressed Enter. AutoCAD assumes that you want to continue with a line from where you last drew an entity. This message indicates that there was no valid last entity from which to continue. Enter a starting point for your line.

`Point or option keyword required.` At a To point: prompt, you entered a character AutoCAD does not understand. Enter a point, or use the option keywords U or C.

Related System Variables

None

Linetype

Creates, loads, and sets linetypes

Syntax

```
Command: Linetype
?/Create/Load/Set:
```

Screen Menu

SETTINGS–LINETYP:

Pull–Down Menu

Utility–Load LTypes

Template Coordinates

Y 15

Description

Linetype enables you to set the current linetype, define linetypes, get linetypes from libraries, and list linetypes available.

The ? option lists the linetypes available in a linetype file on disk. You will be prompted:

```
File to list <ACAD>:
```

Standard linetypes are stored in the default file, ACAD.LIN. If you supply a different file name, there is no need to use the .LIN extension; AutoCAD appends this automatically.

The Create option enables you to create primitive linetypes.

If a linetype is in a file other than ACAD.LIN, you must use the Load option to load it. You will be prompted:

```
Name of linetype to load:
File to search <ACAD>:
```

The Set option sets the linetype with which you will be working. All the entities you draw from this point will be drawn in the linetype you set. If you draw a block with some entities set to layer default linetypes (some with linetype overrides, and some set to linetype by block), there will be confusion when the block is inserted. Some entities retain the linetype you want; other entities change to the layer default. You are prompted:

```
New entity linetype <CONTINUOUS>:
```

Be careful about changing the entities in your drawing. Use overrides with caution.

Possible Responses

Response	Meaning
?	List available linetypes
C	Create linetype
L	Load linetype
S	Set current entity linetype

Hints

Linetype affects only lines, arcs, circles, and polylines.

The following suboptions are available for the Set option:

name	Entity linetype name to set
BYBLOCK	Entity linetype for the block
BYLAYER	Layer's linetype for entities
?	Lists loaded linetypes

Error Messages

`Invalid option keyword.` You did not use a valid option for the Linetype command. Try again.

`Invalid file name.` You entered an invalid file name when trying to use the ? or Load option. Check your entry, and try again.

`Can't open file.` You entered a file name AutoCAD cannot locate. Check your spelling and make sure that you use the full path of the linetype file; try again.

`Linetype _____ not found.` Use the Load option to load it. When setting the linetype, you specified a linetype not currently loaded. Use the Load option to load the linetype, or check the spelling of your entry, and try again.

Related System Variables

CELTYPE

List

Lists information of selected entities in the drawing

Syntax

```
Command: List
Select objects:
```

Screen Menu

INQUIRY–LIST:

Pull–Down Menu

Utility–List

Template Coordinates

T 4
U 4

Description

This command lists information for all the entities in a drawing. Included are entity type, layer, and location relative to the User Coordinate System. Other information is included selectively, based on the entity type.

Hints

To pause the information displayed on your screen, use Ctrl-S or Pause. Press any other key to start the display again.

To echo information to your printer, use Ctrl-Q before the command is executed.

Error Messages

```
*Invalid selection*
Expects a point or Window/Last/Crossing/BOX/Add/
Remove/Multiple/ Previous/Undo/AUto/SIngle.
```
When prompted to select objects, you entered an option keyword that AutoCAD does not understand. Try again.

Related System Variables

None

Load

Loads compiled shape and font files

Syntax

```
Command: Load
Name of shape file to load (or ?):
```

Screen Menu

None

Pull–Down Menu

None

Template Coordinates

None

Description

This command loads shape or font files for use within AutoCAD. Only shape files that have been successfully compiled at the Main Menu can be loaded.

Possible Responses

Response	Meaning
?	List loaded shape files

Hints

When typing the name of a file to be loaded, do not type the .SHX extension; AutoCAD appends this automatically.

Error Messages

Invalid file name. You entered an invalid file name. Check your entry, and try again.

Can't open file. You entered a file name AutoCAD cannot locate. Check your spelling, and make sure that you use the full path of the linetype file; try again.

Related System Variables

None

Ltscale

(Short for Line Type SCALE) Changes the scale of linetypes in your drawing

Syntax

```
Command: Ltscale
New scale factor <1.0>:
```

Screen Menu

SETTINGS–next–LTSCALE:

Pull–Down Menu

Options–Linetype Scale

Template Coordinates

Y 18

Description

Enter a value greater than zero for the scale; the default for new drawings is one. The higher the value of Ltscale, the larger the dashes and spaces between dots and dashes in your line.

If all the lines you draw look similar regardless of the linetype, try increasing the Ltscale value.

For the new scale to take effect, you must execute the Regen command after you set Ltscale.

Hints

You may have to set the scale a few times to get the correct spacing on your linetypes.

If a polyline has closely spaced vertices, the linetype may never show itself at any scale.

Error Messages

`Requires numeric value.` You entered nonnumeric characters when prompted for the scale factor. Check your entry, and try again.

`Value must be positive and nonzero.` When prompted to enter a scale factor, you specified one that is out of range. Enter a value greater than zero.

Related System Variables

LTSCALE

Measure

Places evenly spaced points or markers at intervals along an entity

Syntax

```
Command: Measure
Select object to measure:
<Segment length>/Block:
```

Screen Menu

EDIT–next–MEASURE:

Pull-Down Menu

Modify–Measure

Pull-Down Menu

Options–Measure Distance

Pull-Down Menu

Options–D/M Block Name

Template Coordinates

X 22

Description

Select the object with which you will work. Type the length, or **B** for Block. The lengths will be measured from the end of the entity nearest the point at which you selected that entity.

If you use the Block option instead of specifying a segment length, the following additional prompts will be displayed after the <Segment length>/Block: prompt:

```
Block name to insert:
Align block with object? <default>:
Segment length:
```

Measure can use only a block that has been created and is already in the drawing.

Possible Responses

Response	Meaning
B	Use specified block as marker

Hints

Measure can be used to mark intervals at which you will later insert blocks.

Circles are always measured counterclockwise.

Error Messages

`Value must be positive and nonzero.` You entered a negative, zero, or nonnumeric response to a prompt that requires positive, nonzero responses. Try again.

`Requires numeric distance, two points, or option keyword.` When entering a segment length or the Block option, you entered an illegal character. Check your entry, and try again.

`Object isn't that long.` You entered a number greater than the length of the object you are measuring. Enter a number equal to or smaller than the object's length in current units.

`Cannot measure that entity.` You selected an entity that AutoCAD cannot measure, such as a single point.

Related System Variables

None

Menu

Allows you to load MNU menu files

Syntax

`Command:` **Menu**
`Menu file name or . for none <default>:`

Screen Menu

UTILITY–MENU:

Pull-Down Menu

None

Template Coordinates

X 24

Description

This command lets you use a menu system that you developed yourself or one developed by a third party. When prompted, enter the name of the new menu. AutoCAD supports side screen, button, tablet, aux, and pull-down menus.

Hints

When you are specifying a menu name, omit the .MNU extension; AutoCAD inserts this automatically.

By entering a dot (.) you disable the menu functions. You can bring back the menu supplied with AutoCAD (called ACAD.MNU) with the Menu command, as well.

Error Messages

`Can't open file.` You entered a menu name not in your menu files, or you have not yet created a menu file.

Related System Variables

MENUNAME
MENUECHO

Minsert

(Short for Multiple INSERTion) Makes multiple insertions of a block

Syntax

```
Command: Minsert
Block name (or ?) <default>:
Insertion point:
X scale factor <default>/Corner/XYZ:
Y scale factor <default = X>:
Rotation angle <default>:
```

Screen Menu

BLOCKS–MINSERT:

Pull-Down Menu

None

Template Coordinates

R 3

Description

Minsert lets you insert an array of blocks. You could think of Minsert as a command combining Insert and Array. However, Minsert creates only rectangular arrays, not polar arrays.

The prompts shown are the standard Insert prompts; see Insert in this command reference for an explanation of the options. A difference with Minsert is that you cannot enter a block name with an asterisk (*) to insert an exploded block.

Following are the prompts for the array part of the Minsert command:

```
Number of rows (---) <default>:
Number of columns (|||) <default>:
```

These are the same prompts as for Array. Type the number of rows and the number of columns; responses can be negative. If the number of rows is greater than one, you will be prompted for the distance between the rows or for a unit cell:

```
Unit cell or distance between rows (---)
```

A unit cell includes the block and the distance between the rows. AutoCAD needs to know the distance from one entity in the first block to the same entity in the second block.

Possible Responses

Response	Meaning
name	Load block file name, and form a rectangular array
name=filename	Create block name from file *filename*, and form a rectangular array
?	List names of defined blocks
C	Specify corner of scale
XYZ	Ready Minsert for X, Y, and Z values
~	Displays Select Drawing File dialogue box

Hints

When you specify a rotation angle in response to the `Rotation angle <default>:` prompt, the array (if any) is rotated as well as the blocks it contains.

If you want to insert a drawing file as a block, type a ~ (tilde) at the `Block name (or ?):` prompt. AutoCAD Release 11 will display a dialogue box that lets you pick the file name.

Error Messages

`*Invalid*` You entered an invalid block name. Check the spelling, and try again.

`Point or option keyword required.` You entered an invalid insertion point. Select an insertion point, or enter coordinates separated by commas.

`Requires numeric scale factor,` 2D corner point, or option keyword. Reenter the X-scale factor, a two-dimensional corner point, or an option keyword indicated in the prompt.

`Required numeric angle or second point.` You made a nonnumeric entry when prompted for a rotation angle. Try again, providing a numeric value or a second point that defines the angle.

`Requires an integer value.` When prompted for the number of rows or columns, you entered a value that is not a whole number, is out of bounds, or is nonnumeric. Enter a whole number less than 32,767.

`Value must be positive and nonzero.` When prompted for the number of rows or columns, you entered a number less than one. Try again, using a whole number less than 32,767.

Related System Variables

None

Mirror

Reflects entities about an axis to make a mirror image

Syntax

```
Command: Mirror
Select objects:
First point of mirror line:
Second point:
Delete old objects? <N>:
```

Screen Menu

EDIT–next–MIRROR:

Pull-Down Menu

Modify–Mirror

Template Coordinates

X 12

Description

Mirror allows you to create duplicates of an entity by use of a mirror line. The new entity is created as a reflection of the original as if a mirror had been placed at the mirror line you specify.

At the prompts, select the objects with which you want to work. Because the mirror line is a line of symmetry in the final object, its placement is important. At the next two prompts, specify the first and second points that will define this line.

You can retain the original entities or delete them with the `Delete old objects? <N>:` prompt. If you answer **Y**, only the mirror image will remain.

Hints

You are not limited to using mirror lines on the horizontal or vertical axis. By experimenting with mirror lines at various angles, you can create interesting effects and perhaps save a great deal of drawing time.

Normally, text is also mirrored. If you change the value of system variable MIRRTEXT to 0, text will not be mirrored.

Error Messages

`Invalid 2D point.` When prompted for the first or second point of the mirror line, you entered a single numeric value (two are needed for a coordinate) or a nonnumeric value. Try again, providing a valid coordinate either through numeric input or by picking an on-screen point.

`Yes or No, please.` You entered an invalid character when prompted for a Yes or No response. Try again, using either **Y** or **N**.

`Expects a point or Window/Last/Crossing/BOX/Add/ Remove/Multiple/Previous/Undo/AUto/SIngle.` When prompted to select objects, you entered an option keyword AutoCAD does not understand. Try again.

Related System Variables

MIRRTEXT

Move

Moves objects to a new location in the drawing

Syntax

```
Command: Move
Select objects:
Base point or displacement:
Second point of displacement:
```

Alias

M

Screen Menu

EDIT–next–MOVE:

Pull-Down Menu

Modify–Move

Template Coordinates

W 15

Description

AutoCAD does not limit you to keeping entities where you first create them. This command enables you to change the location of an entity within a drawing.

The Base point option gives AutoCAD a reference for moving the entities. This is equivalent to the insertion base point for blocks.

The displacement option sets the displacements for the entities. You must enter at least an X and Y value; AutoCAD will accept X, Y, and Z values. The displacement should correspond to the X, Y, and Z displacements for the entities.

No matter how you respond to the previous prompt, you will be given the Second point option. If you entered a displacement, press Enter at this prompt. If you indicated a base point, show AutoCAD where you want the entities by dragging them, or indicate the coordinates for the second point.

Hints

You can move entities by dragging them.

If you are moving a group of entities that comprise a larger object (for example, a series of entities that may collectively define a floor plan), make sure you select all the objects to be moved so that they retain their relationship to each other. This is best done by selecting the objects with a window or by crossing.

Error Messages

`Invalid point.` When prompted for the base point or second point of displacement, your response was invalid. Select a point on-screen, or enter two or three coordinates. For the second point, you can show AutoCAD the coordinates by dragging the entity.

Related System Variables

None

Mslide

(Short for Make SLIDE) Makes an SLD slide file of a drawing

Syntax

```
Command: Mslide
Slide file <default>:
```

Screen Menu

UTILITY–SLIDES–MSLIDE:

Pull-Down Menu

None

Template Coordinates

None

Description

Before you execute the Mslide command, bring the drawing into the Drawing Editor and zoom in on the area you want to be the slide.

You must provide the name of the slide file. The name must be a DOS file name—up to eight characters, with the standard DOS limitations. AutoCAD creates the slide from what is currently displayed on-screen.

Hints

If you want to edit the drawing, do so before using Mslide. Slide files cannot be edited.

The Slidelib program, an AutoCAD utility program, can be used to combine many slide files into a slide library.

Error Messages

```
Invalid file name
```
Invalid The file name you entered does not conform to AutoCAD file-naming conventions, or else it exceeds the number of characters allowed by your operating system. Check your spelling and the number of characters you entered, and try again.

Related System Variables

None

Mspace

(Short for Model SPACE) Switches the Drawing Editor to model space

Syntax
Command: **Mspace**

Alias
MS

Screen Menu
MVIEW–MSPACE:

Pull-Down Menu
Display–Mview–Mspace:

Template Coordinates
Q 8

Description
The Mspace command switches the Drawing Editor from paper space to model space.

Hints
You cannot use the Mspace command if no viewports are active. As a work-around, set the system variable TILEMODE to 1.

Error Messages
None

Related System Variables
TILEMODE

Multiple

Repeats the next command until canceled

Syntax
Command: **Multiple**

Screen Menu
None

Pull-Down Menu

None

Template Coordinates

None

Description

This command is used only with another command. It keeps repeating the command until you press Ctrl-C.

For example, if you insert several blocks, you will use the Insert command often. Type **Multiple Insert** at the `Command:` prompt; AutoCAD will keep repeating Insert until you cancel.

Hints

You can type any AutoCAD command following the Multiple command. Multiple only repeats the command, not any associated parameters. For each repetition of the command, you must respond to the prompts.

Multiple saves one keystroke each time you repeat a command because you do not have to press Enter or the space bar.

Error Messages

Error messages vary, depending on the command you are repeating. For help interpreting these messages, refer to the Error Messages section in this Command Reference for the command you are repeating.

`Unknown command. Type ? for list of commands.` The command you entered is invalid. Check your spelling and retype it, or enter **?** to see a list of valid commands.

Related System Variables

None

Mview

(Short for Make VIEWports) Enables you to create and control viewports in paper space

Syntax

```
Command: Mview
ON/OFF/Hideplot/Fit/2/3/4/Restore/<First Point>:
Other corner:
Regenerating drawing
```

Screen Menu
MVIEW

Screen Menu
DISPLAY–MVIEW

Pull-Down Menu
Display–Mview

Template Coordinates
J 8
P 8

Description

The Mview command creates and controls viewports in paper space.

The Off option turns off a viewport. AutoCAD prompts you to `Select objects:` so that you can turn off one or more viewports at a time. When the viewport is off, it displays nothing except the viewport outline.

The On option turns on a viewport. Select the viewports you want turned on when AutoCAD prompts `Select objects:`.

The Fit option inserts a single viewport that fits the drawing screen. AutoCAD responds `Regenerating drawing.`

The 2 option inserts two viewports in one of three configurations. AutoCAD prompts:

```
Horizontal/<Vertical>:
Fit/<first point>: F
Regenerating drawing.
```

You can have AutoCAD split the screen in half vertically or horizontally (when you use the Fit option), or pick the two corners of the new ports.

The 3 option inserts three viewports in one of six configurations. AutoCAD gives the following prompt:

```
Horizontal/Vertical/Above/Below/Left/<Right>:
Fit/<first point>:
Regenerating drawing.
```

The 4 option inserts four viewports in two configurations. The Fit suboption splits the screen into four equal-sized ports. Or you can pick the corners of four viewports:

```
Fit/<first point>:
Second point:
Regenerating drawing.
```

After you pick two corners, AutoCAD splits the rectangle into four windows of equal size.

With the Restore option you can convert a named viewport saved in model space into the equivalent paper-space viewport configuration. AutoCAD prompts `?/Name of window configuration to insert <default>:` If you respond with **?**, AutoCAD lists the named configurations:

```
Viewport configuration(s) to list <*>: Press Enter
Configuration *ACTIVE:
0.0000,0.0000 1.0000,1.0000
?/Name of window configuration to insert <default>:
```

When you enter the name of a model space viewport, AutoCAD creates an equivalent one in paper space.

Hideplot enables you to select which viewports AutoCAD should perform hidden-line removal on when the view is plotted.

The <First Point>: option lets you pick the two corners of a new viewport anywhere on the screen. After picking the first corner, AutoCAD prompts `Other corner:` and then regenerates the drawing.

Possible Responses

Response	Meaning
ON	Turns on specified viewports
OFF	Turns off viewports
H	Tags viewports for hidden-line removal during plotting
F	Fits a viewport to the current view
2	Creates two viewports
3	Creates three viewports
4	Creates four viewports
R	Translates saved model-space viewport configurations into paper-space viewports
<point>	Creates a custom-sized viewport

Hints

If you edit several viewports, turn them off first. This eliminates the wait that normally would accompany a regeneration of the viewports.

If you turn off all viewports, you cannot use the Mspace command to return to model space. Instead, set the system variable TILEMODE to 1.

The Hideplot option does not do a hidden-line removal until plot time. Use the Hide or Shade command instead.

Error Messages

`Grid too dense to display.` The viewport is small enough that AutoCAD will not display the grid. Turn off the grid, use a larger grid spacing, or make the view larger.

`** Command not allowed unless TILEMODE is OFF **`

The Mview command does not work in model space. Set the system variable TILEMODE to 0 or use the Pspace command to change to paper space.

Related System Variables

MAXACTVP
TILEMODE

Offset

Creates a parallel entity next to the original

Syntax

`Command:` **Offset**
`Offset distance or Through <default>:`

Screen Menu

DRAW–OFFSET:

Screen Menu

EDIT–next–OFFSET:

Pull-Down Menu

Modify–Offset

Pull-Down Menu

Options–Offset Distance

Template Coordinates

W 14

Description

When you type an offset distance, all offsets will be that distance. The following set of prompts appears:

```
Select object to offset:
Side to offset:
```

You select the entity to offset and then specify a point on the side of that entity on which you want to place the offset.

If you select the Through option, you will be prompted for the point through which the new entity will pass. The following prompts appear for each entity:

```
Select object to offset:
Through point:
```

AutoCAD looks for the entity to offset and the point through which the new entity will pass.

A problem occurs with Offset when you try to offset complex curves, such as ellipses and other polylines and arc generations. If you offset to the interior of the curve, AutoCAD, reaching a point at which it is not sure how to draw the next curve, improvises.

Possible Responses

Response	Meaning
number	Specify offset distance
T	Specify point through which offset curve will pass

Hints

You can specify only one entity each time you use the command.

Error Messages

`Entity not parallel with UCS.` The extrusion direction of the entity you select is not parallel to the Z axis of the current User Coordinate System. Select another object to offset, making sure its extrusion direction is parallel to the Z axis of the current UCS.

`Invalid through point.` You tried to offset a line that would draw a new line over the original. Select another through point.

`No parallel at that offset.` You tried to offset a circle or arc and specified an offset that would result in a negative radius. Specify an offset with a positive radius.

`Cannot offset that entity.` You tried to offset an entity other than a line, arc, circle, or two-dimensional polyline. Select a line, arc, circle, or two-dimensional polyline.

`Invalid 2D point.` You entered a nonnumeric character, one
coordinate, or more than two coordinates in response to the `Through`
`Point:` prompt. Select a point on-screen, or enter two coordinates.

Related System Variables

None

Oops

Brings back the last group of entities erased

Syntax

Command: **Oops**

Screen Menu

BLOCKS–BLOCK:–OOPS

Pull-Down Menu

Modify # Oops!

Template Coordinates

W 18

Description

Oops is one of several ways within AutoCAD to undo commands. Oops
is used to undo the effects of Erase. It must be used immediately after
you use Erase.

Hints

You can restore only entities erased with the last Erase command. If
you need to restore something prior to the last Erase command, use
the Undo command.

Oops also reverses the effects of the Block and Wblock commands.

Error Messages

`OOPS *Invalid*` You entered the Oops command before erasing
anything during the current work session.

Related System Variables

None

Ortho

(Short for ORTHOgraphic mode) Restricts drawing and editing to horizontal or vertical movement

Syntax

```
Command: Ortho
ON/OFF <default>:
```

Toggle Keys

Ctrl-O or F8

Screen Menu

None

Pull-Down Menu

Settings–Ortho On/Off ^O

Template Coordinates

V 15

Description

When on, Ortho confines lines to the current snap grid's horizontal and vertical directions; you can draw only at right angles.

Pressing Enter at the prompt toggles Ortho on or off.

Possible Responses

Response	Meaning
ON	Turn on horizontal/vertical constraint
OFF	Turn off horizontal/vertical constraint

Hints

Ortho is useful when your drawing consists mainly of horizontal and vertical lines.

You can toggle ortho mode, even in the middle of another command, by pressing the F8 function key or Ctrl-O.

Error Messages

`Ambiguous response, please clarify...` When prompted to enter the Ortho setting, you entered the letter O. Since this could mean either On or Off, you need to spell out as much of the word as necessary to remove ambiguity.

`Invalid option keyword.` You entered a letter that does not correspond to a valid option keyword. Try again.

Related System Variables

ORTHOMODE

Osnap

(Short for Object SNAP modes) Sets object snap modes

Syntax

Command: **Osnap**
Object snap modes:

Screen Menu

***

Screen Menu

SETTINGS–next–OSNAP:

Pull-Down Menu

Assist

Pull-Down Menu

Assist–Osnap: <mode>

Template Coordinates

T 10
U 10

Description

Object snap modes can be used globally, as with the Osnap command, or individually. If the mode is set globally, the mode will be invoked whenever AutoCAD looks for point information.

To use the modes selectively, type the appropriate mode at the prompt for point information, and press Enter. You will be prompted for the entity with which you want to work.

Nearest (template coordinates: T 18) locates a point nearest the center of the box cursor on the entity and snaps to that point.

Endpoint (template coordinates: T 14) is the closest endpoint of a line or arc or the closest defining point of a solid or three-dimensional face. You can snap to the extruded points of these entities.

Midpoint (template coordinates: T 17) snaps to the midpoint of lines, arcs, polyline segments, and the extruded sides of entities. It can be applied to solids and three-dimensional faces by snapping to the midpoint between the two nearest corners.

Center (template coordinates: T 13) snaps to the center of arcs and circles. When using this object snap mode, you must indicate the entity by digitizing the circumference. AutoCAD locates the center; you indicate the entity with which you want to work.

Node (template coordinates: T 19) locks onto a point entity.

Quadrant (template coordinates: T 21) locks onto the closest point on a circle or arc at 0, 90, 180, or 270 degrees. You can use this mode only with entities in the current UCS or entities whose extrusion direction is parallel to the Z axis of the current UCS.

Intersection (template coordinates: T 16) locks onto an intersection only if it is a true intersection in three-dimensional space. For extruded entities, you can lock onto the intersection of the entity and the extrusion lines. If two entities intersect on a UCS and extrude in the same direction, AutoCAD can locate the intersection of the extruded edges. If there is a difference in the amount of extrusion, the shorter extrusion defines the intersection. Make sure that both entities are in the aperture when you indicate the intersection.

Insert (template coordinates: T 15) locks onto the insertion points of blocks, text, and shapes.

Perpendicular (template coordinates: T 20) locks onto an existing entity in such a way that the new entity is perpendicular to the last point entered on the existing entity. The two entities do not have to intersect. Any extrusion must be parallel to the current UCS Z axis. This mode is used in reference to the last point entered.

Tangent (template coordinates: T 22) locks to a point on an entity tangent to the last point entered. Any extrusion must be parallel to the current UCS Z axis.

None (template coordinates: T 12) cancels any globally set object snap modes. Type **none** at the `Object snap modes:` prompt and press Enter.

Possible Responses

Response	Meaning
CEN	Center of arc or circle
END	Closest endpoint of arc or line
INS	Insertion point of text, block, or shape
INT	Intersection of arc, circle, or line

Response	Meaning
MID	Midpoint of arc or line
NEA	Point nearest crosshairs on entity
NOD	Node (point)
NON	None; cancels Osnap mode
PER	Perpendicular to arc, circle, or line
QUA	Quadrant mode of arc or circle
QUI	Quick mode
TAN	Tangent to arc or circle

Hints

Object snap takes place when you answer a `From point:` or `To point:` prompt by picking a point close to an entity. With object snap, you can snap to a particular part of the entity or to a point having a specific spatial relationship to the entity.

When Osnap is enabled, a target box will appear where the crosshairs intersect.

You can execute any Osnap option by typing the first three letters of the option.

It may be easier to use Osnap through the Tools pull-down menu. Each Osnap option is listed, and you can select the one desired with your pointing device.

Error Messages

`Invalid object snap modes.` When prompted for object snap modes you typed an invalid response. Type one of the following: CEN, END, INS, INT, MID, NEA, NOD, NON, PER, QUA, QUI, TAN.

Related System Variables

OSMODE

'Pan

Allows you to move to a new view of the drawing without changing the zoom factor

Syntax

```
Command: 'Pan
Displacement:
Second point:
```

Alias

P

Screen Menu

DISPLAY–PAN:

Pull-Down Menu

Display–Pan

Template Coordinates

Q 9

Description

Pan needs two points to change the view of the drawing. The first is a reference point; the second point indicates the direction and distance you want to pan.

At the Displacement: prompt, type a displacement with X, Y, Z coordinates, or indicate a point. If you type a displacement, press Enter. If you indicate a point, type another point at the Second point: prompt to show the direction and displacement.

You can use Pan as a transparent command within another AutoCAD command by preceding it with an apostrophe: **'Pan**.

Hints

The other way to pan is with Zoom Dynamic.

Instead of indicating the window each time you want to zoom, you can name and save a window as a named view with the View command.

Error Messages

** Requires a regen, cannot be transparent. You tried to use 'Pan within another AutoCAD command. Since the displacement and second points you entered require a regeneration, the Pan command was ignored.

Requires two points, or a displacement followed by RETURN. Your response to the Displacement: or Second point: prompt was inappropriate. Either select a point on-screen, or enter two or three coordinates or a displacement.

Related System Variables

None

Pedit

(Short for Polyline EDIT) Allows you to edit polylines and polymeshes

Syntax

```
Command: Pedit
Select polyline:
```

If the entity you select is not a polyline or polymesh, you see the next prompt:

```
Entity selected is not a polyline.
Do you want to turn it into one? <Y>:
```

A **Y** response turns the entity into a polyline. If the object you select is a polyline, you see the following prompt:

```
Close/Join/Width/Edit vertex/Fit curve/Spline curve/
Decurve/Undo/eXit <X>:
```

Screen Menu

EDIT–next–PEDIT:

Pull-Down Menu

Modify–PolyEdit

Template Coordinates

W 19

Description

If the entity you select is not a polyline, you can make it one by responding **Y** to the `Do you want to turn it into one? <Y>:` prompt.

If the polyline is not closed, you can close it with the Close option.

If the polyline is closed, the Close option becomes the Open option, and you have the option of opening the polyline. These two options toggle to offer you the choice of opening or closing.

The Join option attaches separate line and arc segments to one another, forming a polyline.

The Width option sets a uniform width for the entire polyline.

When you select the Fit curve option, AutoCAD fits a curve to the polyline. The curves are drawn to tangent points and pass through the vertices.

A Spline curve is a best-fit curve to the polyline. This selection uses the vertices of the polyline as a frame to draw the spline. The more vertices there are, the more the curve will be pulled in that direction.

The Decurve option removes the fit curve or the spline from the polyline.

The Undo option will undo the last Pedit operation you performed. You can use it to step to the beginning of the Pedit editing session.

To keep changes you have made, you must use the eXit option to exit the Pedit command.

The Edit vertex option enables you to edit individual segments by using the vertices. When you enter this selection, an X-marker appears at the start of the polyline. The X indicates which segment you will be working with. When you select Edit vertex, AutoCAD displays the following prompt:

```
Next/Previous/Break/Insert/Move/Regen/Straighten/
Tangent/Width/eXit <default>:
```

The Next option moves the indicator to the next vertex.

The Previous option moves the indicator to the previous vertex.

The Break option removes a segment of the polyline or breaks the polyline into separate entities. You will see a new prompt:

```
Next/Previous/Go/eXit <default>:
```

The Next and Previous options move the indicator. The command will be executed for the segments you cross while at this prompt. The Go option executes the selection, and the Exit option leaves the selection without executing.

With Insert you can insert a new vertex between the current vertex and the next vertex. Move the cursor to the vertex directly before the new vertex, then select Insert.

The Move option moves the current vertex to the specified new location.

The Regen option acts like the other Regen command. After you change a segment's width, use Regen to see your changes.

The Straighten option removes all vertices between two indicated vertices. You are prompted:

```
Next/Previous/Go/eXit <default>:
```

The Tangent option provides the polyline tangent information used in the Fit curve option. You can define the angle to which you want the fitted curves to be tangent. Move to the vertex, and enter the tangent angle; an indicator will appear on your screen.

The Width option enables you to change the width of individual segments. You must do a Regen to see the change in the width. You will be prompted for both a new beginning width and a new ending width.

The Exit option returns you to the Pedit prompt.

After you change the polyline, you can use other editing commands. You can copy, move, erase, array, mirror, rotate, and scale the polyline. If these commands are executed, the spline retains its frame. If you break, trim, or explode the polyline, the frame will be deleted. Offset creates a polyline fit to the spline.

Possible Responses

Response	Meaning
C	Close open polyline
D	Decurve polyline
E	Edit vertex
F	Fit curve to polyline (not in 3-D)
J	Join to polyline (not in 3-D)
O	Open polyline
S	Use vertices as frame for spline curve
U	Undo
W	Set uniform width for polyline (not in 3-D)
X	Exit

Options for vertex editing:

B	Set first vertex for break
G	Go
I	Insert new vertex after current vertex
M	Move current vertex
N	Make next vertex current
P	Make previous vertex current
R	Regenerate
S	Set first vertex for straighten
T	Set tangent direction (not in 3-D)
W	Set new width for following segment (not in 3-D)
X	Exit vertex editing; cancel break or straighten

You can also use Pedit to edit three-dimensional polygon meshes. The command options function in the following ways with a three-dimensional polygon mesh:

D restores (decurves) the original mesh.
E edits the mesh vertexes individually.
M opens or closes the mesh in the M direction.
N opens or closes the mesh in the N direction.
S fits a smooth surface, using the SURFTYPE system variable.

Vertex Editing

D moves down in the M direction to the previous vertex.
L moves left in the N direction to the previous vertex.
M moves the indicated vertex.
R moves right in the N direction to the next vertex.
RE redisplays the mesh.
U moves up in the M direction to the next vertex.

Possible Responses

Response	Meaning
D	Desmooth to restore original mesh
E	Edit vertex
M	Open or close mesh in M direction
N	Open or close mesh in N direction
S	Fit a smooth surface
U	Undo
X	Exit

Options for vertex editing:

D	Move down to previous vertex in M direction
L	Move left to previous vertex in N direction
M	Reposition vertex
N	Move to next vertex
P	Move to previous vertex
R	Move right to next vertex in N direction
RE	Redisplay polygon
U	Move up to next vertex in M direction
X	Exit vertex editing

Hints

Pedit toggles between Open and Close. When the polyline is open the prompt displays Close; when it is closed, the prompt displays Open.

Editing polymesh vertices when the M and N factors are small can be difficult. You may want to Zoom in while editing.

Error Messages

`Expects a point or Window/Last/Crossing/BOX` When prompted to select a polyline, you entered an invalid character. Select a point on-screen, enter coordinates, or use the Window, Crossing, or Box methods of entity selection. You can also use the Last option to select the same entity you last selected.

`Yes or No, please.` When prompted to answer whether you want to turn an entity into a polyline, you typed an invalid character. Type **Y** or **N**.

`You cannot join a 3D Polygon Mesh.`
`0 segments added to polyline.` You tried to join a three-dimensional mesh with another entity. Join only line and arc segments.

`Can't join to a closed polyline.` You tried to join an entity with a closed polyline. Join only line and arc segments.

`Requires numeric distance or two points.` Your response to one of the width prompts was invalid. Try again, providing either a numeric distance or picking two on-screen points that define the width.

`Value must be positive.` You entered a negative value in response to one of the width prompts. A segment cannot have a negative width. Enter a positive value.

`Invalid option keyword.` When asked to select an option, you did not give a response that corresponds with a valid option keyword. Select a response from the options shown in the prompt. Pressing Enter when a response is required displays this message.

`Invalid 2D point.` You entered a nonnumeric character, one coordinate, or more than two coordinates in response to one of the location prompts. Select a point on-screen, or enter two coordinates.

`Requires numeric angle or second point.` You gave a nonnumeric response when prompted for the direction of tangent. Try again, providing a numeric value or a second point to define the tangent direction.

`Command has been completely undone.` You selected the Undo option when there was nothing to undo.

Related System Variables
SPLINETYPE
SURFTYPE

Pface

(Short for PolyFACEs) Draws many-sided meshes

Syntax

```
Command: Pface
Vertex 1:
Face 1, vertex 1:
```

Screen Menu

SURFACES–PFACE:

Pull-Down Menu

None

Template Coordinates

None

Description

The Pface command draws meshes out of many-sided faces, unlike the 3Dmesh command, which is limited to three- and four-sided faces. You can change the visibility, color, and layer of any face by preceding the `Face n, vertex n:` prompt with a negative number or the keywords **COLOR** and **LAYER**.

Possible Responses

Response	Meaning
–1	Make the edge invisible
COLOR	Set the polyface color
LAYER	Set the polyface layer

Hints

Polyfaces are meant for use by AutoLISP and ADS programs and by the AME solids modeling add-on. If you want to draw 3-D objects, use the Draw Objects pull-down menu.

Error Messages

None

Related System Variables

PFACEVMAX

Plan

Displays the plan view of the drawing relative to the current UCS, a specified UCS, or the World Coordinate System

Syntax

```
Command: Plan
<Current USC>/Ucs/World:
```

Screen Menu

DISPLAY–PLAN:

Pull-Down Menu

Display–Plan View (UCS)

Pull-Down Menu

Display–Plan View (World)

Template Coordinates

L 2
K 6

Description

The <Current UCS> option provides the plan view with respect to the current User Coordinate System (UCS).

With the UCS option, AutoCAD prompts you for the name of the previously saved UCS for which you want a plan view. You can enter a question mark (?) for a list of currently defined UCSs.

The World option regenerates the drawing to a plan view of the world coordinates.

Possible Responses

Response	Meaning
C	Display plan view of current UCS
U	Display plan view of specified UCS
W	Display plan view of World Coordinate System

Hints

Plan automatically resets the view point to 0,0,1.

Plan turns off perspective and clipping but does not change the current UCS. Consequently, when you enter or display coordinates after the Plan command, they relate to the current UCS rather than to the Plan viewport.

If you want the plan view displayed regardless of the viewport you select, set the UCSFOLLOW system variable to one.

Error Messages

`Invalid option keyword.` When asked to select an option, you gave a response that does not correspond to a valid option keyword. Press Enter to accept the default, or type **C**, **U**, or **W**.

`Regenerating drawing.` AutoCAD is regenerating your drawing to produce the plan view you requested.

Related System Variables

UCSFOLLOW

Pline

(Short for Poly LINE) Draws straight or curved polylines

Syntax

```
Command: Pline
From point:
Current line-width is (default)
Arc/Close/Halfwidth/Length/Undo/Width/<Endpoint of line>:
```

Alias

PL

Screen Menu

DRAW–PLINE:

Pull-Down Menu

Draw–Polyline

Pull-Down Menu

Options–2D Polyline Width

Template Coordinates

K 10

Description

The Pline command needs a starting point for the segments. Indicate a starting point at the `From point:` prompt.

The default drawing segment is a line. You can indicate the <Endpoint of line>:, or select one of the other options.

The Arc option provides a different prompt:

```
Angle/CEnter/CLose/Direction/Halfwidth/Line/Radius/
Second pt/ Undo/Width/<Endpoint of arc>:
```

You can draw arc segments in any of several ways: the Angle, Center, Direction, Radius, and Second pt options all work as they would for the Arc command; see the Arc command for more information.

The Close option closes the current polyline.

The Halfwidth option allows you to specify half the width of a wide polyline. You are prompted:

```
Starting half-width <default>:
Ending half-width <default>:
```

The Length option enables you to enter the length of the segment. AutoCAD draws the segment in the same direction as the last segment.

The Undo option is used to undo the last part of the Pline command. Undo in Pline reacts the same as Undo in the Line command.

The Width option lets you assign widths to polyline segments.

The Endpoint of line option is the default. AutoCAD looks for the end of the line segment.

Possible Responses

Response	Meaning
H	Set new halfwidth
U	Undo last Pline command
W	Set new line width
Enter	Exit

Options for line mode:

A	Change to arc mode
C	Close with straight segment
L	Enter previous segment length

Options for arc mode:

A	Angle
CE	Center point
CL	Close with arc segment
D	Starting direction
L	Length of chord; switch to line mode R Radius
S	Second point of three-point arc

Hints

You can draw lines and arcs with Pline much the same as with the Line and Arc commands, with four important differences:

- ❏ All the prompts display each time you enter a new polyline vertex.
- ❏ Additional prompts, like Halfwidth and Width, control the width of each segment.
- ❏ You can go back and forth between drawing straight and curved segments.
- ❏ Arcs cannot be forced tangent to previous line.

Error Messages

`2D point or option keyword required.` Type one of the choices indicated in the prompt, or select a two-dimensional point as the endpoint of a line or arc.

`Cannot close until two or more segments drawn.` You tried to close an entity with fewer than two segments. Draw another segment, and try again.

`Invalid point.` You responded inappropriately to the `From Point:` prompt. Select a point on-screen, or enter two or three coordinates.

`Requires numeric distance or second point.` When prompted to enter the halfwidth, length, or width, your response was invalid. Enter either a numeric distance representing the halfwidth, length, or width; select on-screen points; or enter coordinates.

`All segments already undone.` You requested Undo when there were no segments to undo.

Related System Variables

None

Plot

Plots a drawing on a pen plotter

Syntax

```
Command: Plot
What to plot -- Display, Extents, Limits, View, or Window:
```

Screen Menu

PLOT–PLOTTER

Pull-Down Menu
File–Plot

Template Coordinates
W 24

Description

The Display option plots the current display, the part of the drawing displayed on the screen when the command is executed.

The Extents option plots the extents of the drawing. Before you plot extents, it is a good idea to Zoom extents. If any entities lie beyond the drawing limits, they are included in the extents.

The Limits option selects the limits you set up for your drawing. If you are using a title block, use this selection.

The View option plots a defined view. Use this for preliminary drawings in large projects.

The Window option plots an area that you window. You are prompted for two corners of the window.

After you specify what you want plotted, you are prompted with the parameter values (similar to the following) established when you last configured AutoCAD:

```
Plot will NOT be written to a selected file.
Sizes are in Inches
Plot origin is at (0.00,0.00)
Plotting area is xx wide by yy high (MAX size)
Plot is NOT rotated 90 degrees
Pen width is 0.010
Area fill will be adjusted for pen width
Hidden lines will NOT be removed
Plot will be scaled to fit available area
Do you want to change anything? <N>
```

Values in these prompts vary depending on how your AutoCAD is configured. To accept the values, press Enter at the prompt. To alter them, press **Y** and then Enter; AutoCAD will prompt you for changes to the parameter values.

At the Do you want to change anything? prompt you can set the speed of your plotting, pen numbers for layers, and linetypes. Pen numbers determine the colors of the entities. If you want to change any of the pen settings, type **Y** at the prompt. You are prompted for the pen number, linetype, and pen speed for entity color 1. You can respond to these prompts in five ways:

❑ Change the value.

❑ Press Enter to retain the current value.

❑ Type **Cn**, where *n* is the pen number to which you want to change.

❑ Type **S** to show the updated table.

❑ Type **X** to resume the Plot prompts.

Entity Color	Pen No.	Line-type	Pen Speed
1 (red)	1	0	38
2 (yellow)	2	0	38
3 (green)	3	0	38
4 (cyan)	4	0	38
5 (blue)	5	0	38
6 (magenta)	6	0	38
7 (white)	7	0	38
8	8	0	38
9	1	0	38
10	1	0	38
11	1	0	38
12	1	0	38
13	1	0	38
14	1	0	38
15	1	0	38

After you enter any changes for the pens, AutoCAD prompts you for basic plotting specifications.

At the Write the plot to a file? prompt, you can send plots to a file instead of to the plotter. This can save time while you are working; plotting can be done later. You can work in inches or millimeters.

The Size units (Inches or Millimeters): prompt enables you to change the size units.

Plot origin in units With pen plotters, the origin is usually the lower left corner of the paper. This is the home position for the pen. For printer plotters, home is the upper left corner. The plot origin corresponds to the lower left corner of the drawing. AutoCAD allows you to move the plot origin. If you are working with D-size paper, you can plot four A-size drawings on the same paper by moving the plot origin.

With the Enter the Size or Width,Height: prompt, AutoCAD enables you to determine the plotting area with which you want to work. The maximum size for plotting depends on the physical size of your plotter. Plotting size is measured from the plot origin; you can create a margin around the drawing by setting a new plot origin.

The `Rotate plot 0/90/180/270:` prompt enables you to rotate the plot. You can answer with the appropriate angle or you can answer Y or N. If you answer Y, the plot is rotated 270 degrees. This means that the point which would have been in the lower left corner will be in the upper left corner, and all other corners will be rotated accordingly. If you answer N, the plot is not rotated.

If you are using wide polylines and solids, you may want to adjust the pen width with the `Pen width:` prompt. This affects the amount of work necessary to fill these areas.

The `Adjust area fill boundaries for pen width?` prompt adjusts the plotting of wide polylines and solids by half a pen width. This adjustment provides a more accurate plot with wide pens. If you are plotting printed circuit artwork, for example, you will want to change the setting by typing **Y**. If you do not need the additional accuracy, respond **N**.

When you are plotting three-dimensional objects, you can remove the hidden lines by entering **Y** at the `Remove hidden lines?` prompt. (You can do this for two-dimensional plots, but it takes a long time and does not change the way the plot looks.)

With the `Specify scale by entering:` prompt, you can set the scale for the plot. This scale is independent of the drawing scale. You can scale either the drawing or the plot. You see this prompt:

```
Specify scale by entering:
Plotted Inches=Drawing Units or Fit or ? <default>:
```

If you are working with millimeters, the prompt says `Plotted Millimeters` instead.

Hints

You can plot from the Main Menu instead of using the Plot command from within a drawing, but you must specify the name of the drawing to plot.

Ctrl-C aborts the plot at any time, plotting only the contents remaining in the plotter's data buffer.

Plan ahead for your title block and border margins when establishing your plotting size, and be sure to leave room for the plotter to grasp the edges of your paper.

Error Messages

`*Invalid*` You responded inappropriately when prompted for what to plot. Press **D**, **E**, **L**, **V**, or **W**, or press Enter to accept the default.

`View not found *Invalid*` You requested a plot of a non-existent view. Retype the view name, or create a view before trying to plot.

`Invalid window specification.` You responded inappropriately to one of the corner prompts for a Window plot. Select a point on-screen, or enter two or three coordinates.

Related System Variables

None

Point

Inserts a point entity into the drawing

Syntax

```
Command: Point
Point:
```

Screen Menu

DRAW–next–POINT:

Pull-Down Menu

Draw–Point

Pull-Down Menu

Options–Point Size

Pull-Down Menu

Options–Point Type...

Template Coordinates

P 10

Description

Any method of indicating point locations is acceptable: object snap modes, absolute coordinates, or relative coordinates. The point will be drawn using the current color on the current layer. How the point appears is determined by system variables PDMODE and PDSIZE.

Hints

To change the size of points, change the value of the PDSIZE system variable.

To specify how points should be displayed, change the PDMODE system variable.

Error Messages

`Invalid point.` You responded inappropriately to the `Point:` prompt. Select a point on-screen, enter two or three coordinates, or use object snap modes.

Related System Variables

PDMODE
PDSIZE

Polygon

Draws multisided Polygons

Syntax

```
Command: polygon
Number of sides:
Edge/<Center of polygon>:
```

Screen Menu

DRAW–next–POLYGON:

Pull-Down Menu

Draw–Polygon

Pull-Down Menu

Options–Polygon Creation

Template Coordinates

O 10

Description

After specifying the number of sides, press **E** if you want to specify the edge, or else select the center point for the polygon. If you select a center point, you receive this prompt:

```
Inscribed in circle/Circumscribed about circle (I/C):
Radius of circle:
```

Type **I** or **C** and then the radius of the circle.

With the Edge option you are indicating one side of the polygon, not the center point and radius. AutoCAD prompts you as follows:

```
First endpoint of edge:
Second endpoint of edge:
```

AutoCAD is looking for two points to define one side of the polygon.

Possible Responses

Response	Meaning
E	Specify edge of polygon
C	Circumscribe (if specifying center point)
I	Inscribe (if specifying center point)

Hints

Use Polygon to help you draw regular polygons. The maximum number of sides is 1,024.

For both the Circumscribe and Inscribe methods of drawing polygons, you can drag the circle radius. For the Edge method, you can drag the second endpoint.

Error Messages

`Requires an integer value.` When prompted for the number of sides for a polygon, you entered a value that is not a whole number, is out of bounds, or is nonnumeric.   Enter a whole number between 3 and 1,024.

`Value must be positive and nonzero.` When prompted for the number of sides for a polygon, you entered zero or a negative number. Type a positive integer between 3 and 1,024.

`Value must be between 3 and 1024.` When prompted for the number of sides for a polygon, you entered a value outside this range. Type a positive integer between 3 and 1,024.

`2D point or option keyword required.` In response to the `Edge/<Center of polygon>:` prompt, you typed something other than the choices allowed. Type E, or specify a two-dimensional point for the center of the polygon.

`Invalid 2D point.` When prompted for one of the endpoints of the edge, you gave an inappropriate response. Select a point on-screen, or enter two coordinates.

`Invalid option keyword.` When asked to select an option, your response did not correspond with a valid option keyword. Select a response from the options shown in the prompt. Pressing Enter when a response is required will also display this message.

Related System Variables

None

Printer Echo

Sends text from the `Command:` prompt area to the printer

Syntax

`Command:` Ctrl-Q

Toggle Key

Ctrl-Q

Screen Menu

None

Pull-Down Menu

None

Template Coordinates

V 17

Description

You can keep a record of what you type at the `Command:` and `Dim:` prompts by pressing Ctrl-Q. AutoCAD echos its prompts and your responses to the printer.

Hints

Printer echoing works only if a printer is connected to the first parallel port.

This is useful for trying to track down bugs or problems you may be having with AutoCAD or AutoLISP. Unfortunately, it can also use up a lot of paper.

Error Messages

None

Related System Variables

None

Prplot

Plots a drawing on a printer plotter

Syntax

```
Command: Prplot
What to plot -- Display, Extents, Limits, View or
Window :
```

Screen Menu

PLOT–PRPLOT:

Pull-Down Menu

File–Print

Template Coordinates

W 25

Description

The Prplot command sends a copy of the drawing to a printer capable of graphics output. The Prplot command is very similar to the Plot command. For information on the options, refer to the Plot command.

Hints

Use your printer instead of your plotter for preliminary plots.

Error Messages

```
*Invalid*
```
You responded inappropriately when prompted for what to plot. Type **D**, **E**, **L**, **V**, or **W**, or press Enter to accept the default.

```
View not found
*Invalid*
```
You requested a plot of a nonexistent view. Retype the view name, or create a view before trying to plot.

```
Invalid window specification.
```
You responded inappropriately to one of the corner prompts for a Window plot. Select a point on-screen, or enter two or three coordinates.

Related System Variables

None

Pspace

(Short for Paper SPACE) Switches the Drawing Editor to paper space

Syntax

Command: **Pspace**

Alias

PS

Screen Menu

MVIEW–PSPACE:

Pull-Down Menu

Mview–Pspace

Template Coordinates

R 8

Description

The Pspace command switches the Drawing Editor from model space to paper space. If the system variable TILEMODE is 1, the Pspace command turns it off (by setting it to 0) before entering paper space.

Hints

Paper space lets you arrange several views of a drawing on a sheet of paper. This greatly simplifies plotting detail and 3-D drawings.

When in paper space, the status line shows the letter P and a triangle icon in the lower left corner.

Error Messages

Already in Paper space. You used the Pspace command while in paper space. Use the Mspace command to switch back to model space.

Number of active viewports exceeded. If you have more than three active viewports, some will disappear from view when you switch to paper space. Increase the value of the system variable MAXACTVP or use the Mview command to change the active viewports.

Related System Variables

MAXACTVP
TILEMODE

Purge

Cleans the drawing database of unused entities

Syntax

```
Command: Purge
Purge unused Blocks/Dimstyles/LAyers/LTypes/SHapes/
STyles/All:
```

Screen Menu

UTILITY–PURGE:

Pull-Down Menu

None

Template Coordinates

None

Description

Unused blocks, dimension styles, layers, linetypes, shapes, and text styles can be purged. The All option searches the database for all unused named objects and presents them for purging.

You must use the Purge command before making any drawing or editing changes to the database.

Layer 0, the continuous linetype, and the standard text style cannot be purged.

Possible Responses

Response	Meaning
A	Purge all unused named objects
B	Purge unused blocks
D	Purge unused dimension styles
LA	Purge unused layers
LT	Purge unused linetypes
SH	Purge unused shapes
ST	Purge unused text styles

Hints

All entities you create while working on a drawing use space in your drawing database and clutter your storage list of names, even if you never use them in your drawing. Use Purge to weed out unnecessary entities.

It is a good idea to use Purge before making backup diskettes.

Using the Wblock command has the same effect, but can be done at the end of the drawing session.

Error Messages

`The PURGE command cannot be used now.`
`*Invalid*` You issued the Purge command when there were no unused blocks, layers, linetypes, shapes, or styles in your drawing. Purge is unnecessary when there are no unused entities.

`Invalid option keyword.` When asked to select an option, you gave a response that did not correspond with a valid option keyword. Select a response from the options shown in the prompt. If you press Enter when there is no default and a response is required, this message is displayed.

Related System Variables

None

Qtext

Replaces all text with a rectangular outline box

Syntax

`Command: `**`Qtext`**
`ON/OFF <default>:`

Screen Menu

SETTINGS–next–QTEXT:

Pull-Down Menu

None

Template Coordinates

V 10
W 8
W 9

Description

Qtext can save time when you work with large drawings that contain large amounts of text. Qtext replaces text with a box, which regenerates faster than the text.

Possible Responses

Response	Meaning
ON	Turn on quick-text mode
OFF	Turn off quick-text mode

Hints

Qtext does not take effect until the next regeneration of the screen.

Another way to speed regeneration of drawings with large amounts of text is to place the text on a separate layer, and then freeze the layer.

Error Messages

`Ambiguous response, please clarify...` When prompted to enter the Qtext setting, you typed the letter O. Since this could mean either On or Off, you need to spell out as much of the word as necessary to remove ambiguity, or press Enter to accept the default.

`Invalid option keyword.` When prompted to enter the Qtext setting, your response was invalid. Try again.

Related System Variables
QTEXTMODE

Quit

Ends the editing session without saving changes to the drawing

Syntax
```
Command: Quit
Really want to discard all changes to drawing? <N>
```

Screen Menu
UTILITY–QUIT

Pull-Down Menu
File–Quit

Template Coordinates
U 25

Description

This is one of two commands you can use to end a session in the Drawing Editor (the other command is End).

Use Quit if you do not want to save changes to your drawing or if you have already used the Save command.

If you respond **Y** when prompted whether you want to discard drawing changes, AutoCAD returns to the Main Menu with no changes saved to your drawing.

If you type **N** or an invalid response to this prompt, the Quit command is cancelled and the AutoCAD `Command:` prompt is displayed.

Possible Responses

Response	Meaning
Y	Discards all changes made during current work session
N	Cancels Quit command

Hints

The .BAK backup file associated with the drawing is preserved unchanged along with the drawing.

Error Messages

None

Related System Variables

None

Redefine

Allows you to reset an undefined AutoCAD command to its original definition

Syntax

```
Command: Redefine
Command name:
```

Screen Menu

None

Pull-Down Menu

None

Template Coordinates

None

Description

Enter the name of the command that has been the subject of the Undefine command. The command will be reset to its original definition.

Hints

You can use a dot (.) in front of an undefined AutoCAD command to redefine it temporarily.

Error Messages

`Unknown command name.` You tried to redefine an unknown command. Check your spelling, and try again.

Related System Variables

None

Redo

Reverses the actions of the Undo command

Syntax

`Command: ` **Redo**

Screen Menu

****–REDO:

Pull-Down Menu

Utility–Redo

Template Coordinates

U 14

Description

This command is especially helpful when you overshoot the commands you want to undo. For this command to work, it must be used immediately after the U or Undo command.

Hints

When you undo more than you planned to undo, you can continue to use Redo repetitively until you enter another command. At this point the commands previously undone are lost.

When you want to show someone else the sequence of steps you went through, you can use Undo to undo a certain number of steps and then Redo them one at a time.

Error Messages

`Previous command did not undo things.` You entered the Redo command without first entering the Undo command. Undo a command, and then try again.

Related System Variables

None

'Redraw

Redraws visible entities in the current viewport

Syntax

Command: **'Redraw**

Alias

R

Screen Menu

DISPLAY–REDRAW:

Screen Menu

****–REDRAW:

Pull-Down Menu

Display–Redraw

Template Coordinate

L 11
P 11

Description

Redraw refreshes the display of the current viewport, cleaning up the display. It takes less time than a Regen command.

You can use Redraw as a transparent command within another AutoCAD command by preceding it with an apostrophe: **'Redraw**.

This command can be used from the normal AutoCAD prompt or within the dimensioning subsystem. It functions the same way in both contexts.

Hints

Redraw reduces screen clutter by erasing any point selection blips.

Error Messages

None

Related System Variables
None

'Redrawall

Redraws visible entities in all viewports

Syntax
Command: **'Redrawall**

Screen Menu
DISPLAY–REDRALL

Pull-Down Menu
None

Template Coordinates
Q 11
R 11

Description
Redrawall is similar to Redraw, except that it refreshes all viewports.

You can use Redrawall as a transparent command within another AutoCAD command by preceding it with an apostrophe: **'Redrawall**.

Hints
In contrast to the Redraw command, Redrawall does not work as a Dim subcommand. However, you can use Redrawall as a transparent command at the Dim: prompt.

Error Messages
None

Related System Variables
None

Regen

Regenerates the drawing in the current viewport

Syntax
Command: **Regen**
Regenerating drawing.

Screen Menu
  DISPLAY–REGEN:

Pull-Down Menu
  None

Template Coordinates
  J 11

Description
  With a regeneration, AutoCAD searches through the drawing database and recalculates the positions of all thawed entities in the drawing. The larger your drawing, the more time Regen takes.

Hints
  To abort Regen, press Ctrl-C.

  When you change system variables, you may want to use Regen to ensure that the entire drawing is current.

  Regen affects only the current viewport.

Error Messages
  None

Related System Variables
  REGENMODE

Regenall

Regenerates visible entities in all viewports

Syntax
  `Command: `**Regenall**
  `Regenerating drawing.`

Screen Menu
  DISPLAY–REGNALL:

Pull-Down Menu
  None

Template Coordinates
  K 11

Description

Regenall is similar to the Regen command, except that it regenerates all viewports.

Hints

To abort Regenall, press Ctrl-C.

Error Messages

None

Related System Variables

REGENMODE

Regenauto

(Short for REGENeration AUTOmatic) When turned off, warns you that a regeneration is about to occur

Syntax

```
Command: Regenauto

ON/OFF <default>:
```

Screen Menu

DISPLAY–RGNAUTO:

Pull-Down Menu

None

Template Coordinates

None

Description

The On option enables automatic regeneration. AutoCAD proceeds without warning you that it is about to regenerate.

The Off option enables the following warning:

```
About to regen--proceed? <Y>
```

Possible Responses

Response	Meaning
ON	Enables automatic regeneration
OFF	Disables automatic regeneration

Hints

The Regen command overrides Regenauto, forcing a regeneration even when Regenauto is turned off.

Error Messages

`Ambiguous response, please clarify...` When prompted to enter the Regenauto setting, you typed the letter O. Since this could mean either On or Off, spell out as much of the word as necessary to remove ambiguity, or press Enter to accept the default.

`Invalid option keyword.` When prompted to enter the Regenauto setting, you gave an invalid response. Try again.

`Yes or No, please.` When prompted to answer whether you want the regeneration to proceed, you responded incorrectly. Type **Y** or **N**.

Related System Variables

REGENMODE

Rename

Renames entities

Syntax

```
Command: Rename
Block/Dimstyle/LAyer/LType/Style/Ucs/VIew/VPort:
Old name:
New name:
```

Screen Menu

UTILITY–RENAME

Pull-Down Menu

None

Template Coordinates

None

Description

This command lets you rename several entities in an AutoCAD drawing. You can rename blocks, dimension styles, layers, linetypes, text styles, coordinate systems, views, and viewports.

When prompted, enter the type of entity you want to rename. Then enter the current name at the `Old name:` prompt and the new name at the `New name:` prompt.

Possible Responses

Response	Meaning
B	Rename block
D	Rename dimension style
LA	Rename layer
LT	Rename linetype
S	Rename text style
U	Rename UCS
VI	Rename view
VP	Rename viewport

Hints

You can use up to 31 characters in a name, including letters, digits, the dollar sign ($), the hyphen (-), and the underscore (_).

If you type a name in lowercase characters, AutoCAD will automatically convert it to uppercase.

Three things cannot be renamed: continuous linetype, layer 0, and shape entities.

Error Messages

`Old name not found.`
`*Invalid*` The object name you entered is invalid. Valid names may contain up to 31 characters including letters, digits, the dollar sign ($), the hyphen (-), and the underscore (_). To see a list of names for blocks, layers, or linetypes, issue the Block, Layer, or Linetype command and then enter a question mark (?).

Related System Variables

None

'Resume

Continues an interrupted script file

Syntax

`Command: `**'Resume**

Screen Menu

UTILITY–SCRIPT–RESUME:

Pull-Down Menu

None

Template Coordinates

None

Description

You can use Resume as a transparent command within another AutoCAD command by preceding it with an apostrophe: **'Resume**.

Hints

To interrupt a script of AutoCAD commands, press Ctrl-C or Backspace. To resume running the script, use Resume (or 'Resume if you interrupted the script in the middle of a command).

Resume also works to resume running a script file that was stopped when an error was encountered.

Error Messages

None

Related System Variables

None

Revsurf

(Short for REVolved SURFace) Generates a surface of revolution by rotating an outline about an axis

Syntax

```
Command: Revsurf
Select path curve:
Select axis of revolution:
Start angle <default>:
Included angle (+=ccw, -=cw) <default>:
```

Screen Menu

SURFACES–REVSURF:

Pull-Down Menu

Draw–Surfaces...

Template Coordinates

N 2

Description

This command creates a surface by revolving a path curve around an axis. It allows you to select the path curve and the axis of revolution. The path curve can be a line, arc, circle, two-dimensional polyline, or three-dimensional polyline. After specifying the path and axis, you indicate the angle to which you want the surface rotated. If the angle is positive, the surface will be created counterclockwise. If the angle is negative, the surface will be generated clockwise. Surfaces are drawn as polygon meshes.

`Select path curve:` prompts for the outline of the object you are drawing, which can be a line, arc, circle, two-dimensional polyline, or three-dimensional polyline. This is the N direction of the resulting mesh.

`Select axis of revolution:` prompts for the axis around which the path curve is revolved. This axis, which can be a line or an open polyline, is the M direction of the resulting mesh.

`Start angle <default>:` allows you to begin the surface at an offset from the defined path curve.

`Included angle (+=ccw, -=cw) <default>:` specifies how far the entities are rotated around the axis.

Hints

The size of the mesh representing a surface is determined by the system variables SURFTAB1 and SURFTAB2. Large numbers for these variables result in small mesh cells but more processing time.

Error Messages

`Entity not usable as a rotation axis.` The entity you selected for the rotation axis is invalid. Select a line or an open polyline.

`Entity not usable to define surface of revolution.` Your response to the `Select path curve:` prompt was invalid. Select a line, arc, circle, two-dimensional polyline, or three-dimensional polyline to determine the N direction of the mesh.

`Invalid point.` Select a point, or enter two or three coordinates.

`Requires numeric angle or two points.` Your response to one of the angle prompts was invalid. Enter a numeric angle, two points, or press Enter to accept the default.

Related System Variables
  SURFTAB1
  SURFTAB2

Rotate

Rotates objects

Syntax
```
Command: Rotate
Select objects:
Base point:
<Rotation Angle>/Reference:
```

Screen Menu
  EDIT–next–ROTATE:

Pull-Down Menu
  Modify–Rotate

Template Coordinates
  W 13

Description
  `Select objects:` prompts for the point around which the entities
  will rotate.

  `Base point:` prompts for the base point.

  The <Rotation angle> option is the default; it defines the rotation
  angle.

  The Reference option allows you to reference an entity in the drawing
  as the current angle and then tell AutoCAD the new rotation. To do
  this, indicate the ends of the source entity, using object snap modes if
  necessary. Then type the angle to which you want the entities rotated.

Possible Responses

Response	Meaning
R	Rotate to referenced angle

Hints
  Rotate lets you turn an entity at a precise angle rather than guessing
  how much to rotate it.

  Negative angles are rotated counterclockwise; positive angles, clockwise.

Error Messages

`Invalid point.` Your response to the `Base point:` prompt was invalid. Select a point on-screen, or enter two or three coordinates.

`Requires numeric angle second point or option keyword.` Your response to the `<Rotation angle>/Reference:` prompt was invalid. Specify the angle, or type **R**.

`Requires numeric angle or two points.` When prompted for the reference angle, you gave an invalid response. Enter a numeric angle or two points that define the angle, or press Enter to accept the default.

Related System Variables

None

Rscript

(Short for Repeat SCRIPT) Rerun the script file

Syntax

`Command:` **Rscript**

Screen Menu

UTILITY–SCRIPT–RSCRIPT:

Pull-Down Menu

None

Template Coordinates

None

Description

This command is used at the end of a script file to rerun the script.

Hints

If the last command in a script is Rscript, it will loop the script to start over.

Error Messages

`*Invalid*` You entered the Rscript command when there were no script files to rerun.

Related System Variables

None

Rulesurf

(Short for RULEd SURFace) Creates a ruled surface between two curves, lines, arcs, circles, or polylines, or between any one of these and a single point

Syntax

```
Command: Rulesurf
Select first defining curve:
Select second defining curve:
```

Screen Menu

SURFACES–RULSURF:

Pull-Down Menu

Draw–Surfaces...

Template Coordinates

N 1

Description

AutoCAD starts the surface from the endpoint of the entity nearest the point used to select the entity. With circles, the start is zero degrees; with polygons, the start is the first vertex. If one of the boundaries is closed, the other must be closed also.

The word curve in the two defining curve prompts may be misleading because you can also select defining lines or polylines and a defining point in addition to arcs and circles.

Hints

You may inadvertently create twisted meshes with closed entities if you do not pick the nearest endpoints on the entities you want to connect with meshing, or if your zero points are not aligned when you try to connect two circles.

Error Messages

`Invalid point.` In response to one of the curve prompts, you selected an invalid point. Select another point, or select a line, arc, circle, or polyline.

`Two points don't define a surface.` You selected points for both defining curves. Select no more than one point and another entity—a line, arc, circle, or polyline.

```
That's the same entity you picked last time. You
```
selected the same invalid entity twice. Select a line, arc, circle, polyline, or point.

Related System Variables

SURFTAB1

Save

Saves the drawing to a DWG file on disk

Syntax

```
Command: Save
File name <default>:
```

Screen Menu

SAVE:

Pull-Down Menu

File–Save

Template Coordinates

T 24
T 25

Description

To increase execution speed, AutoCAD does as much work in the computer's memory (RAM) as possible. If your power fails or the computer is turned off, any changes made since the last save are lost. Save is used to store to disk all drawing and editing changes made since the last time you saved.

Save stores the current state of the drawing in a DWG drawing file. The existing DWG file is renamed as a BAK file.

Hints

It is a good idea to save your work every 10 to 20 minutes, depending on how much time you can afford to spend reconstructing a drawing if you lose it for some reason.

Error Messages

```
A drawing with this name already exists. Do you
want to replace it?
```
When saving a file, you specified a different

output file name and a drawing with a preexisting file name. Consider your naming choice again, and type **Y** only if you want the current drawing to replace the one whose name you specified; otherwise, type **N**, and save the file under another name.

```
Invalid file name
```
Invalid The file name you entered does not conform to AutoCAD file-naming conventions, or else it exceeds the number of characters allowed by your operating system. Check your spelling and the number of characters you entered, and try again.

Related System Variables
None

Scale

Scales objects

Syntax
```
Command: Scale
Select objects:
Base point:
<Scale Factor>/Reference:
```

Screen Menu
EDIT–next–SCALE:

Pull-Down Menu
Modify–Scale

Template Coordinates
W 12

Description
If you want to detail part of the drawing at a different scale, you can draw the detail at full scale and then use the Scale command to scale it up or down. You need a base point, and you can indicate the scale factor, or reference part of the object.

At the `Select objects:` prompt, select the entities you want scaled.

`Base point:` is the point from which AutoCAD will scale the entities. If the base point is inside or on the object, the entity changes size at its present location. If the base point is outside the object, the object moves from its original location in accordance to the scale factor.

The <Scale factor> option is looking for a relative scale factor. All selected entities are multiplied by this factor. A factor of less than one shrinks the entities, whereas a factor greater than one increases the size of the entities.

The Reference option allows you to reference the length of an entity to indicate the new length. All other entities indicated will change size according to the scale generated by the reference. When you select this option, you will see the following prompts:

```
Reference Length <default>:
New Length:
```

Possible Responses

Response	Meaning
R	Scale to referenced length

Hints

Scale lets you change the size of individual entities already in your drawing. It also lets you change the size of the entire drawing.

Error Messages

`Requires numeric distance, second point, or option keyword.` When prompted to enter the scale factor or select the reference option, you entered a nonnumeric value other than the R option keyword (for `Reference`). Enter a scale factor, or type **R** to select the reference option.

`Invalid point.` Your response to the `Base point:` prompt is invalid. Select a point on-screen, or enter two or three coordinates.

`Value must be positive and nonzero.` When prompted for the reference length or new length, you entered zero or a negative number. Enter a positive number.

`Requires numeric distance or second point.` When prompted for the reference length or new length, you entered something other than a numeric distance or second point. Enter a number, or select two points to indicate the length.

Related System Variables

None

Script

Runs an SCR script file from within the Drawing Editor

Syntax

```
Command: Script
Script file <default>:
```

Screen Menu

UTILITY–SCRIPT–SCRIPT:

Pull-Down Menu

None

Template Coordinate

None

Hints

You can write script files with AutoCAD or AutoLISP commands, input, and responses. You run the script with the Script command.

Script files, recognizable by their .SCR extensions, are often useful for demonstrations and presentations. Use the Delay command if you need to slow down the script file. This may be needed so that viewers have time to observe the sequence of commands, input, and responses.

Error Messages

```
Can't open file
```
Invalid You entered a script file name for which no script file exists. Check your file name, and try again. If you have not yet created a script file, do so before using this command.

```
Invalid file name
```
Invalid The file name you entered does not conform to AutoCAD file-naming conventions or exceeds the number of characters allowed by your operating system. Check your spelling and the number of characters you entered, and try again.

Related System Variables

None

Select

Creates a selection set for use in subsequent commands

Syntax

```
Command: Select
Select objects:
```

Screen Menu

EDIT–next–SELECT:

Pull-Down Menu

None

Template Coordinates

None

Description

Select is an alternate way of creating a selection set that can be used by AutoCAD commands.

You specify the predefined selection set with another command by entering **P** when prompted to select objects.

Hints

It is generally safer to build your selection set as you are executing an AutoCAD command. This is because Select allows you to add any entity to the selection set, even those that are not legal for the command with which you subsequently use the selection set.

Error Messages

None

Related System Variables

None

'Setvar

(Short for SET system VARiable) Allows you access to system variables

Syntax

```
Command: 'Setvar
Variable name or ? <default>:
```

Screen Menu

****–SETVAR:

Pull-Down Menu

Settings–Set SysVars...

Template Coordinates

U 1

Description

Setvar lets you read the values of system variables and change many of them. In response to the `Variable name or ?:` prompt, enter the name of the variable you want to view or change. Then enter the new value (if any).

You can use Setvar as a transparent command within another AutoCAD command by preceding it with an apostrophe: **'Setvar**.

Hints

In response to the `Variable name or ?:` prompt, you can type **?** to list variable names available.

Many AutoCAD commands set system variables automatically.

In Release 11, you no longer need to use the Setvar command. You can access system variables by typing their name at the `Command:` prompt.

Error Messages

`(read only)`. You tried to use Setvar to change the value of a read-only system variable. A read-only variable is one that only AutoCAD can change.

`Unknown variable name: Type SETVAR ? for a list of variables.` You entered an invalid variable name. Check the spelling, and retype your entry, or type **?** to see the list of variables.

Related System Variables

All system variables

Sh

(Short for SHell) Allows you to execute a single command in the operating system

Syntax

```
Command: Sh
OS Command:
```

Screen Menu

UTILITY–External Commands–SH:

Pull-Down Menu

None

Template Coordinates
Y 24
Y 25

Description
The Sh command allows you to execute a single command at the system level. It then automatically returns you to AutoCAD, displaying AutoCAD's `Command:` prompt.

Hints
When you are running the Sh command, it may not free up enough memory to run the operating system command or external program. In this case, try the Shell command.

Error Messages
`Bad command or file name` You entered an invalid command at the `OS Command:` prompt. Enter a valid command.

Related System Variables
None

Shade

Does a quick rendering of 3-D objects

Syntax
```
Command: Shade
Regenerating drawing.
Shading 90% done.
Shading complete.
```

Screen Menu
DISPLAY–SHADE:

Pull-Down Menu
Display–Shade:

Pull-Down Menu
Settings–Shade Style...

Template Coordinates
J 1 Quick Hide
J 3 Quick Shade

Description

The Shade command does a quick rendering or hidden-line view of 3-D objects. Autodesk guarantees that Shade takes only twice as long as a regeneration would.

The shaded look is governed by two system variables: SHADEDGE and SHADEDIF. SHADEDGE determines one of four rendering styles:

- ❏ 0: simulates AutoShade-style rendering
- ❏ 1: rendering with outlined faces
- ❏ 2: simulates hidden-line removal
- ❏ 3: flat shading with outlined faces (the default)

SHADEDIF changes the contrast of renderings produced by SHADEDGE 0 and 1. Values closer to 0 reduce contrast; those closer to 100 increase the contrast (and make the rendering look better). The default is 70.

Hints

Shade does its work in the current viewport.

Doing hidden-line removal with SHADEDGE set to 2 is far faster than using the Hide command.

System variable SHADEDGE values 0 and 1 require a graphics board capable of displaying 256 colors.

If you display a slide of a shaded image in a small viewport, some of the detail may be lost.

Error Messages

None

Related System Variables

SHADEDGE
SHADEDIF

Shape

Inserts shapes into a drawing

Syntax

```
Command: Shape
Shape name (or ?):
Starting point:
Height <default>:
Rotation angle <default>:
```

Screen Menu

DRAW–next–SHAPE:

Pull-Down Menu

None

Template Coordinates

None

Description

You must use the Load command to load SHX shape files before you can use the shapes. You can use the question mark (?) to list the shapes already loaded.

The Starting point: prompt is looking for a location at which to insert the shape. This point corresponds to the first vector in the shape definition.

The Height <default> option is used to scale the shape.

With the Rotation angle <default> option a shape can be rotated at a given angle.

Possible Responses

Response	Meaning
?	List shape names

Hints

Shape works only with previously defined shapes you load into the drawing.

Shapes are symbols much like blocks, but shapes display more quickly.

Error Messages

Shape (name) not found. You tried to load a shape name that is not found. The Shape name (or ?): prompt is displayed again so that you can enter a valid shape name.

No default established yet. You pressed Enter at the Shape name (or ?): prompt without first entering a shape name. The shape name you enter here will become the default until you enter another shape name.

Not a valid shape/font file. You tried to load a file that is not a valid shape file. Edit the shape file so that it is valid, and try loading again, or load another valid shape file.

Related System Variables

None

Shell

Allows access to the operating system from inside the Drawing Editor

Syntax

    Command: **Shell**
    OS command:

Screen Menu

UTILITY–External CCommands–SHELL:

Pull-Down Menu

None

Template Coordinates

None

Description

At the OS Command: prompt, you can execute one operating system command, after which AutoCAD will automatically return to the Drawing Editor.

If you press Enter at the OS Command: prompt, you remain in the operating system. Return to AutoCAD by typing **Exit** at the OS prompt.

Hints

Do not try to reexecute AutoCAD while using this command. You can permanently corrupt your AutoCAD files by doing this. You are already in AutoCAD; you have temporarily shelled out to the operating system.

The Shell command may not be available with some operating systems.

Shell can execute utility programs while you are in the Drawing Editor, providing access to all normal operating system commands.

Be sure not to delete any of AutoCAD's temporary files, recognizable by their $AC or $A file type extensions. And do not use the DOS and OS/2 CHKDSK command (which will erase hidden files AutoCAD needs).

Error Messages

Bad command or file name. You entered an invalid command at the OS Command: prompt. Enter a valid command.

Related System Variables

None

Sketch

Allows freehand drawing

Syntax

```
Command: Sketch
Record increment <default>:
Sketch. Pen eXit Quit Record Erase Connect.
```

Screen Menu

DRAW–next–SKETCH:

Pull-Down Menu

None

Template Coordinates

None

Description

Sketch lets you draw as you would on a piece of paper. Use only the Continuous linetype for sketching.

In sketch mode, AutoCAD ignores all input except Sketch options and toggle commands, like Snap and Ortho.

To select an option while you are in Sketch mode, all you need to do is type the capitalized letter. You do not need to press Enter.

The Record increment <default> option helps AutoCAD sketch with line or polyline segments. Record increment is the length of these segments. Both snap mode and ortho affect the way segments are drawn.

The Pen option alternately raises or lowers the pen. If the pen is up, you can move the cursor on the screen without drawing. When the pen is down, AutoCAD accepts cursor movement as the drawing.

The Exit option records the segments permanently and ends Sketch mode.

The Quit option ends Sketch mode without saving any of the work.

The Record option saves the segments without exiting.

The Erase option erases segments as you backtrack through the drawing.

The Connect option connects new segments to existing segments. Make sure that the pen is up, position the cursor next to an existing segment, and then type **C**.

The . (period) option draws a straight line from the last point to the current pen position.

Sketch is not an option. It indicates that you are working in Sketch mode.

Possible Responses

Response	Meaning
C	Connect new segments to existing segments
E	Erase
P	Raise or lower pen
Q	Quit sketch mode without saving
R	Save (record) without exiting
X	Save and exit
.	Draws a straight line from the last point to the current position

Hints

Because freehand drawing generates a large number of lines, it should be used only when AutoCAD's normal data entry is ineffective—for instance with signatures, maps, and other highly irregular shapes.

Error Messages

Requires numeric distance or two points. When specifying the record increment, you gave an invalid response. Try again, entering a numeric distance for the increment or a point. If you select a point, you will be prompted for a second point.

Nothing recorded. You did not sketch anything before recording, or you entered an invalid response to the Sketch. Pen eXit Quit Record Erase Connect. prompt.

n lines recorded. <Pen current> The number of lines you sketched is indicated here. Your response to the Record increment <default>: prompt determines the line length.

Related System Variables
SKETCHINC
SKPOLY

Snap

Sets the drawing increment

Syntax

```
Command: Snap
Snap spacing or ON/OFF/Aspect/Rotate/Style <default>:
```

Toggle Key

Ctrl-B or F9

Screen Menu

SETTINGS–next–SNAP:

Pull-Down Menu

Settings–Drawing Tools...

Pull-Down Menu

Settings–Snap On/Off ^B

Template Coordinates

V 21
Y 12

Description

You can toggle Snap mode on and off inside commands (with Ctrl-B or function key F9) as you are working. You can toggle Snap mode on and start to draw, then toggle Snap mode off while still in the command.

Snap and Grid mode can be compared to using graph paper in your drawings. You can choose to stay on the graph lines or draw between the lines. Staying on the graph lines is like turning snap and grid on; straying off the lines is like turning the modes off.

The snap distance determines the shortest distance AutoCAD will recognize when you move your pointer. Pick points will be limited to the nearest snap point. When you want to pick a point between snap points, use Ctrl-B or F9 to toggle out of Snap mode.

Snap mode has no effect in perspective views.

Like the Grid command, you can set different snap spacings for the X and Y axes. Values may be as large or as small as needed in the drawing. The Aspect option sets the X and Y spacings to different values. AutoCAD prompts you first for the X value and then for the Y value. This option is not available if style is set to isometric.

If you need to draw at an angle other than horizontal, you can rotate the grid and snap to accommodate. The Rotate option affects the visible grid and the invisible snap settings. You are prompted for a base point, around which the grid will be rotated. If you want to align the point with an entity, indicate the entity for the rotation angle. Otherwise, it is a good idea to leave the base point at 0,0.

The Style option enables you to choose between standard drawing mode (the default) or isometric mode. An isometric grid contains angles that are multiples of 60 degrees, in contrast with the normal 90-degree grid for standard drawing mode.

Possible Responses

Response	Meaning
number	Set alignment
ON	Turn on Snap mode
OFF	Turn off Snap mode
A	Change X,Y spacing
R	Rotate snap grid
S	Select standard or isometric style

Hints

The snap setting remains the same when you zoom in or out of the drawing. You may need to change the snap setting when you have zoomed in.

Changes in the snap setting do not affect entities already in the drawing, only the entities or processes that will happen after the snap is set.

Error Messages

`Ambiguous response, please clarify...` When prompted to enter the snap spacing or other options, you typed the letter O. Since this could mean either On or Off, you need to spell out as much of the word as necessary to remove ambiguity, or select one of the other options indicated in the prompt.

`Requires numeric distance, two points, or option keyword.` When prompted for snap spacing, you entered an illegal character. Check your entry, and try again.

`Invalid option keyword.` When prompted to enter snap spacing or another option, your response was invalid. Try again, either indicating spacing or selecting a keyword from the prompt.

`Invalid 2D point.` When prompted for a base point, you entered something invalid. Select a point on-screen, or enter two coordinates.

Requires numeric angle or second point. You responded
with a nonnumeric response when prompted for a rotation angle. Try
again, providing either a numeric value or a second point that defines
the angle.

Related System Variables
SNAPANG
SNAPBASE
SNAPISOPAIR
SNAPMODE
SNAPSTYL
SNAPUNIT

Solid

Draws solid triangular and rectilinear areas

Syntax
```
Command: Solid
First point:
Second point:
Third point:
Fourth point:
Third point:
Fourth point:
```

Screen Menu
DRAW–next–SOLID:

Pull-Down Menu
None

Template Coordinates
None

Description
To draw a solid-filled area, you indicate the corners of the area. You
begin by indicating three or four corners, and continue by indicating
one or two additional corners.

To obtain a rectilinear solid, the points must be selected so that the
first and third points lie on the same edge. If you indicate the points in
a clockwise or counterclockwise direction, you will get a bow-tie
shape.

If you are drawing only a four-point solid, press Enter when prompted the second time for the `Third point:`. If you are drawing a three-point solid, press Enter at the `Fourth point:` prompt. You will still be prompted for the continuation of the command. If you use the continuation, the solids will be connected.

Hints

To terminate the command, press Enter twice.

If you want the figures unfilled, turn off Fill mode. You can fill it by subsequently turning on Fill mode and then using the Regen command. Filled solids increase regeneration time.

Error Messages

`Invalid point.` Your response to one of the point prompts was invalid. Select a point on-screen, or enter two or three coordinates for each point.

Related System Variables

FILLMODE

Status

Displays the status of the current drawing

Syntax

`Command:` **Status**

Screen Menu

INQUIRY–STATUS:

Pull-Down Menu

Utility–Status

Template Coordinates

T 3

Description

Status lists the status of toggles, the drawing extents and limits, the number of entities, insertion base point, snap resolution, grid spacing, disk space, virtual memory, and I/O page space. It also shows current layer, color, linetype, elevation, and the on or off status for axis, fill, grid, ortho, quick text, snap, and the tablet.

Hints

Values displayed by the Status command are expressed in units established with the most recent use of the Units command.

Error Messages

None

Related System Variables

None

Stretch

Changes the length of objects

Syntax

```
Command: Stretch
Select objects to stretch by window...
Select objects:
Base point:
New point:
```

Screen Menu

EDIT–next–STRETCH:

Pull-Down Menu

Modify–Stretch

Template Coordinates

X 17

Description

With Stretch, you can stretch entities to make them smaller or larger or you can realign those entities any way you want.

The first selection must be made by a window or crossing. If you select with a window, you will select all objects contained entirely in the selection box. With crossing, you will select all objects inside or crossing the selection box.

Subsequent selections may be made by pointing. A second window or crossing selection negates the first window or crossing selection.

The Base point: is a reference point for the stretch.

The New point: is the point to which you want the base point moved.

Hints

You can't stretch text, although you can move it with the Stretch command.

Error Messages

`You must select a window to stretch.` You tried to stretch an entity without using a window or crossing when making your selection.

`Invalid window specification.` When using a window to select objects, your selection was invalid. Try again.

`Invalid point.` Your response to one of the point prompts was invalid. Select a point on-screen, or enter two or three coordinates for each point.

`0 found.` No objects were found within the window or crossing you specified. Try again.

`Expects a point or Window/Last/Crossing/BOX/Add/ Remove/Multiple/ Previous/Undo/AUto/SIngle.` When prompted to select objects, you entered an option keyword AutoCAD does not understand. Try again.

Related System Variables

None

Style

Loads a text font into the drawing

Syntax

```
Command: Style
Text style name (or ?) <default>:
New style.
Font file <default>:
Height <default>:
Width factor <default>:
Obliquing angle <default>:
Backwards? <default>:
Upside-down? <default>:
Vertical? <default>:
(name) is now the current text style.
```

Screen Menu

SETTINGS–next–STYLE:

Pull-Down Menu

Options–DText Options...

Template Coordinates

W 10

Description

Style loads a new-text font definition into the drawing. It can be used to modify fonts by changing the height, width, and obliquing angle. You can also specify that the text be drawn backward, upside down, or vertically.

Style names may contain up to 31 characters.

The `Vertical?` prompt appears only if the font you selected allows horizontal and vertical orientation.

When responding to the `Font file:` prompt, omit the .SHX extension.

Possible Responses

Response	Meaning
?	List text styles

Hints

The style you establish with the Style command becomes the current style for Text and Dtext commands.

When you change the font with the Style command, AutoCAD regenerates your screen, replacing all occurrences of the former style name with the new style. Only the font changes.

Error Messages

`Invalid text style name.` The name you entered does not conform to naming conventions. Check your typing, and try again.

`Requires numeric distance or two points.` When specifying the height or obliquing angle, you entered an invalid response. Try again, providing a numeric distance or picking two on-screen points that define the height or angle.

`Requires numeric value.` When prompted for the width factor, you entered one or more nonnumeric characters. Try again with a numeric response.

`Yes or No, please.` When prompted to answer whether you want the text produced backward, upside down, or vertically, you replied incorrectly. Type **Y** or **N**.

`Invalid file name.` The font file name you entered was invalid. Check your spelling, and try again.

`Can't open file.` The file you specified cannot be used by AutoCAD as a font file. Check the file, or specify another font file.

`No such text style. Use main Style command to create it.` You tried to create a new text style at the Dim subcommand level. Instead, use the Style command at the `Command:` prompt to create a new style.

Related System Variables
TEXTSTYLE
TEXTSIZE

Tablet

Allows you to turn the tablet on and off, calibrate the tablet for digitizing drawings, and configure the tablet for a menu

Syntax
`Command: `**Tablet**
`Option (ON/OFF/CAL/CFG):`

Toggle Keys
Ctrl-T or F10

Screen Menu
SETTINGS–next–TABLET:

Pull-Down Menu
None

Template Coordinates
None

Description
The On returns the tablet to menu use after it has been turned off.

The Off option turns off the tablet menu and allows you to use the entire tablet area for digitizing. Use the OFF option before calibrating.

The Cal option allows you to calibrate the tablet to a given paper drawing for the purpose of digitizing the paper drawing into AutoCAD. You are prompted for the following:

```
Digitize first known point:
Enter coordinates for first point:
Digitize second known point:
Enter coordinates for second point:
```

Secure the paper drawing to the digitizing tablet so that it cannot move. On the drawing, select two points you know, and decide what coordinates those two points should have in AutoCAD. These are your first and second points and define the scale of the drawing.

The CFG option enables you to configure the tablet for different menu areas when you switch between menus. If the menus are defined with the same areas and the same number of squares in each area, you do not need to reconfigure the tablet. CFG also enables you to respecify the screen pointing area. Be sure the menu areas and pointing area do not overlap. You are prompted for the following:

```
Enter number of tablet menus desired
(0-4) <4>:
```

If the number you enter is the same as the number of tablet menus you currently have, you will be prompted:

```
Do you want to realign tablet menu areas?
Digitize upper left corner of menu area 1:
Digitize lower left corner of menu area 1:
Digitize lower right corner of menu area 1:
Enter the number of columns for menu area 1:
Enter the number of rows for menu are 1:
Do you want to respecify the screen pointing area?:
Digitize lower left corner of screen pointing area:
Digitize upper right corner of screen pointing area:
```

1 represents the number of the particular tablet area you are defining. If you make a mistake defining one of the corners, you must execute the command again. The screen pointing area specified includes the area used for the screen menu, which can be reached through the tablet or other pointing device.

Possible Responses

Response	Meaning
ON	Turn on tablet mode
OFF	Turn off tablet mode
CAL	Calibrate tablet
CFG	Configure tablet for tablet menus

Hints

If you customize your tablet menu, it is a good idea to work on a copy of TABLET.DWG, give it a new name (such as CUSTOM.DWG), and save the original.

The template coordinates given for each item in this command reference pertain to the command definitions in the AutoCAD TABLET.DWG menu.

When respecifying the screen pointing area, make sure it doesn't overlap tablet menu areas.

See Appendix A for more information on configuring a tablet menu.

Error Messages

`Your pointing device cannot be used as a tablet.` You are using a mouse or another relative pointing device that cannot enter absolute coordinates, as a digitizing tablet does.

`Ambiguous response, please clarify...` When prompted to enter a tablet option, you typed **O** or **C**. Since O could mean either ON or OFF, and C could mean either CAL or CFG, you need to spell out enough of the command to remove ambiguity.

`Invalid option keyword.` When prompted for a tablet option, you entered a response that does not correspond to a valid option keyword. Try again, selecting an option indicated in the prompt.

`Invalid 2D point.` When prompted for a corner, you entered something invalid. Select a point on-screen when digitizing.

`Alarm sounds.` If you try to type coordinates when prompted to digitize a point, the alarm sounds. Digitize by selecting a location on your tablet.

`Value must be between 0 and 4.` When specifying the number of tablet menus, you entered a number outside the range of 0 to 4. Enter a positive integer within this range.

`Requires an integer value.` Your response was not an integer, or it was outside the range of integers allowed. Enter a positive integer within the range indicated in the prompt.

`Points must form a 90 degree angle, try area again...` The points you selected do not form a 90-degree angle. Try again.

`Value must be positive and nonzero.` The value you entered is negative, zero, or nonnumeric. Enter a positive number.

`Too many rows for the selected area.` You specified too many rows to fit in the area you selected. Try again with fewer rows.

Related System Variables

None

Tabsurf

(Short for TABulated SURFace) Creates a tabulated surface from a path curve and a direction vector

Syntax

```
Command: Tabsurf
Select path curve:
Select direction vector:
```

Screen Menu

SURFACES–TABSURF:

Pull-Down Menu

Draw–Surfaces...

Template Coordinates

O 2

Description

Tabsurf extrudes a curve through space along a direction vector. Tabsurf enables you to select the path curve and the direction vector. The path curve can be a line, arc, circle, two-dimensional polyline, or three-dimensional polyline. After you select the curve and direction vector, a tabulated surface is drawn from the point you pick on the curve to the point you pick for the direction vector.

Surface lines are drawn parallel to the direction vector. The tabulated surfaces are created as polygon meshes, with mesh density controlled by the SURFTAB1 system variable.

Select Path curve: is used to define the surface. Lines, arcs, circles, and polylines may be used.

Select direction vector: is a line or an open polyline that indicates the direction and length of the surface.

Hints

Large values for SURFTAB1 will result in dense meshes but longer processing time.

Error Messages

`Invalid point.` Your response to the Select path curve: prompt was invalid. Select a point on-screen, or enter two or three coordinates for each point.

`Entity not usable to define tabulated surface.` The entity you selected for the path curve cannot be used for that purpose. Select a line, arc, circle, or polyline.

`Entity not usable as direction vector.` The entity you selected for the direction vector cannot be used for that purpose. Select a line or open polyline.

Related System Variables

SURFTAB1

Text

Places text in the drawing

Syntax

```
Command: Text
Justify/Style/<Start point>: J
Align/Fit/Center/Middle/Right/TL/TC/TR/ML/MC/MR/BL/
BC/BR:
Height <default>:
Rotation angle <default>:
Text:
```

Screen Menu

DRAW–next–TEXT:

Pull-Down Menu

Draw–Dtext

Template Coordinates

X 8
Y 10

Description

The Text command is used to place text in the drawing. Text can be placed with this or with the Dtext command; they are similar in function and purpose.

Text is treated like another entity; it can later be selected and functioned upon by other AutoCAD commands.

<Start point> is the default justification for the Text command. AutoCAD is looking for the starting point for the text you will insert. The text you enter will be left-justified.

The Justify option enables you to pick one of 14 text-justification options.

The Style option allows you to switch between the loaded text fonts. To load or modify a text font, see the Style command.

If you press Enter at the Text command's prompt, AutoCAD will prompt for text and place any text you enter below the last piece of text entered. The new text will retain all the parameters of the last text including font, height, rotation, and color.

Spaces are allowed for the text you input. When you finish typing text, press Enter.

To insert a paragraph with this command, execute the command and set up the parameters for the text. Then execute the Text command a second time; the parameters default to the last text inserted.

The default text font (called STANDARD) is used unless other fonts have been loaded with the Style command. There are special characters you can insert with your text. These characters are embedded in the text and need codes to activate them. The following table shows the codes and the special characters they activate:

Code	Character
%%o	Overscore
%%u	Underscore
%%d	Degrees symbol
%%p	Plus/minus symbol
%%c	Circle diameter
%%%	Percent sign
%%nnn	ASCII character with decimal code *nnn*

When you have inserted your text in the drawing, you can use the Change command to change everything about the text (except the justification).

Possible Responses

Response	Meaning
A	Align text between two points
BL	Bottom left
BC	Bottom center

Response	Meaning
BR	Bottom right
C	Center text horizontally
F	Fit text between two points
J	Specify justification options
M	Center text horizontally and vertically
ML	Middle left
MC	Middle center
MR	Middle right
R	Right-justify text
S	Select text style
TL	Top left
TC	Top center
TR	Top right

Hints

If you press Enter at the `Start point:` prompt, the next text will start one line below the last text you entered in the drawing and will share the same height, style, justification, and color.

Error Messages

`Invalid point.` Your response to one of the point prompts was invalid. Select a point on-screen, or enter two or three coordinates for each point.

`Requires numeric distance or second point.` When prompted for a distance, you entered something other than a numeric distance or second point. Enter a number, or select two points.

`Value must be positive and nonzero.` The value you entered is negative, zero, or nonnumeric. Enter a positive number.

Related System Variables

TEXTSIZE
TEXTSTYLE

'Textscr

Flips from graphics to text screen on a single-screen system

Syntax

`Command:` **'Textscr**

Toggle Key

F1

Screen Menu

None

Pull-Down Menu

None

Template Coordinates

None

Description

This command is used for single-display systems to switch from the graphics screen to the text screen. See also Graphscr.

Textscr and Graphscr flip back and forth between text and graphics mode. Although you could toggle back and forth on a single-screen system by pressing function key F1, you cannot use F1 in a command script or menu item.

This command has no effect on a dual-screen system.

You can use Textscr as a transparent command within another AutoCAD command by preceding it with an apostrophe: **'Textscr**.

Hints

Using F1 is quicker than typing the command.

Error Messages

None

Related System Variables

None

Time

Keeps track of time spent in a drawing

Syntax

```
Command: Time
Current time:          31 Dec 1990 at 23:59:59.000
Drawing created:       31 Dec 1990 at 23:59:59.000
Drawing last updated:  31 Dec 1990 at 23:59:59.000
Time in drawing editor: 0 days 00:59:59.000
```

```
Elapsed timer:              0 days 00:59:59.000
Timer on.
Display/ON/OFF/Reset:
```

Screen Menu

INQUIRY–TIME:

Pull-Down Menu

None

Template Coordinates

T 1

Description

Time helps you track the times, dates, and durations of edit sessions of the drawing. It can be used for client billing purposes, as well.

You can turn the timer on and off, and reset it.

Drawing created: is the date and time the current drawing was created.

Drawing last updated: is the last time you updated the current file.

Time in drawing editor: is the total amount of time you spent in the Drawing Editor with this drawing.

Elapsed timer: is the time you spent in the Drawing Editor during the current session.

Display/ON/OFF/Reset: The Display option redisplays the time. The On option turns on the timer; The Off option turns off the timer. Reset causes the time to be reset to zero.

Possible Responses

Response	Meaning
D	Display time
ON	Turn on timer
OFf	Turn off timer
R	Reset timer

Hints

Times are expressed to the nearest millisecond in 24-hour format; for example, 13:01:00.000 means 1:01 in the afternoon.

Error Messages

Invalid option keyword. When prompted to select an option, you entered a response that does not correspond to a valid option keyword. Try again, selecting an option indicated in the prompt.

Related System Variables

CDATE
DATE
TDCREATE
TDINDWG
TDUPDATE
TDUSRTIMER

Trace

Draws a line with width

Syntax

```
Command: TRACE
Trace width (default):
From point:
To point:
```

Screen Menu

DRAW–next–TRACE:

Pull-Down Menu

None

Template Coordinates

None

Description

A trace is a line with width. Traces are drawn like lines, by selecting the points where the lines begin and end. Traces can be as wide as you want. They are solid unless fill mode is off; then only the outlines are drawn.

Traces have a number of disadvantages in comparison with polylines: you can't curve, close, continue, or undo a trace or trace segment. These limitations hamper the command's usefulness to the extent that it may be eliminated from future versions of AutoCAD.

Hints

All traces drawn by one Trace command have the same width, and all traces are squared off at both ends.

As an alternative to traces, you should use the Pline command or use wide technical pens for plotting.

Error Messages

`Requires numeric distance or two points.` When prompted for the trace width, you responded with something other than a number or two points. Try again, providing a numeric distance or picking two on-screen points that define the trace width.

`Value must be positive.` A trace cannot have a negative width. Enter a positive value.

`Invalid point.` Your response to one of the point prompts was invalid. Select a point on-screen, or enter coordinates for each point.

`Invalid 2D point.` Your response to the `To Point:` prompt was invalid. Select a point on-screen, or enter two coordinates for the point.

Related System Variables

TRACEWID

Trim

Trims entities back to a boundary

Syntax

```
Command: Trim
Select cutting edge(s)...
Select objects:
Select objects to trim/Undo:
```

Screen Menu

EDIT–next–TRIM:

Pull-Down Menu

Modify–Trim

Template Coordinates

X 18

Description

Trim cuts entities at a boundary. It works with lines, arcs, circles, and polylines. You can also use any of these entities as the boundaries.

When all the boundaries have been selected, you receive this prompt:

```
Select object to trim:/Undo
```

The Undo option reverses the most recent trim.

Hints

You can trim inside or outside the cutting edges, depending on where you select the entity to be trimmed. Select inside the cutting edges to retain what's inside the edges and delete what falls outside. Select the object to trim outside the cutting edges to retain what's outside the edges and delete what falls inside.

Error Messages

`3D Polygon Mesh entities may not be used as edges.` When prompted to select the cutting edge, you selected a three-dimensional polygon mesh. Select a line, arc, circle, or two-dimensional polyline.

`Cannot trim this entity.` The entity you selected cannot be trimmed. Select only lines, arcs, circles, and two-dimensional polylines.

`Select objects: n selected, 0 found,`
`(n) not parallel with UCS)` For your cutting edge you selected an entity whose extrusion direction is not parallel to the Z axis of the current User Coordinate System.

`Entity not parallel with UCS.` You tried to trim an entity whose extrusion direction is not parallel to the Z axis of the current User Coordinate System.

`Entity does not intersect an edge.` The entity you want to trim does not intersect any of the cutting edges.

Related System Variables

None

U

Reverses the effect of the most recent command

Syntax

`Command: U`

Screen Menu

`****–U:`

Pull-Down Menu

Utility–U

Template Coordinates

U 13

Description

This command is one of three methods AutoCAD provides for correcting mistakes. U undoes the most recent command; it has the same effect as Undo 1. It can be used repeatedly to single-step back through previous commands.

Hints

Use Undo if you want to reverse the effects of more than one command at a time.

Error Messages

`Nothing to undo.` U was the first command entered since you accessed this drawing. Type another command before using the U command.

`Everything has been undone.` You have undone all commands entered during this work session.

Related System Variables

None

Ucs

(Short for User Coordinate System) Defines or modifies a user coordinate system

Syntax

```
Command: Ucs
Origin/ZAxis/3point/Entity/View/X/Y/Z/Prev/Restore/Save/Del/?/
<World>:
```

Screen Menu

UCS–UCS:

Pull-Down Menu

Settings and UCS Options...

Pull-Down Menu

Settings–UCS Previous...

Template Coordinates

J 4
K 6　.

Description

Origin defines a new UCS by moving the origin of the current UCS. The orientation of the axis remains the same.

ZAxis defines a new UCS using an origin and a point indicating the positive Z axis. You receive this prompt:

```
Origin point <default>:
Point on positive portion of Z-axis <default>:
```

3point defines a new UCS with three points: origin, positive X axis, and positive Y axis. Object snap modes can be used to indicate a UCS that corresponds to entities in the drawing. You receive this prompt:

```
Origin point <default>:
Point on positive portion of the X-axis <default>:
Point on positive-Y portion of the UCS X-Y plane <default>
```

The three points must not form a straight line.

Entity defines a new UCS using an existing entity. The X,Y plane is parallel to the X,Y plane that was in effect when the entity was drawn and has the same Z direction as that of the indicated entity. The entity must be selected by pointing. The following list describes the process of creating the UCS from each type of entity:

❑ Arc. The center becomes the origin; the X axis passes through the point on the arc closest to the pick point.

❑ Circle. Same as arc.

❑ Dimension. The insertion point is the origin; the X axis is parallel to the UCS of the dimension.

❑ Line. The endpoint nearest the pick point is the new origin; the Y axis is the other end of the line segment indicated.

❑ Point. The origin is the point; the X axis is derived arbitrarily.

❑ Polyline and mesh. The start point is the new origin; the X axis lies between the origin and the next vertex.

❑ Solid. The first point of solid is the origin; the X axis is on the line between the first and second points.

❑ Trace. The first point is the origin; the X axis lies along the center of the trace.

❏ 3D Face. The first point is the origin; the X axis is from the first two points; and the positive Y side is from the first and fourth points.

❏ Shape, text, and block. The origin is the insertion point; the X axis is defined by the rotation.

View defines a new UCS whose Z axis is parallel to the direction of view; that is, perpendicular to the current view.

X/Y/Z rotates the current UCS around the specified axis; enter only one. You are prompted for the rotation around the axis you indicate.

Previous takes you back to the UCS in which you last worked.

Restore restores a named UCS.

Save saves the current UCS by name. You are prompted for a name; the standard conventions apply.

Delete removes the specified UCS from the list. You are prompted for the name of the UCS to delete.

? lists the UCSs that are saved.

World, the default, sets the current coordinate system to the World Coordinate System.

Possible Responses

Response	Meaning
D	Delete specified UCS
E	Use existing entity to define UCS
O	Define new UCS by moving origin of current UCS
P	Make previous UCS current
R	Restore a saved UCS
S	Save current UCS
V	Define new UCS with Z axis parallel to view direction
W	Set current UCS to world coordinate system
X	Rotate current UCS around X axis
Y	Rotate current UCS around Y axis
Z	Rotate current UCS around Z axis
ZA	Define new UCS with specified origin and positive Z axis
3	Define new UCS with specified origin, positive X axis, and positive Y axis
?	List saved UCSs

Hints

When you begin a new drawing, its WCS and UCS are the same, with X, Y, and Z coordinates of zero.

Although UCS was developed for three-dimensional drawing, it can also be used to change the orientation of two-dimensional drawings.

Error Messages

`Invalid option keyword.` When prompted to select an option, you entered a response which does not correspond to a valid option keyword. You may have typed **X/Y/Z** instead of just entering one axis at a time, as AutoCAD requires with the UCS command. Try again, selecting an option indicated in the prompt.

`Invalid point.` Your response to one of the point prompts was invalid. Select a point on-screen, or enter coordinates for each point.

`Coincident with first point.` When specifying the point on the positive-Y portion of the plane, you selected the same point as for the X axis. Select a different point.

`Points are collinear.` You entered points that form a straight line. Select or enter points that do not form a straight line.

`No object found.` You tried to select an entity by some method other than pointing.

`Requires numeric angle or two points.` When prompted for the rotation, your response was invalid. Enter a numeric angle or two points that define the angle.

`Invalid UCS name.` You entered a UCS name that does not conform to AutoCAD file-naming conventions. Try again, using a valid file name.

`____ not found.` You entered a name for which no UCS exists. Enter the name of an existing UCS.

Related System Variables

UCSFOLLOW
UCSICON
UCSNAME
UCSORG
UCSXDIR
UCSYDIR
VIEWMODE
WORLDUCS

Ucsicon

(Short for User Coordinate System ICON) Controls location and visibility of the User Coordinate System icon

Syntax

```
Command: Ucsicon
ON/OFF/All/Noorigin/ORigin <default>:
```

Screen Menu

SETTINGS–next–UCSICON

Pull-Down Menu

Settings–Ucsicon On/Off/OR

Template Coordinates

None

Description

The UCS icon is typically located in the bottom left corner of the viewing screen. It indicates the axis directions for the current User Coordinate System.

The On option turns on the icon.

The Off option turns off the icon.

The All option activates the icon change in all viewports, not just the current port.

The Noorigin option (the default) displays the icon at all times in the screen's lower left corner.

The Origin option displays the icon at the origin of the current UCS, the (0,0,0) position.

Possible Responses

Response	Meaning
A	Change icon in all viewports
N	Display icon in lower left corner of screen
OR	Display icon at origin of current UCS
OFF	Turn off icon
ON	Turn on icon

Hints

The icon shows the current UCS origin and orientation for the current viewport.

If the icon has a plus sign (+) it means that the icon is located at the origin of the current UCS.

The letter W indicates that the current coordinate system is the World Coordinate System (WCS).

A box at the base of the icon that indicates you are looking at the UCS from above; absence of a box indicates that you are looking from below.

Error Messages

`Ambiguous response, please clarify...` When prompted to turn the UCS icon on or off, you pressed the letter O. Because this could mean either ON or OFF, you need to spell out as much of the word as necessary to remove ambiguity, or select one of the other options indicated in the prompt.

`Invalid option keyword.` When prompted to select an option, you entered a response that does not correspond to a valid option keyword. Try again, selecting an option indicated in the prompt.

Related System Variables

UCSICON

Undefine

Allows you to give an AutoCAD command with a new definition

Syntax

```
Command: Undefine
Command name:
```

Screen Menu

None

Pull-Down Menu

None

Template Coordinates

None

Description

This command is used to make an AutoCAD command unavailable. This is desirable if you use AutoLISP to define a function with the same name as an AutoCAD command.

Hints

Undefine works only on commands available from the Command: prompt. It does not work with subcommands, including those in the dimensioning subsystem.

See Redefine in this command reference for restoring AutoCAD's command definitions.

You can execute an AutoCAD command that has been undefined if you precede the command name with a period (.). For example, if you undefine the Line command, you can still use AutoCAD's definition of the Line command by entering the command as **.Redefine**.

The effects of Undefine apply only to the current editing session. All AutoCAD commands return to normal operation the next time you enter the Drawing Editor.

Error Messages

Unknown command name. You tried to undefine an unknown command. Check the spelling, and try again.

Related System Variables

None

Undo

Reverses the effect of previous commands; controls the undo feature

Syntax

Command: **Undo**
Auto/Back/Control/End/Group/Mark/<number>:

Screen Menu

EDIT–next–UNDO:

Pull-Down Menu

Utility–Undo Mark

Pull-Down Menu

Utility–Undo Back

Template Coordinates

Y 14

Description

Undo is another command you can use to correct mistakes. It is similar to the U command but gives you greater control over how many steps you undo at a time.

Undo differs from Erase in that it also undoes zooms and screen settings, whereas Erase only erases entities.

<number>: is the number of commands you want undone at this time.

Auto is the part of Undo that controls how menu selections and other multiple commands are handled. If Auto is on, the menu selections are treated as one command.

The Group option starts the grouping process. When you tell AutoCAD to open a group, the next commands you execute become part of that group. When you have entered all the commands you want in that group, you must End the group.

The End option ends the grouping process. If you start the grouping process, you must end it. When commands have been grouped together, they are undone with one Undo command.

The Mark option allows you to mark a place in your Undo information to return to through the Undo command. You can mark more than one place at a time. When you go back to that mark, the mark is removed. If you want to keep a mark there, you mark the place again. By marking the information, you can experiment in your drawing without worrying about getting back to a particular spot.

The Back option takes you back to the mark you placed in the Undo information. If there are no marks in the Undo information, AutoCAD will undo to the beginning of the editing session.

The Control option allows you to limit the Undo and U commands. AutoCAD prompts you as follows:

    All/None/One:

The All option is the default, allowing you all of the different Undo functions. The None option disables the command, and the One option allows one undo at a time. Both None and One free any disk space used for storing previous Undos.

Possible Responses

Response	Meaning
number	Undo specified number of commands
A	Control treatment of menu selections

Response	Method
B	Undo to previous mark
C	Toggle undo feature off and on
E	End Undo group
G	Group commands
M	Mark a place in Undo information

Hints

If you want to step back through your drawing to a particular point but are not sure how many commands back you need to go, undo a specific number of commands, and then use Redo to undo the effects of the Undo.

The undo feature takes up as much disk space as your drawing file. If you are short on disk space, disable the undo feature.

Error Messages

Requires an integer value or an option keyword. You entered an invalid value or option. Select an option keyword displayed in the prompt, or enter the number of commands to undo. Check your entry, and try again.

Value must be between 1 and 32767. You entered a number outside the valid range. Enter a positive integer between 1 and 32,767.

Nothing to undo. Undo was the first command entered since you accessed this drawing. Type another command before using the Undo command.

Everything has been undone. You have undone all commands entered during this work session.

Yes or No, please. When prompted to answer Yes or No, you typed something else. Type **Y** or **N**.

Ambiguous response, please clarify... When prompted to turn Auto on or off, you typed the letter O. Because this could mean On or Off, you need to spell out as much of the word as necessary to remove ambiguity.

Invalid option keyword. When prompted to select an option, you entered a response that does not correspond to a valid option keyword. Try again, selecting an option indicated in the prompt.

Related System Variables

None

Units

Sets the display format and precision of drawing units

Syntax
```
Command: Units
```

Screen Menu
```
SETTINGS–next–UNITS:
```

Pull-Down Menu
None

Template Coordinates
Y 14

Description

This command allows you to specify your preferences in measurement systems. When you enter the Units command, AutoCAD provides a whole dialogue of prompts to allow you flexibility in entering and viewing coordinates and angles. You have the opportunity to change the following:

❑ How linear measurement units are displayed

❑ The number of decimal digits or fractional divisor displayed

❑ How angular measurements are displayed

❑ The number of decimal digits in angular displays

❑ The angular direction of measurement

You are prompted for each of these areas in turn. The effects of the Units command are global; all measurement displays throughout AutoCAD are affected.

When you enter the Units command, you see the following series of prompts:

```
Report formats:        (Examples)
    1. Scientific      1.55E+01
    2. Decimal         15.50
    3. Engineering     1'-3.50"
    4. Architectural   1'-3 1/2"
    5. Fractional      15 1/2
Enter choice, 1 to 5 <default>:
```

With the exception of engineering and architectural units, these display units can be used with any measurement system. For example, decimal mode is perfect for metric units as well as decimal English units. The fractional selection displays measurements in unitless whole and fraction parts; AutoCAD makes no assumption as to whether the units are inches or millimeters.

The following prompt appears if you choose selection 1, 2, or 3:

```
Number of digits to right of decimal point (0 to 8)
<default>:
```

The following prompt appears for selection 4 or 5:

```
Denominator of smallest fraction to display
(1, 2, 4, 8, 16, 32, or 64) <default>:
```

Next, you are prompted for angle format:

```
Systems of angle measure:
    1.      Decimal degrees    45.5
    2.      Degrees/minutes/seconds 45d00'0.00"
    3.      Grads 50.0000g
    4.      Radians     0.7854r
    5.      Surveyor's units  N 45d00'0" E
Enter choice, 1 to 5 <default>:
```

If the angle you are working with lies on a compass point, simply identify the compass point. For example, zero degrees would be equivalent to E in Surveyor's units. The angle is input the same as Degrees/minutes/seconds.

The precision of the angle measurement is selected next:

```
Number of fractional places for display of angles (0
to 8) <default>:
```

You are then prompted for the direction of angle zero. The default in AutoCAD is for angle zero to be at three o'clock, and for the angles to be figured counterclockwise:

```
Direction for angle 0:
    East   3 o'clock   = 0
    North 12 o'clock  = 90
    West   9 o'clock   = 180
    South  6 o'clock   = 270
Enter direction for angle 0 <default>:
```

If you want to specify an angle other than those listed here, and you have a single-screen system, use function key F1 to flip to the graphics screen. Then indicate the angle with two points. If you indicate an angle in this manner, remember what you have done; you may become confused with a nonstandard angle as your zero angle.

The last prompt in the Units command controls the direction of angles. By default, AutoCAD works counterclockwise. You can work clockwise or counterclockwise:

```
Do you want angles measured clockwise? <N>:
```

Hints

You can create a drawing with one Units setting and then alter the Units later. For instance, you could draw a machine part in decimal notation and later convert to feet and inches.

Any precision you set with the Units command affects only the display of values. AutoCAD internally always keeps track of values to a precision of 16 decimal places.

Error Messages

`Value must be between 1 and 5.` When prompted to select the system of units or of angle measure, you entered something other than an integer between one and five. Type a positive integer within this range.

`Value must be between 0 and 8.` When prompted to select the number of fractional places for display of angles, you entered something other than an integer between zero and eight. Type a positive integer within this range.

`Requires an integer value.` Your response was not an integer or was outside the range of integers allowed. Enter a positive integer within the range indicated in the prompt.

`Invalid choice.` Your response was invalid. Choose from the options in the prompt.

`Yes or No, please.` When prompted to answer Yes or No, you typed something else. Type **Y** or **N**.

Related System Variables

ANGBASE
ANGDIR
AUNITS
AUPREC
LUNITS
LUPREC

'View

Creates named views of the drawing

Syntax

```
Command: 'View
?/Delete/Restore/Save/Window:
View name to save:
```

Screen Menu

DISPLAY–VIEW:

Pull-Down Menu

None

Template Coordinates

None

Description

A view is a named view of a drawing. Using View reduces the number of times you need to pan or zoom.

? lists all the views that currently exist in the drawing.

The Delete option removes from the list the reference for the specified view.

Restore enables you to restore the view to the screen after it has been defined.

The Save option saves the current view by name. You are prompted for a view name, which can be 31 characters long and may contain letters, numbers, dollar signs ($), hyphens (-), and underscores (_). You reference the view by its view name.

The Window option allows you to make several views without zooming in on a view. First you enter the name under which you want the view saved. Then you put a window around the area you want included in the view.

You can use View as a transparent command within another AutoCAD command by preceding it with an apostrophe: 'View.

Possible Responses

Response	Meaning
D	Delete specified view
R	Restore specified view
S	Save current screen display as view
W	Make area in window a view
?	List views

Hints

You can avoid regenerations that normally accompany Zoom All and Zoom Extents by creating a view of the entire drawing.

Error Messages

`Cannot find view.` You tried to delete or restore a nonexistent view.

`Invalid view name.` You tried to save a view under a name that does not conform to AutoCAD file-naming conventions. Rename the view.

Related System Variables

VIEWCTR
VIEWSIZE

Viewports or Vports

Creates viewports in model space

Syntax

`Command:` **Vports**
`Save/Restore/Delete/Join/SIngle/?/2/<3>/4:`

Toggle Key

Ctrl-V

Screen Menu

SETTINGS–VPORTS:

Pull-Down Menu

None

Template Coordinates

None

Description

The rectangular portion of the graphics screen that displays your drawing is called the viewport. You can divide the screen into more than one viewport to display portions of your drawing. You can also set the Snap mode, grid spacing, and three-dimensional view point independently for each viewport. Vport lets you display up to 16 viewports (4, with DOS systems). It also lets you save and restore viewports.

The Save option saves the current viewport configuration by name. You are not limited to the number of viewport configurations that can be saved. You are prompted for viewport names; standard naming requirements apply.

The Restore option restores a named viewport.

The Delete option deletes a named viewport configuration.

The Join option merges two adjacent viewports into one larger viewport. The resulting viewport inherits its characteristics from the current viewport. You are prompted:

```
Select dominant viewport <current>:
Select viewport to join:
```

The Single option returns you to a single viewport.

The ? option lists the names of viewport configurations.

The 2,3,4 option enables you to define two, three, or four viewports:

- ❏ 2: Two viewports are defined with either a vertical or horizontal configuration.
- ❏ 3: Three viewports are defined with one large port next to two small ports.
- ❏ 4: Four viewports divides the screen into four equal areas.

Possible Responses

Response	Meaning
D	Delete named viewport configuration
J	Join two viewports
R	Restore saved viewport
S	Save current viewport by name
SI	Display single viewport, filling the entire graphics area
2	Divide current viewport into two viewports
3	Divide current viewport into three viewports
4	Divide current viewport into four viewports
?	List named viewports

Hints

Viewport names can be up to 31 characters, including letters, numbers, dollar signs, hyphens, and underscores. AutoCAD automatically converts view names to uppercase characters.

Once you have named viewports in a drawing, you can specify a viewport configuration after the Drawing Editor loads the drawing.

When you plot a drawing, only the current viewport is plotted.

Error Messages

`Requires an integer value or an option keyword.` You entered an invalid value or option. Select an option keyword displayed in the prompt, or enter the number of viewports you want to define.

`Cannot find viewport configuration____.` You entered a valid name, but no viewport configuration exists under that name. Check your typing, and try again.

`Invalid viewport configuration name.` You entered an invalid name. Check your typing, and try again.

`Only one viewport is active.` You tried to join two viewports when only one was active. To define additional viewports, use the 2,3,4 option with this command. Then you can join the viewports.

`Invalid viewport I.D.` Your response to one of the select viewport prompts was invalid. Specify a valid name.

`The selected viewports must be distinct.` You selected the same viewport twice when trying to join viewports. Select two different viewports.

Related System Variables

CVPORT

Viewport Switch

Switch between viewports in model space

Syntax

`Command:` Press Ctrl-V

Toggle Key

Ctrl-V

Screen Menu

None

Pull-Down Menu

None

Template Coordinates

V 22

Description

In model space, you have to pick which viewport you want to work in. You can pick the active viewport with your pointing device, or move to the next one by pressing Ctrl-V.

Hints

You can use the Ctrl-V command at the keyboard, in a menu macro, or in an AutoLISP routine.

Error Messages

None

Related System Variables

CVPORT

Viewres

(Short for VIEWing RESolution) Controls AutoCAD's fast regeneration and the resolution of circles and arcs

Syntax

```
Command: Viewres
Do you want fast zooms? <Y>:
Enter circle zoom percent (1-20000) <default>:
Regenerating drawing.
```

Screen Menu

DISPLAY–next–VIEWRES:

Pull-Down Menu

None

Template Coordinates

None

Description

Viewres controls regeneration and the smoothness of curves. The more segments or vectors you specify with `circle zoom percent`, the smoother curves appear. The drawback is that regeneration time increases. The effect of the number of segments drawn becomes increasingly apparent as you zoom in on the curved entity.

If you respond with **Y** to the first prompt, AutoCAD allows fast regenerations.

The `circle zoom percent` is the value that determines the resolution of circles and arcs on your graphics monitor. The default setting is 100. This default value causes AutoCAD to use its internal algorithm to compute the optimum number of vectors for each circle or arc so that it appears smooth at the current zoom magnification.

For faster regenerations, you can set `circle zoom percent` to a number less than 100, such as 15. For zoom circles at zoomed-in views, try a setting of 400.

The circle zoom percent is ignored during plotting and printer plotting (except in version 2.50, because of a bug). Arcs and circles are always plotted at the resolution of the plotter or printer.

Hints

There is a trade-off relationship between resolution and regeneration time. The larger your zoom percentage, the more line segments in a circle and, therefore, the better the resolution. However, regeneration time increases with the number of segments in a circle.

Error Messages

`Yes or No, please.` When prompted to answer `Yes` or `No`, you typed something else. Type **Y** or **N**.

`Value must be between 1 and 20000.` When prompted to enter the center zoom percent, you entered something other than an integer between 1 and 20,000. Type a positive integer within this range.

`Requires an integer value.` When prompted to enter the center zoom percent, you responded with something other than an integer. Enter a positive integer between 1 and 20,000.

Related System Variables

None

Vplayer

(Short for ViewPort LAYER) Controls the visibility of layers in paper space

Syntax

```
Command: Vplayer
?/Freeze/Thaw/Reset/Newfrz/Vpvisdflt:
All/Select/<Current>:
```

Screen Menu

MVIEW–VPLAYER:

Pull-Down Menu

Display–Mview–Vplayer:

Template Coordinates

N 4
O 6

Description

The Vplayer command lets you freeze and thaw layers differently in each viewport. The command works only in paper space.

The ? option lists the frozen layers in a picked viewport. If you use the command in model space, it switches to paper space for the duration of the command:

```
Switching to Paper space.
Select a viewport:
Layers currently frozen in viewport 1:
Switching to Model space
```

The Freeze option changes a layer's status to frozen. AutoCAD prompts you with `Layer(s) to Freeze:` to list one or more layer names to freeze. Separate layer names with a comma and no spaces. After you have specified the layer names, AutoCAD prompts `All/ Select/ <Current>:` to let you specify all viewports, select specific viewports, or select the current viewport.

The Thaw option thaws layers that were frozen in model space (with the Layer command) or in paper space with the Frozen option.

The Reset option changes the visibility of layers in a viewport to the default setting specified by the `Vpvisdflt` option.

The Newfrz option (short for NEW FRoZen) creates new frozen layers in all viewports. AutoCAD prompts `New VPORT frozen layer name(s):` to let you specify the new layer names. AutoCAD creates them as frozen; use the Thaw option to make them visible.

The Vpvisdflt (short for ViewPort VISibility DeFauLT) option enables you to specify which layers you initially want frozen when a new viewport is created. When AutoCAD prompts `Layer name(s) to change default viewport visibility:`, type in the names of the layers you want frozen by default.

Possible Responses

Response	Meaning
?	Use specified block as marker.
F	Freeze layers

Response	Meaning
T	Thaw layers
R	Reset frozen layers to the default setting
N	Create a new frozen layer
V	Create a default set of visible layers

Hints

In paper space, unlike model space, you can set independently the visibility of layers in different viewports. This is useful for plotting views of complex drawings.

Vplayer cannot freeze layers that were not frozen in model space.

Error Messages

None

Related System Variables

None

Vpoint

(Short for View POINT) Allows you to see the drawing in three dimensions

Syntax

```
Command: Vpoint
Rotate/<View point> <default>:
```

Screen Menu

DISPLAY–VPOINT:

Pull-Down Menu

Display–Vpoint 3D...

Template Coordinates

J 2
K 1
M 3

Description

The default viewpoint is plan view with coordinates of 0,0,1. This means that your view is directly over the X,Y plane origin.

Possible Responses

Response	Meaning
R	Select viewpoint by way of rotation angles
Enter	Select viewpoint by way of compass and axes
x,y,z	Specify viewpoint

Hints

You can use the Plan command or Vpoint 0,0,0 to return to the plan view.

You can establish a viewpoint for each viewport. Points and angles entered with this command relate to the current UCS.

If you are unfamiliar with this command, you may find it helpful to establish the X,Y angle first and then adjust the viewpoint.

The drawing is regenerated each time you use the Vpoint command.

Error Messages

`*Invalid*` It may appear that V (for Viewpoint) should be an option keyword in the `Rotate/<Viewpoint> <default>:` prompt, but it isn't. To select this option, you need to press Enter.

`Requires numeric angle or second point.` You responded with a nonnumeric response when prompted for a rotation angle. Try again, providing a numeric value or a second point that defines the angle.

Related System Variables

VPOINTX
VPOINTY
VPOINTZ

Vports

See Viewports

Vslide

(Short for View SLIDE) Allows you to view previously saved SLD slide files

Syntax

```
Command: Vslide
Slide file <default>:
```

Screen Menu
UTILITY–SLIDES–VSLIDE:

Pull-Down Menu
None

Template Coordinates
None

Description
Vslide allows you to view slides you created previously with the Mslide command. When prompted for a slide file, you should enter the name of the singular slide file or (if the slide you want to view is part of a library) the name of the library file followed by the slide name in parentheses.

Possible Responses

Response	Meaning
file	View slide
*file	Load slide, but don't display until the next Vslide command

Hints
To clear a slide from your screen, use Redraw.

You cannot edit or zoom in on a slide.

If you want to see a slide and edit the drawing, display the slide in a separate viewport.

Error Messages
`Can't open file`
`*Invalid*` You entered an unknown Vslide file name. Try again, and be sure not to use the .SLD file extension.

Related System Variables
None

Wblock

(Short for Write BLOCK) Saves a copy of a block (or the entire drawing) on disk

Syntax

```
Command: Wblock
File name:
Block name:
```

Screen Menu

BLOCKS–WBLOCK:

Pull-Down Menu

None

Template Coordinates

R 2

Description

When you create blocks with the Block command, AutoCAD saves the defined block with the current drawing. This means it can be used only within the current drawing. To make the block available for other drawings, you can write the block to a disk file by using the Wblock command.

At the File name prompt AutoCAD requests the name of the file it is creating to hold the block. The file name must comply with DOS conventions.

At the Block name prompt AutoCAD requests the name of the block to write to the file. If the block does not exist yet, press Enter. You will see the usual block-creation prompts for insertion base point and object selection. If the block and the file have the same name, you can type the shorthand character, the equal sign (=); if the entire drawing is being written out, use the asterisk (*); otherwise, type the name of the block to be written to file.

Possible Responses

Response	Meaning
name	Write file name for block
=	Block name is same as file name
*	Write entire drawing
Enter	Write specified block

Hints

After you save the block to disk with Wblock, you can insert it in other drawings. To orient the block appropriately when you insert it, set the UCS for the host drawing before using the Insert command.

Error Messages

`A drawing with this name already exists.`
`Do you want to replace it?` You tried to create a block with the same name as one that already exists. Answer **Yes** only if you want to replace the old block with the new one; otherwise, answer **No**, and rename the new block.

`Yes or No, please.` When prompted to answer `Yes` or `No`, you typed something else. Type **Y** or **N**.

`Block ___ not found.` No block was found under the name you specified. Try again.

`Invalid point.` Your response to the insertion base point prompt was invalid. Select a point on-screen, or enter two or three coordinates.

Related System Variables

None

Xbind

(Short for eXternal BIND) Makes a referenced object part of a drawing

Syntax

`Command: `**`Xbind`**
`Block/Dimstyle/LAyer/LType/Style:`
`Dependent name:`
`Scanning...`

Screen Menu

BLOCKS–XREF:

Pull-Down Menu

None

Template Coordinates

P 3

Description

After you have used the Xref command to reference another drawing, you can use the Xbind command to make any block, dimension style, layer, linetype, or text style part of your current drawing.

Possible Responses

Response	Meaning
B	Bind in a block
D	Bind in a dimension style
LA	Bind in a layer
LT	Bind in a line type
S	Bind in a text style

Hints

If you want to make the entire referenced drawing part of the current drawing, use the Xref Bind command.

Error Messages

`No matching Block names found.` You attempted to bind a block (or dimension style, or layer, or linetype, or text style) that does not exist in the referenced file.

Related System Variables

None

Xref

(Short for eXternal REFerence) Displays another drawing

Syntax

```
Command: Xref
?/Bind/Detach/Path/Reload/<Attach>:
```

Screen Menu

None

Pull-Down Menu

Draw–Xref:

Template Coordinates

P 1
P 2

Description

The Xref command enables you to see another drawing in the current drawing without needing to insert it as a block. You can use the referenced entities for object snaps, set referenced layers and line types, or use referenced dimension and text styles. When you no longer need to see the reference drawing, you can detach it.

If you want to add the referenced drawing permanently, you can bind it in. If you want to bind only parts of the drawing, use the Xbind command.

The ? option lists referenced drawings (and their path names) attached to the current drawing. The list looks similar to the following:

```
Xref(s) to list <*>:
Xref Name       Path

NAME      \PATH
Total Xref(s): 1
```

The Attach option attaches another drawing to the current drawing. Adding it is similar to inserting a block:

```
Xref to Attach: Name
Attach Xref NAME: NAME.dwg
NAME loaded.
Insertion point:
X scale factor <default> / Corner / XYZ:
Y scale factor (default=X):
Rotation angle <default>:
```

The Bind option permanently adds the referenced drawing to the current drawing. When you bind a drawing, it becomes a block in the current drawing:

```
Xref(s) to bind: Name
Scanning...
```

The Detach option removes a referenced drawing from the current drawing:

```
Xref(s) to Detach: Name
Scanning...
```

The Reload option reloads a referenced drawing. You would reload if changes have been made since you attached the reference drawing:

```
Xref to reload: Name
Scanning...
Reload Xref NAME: NAME.dwg
NAME loaded. Regenerating drawing.
```

The Path option changes the OS path name for the referenced drawing. You would use this option if the drawing had been moved to another subdirectory (or to another drive) or if you wanted to reference a different drawing with the same name that resided in another subdirectory. The option prompts you for the old and new path names, and then reloads the drawing:

```
Edit path for which Xref(s): Name
Scanning...
Xref name: NAME
Old path: Name
New path: C:\PATH\NAME
Reload Xref NAME: NAME.dwg
NAME loaded. Regenerating drawing.
```

Possible Responses

Response	Meaning
A	Attach a reference drawing
B	Bind reference drawing to the current drawing
D	Detach a reference drawing
P	Respecify the path to a referenced drawing
R	Reload a referenced drawing
?	List the names of referenced drawings

Hints

Use Xref to view other drawings without inserting them as blocks.

Drawings viewed with Xref are displayed in the current viewport.

Using the asterisk (*) wild-card character affects all referenced drawings. For example, **Detach** * detaches all referenced drawings whereas **Bind** * binds all referenced drawings.

Xref writes information to a file on disk when you use the Attach, Detach, and Reload options. This log file lists the names of blocks, linetypes, layers, styles, registered applications, and dimension styles added to the current drawing. Its contents are similar to the following:

```
==============================
Drawing: NAME
Date/Time: 12/31/90 23:59:59
Operation: Attach Xref
==============================
Attach Xref NAME: NAME.dwg
Update Block symbol table:
  Block update complete.
Update Ltype symbol table:
  Ltype update complete.
Update Layer symbol table:
  Appending symbol: NAME|LINES
NAME loaded.
```

Error Messages

`No matching Xref names found.` You used a drawing-file name that does not exist in the current subdirectory. Check the spelling or include a path name.

Related System Variables

None

'Zoom

Allows you to display an enlarged or condensed view of the drawing

Syntax

```
Command: 'Zoom
All/Center/Dynamic/Extents/Left/Previous/Vmax/
Window/ <Scale(X/XP)>:
```

Alias

Z

Screen Menu

DISPLAY–ZOOM:

Pull-Down Menu

Display–Zoom Window

Pull-Down Menu

Display–Zoom Previous

Pull-Down Menu

Display–Zoom All

Pull-Down Menu

Display–Zoom Dynamic

Pull-Down Menu

Display–Zoom Vmax

Template Coordinates

J 9
P 9

Description

Zoom is one of the most frequently used commands in AutoCAD. It lets you magnify the view of the drawing to make editing easier.

The All option returns you to your drawing limits or the extents, whichever is larger.

The Center option allows you to identify a new center point for the screen and then enter the height. This height is the factor that determines the zoom scale.

The Dynamic option causes a new screen to appear on the monitor.

The extents of the drawing are the precise area in which you have drawn. The X and Y values make up the drawing extents. The Extents option pulls all entities in the drawing onto the screen. This is a good way to see whether any rogue entities are floating around in the drawing.

The Left option enables you to set a new lower left corner and height.

The Previous option returns you to the previous screen. You can restore up to 10 previous views.

The Window option allows you to place a window around the area in which you want to work.

The Scale option allows you to zoom by a scale factor.

You can use Zoom as a transparent command within another AutoCAD command by preceding it with an apostrophe: **'Zoom**. Zoom cannot be used transparently if a regeneration would occur.

Possible Responses

Response	Meaning
number	Zoom by a factor from original scale
numberX	Zoom by a factor from current scale
numberXP	Zoom by a factor relative to paper space
A	All
C	Specify new center point
D	Dynamic
E	Extents
L	Set new lower left corner
P	Return to previous screen
V	Maximum view without regeneration
W	Place window around working area

Hints

The All and Extents options always regenerate your drawing. Use Zoom Vmax whenever appropriate since it does not regenerate the drawing.

Use Zoom Extents to see whether anything was drawn accidently outside of reasonable limits.

Zoom Previous does not restore any entities you erased. Use Undo for this purpose.

Error Messages

`Requires a distance, numberX, or option keyword.` You responded with something other than the options displayed in the prompt. Try again, selecting from the options indicated or specifying the scale.

`Redisplay required by change in drawing extents.` AutoCAD has redisplayed your drawing according to changes you made in the drawing extents.

`Invalid point.` Your response to the center point prompt or a corner point prompt was invalid. Select a point on-screen, or enter two or three coordinates.

`Invalid window specification.` Your response to the corner point prompts for a window was invalid. Either select points on-screen, or enter two or three coordinates for each corner.

Related System Variables

VIEWCTR
VIEWSIZE
VMAX
VMIN

3Dface

(Short for 3-Dimensional FACE) Draws three-dimensional planes

Syntax

```
Command: 3Dface
First point:
Second point:
Third point:
Fourth point:
Third point:
Fourth point:
```

Screen Menu

SURFACES–3DFACE:

Pull-Down Menu

Draw–3D Face

Template Coordinates

N 3

Description

The prompts are similar to those for the Solid command. The difference is in the point input sequence: the points used to define the 3Dface must be indicated clockwise or counterclockwise—not alternately, as with the Solid command.

To make an edge of the 3Dface invisible, type **I** before specifying the first point of that edge in the following format:

```
First point: I 1,2,3
```

You can also type **I** before selecting the point on-screen.

Possible Responses

Response	Meaning
I	Make following edge invisible

Hints

Specify points in clockwise or counterclockwise order.

Error Messages

`Point or option keyword required.` Your response to one of the point prompts was invalid. Select a point on-screen, or enter two or three coordinates for each point.

Related System Variables

SPLFRAME

3Dmesh

(Short for 3-Dimensional MESH) Creates a general polygon mesh

Syntax

```
Command: 3Dmesh
Mesh M size:
Mesh N size:
Vertex (0, 0):
Vertex (0, 1):
```

Screen Menu

SURFACES–3DMESH:

Pull-Down Menu

None

Template Coordinates

None

Description

The 3Dmesh command is used for specifying arbitrary meshes. It is easier to use Rulesurf, Tabsurf, Revsurf, and Edgesurf.

Mesh M size and Mesh N size define how many vertices the mesh will have (M × N vertices).

Default vertices correspond to the current UCS and to the M and N sizes. Vertices may be two- or three-dimensional points.

Error Messages

`Requires an integer value.` When prompted to enter the Mesh M or N size, you responded with something other than an integer. Enter a positive integer between 2 and 256.

`Value must be between 2 and 256.` You entered a value out of range. Enter a positive integer between 2 and 256.

`Value must be positive and nonzero.` The value you entered is negative, zero, or nonnumeric. Enter a positive number.

Related System Variables

None

3Dpoly

(Short for 3-Dimensional POLYline) Draws three-dimensional polylines

Syntax

```
Command: 3Dpoly
From point:
Close/Undo/<Endpoint of line>:
```

Screen Menu

SURFACES–3DPOLY:

Pull-Down Menu

Draw–3D Poly

Template Coordinates

O 3

Description

A three-dimensional polyline is a polyline with independent X, Y, and Z coordinates. Three-dimensional polylines are oriented in space rather than confined to a single X,Y plane, like two-dimensional polylines.

Three-dimensional polylines have no thickness and can be drawn only with straight line segments. Although you can use Pedit to spline-curve-fit a three-dimensional polyline, the curve will actually consist of many short straight segments. Three-dimensional polylines are useful when you want to cross a three-dimensional space in multiple planes.

`From point:` is the start of the polyline.

`Close` closes a polyline with two or more segments.

`Undo` undoes the last segment.

`<Endpoint of line>:` prompts for the next endpoint for the polyline.

Points may be two- or three-dimensional. Use the Pedit command to edit three-dimensional polylines.

Possible Responses

Response	Meaning
C	Close polyline
U	Undo last endpoint
Enter	Exit the 3Dpoly command

Hints

3Dpoly is the three-dimensional counterpart of the two-dimensional command Pline.

Error Messages

`Point or option keyword required.` Your response to one of the point prompts was invalid. Select a point on-screen, or enter two or three coordinates for each point.

`Invalid point.` Your response to the center point or a corner point prompt was invalid. Select a point on-screen, or enter two or three coordinates.

Illustration courtesy of
Autodesk, Inc., Sausalito, CA.

System Variable Reference

This section contains a complete list of AutoCAD's system variables. AutoCAD maintains these variables in order to facilitate execution of the program.

You typically set a system variable in one of the following ways:

❑ By using the Setvar command

❑ By using an AutoCAD command

❑ With AutoLISP

If you use AutoCAD Release 11, you can set many system variables directly at the `Command:` prompt, without using Setvar or any other commands first.

You can use the same methods to read the current value of system variables.

The easiest way to look at a system variable's value, however, is by using the Setvar command, as follows:

```
Command: Setvar
Variable name or ?: ?
Variable(s) to list <*>: Press Enter
```

AutoCAD displays the system variables, 20 at a time. The following system variables are not listed by the Setvar ? command:

System Variable	Meaning
_PKSER	Serial number of your copy of AutoCAD
ERRNO	Error number returned by AutoLISP and ADS
HANDSEED	Starting value for generating handle values
USERI1 *to* USERI5	Stores user-supplied integer values
USERR1 *to* USERR5	Stores user-supplied real values
VISRETAIN	Retain visibility of externally retained drawing layers

This appendix is a variable table that lists the following information about each variable:

❑ The system variable's name

❑ The variable type

❑ Where the variable is stored

❑ The variable's default value

❑ A short description of the variable

The variable's *name* is the name you use to access the variable through the Setvar command, through AutoLISP, or (for Release 11) directly at the Command: prompt.

The variable's *type* has one of the following designations:

Type	Meaning
I	Integer number
R	Real number
S	Text string
2D	Two-dimensional point
3D	Three-dimensional point

All variables are stored somewhere. Most system variables are saved in the drawing. The table shows where system variables are saved, as follows:

Location	Meaning
Acad	Saved in the ACAD.EXE program file
Cfg	Saved in the ACAD.CFG configuration file
Dwg	Saved in the current DWG (drawing) file
Os	Saved in the operating system environment
...	Saved only for the duration of the drawing session

The value listed in the *Default* column is the value of system variables for the prototype drawing ACAD.DWG, straight out of the box. Values that will differ when you use the Setvar ? command on ACAD.DWG are shown in *italic*. For this reason, take the default value as an example of the variable's format.

The *Meaning* column briefly describes the function of the system variable and notes the values of options (if any). You cannot change all system variables. Those you cannot change are called *read-only* variables because you can look at the value but cannot change it. Read-only system variables, such as the data and time, are set by the operating system or by AutoCAD.

Why would you want to change system variables? As you become more adept at using AutoCAD and you begin to "branch out," stretching the limits of built-in AutoCAD functions, you will find that you need to work with system variables.

The table that makes up the bulk of this section lists all AutoCAD Release 11 system variables that the Setvar ? command lists. If you are using an earlier version of AutoCAD, some variables may not be available. The following system variables appear in Release 10 but were dropped in Release 11:

Variable	*Type*	*Saved in*	*Default*	*Meaning*
FLATLAND	I	Dwg	0	Release 9 compatibility mode: 0 = allows 3-D drawing 1 = restricts 3-D drawing
LASTPT3D	3D	...	0.0,0.0,0.0	3-D version of LASTPOINT
VPOINTX	R	Dwg	0	X-component of current viewport's viewing direction, in World coordinates. Describes "camera" point as a 3-D offset from target point. **(Read-only)**
VPOINTY	R	Dwg	0	Y-component of current viewport's viewing direction **(Read-only)**
VPOINTZ	R	Dwg	1	Z-component of current viewport's viewing direction **(Read-only)**

The following listing includes all the system variables available in AutoCAD Release 10 and Release 11:

Variable	Type	Saved in	Default	Meaning
ACADPREFIX	S	Os	C:\ACAD\	Specified by an operating system directory other than the AutoCAD directory for your drawing, that information is stored here. (**Read-only**)
ACADVER	S	Acad	11	The release number of this version of AutoCAD (**Read-only**)
AFLAGS	I	Dwg	0	Determines whether attributes in a block are 1 = invisible 2 = constant 3 = verify 4 = preset
ANGBASE	R	Dwg	0	The direction for angle 0. This is used to calculate all angles in AutoCAD.
ANGDIR	I	Dwg	0	Defines whether angles entered in AutoCAD will default to 0 = counterclockwise 1 = clockwise
APERTURE	I	Cfg	10	Defines the object snap cursor size in pixels
AREA	R	...	0.0	Holds value of the true area from the most recent of Area, List, or Dblist commands (**Read-only**)
ATTDIA	I	Dwg	0	Controls whether the Insert command displays a dialogue box for any attributes defined with a given block: 1 = displays dialogue box 0 = does not
ATTMODE	I	Dwg	1	Holds the value of the Attdisp command: 0 = off 1 = normal 2 = on

Variable	Type	Saved in	Default	Meaning
ATTREQ	I	Dwg	1	Controls whether all attributes are set to their defaults or whether you are prompted for attributes: 0 = defaults 1 = prompted
AUNITS	I	Dwg	0	Holds angular units for Units command: 0 = decimal degrees 1 = degrees/minutes/ seconds 2 = grads 3 = radians 4 = surveyor's units
AUPREC	I	Dwg	0	The precision of the angular units
AXISMODE	I	Dwg	0	Controls axis display (Axis command): 0 = off 1 = on
AXISUNIT	2D	Dwg	0.0,0.0	Tick spacing for the Axis command
BACKZ	R	Dwg	0.0	The offset for back clipping plane, which is set with the Dview command. Units are drawing units. Distance from target to clipping plane can be found by using the formula: camera-to-target distance – BACKZ. (**Read-only**)
BLIPMODE	I	Dwg	1	Determines whether blips appear on-screen: 0 = off 1 = on
CDATE	R	Os	*19901231.235*	Holds current date and time for the drawing. (**Read-only**)
CECOLOR	S	Dwg	BYLAYER	Holds the color with which you currently are drawing (**Read-only**)
CELTYPE	S	Dwg	BYLAYER	Holds the linetype with which you currently are drawing (**Read-only**)
CHAMFERA	R	Dwg	0.0	Holds the first chamfer distance

Variable	Type	Saved in	Default	Meaning
CHAMFERB	R	Dwg	0.0	Holds the second chamfer distance
CLAYER	S	Dwg	0	Holds the name of the current layer (**Read-only**)
CMDECHO	I	...	1	Controls whether commands are echoed to (appear on) the screen during an AutoLISP (command) function: 0 = no echo 1 = echo
COORDS	I	Dwg	0	Controls coordinate display : 0 = updated only when you pick a point 1 = updated as crosshairs travel around screen 2 = relative polar coordinates are displayed after first point requested by AutoCAD command has been picked
CVPORT	I	Dwg	2	Identifies current viewport
CYCLECURR	I	Dwg	1	Reserved by Autodesk for future use (**Read-only**)
CYCLEKEEP	I	Dwg	5	Reserved for future use
DATE	R	Os	2448156.811	Current Julian calendar date and time. Seconds are since midnight. (**Read-only**)
DIASTAT	I	...	1	Sets the exit status of the most-recently exited dialogue box: 0 = exit via Cancel 1 = exit via OK (**Read-only**)
DIMALT	I	Dwg	0	Controls the generation of alternate dimensions: 0 = off 1 = on
DIMALTD	I	Dwg	2	Controls decimal places for alternate dimension value

11

Variable	Type	Saved in	Default	Meaning
DIMALTF	R	Dwg	25.4	AutoCAD multiplies this value (the alternate units scale factor) with value determined by current dimension. If DIMALT is on, alternate value appears with normal value.
DIMAPOST	S	Dwg	""	Holds the suffix for alternate dimensions. Can be set only at the `Dim:` prompt.
DIMASO	I	Dwg	1	Controls the generation of associative dimensions: 1 = dimensions associative 0 = dimensions normal
DIMASZ	R	Dwg	0.18	Controls arrow size. AutoCAD uses this size, that of the text, and a default minimum length for the dimension line to determine whether dimension text will be inside or outside the dimension.
DIMBLK	S	Dwg	""	If you need an indicator instead of the arrows or tick marks, you can create a block and indicate its name here. Can be set only at the `Dim:` prompt.
DIMBLK1	S	Dwg	""	If you want one arrow on the dimension line to be different from the other arrow, DIMBLK1 is placed on the end of the dimension line that extends to the first extension line. Can be set only at the `Dim:` prompt.
DIMBLK2	S	Dwg	""	If you want one arrow on the dimension line to be different from the other arrow, DIMBLK2 is placed on the end of the dimension line that extends to the second extension line. Can be set only at the `Dim:` prompt.

Variable	Type	Saved in	Default	Meaning
DIMCEN	R	Dwg	0.09	Changes the size of the center mark AutoCAD inserts with the Center command. Size is the distance from the center mark along one of the line segments.
DIMCLRD	S	Dwg	BYBLOCK	Sets the color of dimension lines
DIMCLRE	S	Dwg	BYBLOCK	Sets the color of extension lines and leaders
DIMCLRT	S	Dwg	BYBLOCK	Sets the color of dimension text
DIMDLE	R	Dwg	0.0	Extends dimension line past extension lines
DIMDLI	R	Dwg	0.38	Controls the increment size AutoCAD uses to offset dimensions when using the Baseline and Continue subcommands
DIMEXE	R	Dwg	0.18	Controls extension above dimension line of extension lines. If you don't want an extension, set DIMEXE to 0.
DIMEXO	R	Dwg	0.0625	Controls extension line offset from origin. If you don't want an offset, set DIMEXO to 0.
DIMGAP	R	Dwg	0.09	Size of gap between text and dimension lines
DIMLFAC	R	Dwg	1	Sets scale factor for drawing. Default (1) is full scale (one drawing inch equals one object inch). In Release 10, change DIMLFAC only if you need to show a detail at a different scale on the same sheet.
DIMLIM	I	Dwg	0	Generates limits, using the values in DIMTM and DIMTP: 0 = off 1 = on

Variable	Type	Saved in	Default	Meaning
DIMSOXD	I	Dwg	0	Suppresses outside-extension dimension lines: 0 = off 1 = on
DIMPOST	I	Dwg	""	Holds default suffix for dimension text. You can enter a suffix to be attached to dimensions as they are inserted. Can be set only at the `Dim:` prompt.
DIMRND	R	Dwg	0.0	Rounds all dimension values you insert. If you set DIMRND to 0.5, all dimensions will be rounded to nearest half unit.
DIMSAH	I	Dwg	0	Tells AutoCAD to use block names in DIMBLK1 and DIMBLK2 as arrow heads for dimensions: 0 = off 1 = on
DIMSCALE	R	Dwg	1.0	Scales an entire dimension by the same amount. (DIMSCALE is useful for Release 10.)
DIMSE1	I	Dwg	0	Suppresses the first extension line: 0 = don't suppress 1 = suppress
DIMSE2	I	Dwg	0	Suppresses the second extension line: 0 = don't suppress 1 = suppress
DIMSHO	I	Dwg	0	Controls whether dimension values are updated as dimension changes: 0 = off, not updated 1 = on, updated
DIMSTYLE	S	Dwg	"UNNAMED"	Current dimension style name. AutoCAD assigns the dummy name, "*UNNAMED", before you give the dimension style a name. (**Read-only**)

11

Variable	Type	Saved in	Default	Meaning
DIMTAD	I	Dwg	0	Places dimension text above the dimension line: 0 = don't place above 1 = place above
DIMTFAC	R	Dwg	1.0	Text-height scale factor for tolerancing text
DIMTIH	I	Dwg	1	1 = insert text horizontally inside dimensions (parallel to bottom edge of paper) 0 = insert text aligned to dimension line and readable from bottom or right side of drawing
DIMTIX	I	Dwg	0	1 = force dimension text between extension lines, even if dimension line and arrows don't fit 0 = place text outside if not enough room
DIMTM	R	Dwg	0.0	Sets negative tolerances for dimensions
DIMTOFL	I	Dwg	0	1 = draw dimension line between extension lines, even if dimension text is forced outside 0 = place dimension line outside if not enough room
DIMTOH	I	Dwg	1	1 = draw all text horizontally outside dimensions 0 = draw text in alignment with dimension line
DIMTOL	I	Dwg	0	1 = generate tolerances, using the tolerance settings defined in DIMTP and DIMTM 0 = don't insert tolerances
DIMTP	R	Dwg	0.0	Value of positive tolerance

Variable	Type	Saved in	Default	Meaning
DIMTSZ	R	Dwg	0.0	Size of tick marks: 0.0 = standard arrow heads
DIMTVP	R	Dwg	0.0	Places dimension text above or below a dimension line. AutoCAD uses the calculation: *DIMTVP* × *DIMTXT*. (DIMTAD must be off.) *positive* value = place text above dimension line 0 = place text in line *negative* value = place text below line
DIMTXT	R	Dwg	0.18	Controls the text size for dimensions. Type the text size you want, and press Enter.
DIMZIN	I	Dwg	0	Controls AutoCAD's zero-inch editing feature of dimensioning architectural units: 0 = zero feet or zero inches not placed in dimension 1 = zero feet and zero inches placed in dimension 2 = only zero feet placed in dimension 3 = zero inches placed in dimension
DISTANCE	R	...	0.0	Stores the last value computed by the Dist command (**Read-only**)
DRAGMODE	I	Dwg	2	Controls dragging of entities: 0 = no dragging 1 = on, if requested 2 = automatic dragging
DRAGP1	I	Cfg	10	Controls the regen-speed at which entities are dragged
DRAGP2	I	Cfg	25	Controls the redraw-speed at which entities are dragged
DWGNAME	S	Dwg	ACAD	Stores the name of the current drawing (**Read-only**)

Variable	Type	Saved in	Default	Meaning
DWGPREFIX	S	Os	C:\ACAD\	Holds the path for the current drawing (**Read-only**)
ELEVATION	R	Dwg	0.0	Holds the value for the current elevation
EXPERT	I	Dwg	0	Controls the display of `Are you sure?` prompts. When a prompt is suppressed by EXPERT, operation in question is performed as though you had responded **Y** to the prompt.

0 = issue all prompts

1 = suppress `About to regen, proceed?` and `Really want to turn the current layer off?`

2 = suppress preceding prompts, as well as Block command's `Block already defined. Redefine it?` prompt and Save and Wblock commands' `A drawing with this name already exists. Overwrite it?` prompt

3 = suppress preceding prompts and those by Linetype command if a linetype is already loaded or defined

4 = suppress preceding prompts and those by UCS Save and Vports Save if the name already exists

5 = suppress preceding

Variable	Type	Saved in	Default	Meaning
				prompts and those from Dim Style and Dim Save if the dimension style already exists
EXTMAX	3D	Dwg	−1.0E+20, −1.0E+20, −1.0E+20	Upper right coordinate of current extents **(Read-only)**
EXTMIN	3D	Dwg	1.0E+20, 1.0E+20, 1.0E+20	Lower left coordinate of current extents **(Read-only)**
FILEDIA	I	Cfg	1	Controls dialogue box display: 0 = use ~ to display 1 = display whenever possible
FILLETRAD	R	Dwg	0.0	Holds the radius used by the Fillet command
FILLMODE	I	Dwg	1	Controls whether polylines, traces, and solids are filled with color: 0 = not filled 1 = filled
FRONTZ	R	Dwg	0.0	Sets the location of the front clipping plane, defined with the Dview command **(Read-only)**
GRIDMODE	I	Dwg	0	Controls the visibility of the grid: 0 = off 1 = on
GRIDUNIT	2D	Dwg	0.0,0.0	Grid spacing, in X and Y direction
HANDLES	I	Dwg	0	Turns handles on or off: 0 = off 1 = on **(Read-only)**
HIGHLIGHT	I	Cfg	1	Controls whether entities selected for a particular operation are highlighted: 0 = no highlighting 1 = highlighting
INSBASE	3D	Dwg	0.0,0.0,0.0	The insertion base point for the entire drawing

11

Variable	Type	Saved in	Default	Meaning
LASTANGLE	R	...	0	End angle of last arc entered, relative to X, Y plane of current UCS (**Read-only**)
LASTPOINT	3D	...	0.0,0.0,0.0	The last point entered, in UCS coordinates
LENSLENGTH	R	Dwg	50.0	The length of the lens, in millimeters; used in perspective viewing (**Read-only**)

LIMCHECK	I	Dwg	0	Controls the limits-check alarm:
				  0 = off
				  1 = on

LIMMAX	2D	Dwg	12.0,9.0	Upper right drawing limits, in World coordinates
LIMMIN	2D	Dwg	0.0,0.0	Lower left drawing limits, in World coordinates
LTSCALE	R	Dwg	1.0	Global linetype scale factor

LUNITS	I	Dwg	2	Holds the value set for units with the Units command:
				  1 = scientific
				  2 = decimal
				  3 = engineering
				  4 = architectural
				  5 = fractional

LUPREC	I	Dwg	4	Holds decimal places for linear units
MAXACTVP	I	...	4	Maximum number of active viewports visible on-screen
MAXSORT	I	Cfg	200	Maximum number of items in a list to be sorted

MENUECHO	I	...	0	Menu echo and prompt control. Sum of the following bits:
				  0 = display all menu items and system prompts
				  1 = suppress echo of menu items
				  2 = suppress printing of system prompts
				  4 = disable Ctrl-P toggle of menu-item echoing

11

Variable	Type	Saved in	Default	Meaning
MENUNAME	S	Dwg	ACAD	Name of menu file currently in use (**Read-only**)
MIRRTEXT	I	Dwg	1	Controls whether horizontal text is mirrored with the Mirror command: 0 = text not mirrored 1 = text mirrored
ORTHOMODE	I	Dwg	0	Toggle for Ortho mode: 0 = ortho off 1 = ortho on
OSMODE	I	Dwg	0	The current object-snap modes, as the sum of the following bits: 1 = endpoint 2 = midpoint 4 = center 8 = node 16 = quadrant 32 = intersection 64 = insertion 128 = perpendicular 256 = tangent 512 = nearest 1024 = quick
PDMODE	I	Dwg	0	Holds point-entity display value
PDSIZE	R	Dwg	0.0	Holds the current point size
PERIMETER	R	...	0.0	Perimeter computed by Area, List, or Dblist commands (**Read-only**)
PFACEVMAX	I	...	4	Maximum number of vertices per polyface (**Read-only**)
PICKBOX	I	Cfg	3	Object selection target height, in pixels
PLATFORM	S	Acad	""	Hardware platform supported by this copy of AutoCAD (**Read-only**)
POPUPS	I	Cfg	1	Defines whether the graphics card supports dialogue boxes, menu bar, pull-down menus, and icon menus: 0 = not supported 1 = supported (**Read-only**)

Variable	Type	Saved in	Default	Meaning
QTEXTMODE	I	Dwg	0	Toggles quick text mode: 0 = regular text 1 = quick text
REGENMODE	I	Dwg	1	Holds the value for Regenauto: 1 = on 0 = off
SCREENSIZE	2D	Cfg	732.0,533.0	Current viewport size, in pixels (**Read-only**)
SHADEDGE	I	Dwg	3	Determines style of shading: 0 = faces and edges shaded 1 = faces shaded; edges in background color 2 = faces in background color; edges in entity color 3 = faces in entity color; edges in background color
SHADEDIF	I	Dwg	70	Sets the contrast of shaded images: 0 = low contrast 100 = high contrast
SKETCHINC	R	Dwg	0.1	Sketch record increment
SKPOLY	I	Dwg	0	Determines whether lines or polylines are created during Sketch mode: 0 = lines 1 = polylines
SNAPANG	R	Dwg	0	Sets the snap and grid rotation angle for the current viewport
SNAPBASE	2D	Dwg	0.0,0.0	Snap and grid origin point for the current viewport
SNAPISOPAIR	I	Dwg	0	Isoplane currently in use: 0 = left 1 = top 2 = right
SNAPMODE	I	Dwg	0	Snap mode toggle in current viewport: 0 = off 1 = on

Variable	Type	Saved in	Default	Meaning
SNAPSTYL	I	Dwg	0	Holds the value for snap style: 0 = standard 1 = isometric
SNAPUNIT	2D	Dwg	1.0,1.0	Snap spacing
SPLFRAME	I	Dwg	0	Controls the display of spline frames: 0 = don't display 1 = display frame
SPLINESEGS	I	Dwg	8	Sets the number of line segments generated for each spline patch
SPLINETYPE	I	Dwg	6	Determines the type of spline curve generated by Pedit Spline: 5 = quadratic B-spline 6 = cubic B-spline
SURFTAB1	I	Dwg	6	Determines the number of tabulations to be generated for Rulesurf and Tabsurf commands, and the mesh density in the M direction for Revsurf and Edgesurf.
SURFTAB2	I	Dwg	6	Determines the mesh density in the N direction for Revsurf and Edgesurf
SURFTYPE	I	Dwg	6	Sets the type of surface fitting to be performed by Pedit Smooth: 5 = quadratic B-spline surface 6 = cubic B-spline surface 8 = Bezier surface
SURFU	I	Dwg	6	Holds the value for the M-direction density of meshes defined by the 3Dmesh command
SURFV	I	Dwg	6	Holds the value for the N-direction density of meshes defined by the 3Dmesh command
TARGET	3D	Dwg	0.0,0.0,0.0	Holds the target location (**Read-only**)

Variable	Type	Saved in	Default	Meaning
TDCREATE	R	Dwg	2448156.810	Time and date of drawing creation (**Read-only**)
TDINDWG	R	Dwg	0.00056007	Total editing time (**Read-only**)
TDUPDATE	R	Dwg	2448156.810	Time and date of last update or save (**Read-only**)
TDUSRTIMER	R	Dwg	0.00056007	User elapsed time (**Read-only**)
TEMPPREFIX	S	Os	""	Directory name for temporary files (**Read-only**)
TEXTEVAL	I	...	0	Text evaluation: 0 = read all test as literal 1 = treat (and ! as AutoLISP symbols)
TEXTSIZE	R	Dwg	0.2	Default height for new text entities drawn with current text style (Ignored for fixed-height text)
TEXTSTYLE	S	Dwg	"STANDARD"	Current text style (**Read-only**)
THICKNESS	R	Dwg	0.0	Current 3-D thickness
TILEMODE	I	Dwg	1	Release 10 compatibility toggle: 0 = allow paper space 1 = don't allow paper space
TRACEWID	R	Dwg	0.05	Width of trace
UCSFOLLOW	I	Dwg	0	1 = automatic viewing of plan view for new UCS 0 = UCS change does not affect view UCSFOLLOW is ignored in paper space.
UCSICON	I	Dwg	1	Controls the UCS icon's location: 0 = icon turned off 1 = icon displayed in lower left corner 2 = icon displayed at origin
UCSNAME	S	Dwg	""	Holds the name of the current UCS (**Read-only**)

Variable	Type	Saved in	Default	Meaning
UCSORG	3D	Dwg	0.0,0.0,0.0	Holds the origin of the current UCS, World Coordinates (**Read-only**)
UCSXDIR	3D	Dwg	1.0,0.0,0.0	X direction of the current UCS (**Read-only**)
UCSYDIR	3D	Dwg	0.0,1.0,0.0	Y direction of the current UCS (**Read-only**)
VIEWCTR	3D	Dwg	6.2,4.5,0,0	Center of view in the current viewport, in UCS coordinates (**Read-only**)
VIEWDIR	3D	Dwg	0.0,0.0,1.0	Viewing direction of the current viewport, in World coordinates (**Read-only**)
VIEWMODE	I	Dwg	0	Viewing mode for the current viewport. Sum of the following bit codes: 1 = perspective view active 2 = front clipping on 4 = back clipping on 8 = UCS follow mode on 16 = front clip not at eye If on, FRONTZ (front-clip distance) determines the front clipping plane. If off, FRONTZ is ignored and the front clipping plane is set to pass through the camera point (vectors behind the camera are not displayed). This flag is ignored if front clipping (bit 2) is off. (**Read-only**)
VIEWSIZE	R	Dwg	9.0	Height of view in the current viewport, in drawing units (**Read-only**)
VIEWTWIST	R	Dwg	0	Defined in the Dview command (**Read-only**)
VSMAX	3D	...	12.4,9.0,0.0	Upper right corner of the current viewport's "virtual Z=0 screen," in UCS

Variable	Type	Saved in	Default	Meaning
				coordinates (**Read-only**)
VSMIN	3D	...	0.0,0.0,0.0	Lower left corner of the current viewport's virtual-screen coordinates (**Read-only**)
WORLDUCS	I	...	1	1 = current UCS is the same as World Coordinate System 0 = current UCS is not the same as the World Coordinate System (**Read-only**)
WORLDVIEW	I	Dwg	1	Dview and Vpoint command input is relative to current UCS: 1 = current UCS is changed to WCS for duration of Dview or Vpoint command 0 = current UCS is not changed (**Read-only**)

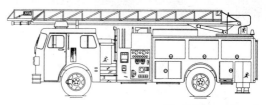

Illustration courtesy of
Autodesk, Inc., Sausalito, CA.

Where To Get Help

This section shows you where to turn when you need extra help with AutoCAD. The AutoCAD Help facility (covered in Chapter 4) can get you through minor problems when you are using the program, but someday you may find yourself faced with a problem not covered by the Help facility or by an AutoCAD manual. When such problems arise, use this part of the book to find extra help.

You already have taken the first step in your search for better AutoCAD support. You are using this book to become more proficient with AutoCAD, and to gain a better understanding of the program than is possible by using only the *AutoCAD Reference Manual*. For more information on AutoCAD, you also can refer to *AutoCAD Advanced Techniques* and *AutoCAD Quick Reference*, 2nd Edition, both published by Que Corporation.

If a tutorial guide or reference manual cannot answer your questions, you should try one of the following options:

❑ Contact your local AutoCAD dealer or Authorized Training Center (ATC).

❑ Join a local AutoCAD Users' Group.

❑ Join the Autodesk forum on CompuServe, or contact one of the many AutoCAD bulletin boards.

If you turn to any of these resources, you will find experienced AutoCAD users. Their knowledge can be invaluable in either helping you solve your problem or directing you to someone who can answer your questions.

AutoCAD Dealers and Authorized Training Centers

Like many CAD programs on the market, AutoCAD is only as good as the people who support it. Autodesk has set up a worldwide network of salespeople and training centers that can help you get the most from the program.

When you have a problem with AutoCAD, talk first to the dealer who sold you the program. Autodesk has always strived to maintain a well-informed sales staff that not only is knowledgeable about AutoCAD but also is willing to steer you toward third-party packages that can make your work with AutoCAD easier.

If you need training, Autodesk maintains authorized training centers across the United States. These centers provide classes that show you how to work from the beginner's level to more advanced levels. Training centers are useful if you want to work with AutoCAD in a short time. Your local AutoCAD dealer should be able to direct you to the nearest Autodesk authorized training center.

AutoCAD Users' Groups

AutoCAD Users' Groups are probably the most enjoyable way to get answers to your AutoCAD problems. Members typically share the same interests and are willing to meet other people and discuss problems, find solutions, and trade tips.

Most users' groups meet informally; they frequently meet at local universities or businesses. A group's membership can range from 10 to more than 100 people. At a meeting, you can find expert users, as well as those who casually dabble in AutoCAD. All of them are there, however, to share their common and unique experiences with the program.

The following list of AutoCAD Users' Groups is current. This list includes the names of local AutoCAD Users' Groups and the names, addresses, and telephone numbers of people to contact if you are interested in joining. When verifiable, each group's meeting schedule is listed, as well. This list includes only groups, names, and numbers that could be verified.

Alabama

Mike Aycock
CAD Users of Birmingham
P.O. Box 43462
Birmingham, AL 35243
(205) 969-1984
Meetings: Monthly; 3rd Tues.

Derrell Dukes
P.O. Drawer 580
Eufaula, AL 36027
(205) 687-3543

James May
2130 Automation Drive
Leeds, AL 35094
(205) 640-7058

Alaska

Robert Posma
Alaska AutoCAD Users' Group
560 E. 34th Avenue
Anchorage, AK 99503
(907) 561-1666
Meetings: Monthly; 4th Thurs. (3rd,
in Nov. and Dec.) 7pm

Arkansas

Michael Stewart
Arkansas MicroCAD Users' Group
2801 S. University Avenue
Little Rock, AR 72204
(501) 569-8222
Meetings: Monthly; 2nd Mon.
(6pm)

Arizona

Brian Goelz
Western Area User Group
4100 East Broadway, Suite 150
Phoenix, AZ 85040-8810
(602) 437-0405
Meetings: Monthly; 2nd Sat. (9am)

Stephanie Kvamme
Phoenix Chapter AutoCAD Users'
Group
4220 W. Northern, Suite 119
Phoenix, AZ 85051
(602) 266-7883
Meetings: Monthly; 3rd Thurs.
(6:30pm)

Jim Reed
Tucson Area AutoCAD Users'
Group
6701 S. Midvale Park Road
Tucson, AZ 85746
(602) 294-5450
Meetings: Varies

California

Bob Dunham
13717 Artesia Blvd.
Cerritos, CA 90701
(213) 926-1511

Andy Khan
AutoCAD User Group
300 West Pontiac Way
Clovis, CA 93613
(209) 275-5561

David L. Wieseler
AUGIE (AutoCAD Users' Group
Inland Empire
900 E. Washington St., Suite 160
Colton, CA 92324
(714) 370-3600
Meetings: Monthly; 4th Wed.

Ronald Lee King
Coachella Valley AutoCAD Users'
Group
66780 E. 4th Street, Suite A
Desert Hot Springs, CA 92240
(619) 329-0055
Meetings: Monthly; 3rd Mon.

Bob Peacock
5055 Santa Teresa Blvd.
Gilroy, CA 95020
(707) 847-1400

Mike Ingram
CAD Group International
13198 Green Horn Road
Grass Valley, CA 95945
(916) 273-9647

George Jones
Healdsburg AutoCAD User Group
6329 West Dry Creek Road
Healdsburg, CA 95448
(707) 433-8954
Meetings: Irregular

Ron Doyle
California Central Coast AutoCAD
    Users
3839 Constellation Road
Lompoc, CA 93436
(805) 928-2794
Meetings: Monthly; 3rd Wed. (7pm)

Michael Berman
Los Angeles Area AutoCAD User
    Group
5301 Laurel Canyon Blvd., #108
North Hollywood, CA 91607-2736
(818) 762-9966
Meetings: Monthly; 4th Thurs.

Genevieve Katz
Oakland Area AutoCAD Users'
    Group
3317 Brundell Drive
Oakland, CA 94602
(415) 530-8870

Lee Walker
Orange County AutoCAD Users
2011 West Chapman, Suite 100
Orange, CA 92668
(714) 385-1132
Meetings: Monthly; 2nd Tues.
    (7pm)

Valerie Newton
Silicon Valley AutoCAD Users'
    Group
777 California Avenue, Suite 100
Palo Alto, CA 94304
(415) 326-8686
Meetings: Bimonthly; 1st Thurs.

Charles Sabah
6695 Owens Drive
Pleasanton, CA 94566
(415) 463-0431

Kathryn Price
San Francisco AutoCAD User Group
662 Bay Street
San Francisco, CA 94133
(415) 923-9228
Meetings: Monthly; 2nd Tues.

Virginia Simoni
AutoCAD Users' Group of Santa
    Cruz
221 20th Avenue
Santa Cruz, CA 95062
(408) 462-0448

John Weitzel
Sonoma County AutoCAD User
    Group
503 Squirrel Court
Santa Rosa, CA 95401
(707) 538-0643
Meetings: Monthly; 3rd Tues.
    (6:30pm)

Betty Menser
Redwood Empire AutoCAD Users
2320 Marinship Way
Sausalito, CA 94965
(707) 762-5772

Christopher DeLucchi
AutoCAD Users' Group of San
    Diego
122 Nardo Avenue
Solana Beach, CA 92075-2021
(619) 755-0854
Meetings: Monthly; 1st Wed.
    (7:30pm)

Ed Thorpe
Sacramento AutoCAD Users' Group
17 North Street, Suite B
Woodland, CA 95695-2931
(916) 666-3187
Meetings: Bimonthly; 2nd and 4th
   Wed. (7pm)

Colorado

Jack Clements
Professional AutoCAD Users' Group
P.O. Box 527
Broomfield, CO 80020-0527
(303) 433-8393
Meetings: Monthly; 1st Wed.
   (6:30pm)

Dennis Kenney
Colorado Springs AutoCAD User
   Group
1303 E. Platte Ave.
Colorado Springs, CO 80909
(303) 603-7066
Meetings: Monthly; 3rd Thurs.

Jeff Serl
Northern Colorado AutoCAD Users'
   Group
P.O. Box 682
Fort Collins, CO 80522
(303) 352-6000
Meetings: Monthly; 3rd Wed.
   (7:30pm)

Julie Evans
Front Range AutoCAD User's Group
10110 Depew Street
Westminster, CO 80020
(303) 465-0413

Connecticut

Jorge Guillen
Greater Hartford AutoCAD Users'
   Group
100 Allyn Street, 4th Floor
Hartford, CT 06103
(203) 525-8651
Meetings: Bimonthly; last Wed.

Dan Cummings
Orange Research Inc.
140 Cascade Blvd.
Milford, CT 06460
(203) 877-5657

Kishin Sujan
Peabody Engineering
39 Maple Tree Avenue
Stamford, CT 06906
(203) 327-7000

Hamid Adib
P.O. Box 1081
West Hartford, CT 06107
(203) 236-2365

Delaware

Mel Sloan
Brandywine Area AutoCAD User
   Group
c/o Gore & Assoc.
750 Otts Chapel Rd.
Newark, DE 19714
(302) 368-2575
Meetings: Monthly; 3rd Thurs.

Florida

John S. Cook
Electro Design Engineering, Inc.
P.O. Box 3270
Brandon, FL 34299
(813) 646-5481
Meetings: Monthly; 3rd Tues.

Todd Maupin
Pensacola AutoCAD User Group
1412 Croquet Drive
Cantonment, FL 32533
(904) 476-1082
Meetings: Bimonthly; 1st and 3rd
   Thurs.

Craig Lojewski
Broward County AutoCAD Users'
  Group
5601 North Powerline Road, Suite
  303
Fort Lauderdale, FL 33309
(305) 791-2900
Meetings: 3rd Tuesday of each
  month

Rich Neiman
Pompano/South Florida Users'
  Group
2003 Cypress Creek Road
Fort Lauderdale, FL 33309
(305) 772-7300
Meetings: Monthly; 1st Tues.

David L. Dennis
NW Florida AutoCAD Professionals
  Assoc.
242 Vicki Leigh Road
Fort Walton Beach, FL 32548-1314
(904) 862-3330
Meetings: Irregular

Chris Favre
Club CADD
6318 Holly Bay Drive
Jacksonville, FL 32211
(904) 396-5583
Meetings: Monthly; 3rd Thurs.

Michael P. Schemer
Central Florida AutoCAD Users'
  Group
P.O. Box 941473
Maitland, FL 32794
(407) 677-5766
Meetings: Monthly; 2nd Tues.
  (7:30pm)

Joe H. Branam
AutoFab with AutoCAD
4730 N.W. 128th Street Rd.
Miami, FL 33054
(305) 685-7978

Tom Celotto
Odessa/Tampa AutoCAD Users'
  Group
2150 Byrd Drive
Odessa, FL 33556
(813) 920-7434
Meetings: Monthly; last Fri. (4pm)

Tom Kaley
Tampa Bay AutoCAD Users' Group
P.O. Box 12248, MS-15
St. Petersburgh, FL 33733
(813) 381-2000
Meetings: Monthly; last Thurs.
  (6:30pm)

Dan E. Dunn
AutoCAD Users of Palm Beaches
P.O. Box 15318
West Palm Beach, FL 33416-5318
(305) 793-3030

Georgia

James Orrison
Southern Electric Users' Group
Bldg. 64A Perimeter Center East,
  Bin 202
Atlanta, GA 30345
(404) 668-2756
Meetings: Quarterly (Atlanta/
  Birmingham/Pensacola/Gulfport)

William Bland
Middle Georgia CAD Group
P.O. Box 110
Macon, GA 31202-0110
(912) 745-4945
Meetings: Monthly; 2nd Thurs.

Ronald Kolman
Savannah Area AutoCAD User
  Group (SAUG)
P.O. Box 23192
Savannah, GA 31403
(912) 233-9003
Meetings: Monthly; 3rd Thurs.

Hawaii

Jim Hogarty
Hawaii AutoCAD Users' Group
(HAUG)
c/o CADTECH, 1188 Bishop Street,
#2206
Honolulu, HI 96813-3309
(808) 526-2886
Meetings: Monthly; 1st Tues. (6pm)

Idaho

Ted A. Corrington
Idaho AutoCAD User's Group
P.O. Box 1059
Caldwell, ID 83606
(208) 454-4572
Meetings: Monthly; 1st Wed. (7pm)

Illinois

Dan Ehrman
Chicago Computer Society
AutoCAD SIG
P.O. Box 8681
Chicago, IL 60680
(312) 942-0705

Leroy Cordes
Greater Chicago AutoCAD Users'
Group Inc.
1412 West Hood
Chicago, IL 60660
(312) 648-1155
Meetings: Monthly; last Wed. (7pm)

R. Dean Williamson
Central Illinois AutoCAD Users
2200 East Eldorado Street
Decatur, IL 62525
(217) 421-2265
Meetings: Bimonthly; 3rd Mon.

Greg Gooch
1600 1st Avenue E.
Milan, IL 61264
(309) 787-1761
Meetings: Quarterly

Phil Hart
Central Illinois AutoCAD Users'
Group
110 East Main Street, Suite 209
Ottawa, IL 61350
(815) 433-5865
Meetings: Monthly; 2nd Mon.
(7pm)

Indiana

Bob Kitt
Dedicated Registered AutoCAD
Workers
701 E. South Street
Albion, IN 46701
(219) 636-2028
Meetings: Monthly; 2nd Tues.
(7pm)

Rick E. Oprisu
Indy AutoCAD Users' Group
122 W. Carmel Drive
Carmel, IN 46032
(317) 575-9606
Meetings: Monthly; 1st Tues. (7pm)

Gary Nemeth
AutoCAD Users and Abusers' Group
1108 S. High St.
P.O. Box 7013
South Bend, IN 46618-1096
(219) 232-3900
Meetings: Monthly; 3rd Fri. (7pm)

Dr. Khosrow Nematollahi
Assoc. of Cen. Indiana Users'
Group
1231 Cumberland Avenue, #A
West Lafayette, IN 47906
(317) 497-1550

Iowa

Norbert Metzler
Mid Iowa AutoCAD Users' Group
P.O. Box 1596
Des Moines, IA 50306
(515) 244-6000
Meetings: Monthly; last Thurs.

John Hendrix
ComputerLand
101 North Court
Ottumwa, IA 52501
(515) 682-5468

Kansas

Brad Swanson
KC-CAD
1250 N. Winchester, Suite D
Olathe, KS 66061
(913) 764-2203
Meetings: Monthly; 3rd Wed.

Kentucky

Dennis Marshall
Bluegrass Area AutoCAD Users'
    Group
237 Moloney Bldg., Cooper Drive
Lexington, KY 40506
(606) 257-3650
Meetings: Monthly; 1st Thurs.
    (7pm)

Deborah Anderson
Kentuckiana AutoCAD Users'
    Group (KAUG)
435 South Third Street
Louisville, KY 40202
(502) 569-3600
Meetings: Monthly; 2nd Thurs.

Louisiana

Renzo Spanhoff
Baton Rouge AutoCAD Users'
    Group
9969 Professional Boulevard
Baton Rouge, LA 70809
(504) 387-0303
Meetings: Monthly; 1st Wed.

Michael Dodson
Lafayette AutoCAD User Group
P.O. Box 51408
Lafayette, LA 70505
(318) 264-4313
Meetings: Monthly; 1st Tues.
    (6:30pm)

Merrie Troxler
CAD Com
3200 Ridgelake Drive, #211
Metairie, LA 70002
(504) 835-4984
Meetings: Monthly; last week

Maine

Daniel C. Moreno
Central Maine AutoCAD Users'
    Group
c/o Platz Assoc., 2 Great Falls Plaza
Auburn, ME 04210
(207) 784-2941

Richard Staples
Eastern Maine ACAD Users' Group
354 Hogan Road
Bangor, ME 04401
(207) 941-4619
Meetings: Monthly; 3rd Thurs.

Greg Keene
Dyer Street
North Berwick, ME 03906
(207) 676-2271

Maryland

Mike Ehrlinger
Baltimore AutoCAD User's Dialog
    (BAUD)
800 S. Rolling Road
Baltimore, MD 21228
(301) 455-4110

David Drazin
CAD/CAM Special Interest Group
15 Orchard Way, North
Rockville, MD 20854
(301) 279-7593

Mark Glick
Baltimore Area AutoCAD Users'
    Group
836 Ritchie Highway
Severna Park, MD 21146
(301) 647-8686
Meetings: Monthly; 2nd Wed.

Massachusetts

The Boston Computer Society
One Center Plaza
Boston, MA 02108
(617) 367-8088

Stephan Mealy
Cape Cod AutoCAD Users' Group
P.O. Box 1430
Buzzards Bay, MA 02532-1430
(508) 888-3841
Meetings: Bimonthly

Bill Abely
Greater Boston AutoCAD Users'
   Group
14 Lowden Avenue
Somerville, MA 02144
(617) 666-2006
Meetings: Monthly; 1st Wed. (6pm)

Michigan

Mike McKelvey
AAAUG: Ann Arbor Area AutoCAD
   Users' Group
P.O. Box 7937
Ann Arbor, MI 48107
(313) 485-0305
Meetings: Monthly; 1st Wed.
   (7:30pm)

Frank Conner
West Michigan AutoCAD Users'
   Group
3310 Eagle Park Drive NE
Grand Rapids, MI 49505
(616) 456-4274
Meetings: Monthly; 1st Mon.

Dave Johnson
Iron Mountain AutoCAD Users'
   Group
P.O. Box 686
Iron Mountain, MI 49801
(906) 774-8000

Jeremy Adcock
Mid-Michigan AutoCAD User Group
123 W. Ottawa Street, 4th Floor
Lansing, MI 48901
(517) 371-6090
Meetings: Monthly; 3rd Tues.
   (7:30)

Thomas Platz
MAIN.MNU Group AutoCAD Users'
   Group
28425 West Eight Mile Road
Livonia, MI 48152
(313) 476-6620
Meetings: Monthly; 2nd Thurs.
   (7pm)

Dennis W. Banaszak
Saginaw Valley AutoCAD Users'
   Group
818 South Michigan Avenue
Saginaw, MI 48602
(517) 799-4717
Meetings: January/April/July/
   October; last Thurs.

Michael McKee
Northeastern Ontario AutoCAD
   User Group
P.O. Box 834
Sault Ste. Marie, MI 49783
(705) 945-3010
Meetings: Quarterly; 3rd Wed.

Kenneth Hornfeld
Main.Mnu
22255 Greenfield, Suite 500
Southfield, MI 48075
(313) 275-5226

Brian Cataldo
AutoCAD User Group
13201 Stevens
Warren, MI 48085
(313) 754-5100

Minnesota

Wayne E. Hobbs
AutoCAD.EXE User Group
416 South 5th Street
Brainerd, MN 56401
(218) 765-3440

Bruce Novotny
CADRE
40 West Highland Park
Hutchinson, MN 55350
(612) 587-3797
Meetings: Monthly; 1st Wed. (1pm)

Hani Ayad
AutoCAD.EXE
P.O. Box 141075
Minneapolis, MN 55414
(612) 379-7543
Meetings: Monthly; 2nd Tues.
   (7pm)

Bob Skaletske
Building 235 - 3F04
St. Paul, MN 55144
(612) 736-2099

Missouri

Skip Smith
1107 S. 291 Highway
Lees Summit, MO 64063
(816) 524-5580

Jerry Craig
Forest Park AutoCAD User Group
5600 Oakland
St. Louis, MO 63110
(314) 644-9291
Meetings: Monthly; 3rd Wed.

Keith Wallis
Ozark AutoCAD User Group
P.O. Box 3499 G.S.
Springfield, MO 65808
(417) 869-7350
Meetings: Bimonthly; 2nd Tues.

Nebraska

Prof. Leendert Kersten
AutoCAD Users of Nebraska
3721 Chapin Circle
Lincoln, NE 68506
(402) 478-4257
Meetings: As announced

Rich Molettiere
Omaha AutoCAD Users' Group
37th and Ames
Omaha, NE 68111
(402) 554-6500

Nevada

Gale Gorman
Las Vegas AutoCAD Users' Group
P.O. Box 27140
Las Vegas, NV 89126-1140
(702) 878-7974

New Hampshire

Brian Morse
State of New Hampshire AutoCAD
   U.G.
100 Saranac Drive (Morse
   Associates)
Nashua, NH 03062
(603) 880-4980
Meetings: Monthly; 2nd Thurs.

Bruce Polderman
State of NH AutoCAD User Group
220 Center Street
Sullivan, NH 03445
(603) 847-3373
Meetings: Monthly; 1st Thurs.

New Jersey

Richard Finch
Southern New Jersey AutoCAD User
   Group
P.O. Box 106
Bordentown, NJ 08505
(609) 298-7449
Meetings: Monthly; 2nd Wed.
   (7pm)

Peter Anger
c/o Olympia & York
395 Lantana Avenue
Englewood, NJ 07631
(201) 494-9708

Art Bianconi
Northeast AutoCAD Users' Group
  (NAUG)
983 Madison Avenue
Plainfield, NJ 07060
(201) 757-9573
Meetings: Monthly; 3rd Thurs.

Mark J. Meara
Princeton Area AutoCAD User
  Group
c/o CUH2A, 600 Alexander Road
Princeton, NJ 08543
(609) 452-1212

Bill Adams
Northeast AutoCAD Users' Group
  (NAUG)
12 Howland Circle
West Caldwell, NJ 07006
(201) 228-3869
Meetings: Monthly; 3rd Thurs.
  (8pm)

New Mexico

Corine Florez Trujillo
Albuquerque AutoCAD Users'
  Group
P.O. Box 80376
Albuquerque, NM 87108
(505) 247-3705
Meetings: Monthly; 3rd Wed.

Millard Edwards
AULA (AutoCAD Users of Los
  Alamos)
P.O. Box 1663, M/S D-410
Los Alamos, NM 87545
(505) 667-2485

New York

Rochelle Borgen
Albany AutoCAD Users' Group
40 Colvin Avenue
Albany, NY 12206
(518) 438-6844

Chris Lanza
Buffalo AutoCAD Users' Group
703 Washington Street
Buffalo, NY 14203
(716) 684-0001
Meetings: Monthly; 3rd Wed. (6pm)

Michael Geyer
Metro NY AutoCAD Users
20 West 20th Street
New York, NY 10011
(212) 691-4722

Frank Munzi
Niagara Frontier AutoCAD Users'
  Group
2400 Buffalo Avenue
Niagara Falls, NY 14303
(716) 278-6428
Meetings: Monthly; 2nd Thurs.
  (7pm)

Bob Schellinger
Rochester Area AutoCAD Users'
  Group
c/o Olin Corporation, P.O. Box 205
Rochester, NY 14601
(716) 436-3030
Meetings: Bimonthly; last Tues.

Diane Eberhard
Long Island AutoCAD Users' Group
27 Pine Ridge Drive
Smithtown, NY 11787
(516) 543-7777
Meetings: Monthly; last Tues.

North Carolina

Paul Aeby
The Charlotte Area AutoCAD User
  Group
2113 Jennie Linn Drive
Charlotte, NC 28215
(704) 525-1088

Doug Willard
Charlotte Area AutoCAD User
  Group
7851 Rainbow Drive
Charlotte, NC 28212
(704) 394-8341
Meetings: Monthly; 2nd Wed.
  (7pm)

Tim Barber
Triangle AutoCAD Users' Group
  (TAG)
Post Office Box 52144
Durham, NC 27717
(919) 490-8977
Meetings: Monthly; last Thurs.

Steve Frick
Piedmont AutoCAD Users' Group
P.O. Box 16341
Greensboro, NC 27406
(919) 674-5372
Meetings: Monthly; 1st Fri.

Beth Robinson
Wilmington AutoCAD Users' Group
243 North Front Street
Wilmington, NC 28401
(919) 343-1048
Meetings: Monthly; 1st Tues.
  (6:30pm)

North Dakota

David Bauman
Mid-Con AutoCad Users' Group
Box 44
Fargo, ND 58107
(701) 232-3271
Meetings: Monthly; 2nd Tues.
  (7:30pm)

Ohio

Janak Dave
Greater Cincinnati AutoCAD User's
  Group
2220 Victory Parkway
Cincinnati, OH 45206-2822
(513) 556-5311
Meetings: Monthly; 2nd Thurs.

Greg Malkin
Northeast Ohio AutoCAD Users'
  Group
4555 Emery Industrial Parkway,
  #102
Cleveland, OH 44128-5767
(216) 765-1133
Meetings: Bimonthly; 1st Wed.

Wes Eichelman
Dayton Area AutoCAD Users' Group
  (DACAD)
1660 Kettering Tower
Dayton, OH 45423
(513) 228-4007
Meetings: Monthly; 2nd Tues.
  (7pm)

Thomas Altman
CADUS
1501 Spring Garden Avenue
Lakewood, OH 44107
(216) 228-9777

David R. Gibson
Tri-County AutoCAD User Group
P.O. Box 385
North Benton, OH 44449
(216) 584-7651
Meetings: Monthly; 4th Wed. (6pm)

Joseph Brancheau
NW Ohio AutoCAD User Group
Caller #10,000, Oregon Road
Toledo, OH 43699
(419) 666-0580
Meetings: Monthly; 1st Wed. (7pm)

Cindy Bedford
North Coast AutoCAD Users' Group
    (NORCAD)
37527 Park Ave.
Willoughby, OH 44094
(216) 951-8070
Meetings: Monthly; last Wed.

Oklahoma

John Helton
Southern Oklahoma AutoCAD User
    Group
P.O. Box 197
Asher, OK 74826
(405) 784-2411
Meetings: Monthly; 3rd Tues.

Skip Bachman
Oklahoma City Metro User's Group
    (OKMUG)
P.O. Box 20400
Oklahoma City, OK 73156-0400
(405) 478-5353
Meetings: Monthly; 2nd Thurs.
    (6pm)

Hugh Earnheart
AutoCAD ACE Users' Group
P.O. Box 32797
Oklahoma City, OK 73123
(405) 949-1442
Meetings: Monthly; 3rd Thurs.

Terry Anderson
Compugraph Professional CAD
    User Group
P.O. Box 3346
Tulsa, OK 74101-3346
(918) 582-4545
Meetings: Quarterly

Jim Surman
3103 N. Hemlock Circle, Suite 110A
Tulsa, OK
(918) 251-4470

Oregon

John Schaeffer
Central Oregon AutoCAD Users'
    Group
Central Oregon Community
    College
Bend, OR 97701
(503) 389-2584

Hans Stangler
P.O. Box 1084
Corvallis, OR 97339
(503) 371-1032

Rusty Gesner
ACADemy User Group
1025 E. Powell, Suite 202
Gresham, OR 97030
(503) 666-5564

Steve Metz
AutoCAD Users' Group of Portland
8339 SW 41st Ave.
Portland, OR 97219
(503) 222-5840
Meetings: Monthly; 4th Tues.
    (6:30pm)

John St. John
Corps of Engineers
20846 SW Martinazzi
Tualatin, OR 97062
(503) 221-3841

Pennsylvania

Nelson Stauffer
P.O. Box 453
Clarks Summit, PA 18411
(717) 586-1488

Kenn Anderson
KEYstone ACADemy AutoCAD
    Users' Group
Box 149
LaPlume, PA 18440
(717) 945-3232
Meetings: Odd-numbered months;
    2nd Thurs.

S.A. Sween
SE Pennsylvania AutoCAD Users'
   Group
Route 2, Box 158
East Earl, PA 17519
(717) 445-6701
Meetings: Monthly; 3rd Mon.

Clem Gordon
Pittsburgh Area AutoCAD Users'
   Group
105 Pine Street
Imperial, PA 15126
(412) 695-3413

Howard Fulmer
Philadelphia AutoCAD Users'
   Group (PAUG)
7500 Germantown Ave.
Spring Garden College
Philadelphia, PA 19119
(215) 275-9866
Meetings: Monthly; 3rd Thurs.
   (5:30pm at Spring Garden
   College)

Les Emerson
Greater Pittsburgh AutoCAD Users'
   Group
104 Julrich Drive
Pittsburgh, PA 15317
(412) 941-7853
Meetings: Monthly; 3rd Wed.
   (6:15pm)

Rhode Island

Nancy Lewis-Lentz
OceanCAD Users' Group
2364 Post Road
Warwick, RI 02886
(401) 732-1123
Meetings: Bimonthly

South Carolina

Richard Tedder
AutoCAD S.I.G., Palmetto P.C. Club

P.O. Box 2046, 1331 Elmwood Ave.
Columbia, SC 29202
(803) 254-6382

Wes McDaniel
Greenville AutoCAD User's Group
P.O. Box 25563
Greenville, SC 29616
(803) 297-9281
Meetings: Monthly; 2nd Tues.
   (6pm)

John R. Watts
Piedmont AutoCAD User Group
Drawer 4386
Spartanburg, SC 29305-4386
(803) 591-3674
Meetings: Monthly; 2nd Tues.
   (7pm)

Gary Wenzel
Sumter AutoCAD Users' Group
P.O. Box 1734
Sumter, SC 29151
(803) 481-6351
Meetings: Quarterly

South Dakota

Gene Murphy
Sioux Falls Area AutoCAD Users'
   Group
600 West Avenue N.
Sioux Falls, SD 57104
(605) 336-3722

Tennessee

Patricia Philips
Dyersburg Area AutoCAD Users'
   Group
P.O. Box 648
Dyersburg, TN 38025
(901) 285-6910

Don Bosten
Jackson Area AutoCAD Users'
    Group
P.O. Box 2468
Jackson, TN 38302-2468
(901) 668-8600
Meetings: Monthly; 3rd Tues.
    (7pm)

Donnia M. Tabor
Smokey Mountain AutoCAD User
    Group
P.O. Box 57
Knoxville, TN 37901
(615) 694-6671
Meetings: Monthly; 1st Tues. (7pm)

Jim Prewett
AutoCAD Users' Group: Memphis
    Chapter
P.O. Box 241938
Memphis, TN 38124
(901) 685-0230
Meetings: Monthly; 2nd Thurs.
    (7pm)

Joe Cook
Nashville AutoCAD Users' Group
    (NAUG)
30 Burton Hills Boulevard, Suite
    230
Nashville, TN 37215
(615) 353-3462
Meetings: Monthly; 3rd Tues.
    (6:30pm)

Mike Nichols
Northwest Tennessee ACAD User
    Group
P.O. Box 550
Paris, TN 38242-0550
(901) 642-4251

Meetings: Monthly; 2nd Tues.
    (5pm)

Texas

Kelly B. Nunn
Austin AutoCAD Users' Group
3636 Executive Center Drive, Suite
    150
Austin, TX 78731
(512) 346-8399
Meetings: Bimonthly; last Tues.

Clyde Brothers
Brazos Valley
Rt. 3, P.O. Box 297
College Station, TX 77840
(409) 776-8820

Jim Patton
AutoCAD User's Goup, Dallas Area
    Chapter
Old Airport Road, P.O. Box 878
Commerce, TX 75428
(214) 220-0222
Meetings: Monthly; 3rd Tues.

Glenn Wells
Dallas-Ft. Worth AutoCAD Users'
    Group
Box 112 HK, Route 3
Farmersville, TX 75031
(214) 782-6660

Bob Mirrielees
El Paso AutoCAD Users' Group
11501 James Watt Dr.
El Paso, TX 79936
(915) 591-5600
Meetings: Monthly; 2nd Wed.
    (7pm)

John Hennessy
Southeast Harris County AutoCAD
    Users' Group
P.O. Box 34311
Houston, TX 77234
(713) 943-5301
Meetings: Bimonthly; 2nd Tues.
    (7pm)

Dan Luce
PRO-CAD Users' Group
12601 High Star
Houston, TX 77072
(713) 463-0196

Glenn A. Seehausen
Northwest Houston AutoCAD User
  Group
P.O. Box 40308
Houston, TX 77240-0308
(713) 890-3300
Meetings: Monthly; 2nd Wed.

Aprim K. Khairo
(AutoCAD Users' Group) City of
  Odessa
411 West Eighth St. (P.O. Box
  4398)
Odessa, TX 79761
(915) 337-7381

Monty Newman
Tyler Area ACAD User's Group
P.O. Box 9020
Tyler, TX 75701
(214) 531-2351
Meetings: Monthly; 3rd Thurs.
  (7pm)

Alan R. Austin
HAL P.C. ACAD S.I.G.
430 Merriweather
Webster, TX 77598
(713) 480-4606
Meetings: Monthly; 3rd Tues.

Utah

Ken Coburn
ACADUSR
9160 South 300 West, #22
Sandy, UT 84070
(801) 561-0525
Meetings: Monthly; 2nd Tues.

Virginia

Dave Morton
Northern Virginia AutoCAD Users'
  Group
7929 Westpark Drive
McLean, VA 22102
(703) 556-0700
Meetings: Monthly; 3rd Thurs.

Dale A. Campbell
Tidewater Area AutoCAD Users'
  Group
c/o Glenn & Assoc., P.O. Box 12154
Norfolk, VA 23502
(804) 461-9130
Meetings: Varies

Michael Farmer
Central Virginia AutoCAD Users'
  Group
P.O. Box 29599
Richmond, VA 23229
(804) 756-7743
Meetings: Monthly; 3rd Wed.

Washington

Dick Vogel
Bellingham User Group (BUG)
Technology Department, Western
  Wash. U.
Bellingham, WA 98225
(206) 676-2976
Meetings: Monthly; 3rd Thurs.
  (7pm)

Dan Flanagan
Seattle Area AutoCAD Users' Group
P.O. Box 6371
Lynnwood, WA 98036
(206) 771-5334
Meetings: Monthly; 3rd Thurs.

Ken Ames
Battelle Blvd.
Richland, WA 99352
(509) 375-3930

Jeff Waymack
Architects Engineers Planners
  Users' Group
2102 North 52nd St.
Seattle, WA 98103
(206) 634-0849
Meetings: Bimonthly; 1st & 3rd
  Tues. (5:30pm)

Dan Stall
West 1720 Fourth Avenue
Spokane, WA 99204
(509) 838-6466

Don Swedberg
Tacoma AutoCAD Users' Group
  (S.I.G.)
1509 N. Juniper
Tacoma, WA 98406
(206) 752-0145
Meetings: Monthly; 2nd Tues.
  (7pm)

Wisconsin

Mark Blaskey
Chippewa Valley AutoCAD Users'
  Group
c/o Envirosystems
1030 Regis Ct.
Eau Claire, WI 54701
(715) 833-2393
Meetings: Monthly; 1st Mon. (7pm)

Dan Schaub
Coulee Region AutoCAD User
  Group
P.O. Box 3206
La Crosse, WI 54602-3206
(608) 788-8451
Meetings: Monthly; 4th Wed. (7pm)

Fred Toney
Greater Madison Area AutoCAD
  User Group
3822 Mineral Point Road
Madison, WI 53705
(608) 238-6761
Meetings: Monthly; 2nd Mon.
  (7pm)

Bill Belson
Wisconsin Local AutoCAD Users'
  Group
P.O. Box 12365
3879 North Richards Street
Milwaukee, WI 53212
(414) 542-6060

Gene Roseburg
NorthStar AutoCAD Users' Group
600 N. Twenty-first St.
Superior, WI 54880
(715) 394-6677

Glenn Furst
Fox Valley AutoCAD User Group
P.O. Box 249
Waupaca, WI 54981
(715) 258-8511
Meetings: Monthly; 1st Mon. (7pm)

Michael R. Clark
Central Wisconsin AutoCAD User's
  Group
1000 Campus Drive
Wausau, WI 54401
(715) 675-3331
Meetings: Monthly; 2nd Tues.
  (7pm)

West Virginia

Max Dent
Greater Tri-State AutoCAD Users'
  Group
200 Ken Lake
Winfield, WV 25213
(304) 755-9677
Meetings: Monthly; 3rd Thurs.
  (7pm)

Argentina

Sergio Levinton
Esrudio Levinton
Lavalle 482 - 8th "A"
Buenos Aires, Argentina 4047
(54) 322-6912

Australia

Ian Batley
Northern Territory AutoCAD User's
    Group
G.P.O. Box 4032
Darwin, NT 0801
Australia
(089) 81 6885
Meetings: Monthly; 1st Thurs.
    (7pm)

Robert Gritsch
1 Colo Place
Pendle Hill, New South Wales 2145
Australia
(02) 818-8245

Tony Studans
99 Nicholson Street
St. Leonards, New South Wales
    2065
Australia
(02) 929-0400

Bob Sunners
Queensland AutoCAD Users' Group
1677 Mt. Cotton Rd.
Burbank, Queensland 4156
Australia
(07) 390-3677
Meetings: Monthly; last Wed.
    (6:30pm)

David Myers
AutoCAD User Group of South
    Australia
Woodford Road
Elizabeth, South Australia 5112
Australia
(08) 255-2044
Meetings: Monthly; 2nd Thurs.

Steve Arnold
AutoCAD Users' Group of SA
P.O. Box 116
Kensington Park, South Australia
    5068
Australia
(08) 277-1711

David Manterfield
P.O. Box 396, Valley Road
Devonport, Tasmania 7310
Australia
(004) 24-4211

Tony Johnston
Tasmanian AutoCAD Users' Group
P.O. Box 88
Moonah, Tasmania 7009
Australia
(002) 78 4512
Meetings: Monthly; 3rd Thurs.

Hal Cutting
Victorian AutoCAD User Group
202 Little Page Street
Middle Park, Victoria 3206
Australia
(03) 690-7494
Meetings: Bimonthly; Monday

John Racovelli
2 Havelock Street
West Perth, West Australia 6005
Australia
(09) 222-5555

Belgium

Jef Schelfhout
Belgium AutoCAD Users' Group
    (UAB)
Rumoldusstraat 66A
Dilbeek B1750
Belgium
(02) 569-4924

Brazil

Joao Augusto Moura Terra
Brazilian AutoCAD Users' Group
Av. Paulista, 1754 Conj. 108
Sao Paulo, SP 01310
Brazil
(011) 287-0764
Meetings: Not yet on regular basis

Canada

Paul Hamonic
Calgary AutoCAD Users' Group
210, 8181 Flint Rd. SE
Calgary, AB T2H 2B8
Canada
(403) 255-5511
Meetings: Monthly; 2nd Tues.

Randy Russell
Edmonton AutoCAD User Group
10248 123 Street NW
Edmonton, AB T5N 1N4
Canada
(403) 424-4756
Meetings: Monthly; 1st Wed. (7pm)

David Toews
Vancouver AutoCAD Users' Society
Box 727-810 West Broadway
Vancouver, BC V57 4C9
Canada
(604) 530-6426
Meetings: Monthly (except July &
    August); 1st Wed. (7:30pm)

Ron Mohr
Kalamalka Computer Users' Group
7000 College Way
Vernon, BC V1T 6Y5
Canada
(604) 545-7291

Brad Blaney
Ministry of Transportation &
    Highways
3C-940 Blanshard Street
Victoria, BC V8W 3E6
Canada
(604) 387-3501
Meetings: Monthly; 2nd Wed.

John McGraw
New Brunswick Area AutoCAD
    Users' Group
102 Queen Street
Fredericton, NB E3B 1A5
Canada
(506) 459-6080

Jeff Morris
Nova Scotia AutoCAD User Group
5251 Duke Street, Suite 1112
Halifax, NS B3J 1P3
Canada
(902) 420-0207
Meetings: Bimonthly

Ryan Monti
Great Slave AutoCAD Users' Group
P.O. Box 1777
Yellowknife, NWT X1A 2P4
Canada
(403) 920-2842

Ted Syme
SCALE
1 Georgian Drive
Barrie, ON L4M 3X9
Canada
(705) 728-1951
Meetings: Irregular basis

Dieter Reisewitz
Northern College AutoCAD Users'
    Group
140 Government Road, East
Kirkland Lake, ON P2N 3L8
Canada
(705) 567-9291
Meetings: Bimonthly; 2nd Mon.

Derek Pearce
Toronto Region AutoCAD Exchange
    (TRACE)
1400 Petrie Way
Mississauga, ON L5J 1G5
Canada
(416) 792-8999
Meetings: Bimonthly; last Tues.
    (7:30pm)

William Smit
39 Glen Manor Drive
Nepean, ON K2G 3E9
Canada
(613) 225-4854

Jamie Monteith
AutoSAR
118 North Victoria Street
Sarnia, ON N7T 5W9
Canada
(519) 332-4400
Meetings: Monthly; last Thurs.

Robert L. Tomlinson
Northern Ontario AutoCAD Users'
 Group
107 Cumberland St. North
Thunderbay, ON P7A 4M3
Canada
(807) 345-6375
Meetings: Monthly; 1st Thurs.

Neil Musson
Windsor AutoCAD User Group
U. of Windsor Phys. Plant, 401
 Sunset Blvd.
Windsor, ON N9B 3P4
Canada
(519) 253-4232
Meetings: Monthly; 1st Wed.

Bill Holden
City of Saskatoon Planning
 Department
City Hall
Saskatoon, SK S7K 0J5
Canada
(306) 975-2684

Cyprus

Christos Pagdatis
Cyprus Association of CAD Users
14 Kefallinias Street, Acropolis
Nicosia, Cyprus
(357) 2-427597
Meetings: Every 2nd Wed. night

England

A. T. Bradbury
Midlands AutoCAD User Group
26 Dam Street

Lichfield, Staffs WS13 6AA
England
(054) 325-1511

Andrew Bichard
AutoCAD Users' Group United
 Kingdom
36 Avenue Road
London N6 5DW
England
(81) 348-3040
Meetings: Monthly (varies)

Phillip Keevil
AUG
53 Derngate
Northampton NN12ET
England
(06) 042-0093

M. Holding
Fitzherbert Road
Farlington, Portsmouth PO6 1RR
England
(070) 537-0961

Clive Meyer
AutoCAD User Group UK
Pelham House, 25 Pelham Square
Brighton, East Sussex BN1 4ET
England
(02) 73-600411
Meetings: Monthly (varies)

France

Jean-Claude Testé
Club Utilisateur AutoCAD
115, Rue de Musselburg
Champigny/Marne 94500
France
(1) 49 83 01 83
Meetings: Twice a year

Greece

Michalis Seitanidis
"ATHENS1" AutoCAD Users' Group
Vriaxidos 18
Athens 116 35
Greece
(01) 701-2284
Meetings: Monthly

India

Rakesh K. Gupta
EAMC (New Delhi AutoCAD Users'
    Group)
50, Kailash Hills, East of Kailash
New Delhi 110024
India
(91)11-684-5184
Meetings: Bimonthly; 2nd & last
    Fri.

Avay Nayak
Bhubaneswar AutoCAD User Group
P.B. No. 82
Bhubaneswar, Orissa 751012
India
0674-53038

Israel

Lee Waldman
Israel AutoCAD User Group
P.O. Box 39079
Tel-Aviv 61390
Israel
(972) 3-5464054
Meetings: Approximately every 6
    weeks

Japan

Takaaki Fujimori
Japan AutoCAD User Group
Unosawa Tokyu Bldg 4F, 1-19-15
    Ebisu
Shibuya-Ku, Tokyo 150
Japan
(03) 473-9511

Masao Okajima
Japan AutoCAD Users' Group
4-6-13-701 Kudan Minami
Chiyoda-ku, Tokyo 102
Japan
(03) 262-4255
Meetings: Monthly; 3rd Fri.

Jordan

Ramzi Kawar
Jordan AutoCAD User Group
P.O. Box 925740
Amman, Jordan
962 6 818360

Lebanon

Gilles Fayad
Lebanese AutoCAD User Group
P.O. Box 16-5182
Beirut, Lebanon
(961) 1-324122

Mexico

Juan Gonzalez
Mexico City AutoCAD Users' Group
50 Munich 142
Vialle Dorado, Mexico 54020
Mexico
391-20-22

Netherlands

Mr. H. Bos
Autocad gebruikers groep VCA
Geestbrugweg 42
Rijswijk 2281 CM
Netherlands
(070) 95-4243
Meetings: Bimonthly

Ko Rinkel
CIAD
P.O. Box 74
Zoetermeer 2700 AB
Netherlands
(31) 79-2193-24

New Zealand

Ken Henry
Auckland AutoCAD Users' Group
P.O. Box 76-128
Manukau City, New Zealand
(09) 267-7531
Meetings: Monthly; 2nd Wed.

Geoff Blokland
Canterbury AutoCAD User Group
Christchurch Polytechnic
P.O. Box 22095
Christchurch, New Zealand
(03) 798 150
Meetings: Bimonthly; 3rd Wed.

Peru

Jaime M. Soldi
AutoCAD Peru
Apartado 18-0934
Lima 18, Peru
(51-14) 45-2394

Scotland

Dr. A. James
Scotland AutoCAD User Group
117 Renfrew Street
Glasgow, Scotland
(041) 332-9797

Spain

Luis Jara
Asicom, SA
c/ Aragon, 264
Barcelona 08007
Spain
(343) 215-9000

Victor M. Gaspar
Club de Usuarios de AutoCAD,
    Editisa
Alda. Recalde 64Bis, EPTA
Bilbao 48010
Spain
(34)4-4435365
Meetings: Not regular

United Arab Emirates

Asif Al-Omari
Abu Dhabi AutoCAD Users' Group
P.O. Box 26562
Abu Dhabi, U.A.E.
9712660543

Yugoslavia

Rok Kolar
AutoCAD User Group
Meza 24
Dravograd
Slovenia, 62 370
Yugoslavia
(602) 83 413
Meetings: Monthly; 1st Fri.

Illustration courtesy of
Autodesk, Inc., Sausalito, CA.

AutoCAD
Troubleshooting Guide

One nice thing about computers is that there is a cause for every effect, even if the cause seems obscure at times. This section describes several pitfalls, their causes, and possible solutions.

AutoCAD is a large program with an impressive range of features and potential applications. But AutoCAD's dynamic nature can create problems for its users. If troubles arise, don't become too distraught. Remember that problems are not unusual when you use a complex computer system. Rather, try to approach your problem from an analytical standpoint, and take the following steps:

1. Identify the nature of the problem.

2. Identify the steps you took that made the problem occur, and determine whether these steps will re-create the problem every time they are followed.

3. Determine the scope of any damage (to your drawing or other files).

4. Note the following: time of day, drawing name, AutoCAD version, command being used, and error message. Keep an error log; it can be especially helpful for finding the cause of intermittent problems.

5. Find a solution.

This process should not be foreign to you: it's a variation of the process used to solve most business problems.

Typically, the errors you encounter will fall into one (or more) of the following general classifications:

❑ **Configuration errors.** These errors are symptomatic of an improperly installed system or a system that has been upgraded without changing AutoCAD's configuration. Otherwise, AutoCAD may be looking for a file that is not where it is supposed to be.

❑ **Hardware errors.** These errors can be caused by hardware that is not suited to the task, is improperly installed, or is just plain faulty.

❑ **Input errors.** These errors occur when you input misspelled commands or invalid data into the computer. The solution generally involves changing the input to something that AutoCAD understands.

❑ **Software bugs.** These can be errors with AutoCAD itself, with a software add-on package used with AutoCAD, or with an AutoLISP program written to work with AutoCAD.

❑ **System errors.** These errors are caused by the operating system you are using. Your options here may be limited and generally are outside the scope of this chapter. System errors may require that your computer or its operating system be repaired.

❑ **Environmental errors.** These errors are caused by external sources, such as voltage drops caused by other equipment, monitor interference caused by an adjacent monitor or other device radiating radio frequencies, and so on.

Although determining which type of error has occurred can be difficult, figuring out the problem is usually easy. You should be able to fit an error condition pretty quickly into one of the preceding categories.

Consider the nature of the problem. Ask yourself questions like:

❑ Am I able to enter AutoCAD, and does the Main Menu appear correctly?

❑ Am I able to enter the Drawing Editor? With a previous drawing? With a new drawing?

❑ Am I able to enter commands from the keyboard, but not from the menu?

This kind of questioning will lead you to the appropriate area of your computer's hardware or software, where you can investigate further.

The preceding paragraph gave you an example of a logical train of thought. Clearly, you cannot enter the Drawing Editor if you cannot even enter AutoCAD. If you hop around from one possibility to another, you probably will waste valuable time looking in the wrong place for your answer.

Your best bet for finding the problem is to keep a cool head and try to re-create the problem. Start at the point at which the problem may have occurred, or do something that may cause the problem to occur. Then move ahead in a linear fashion. Only then, with these facts in mind, can you arrive at a solution.

You should get into the habit of frequently backing up your work. This means taking the time to save the drawing to the hard drive, with a copy on a floppy disk. Store a second copy of valuable work in another location outside your office.

Troubleshooting Configuration Errors

CONFIGURATION PROBLEM #1:

My display screen does not make any sense when I enter the Drawing Editor. It is full of squiggly lines, and I cannot read any text on the screen.

Possible Cause: AutoCAD is configured for the wrong display device.

Solution: Flip to the text screen (press F1). Return to the Main Menu, and choose Option 5 to reconfigure the system. Specify the display device option that represents your hardware.

CONFIGURATION PROBLEM #2:

When I reconfigured AutoCAD, I could not find my device listed in the configuration choices.

Possible Cause: The appropriate driver is either missing from the directory in which you are keeping drivers or has been discontinued, or you have a device that uses an ADI (Autodesk Device Interface) driver.

Solution: Ask your supplier for the name of the driver you need; then check for the file on your original AutoCAD disks. If you do not find it, look in a directory (called \OBSOLETE) on the AutoCAD Drivers disk.

CONFIGURATION PROBLEM #3:

When I run AutoCAD, I see a message that indicates I am out of RAM.

Possible Cause: The Acadfreeram variable in your AUTOEXEC.BAT file is not set or is set improperly.

Solution: In the AUTOEXEC.BAT file, change the line that controls the Acadfreeram variable. This line looks like the following:

```
SET ACADFREERAM=24
```

Experiment with the value to the right of the equal sign, alternately increasing or decreasing it until the error message disappears. The number tells AutoCAD to set aside the number times 1,000. In this case, AutoCAD will set aside 24,000 bytes of RAM (the maximum). Acadfreeram does not apply to DOS extender versions of AutoCAD.

CONFIGURATION PROBLEM #4:

I have extra memory installed in my computer system; but when I run AutoCAD, I get a message indicating that extra memory is disabled.

Possible Cause: A variety of factors can cause this message to appear.

Solution: Review the settings for Acadxmem, Acadlimem, and Lispxmem in the AUTOEXEC.BAT file. The use of extra memory is covered in Chapter 4 of the *AutoCAD Installation and Performance Guide.*

CONFIGURATION PROBLEM #5:

AutoCAD cannot find the overlay (.OVL), shape (.SHX), or menu (.MNX) files.

Possible Cause: Either the files have been erased from the \ACAD directory, or the environment variable SET ACAD= is missing from the AUTOEXEC.BAT or ACAD.BAT file.

Solution: If you are using a third-party menu system or loading AutoCAD onto a RAM disk, you may have to provide an environment setting for the directory that contains these files. Review the literature from the menu system you are using, or ask your dealer about the RAM disk installation.

CONFIGURATION PROBLEM #6:

My digitizer menu does not work in the proper squares.

Possible Cause: The menu overlay on your digitizer has moved.

Solution: Using the Tablet command, reconfigure your digitizer.

CONFIGURATION PROBLEM #7:

My cursor freezes on-screen, or my keyboard seems sluggish.

Possible Cause: An interrupt conflict or more than one device assigned to the same communications port, or the snap setting is larger than the current view.

Solution: First, try turning snap off with function key F9. Check the AutoCAD configuration and any driver addresses you may have provided, to see whether the digitizer is installed properly.

CONFIGURATION PROBLEM #8:

The text I had in a drawing will not display on-screen.

Possible Cause: AutoCAD uses a shape file (.SHX) to create the text style in your drawing. This file is missing.

Solution: Recopy the required .SHX file from the AutoCAD Support disk to the computer's /ACAD directory.

CONFIGURATION PROBLEM #9:

I receive a message stating that my AutoCAD prototype drawing is not on file.

Possible Cause: You attempted to begin a new drawing from the AutoCAD Main Menu when ACAD.DWG was not stored in the proper directory.

Solution: In the configuration section, specify the ACAD.DWG file's location, or copy ACAD.DWG to the current subdirectory.

CONFIGURATION PROBLEM #10:

I receive a message indicating that setup is not loaded.

Possible Cause: AutoCAD cannot locate the file SETUP.LSP while loading AutoLISP.

Solution: Make sure that SETUP.LSP is available in the current subdirectory or that your DOS PATH is set to include the subdirectory in which SETUP.LSP is located.

CONFIGURATION PROBLEM #11:

I am using an extended DOS version of AutoCAD but it is very sluggish. Every keystroke takes several seconds to appear in the command prompt area and the hard drive seems to be doing lots of work.

Possible Cause: This version of AutoCAD needs a great deal of memory. The minimum required is 2M of RAM, but even 4M is only good enough to hold a 400K drawing.

Solution: Install more memory in your computer. As a guideline, you computer should have

- ❏ 4M to run AutoCAD
- ❏ 1M extra to run AME also
- ❏ 1M extra for each megabyte of drawing size

Troubleshooting Hardware Errors

Two types of hardware generally cause problems in the use of AutoCAD: plotters (or printer/plotters) and display devices. These devices use drivers, written by Autodesk or the manufacturers of the devices, that determine AutoCAD's output format. If there are bugs in the drivers themselves, strange things can happen to your display or plots.

Display Device Errors

Display devices arc graphics cards and monitors. The graphics card may not be totally compatible with the computer or the software. Normal software (such as a word processor or spreadsheet) will not point out these discrepancies, but AutoCAD will.

AutoCAD is a demanding program, especially where visual graphics are concerned. Your display device may need a newer driver in order to work with a new version of AutoCAD. Contact the supplier for an update.

When a display adapter conflicts with AutoCAD, the problem may show up as a locked-up display, an inactive Advanced User Interface, a malfunctioning digitizer or mouse (due to interrupt problems), colors that do not display properly, or a cursorless or blank screen.

Some graphics cards have a feature called *display-list processing*. The display list, which holds a virtual screen of the AutoCAD drawing, is stored in extra memory. These cards require drivers that use a great deal of RAM and they can have a variety of bugs in their software. Problems with display-list processing cards should be taken up directly with the manufacturer.

DISPLAY DEVICE PROBLEM #1:

My display screen does not make any sense when I start my computer. It is blank or full of gibberish.

Possible Cause: Generally, this is due to improperly installed or faulty hardware.

Solution: Refer to your computer system manuals for a possible solution. If this does not help, consult the dealer who provided you with the system.

DISPLAY DEVICE PROBLEM #2:

My system has two monitors, but the drawing does not come up on either monitor or comes up only on the smaller of the two.

Possible Cause: Improper configuration of the software or hardware.

Solution: If you can, have the dealer perform the installation. If this is not possible, check the graphics board's installation manual. If your graphics card uses the ADI interface, the card's manufacturer should have instructions on how to set it up correctly for dual-screen operation. If necessary, ask someone who is using the same setup.

Plotter or Printer/Plotter Errors

Plotters use a method called "handshaking" to let the computer know that the plotter is ready to receive data. You must know how the system is set up, which communications port the plotter is connected to, and other factors such as parity, baud rate, and stop bits. For proper handshaking to occur, the correct lines within the plotter cable must be connected to the computer's communications port, and the wires must be shielded from outside electrical interference.

Problems with drivers and cables can show up as loss of plot origin, lack of activity, erratic pen behavior, and failure to respond to pen-change commands from AutoCAD. If you have such problems, check the cable wiring. It should be the same as that shown in the AutoCAD *Installation and Performance Guide*.

PLOTTER PROBLEM #1:

The plotter seems to skip over certain lines and text on my plots.

Possible Cause: AutoCAD's pen-width setting does not match the actual width of your plotter's pens.

Solution: Try to plot again, but change the pen width to one that is equal to (or smaller than) the actual pen width.

PLOTTER PROBLEM #2:

While attempting to plot, I receive a message indicating that there is no response from the controller (or plotter) and that my plot is canceled.

Possible Causes: The plotter is not connected or has not had time to warm up.

Solution: Check the plotter connections to make sure that they are firm and secure. Some plotters also require a warm-up period before plotting can begin. Check your plotter manual to see whether this is necessary. If all else fails, check the actual cable connected to the plotter; it may be wired incorrectly.

PLOTTER PROBLEM #3:

My plots are fine if they are smaller than a certain size; a larger plot will start drawing unwanted lines in unwanted places while skipping other lines that should be there.

Probable Cause: The plotter driver has become scrambled.

Solution: Recopy the plotter driver from the proper AutoCAD distribution disk to your hard disk and reconfigure AutoCAD to use the new copy of the driver.

PRINTER/PLOTTER PROBLEM #1:

When I attempt to use a printer plotter, I receive a message stating that the printer is not ready.

Possible Causes: The printer is not connected properly, is not turned on, is out of paper, or is off-line.

Solution: Check the printer to make sure that it is correctly set up and connected to the computer. Try the plot again.

Other Hardware Errors

HARDWARE PROBLEM #1:

When running AutoCAD, I see a message similar to `Error: FMTOUT`.

Possible Cause: Your math coprocessor is not installed correctly or is faulty.

Solution: Check your math coprocessor. It may not be seated properly. If this does not seem to be the case, replace it and try again. If the error goes away, the first math coprocessor is bad and should be retired.

Troubleshooting Input Errors

INPUT PROBLEM #1:

When I insert a block into my drawing, nothing appears.

Possible Cause: The block contains entities that are on a layer which currently is turned off or frozen.

Solution: Check to see which layers are off or frozen. Entities will not appear if they are in a block on a layer that is off or frozen.

If no layers are off or frozen, you may have made a common mistake when creating the block. When you were prompted for an insertion point, you may have failed to specify the entities to be defined as a block. This results in a block of "nothing." In this case, you will need to define the block again.

INPUT PROBLEM #2:

When I insert a block, I get an old version rather than the latest version that's stored on disk.

Possible Cause: Your drawing has not been updated to include the current disk version of your block.

Solution: To force the Drawing Editor to redefine the block by reading the new one from the disk, use the following command:

    Insert *Oldblock Newblock*

Oldblock is the name of the block definition you want to update with *Newblock*.

INPUT PROBLEM #3:

When AutoCAD tries to load the menu file I have been using, the program reports Incompatible Menu File.

Possible Cause: The proper .MNX file was erased, and you copied an out-of-date .MNX file to the hard disk.

Solution: Erase the .MNX file, and have AutoCAD recompile the .MNU file.

INPUT PROBLEM #4:

When I pick a menu choice, some of the prompts are out of sequence, or the commands do not work.

Possible Cause: You are using a menu from an earlier version of AutoCAD.

Solution: AutoCAD redesigned the prompting sequence order for some commands in Release 11. In the event that you are using a menu from Release 10 or earlier, you must reprogram your menu to match the current prompting sequence.

INPUT PROBLEM #5:

When I Zoom All, my drawing appears (very small) in one corner of the screen, but I cannot find anything else on the screen.

Possible Cause: When you did a Copy or Move, you picked a Base Displacement Point and then pressed Enter, rather than Ctrl-C, to cancel the command. This sent the objects off into space a distance equal to the value of the point you picked for the Base point. Later, you froze or turned off a layer with that object on it.

Solution: Thaw and turn on all layers, and execute a Regen command. Then erase the offending entity (which may be impossible to see if you are zoomed way out) and execute another Zoom All.

INPUT PROBLEM #6:

When I switch to paper space, the drawing disappears.

Possible Cause: You need to use the Mview command to create paper space viewports.

Solution: Use the Mview command to create one (or more) viewports. Then return to model space (with the Mspace command) and use the Zoom command to size the view in each viewport.

INPUT PROBLEM #7:

I cannot find the proper divisions using the Divide command.

Possible Cause: Your point-type setting is not visible at the drawing scale you are using.

Solution: Using Pdmode and Pdsize, reset the point type.

INPUT PROBLEM #8:

The circles on my screen seem to be many-sided polygons. Sometimes, my picks do not find them.

Possible Cause: The Viewres setting is too low.

Solution: Change Viewres to 400. You might experiment with this value. A higher number will slow down redraw and regeneration times.

INPUT PROBLEM #9:

My polylines are hollow.

Possible Cause: Fillmode is set to Off.

Solution: Turn on Fillmode.

INPUT PROBLEM #10:

My drawing contains unnamed user blocks, and I cannot purge them from the drawing.

Possible Cause: Hatch patterns and associative dimensions are the unnamed blocks.

Solution: You shouldn't want to purge them. If, however, you really do want to, then either erase or explode the Hatch pattern or Dimension block.

INPUT PROBLEM #11:

I cannot purge a block from a drawing even though I am not using the block.

Possible Cause: The block is nested within another block you are using.

Solution: By extension, you are using the block in question. If you believe that this block does not enhance the value of the drawing, explode the block that contains the block you don't want, erase the unwanted block, and redefine the first block.

INPUT PROBLEM #12:

AutoCAD does not change some items I select with the Stretch command.

Possible Cause: The items to be stretched must be within the Last window with which you select them. If they are part of a block, they will not move unless the block's insertion point is within the stretch window.

Solution: Make sure that you use the proper stretch window, or use more than one Stretch command.

INPUT PROBLEM #13:

When I change an object to a different layer, its linetype or color doesn't change.

Possible Cause: The objects are not colored or linetyped BYLAYER.

Solution: Use the Chprop command to make the object's property definition BYLAYER.

INPUT PROBLEM #14:

I cannot get any objects on my screen with the Dview command.

Possible Cause: The target and camera positions are not located properly to display drawing objects.

Solution: Use the Dview command's Points option.

INPUT PROBLEM #15:

When I use a particular AutoLISP routine, AutoCAD locks up and displays a 1>.

Possible Cause: The LISP routine is missing either a right parenthesis or a quotation mark (").

Solution: Enter a quotation mark and then a right parenthesis from the keyboard. Then press Enter.

INPUT PROBLEM #16:

Some of the AutoLISP routines I use abort, saying that they cannot find a specific layer.

Possible Cause: You have renamed or purged from your drawing a layer that the LISP routine expects to find.

Solution: Review the LISP routine's requirements, or insert a new copy of your prototype drawing by typing **Insert *xxx=xxx***, where *xxx* is the name of your prototype drawing.

INPUT PROBLEM #17:

When loading the AutoLISP file ACAD.LSP, AutoCAD reports an unrecognized character and displays the message `Unable to enter AutoLISP`.

Possible Cause: The file has been edited by a word processor that leaves high-order ASCII characters in the file; although you cannot see these characters, AutoLISP can.

Solution: Save the file, using the word processor's ASCII mode (called "nondocument mode" in WordStar and "DOS text" in WordPerfect).

INPUT PROBLEM #18:

When I use the Igesin command, I get a drawing that does not resemble the original in any way.

Possible Cause: The IGES file was written by another CAD system that didn't implement the IGES standard correctly.

Solution: Although there is an IGES standard, many CAD systems implement it differently because they have different definitions of entities. You will have to perform some manual clean-up after you import a drawing from such a system. Look for blocks that are not defined correctly, layers that are not named correctly, incorrect linetypes, circles and arcs that actually are many short line segments, text that is the wrong style or size, etc.

INPUT PROBLEM #19:

When I build a block with attributes for later extraction, the Attext commands put the information into a file in an incorrect order.

Possible Cause: The Attext command is using a template file that is not designed correctly.

Solution: Check the template file you have designed for this particular use. You may have specified extraction of an attribute that does not exist in a given block, thereby causing a skipped field.

Troubleshooting Environmental Errors

Environmental errors occur when computer components do not relate to each other well in an indirect manner. The electromagnetic radiation that computers and monitors emit can interfere with each other. Computers sold in the United States must be approved by the Federal Communications Commission. If the computer passes the FCC test, it is given one of two ratings:

❑ **Class A.** The computer emits some electromagnetic radiation but is suitable for use in office environments. Since the radiation caused may be strong enough to create noise on nearby radios and decrease image quality on nearby television sets, Class-A-rated computers are not suited for home use.

❑ **Class B.** The computer emits very little electromagnetic radiation and is suitable for office and home use.

Not all aspects of computer design can be regulated. Here are some environmental problems you may come across.

ENVIRONMENTAL PROBLEM #1

The image on my color monitor is wavy or has patches of incorrect colors.

Possible cause: There is a strong source of electromagnetic radiation near the monitor.

Solution: If a second monitor is located nearby, move it farther away. The problem may go away. High voltage power lines in a nearby wall are another source of electromagnetic radiation. Move the entire computer away from the wall to see whether the problem goes away.

ENVIRONMENTAL PROBLEM #2

When I use a digitizer with AutoCAD, the crosshair cursor jumps around on the screen.

Possible cause: There is a strong source of electromagnetic radiation near the digitizer.

Solution: If the monitor is located too close to the digitizing tablet, the electromagnetic radiation emitted by the monitor can interfere with a sensitive digitizer. Move the monitor farther away from the digitizer.

ENVIRONMENTAL PROBLEM #3

When I use AutoCAD for long periods of time my eyes begin to hurt.

Possible cause: Your computer is displaying the AutoCAD graphics on an *interlaced* monitor. Interlaced monitors tend to exhibit more flicker problems.

ENVIRONMENTAL PROBLEM #4

The office building I work in has frequent brownouts and occasional blackouts.

Possible cause: Many older buildings were not designed with sufficient power capacity to handle a computer, printer, and monitor on every desk.

Solution: Purchase an uninterruptable power supply (called a *UPS*). The UPS is a continuously recharged battery that takes over powering the computer during a brownout or blackout. Most UPSes have sufficient capacity to power your computer system for 5 to 10 minutes, which is long enough for you to save your work on the hard disk.

ENVIRONMENTAL PROBLEM #5

I worry about the effects of the computer (or VDT screen) on my body.

Possible cause: Many stories have been printed about VDT (video display terminal) screens emitting several forms of harmful radiation. Researchers have not found a direct link between radiation from computers and disease of the human body. The most recent research suggests that very-low frequency (VLF) and extremely-low frequency (ELF) radiation emitted from the sides of *color* monitors may cause damage to cells in the body. The problem in pinning down a link is that different frequencies affect different people in different ways.

Solution: If you use a color monitor, try switching to a monochrome one. If you must use a color monitor, buy one that conforms to the Swedish environmental design. If your coworkers use color monitors, make sure that you are not sitting behind or to the side of their monitors. (This may require some creative office layouts.)

Troubleshooting System Errors

Operating system errors generally are similar to those that arise from system configuration conflicts, except that their cause may require the manufacturer of your computer to do some redesigning and rewriting of the operating system. As you can imagine, the manufacturer may not choose to follow through on this solution. Your only recourse may be to swap your system for a different computer.

SYSTEM PROBLEM #1:

My computer locks up when I try to use AutoCAD.

Possible Cause: This is a tough one because there are hundreds of possible causes.

Solution: Because there are so many possible reasons for this error, the best solution is to contact someone who is extremely knowledgeable about AutoCAD and your type of computer system. That person will need to perform some tests on your computer, but probably will come up with a solution quickly. Perhaps your AutoCAD dealer can help you or give you the name of someone who can.

SYSTEM PROBLEM #2:

When I start my computer (or AutoCAD), I see a message that says I am out of environment space.

Possible Cause: The normal memory area used by your operating system for environmental variables is too small.

Solution: Increase the environment space by using the appropriate command in your CONFIG.SYS file. With DOS V3.2 or later, use

SHELL=c:\command.com /p /e:512

With DOS V3.0 or V3.1, use

SHELL=c:\command.com /p /e:32

Both of these statements expand the area for storing environment variables to 512 bytes. For more information, refer to AutoCAD's *Installation and Performance Guide* and the OS manual.

Troubleshooting Software Bugs

If you suspect that you have encountered a software bug, double-check your reasoning. It is easy to fall into the trap of blaming errors on the software, when in fact the error falls into a different category, such as an input error. If, after careful analysis, you determine that you have a real software bug, you should do the following:

1. Make a detailed, written list of your system hardware, software, any TSR programs you may have installed, memory configuration, etc. Include anything that affects your computer environment.

2. Write down every step you took that led to the error. These should be steps that other users can take to make the error occur on their system.

3. Contact the software authors (either Autodesk or a third-party software vendor) to let them know of the bug. They will want all the information you have detailed in Steps 1 and 2.

4. Sit back and wait. Fixing software errors takes time. You should, however, expect the software authors to give you an estimate of when they will have a fix; then you should expect them to perform accordingly.

Troubleshooting Error Messages

AutoCAD issues a variety of error messages from a continually evolving list of messages. Some of those messages and their possible causes are listed in this section. Many of the messages can be triggered by a number of situations, including file corruption.

INTERNAL ERROR: FREE

`Internal error: FREE` indicates that AutoCAD is trying to free a temporary work buffer but cannot do so. This message can be caused by a software bug or by faulty memory (parity error).

SMIO 1 or GETSM

This message can indicate an Input/Output (I/O) error when reading one of the drawing's layer, linetype, text style, view, or other tables. It could indicate corruption of the drawing file or of a temporary file maintained either in I/O page space or on the hard disk by AutoCAD.

FMTOUT 2

This error is typical of hardware in which the coprocessor switches are not set correctly. Check the switches on the motherboard, and make sure that the coprocessor is seated correctly.

FMTOUT 1

`FMTOUT 1` is issued by some initialization code that is trying to compute various constants based on the computer's mathematical precision. The message usually indicates a problem with the math coprocessor.

HMATH

This message indicates that the database contains an inappropriate number, which AutoCAD does not know how to use. Negative radii, coordinates such as 1e+98, can cause this to occur. You may be able to find the problem by editing a DXF file and looking for the offending digits.

MWRITE

An `MWRITE failed m,n` error indicates that AutoCAD was trying to write the header portion of the drawing file to disk (as for Save, End, or Wblock), but that the operation failed for some reason. The numbers indicate the expected file position following the write (the drawing file header's length) and the actual file position.

SCANDR

This error message indicates a corrupted file that was improperly written to disk. As was mentioned earlier, you may be able to save the drawing with a third-party software package.

DISK FULL

The DISK FULL error message indicates that your hard disk is full or that AutoCAD cannot handle the number of available files in the File Allocation Table (an AutoCAD Release 10 bug for large hard disks of 100M or more). Although you may have thought that you had plenty of space when you started the drawing, you must realize that AutoCAD also opens many temporary files. If you do not get any error message, but the Drawing Editor is locked up, the disk was filled when a temporary file was opened.

EREAD

EREAD errors occur when AutoCAD tries to read the drawing file and encounters some type of file or data error when reading entities from the file. In other words, the file was stored with unreadable data or data that AutoCAD does not know how to interpret. The data may be garbled because of extended memory handling problems, hard disk error, power surge, damaged floppy disk, or some other factor.

TCODE

This indicates a bad header record written in the drawing file. You may be able to insert the drawing into another drawing and create a DXF file that can be edited with a text editor to correct the problem.

LTINIT

The linetype table section of the drawing database has improper definitions.

RFSubs

This message indicates faulty handling of on-screen image refreshing. It indicates a hardware problem in the storage of the temporary file containing the virtual screen image. Faulty memory boards or bad hard disk controllers can cause this message to appear.

EREGEN

This message shows that errors were encountered while obtaining an entity definition for display purposes from the temporary drawing files. EREGEN is similar to RFSubs.

SHELL: "Insufficient memory to continue"

This message appears if AutoCAD detects a conflicting interrupt in RAM while paging to disk during execution of the Shell command. This can indicate a problem with a terminate-and-stay-resident program.

SHELL: "Error swapping temp file"

This message indicates that a hardware error was encountered while you paged out to extended or expanded memory—or to the hard disk during execution of the Shell command.

Summary

Many errors can occur while you use AutoCAD. This chapter has introduced you to some of them and to their possible causes and solutions.

Remember that when a problem occurs you should use the information in this chapter to determine the nature of that problem. Stop what you are doing and think back through the steps you have taken recently. In this way, you can determine not only the precise cause of the problem but also a solution.

As your AutoCAD skills grow, your problems will become more complex. The more experienced you are, the harder you will push AutoCAD; problems increase when the limits of a system are pushed.

Installing AutoCAD Release 11

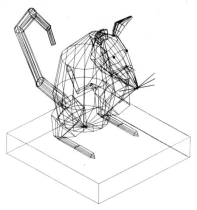

This appendix explains how to install AutoCAD Release 11 on your computer system. If your system already has been set up, and the software has been installed by someone else, this appendix probably will be of little interest to you. You should familiarize yourself with the AutoCAD installation procedures, however, in case you ever need to install the program yourself. This may be necessary after a hard disk failure, if your program files become corrupted, or for many other reasons. You also should carefully read the following sections on configuration; eventually, you may want to change your AutoCAD configuration.

In addition to explaining *installation* (the process of transferring the software to your computer system), this appendix explains the steps involved in configuring the software. *Configuration* means telling AutoCAD what kind of peripheral equipment is attached to the computer.

Many of these hardware devices were described in Chapter 2. Your collection of peripherals may include a graphics adapter, mouse, digitizer, plotter, or printer plotter. This appendix also addresses memory (RAM) usage and ADI (Autodesk Device Interface) considerations for your peripherals.

Before Installation

Chapter 2 focused on the various types of computer hardware and peripherals you could have attached to your system. What follows is a list of the minimum basic hardware components you *must* have in order to

897

run the 386 DOS Extender version of AutoCAD Release 11. (Refer to Chapter 2 if you need more information on a specific piece of equipment.)

❑ **Computer.** AutoCAD Release 11 requires a true PC-compatible 80386SX-, 80386- or 80486-based computer. Specifically, Autodesk supports the IBM PS/2 Model 70 and 80; the COMPAQ Deskpro 386SX, 386, and 486; and Hewlett-Packard 386 and 486 systems.

❑ **Math coprocessor.** AutoCAD cannot run without a math coprocessor. Make sure that your system has a coprocessor, such as Intel's 80287, 80387, and 80387SX math coprocessor (the 80486 chip includes the math chip circuitry).

❑ **Memory.** AutoCAD needs a minimum of 2M of RAM; 4M is recommended. AutoCAD can access up to 4 gigabytes (4,000 megabytes) of memory.

❑ **Hard disk.** Your system should have at least a 20M hard disk drive with 3.7M of storage space available for AutoCAD's program files.

❑ **Floppy disk drive.** You should have at least one 1.2M (5 1/4") or 720K (3 1/2") floppy disk drive.

❑ **Operating system.** For the version of AutoCAD used in this text, DOS V3.3 or later is required.

❑ **Graphics display.** AutoCAD can utilize a graphics board (and monitor) compatible with one of the following (optionally, you can install a text card and monitor for a two-monitor setup):

IBM VGA (Video Graphics Array)
IBM EGA (Enhanced Graphics Adapter)
IBM 8514/A
Hercules Graphics Card
COMPAQ Portable III plasma display
ADI real-mode V4.0 and V4.1
ADI protected-mode V4.0 and V4.1

❑ **Input device.** AutoCAD can use a digitizer, mouse, or other input device compatible with one of the following:

IBM PS/2 mouse
Logitech Logimouse
Microsoft serial or bus mouse
Mouse Systems mouse
CalComp 2500, 9000, and 9100 series tablets
GTCO Digi-Pad 5 tablets
Hitachi HICOMSCAN HDG series tablets

Houston Instruments HIPAD DT11AA and True Grid 8000
series tablets
Kurta Series I, II, and III tablets
Numonics 2200 Series tablets
Summagraphics SummaSketch MM and MicroGrid tablets
ADI real-mode
ADI protected-mode

❏ **Output device** (optional). AutoCAD can use a plotter or
printer plotter that is compatible with one or two of the
following:

Alpha Merics Alphaplot pen plotter
CalComp 906/907/PCI plotter controllers
Hewlett-Packard pen and electrostatic plotters
Houston Instrument DMP-series pen plotters
IBM 3700 series pen plotters
PostScript laser printers
Epson FX-80, FX-100, and FX-286 dot-matrix printer
Hewlett-Packard LaserJet laser printer and PaintJet ink jet
printer
IBM Graphics and ProPrinter dot-matrix printers
JDL 750 dot-matrix printer
NEC Pinwriter P5, P5XL, and P9XL dot-matrix printers
Okidata 84 and 85 dot-matrix printers
ADI real-mode
ADI protected-mode
UNIX plot file

❏ **Serial port.** This type of connector is required for the
pointing device and plotters.

❏ **Parallel port.** This type of connector is required for
printer plotters and the hardware lock (on international
versions of AutoCAD).

Other versions of AutoCAD, such as for 286 DOS Extender, Macintosh,
and so on, have other hardware requirements and supported hardware.
See the AutoCAD *Installation and Performance Guide* for the complete
list.

AutoCAD's productivity improves with faster hardware, but only to a
point. Do not skimp on any part of your system, to the extent your
budget allows. In time you will learn that the benefits of increased
productivity outweigh the dollars you might have saved by buying slower
or inferior equipment. An authorized AutoCAD dealer can help you select
the hardware that best meets your requirements.

Regardless of the type of hardware you choose, you should remember
that real productivity improvements come from spending the time
needed to customize AutoCAD. You can increase your work efficiency far

more by using prototype drawings, block libraries, menu macros, and AutoLISP routines than by buying the fastest computer.

The Installation Process

This appendix deals with installing AutoCAD Release 11 on IBM-compatible 386 and 486 computers. To begin, remove the shrink wrap from the AutoCAD program diskettes.

Running the Install Program

Installation is done by an installation program that creates appropriate subdirectories on your computer's hard disk and copies files from the master diskettes to the hard drive. The copy of AutoCAD on the hard disk is the one you will use daily; it is the only copy you legally are allowed to have.

Starting the installation procedure is simple. Insert diskette #1 (called *Executables-1*) into drive A. At the DOS prompt, type the following command:

A:INSTALL

The opening screen (see fig. A.1) tells you about the Install program and which keys you can use.

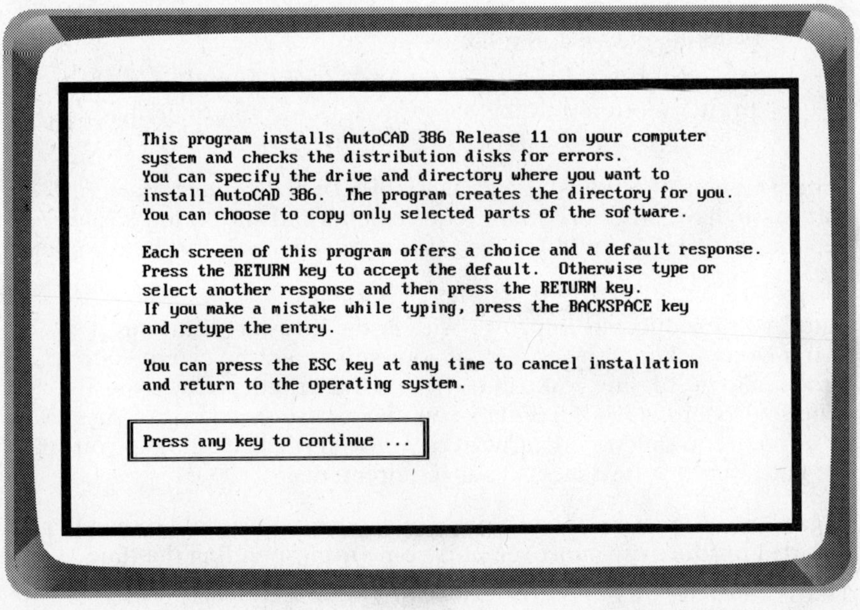

Fig. A.1.
The Install program's opening screen.

```
This program installs AutoCAD 386 Release 11 on your computer
system and checks the distribution disks for errors.
You can specify the drive and directory where you want to
install AutoCAD 386.  The program creates the directory for you.
You can choose to copy only selected parts of the software.

Each screen of this program offers a choice and a default response.
Press the RETURN key to accept the default.  Otherwise type or
select another response and then press the RETURN key.
If you make a mistake while typing, press the BACKSPACE key
and retype the entry.

You can press the ESC key at any time to cancel installation
and return to the operating system.

Press any key to continue ...
```

Next, you are asked to type in your name to personalize this copy of AutoCAD (see fig. A.2). This ensures that your name appears if others take your copy of AutoCAD. The Install program expects you to type at least four characters on each line.

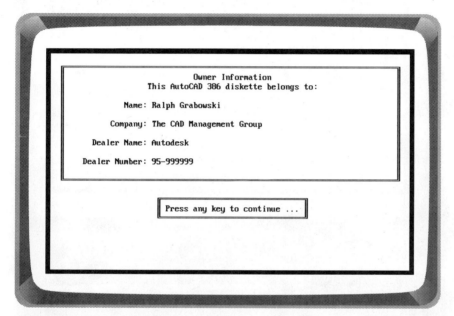

```
                        Owner Information
              This AutoCAD 386 diskette belongs to:

         Name: Ralph Grabowski

      Company: The CAD Management Group

  Dealer Name: Autodesk

Dealer Number: 95-999999




              ┌─────────────────────────────────┐
              │ Press any key to continue ...    │
              └─────────────────────────────────┘
```

Fig. A.2. Personalizing AutoCAD makes it harder for others to take a copy.

After confirming your personalization, the Install program asks where (which drive and subdirectory) you want to install AutoCAD (see fig. A.3). By default, AutoCAD is stored on drive C; the default AutoCAD subdirectory is C:\ACAD.

Before copying files from the diskettes to the hard drive, the Install program asks which files you want installed (see fig. A.4). You have the option of installing all or some of the files. If your hard disk has enough space, choose the Install all files option. If you have limited space, pick the Executable/Support files only option.

The Install program then takes about 10 minutes to copy files from the diskettes onto the hard drive. The screen displays the program's progress (see fig. A.5). When the program needs a new diskette, it asks for that diskette by name. Simply remove the diskette that is no longer needed, insert the new diskette, and press Enter.

Fig. A.3.
You can
install
AutoCAD in
any
subdirectory.

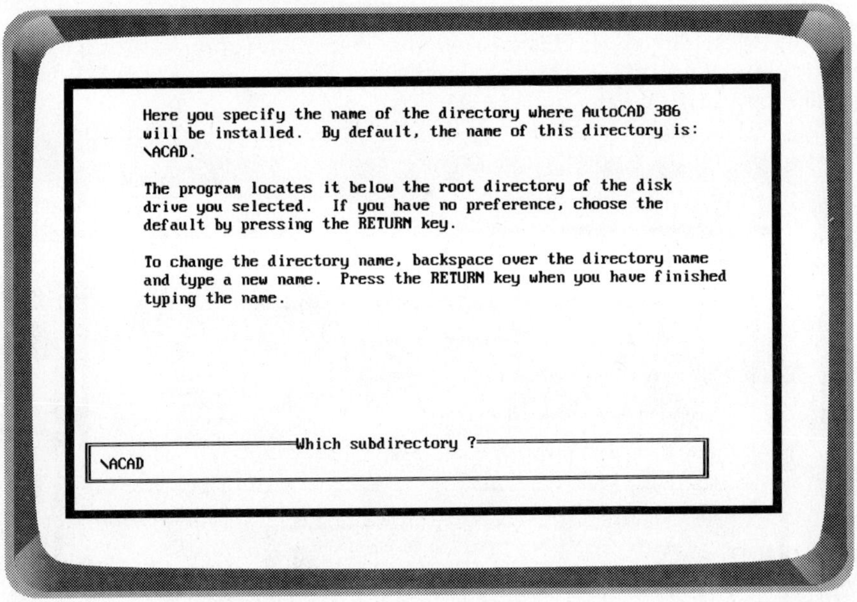

```
Here you specify the name of the directory where AutoCAD 386
will be installed.  By default, the name of this directory is:
\ACAD.

The program locates it below the root directory of the disk
drive you selected.  If you have no preference, choose the
default by pressing the RETURN key.

To change the directory name, backspace over the directory name
and type a new name.  Press the RETURN key when you have finished
typing the name.




                          =Which subdirectory ?=
\ACAD
```

Fig. A.4.
The Install
program lets
you choose
which files
you want
installed.

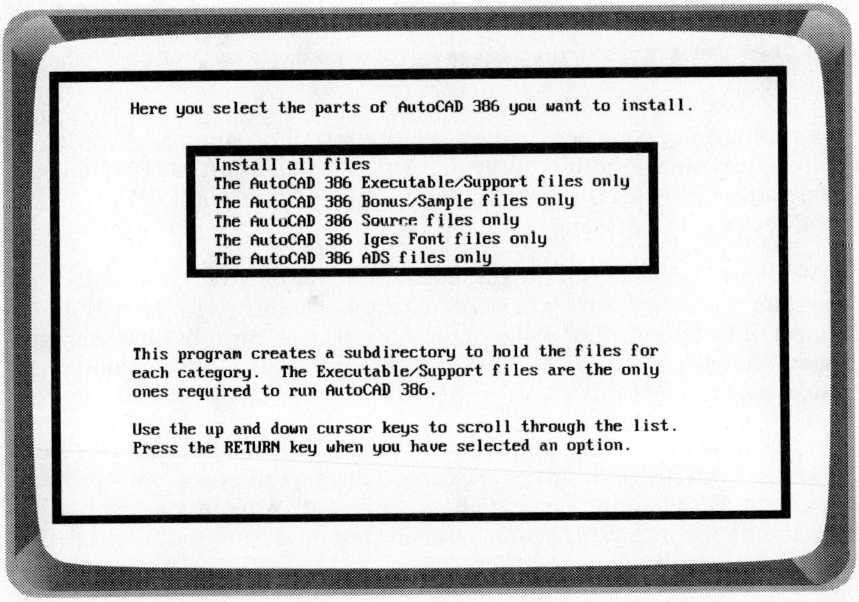

```
Here you select the parts of AutoCAD 386 you want to install.


       Install all files
       The AutoCAD 386 Executable/Support files only
       The AutoCAD 386 Bonus/Sample files only
       The AutoCAD 386 Source files only
       The AutoCAD 386 Iges Font files only
       The AutoCAD 386 ADS files only



This program creates a subdirectory to hold the files for
each category.  The Executable/Support files are the only
ones required to run AutoCAD 386.

Use the up and down cursor keys to scroll through the list.
Press the RETURN key when you have selected an option.
```

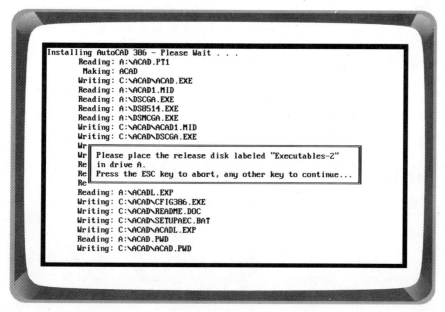

Fig. A.5.
The Install program reports its progress while copying files.

After all the files have been copied, the Install program asks if you want it to create a batch file called ACAD386.BAT (see fig. A.6). This file sets up the DOS environment, changes to the ACAD subdirectory, and starts AutoCAD. Answer **Y** to create the file.

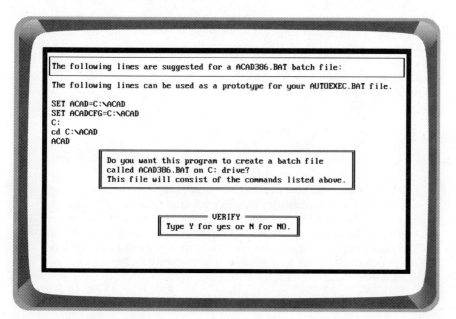

Fig. A.6.
This batch file starts AutoCAD.

After you have installed AutoCAD, store the master diskettes in a safe, static-free, antimagnetic environment. A disk holder is ideal. Take care not to place disks on your digitizing tablet; the digitizer creates a magnetic field that can destroy data stored on the disk.

Remember to send in your registration card, if your dealer has not already done so. You will receive a plastic overlay for your digitizer, a copy of *CADalyst* magazine, a list of Authorized Training Centers, and other information.

Configuring AutoCAD for Your Hardware

Configuration is the most imposing task in the AutoCAD installation process. There are hundreds of AutoCAD-compatible hardware devices and thousands of variations that can be made in the configuration. This appendix uses a sample configuration which assumes that you have the following equipment:

❑ A computer from the recommended list

❑ A Video Graphics Array adapter (VGA)

❑ A Summagraphics SummaSketch digitizing tablet

❑ A Hewlett-Packard Draftmaster E-sized pen plotter

❑ An Epson FX-80 printer plotter

You should not interpret this list as a shopping list. Rather, the list represents commonly used equipment and is intended to familiarize you with the configuration process. If your hardware is different from that in the sample configuration, refer to the hardware manuals and installation documentation for specific instructions. Substitute those instructions for the ones given here.

 AutoCAD provides *driver files* (a program that lets AutoCAD interface with a particular piece of hardware) for most standard pieces of equipment. AutoCAD also features its own driver file around which other hardware manufacturers can write their own driver files for certain pieces of equipment. This standard driver file is called the ADI (Autodesk Device Interface). All display-list graphics board manufacturers and some plotter and digitizer manufacturers take advantage of this feature to provide additional enhancements. This book cannot attempt to address every kind of ADI interface. Refer to your equipment manuals for specific instructions concerning your hardware.

Starting AutoCAD for the First Time

Before you can use AutoCAD, you must configure the program to recognize your hardware. But before you can configure AutoCAD, you must start the program for the first time. To start AutoCAD, type the following command at the DOS prompt:

ACAD386

This command runs the ACAD386.BAT batch file, which was created by the installation program. The batch file, in turn, loads AutoCAD. You should see a screen of information concerning AutoCAD and first-time users (see fig. A.7). The text is contained in the ACAD.MSG file, and appears whenever you execute AutoCAD. You should read, heed, and delete it.

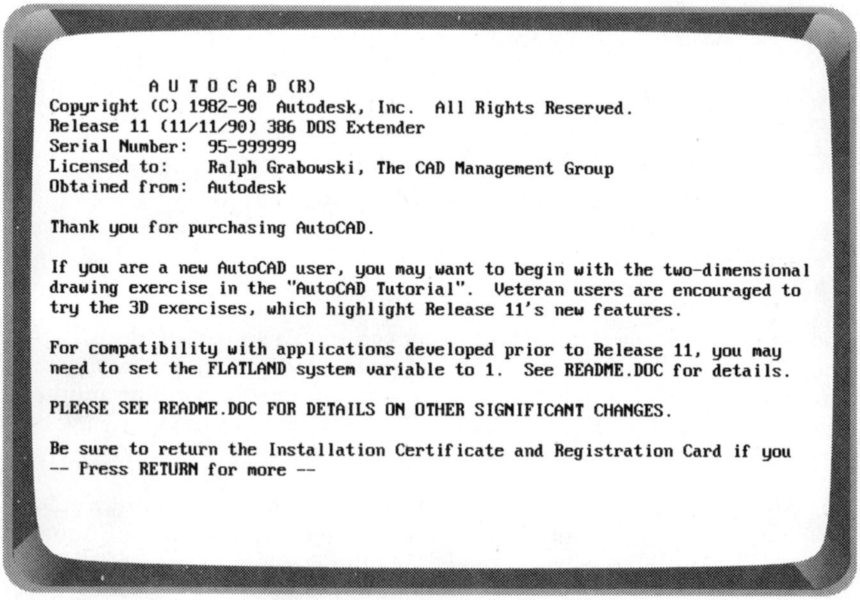

```
            A U T O C A D  (R)
Copyright (C) 1982-90  Autodesk, Inc.  All Rights Reserved.
Release 11 (11/11/90) 386 DOS Extender
Serial Number:  95-999999
Licensed to:     Ralph Grabowski, The CAD Management Group
Obtained from:  Autodesk

Thank you for purchasing AutoCAD.

If you are a new AutoCAD user, you may want to begin with the two-dimensional
drawing exercise in the "AutoCAD Tutorial".  Veteran users are encouraged to
try the 3D exercises, which highlight Release 11's new features.

For compatibility with applications developed prior to Release 11, you may
need to set the FLATLAND system variable to 1.  See README.DOC for details.

PLEASE SEE README.DOC FOR DETAILS ON OTHER SIGNIFICANT CHANGES.

Be sure to return the Installation Certificate and Registration Card if you
-- Press RETURN for more --
```

Fig. A.7. The opening AutoCAD screen displays a message welcoming you to AutoCAD.

After you read the ACAD.MSG file, press Enter twice. At the top of the screen, the AutoCAD copyright information appears along with the following message:

AutoCAD is not yet configured.

You must specify the devices to which AutoCAD will interface. Press RETURN to continue:

Press Enter. AutoCAD then prompts you to begin the configuration process.

Configuring AutoCAD for the Display Adapter

The next screen lists the eight graphics boards and drivers that AutoCAD Release 11 supports. The first three selections are ADI drivers that let AutoCAD work with any graphics board that has its own ADI driver. The last selection, Null display, enables you to use AutoCAD with no graphics display.

After the list is displayed, you are prompted to enter the number that corresponds to your video display adapter:

```
Select device number or ? to repeat list <1>:
```

For this example, press **8** to select the IBM Video Graphics Array.

After you have selected the graphics board, AutoCAD asks you several questions about how you want AutoCAD to display its graphics.

AutoCAD gives you the opportunity to adjust a square on your graphics screen, as follows:

```
If you have previously measured the height and
width of a "square" on your graphics screen, you
may use these measurements to correct the aspect
ratio.
Would you like  to do so? <N>
```

Since in this example you have not yet even seen a square on the screen, type **N** or press Enter. Later, when you get to the Drawing Editor, if you notice that squares and circles are elongated in one direction or another, measure the dimensions of a square on the screen. You can come back to the Configuration Menu and adjust the aspect ratio.

An incorrect aspect ratio does not affect the accuracy of AutoCAD, nor is the plotted output adversely affected. Squares are still square in the drawing database. The elongation is the result of a (slightly) mismatched graphics board and monitor.

Many monitors let you adjust the width and height of the screen image. You can use the monitor's controls to correct squares and circles, instead of using AutoCAD's aspect ratio correction.

Continue the configuration by answering yes to the following prompts (type **Y** or press Enter):

```
Do you want a status line? <Y>
Do you want a command prompt area? <Y>
Do you want a screen menu area? <Y>
```

By answering yes, you define the normal AutoCAD drawing screen. If you find that you don't use the screen menu, you can come back to the Configuration Menu to turn it off. This frees up a bit of the drawing area on the graphics screen.

If you have a dual-screen setup, you do not need the command prompt area because it is displayed on the text screen. You can turn off the command prompt area to free up additional drawing space.

Your answer to the next prompt is based on your preference:

```
You may select either a dark (black) or a light
graphics area background. If you select a light
graphics area background, then lines drawn in color
7 will be drawn in black instead. This choice most
closely resembles a black ink drawing on paper.

Do you want dark vectors on a light background
field? <Y>
```

AutoCAD can display a black or light gray background screen. Many people find the black background easier on their eyes, especially with interlaced video boards. Colored lines also show up better against the black. Other people prefer the simulated black-ink-on-paper that the light gray background provides. As before, if you change your mind, you can always come back later and change the screen.

AutoCAD then displays the following prompt:

```
Do you want to supply individual colors for parts
of the graphics screen? <N>:
```

Press Enter in response to this prompt. If you answer yes to the prompt, AutoCAD lets you customize the colors used to display the menus and command prompt area. At this time, diddling with the many color options would be a great waste of time. The default colors selected by Autodesk are quite attractive; if a color combination really annoys you, you can change it later.

The final screen shows the available colors and the number that corresponds to each. If you specified a monochrome monitor earlier, you will be prompted for color assignments using shades of gray.

The video display portion of the configuration process is complete. You are prompted to press Enter to continue.

Configuring AutoCAD for the Digitizer

Next, you should see a list of digitizers, including two ADI options, many digitizing tablets, and several mice. There is also a None option, in case you are using only the keyboard. AutoCAD then displays the following prompt:

```
Select device number or ? to repeat list <1>:
```

Enter the number that corresponds to your pointing device. For this example, type **16** for the Summagraphics SummaSketch digitizer. Depending on the type of pointing device you select, you may see the following display on your screen:

```
Connects to Asynchronous Communications Adapter port.

Standard ports are:
COM1
COM2

Enter port name, or address in hexadecimal <COM1>:
```

Type the name of the communications port used by your digitizer tablet. (If you are not sure about what to enter here, it can be determined by whoever connected the digitizer to the computer.) For the example, assume that the default, COM1 (serial port #1), is acceptable. Press Enter to select the default.

Next, you may see a prompt similar to the following:

```
You may configure one of two different digitizers

0 - 8.5 x 11
1 - 12 x 12

Select your digitizer size, 0 or 1 <0>:
```

Digitizing tablets come in a variety of sizes, from the size of a sheet of paper to E-size. Your response should be consistent with the equipment you actually have. For this example, type **1** to specify the 12-by-12-inch tablet.

At this point AutoCAD may display additional prompts for information about your pointing device. If so, answer each question as it appears. When the pointing-device portion of the configuration process is complete, you are prompted to press Enter to continue.

Configuring AutoCAD for the Plotter

Next you see a list of plotters. The list includes a half-dozen pen plotters, the ADI and UNIX plotter drivers, and the None option (in case no plotter is attached to the computer). The following prompt appears at the end of the list:

```
Select device number or ? to repeat list <1>:
```

Enter the number that corresponds to your plotter. For the example,
press **6**, which corresponds to the Hewlett-Packard brand of plotter.
AutoCAD often needs to know which model of plotter you want to use,
and displays the following list of available models:

```
Supported models:
1.  7220
2.  7470
3.  7475
4.  7550
5.  7580
6.  7585
7.  7586
8.  7600 240D
9.  7600 240E
10. Colorpro
11. Draftpro
12. Draftpro DXL
13. Draftpro EXL
14. Draftmaster

Enter selection, 1 to 14 <1>:
```

Enter **14** for the Draftmaster E-size pen plotter. Most plotters are
compatible with Hewlett-Packard; read the plotter's manual to find out
which Hewlett-Packard model your plotter most closely resembles.

AutoCAD then asks you to designate the communications port to which
the plotter is connected:

```
Connects to Asynchronous Communications Adapter port.
Standard ports are:

COM1
COM2

Enter port name, or address in hexadecimal <COM1>:
```

Here you type the name of the second serial port, which usually is COM2.
This port typically is the next port available. For the sample configuration,
specify **COM2**, because the digitizer is connected to the first serial port,
COM1.

If your computer has only one serial port, AutoCAD lets you connect both the digitizer and the plotter to the same port. However, you will have to do a great deal of cable swapping or use an A-B selector switch. Whenever you want to plot a drawing, you will have to unplug the digitizer and plug in the plotter. The cost of a serial expansion board is less than the switch; you should consider installing a second serial port.

You can adjust the aspect ratio of the plotted output, just as with the video display. AutoCAD prompts as follows:

```
If you have previously measured the lengths of a horizontal
and a vertical line that were plotted to a specific scale,
you may use these measurements to calibrate your plotter.

Would you like to calibrate your plotter? <N>
```

Press Enter; you answer no because you haven't used the plotter with AutoCAD yet. As with the other configuration items, you can always change your responses later if you need to.

The next series of questions deals with the default values AutoCAD uses when doing a plot. You can change the values when you use the Plot command. In the meantime, AutoCAD wants to know what to use as defaults:

```
Write the plot to a file? <N>
```

If you plan to plot AutoCAD drawings directly to the plotter, answer no (press Enter). If you use a plot spooler or need to plot the drawing to disk, answer **Y**. The disk file will have the name of the drawing file with the PLT extension, by default. At plot time, AutoCAD lets you use any file name and extension you like.

Some plotters, such as electrostatic plotters and PostScript laser printers, have a parallel port. By using a file name of PRN, you can force AutoCAD to use the parallel port, which is much faster than the serial port.

Next, you indicate whether you want to use metric or English units of measure:

```
Size units (Inches or Millimeters) <I>:
```

Press Enter. The selection affects only the remaining prompts, not the scale of the drawing. Next, AutoCAD lets you change the plot's origin:

```
Plot origin in Inches <0.00,0.00>:
```

Plot origin indicates the position on the drawing at which AutoCAD should begin plotting. AutoCAD usually places the lower left corner in the lower left corner of the paper (0,0). Press Enter now to accept the default. You can change the origin if you want to plot several drawings on one sheet or to avoid plotting on a title block.

Because the HP Draftmaster can plot on all sizes of paper, from smaller than A-size to larger than E-size, AutoCAD asks what size paper you will be using:

```
Standard values for plotting size

Size    Width    Height
A       10.50      8.50
B       16.00     10.00
C       21.00     16.00
D       33.00     21.00
E       43.00     33.00
MAX     44.72     35.31

Enter the Size or Width,Height (in Inches) <MAX>:
```

Type the letter associated with the paper size; in this example, type **E** for E-size. AutoCAD also lets you rotate the paper in 90-degree increments. Pressing Enter does not rotate the plot:

```
Rotate plot 0/90/180/270 <0>
```

There may be times when you want to rotate the plot. For example, if you plot to a PostScript laser printer, you will answer **90** to the question. For this example, press Enter.

Next, AutoCAD asks about the width of the plotting pens:

```
Pen Width <0.010>:
```

Press Enter for the default pen size (0.01" matches the most common pen width). If you use a different width pen, type the size in inches. For PostScript plotters, reduce the number to 0.001"; otherwise the lines will look too chunky.

If your plotter uses normal-width pens (such as 0.01"), you don't need to have AutoCAD adjust for that.

Next, AutoCAD needs to know how to deal with solid-filled areas in plots:

```
Adjust area fill boundaries for pen width? <N>
```

Press Enter. When AutoCAD fills a solid area, it moves the plotter pen back and forth to fill the area and then outlines the area for a neater finish. If you are using a very wide pen, the outline can be too large. If you answer **Y** to the preceding prompt, AutoCAD compensates for the wide pen by moving the outline inward.

AutoCAD then asks if you want hidden lines to be removed from the drawing when plotting:

```
Remove hidden lines? <N>
```

For two-dimensional drawings, AutoCAD should not remove hidden lines. Press Enter to keep hidden lines. If you specify that hidden lines should be removed, AutoCAD will calculate and remove (from the plotted image only) lines that normally would not be seen.

Finally, you are asked to do the following:

```
Specify scale by entering:
Plotted Inches=Drawing Units or Fit or ? <F>:
```

At this point, type **F** to select the default response of F (for Fit) to make the drawing fit the paper, regardless of scale. This ensures that your first plotted drawing will fit the paper exactly. Chapter 8 discusses plotting in detail. You can change this response whenever you use the Plot command, however, so your answer here is not critical.

Now the plotter portion of the configuration process is complete. You are prompted to press Enter to continue.

Configuring AutoCAD for a Printer Plotter

You should now see a list of printer plotters. Again, you have a half-dozen choices, plus the ADI driver and None options. At the end of the list, AutoCAD displays this prompt:

```
Select device number or ? to repeat list <1>:
```

For the sample configuration, select **3** for Epson-brand dot-matrix printers. Next, AutoCAD wants to know which parallel port the printer is connected to:

```
Connects to Parallel Communications Port:
Standard ports are:

LPT1

Enter port name, or address in hexadecimal <LPT1>:
```

Press Enter in response to the prompt, to specify the LPT1 port.

Next, depending on the type of printer plotter you specified, AutoCAD may display a prompt similar to the following:

```
The following printer models are supported:
```

```
1.   Epson FX-80
2.   Epson FX-100 or 286

Select desired model <1>:
```

For the sample configuration, type **1**. Your response should match the printer attached to the computer. Many printers are compatible with one of these models; consult the manual.

Next, AutoCAD poses the same series of questions that you answered to configure the program for your plotter. Answer them using the guidelines provided earlier in this appendix for configuring AutoCAD for a plotter.

The Main Configuration Menu

After you finish configuring AutoCAD for your hardware, you are returned to the main Configuration Menu. As you can see from figure A.8, the menu includes nine options (counting Option 0), each of which is described briefly in the following sections.

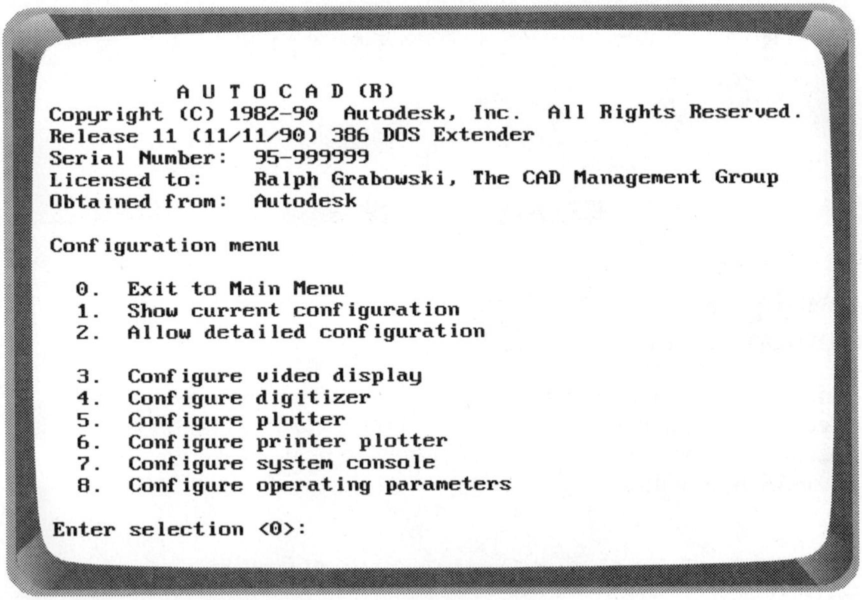

```
        A U T O C A D (R)
Copyright (C) 1982-90  Autodesk, Inc.  All Rights Reserved.
Release 11 (11/11/90) 386 DOS Extender
Serial Number:   95-999999
Licensed to:     Ralph Grabowski, The CAD Management Group
Obtained from:   Autodesk

Configuration menu

   0.   Exit to Main Menu
   1.   Show current configuration
   2.   Allow detailed configuration

   3.   Configure video display
   4.   Configure digitizer
   5.   Configure plotter
   6.   Configure printer plotter
   7.   Configure system console
   8.   Configure operating parameters

Enter selection <0>:
```

Fig. A.8.
The main
Configuration
Menu.

Configuration Menu Option 0 — Exit to Main Menu

This option does two things. It lets you save the changes you have made during your configuration session; it also is the only way to return to AutoCAD's Main Menu. You should choose this option when you have finished configuring AutoCAD.

Configuration Menu Option 1 — Show Current Configuration

This option displays the current configuration settings used by AutoCAD (see fig. A.9). It displays the video display adapter, digitizer, plotter, and printer plotter configurations, and prompts you to press Enter to return to the main Configuration Menu.

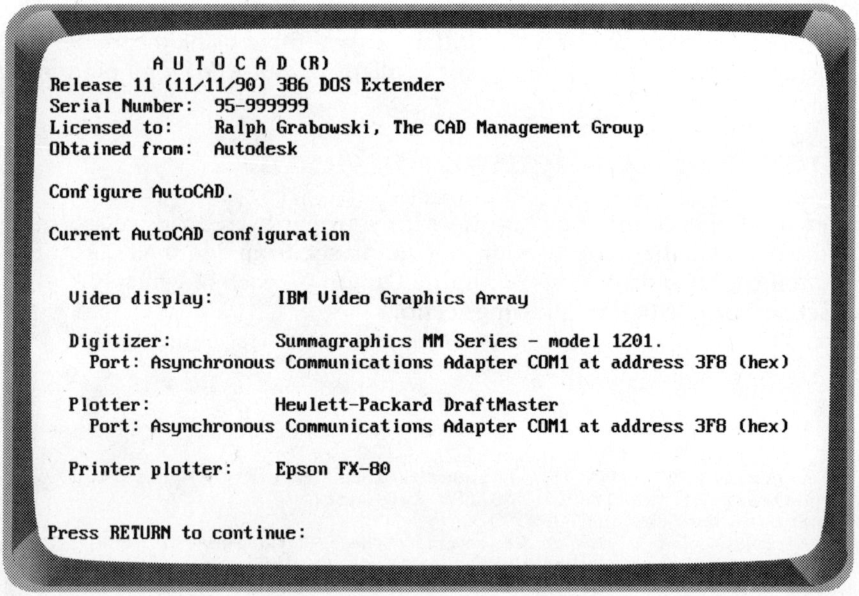

Fig. A.9.
The current
configuration.

```
          A U T O C A D  (R)
Release 11 (11/11/90) 386 DOS Extender
Serial Number:  95-999999
Licensed to:    Ralph Grabowski, The CAD Management Group
Obtained from:  Autodesk

Configure AutoCAD.

Current AutoCAD configuration


  Video display:     IBM Video Graphics Array

  Digitizer:         Summagraphics MM Series - model 1201.
    Port: Asynchronous Communications Adapter COM1 at address 3F8 (hex)

  Plotter:           Hewlett-Packard DraftMaster
    Port: Asynchronous Communications Adapter COM1 at address 3F8 (hex)


  Printer plotter:   Epson FX-80


Press RETURN to continue:
```

Configuration Menu Option 2 — Allow Detailed Configuration

Some devices have additional prompts that let you fine-tune their operation. An example is pen-motion optimization for plotters. By selecting Option 2, you can change the default values preselected by AutoCAD to enhance the plotter's performance.

Configuration Menu Option 3 — Configure Video Display

Select this option if you want to change the driver used for your graphics board, or if you change graphics boards. The procedure is the same as described earlier in this chapter.

Configuration Menu Option 4 — Configure Digitizer

Use this option to configure a different digitizer driver or to change the default settings for your digitizer. The procedure is the same as that described earlier in this chapter.

Configuration Menu Option 5 — Configure Plotter

Use this option to select a different plotter driver or to change the default plotting parameters AutoCAD uses with your plotter. The prompts are the same as those mentioned previously, depending on the plotter option you choose.

Configuration Menu Option 6 — Configure Printer Plotter

This option lets you select a different printer plotter or change the default parameters used with your printer plotter. The prompts will be the same as those indicated previously, depending on the printer plotter you select.

Configuration Menu Option 7 — Configure System Console

This option does not apply to PC compatibles because there are no options to change. Some of the other hardware platforms, such as the Sun 386, have configurable system console parameters.

Configuration Menu Option 8 — Configure Operating Parameters

This option takes you to a secondary configuration menu (see fig. A.10). These options are described separately.

Option 0 — Exit to Configuration Menu

This option takes you back to the main Configuration Menu.

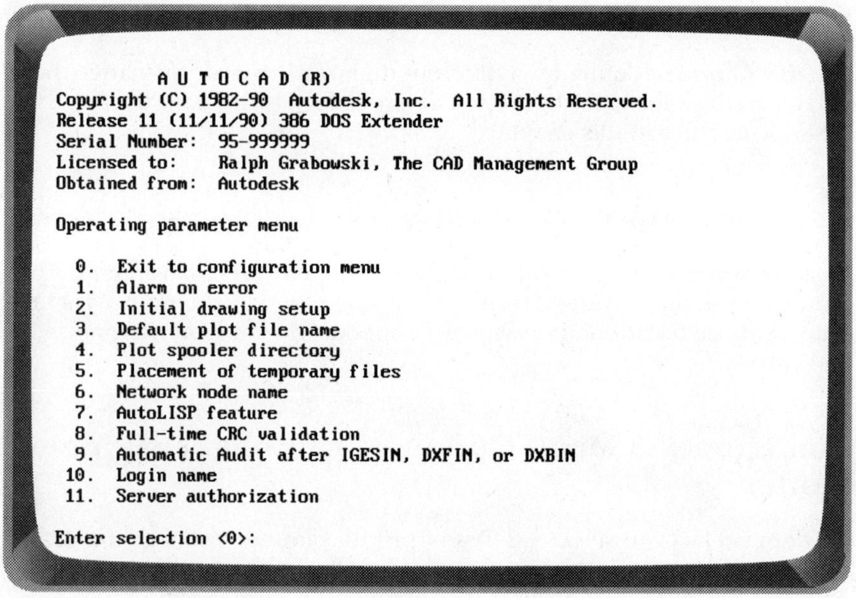

Fig. A.10.
The menu for
configuring
operating
parameters.

```
          A U T O C A D (R)
Copyright (C) 1982-90  Autodesk, Inc.  All Rights Reserved.
Release 11 (11/11/90) 386 DOS Extender
Serial Number:  95-999999
Licensed to:    Ralph Grabowski, The CAD Management Group
Obtained from:  Autodesk

Operating parameter menu

    0.  Exit to configuration menu
    1.  Alarm on error
    2.  Initial drawing setup
    3.  Default plot file name
    4.  Plot spooler directory
    5.  Placement of temporary files
    6.  Network node name
    7.  AutoLISP feature
    8.  Full-time CRC validation
    9.  Automatic Audit after IGESIN, DXFIN, or DXBIN
   10.  Login name
   11.  Server authorization

Enter selection <0>:
```

Option 1 — Alarm on Error

If you select this option, AutoCAD displays the following prompt:

```
Do you want the console alarm to sound when you
make an input error? <N>
```

Answer **Y**. If you make an AutoCAD error, the computer beeps to bring
errors to your attention. If the beeping drives you crazy, you can come
back later and change the answer to no.

Option 2 — Initial Drawing Setup

When you choose this option, AutoCAD displays the following prompt:

```
Enter name of default prototype file for new
drawings or . for none <acad>:
```

If you have a drawing that you want to use as the prototype for all
drawing work, it is useful to type its file name here (including the path, if
necessary). By doing so, you eliminate much of the repetitive work (such
as standardized layers, grid aspect, snap ratio, and other functions)
needed to set up the drawing environment. If you do not specify a

drawing along with the correct path, ACAD.DWG is used as the default prototype drawing. Press Enter to accept the default. You can change it at any time.

Option 3 — Default Plot File Name

If you choose Option 3, you will see the following prompt:

```
Enter default plot file name (for plot to file)
or . for none <.>:
```

Press Enter at this prompt. If you want to use a common plot file name for all drawings you plot, enter the name here. If you commonly plot to the parallel port, enter the file name PRN here. Otherwise, AutoCAD will prompt you for a name as the last step before the plotter does its job.

Option 4 — Plot Spooler Directory

Choosing this menu option causes the following message and prompts to be displayed:

```
When plotting to a file, AutoCAD writes the output
to the plot spooler directory if the special name
AUTOSPOOL is given as the plot file name. The plot
spooler directory is ignored for normal plotting.

Enter plot spooler directory name <\spfiles\>:
```

This feature is handy if you are using a plot spooler. Otherwise, ignore the option.

Option 5 — Placement of Temporary Files

By choosing this option you receive the following prompt:

```
Enter directory name for temporary files, or
DRAWING to place them in the same directory as the
drawing being edited.<DRAWING>:
```

Press Enter at this prompt. AutoCAD creates many temporary files while it is working. If you are using a network, you must specify a subdirectory to hold the temporary files. Otherwise, your copy of AutoCAD's temporary files will be confused for another operator's copy.

Option 6 — Network Node Name

When you select Option 6, AutoCAD displays this prompt:

```
On network and multiuser systems, a unique "network
node name" should be specified for each user. This
name is added to certain temporary files and to
plot spooler output files to ensure uniqueness.

Enter network node name (1 to 3 characters) <AC$>:
```

Press Enter at this prompt. For instructional purposes, ignore this option. Some CAD environments are networked, but networking is beyond the scope of this book.

Option 7 — AutoLISP Feature

When you select Option 7, you are asked:

```
Do you want AutoLISP enabled? <Y>
```

Press **N** to answer no if your computer lacks enough RAM to hold all of AutoCAD, AutoLISP, and the drawing. You must press **Y** to answer yes if you use AutoLISP, ADS, or AME.

Option 8 — Full-time CRC Validation

AutoCAD can check the validity (via cyclic redundancy checking) of a DWG file when you load it into the Drawing Editor:

```
Do you want full-time CRC validation? <N> Y
```

Answer by pressing **Y**.

Option 9 — Automatic Audit after IGESIN, DXFIN, or DXBIN

AutoCAD also can check the validity of IGES, DXF, and DXB files when you import them into the Drawing Editor. If you want AutoCAD to do this automatically, select option 9 and type **Y** at the following prompt:

```
Do you want an automatic audit after IGESIN, DXFIN
or DXBIN? <N>
```

Option 10 — Login Name

Option 10 prompts you to enter a login name:

```
Enter default login name or . for none <Your name here:>
```

Press Enter at this prompt. AutoCAD uses the *login* name to determine
who is currently using the program (this is important in networked
installations). If you enter a default name, AutoCAD won't prompt you for
a login name each time you enter the Drawing Editor.

Option 11 — Server Authorization

This option sets the number of networked users who can access this copy
of AutoCAD:

```
AutoCAD's serial number is 95-999999
Enter the maximum number of users for this package <1>:
Do you wish to enable file-locking? <Y>
```

Press Enter to accept the default number of users. If you enter a number
larger than one, AutoCAD prompts for the authorization number that you
obtained from your dealer.

If you are the only person using this copy of AutoCAD, type **N** to disable
file locking; otherwise, AutoCAD will lock you out of your own drawing if
the computer crashes.

Saving Your Configuration Changes

As was stressed earlier, it is important that you save the changes you
make to AutoCAD's configuration. To save changes, select Option 0, Exit
to Main Menu. You will see the following prompts:

```
If you answer N to the following question, all configuration
changes you have just made will be discarded.
Keep configuration changes? <Y>
```

If you want to save your changes (AutoCAD assumes that you do),
simply press Enter. If you made a mistake or don't want to save the
configuration, type **N**. This completes the configuration of AutoCAD on
your computer.

Setting Up Your Digitizer Overlay

If you do not have an overlay for your digitizer tablet, this section will be of little use. If you have registered your copy of AutoCAD, you will receive an overlay in the mail. If you have a tablet overlay, follow these steps to set it up:

1. Place the digitizer overlay on your tablet.

2. Fasten the overlay to the tablet with the fasteners provided.

3. Start AutoCAD normally. If you need help, refer to the beginning of this appendix or to Chapter 4.

4. Choose to edit an existing drawing by selecting Option 2 from the Main Menu. Specify the drawing name as **ACAD**.

5. Once you are in the Drawing Editor, move your puck or pen around a bit. You should see the crosshairs move across the screen. If the crosshair cursor does not appear, something probably is wrong with your configuration of AutoCAD. Proceeding from this point will be useless; you should not go any further until you can find and correct the problem.

6. The screen menu is at the screen's right side. Highlight the SETTINGS option and press Enter.

7. A new set of screen menu options appears. Pick the NEXT option.

8. Another set of screen menu options appears. Pick the TABLET option.

9. Again, the screen menu options change. This time, pick the CONFIG option.

10. Following the diagram shown in figure A.11, configure your tablet by answering the questions presented on the screen.

11. When you have finished answering the questions, type **Save** at the `Command:` prompt to save your changes to disk.

12. Use the End command to leave the Drawing Editor.

If you ever change your template, or if you move the template on your digitizer, you must repeat these steps to reconfigure the tablet. The process may seem long, but the results are well worth the trouble.

AutoCAD Support

When you first begin using AutoCAD, you may be puzzled about how to do something or you may run into other problems. If so, call your dealer;

any questions your dealer can't answer will be referred to Autodesk. By using a modem, you can contact Autodesk on CompuServe's Autodesk Forum (a response within 24 hours is guaranteed.)

The best place to get an answer is from a more experienced user. Most urban areas in North America have an AutoCAD users' group, where AutoCAD users meet monthly to exchange ideas and help each other. For help with complicated problems, you may have to hire a consultant with several years' experience with AutoCAD. Your dealer may be able to give you information about a users' group and the names of consultants.

Additionally, there are service bureaus that provide a variety of services, such as digitizing paper drawings into AutoCAD, plotting AutoCAD drawings, training, and consulting. Fees and turn-around times for these services vary; if possible, get a quote and references from several bureaus before you select the one you will work with.

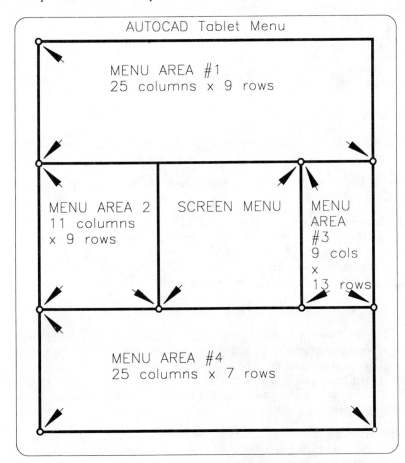

Fig. A.11. You must pick 14 points for AutoCAD to know where the four menus and screen area are.

Networking AutoCAD

If your firm has a networked computing environment, you can install AutoCAD Release 11 on the network in two different ways: on each local workstation or on the central file server.

Installing AutoCAD on Local Workstations

To install AutoCAD on local workstations, you need to purchase one copy of AutoCAD for each workstation. The installation procedure is the same as noted in earlier sections. This is the only approach that works with AutoCAD Release 10.

In this approach, each workstation is independent and can customize the AutoCAD environment—you don't even need to upgrade all workstations from Release 10 at once—you only use the network to share drawing files and peripheral devices (such as plotters and mass storage units).

Installing AutoCAD on Central File Server

To install AutoCAD on a central file server, you need to purchase only one copy of AutoCAD. Installing AutoCAD on the central file server is more complex than on individual workstations, but the total installation time is greatly reduced.

Release 11 has features that allow several users to run the single copy of AutoCAD:

File locking. If a user accesses an AutoCAD-related file, AutoCAD *locks* the file for the duration of its use. Locking a file means that no other AutoCAD user can access the file. AutoCAD prints a warning message on the screen that another person is using the file. AutoCAD locks a file by changing the last letter of the filename extension to K. For example, AutoCAD renames drawing file extension DWG to DWK. See Appendix G for the complete list of locked-file extension names.

 The file-locking feature is AutoCAD-specific. It is not implemented at the operating system level. You can still use the DOS Copy command to get a copy of a locked drawing file. Since the possibility exists that you may have made a copy of an old version of the drawing file, you should check first for the existence of the accompanying DWK file.

Multiple user authorization. When you purchase AutoCAD Release 11, you have the option of purchasing additional user authorizations. AutoCAD can tell how often it has been loaded into the memory of a computer. To let more than one workstation load AutoCAD from the central file server, you need to enter an eight-digit code number that permits multiple users. The maximum is 128 users at one time.

Password protection. To prevent unauthorized use of AutoCAD at a workstation, AutoCAD Release 11 implements a password-protection feature. You can type in a secret word that prevents others from using AutoCAD.

The benefit of a single, central copy of AutoCAD is that you need to buy only as many authorizations as there are likely to be users accessing AutoCAD at one time. If your firm has 25 workstations, but only 18 that use AutoCAD at any one time, you only need to buy 18 authorizations. If the need for AutoCAD increases, you can purchase additional authorizations over the phone.

Temporary files. In configuring AutoCAD on a central file server, you will need to create a separate start-up batch file for each workstation. The batch file specifies the working directory for that workstation, including the location of the ACAD.CFG file. This file contains the name of the subdirectory where AutoCAD's temporary files should be located. If this is not done, then every workstation will store the temporary files in the same place, corrupting the drawing files.

AutoCAD Release 11 is more friendly toward networked environments, but still requires the knowledge of a network manager if it is to be installed and maintained correctly. Installing AutoCAD on a network is not recommended for someone new to computers.

Summary

The AutoCAD installation and configuration is over. As you have seen, the process can be confusing. If you get in a hurry or let it get the best of you, you will feel frustrated. Take your time, and enjoy learning about your equipment and software; they will reward you with years of productivity.

To recap a few important points about installing AutoCAD Release 11:

- ❏ Make sure that you have the proper equipment for using AutoCAD.
- ❏ Be sure to read the instructions for your peripheral equipment before you install AutoCAD.
- ❏ Read the README.DOC document that came with your AutoCAD disks. These files contain additional last-minute information.
- ❏ Send in your registration card.
- ❏ Most of all, enjoy your equipment and software and have fun.

Now you are ready to use AutoCAD. Turn to Chapter 4 to get a feel for your new software.

B

Useful Additional Programs

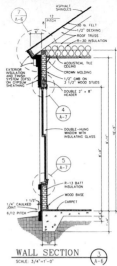

WALL SECTION
SCALE: 3/4"=1'-0"

Illustration courtesy of
Autodesk, Inc., Sausalito, CA.

One reason for AutoCAD's tremendous success is the ease it affords third-party developers in creating add-on programs and enhancement packages for use with AutoCAD. Further, AutoCAD provides drafting and design utilities that are not aimed at any one discipline.

Third-party software can range from a simple AutoLISP routine written by a friend to a complete customization package for numerically controlled (NC) programming. The AutoLISP routine might do something as simple as inserting the coordinate text next to a point (something that AutoCAD itself does not do). The NC package might determine automatically the six-axis milling path of your three-dimensional drawing, convert the drawing to NC machine code, and convert the code back into an AutoCAD drawing for checking.

Because there are nearly 1,000 third-party developers, Autodesk has implemented four programs to certify developers. A *Registered Developer* has proven to Autodesk that its add-on software has at least 10 customers. *Strategic Developers* have products for key markets (such as NC programming, A/E/C, facilities management, geographical information systems, and mapping). The software is of high quality and has worldwide support. *Corporate Developers* are corporations, with at least 100 AutoCAD stations, that develop in-house software. The *Future Registered Developer Program* is for developers who have no product yet; Autodesk reviews the research-and-development plans of such developers to see whether the developers are on the right track.

The packages described here customize AutoCAD by way of menu macros, tablet overlays, AutoLISP routines, block libraries, and file connections to other programs. You could do exactly the same thing

925

yourself (AutoCAD includes most of the tools you need) but not as cost-effectively. The *AutoCAD Sourcebook* and *AutoCAD Sourcebook Supplement* (both published by Que Corporation) list information on hundreds of third-party packages.

Other software add-ons described here are more general in nature. They make using AutoCAD (and computers) easier for anyone, regardless of the user's discipline. This appendix lists several packages, available both commercially and as shareware, that enhance AutoCAD's effectiveness.

Application-Specific Software

These add-on software packages help customize AutoCAD for specific applications. These packages contain many library symbols and AutoLISP routines to make your design work easier.

ASG Architectural

For several years, Autodesk sold an architectural add-on package called AutoCAD AEC Architectural. The software has returned to its originators, the Archsoft Group, and is now being sold as ASG Architectural. The package enables architects to create architectural plans more easily with AutoCAD. The program features automatic wall-drawing and door/window-insertion routines. ASG Architectural toggles between 2-D and 3-D modes, and includes a large library of predrawn figures.

DCA Engineering Software

The DCA Civil Engineering package by DCA Engineering, Inc., is a group of programs that run from within AutoCAD and customize AutoCAD for civil engineers. The different modules allow for profile and cross-section generation, three-dimensional mesh creation from points, lot sizing, complete drawing annotation, and other specific civil engineering requirements.

NC Polaris

NC Polaris, from NC Microproducts, enables NC (numerical control) programmers to use AutoCAD to control lathe and milling machines. After creating a design in AutoCAD, the operator instructs NC Polaris to determine the tool path that would create the object. After you are satisfied with the path, NC Polaris converts the AutoCAD drawing into a format the machine tool understands.

LandCADD Professional Land Planner

The LandCADD Professional Land Planner package by LandCADD, Inc., enables landscape designers to perform site design and land planning from within AutoCAD. The template contains a complete symbol library of plants and trees as well as routines to simulate growth of the flora over extended periods. These simulation capabilities, coupled with routines for landscaping design, irrigation design, and many standard construction details, make the package extremely helpful to the landscape architect.

FMS/AC Facilities Management Systems

FMS/AC, from Facilities Management Systems, lets you create maps from data input into AutoCAD. A municipality, for example, can quickly get a list of all water lines older than 25 years, or all properties with a value of over $1 million.

Andersen Windows CADD-I

One of the newer generation of computerized product lines available from a manufacturer, the CADD-I template contains window details, elevations, and sections that help shorten your design time. This package contains the same information found in the Andersen specifications booklets as well as routines for insertion of custom windows and doors, and storefront design.

General Utility Programs

The following programs are useful for all AutoCAD users, no matter what their discipline.

AutoManager

AutoManager, by CYCO International, is a drawing-management program for AutoCAD. The program enables you to open DWG files, turn layers on and off, and even view blocks within a drawing—without ever entering the AutoCAD program. AutoManager contains super-fast routines for erasing, copying, and renaming multiple files across different directories. The program's capabilities make CAD workstation management easier.

AutoSave

Although AutoCAD Release 11 can recover damaged drawing files, you need a third-party program if you need to recover damaged Release 10 drawings. AutoSave, from CYCO International, reads a DWG file, makes sure that the file's format makes sense, and writes the result as a DXF file. You can then read the DXF file into AutoCAD and redraw the missing or incorrect parts of the drawing.

CAD LETTEREASE

AutoCAD can use multiple text styles within a drawing. The CAD LETTEREASE template, developed by CAD Lettering Systems, Inc., is a series of custom-designed fonts that mimic many of the typefaces available in press-on lettering. This add-in program enables you to place lettering along arcs and polylines and to control the spacing between individual letters. Each LETTEREASE lettering style comes in 5 different forms that can be reproduced accurately (from 1/16 inch up to 5 feet high) with no distortion.

QuickSurf

If you need to create 3-D meshes from a series of random points within a drawing, QuickSurf is the fastest method available. The QuickSurf program by Schreiber Instruments is available as a demo version from many bulletin boards. The program can read random points or contour lines and create the matching 3-D mesh surface model. Its speed comes from the use of an external module to perform all calculations; QuickSurf does not rely on AutoLISP routines, as many other surface-modeling packages do.

Plump RX

Plotting a large drawing can take a long time. AutoCAD can send the plot data far faster than the pen plotter can accept it. A fast solution is a plot spooler. You can quickly plot the drawing to disk and return to the Drawing Editor, but Plump RX (memory-resident software from SSC Softsystems, Inc.) *spools* the plot data from a disk file to the pen plotter (or printer plotter) in the background. The plotter continues to receive data and plot the drawing while you work on the next drawing in AutoCAD.

Shareware Software

All the preceding software add-ons are commercial packages that cost between $100 and $3,000. *Shareware* is software you can obtain free or at little cost. If you find the product useful, the programmer requests a nominal fee, such as $10 to $50.

TED

TED (for Text EDitor) is a shareware product that can be found on CompuServe. TED was designed from the ground up to be as similar as possible to a normal full-screen text editor that you would use when you are not in AutoCAD. TED has color capabilities, can do search-and-replace, can break apart lines of text or put two lines together, can cut and paste from the middle of one line to the middle of another, and uses intuitive cursor-control keys. In addition, TED can import text from outside AutoCAD. And, by using the SHELL command, you can do all this without leaving AutoCAD. TED is not a TSR; it requires no additional memory.

DXFer

AutoCAD lets you read drawing files created by earlier versions but won't create a new drawing for the older version. DXFer, from Tangent Graphics, is a shareware product that translates Release 10 drawings to earlier versions, including Release 9. It has several options that let you control the output, which is useful for translating AutoCAD drawings into the format needed by another CAD package. DXFer is available on CompuServe's Autodesk Forum.

General Software

The following software can be useful for any computer user—even those who don't use AutoCAD. However, these two packages are particularly well suited for AutoCAD.

PC Tools

PC Tools, from Central Point Software, is a large collection of utility programs that work with any DOS, OS/2, or Macintosh computer. It includes several programs essential for AutoCAD users. One is a memory-resident text editor that shows spaces and carriage returns (as dots and arrows), making it easier for you to write error-free script files. The text editor also does automatic indentation and saves, which is useful for AutoLISP programming.

The file-recovery program undeletes files you have accidentally erased. The back up program quickly saves all files on the hard disk to floppy disks or to a tape drive. The DOS shell lets you "point and shoot" your way around subdirectories; you don't need to type any DOS commands.

Hijaak

If you need to insert AutoCAD drawings into word-processing documents, or convert graphical file formats, screen-capture software like Hijaak, from Inset Systems, enables you to do that. Hijaak captures screens from several graphics boards, including VGA. It can then print the screen to a printer or convert the format to that used by paint programs or word processing software.

Summary

The many products available to enhance AutoCAD are too numerous to mention here. The products listed in this section should give you an idea of the diverse programs available to make AutoCAD more productive for you.

C

Hatch Patterns

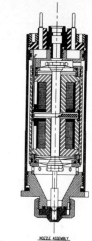

AutoCAD Release 11 comes with 52 hatch patterns (Release 10 has 43) defined in file ACAD.PAT. Figure C.1 shows the pattern associated with each name.

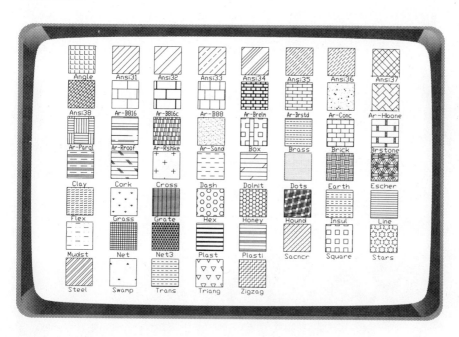

*Fig. C.1.
AutoCAD
Release 11
has many
hatch
patterns.*

931

D

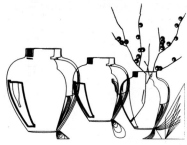

Illustration courtesy of
Autodesk, Inc., Sausalito, CA.

Linetypes

AutoCAD features 25 built-in linetypes, which are defined in the file ACAD.LIN. In addition to the continuous linetype, AutoCAD includes eight basic patterns plus two scaled versions of each. The *name*2 linetype is double-scale, whereas the *name*X2 linetype is half-scale. (Release 10 does not include the scaled linetypes.)

Figure D.1 shows the name and pattern associated with each linetype.

CONTINUOUS _____

BORDER _ _ . _ _ . _ _ . _ _ . _ _ . _ _ . _ _ . _ _ .

BORDER2 _._._._._._._._._._._._._._._._._._

BORDERX2 __ __ . __ __ . __ __ . __ __ .

CENTER ___ _ ___ _ ___ _ ___ _ ___ _ ___ _ ___ _

CENTER2 __ _ __ _ __ _ __ _ __ _ __ _ __ _ __ _ __ _ __

CENTERX2 _____ _ _____ _ _____ _ _____ _

DASHDOT _ . _ . _ . _ . _ . _ . _ . _ . _ . _ . _ .

DASHDOT2 _._._._._._._._._._._._._._._._.

DASHDOTX2 __ . __ . __ . __ . __ . __ . __

DASHED _

DASHED2 _

DASHEDX2 __ __ __ __ __ __ __ __ __ __ __

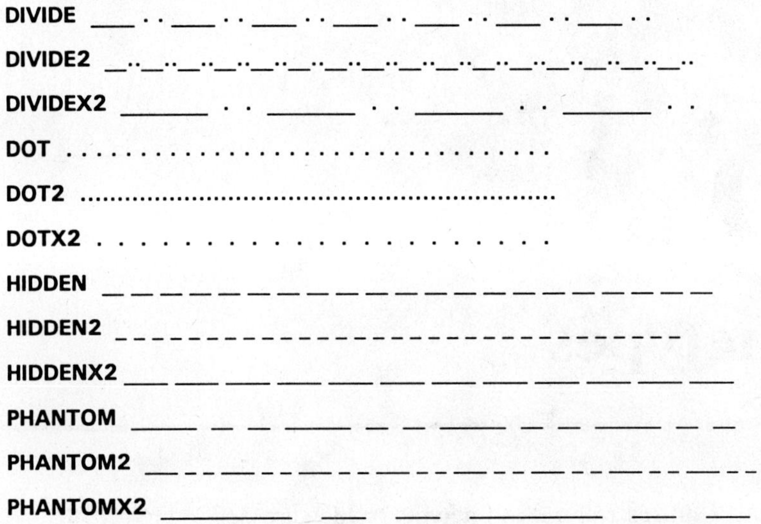

Fig. D.1.
AutoCAD's
linetypes are
defined in the
file ACAD.LIN.

DIVIDE ___ · · ___ · · ___ · · ___ · · ___ · · ___ · · ___ · ·

DIVIDE2 _·_·_·_·_·_·_·_·_·_·_·_·_·_·_·_·_·_·_··

DIVIDEX2 _____ · · _____ · · _____ · · _____ · ·

DOT ·

DOT2 ·

DOTX2 · · · · · · · · · · · · · · · ·

HIDDEN _

HIDDEN2 _

HIDDENX2 ___ ___ ___ ___ ___ ___ ___ ___ ___ ___ ___

PHANTOM ____ _ _ ____ _ _ ____ _ _ ____ _ _

PHANTOM2 __ _ _ __ _ _ __ _ _ __ _ _ __ _ _ __ _ _ __ _ _ __ _ _

PHANTOMX2 _____ ___ ___ _____ ___ ___

E

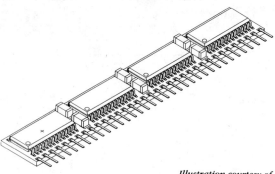

*Illustration courtesy of
Autodesk, Inc., Sausalito, CA.*

Text Fonts

AutoCAD features 29 built-in text fonts, each of which is defined in a separate SHX font file. All fonts, except Monotxt, are *proportionately* spaced like the text in this book, which means that the letter I takes less space than the letter W. Proportional spacing makes the text easier to read.

The Monotxt font is meant for tabular text, where the spacing of each letter must be the same. The four IGES fonts include symbols for drawings translated into IGES format. The five symbol fonts enable you to add discipline-specific symbols (astronomy, mathematics, cartography, meteorology, and music) by simply pressing a key. The Greek fonts are also useful for symbols. The CyrilLic font is true Cyrillic; the CyrilTlc is a transliteration.

TIP

Complex-looking fonts, such as RomanT and GothicE, take much longer to regenerate and redraw on the screen than simple-looking fonts, like Txt and RomanS. Enter text into the drawing with the appropriate font, then use the Style command to redefine the text style to a simple font. When it comes time to plot, change the text style back again.

Some fonts with different names look the same. They are from earlier versions of AutoCAD and are included for compatibility, as follows:

Old Name	New Name
Simplex	RomanS
Complex	RomanC
Italic	ItalicC

Figure E.1 shows the text font names and a sample of the styles.

935

Fig. E.1.
AutoCAD
has 29
built-in
text fonts.

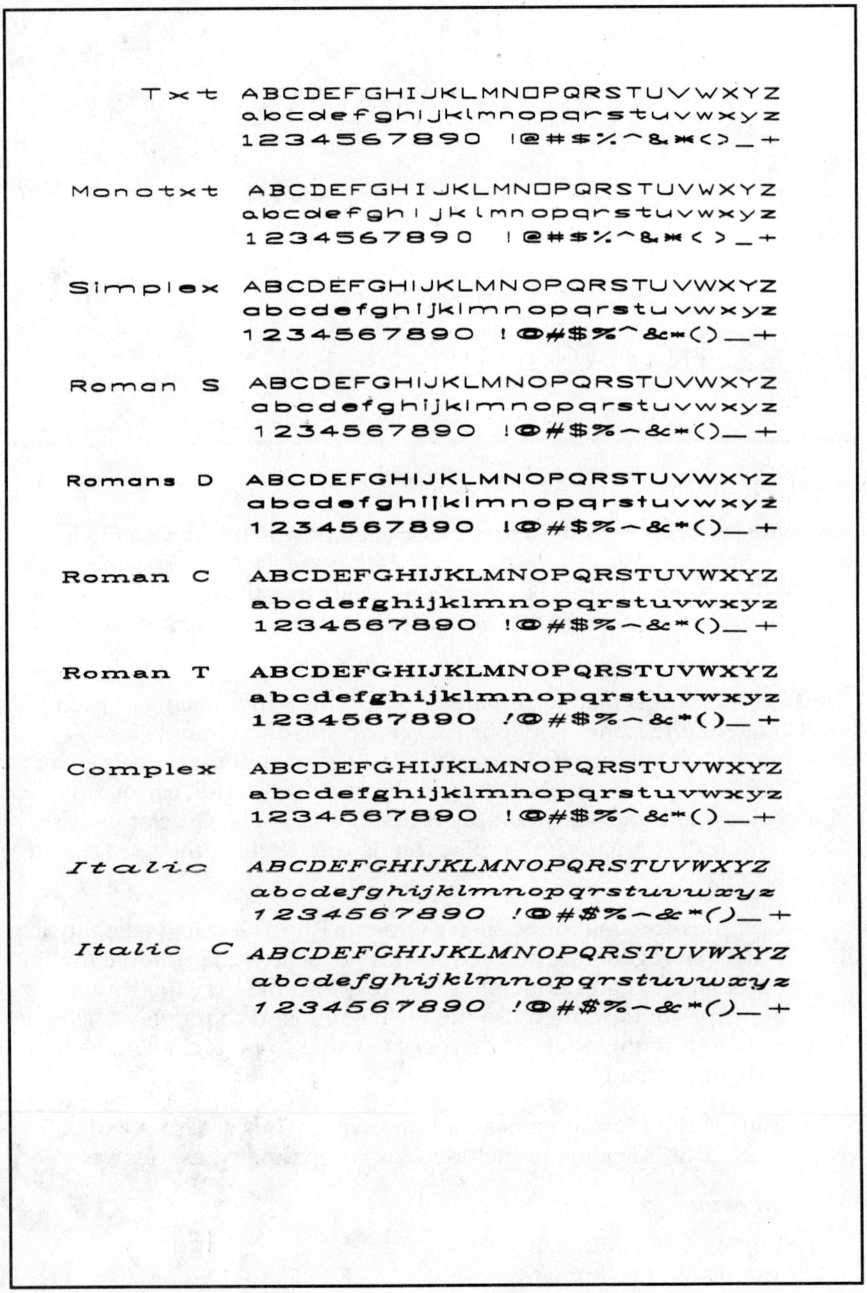

Txt
ABCDEFGHIJKLMNOPQRSTUVWXYZ
abcdefghijklmnopqrstuvwxyz
1234567890 !@#$%^&*<>_+

Monotxt
ABCDEFGHIJKLMNOPQRSTUVWXYZ
abcdefghijklmnopqrstuvwxyz
1234567890 !@#$%^&*<>_+

Simplex
ABCDEFGHIJKLMNOPQRSTUVWXYZ
abcdefghijklmnopqrstuvwxyz
1234567890 !@#$%^&*()_+

Roman S
ABCDEFGHIJKLMNOPQRSTUVWXYZ
abcdefghijklmnopqrstuvwxyz
1234567890 !@#$%~&*()_+

Romans D
ABCDEFGHIJKLMNOPQRSTUVWXYZ
abcdefghijklmnopqrstuvwxyz
1234567890 !@#$%~&*()_+

Roman C
ABCDEFGHIJKLMNOPQRSTUVWXYZ
abcdefghijklmnopqrstuvwxyz
1234567890 !@#$%~&*()_+

Roman T
ABCDEFGHIJKLMNOPQRSTUVWXYZ
abcdefghijklmnopqrstuvwxyz
1234567890 !@#$%~&*()_+

Complex
ABCDEFGHIJKLMNOPQRSTUVWXYZ
abcdefghijklmnopqrstuvwxyz
1234567890 !@#$%^&*()_+

Italic
ABCDEFGHIJKLMNOPQRSTUVWXYZ
abcdefghijklmnopqrstuvwxyz
1234567890 !@#$%~&()_+*

Italic C
ABCDEFGHIJKLMNOPQRSTUVWXYZ
abcdefghijklmnopqrstuvwxyz
1234567890 !@#$%~&()_+*

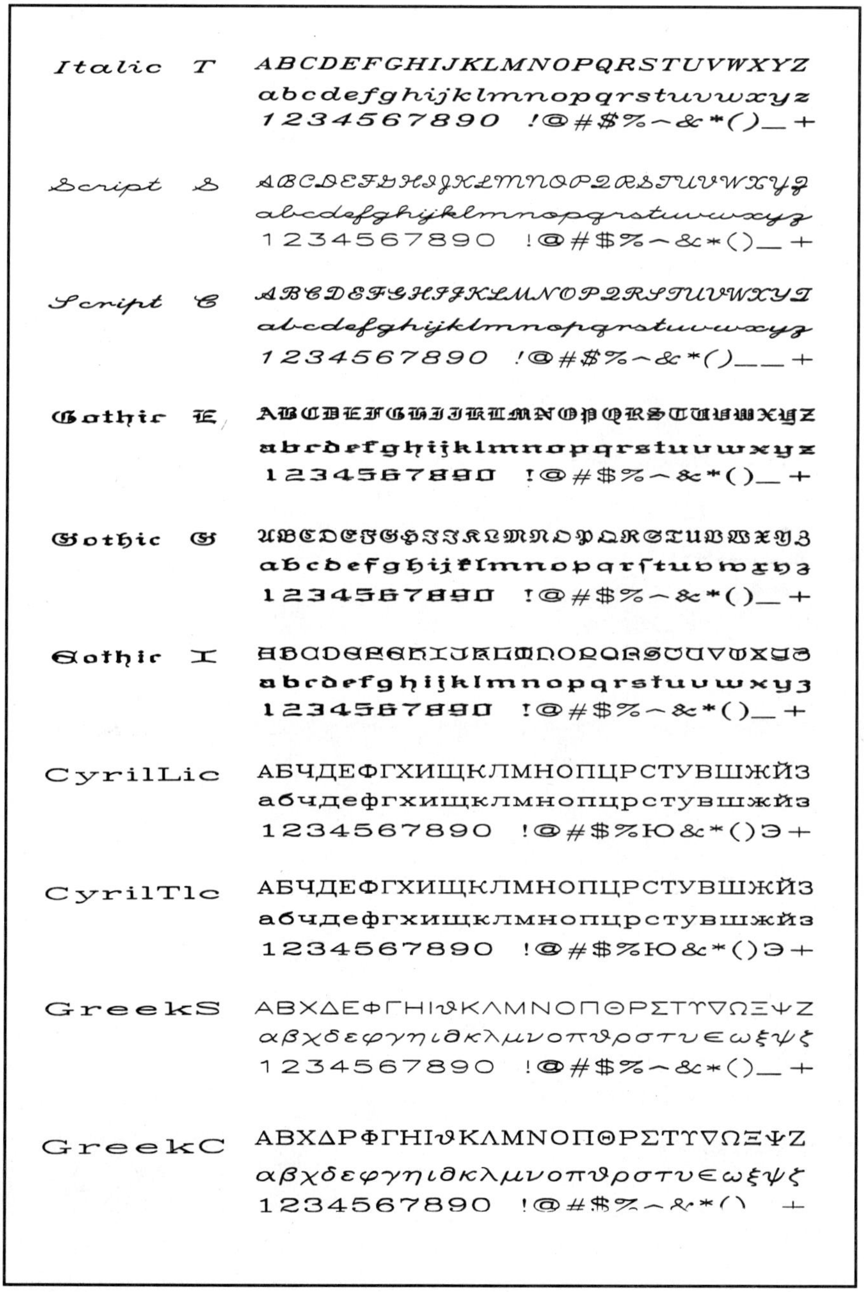

Italic	T	ABCDEFGHIJKLMNOPQRSTUVWXYZ
		abcdefghijklmnopqrstuvwxyz
		1234567890 !@#$%~&*()_+

Fig. E.1.
(continued).

Script	S	ABCDEFGHIJKLMNOPQRSTUVWXYZ
		abcdefghijklmnopqrstuvwxyz
		1234567890 !@#$%~&*()_+

Script	C	ABCDEFGHIJKLMNOPQRSTUVWXYZ
		abcdefghijklmnopqrstuvwxyz
		1234567890 !@#$%~&*()__+

Gothic	E	ABCDEFGHIJKLMNOPQRSTUVWXYZ
		abcdefghijklmnopqrstuvwxyz
		1234567890 !@#$%~&*()_+

Gothic	G	ABCDEFGHIJKLMNOPQRSTUVWXYZ
		abcdefghijklmnopqrstuvwxyz
		1234567890 !@#$%~&*()_+

Gothic	I	ABCDEFGHIJKLMNOPQRSTUVWXYZ
		abcdefghijklmnopqrstuvwxyz
		1234567890 !@#$%~&*()_+

CyrilLic		АБЧДЕФГХИЩКЛМНОПЦРСТУВШЖЙЗ
		абчдефгхищклмнопцрстувшжйз
		1234567890 !@#$%Ю&*()Э+

CyrilTlc		АБЧДЕФГХИЩКЛМНОПЦРСТУВШЖЙЗ
		абчдефгхищклмнопцрстувшжйз
		1234567890 !@#$%Ю&*()Э+

GreekS		ΑΒΧΔΕΦΓΗΙϑΚΛΜΝΟΠΘΡΣΤΥϒΩΞΨΖ
		αβχδεφγηιϑκλμνοπϖρστυ∈ωξψζ
		1234567890 !@#$%~&*()_+

GreekC		ΑΒΧΔΡΦΓΗΙϑΚΛΜΝΟΠΘΡΣΤΥϒΩΞΨΖ
		αβχδεφγηιϑκλμνοπϖρστυ∈ωξψζ
		1234567890 !@#$%~&*() +

Fig. E.1.
(continued).

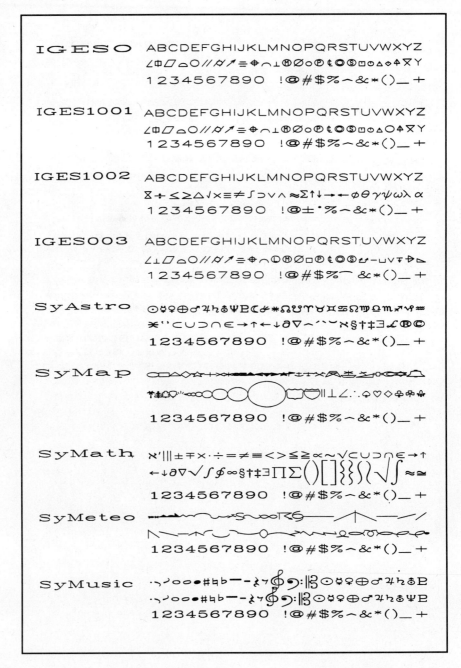

F

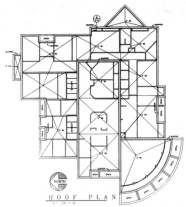

*Illustration courtesy of
Autodesk, Inc., Sausalito, CA.*

Button Assignments

AutoCAD refers to the first button on your pointing device as button 0 and defines it as the pick button. The ACAD.MNU menu file defines the remaining buttons, up to a total of 10 (some digitizing tablets have 16-button pucks). You can redefine the meaning of any button (except button 0) in the menu file.

The meanings of the buttons change when you enter the Sketch command; you cannot use customized buttons while in Sketch mode. Both sets of definitions follow:

Button Number	AutoCAD Meaning	Sketch-Command Meaning
0	Pick	Raise/ower pen (P)
1	Return	Line to point (.)
2	Display Assist menu	Record sketch (R)
3	Cancel	Record and exit (X)
4	Snap toggle	Discard and quit (Q)
5	Ortho toggle	Erase (E)
6	Grid toggle	Connect (C)
7	Coordinate display	Not defined
8	Isoplane toggle	Not defined
9	Toggle tablet mode	Not defined
10–15	Not defined	Not defined

If you have no menu loaded into the current drawing, only button 0 will work as expected. The work-around is to load a menu file with the Menu command.

G

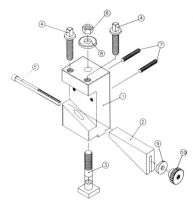

File-Name Extensions

Most computer programs reserve several file-name extensions for
themselves. The three-letter extension tells you the purpose of the file.
For example, ACAD.EXE is the AutoCAD program (*EXE* stands for
executable), ACAD.DWG is the prototype drawing file, and ACAD.PAT is
the hatch-pattern file.

AutoCAD uses a total of 46 extension names. Periodically, you may want
to erase unnecessary files, such as those ending with BAK, XLG, and $AC.

AutoCAD Release 11 implements *file locking*, a feature meant for
networked CAD stations. File locking prevents other users from accessing
an AutoCAD-related file while your copy of AutoCAD is using it. The
locked file name exists only while AutoCAD is actually using that file.

11

AutoCAD locks a file by changing the last character of the three-letter
extension to *K*. For example, a locked drawing file (DWK) exists the
entire time you are editing that drawing. A locked (MNK) menu file exists
only while AutoCAD compiles and loads it; the MNK file is erased once
the menu is loaded.

Table G.1 lists the file extensions AutoCAD uses, the locked-menu
version, and the meaning of the extension.

Table G.1
AutoCAD File Extensions

Extension Name	Locked Name	Meaning
ADS		ADS load file
ADT		Release 11 Audit-command log
ASM		AutoSolid model
BAK	BKK	Backup of a saved drawing file
BK0		Emergency backup file
C		ADS program source code
CFG	CFK	Configuration file
DFS		Release 11 Mview-command setup defaults
DWG	DWK	Drawing file
DXB	DBK	DXB Binary drawing exchange file
DXF	DFK	DXF ASCII drawing exchange file
DXX	DXK	Extracted attribute data
ERR		Error-message log
EXE		AutoCAD program
EXP		Extended-memory programs
FLM	FLK	Filmroll file for AutoShade
H		ADS header source code
HLP		Help file
HDX		Help file index
IGS	IGK	IGES drawing exchange file
LIB		ADS library file
LIN	LIK	Linetype definition
LSP		AutoLISP source code
LST	LTK	Plot file created by Prplot command
MAT		Release 11 material property definitions
MND		Menu file source for the MC.EXE menu compiler
MNU		Menu file source
MNX	MXK	Compiled menu
MSG		Main Menu message
OBJ		ADS object code
OLD	OLK	Converted old-format drawing file
OVL		AutoCAD Release 10 program overlay
PAT		Hatch-pattern definitions
PGP		External program parameters
PLT	PLK	Plot file created by Plot command
PRP	PRK	Plot file created by ADI printer plotter
PWD	PWK	Release 11 password
SCR		Script file source code
SHP		Shape and text source code
SHX	SHK	Shape and text compiled code
SLB		Slide library
SLD	SDK	Slide file
TXT		Attribute extract template file
UNT		Release 11 unit translations used by AutoLISP
XLG		Release 11 Xref-command log
$AC	$AK	Temporary working file

*Illustration courtesy of
Autodesk, Inc., Sausalito, CA.*

Glossary

Words set in *italic* are defined elsewhere in the Glossary.

A

Absolute coordinate. The location of a point with reference to a fixed origin point. Can be *Cartesian*, *polar*, cylindrical, or spherical. These coordinates are treated as X,Y,Z displacements from 0,0,0.

Aperture. A target box surrounding the *crosshair's* intersection; used to select objects quickly on-screen.

Array. Multiple copies of entities in rows and columns, arranged in a *rectangular* or *polar* pattern.

Associative dimension. A dimension stored as a single object rather than as a collection of individual lines, areas, solids, and dimension text. The associated values are updated automatically to reflect modifications to a dimensioned object.

Attribute. An object that stores any type of information associated with a *block*.

Attribute mode. Four attribute-mode toggles control the handling of *attribute*s: Invisible, Constant, Verify, and Preset.

Attribute tag. A one-word label for the *attribute* being defined.

Axis of revolution. The axis around which a *path curve* revolves.

B

Base point. A reference point, located anywhere in a drawing, that AutoCAD uses when copying or moving entities to a second point.

Blip. A symbol—usually a small cross (+)—that AutoCAD places on the screen to indicate puck points. Although they appear on the screen whenever you select a point, blips are not part of your drawing and are erased with the next redraw.

Block. A group of objects that are treated as a single object. A block can contain part or all of a drawing. Blocks are used to insert components of one drawing into another drawing or to make copies of a component in the same drawing.

Boundary. The outline of an area to be hatched, including any internal outlines of areas that should not be hatched. Boundaries must be closed figures.

C

CAD. An acronym for *computer-aided design* or *computer-aided drafting*.

CAM. An acronym for *computer-aided manufacturing*.

Camera. The location from which you look at an object.

Cartesian coordinate system. A coordinate system that uses two or three axes to locate any given point in three dimensions. The origin of this system is 0,0 (X=0, Y=0) or 0,0,0 (X=0, Y=0, and Z=0).

Cell. See *unit cell*.

Chamfer. A beveled edge between two intersecting lines.

Chord. A straight line segment connecting the endpoints of an arc.

Clipping plane. A plane, perpendicular to the line of sight, which can be applied anywhere between the *camera* and *target point* so that it blocks whatever is behind it or in front of it. Two clipping planes show only objects between them. Clipping planes are used to show *views* that would otherwise be hidden by objects in the foreground.

Construction plane. The X-Y plane at the current *elevation*.

Continuation. The process of drawing a second line or arc that starts at the end of the most recently drawn line or arc.

Coons surface patch. The surface created by using the Edgesurf command. An interpolated bicubic surface between four adjoining curves; the curves may be in any alignment in the drawing.

Coordinate system icon. An on-screen symbol that indicates the *orientation* of the X and Y axes as you change coordinate systems.

Corrupt. To change or partially erase information in a file so that your computer no longer understands it.

Crosshairs. A cursor drawn as two perpendicular crossed lines; used to select coordinate locations on-screen.

D

Delta. The change in the X, Y, and Z values from one point to another (*delta x*, *delta y*, and *delta z*); the change in distance in the X, Y, and Z directions.

Dialogue box. A temporary overlay that provides prompts with which you can respond to a command.

Digitizing. The process of accurately indicating points in a drawing or selecting coordinates on an AutoCAD template.

Digitizing tablet. A flat, electronic surface used in conjunction with a *stylus* or *puck* to enter commands and select points on-screen.

Dimensions. Measurements in the form of extension lines of the angles and distances between points in a drawing.

Dimension line. A line showing the distance or angle the *dimension* measures.

Dimension styles. A set of standards applying to *dimensions* that can be referred to by name.

Dimension variables. System variables that affect the way *dimensions* act and appear.

Dimensioning commands. Commands that add dimensioning to a drawing.

Direction vector. A line or an open *polyline* with an exact direction and length but without a specific location.

Displacement. The distance an object moves along the X, Y, and Z axes. The distance is expressed as *delta x*, *delta y*, and *delta z*.

Dragging. The process in which AutoCAD draws a ghosted or temporary image of an object as it is drawn or edited; enables you to see the effect of the change before it takes place.

Drawing commands. Commands used to create an object.

E

Editing commands. Commands that modify or change previously created objects.

Elevation. The location of objects on the Zaxis.

Entity. The basic graphic elements in a drawing. AutoCAD entities include: point, line, circle, arc, trace, solid, *polyline*, text, *attribute*, *associative dimension*, *block*, 3-D polyline, 3-D face, 3-D*mesh*, polymesh, and *viewports*.

Extents. The area in which you have drawn; the extents indicate the drawing's actual size.

Extrusion. An object's thickness or extension from its X-Y plane along the Z axis of the *UCS*. The extrusion's direction is always parallel to the Z axis of the *UCS* in which the object was created.

F

Fillet. The rounded intersection of two intersecting objects. (See *Chamfer*.)

Flip screen key. On a PC keyboard, the F1 function key, which "flips"— or switches—between the AutoCAD text screen and graphics screen on a single-screen system.

G

Global editing. The process of editing all *attributes* at one time.

Grid. A rectangular *array* of reference points that lie within a drawing's limits. Grid points are not part of the drawing.

H

Hatching. The process of filling an area with a design for purposes of identification.

I

Insertion base point. A reference point used as the 0,0 origin point when a *block*, object, or another drawing is inserted into or edited in a drawing. Inserting, scaling, and rotating are relative to the insertion point.

Isometric. A two-dimensional representation of a three-dimensional object.

L

Layer. In a drawing, an overlay on which specific data can be stored.

Leader. A *dimension line* that connects the dimension text with the object being dimensioned or labeled.

Library part. (Also called *block*.) An object created from other objects or blocks. Several add-on software packages provide symbol libraries for use with AutoCAD.

Limits. The boundaries that determine the potential size of a drawing. (See *Extents*.)

M

Menu. A list of options presented by a program; enables you to select the option by specifying a single number or name.

Mesh. A pattern of intersecting lines indicating a three-dimensional surface.

Mirroring. The process of producing a mirror image of an object.

Model Space. The AutoCAD drawing environment.

Mouse. A pointing device with one or more buttons that positions the cursor on the computer screen.

Multiple insert. The process of inserting more than one copy of a *block* at a time.

N

Nest. To place one *block* inside another. Several simple blocks can be combined into a single complex block.

O

Object pointing. The use of the pointing device to move the *pickbox* cursor until the cursor rests on the object to be selected.

Obliquing angle. An angle, taken from the vertical, that determines the slant of letters for a text font.

Orientation. The location or position of an object. The *UCS icon* shows the orientation for the current *viewport*.

Ortho. (Short for ORTHOgonal.) A mode that permits only horizontal or vertical pointer movement and input.

P

Paper space. The AutoCAD plotting environment.

Path curve. The arc, circle, line, or *polyline* revolved around an axis to define a surface; the outline of the object you are drawing.

Picking. The process of using a pointing device to select commands from the tablet or screen and to indicate objects or locations on-screen.

Pickbox. A small box that appears on-screen at the intersection of the *crosshairs*. The pickbox appears when AutoCAD prompts you to select objects.

Plan view. The view of the current *construction plane* from the positive Z axis. The plan view is determined by the coordinate system.

Pointing device. A hand-held device (a *puck*, *mouse*, or *stylus*) used for *digitizing*.

Point filter. Selecting a point by entering a single coordinate preceded by a period (.*x*, for example) and then responding to prompts for the other coordinate points. Used to align new parts of a drawing with existing objects in the current *construction plane*.

Polar. Resembling a pole or axis; relating to *polar coordinates*.

Polar coordinate. A 2-D coordinate system defined by a distance and an angle. The angles are relative to 0 degrees, with positive angles measured counterclockwise.

Polyline. A connected line composed of variable-width lines and arcs.

Primitive. A simple object (such as a line, circle, or arc) on which other, more complex objects are based; also known as an *entity*.

Profile. Synonymous with *path curve*.

Properties. Characteristic qualities of an object; in AutoCAD, properties include color, linetype, *layer*, and *thickness*.

Prototype drawing. The drawing that stores the default information used by AutoCAD in the creation of new drawings.

Puck. A pointing device, resembling a *mouse*, with one or more buttons. Used with a *digitizing tablet* to move *crosshairs* on-screen and execute commands.

R

Record increment. The distance the pointing device travels to draw a line or *polyline* in Sketch mode. The smaller the increment, the shorter the line segments, which makes a smoother curve but takes up more memory.

Rectangular. One of two types of AutoCAD *arrays*: rectangular and *polar*. Rectangular arrays are composed of repetitive objects arranged in rows and columns.

Relative coordinates. Points located in relation to another (often the last point entered).

Right-hand rule. A method of determining the direction of the positive Z axis. Extend your right thumb along the positive X axis and point your index finger in the positive Y direction. When you curl your remaining fingers, they point along the positive Z axis. Useful for visualizing *UCS orientation*.

Rotation factor. The number of degrees an object is rotated.

Rubber-band effect. The stretching and movement of a line as it follows the cursor from a fixed point when the cursor moves the line's endpoint.

S

Selection set. A collection of one or more objects to be processed by an AutoCAD command.

Shading. The alteration of a drawing to suggest three-dimensionality or shadows.

Slide. A snapshot of the screen; often used for presentations.

Slider bar. Adjustment controls presented on-screen by the Dview command. The slider bars enable you to adjust your view.

Snap. To lock on to an object or *grid* at a snap point. The Snap command establishes the smallest increment AutoCAD moves the pointer.

Stylus. A hand-held pointing device resembling a pen with a spring-loaded or electronic tip. Used like a *puck* to enter commands or points from a *digitizing tablet*.

System variable. A variable that contains information (*grid*, *snap*, and axis information, for example) about a drawing's environment settings and their values.

T

Tabulated surface. A surface defined by a *path curve* and a *direction vector*. These surfaces are represented as polygon *meshes*.

Tangent. A line through a point on the circumference of a circle (or other curved line) perpendicular to the radius at that point.

Target point. The point at which you are looking.

Template coordinates. X and Y coordinates for a menu item on a template for a *digitizing tablet*.

Thickness. The distance an object extends from its X-Y plane.

Three-dimensional face. A flat plane in three-dimensional space.

Three-point definition. A method of defining a *UCS* with an origin, a positive X axis, and a positive Y axis.

Torus. A 3-D surface shaped like a doughnut; generated by rotating a circle around an axis in a plane that doesn't intersect the circle.

Transparent command. An AutoCAD command that can be used within another AutoCAD command. Transparent commands are invoked by preceding the command name with an apostrophe ('). The transparent commands are 'Ddemodes, 'Ddlmodes, 'Ddrmodes, 'Graphscr, 'Help, '?, 'Pan, 'Redraw, 'Redrawall, 'Resume, 'Setvar, 'Textscr, 'View, and 'Zoom.

U

UCS. An acronym for *user coordinate system*.

UCS icon. See *coordinate system icon*.

Unit. The distance from one point to another; such as one inch or one centimeter. Also refers to the system of measurement with which you are working (metric, for example).

Unit cell. In an *array*, the area between row and column distances.

User Coordinate System (UCS). A user-defined coordinate system (or plane), defined within the *World Coordinate System* used by AutoCAD. Can be at any angle in space.

V

View. A graphical representation of a drawing from a specific location (*viewpoint*) in space.

Viewpoint. The direction and *elevation* from which you view a drawing; your location in relation to the object you are drawing.

Viewport. The screen's graphics area; different views of a drawing may be displayed simultaneously in multiple view ports.

W

WCS. An acronym for *world coordinate system*.

Wild-card character. A symbol, such as * or ?. In AutoCAD and some operating systems, * represents any characters; ? represents a single character.

Window. A framed area on the drawing screen that encloses a part of the drawing for modification or zooming.

World Coordinate System (WCS). In AutoCAD, a fixed *Cartesian coordinate system* consisting of *absolute coordinates*: a horizontal X *displacement*, a vertical Y displacement, and a positive Z displacement for 3-D. The WCS is the default User Coordinate System, but you can create other *UCSs* at any angle or location in 3-D space relative to the WCS.

X

X-Y plane. (See *Construction plane*.)

Xref. (Short for *eXternal REFerence*). Has entered the working vocabulary through AutoCAD Release 11. Pertains, although not exclusively, to the immediate regional whereabouts of a necessarily different drawing file. May include a path name.

Index

B

E

F

U

Computer Books From Que Mean PC Performance!

Spreadsheets

1-2-3 Database Techniques	$29.95
1-2-3 Graphics Techniques	$24.95
1-2-3 Macro Library, 3rd Edition	$39.95
1-2-3 Release 2.2 Business Applications	$39.95
1-2-3 Release 2.2 Quick Reference	$ 7.95
1-2-3 Release 2.2 QuickStart	$19.95
1-2-3 Release 2.2 Workbook and Disk	$29.95
1-2-3 Release 3 Business Applications	$39.95
1-2-3 Release 3 Quick Reference	$ 7.95
1-2-3 Release 3 QuickStart	$19.95
1-2-3 Release 3 Workbook and Disk	$29.95
1-2-3 Tips, Tricks, and Traps, 3rd Edition	$24.95
Excel Business Applications: IBM Version	$39.95
Excel Quick Reference	$ 7.95
Excel QuickStart	$19.95
Excel Tips, Tricks, and Traps	$22.95
Using 1-2-3, Special Edition	$26.95
Using 1-2-3 Release 2.2, Special Edition	$26.95
Using 1-2-3 Release 3	$27.95
Using Excel: IBM Version	$29.95
Using Lotus Spreadsheet for DeskMate	$19.95
Using Quattro Pro	$24.95
Using SuperCalc5, 2nd Edition	$29.95

Databases

dBASE III Plus Handbook, 2nd Edition	$24.95
dBASE III Plus Tips, Tricks, and Traps	$24.95
dBASE III Plus Workbook and Disk	$29.95
dBASE IV Applications Library, 2nd Edition	$39.95
dBASE IV Programming Techniques	$24.95
dBASE IV QueCards	$21.95
dBASE IV Quick Reference	$ 7.95
dBASE IV QuickStart	$19.95
dBASE IV Tips, Tricks,and Traps, 2nd Ed.	$24.95
dBASE IV Workbook and Disk	$29.95
R:BASE User's Guide, 3rd Edition	$22.95
Using Clipper	$24.95
Using DataEase	$24.95
Using dBASE IV	$27.95
Using FoxPro	$26.95
Using Paradox 3	$24.95
Using Reflex, 2nd Edition	$22.95
Using SQL	$24.95

Business Applications

Introduction to Business Software	$14.95
Introduction to Personal Computers	$19.95
Lotus Add-in Toolkit Guide	$29.95
Norton Utilities Quick Reference	$ 7.95
PC Tools Quick Reference, 2nd Edition	$ 7.95
Q&A Quick Reference	$ 7.95
Que's Computer User's Dictionary	$9.95
Que's Wizard Book	$ 9.95
Smart Tips, Tricks, and Traps	$24.95
Using Computers in Business	$22.95
Using DacEasy, 2nd Edition	$24.95
Using Dollars and Sense: IBM Version, 2nd Edition	$19.95
Using Enable/OA	$29.95
Using Harvard Project Manager	$24.95
Using Lotus Magellan	$21.95
Using Managing Your Money, 2nd Edition	$19.95
Using Microsoft Works: IBM Version	$22.95

Using Norton Utilities	$24.95
Using PC Tools Deluxe	$24.95
Using Peachtree	$22.95
Using PFS: First Choice	$22.95
Using PROCOMM PLUS	$19.95
Using Q&A, 2nd Edition	$23.95
Using Quicken	$19.95
Using Smart	$22.95
Using SmartWare II	$29.95
Using Symphony, Special Edition	$29.95

CAD

AutoCAD Advanced Techniques	$34.95
AutoCAD Quick Reference	$ 7.95
AutoCAD Sourcebook	$24.95
Using AutoCAD, 2nd Edition	$24.95
Using Generic CADD	$24.95

Word Processing

DisplayWrite QuickStart	$19.95
Microsoft Word 5 Quick Reference	$ 7.95
Microsoft Word 5 Tips, Tricks, and Traps: IBM Version	$22.95
Using DisplayWrite 4, 2nd Edition	$24.95
Using Microsoft Word 5: IBM Version	$22.95
Using MultiMate	$22.95
Using Professional Write	$22.95
Using Word for Windows	$22.95
Using WordPerfect, 3rd Edition	$21.95
Using WordPerfect 5	$24.95
Using WordPerfect 5.1, Special Edition	$24.95
Using WordStar, 2nd Edition	$21.95
WordPerfect QueCards	$21.95
WordPerfect Quick Reference	$ 7.95
WordPerfect QuickStart	$19.95
WordPerfect Tips, Tricks, and Traps, 2nd Edition	$22.95
WordPerfect 5 Workbook and Disk	$29.95
WordPerfect 5.1 Quick Reference	$ 7.95
WordPerfect 5.1 QuickStart	$19.95
WordPerfect 5.1 Tips, Tricks, and Traps	$22.95
WordPerfect 5.1 Workbook and Disk	$29.95

Hardware/Systems

DOS Power Techniques	$29.95
DOS Tips, Tricks, and Traps	$24.95
DOS Workbook and Disk, 2nd Edition	$29.95
Hard Disk Quick Reference	$ 7.95
MS-DOS Quick Reference	$ 7.95
MS-DOS QuickStart	$21.95
MS-DOS User's Guide, Special Edition	$29.95
Networking Personal Computers, 3rd Edition	$24.95
The Printer Bible	$29.95
Que's Guide to Data Recovery	$24.95
Understanding UNIX, 2nd Edition	$21.95
Upgrading and Repairing PCs	$29.95
Using DOS	$22.95
Using Microsoft Windows 3, 2nd Edition	$22.95
Using Novell NetWare	$29.95
Using OS/2	$29.95
Using PC DOS, 3rd Edition	$24.95
Using UNIX	$24.95
Using Your Hard Disk	$29.95
Windows 3 Quick Reference	$ 7.95

Desktop Publishing/Graphics

Harvard Graphics Quick Reference	$ 7.95
Using Animator	$24.95
Using Harvard Graphics	$24.95
Using Freelance Plus	$24.95
Using PageMaker: IBM Version, 2nd Edition	$24.95
Using PFS: First Publisher	$22.95
Using Ventura Publisher, 2nd Edition	$24.95
Ventura Publisher Tips, Tricks, and Traps,	$24.95

Macintosh/Apple II

AppleWorks QuickStart	$19.95
The Big Mac Book	$27.95
Excel QuickStart	$19.95
Excel Tips, Tricks, and Traps	$22.95
Que's Macintosh Multimedia Handbook	$22.95
Using AppleWorks, 3rd Edition	$21.95
Using AppleWorks GS	$21.95
Using Dollars and Sense: Macintosh Version	$19.95
Using Excel: Macintosh Version	$24.95
Using FileMaker	$24.95
Using MacroMind Director	$29.95
Using MacWrite	$22.95
Using Microsoft Word 4: Macintosh Version	$24.95
Using Microsoft Works: Macintosh Version, 2nd Edition	$24.95
Using PageMaker: Macintosh Version	$24.95

Programming/Technical

Assembly Language Quick Reference	$ 7.95
C Programmer's Toolkit	$39.95
C Programming Guide, 3rd Edition	$24.95
C Quick Reference	$ 7.95
DOS and BIOS Functions Quick Reference	$ 7.95
DOS Programmer's Reference, 2nd Edition	$29.95
Oracle Programmer's Guide	$24.95
Power Graphics Programming	$24.95
QuickBASIC Advanced Techniques	$22.95
QuickBASIC Programmer's Toolkit	$39.95
QuickBASIC Quick Reference	$ 7.95
QuickPascal Programming	$22.95
SQL Programmer's Guide	$29.95
Turbo C Programming	$22.95
Turbo Pascal Advanced Techniques	$22.95
Turbo Pascal Programmer's Toolkit	$39.95
Turbo Pascal Quick Reference	$ 7.95
UNIX Programmer's Quick Reference	$ 7.95
Using Assembly Language, 2nd Edition	$29.95
Using BASIC	$19.95
Using C	$27.95
Using QuickBASIC 4	$24.95
Using Turbo Pascal	$29.95

For More Information, Call Toll Free!
1-800-428-5331

All prices and titles subject to change without notice. Non-U.S. prices may be higher. Printed in the U.S.A.

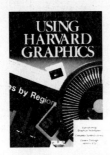